HIGH-SPEED NETWORKS: TCP/IP AND ATM DESIGN PRINCIPLES

state-of-the art survey of high-speed networks. Topics covered include TCP congestion ontrol, ATM traffic management, internet traffic management and the Internet Services rchitecture (ISA), internet routing protocols and multicast routing protocols, resource eservation and RSVP, and lossless and lossy compression. Examines important topic of self-milar data traffic. ISBN 0-13-525965-7

LOCAL AND METROPOLITAN AREA NETWORKS, SIXTH EDITION

n in-depth presentation of the technology and architecture of local and metropolitan area etworks. Covers topology, transmission media, medium access control, standards, iternetworking, and network management. Provides an up-to-date coverage of LAN/MAN ystems, including Fast Ethernet, Fibre Channel, and wireless LANs, plus LAN QoS. **eceived the 2001 TAA award for long-term excellence in a Computer Science Textbook.** BN 0-13-012939-9

ISDN AND BROADBAND ISDN, WITH FRAME RELAY AND ATM: FOURTH EDITION

n in-depth presentation of the technology and architecture of integrated services digital etworks (ISDN). Covers the integrated digital network (IDN), xDSL, ISDN services and rchitecture, signaling system no. 7 (SS7) and provides detailed coverage of the ITU-T rotocol standards. Also provides detailed coverage of protocols and congestion control rategies for both frame relay and ATM. ISBN 0-13-973744-8

BUSINESS DATA COMMUNICATIONS, FOURTH EDITION

comprehensive presentation of data communications and telecommunications from a usiness perspective. Covers voice, data, image, and video communications and applications echnology and includes a number of case studies. ISBN 0-13-088263-1

NETWORK SECURITY ESSENTIALS

tutorial and survey on network security technology. The book covers important network ecurity tools and applications, including S/MIME, IP Security, Kerberos, SSL/TLS, SET, nd X509v3. In addition, methods for countering hackers and viruses are explored. SBN 0-13-016093-8

ngs   telephone: 800-526-0485

WIRELESS COMMUNICATIONS AND NETWORKING

WIRELESS COMMUNICATIONS AND NETWORKING

William Stallings

Prentice Hall
Upper Saddle River, New Jersey 07458

Library of Congress Cataloging-in-Publication Data

Stallings, William.
    Wireless Communications and Networking / William Stallings.
      p. cm.
    Includes bibliographical references.
    ISBN 0-13-040864-6
    1. Wireless networks. 2. Communications. I. Title.

    TK5106.3.L28 2001
    005.8—dc21
                                   2001035756
                                     CIP

Vice-president of editorial development, ECS: Marcia Horton
Publisher: Alan Apt
Associate editor: Toni Holm
Editorial assistant: Amy K. Todd
Executive managing editor: Vince O'Brien
Managing editor: David A. George
Vice-president of production and manufacturing: David W. Riccardi
Production editor: Rose Kernan
Art director: Heather Scott
Manufacturing buyers: Lisa McDowell and Pat Brown
Marketing manager: Jennie Burger

 © 2002 by Prentice-Hall, Inc.
Upper Saddle River, New Jersey 07458

The author and publisher of this book have used their best efforts in preparing this book. These efforts include the
development, research, and testing of the theories and programs to determine their effectiveness. The author and
publisher make no warranty of any kind, expressed or implied, with regard to these programs or the documentation
contained in this book. The author and publisher shall not be liable in any event for incidental or consequential
damages in connection with, or arising out of, the furnishing, performance, or use of these programs.

Printed in the United States of America

10 9 8 7 6 5 4 3 2 1

ISBN 0-13-040864-6

Prentice-Hall International (UK) Limited, *London*
Prentice-Hall of Australia Pty. Limited, *Sydney*
Prentice-Hall Canada, Inc., *Toronto*
Prentice-Hall Hispanoamericana, S. A., *Mexico*
Prentice-Hall of India Private Limited, *New Delhi*
Prentice-Hall of Japan, Inc., *Tokyo*
Pearson Education Asia Pte. Ltd., *Singapore*
Editora Prentice-Hall do Brasil, Ltda., *Rio de Janeiro*

As Always,
for A.

CONTENTS

PART TWO   WIRELESS COMMUNICATION TECHNOLOGY 99

CHAPTER 5   Antennas and Propagation 99

CHAPTER 6   Signal Encoding Techniques 131

CHAPTER 7   Spread Spectrum 167

CHAPTER 8   Coding and Error Control 203

PART THREE   WIRELESS NETWORKING 255

CHAPTER 9   Satellite Communications 255

APPENDICES

PREFACE

Objectives

Wireless technology has become the most exciting area in telecommunications and networking. The rapid growth of mobile telephone use, various satellite services, and now the wireless Internet are generating tremendous changes in telecommunications and networking. This book explores the key topics in the field in the following general categories:

- **Technology and architecture:** There is a small collection of ingredients that serves to characterize and differentiate wireless communication and networking, including frequency band, signal encoding technique, error correction technique, and network architecture.
- **Network type:** This book covers the important types of wireless networks, including satellite, cellular, fixed wireless access, and wireless LANs.
- **Design approaches:** The book examines alternative design choices and assesses their relative merits.
- **Applications:** A number of key technologies and applications have been developed on top of wireless infrastructures, especially mobile IP and wireless Web access.

The book includes an extensive glossary, a list of frequently used acronyms, and a bibliography. Each chapter includes problems, suggestions for further reading, and a list of relevant Web sites. Each chapter also includes, for review, a list of key words and a number of review questions.

Throughout, there is an emphasis on both technology and on standards. The book provides a comprehensive guide to understanding specific wireless standards, such as those promulgated by ITU and IEEE 802, as well as standards developed by other organizations. This emphasis reflects the importance of such standards in defining the available products and future research directions in this field.

Intended Audience

This book is intended for a broad range of readers who will benefit from an understanding of wireless communications and networks, and the associated technologies. This includes students and professionals in the fields of data processing and data communications, designers and implementers, and data communication and networking customers and managers. The book is designed to be self-contained. For the reader with little or no background in data communications, Part One and the appendices cover a number of basic topics.

Internet Services for Instructors and Students

There is a Web site for this book that provides support for students and instructors. The site includes links to other relevant sites, transparency masters of figures and tables in the book in PDF (Adobe Acrobat) format, and sign-up information for the book's Internet mailing list. The Web page is at WilliamStallings.com/Wireless1e.html; see Section 1.7 for more information. An Internet mailing list has been set up so that instructors using this book can exchange information, suggestions, and questions with each other and with the author. As soon as typos or other errors are discovered, an errata list for this book will be available at WilliamStallings.com.

Acknowledgments

This book has benefited from review by a number of people, who gave generously of their time and expertise. These include the following, who reviewed all or part of the manuscript as well as the book's proposal: Mario Gerla (UCLA), Jerry Place (U. of Missouri—KC), John Metzner (Penn State), Upkar Varshney (Georgia State), Peter Rha (San Francisco State), and Arthur Werbner.

Thanks also to the many people who provided detailed technical reviews of a single chapter: Lars Poulsen, Howard Eisenhauer, D. E. Jennings, Paul Robichaux, John Adams, Jerry Huang, Andreas Kasenides, Munira Ahmed, Hossein Izadpanah, Aaron King, Benoit d'Udekem, Marco Casole, Kevin Peterson, Dinesh Lal Pradhan, and Cathal Mc Daid.

Steven Kilby contributed Chapter 1 and reviewed a number of chapters. His contribution is greatly appreciated. Thanks also to Richard Van Slyke of Polytechnic University of Brooklyn, who supplied many of the review questions. Tom Fronckowiak developed the PowerPoint slides for the book.

Finally, I would like to thank the many people responsible for the publication of the book, all of whom did their usual excellent job. This includes the staff at Prentice Hall, particularly my editors Toni Holm and Alan Apt and production manager Rose Kernan. Also, Jake Warde of Warde Publishers managed the supplements and reviews; Joanna V. Pomeranz at V&M managed the book's printing; and Patricia P. Daly did the copy editing.

WIRELESS COMMUNICATIONS AND NETWORKING

CHAPTER 1

INTRODUCTION[1]

---

[1]This chapter, with the exception of Section 1.7, was contributed by Steven Kilby.

T his book is a survey of wireless communications and networks. Many factors, including increased competition and the introduction of digital technology, have led to unprecedented growth in the wireless market. In this chapter, we discuss some of the key factors driving this new telecommunications revolution.

This book, and the accompanying Web site, cover a lot of material. Following the general discussion, this chapter gives the reader an overview of the book.

1.1   WIRELESS COMES OF AGE

Guglielmo Marconi invented the wireless telegraph in 1896.[2] In 1901, he sent telegraphic signals across the Atlantic Ocean from Cornwall to St. John's Newfoundland; a distance of 1800 miles. His invention allowed two parties to communicate by sending each other alphanumeric characters encoded in an analog signal. Over the last century, advances in wireless technologies have led to the radio, the television, the mobile telephone, and communications satellites. All types of information can now be sent to almost every corner of the world. Recently, a great deal of attention has been focused on satellite communications, wireless networking, and cellular technology.

Communications satellites were first launched in the 1960s. Those first satellites could only handle 240 voice circuits. Today, satellites carry about one-third of the voice traffic and all of the television signals between countries [EVAN98]. Modern satellites typically introduce a quarter-second propagation delay to the signals they handle. Newer satellites in lower orbits, with less inherent signal delay, will soon be deployed to provide data services such as Internet access.

Wireless networking is allowing businesses to develop WANs, MANs, and LANs without a cable plant. The IEEE has developed 802.11 as a standard for wireless LANs. The Bluetooth industry consortium is also working to provide a seamless wireless networking technology.

The cellular or mobile telephone is the modern equivalent of Marconi's wireless telegraph, offering two-party, two-way communication. The first-generation wireless phones used analog technology. These devices were heavy and coverage was patchy, but they successfully demonstrated the inherent convenience of mobile communications. The current generation of wireless devices are built using digital technology instead of analog. Digital networks can carry much more traffic and provide better reception and security than analog networks. In addition, digital technology has made possible value-added services such as caller identification. The next-generation wireless device will also be digital and will connect to the Internet using new frequency ranges at higher information rates.

The impact of wireless communications has been and will continue to be profound. Very few inventions have been able to "shrink" the world in such a manner.

---

[2]The actual invention of radio communications more properly should be attributed to Nikola Tesla, who gave a public demonstration in 1893. Marconi's patents were overturned in favor of Tesla in 1943 [ENGE00].

The standards that define how wireless communication devices interact are quickly converging and soon will allow the creation of a global wireless network that will deliver a wide variety of services.

1.2 THE CELLULAR REVOLUTION

The cellular revolution is intuitively apparent in the growth of the mobile phone market alone. In 1990, the number of users was approximately 11 million. By 2004, the number will likely be 1 billion [ECON99]. The next-generation devices, with access to the Internet, are sure to add to this momentum. One estimate is that the number of wireless Internet devices will exceed the number of wired Internet devices by 2005 [ECON99].

Phones are currently the most obvious sign of the success of wireless. Since 1996, the number of new mobile phone subscribers has exceeded the number of new fixed telephone subscribers [ECON99]. There are many reasons why this has happened. Mobile phones are convenient; they move with people. In addition, by their nature, they are location aware. A mobile phone communicates with regional base stations that are at fixed locations.

Technical innovations have contributed to the success of mobile phones. The handsets have become smaller and lighter, battery life has increased, and digital technology has improved reception and allowed better use of a finite spectrum. As with many types of digital equipment, the costs associated with mobile telephones have been decreasing. In areas where competition flourishes, prices have dropped dramatically since 1996.

In many geographic areas, mobile telephones are the only economical way to provide phone service to the population. Operators can erect base stations quickly and inexpensively when compared with digging up ground to lay copper in harsh terrain.

Mobile telephones are only the tip of the cellular revolution. Increasingly, new types of wireless devices are being introduced. These new devices have access to the Internet. They include personal organizers and telephones, but now they have Web access, instant messaging, e-mail, and other services available on the Internet. Wireless devices in automobiles allow users to download maps and directions on demand. Soon, the devices may be able to call for help when an accident has occurred or perhaps notify the user of the lowest-priced fuel in the immediate area. Other conveniences will be available as well. For example, refrigerators may one day be able to order groceries over the Internet to replace consumed items.

The first rush to wireless was for voice. Now, the attention is on data. Within five years wireless data service is projected to be a multibillion-dollar market [AGRA99]. A big part of this market is the "wireless" Internet. Wireless users will use the Internet differently than fixed users. Wireless devices have limited displays and input capabilities compared with typical fixed devices such as the PC. Transactions and messaging will be the rule instead of lengthy browsing sessions. Because wireless devices are location aware, information can be tailored to the geographic location of the user. Information will be able to find users, instead of users searching for information.

1.3 THE GLOBAL CELLULAR NETWORK

Today there is no single cellular network. Devices support one or two of a myriad of technologies and generally work only within the confines of a single operator's network. To move beyond this model, more work must be done to define and implement standards.

The International Telecommunication Union (ITU) is working to develop a family of standards for the next-generation wireless devices. The new standards will use higher frequencies to increase capacity. The new standards will also help overcome the incompatibilities introduced as the different first- and second-generation networks were developed and deployed over the last decade.

The dominant first-generation digital wireless network in North America was the Advanced Mobile Phone System (AMPS). This network offers a data service using the Cellular Digital Packet Data (CDPD) overlay network, which provides a 19.2-kbps data rate. The CPDP uses idle periods on regular voice channels to provide the data service.

The key second-generation wireless systems are the Global System for Mobile Communications (GSM), Personal Communications Service (PCS) IS-136, and PCS IS-95. The PCS standard IS-136 uses time division multiple access (TDMA) while IS-95 uses code division multiple access (CDMA). The GSM and PCS IS-136 use dedicated channels at 9.6 kbps to deliver the data service.

The ITU is developing International Mobile Telecommunications-2000 (IMT-2000). This family of standards is intended to provide a seamless global network. The standards are being developed around the 2-GHz frequency band. The new standards and frequency band will provide data rates up to 2 Mbps.

In addition to defining frequency usage, encoding techniques, and transmission, standards also need to define how mobile devices will interact with the Internet. Several standards bodies and industry consortiums are working to that end. The Wireless Application Protocol (WAP) Forum is developing a common protocol that allows devices with limited display and input capabilities to access the Internet. The Internet Engineering Task Force (IETF) is developing a mobile IP standard that adapts the ubiquitous IP protocol to work within a mobile environment.

1.4 BROADBAND

The Internet is increasingly a multimedia experience. Graphics, video, and audio abound on the pages of the World Wide Web. Business communications are following the same trend. For example, e-mail frequently includes rich multimedia attachments. In order to participate fully, wireless networks require the same high data rates as their fixed counterparts. The higher data rates are obtainable with broadband wireless technology.

Broadband wireless service shares the same advantages of all wireless services: convenience and reduced cost. Operators can deploy the service faster than a fixed service and without the cost of a cable plant. The service is also mobile and can be deployed almost anywhere.

There are many initiatives developing broadband wireless standards around many different applications. The standards cover everything from the wireless LAN to the small wireless home network. Data rates vary from 2 Mbps to well over 100 Mbps. Many of these technologies are available now and many more will become available in the next several years.

Wireless LANs (WLANs) provide network services where it is difficult or too expensive to deploy a fixed infrastructure. The primary WLAN standards are IEEE 802.11b and Europe's HiperLAN. The IEEE initiative provides for data rates as high as 11 Mbps. The European standard defines a maximum rate of 24 Mbps and a future revision will operate up to 54 Mbps.

A potential problem with 802.11b is compatibility with Bluetooth. Bluetooth is a wireless networking specification that defines wireless communications between devices such as laptops, PDAs, and mobile phones. Bluetooth and 802.11b use the same frequency band. The technologies would most likely interfere with each other if deployed in the same device.

The HomeRF initiative is developing standards to define wireless communications between products such as home computers and peripherals. HomeRF currently operates up to 2 Mbps but a new revision will operate near 10 Mbps.

1.5   THE TROUBLE WITH WIRELESS

Wireless is convenient and often less expensive to deploy than fixed services, but wireless is not perfect. There are limitations, political and technical difficulties that may ultimately prevent wireless technologies from reaching their full potential. Two issues are incompatible standards and device limitations.

As mentioned previously, in North America there are two standards for digital cellular service. Internationally, there is at least one more. A device using PCS IS-136 will not work in an area where the deployed technology is PCS IS-95. Also mentioned previously is the inability to use Bluetooth and 802.11b in the same device. These are just two examples of problems that arise when industrywide standards do not exist. The lack of an industrywide standard holds the technologies back from delivering one of the true ideals of wireless: ubiquitous access to data.

Device limitations also restrict the free flow of data. The small LCD on a mobile telephone is inadequate for displaying more than a few lines of text. In addition, most mobile wireless devices cannot access the vast majority of WWW sites on the Internet. The browsers use a special language, wireless markup language (WML), instead of the de facto standard HTML.

Most likely, no one wireless device will be able to meet every need. The potential of wireless can be met but not with a single product. Wireless will succeed because it will be integrated into a variety of devices that can meet a variety of needs.

1.6   OUTLINE OF THE BOOK

The objective of this book is to provide a comprehensive technical survey of wireless communications fundamentals, wireless networks, and wireless applications. The book is organized into four parts. The reader who is already familiar with data communications and networking technology can safely skip or just skim Part One. Part Two discusses underlying principles common to all of the material covered in the remainder of the book and should be read next. Parts Three and Four are independent and may be covered in either order. Within Part Three, all of the chapters are more or less independent and can be read in any order depending on your level of interest. The same is true of Chapters 14 and 15 in Part Five.

Part One: Background

This part provides a preview and context for the remainder of the book, covering basic topics in data communications as well as TCP/IP. Part One, together with the appendices at the end of the book, is intended to make the book as self-contained as possible.

Chapter 2: Transmission Fundamentals

Chapter 2 provides a basic overview of transmission topics. The chapter begins with a look at some data communications concepts, including signaling techniques and analog and digital data transmission. The chapter then covers channel capacity, transmission media, and the concept of multiplexing.

Chapter 3: Communication Networks

This chapter provides an overview of comparison of basic communication network technologies, including circuit switching, packet switching, and ATM.

Chapter 4: Protocols and the TCP/IP Protocol Suite

Data network communication and distributed applications rely on underlying communications software that is independent of application and relieves the application of much of the burden of reliably exchanging data. This communications software is organized into a protocol architecture, the most important incarnation of which is the TCP/IP protocol suite. Chapter 4 introduces the concept of a protocol architecture and provides an overview of TCP/IP. Another architecture, the Open Systems Interconnection (OSI) reference model, is briefly described. Finally, the concept of internetworking and the use of TCP/IP to achieve internetworking are discussed.

Part Two: Wireless Communication Technology

This part is concerned with the underlying technology of wireless transmission and the encoding of analog and digital data for wireless transmission.

Chapter 5: Antennas and Propagation

Chapter 5 examines the fundamental principles of radio and microwave. The chapter discusses relevant aspects of antenna performance, then looks at wireless transmission modes, and finally examines the key issue of fading.

Chapter 6: Signal Encoding Techniques

Data come in both analog (continuous) and digital (discrete) form. For transmission, input data must be encoded as an electrical signal that is tailored to the characteristics of the transmission medium. Both analog and digital data can be represented by either analog or digital signals; the relevant cases for wireless transmission are discussed in Chapter 6.

Chapter 7: Spread Spectrum

An increasingly popular form of wireless communications is known as spread spectrum. Two general approaches are used: frequency hopping and direct sequence spread spectrum. Chapter 7 provides an overview of both techniques. The chapter also looks at the concept of code division multiple access (CDMA), which is an application of spread spectrum to provide multiple access.

Chapter 8: Coding and Error Control

Wireless communications systems are highly prone to error, and virtually all wireless transmission schemes include techniques for forward error correction (FEC) by adding redundancy to the transmitted data so that bit errors can be corrected at the receiver. Chapter 8 examines FEC in detail. In addition, Chapter 8 looks at the use of redundancy for error detection, which is also found in many wireless schemes. Finally, error detection is often combined with automatic repeat request (ARQ) techniques the enable a transmitter to retransmit blocks of data in which the receiver has detected an error.

Part Three: Wireless Networking

This part examines the major types of wireless networks. These include satellite-based networks, cellular networks, cordless systems, fixed wireless access schemes, and the use of mobile IP and the Wireless Application Protocol (WAP) to provide Internet and Web access.

Chapter 9: Satellite Communications

This chapter covers the basic principles of satellite communications. It looks at geostationary satellites (GEOS), low-earth orbiting satellites (LEOS), and medium-earth orbiting satellites (MEOS). The key design issue of capacity allocation is examined in detail.

Chapter 10: Cellular Wireless Networks

Chapter 10 begins with a discussion of the important design issues related to cellular wireless networks. Next, the chapter covers the traditional mobile telephony service, now know as first-generation analog. Chapter 10 then examines second-generation digital cellular networks, looking at the two principal approaches: time division multiple access (TDMA) and code division multiple access (CDMA). Finally, an overview of third-generation networks is provided.

Chapter 11: Cordless Systems and Wireless Local Loop

Chapter 11 looks at two technologies that bring wireless access into the residence and office: cordless systems and wireless local loop (WLL). Cordless systems have evolved from the simple single-user cordless telephones used within the home to accommodate multiple users over much larger ranges. Sometimes called radio in the loop (RITL) or fixed wireless access (FWA), WLL is a system that connects subscribers to the public switched telephone network (PSTN) using radio signals as a substitute for copper for all or part of the connection between the subscriber and the switch. Chapter 11 looks at the design issues related to WLL and then examines the IEEE 802.16 standard.

Chapter 12: Mobile IP and Wireless Access Protocol

Chapter 12 examines the modifications to IP to accommodate wireless access to the Internet. The chapter then examines the Wireless Application Protocol (WAP). WAP provides mobile users of wireless phones and other wireless terminals, such as pagers and personal digital assistants (PDAs), access to telephony and information services, including the Internet and the Web.

Part Four: Wireless Local Area Networks

In recent years, a whole new class of local area networks have arrived to provide an alternative to LANs based on twisted pair, coaxial cable, and optical fiber—wireless LANs. The key advantages of the wireless LAN are that it eliminates the wiring cost, which is often the most costly component of a LAN, and that it accommodates mobile workstations. This part examines underlying wireless LAN technology and then examines two standardized approaches to local wireless networking.

Chapter 13: Wireless LAN Technology

Wireless LANs use one of three transmission techniques: spread spectrum, narrowband microwave, and infrared. Chapter 13 provides an overview of LANs and wireless LAN technology and applications.

Chapter 14: IEEE 802.11 Wireless LAN Standard

The most significant set of standards defining wireless LANs are those defined by the IEEE 802.11 committee. Chapter 14 examines this set of standards in depth.

Chapter 15: Bluetooth

Bluetooth is an open specification for wireless communication and networking among PCs, mobile phones, and other wireless devices. Bluetooth is one of the fastest growing technology standards ever. It is intended for use within a local area. Chapter 15 examines this specification in depth.

1.7 INTERNET AND WEB RESOURCES

There are a number of resources available on the Internet and the Web to support this book and to help one keep up with developments in this field.

Web Sites for This Book

A special Web page has been set up for this book at WilliamStallings.com/
Wireless1e.html. The site includes the following:

- **Useful Web sites:** There are links to other relevant Web sites, including the sites listed in this appendix and throughout this book.
- **Errata sheet:** An errata list for this book will be maintained and updated as needed. Please e-mail any errors that you spot to me. Errata sheets for my other books are at WilliamStallings.com.
- **Figures:** All of the figures in this book in PDF (Adobe Acrobat) format.
- **Tables:** All of the tables in this book in PDF format.
- **Slides:** A set of PowerPoint slides, organized by chapter.
- **Internet mailing list:** The site includes sign-up information for the book's Internet mailing list.
- **Wireless courses:** There are links to home pages for courses based on this book; these pages may be useful to other instructors in providing ideas about how to structure their course.

I also maintain the Computer Science Student Resource Site, at WilliamStallings.com/StudentSupport.html; the purpose of this site is to provide documents, information, and links for computer science students and professionals. Links are organized into four categories:

- **Math:** Includes a basic math refresher, a queuing analysis primer, a number system primer, and links to numerous math sites
- **How-to:** Advice and guidance for solving homework problems, writing technical reports, and preparing technical presentations
- **Research resources:** Links to important collections of papers, technical reports, and bibliographies
- **Miscellaneous:** A variety of useful documents and links

Other Web Sites

There are numerous Web sites that provide information related to the topics of this book. In subsequent chapters, pointers to specific Web sites can be found in the "Recommended Reading and Web Sites" section. Because the addresses for Web sites tend to change frequently, I have not included these in the book. For all of the Web sites listed in the book, the appropriate link can be found at this book's Web site.

The following Web sites are of general interest related to wireless communications:

- **Telecommunications Technology Resources Page:** Excellent source of links covering numerous topics

- **Vendors:** Links to thousands of hardware and software vendors who currently have WWW sites, as well as a list of thousands of computer and networking companies in a Phone Directory
- **Mobile and Wireless Computing Index:** Source of information about wireless technology, products, conferences, and publications
- **Wireless Developer Network:** News, tutorials, and discussions on wireless topics
- **Wireless Technology:** An amazing list of links to all aspects or wireless communications, networking, and standards

USENET Newsgroups

A number of USENET newsgroups are devoted to some aspect of data communications or networking. As with virtually all USENET groups, there is a high noise-to-signal ratio, but it is worth experimenting to see if any meet your needs. The most relevant are as follows:

- **comp.std.wireless:** General discussion of wireless standards for wide area and local area networks. This is a moderated group, which keeps the discussion focused.
- **comp.dcom.*:** There are a number of data communications related newsgroups that begin with "comp.dcom."

The purpose of this chapter is to make this book self-contained for the reader with little or no background in data communications. For the reader with greater interest, references for further study are supplied at the end of the chapter.

2.1 SIGNALS FOR CONVEYING INFORMATION

In this book, we are concerned with electromagnetic signals used as a means to transmit information. An electromagnetic signal is a function of time, but it can also be expressed as a function of frequency; that is, the signal consists of components of different frequencies. It turns out that the frequency domain view of a signal is far more important to an understanding of data transmission than a time domain view. Both views are introduced here.

Time Domain Concepts

Viewed as a function of time, an electromagnetic signal can be either analog or digital. An **analog signal** is one in which the signal intensity varies in a smooth fashion over time. In other words, there are no breaks or discontinuities in the signal. A **digital signal** is one in which the signal intensity maintains a constant level for some period of time and then changes to another constant level.[1] Figure 2.1

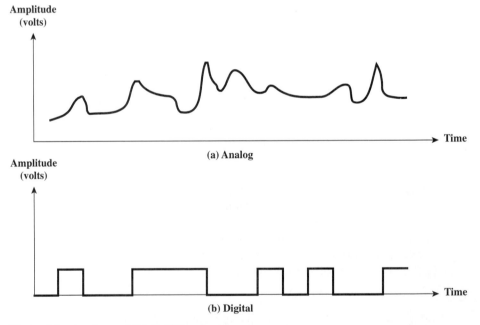

Figure 2.1   Analog and Digital Waveforms

---

[1]This is an idealized definition. In fact, the transition from one voltage level to another will not be instantaneous, but there will be a small transition period. Nevertheless, an actual digital signal approximates closely the ideal model of constant voltage levels with instantaneous transitions.

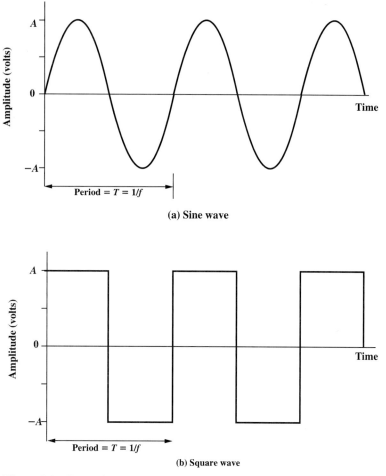

Figure 2.2 Examples of Periodic Signals

shows examples of both kinds of signals. The analog signal might represent speech, and the digital signal might represent binary 1s and 0s.

The simplest sort of signal is a **periodic signal**, in which the same signal pattern repeats over time. Figure 2.2 shows an example of a periodic analog signal (sine wave) and a periodic digital signal (square wave). Mathematically, a signal $s(t)$ is defined to be periodic if and only if

$$s(t + T) = s(t) \qquad -\infty < t < +\infty$$

where the constant T is the period of the signal (T is the smallest value that satisfies the equation). Otherwise, a signal is **aperiodic**.

The sine wave is the fundamental analog signal. A general sine wave can be represented by three parameters: peak amplitude (A), frequency (f), and phase (ϕ). The **peak amplitude** is the maximum value or strength of the signal over time; typically, this value is measured in volts. The **frequency** is the rate [in cycles per second, or Hertz (Hz)] at which the signal repeats. An equivalent parameter is the **period** (T) of a signal, which is the amount of time it takes for one repetition; therefore, $T = 1/f$. **Phase** is a measure of the relative position in time within a single period of a signal, as illustrated later.

The general sine wave can be written

$$s(t) = A \sin(2\pi ft + \phi)$$

Figure 2.3 shows the effect of varying each of the three parameters. In part (a) of the figure, the frequency is 1 Hz; thus the period is $T = 1$ second. Part (b) has the same frequency and phase but a peak amplitude of 0.5. In part (c) we have $f = 2$, which is equivalent to $T = 1/2$. Finally, part (d) shows the effect of a phase shift of $\pi/4$ radians, which is 45 degrees (2π radians = $360° = 1$ period).

In Figure 2.3 the horizontal axis is time; the graphs display the value of a signal at a given point in space as a function of time. These same graphs, with a change of scale, can apply with horizontal axes in space. In that case, the graphs display the value of a signal at a given point in time as a function of distance. For example, for a sinusoidal transmission (say, an electromagnetic radio wave some distance from a radio antenna or sound some distance from loudspeaker) at a particular instant of time, the intensity of the signal varies in a sinusoidal way as a function of distance from the source.

There is a simple relationship between the two sine waves, one in time and one in space. Define the **wavelength** (λ) of a signal as the distance occupied by a single cycle, or, put another way, the distance between two points of corresponding phase of two consecutive cycles. Assume that the signal is traveling with a velocity v. Then the wavelength is related to the period as follows: $\lambda = vT$. Equivalently, $\lambda f = v$. Of particular relevance to this discussion is the case where $v = c$, the speed of light in free space, which is approximately 3×10^8 m/s.

Frequency Domain Concepts

In practice, an electromagnetic signal will be made up of many frequencies. For example, the signal

$$s(t) = (4/\pi) \times (\sin(2\pi ft) + (1/3)\sin(2\pi(3f)t))$$

is shown in Figure 2.4c. The components of this signal are just sine waves of frequencies f and $3f$; parts (a) and (b) of the figure show these individual components. There are two interesting points that can be made about this figure:

- The second frequency is an integer multiple of the first frequency. When all of the frequency components of a signal are integer multiples of one frequency, the latter frequency is referred to as the **fundamental frequency**.
- The period of the total signal is equal to the period of the fundamental frequency. The period of the component $\sin(2\pi ft)$ is $T = 1/f$, and the period of $s(t)$ is also T, as can be seen from Figure 2.4c.

It can be shown, using a discipline known as Fourier analysis, that any signal is made up of components at various frequencies, in which each component is a

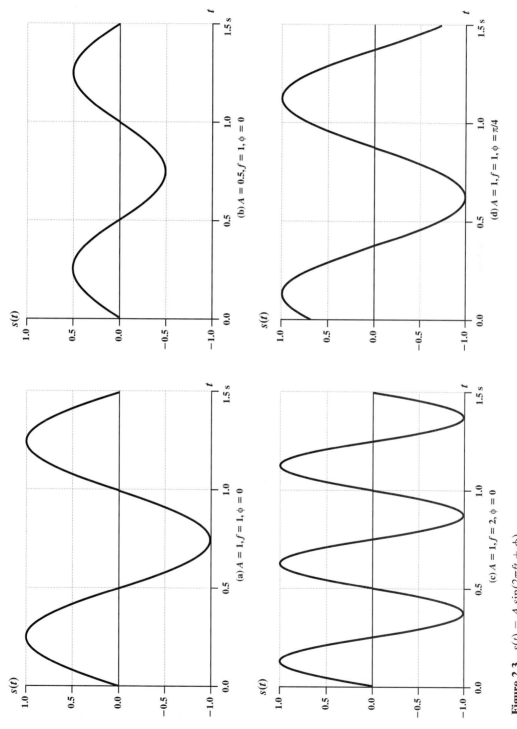

Figure 2.3 $s(t) = A \sin(2\pi f t + \phi)$

(a) $A = 1, f = 1, \phi = 0$

(b) $A = 0.5, f = 1, \phi = 0$

(c) $A = 1, f = 2, \phi = 0$

(d) $A = 1, f = 1, \phi = \pi/4$

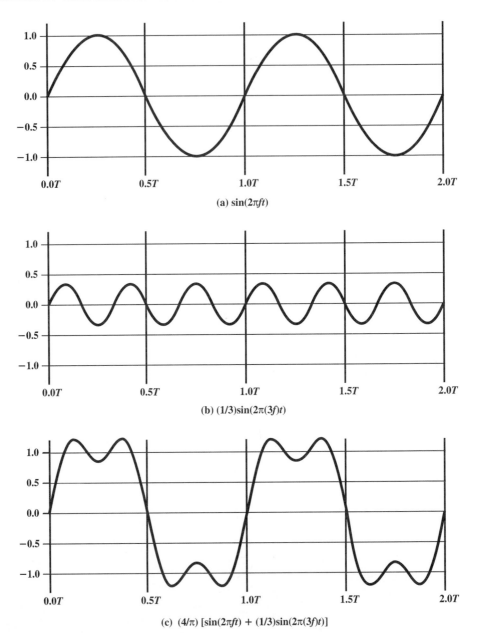

Figure 2.4 Addition of Frequency Components ($T = 1/f$)

sinusoid. By adding together enough sinusoidal signals, each with the appropriate amplitude, frequency, and phase, any electromagnetic signal can be constructed. Put another way, any electromagnetic signal can be shown to consist of a collection of periodic analog signals (sine waves) at different amplitudes, frequencies, and phases.

The importance of being able to look at a signal from the frequency perspective (frequency domain) rather than a time perspective (time domain) should become clear as the discussion proceeds. For the interested reader, the subject of Fourier analysis is introduced in Appendix C.

The **spectrum** of a signal is the range of frequencies that it contains. For the signal of Figure 2.4c, the spectrum extends from f to $3f$. The **absolute bandwidth** of a signal is the width of the spectrum. In the case of Figure 2.4c, the bandwidth is $3f - f = 2f$. Many signals have an infinite bandwidth, but with most of the energy contained in a relatively narrow band of frequencies. This band is referred to as the **effective bandwidth**, or just **bandwidth**.

Relationship between Data Rate and Bandwidth

There is a direct relationship between the information-carrying capacity of a signal and its bandwidth: The greater the bandwidth, the higher the information-carrying capacity. As a very simple example, consider the square wave of Figure 2.2b. Suppose that we let a positive pulse represent binary 0 and a negative pulse represent binary 1. Then the waveform represents the binary stream 0101. . . . The duration of each pulse is $1/(2f)$; thus the data rate is $2f$ bits per second (bps). What are the frequency components of this signal? To answer this question, consider again Figure 2.4. By adding together sine waves at frequencies f and $3f$, we get a waveform that begins to resemble the square wave. Let us continue this process by adding a sine wave of frequency $5f$, as shown in Figure 2.5a, and then adding a sine wave of frequency $7f$, as shown in Figure 2.5b. As we add additional odd multiples of f, suitably scaled, the resulting waveform approaches that of a square wave more and more closely.

Indeed, it can be shown that the frequency components of the square wave with amplitudes A and $-A$ can be expressed as follows:

$$s(t) = A \times \frac{4}{\pi} \times \sum_{k\,\text{odd},k\,=\,1}^{\infty} \frac{\sin(2\pi k f t)}{k}$$

This waveform has an infinite number of frequency components and hence an infinite bandwidth. However, the peak amplitude of the kth frequency component, kf, is only $1/k$, so most of the energy in this waveform is in the first few frequency components. What happens if we limit the bandwidth to just the first three frequency components? We have already seen the answer, in Figure 2.5a. As we can see, the shape of the resulting waveform is reasonably close to that of the original square wave.

We can use Figures 2.4 and 2.5 to illustrate the relationship between data rate and bandwidth. Suppose that we are using a digital transmission system that is capable of transmitting signals with a bandwidth of 4 MHz. Let us attempt to transmit a sequence of alternating 0s and 1s as the square wave of Figure 2.5c. What data rate can be achieved? We look at three cases.

Case I. Let us approximate our square wave with the waveform of Figure 2.5a. Although this waveform is a "distorted" square wave, it is sufficiently close to

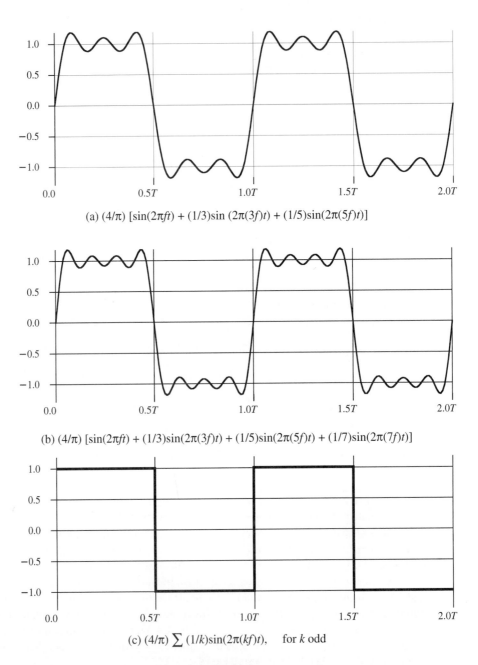

(a) $(4/\pi) [\sin(2\pi ft) + (1/3)\sin (2\pi(3f)t) + (1/5)\sin(2\pi(5f)t)]$

(b) $(4/\pi) [\sin(2\pi ft) + (1/3)\sin(2\pi(3f)t) + (1/5)\sin(2\pi(5f)t) + (1/7)\sin(2\pi(7f)t)]$

(c) $(4/\pi) \sum (1/k)\sin(2\pi(kf)t)$,   for k odd

Figure 2.5   Frequency Components of Square Wave ($T = 1/f$)

the square wave that a receiver should be able to discriminate between a binary 0 and a binary 1. If we let $f = 10^6$ cycles/second = 1 MHz, then the bandwidth of the signal

$$s(t) = \frac{4}{\pi} \times \left[\sin((2\pi \times 10^6)t) + \frac{1}{3} \sin((2\pi \times 3 \times 10^6)t) + \frac{1}{5} \sin((2\pi \times 5 \times 10^6)t) \right]$$

is $(5 \times 10^6) - 10^6 = 4$ MHz. Note that for $f = 1$ MHz, the period of the fundamental frequency is $T = 1/10^6 = 10^{-6} = 1$ μs. If we treat this waveform as a bit string of 1s and 0s, one bit occurs every 0.5 μs, for a data rate of $2 \times 10^6 = 2$ Mbps. Thus, for a bandwidth of 4 MHz, a data rate of 2 Mbps is achieved.

Case II. Now suppose that we have a bandwidth of 8 MHz. Let us look again at Figure 2.5a, but now with $f = 2$ MHz. Using the same line of reasoning as before, the bandwidth of the signal is $(5 \times 2 \times 10^6) - (2 \times 10^6) = 8$ MHz. But in this case $T = 1/f = 0.5$ μs. As a result, one bit occurs every 0.25 μs for a data rate of 4 Mbps. Thus, other things being equal, by doubling the bandwidth, we double the potential data rate.

Case III. Now suppose that the waveform of Figure 2.4c is considered adequate for approximating a square wave. That is, the difference between a positive and negative pulse in Figure 2.4c is sufficiently distinct that the waveform can be used successfully to represent a sequence of 1s and 0s. Assume as in Case II that $f = 2$ MHz and $T = 1/f = 0.5$ μs, so that one bit occurs every 0.25 μs for a data rate of 4 Mbps. Using the waveform of Figure 2.4c, the bandwidth of the signal is $(3 \times 2 \times 10^6) - (2 \times 10^6) = 4$ MHz. Thus, a given bandwidth can support various data rates depending on the ability of the receiver to discern the difference between 0 and 1 in the presence of noise and other impairments.

To summarize,

- **Case I:** Bandwidth = 4 MHz; data rate = 2 Mbps
- **Case II:** Bandwidth = 8 MHz; data rate = 4 Mbps
- **Case III:** Bandwidth = 4 MHz; data rate = 4 Mbps

We can draw the following conclusions from the preceding discussion. In general, any digital waveform will have infinite bandwidth. If we attempt to transmit this waveform as a signal over any medium, the transmission system will limit the bandwidth that can be transmitted. Furthermore, for any given medium, the greater the bandwidth transmitted, the greater the cost. Thus, on the one hand, economic and practical reasons dictate that digital information be approximated by a signal of limited bandwidth. On the other hand, limiting the bandwidth creates distortions, which makes the task of interpreting the received signal more difficult. The more limited the bandwidth, the greater the distortion and the greater the potential for error by the receiver.

2.2 ANALOG AND DIGITAL DATA TRANSMISSION

The terms *analog* and *digital* correspond, roughly, to *continuous* and *discrete*, respectively. These two terms are used frequently in data communications in at least three contexts: data, signals, and transmission.

Briefly, we define **data** as entities that convey meaning, or information. **Signals** are electric or electromagnetic representations of data. **Transmission** is the communication of data by the propagation and processing of signals. In what follows, we try to make these abstract concepts clear by discussing the terms *analog* and *digital* as applied to data, signals, and transmission.

Analog and Digital Data

The concepts of analog and digital data are simple enough. Analog data take on continuous values in some interval. For example, voice and video are continuously varying patterns of intensity. Most data collected by sensors, such as temperature and pressure, are continuous valued. Digital data take on discrete values; examples are text and integers.

The most familiar example of analog data is **audio**, which, in the form of acoustic sound waves, can be perceived directly by human beings. Figure 2.6 shows the acoustic spectrum for human speech and for music. Frequency components of typical speech

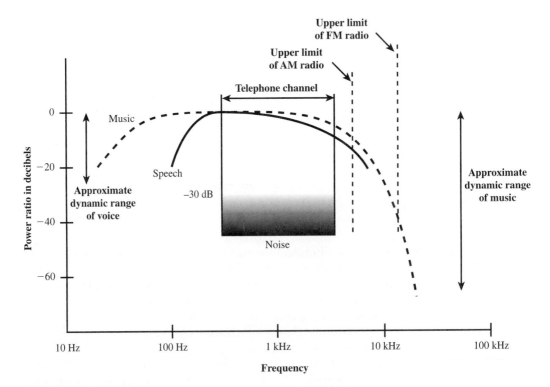

Figure 2.6 Acoustic Spectrum of Speech and Music [CARN99]

Figure 2.7   Attenuation of Digital Signals

may be found between approximately 100 Hz and 7 kHz. Although much of the energy in speech is concentrated at the lower frequencies, tests have shown that frequencies up to 600 to 700 Hz add very little to the intelligibility of speech to the human ear. Typical speech has a dynamic range of about 25 dB;[2] that is, the power produced by the loudest shout may be as much as 300 times greater than the least whisper. Figure 2.6 also shows the acoustic spectrum and dynamic range for music.

Analog and Digital Signaling

In a communications system, data are propagated from one point to another by means of electric signals. An **analog signal** is a continuously varying electromagnetic wave that may be propagated over a variety of media, depending on frequency; examples are copper wire media, such as twisted pair and coaxial cable; fiber optic cable; and atmosphere or space propagation (wireless). A **digital signal** is a sequence of voltage pulses that may be transmitted over a copper wire medium; for example, a constant positive voltage level may represent binary 0 and a constant negative voltage level may represent binary 1.

The principal advantages of digital signaling are that it is generally cheaper than analog signaling and is less susceptible to noise interference. The principal disadvantage is that digital signals suffer more from attenuation than do analog signals. Figure 2.7 shows a sequence of voltage pulses, generated by a source using two voltage levels, and the received voltage some distance down a conducting medium. Because of the attenuation, or reduction, of signal strength at higher frequencies, the pulses become rounded and smaller. It should be clear that this attenuation can lead rather quickly to the loss of the information contained in the propagated signal.

Both analog and digital data can be represented, and hence propagated, by either analog or digital signals. This is illustrated in Figure 2.8. Generally, analog data are a function of time and occupy a limited frequency spectrum. Such data can be directly represented by an electromagnetic signal occupying the same spectrum. The best example of this is voice data. As sound waves, voice data have frequency components in the range 20 Hz to 20 kHz. However, most of the speech energy is in a much narrower range. The standard spectrum of voice signals is 300 to 3400 Hz, and this is quite adequate to propagate speech intelligibly and clearly. The telephone instrument does just that. For all sound input in the range of 300 to 3400 Hz, an electromagnetic signal with the same frequency–amplitude pattern is produced. The process is performed in reverse to convert the electromagnetic energy back into sound.

---

[2]The concept of decibels is explained in Appendix 2A.

Digital data can also be represented by analog signals by use of a modem (modulator-demodulator). The modem converts a series of binary (two-valued) voltage pulses into an analog signal by modulating a carrier frequency. The resulting signal occupies a certain spectrum of frequency centered about the carrier and may be propagated across a medium suitable for that carrier. The most common modems represent digital data in the voice spectrum and hence allow those data to be propagated over ordinary voice-grade telephone lines. At the other end of the line, a modem demodulates the signal to recover the original data.

In an operation very similar to that performed by a modem, analog data can be represented by digital signals. The device that performs this function for voice data is a codec (coder-decoder). In essence, the codec takes an analog signal that directly represents the voice data and approximates that signal by a bit stream. At the other end of the line, a codec uses the bit stream to reconstruct the analog data. This topic is explored subsequently.

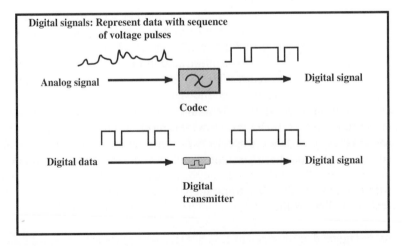

Figure 2.8   Analog and Digital Signaling of Analog and Digital Data

Table 2.1 Analog and Digital Transmission

(a) Data and Signals

	Analog Signal	**Digital Signal**
Analog Data	Two alternatives: (1) signal occupies the same spectrum as the analog data; (2) analog data are encoded to occupy a different portion of spectrum.	Analog data are encoded using a codec to produce a digital bit stream.
Digital Data	Digital data are encoded using a modem to produce analog signal.	Two alternatives: (1) signal consists of a two voltage levels to represent the two binary values; (2) digital data are encoded to produce a digital signal with desired properties.

(b) Treatment of Signals

	Analog Transmission	**Digital Transmission**
Analog Signal	Is propagated through amplifiers; same treatment whether signal is used to represent analog data or digital data.	Assumes that the analog signal represents digital data. Signal is propagated through repeaters; at each repeater, digital data are recovered from inbound signal and used to generate a new analog outbound signal.
Digital Signal	Not used	Digital signal represents a stream of 1s and 0s, which may represent digital data or may be an encoding of analog data. Signal is propagated through repeaters; at each repeater, stream of 1s and 0s is recovered from inbound signal and used to generate a new digital outbound signal.

Finally, digital data can be represented directly, in binary form, by two voltage levels. To improve propagation characteristics, however, the binary data are often encoded into a more complex form of digital signal, as explained subsequently.

Each of the four combinations (Table 2.1a) just described is in widespread use. The reasons for choosing a particular combination for any given communications task vary. We list here some representative reasons:

- **Digital data, digital signal:** In general, the equipment for encoding digital data into a digital signal is less complex and less expensive than digital-to-analog equipment.

- **Analog data, digital signal:** Conversion of analog data to digital form permits the use of modern digital transmission and switching equipment.
- **Digital data, analog signal:** Some transmission media, such as optical fiber and satellite, will only propagate analog signals.
- **Analog data, analog signal:** Analog data are easily converted to an analog signal.

Analog and Digital Transmission

Both analog and digital signals may be transmitted on suitable transmission media. The way these signals are treated is a function of the transmission system. Table 2.1b summarizes the methods of data transmission. **Analog transmission** is a means of transmitting analog signals without regard to their content; the signals may represent analog data (e.g., voice) or digital data (e.g., data that pass through a modem). In either case, the analog signal will suffer attenuation that limits the length of the transmission link. To achieve longer distances, the analog transmission system includes amplifiers that boost the energy in the signal. Unfortunately, the amplifier also boosts the noise components. With amplifiers cascaded to achieve long distance, the signal becomes more and more distorted. For analog data, such as voice, quite a bit of distortion can be tolerated and the data remain intelligible. However, for digital data transmitted as analog signals, cascaded amplifiers will introduce errors.

Digital transmission, in contrast, is concerned with the content of the signal. We have mentioned that a digital signal can be propagated only a limited distance before attenuation endangers the integrity of the data. To achieve greater distances, repeaters are used. A repeater receives the digital signal, recovers the pattern of ones and zeros, and retransmits a new signal. Thus, the attenuation is overcome.

The same technique may be used with an analog signal if the signal carries digital data. At appropriately spaced points, the transmission system has retransmission devices rather than amplifiers. The retransmission device recovers the digital data from the analog signal and generates a new, clean analog signal. Thus, noise is not cumulative.

2.3 CHANNEL CAPACITY

A variety of impairments can distort or corrupt a signal. A common impairment is noise, which is any unwanted signal that combines with and hence distorts the signal intended for transmission and reception. Noise and other impairments are discussed in Chapter 5. For the purposes of this section, we simply need to know that noise is something that degrades signal quality. For digital data, the question that then arises is to what extent these impairments limit the data rate that can be achieved. The maximum rate at which data can be transmitted over a given communication path, or channel, under given conditions, is referred to as the **channel capacity**.

There are four concepts here that we are trying to relate to one another:

- **Data rate:** This is the rate, in bits per second (bps), at which data can be communicated.

- **Bandwidth:** This is the bandwidth of the transmitted signal as constrained by the transmitter and the nature of the transmission medium, expressed in cycles per second, or Hertz.
- **Noise:** This is the average level of noise over the communications path.
- **Error rate:** This is the rate at which errors occur, where an error is the reception of a 1 when a 0 was transmitted or the reception of a 0 when a 1 was transmitted.

The problem we are addressing is this: Communications facilities are expensive and, in general, the greater the bandwidth of a facility, the greater the cost. Furthermore, all transmission channels of any practical interest are of limited bandwidth. The limitations arise from the physical properties of the transmission medium or from deliberate limitations at the transmitter on the bandwidth to prevent interference from other sources. Accordingly, we would like to make as efficient use as possible of a given bandwidth. For digital data, this means that we would like to get as high a data rate as possible at a particular limit of error rate for a given bandwidth. The main constraint on achieving this efficiency is noise.

Nyquist Bandwidth

To begin, let us consider the case of a channel that is noise free. In this environment, the limitation on data rate is simply the bandwidth of the signal. A formulation of this limitation, due to Nyquist, states that if the rate of signal transmission is $2B$, then a signal with frequencies no greater than B is sufficient to carry the signal rate. The converse is also true: Given a bandwidth of B, the highest signal rate that can be carried is $2B$. This limitation is due to the effect of intersymbol interference, such as is produced by delay distortion.[3] The result is useful in the development of digital-to-analog encoding schemes and is derived in Appendix 6A.

Note that in the preceding paragraph, we referred to signal rate. If the signals to be transmitted are binary (two voltage levels), then the data rate that can be supported by B Hz is $2B$ bps. As an example, consider a voice channel being used, via modem, to transmit digital data. Assume a bandwidth of 3100 Hz. Then the capacity, C, of the channel is $2B = 6200$ bps. However, as we shall see in Chapter 6, signals with more than two levels can be used; that is, each signal element can represent more than one bit. For example, if four possible voltage levels are used as signals, then each signal element can represent two bits. With multilevel signaling, the Nyquist formulation becomes

$$C = 2B \log_2 M$$

where M is the number of discrete signal or voltage levels. Thus, for $M = 8$, a value used with some modems, a bandwidth of $B = 3100$ Hz yields a capacity $C = 18,600$ bps.

So, for a given bandwidth, the data rate can be increased by increasing the number of different signal elements. However, this places an increased burden on

---

[3]Delay distortion of a signal occurs when the propagation delay for the transmission medium is not constant over the frequency range of the signal.

the receiver: Instead of distinguishing one of two possible signal elements during each signal time, it must distinguish one of M possible signals. Noise and other impairments on the transmission line will limit the practical value of M.

Shannon Capacity Formula

Nyquist's formula indicates that, all other things being equal, doubling the bandwidth doubles the data rate. Now consider the relationship among data rate, noise, and error rate. The presence of noise can corrupt one or more bits. If the data rate is increased, then the bits become "shorter" so that more bits are affected by a given pattern of noise. Thus, at a given noise level, the higher the data rate, the higher the error rate.

Figure 2.9 is an example of the effect of noise on a digital signal. Here the noise consists of a relatively modest level of background noise plus occasional larger spikes of noise. The digital data can be recovered from the signal by sampling the received waveform once per bit time. As can be seen, the noise is occasionally sufficient to change a 1 to a 0 or a 0 to a 1.

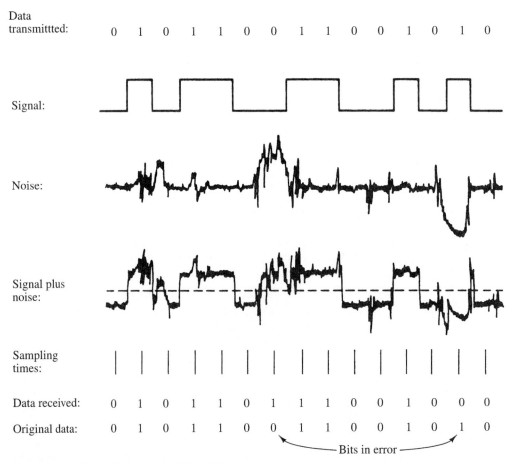

Figure 2.9 Effect of Noise on a Digital Signal

All of these concepts can be tied together neatly in a formula developed by the mathematician Claude Shannon. As we have just illustrated, the higher the data rate, the more damage that unwanted noise can do. For a given level of noise, we would expect that a greater signal strength would improve the ability to receive data correctly in the presence of noise. The key parameter involved in this reasoning is the signal-to-noise ratio (SNR, or S/N),[4] which is the ratio of the power in a signal to the power contained in the noise that is present at a particular point in the transmission. Typically, this ratio is measured at a receiver, because it is at this point that an attempt is made to process the signal and eliminate the unwanted noise. For convenience, this ratio is often reported in decibels:

$$\text{SNR}_{dB} = 10 \log_{10} \frac{\text{signal power}}{\text{noise power}}$$

This expresses the amount, in decibels, that the intended signal exceeds the noise level. A high SNR will mean a high-quality signal and a low number of required intermediate repeaters.

The signal-to-noise ratio is important in the transmission of digital data because it sets the upper bound on the achievable data rate. Shannon's result is that the maximum channel capacity, in bits per second, obeys the equation

$$C = B \log_2(1 + \text{SNR})$$

where C is the capacity of the channel in bits per second and B is the bandwidth of the channel in Hertz. The Shannon formula represents the theoretical maximum that can be achieved. In practice, however, only much lower rates are achieved. One reason for this is that the formula assumes white noise (thermal noise). Impulse noise is not accounted for, nor are attenuation distortion or delay distortion.

The capacity indicated in the preceding equation is referred to as the error-free capacity. Shannon proved that if the actual information rate on a channel is less than the error-free capacity, then it is theoretically possible to use a suitable signal code to achieve error-free transmission through the channel. Shannon's theorem unfortunately does not suggest a means for finding such codes, but it does provide a yardstick by which the performance of practical communication schemes may be measured.

Several other observations concerning the preceding equation may be instructive. For a given level of noise, it would appear that the data rate could be increased by increasing either signal strength or bandwidth. However, as the signal strength increases, so do the effects of nonlinearities in the system, leading to an increase in intermodulation noise. Note also that, because noise is assumed to be white, the wider the bandwidth, the more noise is admitted to the system. Thus, as B increases, SNR decreases.

---

[4]Some of the literature uses SNR, others use S/N. Also, in some cases the dimensionless quantity is referred to as SNR or S/N and the quantity in decibels is referred to as SNR_{db} or $(\text{S/N})_{db}$. Others use just SNR or S/N to mean the dB quantity. This text uses SNR and SNR_{db}.

Example. Let us consider an example that relates the Nyquist and Shannon formulations. Suppose that the spectrum of a channel is between 3 MHz and 4 MHz and $SNR_{dB} = 24$ dB. Then

$$B = 4 \text{ MHz} - 3 \text{ MHz} = 1 \text{ MHz}$$
$$SNR_{dB} = 24 \text{ dB} = 10 \log_{10}(SNR)$$
$$SNR = 251$$

Using Shannon's formula,

$$C = 10^6 \times \log_2(1 + 251) \approx 10^6 \times 8 = 8 \text{ Mbps}$$

This is a theoretical limit and, as we have said, is unlikely to be reached. But assume we can achieve the limit. Based on Nyquist's formula, how many signaling levels are required? We have

$$C = 2B \log_2 M$$
$$8 \times 10^6 = 2 \times (10^6) \times \log_2 M$$
$$4 = \log_2 M$$
$$M = 16$$

2.4 TRANSMISSION MEDIA

In a data transmission system, the **transmission medium** is the physical path between transmitter and receiver. Transmission media can be classified as guided or unguided. In both cases, communication is in the form of electromagnetic waves. With **guided media**, the waves are guided along a solid medium, such as copper twisted pair, copper coaxial cable, or optical fiber. The atmosphere and outer space are examples of **unguided media**, which provide a means of transmitting electromagnetic signals but do not guide them; this form of transmission is usually referred to as **wireless transmission**.

The characteristics and quality of a data transmission are determined both by the characteristics of the medium and the characteristics of the signal. In the case of guided media, the medium itself is more important in determining the limitations of transmission. For unguided media, the bandwidth of the signal produced by the transmitting antenna is more important than the medium in determining transmission characteristics. One key property of signals transmitted by antenna is directionality. In general, signals at lower frequencies are omnidirectional; that is, the signal propagates in all directions from the antenna. At higher frequencies, it is possible to focus the signal into a directional beam.

Figure 2.10 depicts the electromagnetic spectrum and indicates the frequencies at which various guided media and unguided transmission techniques operate.[5] In the remainder of this section, we provide a brief overview of unguided, or wireless, media.

For unguided media, transmission and reception are achieved by means of an antenna. For transmission, the antenna radiates electromagnetic energy into the medium (usually air), and for reception, the antenna picks up electromagnetic waves

---

[5]Note the use of a log scale. A basic review of log scales is in the math refresher document at the Computer Science Student Resource Site at WilliamStallings.com/Student.Support.html.

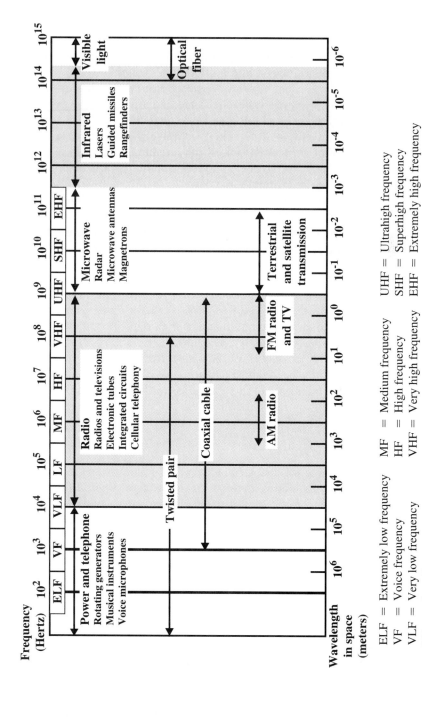

Figure 2.10 Electromagnetic Spectrum for Telecommunications

ELF = Extremely low frequency   MF = Medium frequency   UHF = Ultrahigh frequency
VF = Voice frequency   HF = High frequency   SHF = Superhigh frequency
VLF = Very low frequency   VHF = Very high frequency   EHF = Extremely high frequency
LF = Low frequency

29

from the surrounding medium. There are basically two types of configurations for wireless transmission: directional and omnidirectional. For the directional configuration, the transmitting antenna puts out a focused electromagnetic beam; the transmitting and receiving antennas must therefore be carefully aligned. In the omnidirectional case, the transmitted signal spreads out in all directions and can be received by many antennas. In general, the higher the frequency of a signal, the more it is possible to focus it into a directional beam.

Three general ranges of frequencies are of interest in our discussion of wireless transmission. Frequencies in the range of about 1 GHz (gigahertz = 10^9 Hz) to 40 GHz are referred to as **microwave frequencies**. At these frequencies, highly directional beams are possible, and microwave is quite suitable for point-to-point transmission. Microwave is also used for satellite communications. Frequencies in the range 30 MHz to 1 GHz are suitable for omnidirectional applications. We refer to this range as the radio range.

Another important frequency range, for local applications, is the infrared portion of the spectrum. This covers, roughly, from 3×10^{11} to 2×10^{14} Hz. Infrared is useful in local point-to-point and multipoint applications within confined areas, such as a single room.

Terrestrial Microwave

Physical Description

The most common type of microwave antenna is the parabolic "dish." A typical size is about 3 m in diameter. The antenna is fixed rigidly and focuses a narrow beam to achieve line-of-sight transmission to the receiving antenna. Microwave antennas are usually located at substantial heights above ground level to extend the range between antennas and to be able to transmit over intervening obstacles. To achieve long-distance transmission, a series of microwave relay towers is used, and point-to-point microwave links are strung together over the desired distance.

Applications

A primary use for terrestrial microwave systems is in long-haul telecommunications service, as an alternative to coaxial cable or optical fiber. The microwave facility requires far fewer amplifiers or repeaters than coaxial cable over the same distance but requires line-of-sight transmission. Microwave is commonly used for both voice and television transmission.

Another increasingly common use of microwave is for short point-to-point links between buildings. This can be used for closed-circuit TV or as a data link between local area networks. Short-haul microwave can also be used for the so-called bypass application. A business can establish a microwave link to a long-distance telecommunications facility in the same city, bypassing the local telephone company.

Two other important uses of microwave are examined in some detail in Part Three: cellular systems and fixed wireless access.

Transmission Characteristics

Microwave transmission covers a substantial portion of the electromagnetic spectrum. Common frequencies used for transmission are in the range 2 to 40 GHz.

Table 2.2 Typical Digital Microwave Performance

Band (GHz)	Bandwidth (MHz)	Data Rate (Mbps)
2	7	12
6	30	90
11	40	135
18	220	274

The higher the frequency used, the higher the potential bandwidth and therefore the higher the potential data rate. Table 2.2 indicates bandwidth and data rate for some typical systems.

As with any transmission system, a main source of loss is attenuation. For microwave (and radio frequencies), the loss can be expressed as

$$L = 10 \log\left(\frac{4\pi d}{\lambda}\right)^2 \text{dB} \tag{2.1}$$

where d is the distance and λ is the wavelength, in the same units. Thus, loss varies as the square of the distance. In contrast, for twisted pair and coaxial cable, loss varies logarithmically with distance (linear in decibels). Thus repeaters or amplifiers may be placed farther apart for microwave systems—10 to 100 km is typical. Attenuation is increased with rainfall. The effects of rainfall become especially noticeable above 10 GHz. Another source of impairment is interference. With the growing popularity of microwave, transmission areas overlap and interference is always a danger. Thus the assignment of frequency bands is strictly regulated.

The most common bands for long-haul telecommunications are the 4 GHz to 6 GHz bands. With increasing congestion at these frequencies, the 11 GHz band is now coming into use. The 12 GHz band is used as a component of cable TV systems. Microwave links are used to provide TV signals to local cable TV (CATV) installations; the signals are then distributed to individual subscribers via coaxial cable. Higher-frequency microwave is being used for short point-to-point links between buildings; typically, the 22 GHz band is used. The higher microwave frequencies are less useful for longer distances because of increased attenuation but are quite adequate for shorter distances. In addition, at the higher frequencies, the antennas are smaller and cheaper.

Satellite Microwave

Physical Description

A communication satellite is, in effect, a microwave relay station. It is used to link two or more ground-based microwave transmitter/receivers, known as earth stations, or ground stations. The satellite receives transmissions on one frequency band (uplink), amplifies or repeats the signal, and transmits it on another frequency (downlink). A single orbiting satellite will operate on a number of frequency bands, called *transponder channels*, or simply *transponders*.

Applications

The communication satellite is a technological revolution as important as fiber optics. Among the most important applications for satellites are the following are the following:

- Television distribution
- Long-distance telephone transmission
- Private business networks

Because of their broadcast nature, satellites are well suited to television distribution and are being used extensively in the United States and throughout the world for this purpose. In its traditional use, a network provides programming from a central location. Programs are transmitted to the satellite and then broadcast down to a number of stations, which then distribute the programs to individual viewers. One network, the Public Broadcasting Service (PBS), distributes its television programming almost exclusively by the use of satellite channels. Other commercial networks also make substantial use of satellite, and cable television systems are receiving an ever-increasing proportion of their programming from satellites. The most recent application of satellite technology to television distribution is direct broadcast satellite (DBS), in which satellite video signals are transmitted directly to the home user. The dropping cost and size of receiving antennas have made DBS economically feasible, and a number of channels are either already in service or in the planning stage.

Satellite transmission is also used for point-to-point trunks between telephone exchange offices in public telephone networks. It is the optimum medium for high-usage international trunks and is competitive with terrestrial systems for many long-distance intranational links.

Finally, there are a number of business data applications for satellite. The satellite provider can divide the total capacity into a number of channels and lease these channels to individual business users. A user equipped with antennas at a number of sites can use a satellite channel for a private network. Traditionally, such applications have been quite expensive and limited to larger organizations with high-volume requirements.

Transmission Characteristics

The optimum frequency range for satellite transmission is in the range 1 to 10 GHz. Below 1 GHz, there is significant noise from natural sources, including galactic, solar, and atmospheric noise, and human-made interference from various electronic devices. Above 10 GHz, the signal is severely attenuated by atmospheric absorption and precipitation.

Most satellites providing point-to-point service today use a frequency bandwidth in the range 5.925 to 6.425 GHz for transmission from earth to satellite (uplink) and a bandwidth in the range 3.7 to 4.2 GHz for transmission from satellite to earth (downlink). This combination is referred to as the 4/6 GHz band. Note that the uplink and downlink frequencies differ. For continuous operation without interference, a satellite cannot transmit and receive on the same frequency. Thus signals received from a ground station on one frequency must be transmitted back on another.

The 4/6 GHz band is within the optimum zone of 1 to 10 GHz but has become saturated. Other frequencies in that range are unavailable because of sources of interference operating at those frequencies, usually terrestrial microwave. Therefore, the 12/14 GHz band has been developed (uplink: 14 to 14.5 GHz; downlink: 11.7 to 14.2 GHz). At this frequency band, attenuation problems must be overcome. However, smaller and cheaper earth-station receivers can be used. It is anticipated that this band will also saturate, and use is projected for the 19/29 GHz band (uplink: 27.5 to 31.0 GHz; downlink: 17.7 to 21.2 GHz). This band experiences even greater attenuation problems but will allow greater bandwidth (2500 MHz versus 500 MHz) and even smaller and cheaper receivers.

Several properties of satellite communication should be noted. First, because of the long distances involved, there is a propagation delay of about a quarter second from transmission from one earth station to reception by another earth station. This delay is noticeable in ordinary telephone conversations. It also introduces problems in the areas of error control and flow control, which we discuss in later chapters. Second, satellite microwave is inherently a broadcast facility. Many stations can transmit to the satellite, and a transmission from a satellite can be received by many stations.

Broadcast Radio

Physical Description

The principal difference between broadcast radio and microwave is that the former is omnidirectional and the latter is directional. Thus broadcast radio does not require dish-shaped antennas, and the antennas need not be rigidly mounted to a precise alignment.

Applications

Radio is a general term used to encompass frequencies in the range of 3 kHz to 300 GHz. We are using the informal term *broadcast radio* to cover the VHF and part of the UHF band: 30 MHz to 1 GHz. This range covers FM radio and UHF and VHF television. This range is also used for a number of data networking applications.

Transmission Characteristics

The range 30 MHz to 1 GHz is an effective one for broadcast communications. Unlike the case for lower-frequency electromagnetic waves, the ionosphere is transparent to radio waves above 30 MHz. Thus transmission is limited to the line of sight, and distant transmitters will not interfere with each other due to reflection from the atmosphere. Unlike the higher frequencies of the microwave region, broadcast radio waves are less sensitive to attenuation from rainfall.

As with microwave, the amount of attenuation due to distance for radio obeys Equation (2.1), namely $10 \log \left(\dfrac{4\pi d}{\lambda} \right)^2$. Because of the longer wavelength, radio waves suffer relatively less attenuation.

A prime source of impairment for broadcast radio waves is multipath interference. Reflection from land, water, and natural or human-made objects can create multiple paths between antennas. This effect is frequently evident when TV reception displays multiple images as an airplane passes by.

Infrared

Infrared communications is achieved using transmitters/receivers (transceivers) that modulate noncoherent infrared light. Transceivers must be within the line of sight of each other either directly or via reflection from a light-colored surface such as the ceiling of a room.

One important difference between infrared and microwave transmission is that the former does not penetrate walls. Thus the security and interference problems encountered in microwave systems are not present. Furthermore, there is no frequency allocation issue with infrared, because no licensing is required.

2.5 MULTIPLEXING

In both local and wide area communications, it is almost always the case that the capacity of the transmission medium exceeds the capacity required for the transmission of a single signal. To make efficient use of the transmission system, it is desirable to carry multiple signals on a single medium. This is referred to as *multiplexing*.

Figure 2.11 depicts the multiplexing function in its simplest form. There are *n* inputs to a multiplexer. The multiplexer is connected by a single data link to a demultiplexer. The link is able to carry *n* separate channels of data. The multiplexer combines (multiplexes) data from the *n* input lines and transmits over a higher-capacity data link. The demultiplexer accepts the multiplexed data stream, separates (demultiplexes) the data according to channel, and delivers them to the appropriate output lines.

The widespread use of multiplexing in data communications can be explained by the following:

1. The higher the data rate, the more cost effective the transmission facility. That is, for a given application and over a given distance, the cost per kbps declines with an increase in the data rate of the transmission facility. Similarly,

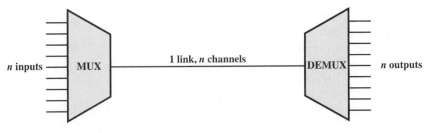

Figure 2.11 Multiplexing

the cost of transmission and receiving equipment, per kbps, declines with increasing data rate.

2. Most individual data communicating devices require relatively modest data rate support. For example, for most client/server applications, a data rate of up to 64 kbps is generally more than adequate.

The preceding statements were phrased in terms of data communicating devices. Similar statements apply to voice communications. That is, the greater the capacity of a transmission facility, in terms of voice channels, the less the cost per individual voice channel, and the capacity required for a single voice channel is modest.

Two techniques for multiplexing in telecommunications networks are in common use: **frequency division multiplexing (FDM)** and **time division multiplexing (TDM)**.

FDM takes advantage of the fact that the useful bandwidth of the medium exceeds the required bandwidth of a given signal. A number of signals can be carried simultaneously if each signal is modulated onto a different carrier frequency and the carrier frequencies are sufficiently separated so that the bandwidths of the signals do not overlap. Figure 2.12.a depicts a simple case. Six signal sources are fed into a multiplexer that modulates each signal onto a different frequency (f_1, ..., f_6). Each signal requires a certain bandwidth centered around its carrier frequency, referred to as a **channel**. To prevent interference, the channels are separated by **guard bands**, which are unused portions of the spectrum (not shown in the figure).

An example is the multiplexing of voice signals. We mentioned that the useful spectrum for voice is 300 to 3400 Hz. Thus, a bandwidth of 4 kHz is adequate to carry the voice signal and provide a guard band. For both North America (Bell System standard) and internationally (International Telecommunication Union Telecommunication Standardization Sector [ITU-T] standard), a standard voice multiplexing scheme is twelve 4-kHz voice channels from 60 to 108 kHz. For higher-capacity links, both Bell and ITU-T define larger groupings of 4-kHz channels.

TDM takes advantage of the fact that the achievable bit rate (sometimes, unfortunately, called bandwidth) of the medium exceeds the required data rate of a digital signal. Multiple digital signals can be carried on a single transmission path by interleaving portions of each signal in time. The interleaving can be at the bit level or in blocks of bytes or larger quantities. For example, the multiplexer in Figure 2.12b has six inputs that might each be, say, 9.6 kbps. A single line with a capacity of 57.6 kbps could accommodate all six sources. Analogously to FDM, the sequence of time slots dedicated to a particular source is called a channel. One cycle of time slots (one per source) is called a frame.

The TDM scheme depicted in Figure 2.12b is also known as synchronous TDM, referring to the fact that time slots are preassigned and fixed. Hence the timing of transmission from the various sources is synchronized. In contrast, asynchronous TDM allows time on the medium to be allocated dynamically. Unless otherwise noted, the term *TDM* will be used to mean synchronous TDM.

A generic depiction of a synchronous TDM system is provided in Figure 2.13. A number of signals [$m_i(t)$, $i = 1, n$] are to be multiplexed onto the same transmission medium. The signals carry digital data and are generally digital signals. The incoming data from each source are briefly buffered. Each buffer is typically one bit

(a) Frequency division multiplexing

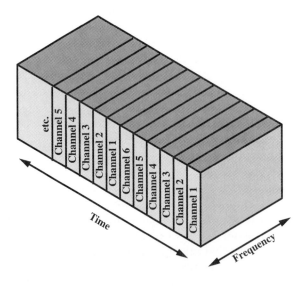

(b) Time division multiplexing

Figure 2.12   FDM and TDM

or one character in length. The buffers are scanned sequentially to form a composite digital data stream $m_c(t)$. The scan operation is sufficiently rapid so that each buffer is emptied before more data can arrive. Thus, the data rate of $m_c(t)$ must at least equal the sum of the data rates of the $m_i(t)$. The digital signal $m_c(t)$ may be transmitted directly, or passed through a modem so that an analog signal is transmitted. In either case, transmission is typically synchronous.

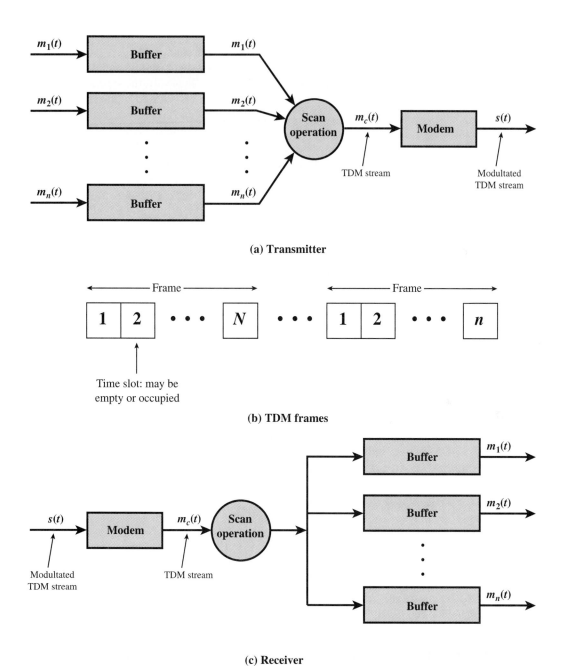

(a) Transmitter

(b) TDM frames

(c) Receiver

Figure 2.13 Synchronous TDM System

The transmitted data may have a format something like Figure 2.13b. The data are organized into frames. Each frame contains a cycle of time slots. In each frame, one or more slots is dedicated to each data source. The sequence of slots dedicated to one source, from frame to frame, is called a channel. The slot length equals the transmitter buffer length, typically a bit or a byte (character).

The byte-interleaving technique is used with asynchronous and synchronous sources. Each time slot contains one character of data. Typically, the start and stop bits of each character are eliminated before transmission and reinserted by the receiver, thus improving efficiency. The bit-interleaving technique is used with synchronous sources and may also be used with asynchronous sources. Each time slot contains just one bit.

At the receiver, the interleaved data are demultiplexed and routed to the appropriate destination buffer. For each input source $m_i(t)$, there is an identical output source that will receive the input data at the same rate at which it was generated.

Synchronous TDM is called synchronous not because synchronous transmission is used, but because the time slots are preassigned to sources and fixed. The time slots for each source are transmitted whether or not the source has data to send. This is, of course, also the case with FDM. In both cases, capacity is wasted to achieve simplicity of implementation. Even when fixed assignment is used, however, it is possible for a synchronous TDM device to handle sources of different data rates. For example, the slowest input device could be assigned one slot per cycle, while faster devices are assigned multiple slots per cycle.

One example of TDM is the standard scheme used for transmitting PCM voice data, known in AT&T parlance as T1 carrier. Data are taken from each source, one sample (7 bits) at a time. An eighth bit is added for signaling and supervisory functions. For T1, 24 sources are multiplexed, so there are $8 \times 24 = 192$ bits of data and control signals per frame. One final bit is added for establishing and maintaining synchronization. Thus a frame consists of 193 bits and contains one 7-bit sample per source. Since sources must be sampled 8000 times per second, the required data rate is $8000 \times 193 = 1.544$ Mbps. As with voice FDM, higher data rates are defined for larger groupings.

TDM is not limited to digital signals. Analog signals can also be interleaved in time. Also, with analog signals, a combination of TDM and FDM is possible. A transmission system can be frequency divided into a number of channels, each of which is further divided via TDM.

2.6 RECOMMENDED READING

[STAL00] covers all of the topics in this chapter in greater detail. [FREE99] is also a readable and rigorous treatment of the topics of this chapter. A thorough treatment of both analog and digital communication is provided in [COUC01].

COUC01 Couch, L. *Digital and Analog Communication Systems.* Upper Saddle River, NJ: Prentice Hall, 2001.

FREE99 Freeman, R. *Fundamentals of Telecommunications.* New York: Wiley, 1999.

STAL00 Stallings, W. *Data and Computer Communications, 6th ed.* Upper Saddle River: NJ: Prentice Hall, 2000.

2.7 KEY TERMS, REVIEW QUESTIONS, AND PROBLEMS

Key Terms

analog data	frequency division	phase
analog signal	multiplexing (FDM)	radio
analog transmission	frequency domain	satellite microwave
aperiodic	fundamental frequency	spectrum
bandwidth	guided media	synchronous TDM
broadcast radio	infrared	terrestrial microwave
channel capacity	microwave	time division multiplexing (TDM)
decibel (dB)	multiplexing	time domain
digital data	noise	transmission media
digital signal	peak amplitude	unguided media
digital transmission	period	wavelength
frequency	periodic	wireless

Review Questions

1 Differentiate between an analog and a digital electromagnetic signal.
2 What are three important characteristics of a periodic signal?
3 How many radians are there in a complete circle of 360 degrees?
4 What is the relationship between the wavelength and frequency of a sine wave?
5 What is the relationship between a signal's spectrum and its bandwidth?
6 What is attenuation?
7 Define channel capacity.
8 What key factors affect channel capacity?
9 Differentiate between guided media and unguided media.
10 What are some major advantages and disadvantages of microwave transmission?
11 What is direct broadcast satellite (DBS)?
12 Why must a satellite have distinct uplink and downlink frequencies?
13 Indicate some significant differences between broadcast radio and microwave.
14 Why is multiplexing so cost-effective?
15 How is interference avoided by using frequency division multiplexing?
16 Explain how synchronous time division multiplexing (TDM) works.

Problems

1 A signal has a fundamental frequency of 1000 Hz. What is its period?
2 Express the following in the simplest form you can:
   a. $\sin(2\pi ft - \pi) + \sin(2\pi ft + \pi)$
   b. $\sin 2\pi ft + \sin(2\pi ft - \pi)$
3 Sound may be modeled as sinusoidal functions. Compare the wavelength and relative frequency of musical notes. Use 330 m/s as the speed of sound and the following frequencies for the musical scale.

Note	C	D	E	F	G	A	B	C
Frequency	264	297	330	352	396	440	495	528

4 If the solid curve in Figure 2.14 represents $\sin(2\pi t)$, what does the dotted curve represent? That is, the dotted curve can be written in the form $A \sin(2\pi ft + \phi)$; what are A, f, and ϕ?

5 Decompose the signal $(1 + 0.1 \cos 5t) \cos 100t$ into a linear combination of sinusoidal function, and find the amplitude, frequency, and phase of each component. *Hint:* Use the identity for $\cos a \cos b$.

6 Figure 2.5 shows the effect of eliminating higher-harmonic components of a square wave and retaining only a few lower-harmonic components. What would the signal look like in the opposite case; that is, retaining all higher harmonics and eliminating a few lower harmonics?

7 What is the channel capacity for a teleprinter channel with a 300-Hz bandwidth and a signal-to-noise ratio of 3 dB?

8 A digital signaling system is required to operate at 9600 bps.
   a. If a signal element encodes a 4-bit word, what is the minimum required bandwidth of the channel?
   b. Repeat part (a) for the case of 8-bit words.

9 Study the works of Shannon and Nyquist on channel capacity. Each places an upper limit on the bit rate of a channel based on two different approaches. How are the two related?

10 Given a channel with an intended capacity of 20 Mbps, the bandwidth of the channel is 3 MHz. What signal-to-noise ratio is required to achieve this capacity?

11 Show that doubling the transmission frequency or doubling the distance between transmitting antenna and receiving antenna attenuates the power received by 6 dB.

12 Fill in the missing elements in the following table of approximate power ratios for various dB levels.

Decibels	1	2	3	4	5	6	7	8	9	10
Losses			0.5							0.1
Gains			2							10

13 If an amplifier has a 30-dB voltage gain, what voltage ratio does the gain represent?
14 An amplifier has an output of 20 W. What is its output in dBW?

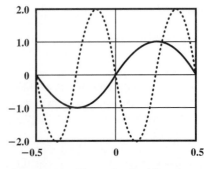

Figure 2.14 Figure for Problem 4

APPENDIX 2A DECIBELS AND SIGNAL STRENGTH

An important parameter in any transmission system is the signal strength. As a signal propagates along a transmission medium, there will be a loss, or *attenuation*, of signal strength. To compensate, amplifiers may be inserted at various points to impart a gain in signal strength.

It is customary to express gains, losses, and relative levels in decibels because

- Signal strength often falls off logarithmically, so loss is easily expressed in terms of the decibel, which is a logarithmic unit.
- The net gain or loss in a cascaded transmission path can be calculated with simple addition and subtraction.

The decibel is a measure of the ratio between two signal levels. The decibel gain is given by

$$G_{dB} = 10 \log_{10} \frac{P_{out}}{P_{in}}$$

where

$$
\begin{aligned}
G_{dB} &= \text{gain, in decibels} \\
P_{in} &= \text{input power level} \\
P_{out} &= \text{output power level} \\
\log_{10} &= \text{logarithm to the base 10 (from now on,} \\
&\quad \text{we will simply use log to mean } \log_{10})
\end{aligned}
$$

Table 2.3 shows the relationship between decibel values and powers of 10.

There is some inconsistency in the literature over the use of the terms *gain* and *loss*. If the value of G_{dB} is positive, this represents an actual gain in power. For example, a gain of 3 dB means that the power has doubled. If the value of G_{dB} is negative, this represents an actual loss in power. For example, a gain of -3 dB means that the power has halved, and this is a loss of power. Normally, this is expressed by saying there is a loss of 3 dB. However, some of the literature would

Table 2.3 Decibel Values

Power Ratio	dB	Power Ratio	dB
10^1	10	10^{-1}	-10
10^2	20	10^{-2}	-20
10^3	30	10^{-3}	-30
10^4	40	10^{-4}	-40
10^5	50	10^{-5}	-50
10^6	60	10^{-6}	-60

say that this is a loss of -3 dB. It makes more sense to say that a negative gain corresponds to a positive loss. Therefore, we define a decibel loss as

$$L_{dB} = -10 \log_{10} \frac{P_{out}}{P_{in}} = 10 \log_{10} \frac{P_{in}}{P_{out}} \qquad (2.2)$$

> **Example.** If a signal with a power level of 10 mW is inserted onto a transmission line and the measured power some distance away is 5 mW, the loss can be expressed as
>
> $$L_{dB} = 10 \log(10/5) = 10(0.3) = 3 \text{ dB}.$$

Note that the decibel is a measure of relative, not absolute, difference. A loss from 1000 mW to 500 mW is also a loss of 3 dB.

The decibel is also used to measure the difference in voltage, taking into account that power is proportional to the square of the voltage:

$$P = \frac{V^2}{R}$$

where

P = power dissipated across resistance R
V = voltage across resistance R

Thus

$$L_{dB} = 10 \log \frac{P_{in}}{P_{out}} = 10 \log \frac{V_{in}^2/R}{V_{out}^2/R} = 20 \log \frac{V_{in}}{V_{out}}$$

> **Example.** Decibels are useful in determining the gain or loss over a series of transmission elements. Consider a series in which the input is at a power level of 4 mW, the first element is a transmission line with a 12-dB loss (-12-dB gain), the second element is an amplifier with a 35-dB gain, and the third element is a transmission line with a 10-dB loss. The net gain is $(-12 + 35 - 10) = 13$ dB. To calculate the output power P_{out},
>
> $$G_{db} = 13 = 10 \log(P_{out}/4 \text{ mW})$$
> $$P_{out} = 4 \times 10^{1.3} \text{ mW} = 79.8 \text{ mW}$$

Decibel values refer to relative magnitudes or changes in magnitude, not to an absolute level. It is convenient to be able to refer to an absolute level of power or voltage in decibels so that gains and losses with reference to an initial signal level may be calculated easily. The **dBW (decibel-Watt)** is used extensively in microwave applications. The value of 1 W is selected as a reference and defined to be 0 dBW. The absolute decibel level of power in dBW is defined as

$$\text{Power}_{dBW} = 10 \log \frac{\text{Power}_W}{1 \text{ W}}$$

Example. A power of 1000 W is 30 dBW, and a power of 1 mW is −30 dBW.

Another common unit is the **dBm (decibel-milliWatt)**, which uses 1 mW as the reference. Thus 0 dBm = 1 mW. The formula is

$$\text{Power}_{dBm} = 10 \log \frac{\text{Power}_{mW}}{1mW}$$

Note the following relationships:

$$+30 \text{ dBm } = 0 \text{ dBW}$$
$$0 \text{ dBm } = -30 \text{ dBW}$$

CHAPTER 3

COMMUNICATION NETWORKS

T his chapter provides an overview of various approaches to communication networking. The chapter begins with a survey of different type of networks based on geographic extent. Then circuit switching, packet switching, and ATM (asynchronous transfer mode) networks are examined.

3.1 LANs, MANs, AND WANs

Local area networks (LANs), metropolitan area networks (MANs), and wide area networks (WANs) are all examples of communications networks. Figure 3.1 illustrates these categories, plus some special cases. By way of contrast, the typical range of parameters for a multiple-processor computer is also depicted.

Wide Area Networks

WANs cover a large geographical area, may require the crossing of public right-of-ways, and may rely at least in part on circuits provided by a common carrier. Typically, a WAN consists of a number of interconnected switching nodes. A transmission from any one device is routed through these internal nodes to the specified destination device.

Traditionally, WANs have provided only relatively modest capacity to subscribers. For data attachment, either to a data network or to a telephone network

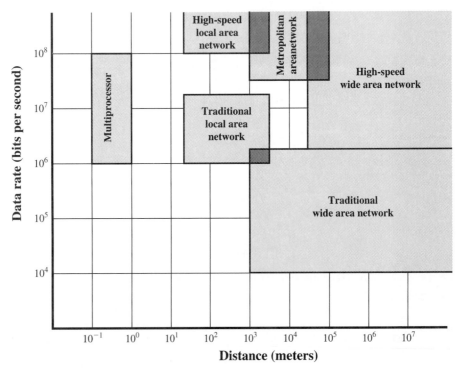

Figure 3.1 Comparison of Multiprocessor Systems, LANs, MANs, and WANs

by means of a modem, data rates of 64,000 bps or less have been common. Business subscribers have been able to obtain higher rates, with a service known as T1, which operates at 1.544 Mbps, being common.

The continuing development of practical optical fiber facilities has led to the standardization of much higher data rates for WANs, and these services are becoming more widely available. These high-speed WANs provide user connections in the 10s and 100s of Mbps, using a transmission techniques known asynchronous transfer mode (ATM).

Local Area Networks

As with WANs, a LAN is a communications network that interconnects a variety of devices and provides a means for information exchange among those devices. There are several key distinctions between LANs and WANs:

1. The scope of the LAN is small, typically a single building or a cluster of buildings. This difference in geographic scope leads to different technical solutions, as we shall see.

2. It is usually the case that the LAN is owned by the same organization that owns the attached devices. For WANs, this is less often the case, or at least a significant fraction of the network assets are not owned. This has two implications. First, care must be taken in the choice of LAN, since there may be a substantial capital investment (compared with dial-up or leased charges for WANs) for both purchase and maintenance. Second, the network management responsibility for a LAN falls solely on the user.

3. The internal data rates of LANs are typically much greater than those of WANs.

A simple example of a LAN that highlights some of its characteristics is shown in Figure 3.2. All of the devices are attached to a shared transmission medium. A transmission from any one device can be received by all other devices attached to the same network.

Traditional LANs have provided data rates in a range from about 1 to 20 Mbps. These data rates, though substantial, have become increasingly inadequate with the proliferation of devices, the growth in multimedia applications, and the increased use of the client/server architecture. As a result, much of the effort in

Figure 3.2   A Simple Local Area Network

LAN development has been in the development of high-speed LANs, with data rates of 100 Mbps to 10 Gbps.

Metropolitan Area Networks

As the name suggests, a MAN occupies a middle ground between LANs and WANs. Interest in MANs has come about as a result of a recognition that the traditional point-to-point and switched network techniques used in WANs may be inadequate for the growing needs of organizations. While ATM promises to meet a wide range of high-speed needs, there is a requirement now for both private and public networks that provide high capacity at low costs over a large area. The high-speed shared-medium approach of the LAN standards provides a number of benefits that can be realized on a metropolitan scale. As Figure 3.1 indicates, MANs cover greater distances at higher data rates than LANs, although there is some overlap in geographical coverage.

The primary market for MANs is the customer that has high-capacity needs in a metropolitan area. A MAN is intended to provide the required capacity at lower cost and greater efficiency than obtaining an equivalent service from the local telephone company.

3.2 SWITCHING TECHNIQUES

For transmission of data beyond a local area, communication is typically achieved by transmitting data from source to destination through a network of intermediate switching nodes; this switched network design is sometimes used to implement LANs and MANs as well. The switching nodes are not concerned with the content of the data; rather their purpose is to provide a switching facility that will move the data from node to node until they reach their destination. The end devices that wish to communicate may be referred to as stations. The stations may be computers, terminals, telephones, or other communicating devices. We will refer to the switching devices whose purpose is to provide communication as *nodes*. The nodes are connected to each other in some topology by transmission links. Each station attaches to a node, and the collection of nodes is referred to as a *communications network*.

Figure 3.3 illustrates a simple network. Signals entering the network from a station are routed to the destination by being switched from node to node. For example, information from station A intended for station F is sent to node 4. It may then be routed via nodes 5 and 6 or nodes 7 and 6 to the destination. Several observations are in order:

1. Some nodes connect only to other nodes (e.g., 5 and 7). Their sole task is the internal (to the network) switching of information. Other nodes have one or more stations attached as well; in addition to their switching functions, such nodes accept information from and deliver information to the attached stations.
2. Node-station links are generally dedicated point-to-point links. Node-node links are usually multiplexed links, using either frequency division multiplexing (FDM) or some form of time division multiplexing (TDM).

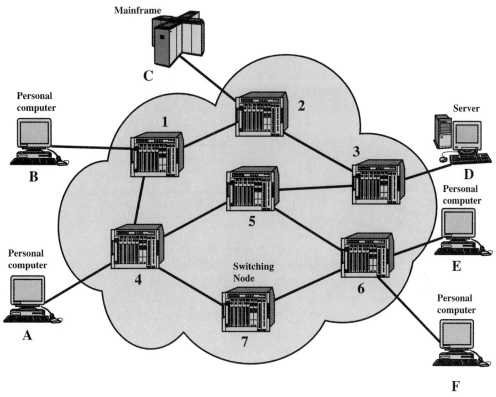

Figure 3.3 Simple Switching Network

3. Usually, the network is not fully connected; that is, there is not a direct link between every possible pair of nodes. However, it is always desirable to have more than one possible path through the network for each pair of stations. This enhances the reliability of the network.

Two quite different technologies are used in wide area switched networks: circuit switching and packet switching. These two technologies differ in the way the nodes switch information from one link to another on the way from source to destination. In the remainder of this chapter, we look at the details of both of these technologies and then look at an important special case of packet switching known as cell relay, or ATM.

3.3 CIRCUIT SWITCHING

Circuit switching is the dominant technology for both voice and data communications today and will remain so for the foreseeable future. Communication via circuit switching implies that there is a dedicated communication path between two stations. That path is a connected sequence of links between network nodes. On each physical link, a channel is dedicated to the connection. The most common example of circuit switching is the telephone network.

Communication via circuit switching involves three phases, which can be explained with reference to Figure 3.3.

1. **Circuit establishment.** Before any signals can be transmitted, an end-to-end (station-to-station) circuit must be established. For example, station A sends a request to node 4 requesting a connection to station E. Typically, the link from A to 4 is a dedicated line, so that part of the connection already exists. Node 4 must find the next leg in a route leading to node 6. Based on routing information and measures of availability and perhaps cost, node 4 selects the link to node 5, allocates a free channel (using frequency division multiplexing, FDM, or time division multiplexing, TDM) on that link and sends a message requesting connection to E. So far, a dedicated path has been established from A through 4 to 5. Because a number of stations may attach to 4, it must be able to establish internal paths from multiple stations to multiple nodes. How this is done is discussed later in this section. The remainder of the process proceeds similarly. Node 5 dedicates a channel to node 6 and internally ties that channel to the channel from node 4. Node 6 completes the connection to E. In completing the connection, a test is made to determine if E is busy or is prepared to accept the connection.

2. **Information transfer.** Information can now be transmitted from A through the network to E. The transmission may be analog voice, digitized voice, or binary data, depending on the nature of the network. As the carriers evolve to fully integrated digital networks, the use of digital (binary) transmission for both voice and data is becoming the dominant method. The path is A-4 link, internal switching through 4, 4-5 channel, internal switching through 5, 5-6 channel, internal switching through 6, 6-E link. Generally, the connection is full duplex, and signals may be transmitted in both directions simultaneously.

3. **Circuit disconnect.** After some period of information transfer, the connection is terminated, usually by the action of one of the two stations. Signals must be propagated to nodes 4, 5, and 6 to deallocate the dedicated resources.

Note that the connection path is established before data transmission begins. Thus, channel capacity must be reserved between each pair of nodes in the path and each node must have available internal switching capacity to handle the requested connection. The switches must have the intelligence to make these allocations and to devise a route through the network.

Circuit switching can be rather inefficient. Channel capacity is dedicated for the duration of a connection, even if no data are being transferred. For a voice connection, utilization may be rather high, but it still does not approach 100%. For a terminal-to-computer connection, the capacity may be idle during most of the time of the connection. In terms of performance, there is a delay prior to signal transfer for call establishment. However, once the circuit is established, the network is effectively transparent to the users. Information is transmitted at a fixed data rate with no delay other than the propagation delay through the transmission links. The delay at each node is negligible.

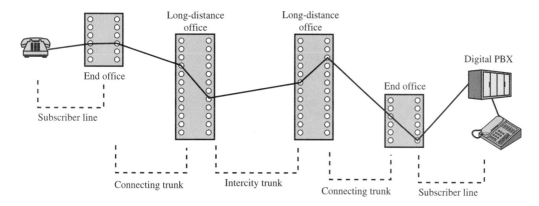

Figure 3.4   Example Connection over a Public Circuit-Switching Network

Circuit switching was developed to handle voice traffic but is now also used for data traffic. The best-known example of a circuit-switching network is the public telephone network (Figure 3.4). This is actually a collection of national networks interconnected to form the international service. Although originally designed and implemented to service analog telephone subscribers, it handles substantial data traffic via modem and is well on its way to being converted to a digital network. Another well-known application of circuit switching is the private branch exchange (PBX), used to interconnect telephones within a building or office. Circuit switching is also used in private networks. Typically, such a network is set up by a corporation or other large organization to interconnect its various sites. Such a network usually consists of PBX systems at each site interconnected by dedicated, leased lines obtained from one of the carriers, such as AT&T. A final common example of the application of circuit switching is the data switch. The data switch is similar to the PBX but is designed to interconnect digital data processing devices, such as terminals and computers.

A public telecommunications network can be described using four generic architectural components:

- **Subscribers:** The devices that attach to the network. It is still the case that most subscriber devices to public telecommunications networks are telephones, but the percentage of data traffic increases year by year.
- **Subscriber line:** The link between the subscriber and the network, also referred to as the local loop. Almost all subscriber line connections use twisted pair wire. The length of a subscriber line is typically in a range from a few kilometers to a few tens of kilometers. The subscriber line is also known as a **subscriber loop**, or a **local loop**.
- **Exchanges:** The switching centers in the network. A switching center that directly supports subscribers is known as an end office. Typically, an end office will support many thousands of subscribers in a localized area. There are over 19,000 end offices in the United States, so it is clearly impractical for each end office to have a direct link to each of the other end offices; this would require on the order of 2×10^8 links. Rather, intermediate switching nodes are used.

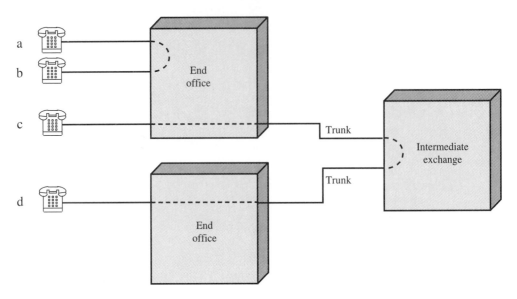

Figure 3.5 Circuit Establishment

- **Trunks:** The branches between exchanges. Trunks carry multiple voice-frequency circuits using either FDM or synchronous TDM. Earlier, these were referred to as carrier systems.

Subscribers connect directly to an end office, which switches traffic between subscribers and between a subscriber and other exchanges. The other exchanges are responsible for routing and switching traffic between end offices. This distinction is shown in Figure 3.5. To connect two subscribers attached to the same end office, a circuit is set up between them in the same fashion as described before. If two subscribers connect to different end offices, a circuit between them consists of a chain of circuits through one or more intermediate offices. In the figure, a connection is established between lines a and b by simply setting up the connection through the end office. The connection between c and d is more complex. In c's end office, a connection is established between line c and one channel on a TDM trunk to the intermediate switch. In the intermediate switch, that channel is connected to a channel on a TDM trunk to d's end office. In that end office, the channel is connected to line d.

Circuit-switching technology has been driven by its use to carry voice traffic. One of the key requirements for voice traffic is that there must be virtually no transmission delay and certainly no variation in delay. A constant signal transmission rate must be maintained, because transmission and reception occur at the same signal rate. These requirements are necessary to allow normal human conversation. Further, the quality of the received signal must be sufficiently high to provide, at a minimum, intelligibility.

Circuit switching achieved its widespread, dominant position because it is well suited to the analog transmission of voice signals. In today's digital world, its inefficiencies are more apparent. However, despite the inefficiency, circuit switching is and will remain an attractive choice for both local area and wide area networking.

One of its key strengths is that it is transparent. Once a circuit is established, it appears like a direct connection to the two attached stations; no special networking logic is needed at the station.

3.4 PACKET SWITCHING

Long-haul circuit-switching telecommunications networks were originally designed to handle voice traffic, and the majority of traffic on these networks continues to be voice. A key characteristic of circuit-switching networks is that resources within the network are dedicated to a particular call. For voice connections, the resulting circuit will enjoy a high percentage of utilization since, most of the time, one party or the other is talking. However, as the circuit-switching network began to be used increasingly for data connections, two shortcomings became apparent:

- In a typical terminal-to-host data connection, much of the time the line is idle. Thus, with data connections, a circuit-switching approach is inefficient.
- In a circuit-switching network, the connection provides for transmission at a constant data rate. Thus each of the two devices that are connected must transmit and receive at the same data rate as the other, which limits the utility of the network in interconnecting a variety of host computers and terminals.

To understand how packet switching addresses these problems, let us briefly summarize packet-switching operation. Data are transmitted in blocks, called packets. A typical upper bound on packet length is 1000 octets (bytes). If a source has a longer message to send, the message is broken up into a series of packets (Figure 3.6). Each packet consists of a portion of the data (or all of the data for a short message) that a station wants to transmit, plus a packet header that contains control information. The control information, at a minimum, includes the information that the network requires in order to be able to route the packet through the network and deliver it to the intended destination. At each node en route, the packet is received, stored briefly, and passed on to the next node.

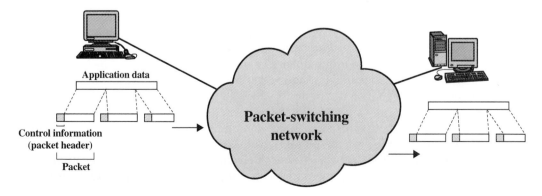

Figure 3.6   The Use of Packets

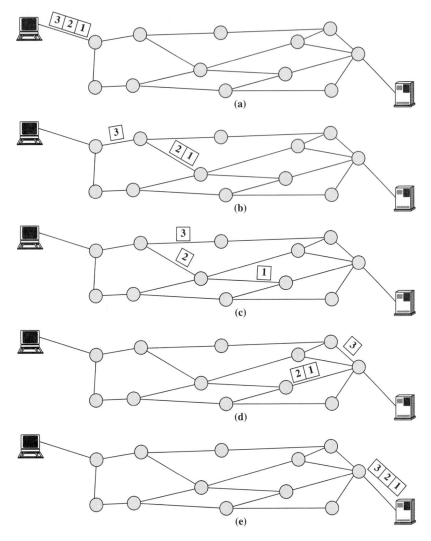

Figure 3.7 Packet Switching: Datagram Approach

Figure 3.7 illustrates the basic operation. A transmitting computer or other device sends a message as a sequence of packets (a). Each packet includes control information indicating the destination station (computer, terminal, etc.). The packets are initially sent to the node to which the sending station attaches. As each packet arrives at this node, it stores the packet briefly, determines the next leg of the route, and queues the packet to go out on that link. Each packet is transmitted to the next node (b) when the link is available. All of the packets eventually work their way through the network and are delivered to the intended destination.

The packet-switching approach has a number of advantages over circuit switching:

- Line efficiency is greater, since a single node-to-node link can be dynamically shared by many packets over time. The packets are queued up and transmitted as rapidly as possible over the link. By contrast, with circuit switching, time on a node-to-node link is preallocated using synchronous time division multiplexing. Much of the time, such a link may be idle because a portion of its time is dedicated to a connection that is idle.

- A packet-switching network can carry out data-rate conversion. Two stations of different data rates can exchange packets, since each connects to its node at its proper data rate.

- When traffic becomes heavy on a circuit-switching network, some calls are blocked; that is, the network refuses to accept additional connection requests until the load on the network decreases. On a packet-switching network, packets are still accepted, but delivery delay increases.

- Priorities can be used. Thus, if a node has a number of packets queued for transmission, it can transmit the higher-priority packets first. These packets will therefore experience less delay than lower-priority packets.

Packet switching also has disadvantages relative to circuit switching:

- Each time a packet passes through a packet-switching node it incurs a delay not present in circuit switching. At a minimum, it incurs a transmission delay equal to the length of the packet in bits divided by the incoming channel rate in bits per second; this is the time it takes to absorb the packet into an internal buffer. In addition, there may be a variable delay due to processing and queuing in the node.

- Because the packets between a given source and destination may vary in length, may take different routes, and may be subject to varying delay in the switches they encounter, the overall packet delay can vary substantially. This phenomenon, called jitter, may not be desirable for some applications (for example, in real-time applications, including telephone voice and real-time video).

- To route packets through the network, overhead information, including the address of the destination, and often sequencing information must be added to each packet, which reduces the communication capacity available for carrying user data. This is not needed in circuit switching once the circuit is set up.

- More processing is involved in the transfer of information using packet switching than in circuit switching at each node. In the case of circuit switching, there is virtually no processing at each switch once the circuit is set up.

Basic Operation

A station has a message to send through a packet-switching network that is of greater length than the maximum packet size. It therefore breaks the message into packets and sends these packets, one at a time, to the network. A question arises as to how the network will handle this stream of packets as it attempts to route them through the network and deliver them to the intended destination. Two approaches are used in contemporary networks: datagram and virtual circuit.

In the **datagram** approach, each packet is treated independently, with no reference to packets that have gone before. This approach is illustrated in Figure 3.7. Each node chooses the next node on a packet's path, taking into account information received from neighboring nodes on traffic, line failures, and so on. So the packets, each with the same destination address, do not all follow the same route (c), and

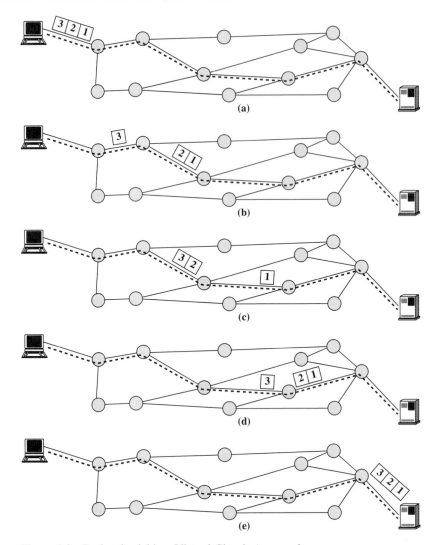

Figure 3.8 Packet Swtiching: Virtual Circuit Approach

they may arrive out of sequence at the exit point. In this example, the exit node restores the packets to their original order before delivering them to the destination. In some datagram networks, it is up to the destination rather than the exit node to do the reordering. Also, it is possible for a packet to be destroyed in the network. For example, if a packet-switching node crashes momentarily, all of its queued packets may be lost. Again, it is up to either the exit node or the destination to detect the loss of a packet and decide how to recover it. In this technique, each packet, treated independently, is referred to as a datagram.

In the **virtual circuit** approach, a preplanned route is established before any packets are sent. Once the route is established, all the packets between a pair of communicating parties follow this same route through the network. This is illustrated in Figure 3.8. Because the route is fixed for the duration of the logical connection, it is somewhat similar to a circuit in a circuit-switching network and is referred to as a virtual circuit. Each packet contains a virtual circuit identifier as well as data. Each node on the preestablished route knows where to direct such packets; no routing decisions are required. At any time, each station can have more than one virtual circuit to any other station and can have virtual circuits to more than one station.

So the main characteristic of the virtual circuit technique is that a route between stations is set up prior to data transfer. Note that this does not mean that this is a dedicated path, as in circuit switching. A packet is still buffered at each node and queued for output over a line. The difference from the datagram approach is that, with virtual circuits, the node need not make a routing decision for each packet. It is made only once for all packets using that virtual circuit.

If two stations wish to exchange data over an extended period of time, there are certain advantages to virtual circuits. First, the network may provide services related to the virtual circuit, including sequencing and error control. Sequencing refers to the fact that, because all packets follow the same route, they arrive in the original order. Error control is a service that assures not only that packets arrive in proper sequence, but that all packets arrive correctly. For example, if a packet in a sequence from node 4 to node 6 fails to arrive at node 6, or arrives with an error, node 6 can request a retransmission of that packet from node 4 (Figure 3.3). Another advantage is that packets should transit the network more rapidly with a virtual circuit; it is not necessary to make a routing decision for each packet at each node.

One advantage of the datagram approach is that the call setup phase is avoided. Thus, if a station wishes to send only one or a few packets, datagram delivery will be quicker. Another advantage of the datagram service is that, because it is more primitive, it is more flexible. For example, if congestion develops in one part of the network, incoming datagrams can be routed away from the congestion. With the use of virtual circuits, packets follow a predefined route, and thus it is more difficult for the network to adapt to congestion. A third advantage is that datagram delivery is inherently more reliable. With the use of virtual circuits, if a node fails, all virtual circuits that pass through that node are lost. With datagram delivery, if a node fails, subsequent packets may find an alternate route that bypasses that node.

Packet Size

There is a significant relationship between packet size and transmission time, as shown in Figure 3.9. In this example, it is assumed that there is a virtual circuit from station A through nodes 4 and 1 to station B (Figure 3.3). The message to be sent comprises 40 octets, and each packet contains 3 octets of control information, which is placed at the beginning of each packet and is referred to as a header. If the entire message is sent as a single packet of 43 octets (3 octets of header plus 40 octets of data), then the packet is first transmitted from station A to node 4 (Figure 3.9a). When the entire packet is received, it can then be transmitted from 4 to 1. When the entire packet is received at node 1, it is then transferred to station B. Ignoring switching time, total transmission time is 129 octet-times (43 octets $\times$ 3 packet transmissions).

Suppose now that we break the message up into two packets, each containing 20 octets of the message and, of course, 3 octets each of header, or control information. In this case, node a can begin transmitting the first packet as soon as it has arrived from A, without waiting for the second packet. Because of this overlap in

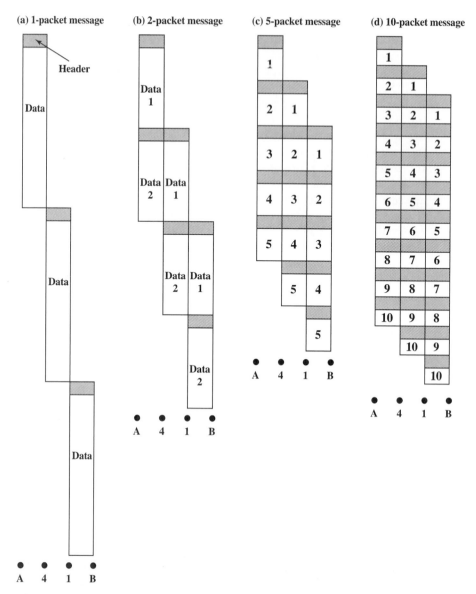

Figure 3.9 Effect of Packet Size on Transmission Time

transmission, the total transmission time drops to 92 octet-times. By breaking the message up into five packets, each intermediate node can begin transmission even sooner and the savings in time is greater, with a total of 77 octet-times for transmission. However, this process of using more and smaller packets eventually results in increased, rather than reduced delay as illustrated in Figure 3.9d. This is because each packet contains a fixed amount of header, and more packets mean more of these headers. Furthermore, the example does not show the processing and queuing delays at each node. These delays are also greater when more packets are handled for a single message. However, we shall see in the next section that an extremely small packet size (53 octets) can result in an efficient network design.

3.5 ASYNCHRONOUS TRANSFER MODE

Asynchronous transfer mode (ATM), also known as cell relay, is in some ways similar to packet switching. Like packet switching, ATM involves the transfer of data in discrete chunks. Also, like packet switching, ATM allows multiple logical connections to be multiplexed over a single physical interface. In the case of ATM, the information flow on each logical connection is organized into fixed-size packets, called cells.

ATM is a streamlined protocol with minimal error and flow control capabilities. This reduces the overhead of processing ATM cells and reduces the number of overhead bits required with each cell, thus enabling ATM to operate at high data rates. Further, the use of fixed-size cells simplifies the processing required at each ATM node, again supporting the use of ATM at high data rates.

ATM Logical Connections

Logical connections in ATM are referred to as virtual channel connections (VCCs). A VCC is analogous to a virtual circuit in a packet-switching network; it is the basic unit of switching in an ATM network. A VCC is set up between two end users through the network, and a variable-rate, full-duplex flow of fixed-size cells is exchanged over the connection. VCCs are also used for user-network exchange (control signaling) and network-network exchange (network management and routing).

For ATM, a second sublayer of processing has been introduced that deals with the concept of virtual path (Figure 3.10). A virtual path connection (VPC) is a bundle of VCCs that have the same end points. Thus all of the cells flowing over all of the VCCs in a single VPC are switched together.

The virtual path concept was developed in response to a trend in high-speed networking in which the control cost of the network is becoming an increasingly higher proportion of the overall network cost. The virtual path technique helps contain the control cost by grouping connections sharing common paths through the network into a single unit. Network management actions can then be applied to a small number of groups of connections instead of a large number of individual connections.

Several advantages can be listed for the use of virtual paths:

Figure 3.10 ATM Connection Relationships

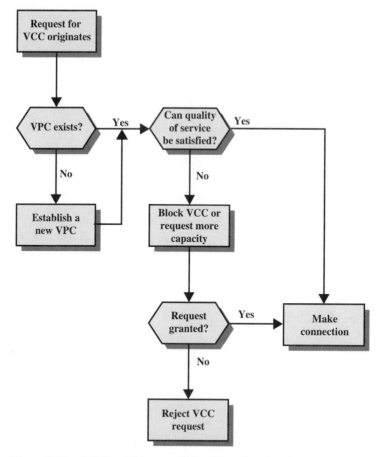

Figure 3.11 Call Establishment Using Virtual Paths

- **Simplified network architecture:** Network transport functions can be separated into those related to an individual logical connection (virtual channel) and those related to a group of logical connections (virtual path).
- **Increased network performance and reliability:** The network deals with fewer, aggregated entities.
- **Reduced processing and short connection setup time:** Much of the work is done when the virtual path is set up. By reserving capacity on a virtual path connection in anticipation of later call arrivals, new virtual channel connections can be established by executing simple control functions at the end points of the virtual path connection; no call processing is required at transit nodes. Thus, the addition of new virtual channels to an existing virtual path involves minimal processing.
- **Enhanced network services:** The virtual path is used internal to the network but is also visible to the end user. Thus, the user may define closed user groups or closed networks of virtual channel bundles.

Figure 3.11 suggests in a general way the call establishment process using virtual channels and virtual paths. The process of setting up a virtual path connection is decoupled from the process of setting up an individual virtual channel connection:

- The virtual path control mechanisms include calculating routes, allocating capacity, and storing connection state information.
- For an individual virtual channel setup, control involves checking that there is a virtual path connection to the required destination node with sufficient available capacity to support the virtual channel, with the appropriate quality of service, and then storing the required state information (virtual channel/virtual path mapping).

The terminology of virtual paths and virtual channels used in the standards is a bit confusing and is summarized in Table 3.1.

Virtual Channel Connection Uses

The end points of a VCC may be end users, network entities, or an end user and a network entity. In all cases, cell sequence integrity is preserved within a VCC: that is, cells are delivered in the same order in which they are sent. Let us consider examples of the three uses of a VCC:

- **Between end users:** Can be used to carry end-to-end user data; can also be used to carry control signaling between end users, as explained later. A VPC between end users provides them with an overall capacity; the VCC organization of the VPC is up to the two end users, provided the set of VCCs does not exceed the VPC capacity.

Table 3.1 Virtual Path/Virtual Channel Terminology

Virtual Channel (VC)   A generic term used to describe unidirectional transport of ATM cells associated by a common unique identifier value.
Virtual Channel Link   A means of unidirectional transport of ATM cells between a point where a VCI value is assigned and the point where that value is translated or terminated.
Virtual Channel Identifier (VCI)   A unique numerical tag that identifies a particular VC link for a given VPC.
Virtual Channel Connection (VCC)   A concatenation of VC links that extends between two points where ATM service users access the ATM layer. VCCs are provided for the purpose of user-user, user-network, or network-network information transfer. Cell sequence integrity is preserved for cells belonging to the same VCC.
Virtual Path   A generic term used to describe unidirectional transport of ATM cells belonging to virtual channels that are associated by a common unique identifier value.
Virtual Path Link   A group of VC links, identified by a common value of VPI, between a point where a VPI value is assigned and the point where that value is translated or terminated.
Virtual Path Identifier (VPI)   Identifies a particular VP link.
Virtual Path Connection (VPC)   A concatenation of VP links that extends between the point where the VCI values are assigned and the point where those values are translated or removed (i.e., extending the length of a bundle of VC links that share the same VPI). VPCs are provided for the purpose of user-user, user-network, or network-network information transfer.

- **Between an end user and a network entity:** Used for user-to-network control signaling, as discussed later. A user-to-network VPC can be used to aggregate traffic from an end user to a network exchange or network server.
- **Between two network entities:** Used for network traffic management and routing functions. A network-to-network VPC can be used to define a common route for the exchange of network management information.

Virtual Path/Virtual Channel Characteristics

ITU-T Recommendation I.150 lists the following as characteristics of virtual channel connections:

- **Quality of service:** A user of a VCC is provided with a quality of service specified by parameters such as cell loss ratio (ratio of cells lost to cells transmitted) and cell delay variation.
- **Switched and semipermanent virtual channel connections:** Both switched connections, which require call-control signaling, and dedicated channels can be provided.
- **Cell sequence integrity:** The sequence of transmitted cells within a VCC is preserved.
- **Traffic parameter negotiation and usage monitoring:** Traffic parameters can be negotiated between a user and the network for each VCC. The input of cells to the VCC is monitored by the network to ensure that the negotiated parameters are not violated.

The types of traffic parameters that can be negotiated include average rate, peak rate, burstiness, and peak duration. The network may need a number of strategies to deal with congestion and to manage existing and requested VCCs. At the crudest level, the network may simply deny new requests for VCCs to prevent congestion. Additionally, cells may be discarded if negotiated parameters are violated or if congestion becomes severe. In an extreme situation, existing connections might be terminated.

I.150 also lists characteristics of VPCs. The first four characteristics listed are identical to those for VCCs. That is, quality of service, switched and semipermanent VPCs, cell sequence integrity, and traffic parameter negotiation and usage monitoring are all also characteristics of a VPC. There are a number of reasons for this duplication. First, this provides some flexibility in how the network service manages the requirements placed on it. Second, the network must be concerned with the overall requirements for a VPC, and within a VPC may negotiate the establishment of virtual channels with given characteristics. Finally, once a VPC is set up, it is possible for the end users to negotiate the creation of new VCCs. The VPC characteristics impose a discipline on the choices that the end users may make.

In addition, a fifth characteristic is listed for VPCs:

- **Virtual channel identifier restriction within a VPC:** One or more virtual channel identifiers, or numbers, may not be available to the user of the VPC but may be reserved for network use. Examples include VCCs used for network management.

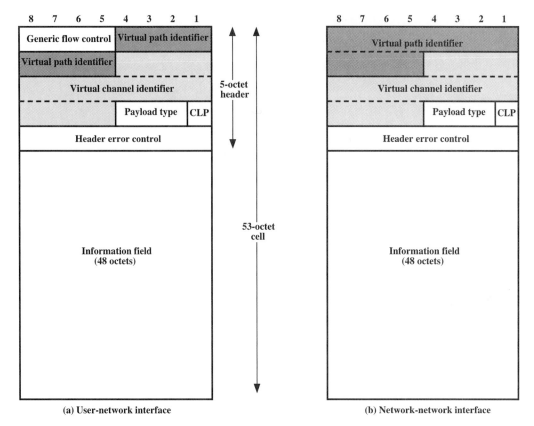

Figure 3.12   ATM Cell Format

ATM Cells

ATM uses fixed-size cells, consisting of a 5-octet header and a 48-octet information field. There are several advantages to the use of small, fixed-size cells. First, the use of small cells may reduce queuing delay for a high-priority cell, because it waits less if it arrives slightly behind a lower-priority cell that has gained access to a resource (e.g., the transmitter). Second, it appears that fixed-size cells can be switched more efficiently, which is important for the very high data rates of ATM. With fixed-size cells, it is easier to implement the switching mechanism in hardware.

Header Format

Figure 3.12a shows the header format at the user-network interface. Figure 3.12b shows the cell header format internal to the network. Internal to the network, the Generic Flow Control field, which performs end-to-end functions, is not retained. Instead, the Virtual Path Identifier field is expanded from 8 to 12 bits. This allows support for an expanded number of VPCs internal to the network, to include those supporting subscribers and those required for network management.

The **Generic Flow Control** (GFC) field can be used for control of cell flow at the local user-network interface. The details of its application are for further study.

Table 3.2 Payload Type (PT) Field Coding

PT Coding	Interpretation	
0 0 0	User data cell, congestion not experienced,	SDU-type = 0
0 0 1	User data cell, congestion not experienced,	SDU-type = 1
0 1 0	User data cell, congestion experienced,	SDU-type = 0
0 1 1	User data cell, congestion experienced,	SDU-type = 1
1 0 0	OAM segment associated cell	
1 0 1	OAM end-to-end associated cell	
1 1 0	Resource management cell	
1 1 1	Reserved for future function	

SDU = service data unit
OAM = operations, administration, and maintenance

The field could be used to assist the customer in controlling the flow of traffic for different qualities of service. One candidate for the use of this field is a multiple-priority level indicator to control the flow of information in a service-dependent manner. In any case, the GFC mechanism is used to alleviate short-term overload conditions in the network.

The **Virtual Path Identifier** (VPI) field constitutes a routing field for the network. It is 8 bits at the user-network interface and 12 bits at the network-network interface, allowing for more virtual paths to be supported within the network. The **Virtual Channel Identifier** (VCI) field is used for routing to and from the end user. Thus, it functions much as a service access point.

The **Payload Type** (PT) field indicates the type of information in the information field. Table 3.2 shows the interpretation of the PT bits. A value of 0 in the first bit indicates user information (that is, information from the next higher layer). In this case, the second bit indicates whether congestion has been experienced; the third bit, known as the service data unit (SDU)[1] type bit, is a one-bit field that can be used to discriminate two types of ATM SDUs associated with a connection. The term *SDU* refers to the 48-octet payload of the cell. A value of 1 in the first bit of the payload type field indicates that this cell carries network management or maintenance information. This indication allows the insertion of network-management cells onto a user's VCC without impacting the user's data. Thus, the PT field can provide inband control information.

The **Cell Loss Priority** (CLP) field is used to provide guidance to the network in the event of congestion. A value of 0 indicates a cell of relatively higher priority, which should not be discarded unless no other alternative is available. A value of 1 indicates that this cell is subject to discard within the network. The user might employ this field so that extra information may be inserted into the network, with a CLP of 1, and delivered to the destination if the network is not congested. The network may set this field to 1 for any data cell that is in violation of a agreement between the user and the network concerning traffic parameters. In this case, the switch that does the setting realizes that the cell exceeds the agreed traffic parameters

---

[1]This is the term used in ATM Forum documents. In ITU-T documents, this bit is referred to as the ATM-user-to-ATM-user (AAU) indication bit. The meaning is the same.

but that the switch is capable of handling the cell. At a later point in the network, if congestion is encountered, this cell has been marked for discard in preference to cells that fall within agreed traffic limits.

The **Header Error Control** (HEC) field is an 8-bit error code that can be used to correct single-bit errors in the header and to detect double-bit errors. In the case of most existing protocols the data that serve as input to the error code calculation are in general, much longer than the size of the resulting error code. This allows for error detection. In the case of ATM, the input to the calculation is only 32 bits, compared with 8 bits for the code. The fact that the input is relatively short allows the code to be used not only for error detection but, in some cases, for actual error correction. This is because there is sufficient redundancy in the code to recover from certain error patterns.

The error protection function provides both recovery from single-bit header errors and a low probability of the delivery of cells with errored headers under bursty error conditions. The error characteristics of fiber-based transmission systems appear to be a mix of single-bit errors and relatively large burst errors. For some transmission systems, the error correction capability, which is more time consuming, might not be invoked.

ATM Service Categories

An ATM network is designed to be able to transfer many different types of traffic simultaneously, including real-time flows such as voice, video, and bursty TCP flows. Although each such traffic flow is handled as a stream of 53-octet cells traveling through a virtual channel, the way in which each data flow is handled within the network depends on the characteristics of the traffic flow and the requirements of the application. For example, real-time video traffic must be delivered within minimum variation in delay.

In this subsection, we summarize ATM service categories, which are used by an end system to identify the type of service required. The following service categories have been defined by the ATM Forum:

- **Real-time service**
    —Constant bit rate (CBR)
    —Real-time variable bit rate (rt-VBR)
- **Non-real-time service**
    —Non-real-time variable bit rate (nrt-VBR)
    —Available bit rate (ABR)
    —Unspecified bit rate (UBR)

Real-Time Services

The most important distinction among applications concerns the amount of delay and the variability of delay, referred to as jitter, that the application can tolerate. Real-time applications typically involve a flow of information to a user that is intended to reproduce that flow at a source. For example, a user expects a flow of audio or video information to be presented in a continuous, smooth fashion. A lack of continuity or excessive loss results in significant loss of quality. Applications that involve interaction between people have tight constraints on delay. Typically, any delay above a few hundred milliseconds becomes noticeable and annoying. Accordingly, the demands in the ATM network for switching and delivery of real-time data are high.

The **constant bit rate (CBR)** service is perhaps the simplest service to define. It is used by applications that require a fixed data rate that is continuously available during the connection lifetime and a relatively tight upper bound on transfer delay. CBR is commonly used for uncompressed audio and video information. Examples of CBR applications include

- Videoconferencing
- Interactive audio (e.g., telephony)
- Audio/video distribution (e.g., television, distance learning, pay-per-view)
- Audio/video retrieval (e.g., video-on-demand, audio library)

The **real-time variable bit rate (rt-VBR)** category is intended for time-sensitive applications; that is, those requiring tightly constrained delay and delay variation. The principal difference between applications appropriate for rt-VBR and those appropriate for CBR is that rt-VBR applications transmit at a rate that varies with time. Equivalently, an rt-VBR source can be characterized as somewhat bursty. For example, the standard approach to video compression results in a sequence of image frames of varying sizes. Because real-time video requires a uniform frame transmission rate, the actual data rate varies.

The rt-VBR service allows the network more flexibility than CBR. The network is able to statistically multiplex a number of connections over the same dedicated capacity and still provide the required service to each connection.

Non-Real-Time Services

Non-real-time services are intended for applications that have bursty traffic characteristics and do not have tight constraints on delay and delay variation. Accordingly, the network has greater flexibility in handling such traffic flows and can make greater use of statistical multiplexing to increase network efficiency.

For some non-real-time applications, it is possible to characterize the expected traffic flow so that the network can provide substantially improved quality of service (QoS) in the areas of loss and delay. Such applications can use the **non-real-time variable bit rate (nrt-VBR)** service. With this service, the end system specifies a peak cell rate, a sustainable or average cell rate, and a measure of how bursty or clumped the cells may be. With this information, the network can allocate resources to provide relatively low delay and minimal cell loss.

The nrt-VBR service can be used for data transfers that have critical response-time requirements. Examples include airline reservations, banking transactions, and process monitoring.

At any given time, a certain amount of the capacity of an ATM network is consumed in carrying CBR and the two types of VBR traffic. Additional capacity is available for one or both of the following reasons: (1) Not all of the total resources have been committed to CBR and VBR traffic, and (2) the bursty nature of VBR traffic means that at some times less than the committed capacity is being used. All of this unused capacity could be made available for the **unspecified bit rate (UBR)** service. This service is suitable for applications that can tolerate variable delays and some cell losses, which is typically true of TCP-based traffic. With UBR, cells are forwarded on a first-in-first-out (FIFO) basis using the capacity not consumed by other services; both delays and variable losses are possible. No initial commitment is made to a UBR source and no feedback concerning congestion is provided; this is referred to as a **best-effort service**. Examples of UBR applications include

- Text/data/image transfer, messaging, distribution, retrieval
- Remote terminal (e.g., telecommuting)

Bursty applications that use a reliable end-to-end protocol such as TCP can detect congestion in a network by means of increased round-trip delays and packet discarding. However, TCP has no mechanism for causing the resources within the network to be shared fairly among many TCP connections. Further, TCP does not minimize congestion as efficiently as is possible using explicit information from congested nodes within the network.

To improve the service provided to bursty sources that would otherwise use UBR, the **available bit rate (ABR)** service has been defined. An application using ABR specifies a peak cell rate (PCR) that it will use and a minimum cell rate (MCR) that it requires. The network allocates resources so that all ABR applications receive at least their MCR capacity. Any unused capacity is then shared in a fair and controlled fashion among all ABR sources. The ABR mechanism uses explicit feedback to sources to assure that capacity is fairly allocated. Any capacity not used by ABR sources remains available for UBR traffic.

An example of an application using ABR is LAN interconnection. In this case, the end systems attached to the ATM network are routers.

Figure 3.13 suggests how a network allocates resources during a steady-state period of time (no additions or deletions of virtual channels).

Figure 3.13 ATM Bit Rate Services

3.6 RECOMMENDED READING AND WEB SITES

As befits its age, circuit switching has inspired a voluminous literature. Two good books on the subject are [BELL00] and [FREE96]. The literature on packet switching is also enormous. Books with good treatments of this subject include [SPOH97], [BERT92], and [SPRA91]. [MCDY99] and [BLAC99] provide good coverage of ATM.

[STAL00] covers all of the topics in this chapter in greater detail.

BELL00   Bellamy, J. *Digital Telephony.* New York: Wiley, 2000.

BERT92   Bertsekas, D., and Gallager, R. *Data Networks.* Englewood Cliffs, NJ: Prentice Hall, 1992.

BLAC99   Black, U. *ATM Volume I: Foundation for Broadband Networks.* Upper Saddle River, NJ: Prentice Hall, 1992.

FREE96   Freeman, R. *Telecommunication System Engineering.* New York: Wiley, 1996.

MCDY99   McDysan, D., and Spohn, D. *ATM: Theory and Application.* New York: McGraw-Hill, 1999.

SPOH97   Spohn, D. *Data Network Design.* New York: McGraw-Hill, 1997.

SPRA91   Spragins, J.; Hammond, J.; and Pawlikowski, K. *Telecommunications Protocols and Design.* Reading, MA: Addison-Wesley, 1991.

STAL00   Stallings, W. *Data and Computer Communications, 6th ed.* Upper Saddle River: NJ: Prentice Hall, 2000.

 Recommended Web sites:

- **ATM Forum Web Site:** Contains technical specifications, white papers, and online copies of the Forum's publication, *53 Bytes*
- **Cell Relay Retreat:** Contains archives of the cell-relay mailing list, links to numerous ATM-related documents, and links to many ATM-related Web sites

3.7 KEY TERMS, REVIEW QUESTIONS, AND PROBLEMS

Key Terms

asynchronous transfer mode (ATM)	local area network (LAN)	subscriber loop
cell	local loop	virtual channel
cell relay	metropolitan area network (MAN)	virtual circuit
circuit switching	packet	virtual path
datagram	packet switching	wide area network (WAN)
header		

Review Questions

1 Differentiate between WANs and LANs.
2 Why is it useful to have more than one possible path through a network for each pair of stations?
3 What is the principal application that has driven the design of circuit-switching networks?
4 Distinguish between static and alternate routing in a circuit-switching network.
5 What is a semipermanent connection?
6 What data rates are offered for ISDN primary access?
7 Explain the difference between datagram and virtual circuit operation.
8 What are some of the limitations of using a circuit-switching network for data transmission?
9 What is the difference between a virtual channel and a virtual path?

Problems

1 Define the following parameters for a switching network:

N = number of hops between two given end systems
L = message length in bits
B = data rate, in bits per second (bps), on all links
P = fixed packet size, in bits
H = overhead (header) bits per packet
S = call setup time (circuit switching or virtual circuit) in seconds
D = propagation delay per hop in seconds

  a. For $N = 4$, $L = 3200$, $B = 9600$, $P = 1024$, $H = 16$, $S = 0.2$, $D = 0.001$, compute the end-to-end delay for circuit switching, virtual circuit packet switching, and datagram packet switching. Assume that there are no acknowledgments. Ignore processing delay at the nodes.
  b. Derive general expressions for the three techniques of part (a), taken two at a time (three expressions in all), showing the conditions under which the delays are equal.

2 What value of P, as a function of N, L, and H, results in minimum end-to-end delay on a datagram network? Assume that L is much larger than P, and D is zero.

3 Consider a simple telephone network consisting of two end offices and one intermediate switch with a 1-MHz full-duplex trunk between each end office and the intermediate switch. The average telephone is used to make four calls per 8-hour workday, with a mean call duration of six minutes. Ten percent of the calls are long distance. What is the maximum number of telephones an end office can support?

4 Explain the flaw in the following reasoning: Packet switching requires control and address bits to be added to each packet. This introduces considerable overhead in packet switching. In circuit switching, a transparent circuit is established. No extra bits are needed.

  a. Therefore, there is no overhead in circuit switching.
  b. Because there is no overhead in circuit switching, line utilization must be more efficient than in packet switching.

5 Assuming no malfunction in any of the stations or nodes of a network, is it possible for a packet to be delivered to the wrong destination?

6 Consider a packet-switching network of N nodes, connected by the following topologies:

  a. Star: One central node with no attached station; all other nodes attach to the central node.
  b. Loop: Each node connects to two other nodes to form a closed loop.
  c. Fully Connected: Each node is directly connected to all other nodes.

  For each case, give the average number of hops between stations.

7 One key design decision for ATM was whether to use fixed- or variable-length cells. Let us consider this decision from the point of view of efficiency. We can define transmission efficiency as

$$N = \frac{\text{Number of information octets}}{\text{Number of information octets} + \text{Number of overhead octets}}$$

a. Consider the use of fixed-length packets. In this case the overhead consists of the header octets. Define

L = Data field size of the cell in octets
H = Header size of the cell in octets
X = Number of information octets to be transmitted as a single message

Derive an expression for N. *Hint:* The expression will need to use the operator $\lceil \bullet \rceil$, where $\lceil Y \rceil$ = the smallest integer greater than or equal to Y.

b. If cells have variable length, then overhead is determined by the header, plus the flags to delimit the cells or an additional length field in the header. Let Hv = additional overhead octets required to enable the use of variable-length cells. Derive an expression for N in terms of X, H, and Hv.

c. Let $L = 48$, $H = 5$, and $Hv = 2$. Plot N versus message size for fixed- and variable-length cells. Comment on the results.

8 Another key design decision for ATM is the size of the data field for fixed-size cells. Let us consider this decision from the point of view of efficiency and delay.

a. Assume that an extended transmission takes place, so that all cells are completely filled. Derive an expression for the efficiency N as a function of H and L.

b. Packetization delay is the delay introduced into a transmission stream by the need to buffer bits until an entire packet is filled before transmission. Derive an expression for this delay as a function of L and the data rate R of the source.

c. Common data rates for voice coding are 32 kbps and 64 kbps. Plot packetization delay as a function of L for these two data rates; use a left-hand y-axis with a maximum value of 2 ms. On the same graph, plot transmission efficiency as a function of L; use a right-hand y-axis with a maximum value of 100%. Comment on the results.

9 Consider compressed video transmission in an ATM network. Suppose standard ATM cells must be transmitted through 5 switches. The data rate is 43 Mbps.

a. What is the transmission time for one cell through one switch?

b. Each switch may be transmitting a cell from other traffic, all of which we assume to have lower (non-preemptive for the cell) priority. If the switch is busy transmitting a cell, our cell has to wait until the other cell completes transmission. If the switch is free, our cell is transmitted immediately. What is the maximum time from when a typical video cell arrives at the first switch (and possibly waits) until it is finished being transmitted by the fifth and last one? Assume that you can ignore propagation time, switching time, and everything else but the transmission time and the time spent waiting for another cell to clear a switch.

c. Now suppose we know that each switch is utilized 60% of the time with the other low-priority traffic. By this we mean that with probability 0.6 when we look at a switch it is busy. Suppose that if there is a cell being transmitted by a switch, the average delay spent waiting for a cell to finish transmission is one-half a cell transmission time. What is the average time from the input of the first switch to clearing the fifth?

d. However, the measure of most interest is not delay but jitter, which is the variability in the delay. Use parts (b) and (c) to calculate the maximum and average variability, respectively, in the delay.

In all cases assume that the various random events are independent of one another; for example, we ignore the burstiness typical of such traffic.

CHAPTER 4

PROTOCOLS AND THE TCP/IP SUITE

We begin this chapter by introducing the concept of a layered protocol architecture. We then examine the most important such architecture, the TCP/IP protocol suite. TCP/IP is an Internet-based concept and is the framework for developing a complete range of computer communications standards. Virtually all computer vendors now provide support for this architecture. Another well-known architecture is the Open Systems Interconnection (OSI) reference model. OSI is a standardized architecture that is often used to describe communications functions but that is now rarely implemented.

Following a discussion of protocol architectures, the important concept of internetworking is examined. Inevitably, an organization will require the use of more than one communication network. Some means of interconnecting these networks is required, and this raises issues that relate to the protocol architecture.

4.1 THE NEED FOR A PROTOCOL ARCHITECTURE

When computers, terminals, and/or other data processing devices exchange data, the procedures involved can be quite complex. Consider, for example, the transfer of a file between two computers. There must be a data path between the two computers, either directly or via a communication network. But more is needed. Typical tasks to be performed include the following:

1. The source system must either activate the direct data communication path or inform the communication network of the identity of the desired destination system.
2. The source system must ascertain that the destination system is prepared to receive data.
3. The file transfer application on the source system must ascertain that the file management program on the destination system is prepared to accept and store the file for this particular user.
4. If the file formats used on the two systems are incompatible, one or the other system must perform a format translation function.

It is clear that there must be a high degree of cooperation between the two computer systems. Instead of implementing the logic for this as a single module, the task is broken up into subtasks, each of which is implemented separately. In a protocol architecture, the modules are arranged in a vertical stack. Each layer in the stack performs a related subset of the functions required to communicate with another system. It relies on the next lower layer to perform more primitive functions and to conceal the details of those functions. It provides services to the next higher layer. Ideally, layers should be defined so that changes in one layer do not require changes in other layers.

Of course, it takes two to communicate, so the same set of layered functions must exist in two systems. Communication is achieved by having the corresponding, or *peer*, layers in two systems communicate. The peer layers communicate by means of formatted blocks of data that obey a set of rules or conventions known as a *protocol*. The key features of a protocol are as follows:

- **Syntax:** Concerns the format of the data blocks
- **Semantics:** Includes control information for coordination and error handling
- **Timing:** Includes speed matching and sequencing

4.2   THE TCP/IP PROTOCOL ARCHITECTURE

The TCP/IP protocol architecture is a result of protocol research and development conducted on the experimental packet-switched network, ARPANET, funded by the Defense Advanced Research Projects Agency (DARPA), and is generally referred to as the TCP/IP protocol suite. This protocol suite consists of a large collection of protocols that have been issued as Internet standards by the Internet Architecture Board (IAB).

The TCP/IP Layers

In general terms, communications can be said to involve three agents: applications, computers, and networks. Examples of applications include file transfer and electronic mail. The applications that we are concerned with here are distributed applications that involve the exchange of data between two computer systems. These applications, and others, execute on computers that can often support multiple simultaneous applications. Computers are connected to networks, and the data to be exchanged are transferred by the network from one computer to another. Thus, the transfer of data from one application to another involves first getting the data to the computer in which the application resides and then getting the data to the intended application within the computer.

With these concepts in mind, it appears natural to organize the communication task into five relatively independent layers:

- Physical layer
- Network access layer
- Internet layer
- Host-to-host, or transport layer
- Application layer

The **physical layer** covers the physical interface between a data transmission device (e.g., workstation, computer) and a transmission medium or network. This layer is concerned with specifying the characteristics of the transmission medium, the nature of the signals, the data rate, and related matters.

The **network access layer** is concerned with the exchange of data between an end system (server, workstation, etc.) and the network to which it is attached. The sending computer must provide the network with the address of the destination computer, so that the network may route the data to the appropriate destination. The sending computer may wish to invoke certain services, such as priority, that might be provided by the network. The specific software used at this layer depends on the type of network to be used; different standards have been developed for circuit switching, packet switching (e.g., X.25), LANs (e.g., Ethernet), and others. Thus it makes sense to separate those functions having to do with network access into a separate layer. By doing this, the remainder of the communications software, above the network access layer, need not be concerned about the specifics of the network to be used. The same higher-layer software should function properly regardless of the particular network to which the computer is attached.

The network access layer is concerned with access to and routing data across a network for two end systems attached to the same network. In those cases where two devices are attached to different networks, procedures are needed to allow data to traverse multiple interconnected networks. This is the function of the **internet layer**. The Internet Protocol (IP) is used at this layer to provide the routing function across multiple networks. This protocol is implemented not only in the end systems but also in routers. A router is a processor that connects two networks and whose primary function is to relay data from one network to the other on its route from the source to the destination end system.

Regardless of the nature of the applications that are exchanging data, there is usually a requirement that data be exchanged reliably. That is, we would like to be assured that all of the data arrive at the destination application and that the data arrive in the same order in which they were sent. As we shall see, the mechanisms for providing reliability are essentially independent of the nature of the applications. Thus, it makes sense to collect those mechanisms in a common layer shared by all applications; this is referred to as the **host-to-host layer**, or **transport layer**. The Transmission Control Protocol (TCP) is the most commonly used protocol to provide this functionality.

Finally, the **application layer** contains the logic needed to support the various user applications. For each different type of application, such as file transfer, a separate module is needed that is peculiar to that application.

Operation of TCP and IP

Figure 4.1 indicates how these protocols are configured for communications. To make clear that the total communications facility may consist of multiple networks, the constituent networks are usually referred to as *subnetworks*. Some sort of network access protocol, such as the Ethernet logic, is used to connect a computer to a subnetwork. This protocol enables the host to send data across the subnetwork to another host or, in the case of a host on another subnetwork, to a router. IP is implemented in all of the end systems and the routers. It acts as a relay to move a block of data from one host, through one or more routers, to another host. TCP is implemented only in the end systems; it keeps track of the blocks of data to assure that all are delivered reliably to the appropriate application.

For successful communication, every entity in the overall system must have a unique address. Actually, two levels of addressing are needed. Each host on a subnetwork must have a unique global internet address; this allows the data to be delivered to the proper host. Each process with a host must have an address that is unique within the host; this allows the host-to-host protocol (TCP) to deliver data to the proper process. These latter addresses are known as ports.

Let us trace a simple operation. Suppose that a process, associated with port 1 at host A, wishes to send a message to another process, associated with port 3 at host B. The process at A hands the message down to TCP with instructions to send it to host B, port 3. TCP hands the message down to IP with instructions to send it

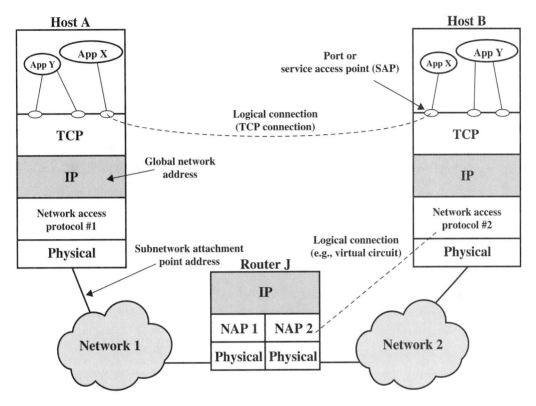

Figure 4.1 TCP/IP Concepts

to host B. Note that IP need not be told the identity of the destination port. All it needs to know is that the data are intended for host B. Next, IP hands the message down to the network access layer (e.g., Ethernet logic) with instructions to send it to router J (the first hop on the way to B).

To control this operation, control information as well as user data must be transmitted, as suggested in Figure 4.2. Let us say that the sending process generates a block of data and passes this to TCP. TCP may break this block into smaller pieces to make it more manageable. To each of these pieces, TCP appends control information known as the TCP header, forming a *TCP segment*. The control information is to be used by the peer TCP protocol entity at host B. Examples of items in this header include the following:

- **Destination port:** When the TCP entity at B receives the segment, it must know to whom the data are to be delivered.
- **Sequence number:** TCP numbers the segments that it sends to a particular destination port sequentially, so that if they arrive out of order, the TCP entity at B can reorder them.
- **Checksum:** The sending TCP includes a code that is a function of the contents of the remainder of the segment. The receiving TCP performs the same calculation and compares the result with the incoming code. A discrepancy results if there has been some error in transmission.

Next, TCP hands each segment over to IP, with instructions to transmit it to B. These segments must be transmitted across one or more subnetworks and relayed through one or more intermediate routers. This operation, too, requires the use of control information. Thus IP appends a header of control information to each segment to form an *IP datagram*. An example of an item stored in the IP header is the destination host address (in this example, B).

Finally, each IP datagram is presented to the network access layer for transmission across the first subnetwork in its journey to the destination. The network access layer appends its own header, creating a packet, or frame. The packet is transmitted across the subnetwork to router J. The packet header contains the information that the subnetwork needs to transfer the data across the subnetwork. Examples of items that may be contained in this header include the following:

- **Destination subnetwork address:** The subnetwork must know to which attached device the packet is to be delivered.
- **Facilities requests:** The network access protocol might request the use of certain subnetwork facilities, such as priority.

At router J, the packet header is stripped off and the IP header examined. On the basis of the destination address information in the IP header, the IP module in the router directs the datagram out across subnetwork 2 to B. To do this, the datagram is again augmented with a network access header.

When the data are received at B, the reverse process occurs. At each layer, the corresponding header is removed, and the remainder is passed on to the next higher layer, until the original user data are delivered to the destination process.

As an aside, the generic name for a block of data exchanged at any protocol level is referred to as a **protocol data unit** (PDU). Thus, a TCP segment is a TCP PDU.

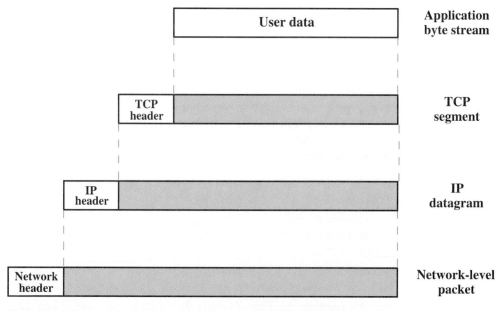

Figure 4.2   Protocol Data Units (PDUs) in the TCP/IP Architecture

TCP/IP Applications

A number of applications have been standardized to operate on top of TCP. We mention three of the most common here.

The **Simple Mail Transfer Protocol (SMTP)** provides a basic electronic mail facility. It provides a mechanism for transferring messages among separate hosts. Features of SMTP include mailing lists, return receipts, and forwarding. The SMTP protocol does not specify the way in which messages are to be created; some local editing or native electronic mail facility is required. Once a message is created, SMTP accepts the message and makes use of TCP to send it to an SMTP module on another host. The target SMTP module will make use of a local electronic mail package to store the incoming message in a user's mailbox.

The **File Transfer Protocol (FTP)** is used to send files from one system to another under user command. Both text and binary files are accommodated, and the protocol provides features for controlling user access. When a user wishes to engage in file transfer, FTP sets up a TCP connection to the target system for the exchange of control messages. These allow user ID and password to be transmitted, and allow the user to specify the file and file actions desired. Once a file transfer is approved, a second TCP connection is set up for the data transfer. The file is transferred over the data connection, without the overhead of any headers or control information at the application level. When the transfer is complete, the control connection is used to signal the completion and to accept new file transfer commands.

TELNET provides a remote logon capability, which enables a user at a terminal or personal computer to logon to a remote computer and function as if directly connected to that computer. The protocol was designed to work with simple scroll-mode terminals. TELNET is actually implemented in two modules: User TELNET interacts with the terminal I/O (input/output) module to communicate with a local terminal. It converts the characteristics of real terminals to the network standard and vice versa. Server TELNET interacts with an application, acting as a surrogate terminal handler so that remote terminals appear as local to the application. Terminal traffic between user and server TELNET is carried on a TCP connection.

4.3 THE OSI MODEL

The Open Systems Interconnection (OSI) reference model was developed by the International Organization for Standardization (ISO)[1] as a model for a computer protocol architecture and as a framework for developing protocol standards.

Protocol Layers

The OSI model consists of seven layers:

- Application
- Presentation

---

[1]ISO is not an acronym (in which case it would be IOS), but a word, derived from the Greek *isos*, meaning *equal*.

- Session
- Transport
- Network
- Data link
- Physical

Figure 4.3 illustrates the OSI model and provides a brief definition of the functions performed at each layer. The intent of the OSI model is that protocols be developed to perform the functions of each layer.

The designers of OSI assumed that this model and the protocols developed within this model would come to dominate computer communications, eventually

Application

Provides access to the OSI environment for users and also provides distributed information services.

Presentation

Provides independence to the application processes from differences in data representation (syntax).

Session

Provides the control structure for communication between applications; establishes, manages, and terminates connections (sessions) between cooperating applications.

Transport

Provides reliable, transparent transfer of data between end points; provides end-to-end error recovery and flow control.

Network

Provides upper layers with independence from the data transmission and switching technologies used to connect systems; responsible for establishing, maintaining, and terminating connections.

Data Link

Provides for the reliable transfer of information across the physical link; sends blocks (frames) with the necessary synchronization, error control, and flow control.

Physical

Concerned with transmission of unstructured bit stream over physical medium; deals with the mechanical, electrical, functional, and procedural characteristics to access the physical medium.

Figure 4.3   The OSI Layers

OSI   TCP/IP

OSI	TCP/IP
Application	Application
Presentation	
Session	
Transport	Transport (host-to-host)
Network	Internet
Data link	Network access
Physical	Physical

Figure 4.4   A Comparison of the OSI and TCP/IP Protocol Architectures

replacing proprietary protocol implementations and rival multivendor models such as TCP/IP. This has not happened. Although many useful protocols have been developed in the context of OSI, the overall seven-layer model has not flourished. Instead, the TCP/IP architecture has come to dominate. There are a number of reasons for this outcome. Perhaps the most important is that the key TCP/IP protocols were mature and well tested at a time when similar OSI protocols were in the development stage. When businesses began to recognize the need for interoperability across networks, only TCP/IP was available and ready to go. Another reason is that the OSI model is unnecessarily complex, with seven layers to accomplish what TCP/IP does with fewer layers.

Figure 4.4 illustrates the layers of the TCP/IP and OSI architectures, showing roughly the correspondence in functionality between the two.

Standardization within the OSI Framework[2]

The principal motivation for the development of the OSI model was to provide a framework for standardization. Within the model, one or more protocol standards can be developed at each layer. The model defines in general terms the functions to be performed at that layer and facilitates the standards-making process in two ways:

- Because the functions of each layer are well defined, standards can be developed independently and simultaneously for each layer. This speeds up the standards-making process.
- Because the boundaries between layers are well defined, changes in standards in one layer need not affect already existing software in another layer. This makes it easier to introduce new standards.

[2]The concepts introduced in this subsection apply as well to the TCP/IP architecture.

Figure 4.5 illustrates the use of the OSI model as such a framework. The overall communications function is decomposed into seven distinct layers, using modular design. That is, the overall function is broken up into a number of modules, making the interfaces between modules as simple as possible. In addition, the design principle of information hiding is used: Lower layers are concerned with greater levels of detail; upper layers are independent of these details. Within each layer, both the service provided to the next higher layer and the protocol to the peer layer in other systems are provided.

Figure 4.6 shows more specifically the nature of the standardization required at each layer. Three elements are key:

- **Protocol specification:** Two entities at the same layer in different systems cooperate and interact by means of a protocol. Because two different open systems are involved, the protocol must be specified precisely. This includes the format of the protocol data units exchanged, the semantics of all fields, and the allowable sequence of PDUs.
- **Service definition:** In addition to the protocol or protocols that operate at a given layer, standards are needed for the services that each layer provides to

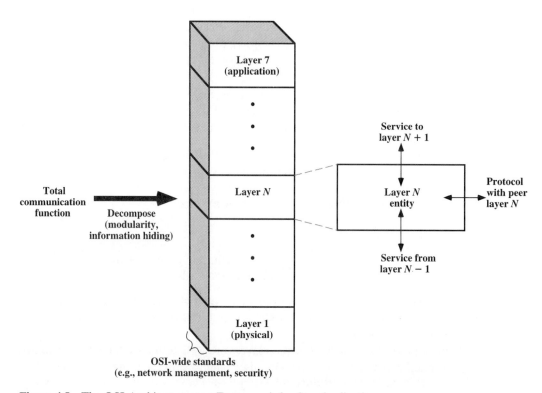

Figure 4.5   The OSI Architecture as a Framework for Standardization

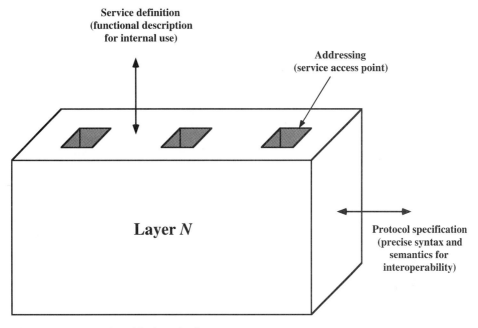

Figure 4.6 Layer-Specific Standards

the next higher layer. Typically, the definition of services is equivalent to a functional description that defines what services are provided, but not how the services are to be provided.

- **Addressing:** Each layer provides services to entities at the next higher layer. These entities are referenced by means of a service access point (SAP). Thus, a network service access point (NSAP) indicates a transport entity that is a user of the network service.

The need to provide a precise protocol specification for open systems is self-evident. The other two items listed warrant further comment. With respect to service definitions, the motivation for providing only a functional definition is as follows. First, the interaction between two adjacent layers takes place within the confines of a single open system and is not the concern of any other open system. Thus, as long as peer layers in different systems provide the same services to their next higher layers, the details of how the services are provided may differ from one system to another without loss of interoperability. Second, it will usually be the case that adjacent layers are implemented on the same processor. In that case, we would like to leave the system programmer free to exploit the hardware and operating system to provide an interface that is as efficient as possible.

With respect to addressing, the use of an address mechanism at each layer, implemented as a service access point, allows each layer to multiplex multiple users from the next higher layer. Multiplexing may not occur at each layer, but the model allows for that possibility.

4.4 INTERNETWORKING

In most cases, a LAN or WAN is not an isolated entity. An organization may have more than one type of LAN at a given site to satisfy a spectrum of needs. An organization may have multiple LANs of the same type at a given site to accommodate performance or security requirements. And an organization may have LANs at various sites and need them to be interconnected via WANs for central control of distributed information exchange.

Table 4.1 lists some commonly used terms relating to the interconnection of networks, or internetworking. An interconnected set of networks, from a user's point of view, may appear simply as a larger network. However, if each of the constituent networks retains its identity, and special mechanisms are needed for communicating across multiple networks, then the entire configuration is often referred to as an **internet**. The most important example of an internet is referred to simply as the Internet. As the Internet has evolved from its modest beginnings as a research-oriented packet-switching network, it has served as the basis for the development of internetworking technology and as the model for private internets within organizations. These latter are also referred to as **intranets**.

Each constituent subnetwork in an internet supports communication among the devices attached to that subnetwork; these devices are referred to as **end sys-**

Table 4.1 Internetworking Terms

Communication Network
A facility that provides a data transfer service among devices attached to the network.
Internet
A collection of communication networks interconnected by bridges and/or routers.
Intranet
An internet used by a single organization that provides the key Internet applications, especially the World Wide Web. An intranet operates within the organization for internal purposes and can exist as an isolated, self-contained internet, or may have links to the Internet.
End System (ES)
A device attached to one of the networks of an internet that is used to support end-user applications or services.
Intermediate System (IS)
A device used to connect two networks and permit communication between end systems attached to different networks.
Bridge
An IS used to connect two LANs that use similar LAN protocols. The bridge acts as an address filter, picking up packets from one LAN that are intended for a destination on another LAN and passing those packets on. The bridge does not modify the contents of the packets and does not add anything to the packet. The bridge operates at layer 2 of the OSI model.
Router
An IS used to connect two networks that may or may not be similar. The router employs an internet protocol present in each router and each end system of the network. The router operates at layer 3 of the OSI model.

tems (ESs). In addition, subnetworks are connected by devices referred to in the ISO documents as **intermediate systems** (ISs). ISs provide a communications path and perform the necessary relaying and routing functions so that data can be exchanged between devices attached to different subnetworks in the internet.

Two types of ISs of particular interest are bridges and routers. The differences between them have to do with the types of protocols used for the internetworking logic. In essence, a **bridge** operates at layer 2 of the OSI seven-layer architecture and acts as a relay of frames between like networks. A **router** operates at layer 3 of the OSI architecture and routes packets between potentially different networks. Both the bridge and the router assume that the same upper-layer protocols are in use.

The roles and functions of routers were introduced in the context of IP earlier in this chapter. However, because of the importance of routers in the overall networking scheme, it is worth providing additional comment in this section.

Routers

Internetworking among dissimilar subnetworks is achieved by using routers to interconnect the subnetworks. Essential functions that the router must perform include the following:

1. Provide a link between networks.
2. Provide for the routing and delivery of data between processes on end systems attached to different networks.
3. Provide these functions in such a way as not to require modifications of the networking architecture of any of the attached subnetworks.

The third point implies that the router must accommodate a number of differences among networks, such as the following:

- **Addressing schemes:** The networks may use different schemes for assigning addresses to devices. For example, an IEEE 802 LAN uses a 48-bit binary address for each attached device; an ATM network typically uses 15-digit decimal addresses (encoded as 4 bits per digit for a 60-bit address). Some form of global network addressing must be provided, as well as a directory service.

- **Maximum packet sizes:** Packets from one network may have to be broken into smaller pieces to be transmitted on another network, a process known as *segmentation*. For example, Ethernet imposes a maximum packet size of 1500 bytes; a maximum packet size of 1000 bytes is common on X.25 networks. A packet that is transmitted on an Ethernet system and picked up by a router for retransmission on an X.25 network may have to be fragmented into two smaller ones.

- **Interfaces:** The hardware and software interfaces to various networks differ. The concept of a router must be independent of these differences.

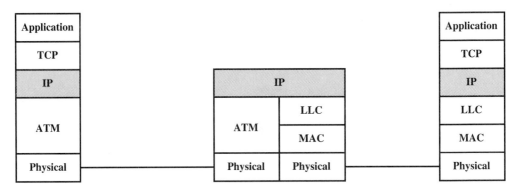

Figure 4.7 Configuration for TCP/IP Example

- **Reliability:** Various network services may provide anything from a reliable end-to-end virtual circuit to an unreliable service. The operation of the routers should not depend on an assumption of network reliability.

The preceding requirements are best satisfied by an internetworking protocol, such as IP, that is implemented in all end systems and routers.

Internetworking Example

Figure 4.7 depicts a configuration that we will use to illustrate the interactions among protocols for internetworking. In this case, we focus on a server attached to an ATM WAN and a workstation attached to an IEEE 802 LAN, with a router connecting the two networks.[3] The router will provide a link between the server and the workstation that enables these end systems to ignore the details of the intervening networks.

Figures 4.8 through 4.10 outline typical steps in the transfer of a block of data, such as a file or a Web page, from the server, through an internet, and ultimately to

---

[3]Section 14.1 describes the IEEE 802 protocol architecture. For now, you need to know that the architecture consists of a physical layer; a medium access control (MAC) layer concerned with addressing and error control, and a logical link control (LLC) layer, concerned with logical connections and identifying the user of LLC.

1. Preparing the data. The application protocol prepares a block of data for transmission. For example, an email message (SMTP), a file (FTP), or a block of user input (TELNET).

2. Using a common syntax. If necessary, the data are converted to a form expected by the destination. This may include a different character code, the use of encryption, and/or compression.

3. Segmenting the data. TCP may break the data block into a number of segments, keeping track of their sequence. Each TCP segment includes a header containing a sequence number and a frame check sequence to detect errors.

4. Duplicating segments. A copy is made of each TCP segment, in case the loss or damage of a segment necessitates retransmission. When an acknowledgment is received from the other TCP entity, a segment is erased.

5. Fragmenting the segments. IP may break a TCP segment into a number of datagrams to meet size requirements of the intervening networks. Each datagram includes a header containing a destination address, a frame check sequence, and other control information.

6. Framing. An ATM header is added to each IP datagram to form an ATM cell. The header contains a connection identifier and a header error control field

Peer-to-peer dialogue. Before data are sent, the sending and receiving applications agree on format and encoding and agree to exchange data.

Peer-to-peer dialogue. The two TCP entities agree to open a connection.

Peer-to-peer dialogue. Each IP datagram is forwarded through networks and routers to the destination system.

Peer-to-peer dialogue. Each cell is forwarded through the ATM network.

7. Transmission. Each cell is transmitted over the medium as a sequence of bits.

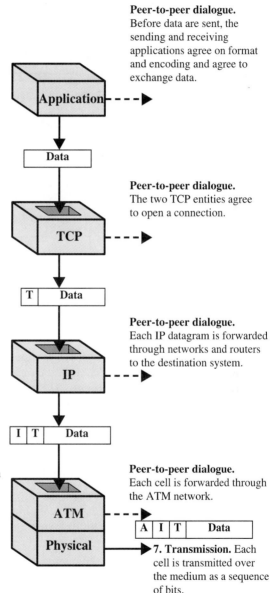

Figure 4.8 Operation of TCP/IP: Action at Sender

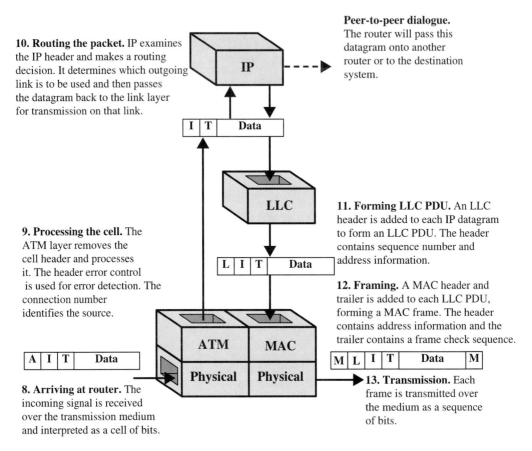

10. Routing the packet. IP examines the IP header and makes a routing decision. It determines which outgoing link is to be used and then passes the datagram back to the link layer for transmission on that link.

Peer-to-peer dialogue. The router will pass this datagram onto another router or to the destination system.

9. Processing the cell. The ATM layer removes the cell header and processes it. The header error control is used for error detection. The connection number identifies the source.

11. Forming LLC PDU. An LLC header is added to each IP datagram to form an LLC PDU. The header contains sequence number and address information.

12. Framing. A MAC header and trailer is added to each LLC PDU, forming a MAC frame. The header contains address information and the trailer contains a frame check sequence.

8. Arriving at router. The incoming signal is received over the transmission medium and interpreted as a cell of bits.

13. Transmission. Each frame is transmitted over the medium as a sequence of bits.

Figure 4.9 Operation of TCP/IP: Action at Router

an application in the workstation. In this example, the message passes through just one router. Before data can be transmitted, the application and transport layers in the server establish, with the corresponding layer in the workstation, the applicable ground rules for a communication session. These include character code to be used, error-checking method, and the like. The protocol at each layer is used for this purpose and then is used in the transmission of the message.

20. Delivering the data. The application performs any needed transformations, including decompression and decryption, and directs the data to the appropriate file or other destination.

19. Reassembling user data. If TCP has broken the user data into multiple segments, these are reassembled and the block is passed up to the application.

18. Processing the TCP segment. TCP removes the header. It checks the frame check sequence and acknowledges if there is a match and discards for mismatch. Flow control is also performed.

17. Processing the IP datagram. IP removes the header. The frame check sequence and other control information are processed.

16. Processing the LLC PDU. The LLC layer removes the header and processes it. The sequence number is used for flow and error control.

15. Processing the frame. The MAC layer removes the header and trailer and processes them. The frame check sequence is used for error detection.

14. Arriving at destination. The incoming signal is received over the transmission medium and interpreted as a frame of bits.

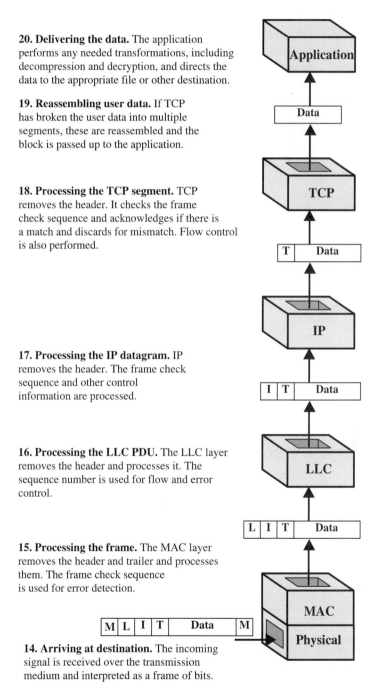

Figure 4.10   Operation of TCP/IP: Action at Receiver

4.5   RECOMMENDED READING

[STAL00] covers all of the topics in this chapter in greater detail. A very useful reference work on TCP/IP is [MURH98], which covers the spectrum of TCP/IP-related protocols in a technically concise but thorough fashion.

MURH98 Murhammer, M., et al. *TCP/IP: Tutorial and Technical Overview.* Upper Saddle River: NJ: Prentice Hall, 1998.

STAL00   Stallings, W. *Data and Computer Communications, 6th ed.* Upper Saddle River, NJ: Prentice Hall, 2000.

4.6   KEY TERMS, REVIEW QUESTIONS, AND PROBLEMS

Key Terms

application layer	IPv6	protocol data unit (PDU)
checksum	Internetworking	router
frame check	network layer	service access point (SAP)
sequence (FCS)	physical layer	Transmission Control
header	port	Protocol (TCP)
internet	protocol	transport layer
Internet Protocol (IP)	protocol	User Datagram Protocol
Intranet	architecture	(UDP)

Review Questions

1 What is the major function of the network access layer?
2 What tasks are performed by the transport layer?
3 What is a protocol?
4 What is a protocol data unit (PDU)?
5 What is a protocol architecture?
6 What is TCP/IP?
7 What are some advantages to layering as seen in the TCP/IP architecture?
8 What is a router?

Problems

1 Using the layer models in Figure 4.11, describe the ordering and delivery of a pizza, indicating the interactions at each level.
2 **a.** The French and Chinese prime ministers need to come to an agreement by telephone, but neither speaks the other's language. Further, neither has on hand a translator that can translate to the language of the other. However, both prime ministers have English translators on their staffs. Draw a diagram similar to Figure 4.11 to depict the situation, and describe the interaction and each level.

Figure 4.11   Architecture for Problem 4.11

b. Now suppose that the Chinese prime minister's translator can translate only into Japanese and that the French prime minister has a German translator available. A translator between German and Japanese is available in Germany. Draw a new diagram that reflects this arrangement and describe the hypothetical phone conversation.

3 List the major disadvantages with the layered approach to protocols.

4 Two blue armies are each poised on opposite hills preparing to attack a single red army in the valley. The red army can defeat either of the blue armies separately but will fail to defeat both blue armies if they attack simultaneously. The blue armies communicate via an unreliable communications system (a foot soldier). The commander with one of the blue armies would like to attack at noon. His problem is this: If he sends a message to the other blue army, ordering the attack, he cannot be sure it will get through. He could ask for acknowledgment, but that might not get through. Is there a protocol that the two blue armies can use to avoid defeat?

5 A broadcast network is one in which a transmission from any one attached station is received by all other attached stations over a shared medium. Examples are a bus-topology local area network, such as Ethernet, and a wireless radio network. Discuss the need or lack of need for a network layer (OSI layer 3) in a broadcast network.

6 Among the principles used by ISO to define the OSI layers were the following:

- The number of layers should be small enough to avoid unwieldy design and implementation, but large enough so that separate layers handle functions that are different in process or technology.
- Layer boundaries should be chosen to minimize the number and size of interactions across boundaries.

Based on these principles, design an architecture with eight layers and make a case for it. Design one with six layers and make a case for that.

7 In Figure 4.2, exactly one protocol data unit (PDU) in layer N is encapsulated in a PDU at layer $(N - 1)$. It is also possible to break one N-level PDU into multiple $(N - 1)$-level PDUs (segmentation) or to group multiple N-level PDUs into one $(N - 1)$-level PDU (blocking).

a. In the case of segmentation, is it necessary that each $(N - 1)$-level segment contain a copy of the N-level header?

b. In the case of blocking, is it necessary that each N-level PDU retain its own header, or can the data be consolidated into a single N-level PDU with a single N-level header?

8 Why is UDP needed? Why can't a user program directly access IP?

APPENDIX 4A INTERNET PROTOCOL

Within the TCP/IP protocol suite, perhaps the most important protocol is the Internet Protocol (IP). The version that has been use for decades is known as IPv4. Recently, a new version, IPv6, has been standardized, although it is not yet widely deployed.

IPv4

Figure 4.12a shows the IP header format, which is a minimum of 20 octets, or 160 bits. The fields are as follows:

- **Version (4 bits):** Indicates version number, to allow evolution of the protocol; the value is 4.
- **Internet Header Length (IHL) (4 bits):** Length of header in 32-bit words. The minimum value is five, for a minimum header length of 20 octets.
- **Type of Service (8 bits):** Provides guidance to end system IP modules and to routers along the packet's path, in terms of the packet's relative priority.
- **Total Length (16 bits):** Total IP packet length, in octets.
- **Identification (16 bits):** A sequence number that, together with the source address, destination address, and user protocol, is intended to identify a packet uniquely. Thus, the identifier should be unique for the packet's source address, destination address, and user protocol for the time during which the packet will remain in the internet.
- **Flags (3 bits):** Only two of the bits are currently defined. When a packet is fragmented, the More bit indicates whether this is the last fragment in the original packet. The Don't Fragment bit prohibits fragmentation when set. This bit may be useful if it is known that the destination does not have the capability to reassemble fragments. However, if this bit is set, the packet will be discarded if it exceeds the maximum size of an en route subnetwork. Therefore, if the bit is set, it may be advisable to use source routing to avoid subnetworks with small maximum packet size.
- **Fragment Offset (13 bits):** Indicates where in the original packet this fragment belongs, measured in 64-bit units. This implies that fragments other than the last fragment must contain a data field that is a multiple of 64 bits in length.
- **Time to Live (8 bits):** Specifies how long, in seconds, a packet is allowed to remain in the internet. Every router that processes a packet must decrease the TTL by at least one, so the TTL is somewhat similar to a hop count.
- **Protocol (8 bits):** Indicates the next higher level protocol, which is to receive the data field at the destination; thus, this field identifies the type of the next header in the packet after the IP header.
- **Header Checksum (16 bits):** An error-detecting code applied to the header only. Because some header fields may change during transit (e.g., time to live, segmentation-related fields), this is reverified and recomputed at each router. The checksum field is the 16-bit ones complement addition of all 16-bit words in the header. For purposes of computation, the checksum field is itself initialized to a value of zero.

(a) IPv4 header

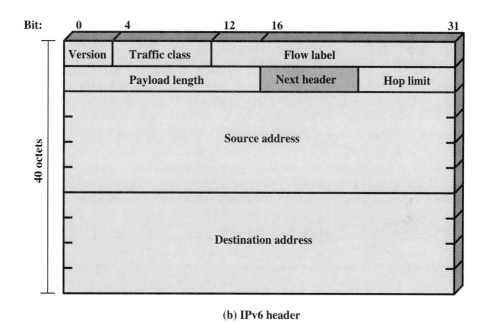

(b) IPv6 header

Figure 4.12 IP Headers

- **Source Address (32 bits):** Coded to allow a variable allocation of bits to specify the network and the end system attached to the specified network (7 and 24 bits, 14 and 16 bits, or 21 and 8 bits).
- **Destination Address (32 bits):** Same characteristics as source address.
- **Options (variable):** Encodes the options requested by the sending user; these may include security label, source routing, record routing, and timestamping.
- **Padding (variable):** Used to ensure that the packet header is a multiple of 32 bits in length.

The source and destination address fields in the IP header each contain a 32-bit global internet address, generally consisting of a network identifier and a host identifier. The address is coded to allow a variable allocation of bits to specify network and host, as depicted in Figure 4.13. This encoding provides flexibility in assigning addresses to hosts and allows a mix of network sizes on an internet. The three principal network classes are best suited to the following conditions:

- **Class A:** Few networks, each with many hosts
- **Class B:** Medium number of networks, each with a medium number of hosts
- **Class C:** Many networks, each with a few hosts

In a particular environment, it may be best to use addresses all from one class. For example, a corporate internetwork that consist of a large number of departmental local area networks may need to use Class C addresses exclusively. However, the format of the addresses is such that it is possible to mix all three classes of addresses on the same internetwork; this is what is done in the case of the Internet itself. A mixture of classes is appropriate for an internetwork consisting of a few large networks, many small networks, plus some medium-sized networks.

IP addresses are usually written in what is called *dotted decimal notation*, with a decimal number representing each of the octets of the 32-bit address. For example, the IP address 11000000 11100100 00010001 00111001 is written as 192.228.17.57.

Figure 4.13 IP Address Formats

Note that all Class A network addresses begin with a binary 0. Network addresses with a first octet of 0 (binary 00000000) and 127 (binary 01111111) are reserved, so there are 126 potential Class A network numbers, which have a first dotted decimal number in the range 1 to 126. Class B network addresses begin with a binary 10, so that the range of the first decimal number in a Class B address is 128 to 191(binary 10000000 to 10111111). The second octet is also part of the Class B address, so that there are $2^{14} = 16,384$ Class B addresses. For Class C addresses, the first decimal number ranges from 192 to 223 (11000000 to 11011111). The total number of Class C addresses is $2^{21} = 2,097,152$.

IPv6

In 1995, the Internet Engineering Task Force (IETF), which develops protocol standards for the Internet, issued a specification for a next-generation IP, known then as IPng (RFC 1752). This specification led to the development of a standard known as IPv6 (RFC 2460). IPv6 provides a number of functional enhancements over the existing IP (known as IPv4), designed to accommodate the higher speeds of today's networks and the mix of data streams, including graphic and video, that are becoming more prevalent. But the driving force behind the development of the new protocol was the need for more addresses. IPv4 uses a 32-bit address to specify a source or destination. With the explosive growth of the Internet and of private networks attached to the Internet, this address length became insufficient to accommodate all systems needing addresses. As Figure 4.12b shows, IPv6 includes 128-bit source and destination address fields. Ultimately, all installations using TCP/IP are expected to migrate from the current IP to IPv6, but this process will take many years, if not decades.

APPENDIX 4B TRANSMISSION CONTROL PROTOCOL

For most applications that make use of the TCP/IP protocol suite, the application relies on TCP to assure reliable delivery of data; TCP in turn relies on IP to handle addressing and routing chores.

We begin with a discussion of one of the central mechanisms of TCP: flow control. The functionality of TCP is then summarized by discussing the elements in the TCP header.

TCP Flow Control

As with most protocols that provide flow control, TCP uses a form of sliding-window mechanism. It differs from the mechanism used in many other protocols, such as LLC, HDLC, and X.25, in that it decouples acknowledgment of received data units from the granting of permission to send additional data units.

The flow control mechanism used by TCP is known as a credit allocation scheme. For the credit scheme, each individual octet of data that is transmitted is considered to have a sequence number. In addition to data, each transmitted segment includes in its header three fields related to flow control: sequence number (SN), acknowledgment number (AN), and window (W). When a transport entity sends a segment, it includes the sequence number of the first octet in the segment data field. A transport entity acknowledges an incoming segment with a return segment that includes ($AN = i, W = j$), with the following interpretation:

- All octets through sequence number $SN = i - 1$ are acknowledged; the next expected octet has sequence number i.
- Permission is granted to send an additional window of $W = j$ octets of data; that is, the j octets corresponding to sequence numbers i through $i + j - 1$.

Figure 4.14 illustrates the mechanism. For simplicity, we show data flow in one direction only and assume that 200 octets of data are sent in each segment. Initially, through the connection establishment process, the sending and receiving sequence numbers are synchronized and A is granted an initial credit allocation of 1400 octets, beginning with octet number 1001. After sending 600 octets in three segments, A has shrunk its window to a size of 800 octets (numbers 1601 through 2400). Following receipt of these segments, B acknowledges receipt of all octets through 1601 and issues a credit of 1000 octets. This means that A can send octets 1601 through 2600 (5 segments). However, by the time that B's message has arrived at A, A has already sent two segments, containing octets 1601 through 2000 (which was permissible under the initial allocation). Thus, A's remaining credit at this point is only 400 octets (2 segments). As the exchange proceeds, A advances the trailing edge of its window each time that it transmits and advances the leading edge only when it is granted credit.

The credit allocation mechanism is quite flexible. For example, consider that the last message issued by B was ($AN = i$, W = j) and that the last octet of data received by B was octet number $i - 1$. Then

- To increase credit to an amount k ($k > j$) when no additional data have arrived, B issues ($AN = i, W = k$).
- To acknowledge an incoming segment containing m octets of data ($m < j$) without granting additional credit, B issues ($AN = i + m$, $W = j - m$).

TCP Segment Format

TCP uses only a single type of protocol data unit, called a TCP segment. The header is shown in Figure 4.15a. Because one header must serve to perform all protocol mechanisms, it is rather large, with a minimum length of 20 octets. The fields are as follows:

- **Source Port (16 bits):** Source TCP user.
- **Destination Port (16 bits):** Destination TCP user.
- **Sequence Number (32 bits):** Sequence number of the first data octet in this segment except when the SYN flag is set. If SYN is set, it is the initial sequence number (ISN) and the first data octet is ISN + 1.
- **Acknowledgment Number (32 bits):** A piggybacked acknowledgment. Contains the sequence number of the next data octet that the TCP entity expects to receive.

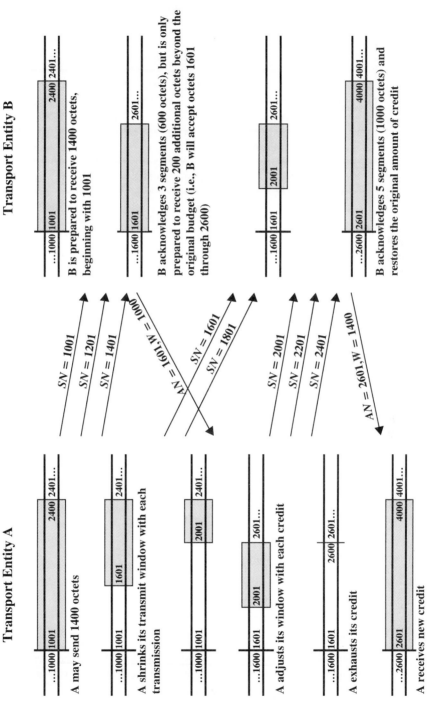

Figure 4.14 Example of TCP Credit Allocation Mechanism

(a) TCP header

(b) UDP header

Figure 4.15 TCP and UDP Headers

- **Data Offset (4 bits):** Number of 32-bit words in the header.
- **Reserved (6 bits):** Reserved for future use.
- **Flags (6 bits):**
  URG: Urgent pointer field significant.
  ACK: Acknowledgment field significant.
  PSH: Push function.
  RST: Reset the connection.
  SYN: Synchronize the sequence numbers.
  FIN: No more data from sender.
- **Window (16 bits):** Flow control credit allocation, in octets. Contains the number of data octets, beginning with the one indicated in the acknowledgment field that the sender is willing to accept.
- **Checksum (16 bits):** The ones complement of the sum modulo $2^{16} - 1$ of all the 16-bit words in the segment plus a pseudoheader, described later.

- **Urgent Pointer (16 bits):** Points to the last octet in a sequence of urgent data. This allows the receiver to know how much urgent data are coming.
- **Options (Variable):** An example is the option that specifies the maximum segment size that will be accepted.

The *sequence number* and *acknowledgment number* are bound to octets rather than to entire segments. For example, if a segment contains sequence number 1001 and includes 600 octets of data, the sequence number refers to the first octet in the data field; the next segment in logical order will have sequence number 1601. Thus, TCP is logically stream oriented: It accepts a stream of octets from the user, groups them into segments as it sees fit, and numbers each octet in the stream.

The *checksum* field applies to the entire segment plus a pseudoheader prefixed to the header at the time of calculation (at both transmission and reception). The pseudoheader includes the following fields from the IP header: source and destination internet address and protocol, plus a segment length field. By including the pseudoheader, TCP protects itself from misdelivery by IP. That is, if IP delivers a segment to the wrong host, even if the segment contains no bit errors, the receiving TCP entity will detect the delivery error.

APPENDIX 4C USER DATAGRAM PROTOCOL

In addition to TCP, there is one other transport-level protocol that is in common use as part of the TCP/IP protocol suite: the User Datagram Protocol (UDP), specified in RFC 768. UDP provides a connectionless service for application-level procedures. Thus, UDP is basically an unreliable service; delivery and duplicate protection are not guaranteed. However, this does reduce the overhead of the protocol and may be adequate in many cases.

The strengths of the connection-oriented approach are clear. It allows connection-related features such as flow control, error control, and sequenced delivery. Connectionless service, however, is more appropriate in some contexts. At lower layers (internet, network), connectionless service is more robust. An example of this is the datagram approach to packet switching, discussed in Chapter 3. When each packet is treated independently and routed independently, the impact of congestion or loss in the network is less than if there is a predefined route or connection over which all packets travel.

In addition, a connectionless service represents a "least common denominator" of service to be expected at higher layers. Further, even at transport and above there is justification for a connectionless service. There are instances in which the overhead of connection establishment and maintenance is unjustified or even counterproductive. Examples include the following:

- **Inward data collection:** Involves the periodic active or passive sampling of data sources, such as sensors, and automatic self-test reports from security equipment or network components. In a real-time monitoring situation, the loss of an occasional data unit would not cause distress, because the next report should arrive shortly.

- **Outward data dissemination:** Includes broadcast messages to network users, the announcement of a new node or the change of address of a service, and the distribution of real-time clock values.

- **Request-response:** Applications in which a transaction service is provided by a common server to a number of distributed transport service users, and for which a single request-response sequence is typical. Use of the service is regulated at the application level, and lower-level connections are often unnecessary and cumbersome.

- **Real-time applications:** Such as voice and telemetry, involving a degree of redundancy and/or a real-time transmission requirement. These must not have connection-oriented functions such as retransmission.

Thus, there is a place at the transport level for both a connection-oriented and a connectionless type of service.

UDP sits on top of IP. Because it is connectionless, UDP has very little to do. Essentially, it adds a port addressing capability to IP. This is best seen by examining the UDP header, shown in Figure 4.15b. The header includes a source port and destination port. The length field contains the length of the entire UDP segment, including header and data. The checksum is the same algorithm used for TCP and IP. For UDP, the checksum applies to the entire UDP segment plus a pseudoheader prefixed to the UDP header at the time of calculation and is the same pseudoheader used for TCP. If an error is detected, the segment is discarded and no further action is taken.

The checksum field in UDP is optional. If it is not used, it is set to zero. However, it should be pointed out that the IP checksum applies only to the IP header and not to the data field, which in this case consists of the UDP header and the user data. Thus, if no checksum calculation is performed by UDP, then no check is made on the user data.

Wireless Communication Technology

CHAPTER **5**

ANTENNAS AND PROPAGATION

T his chapter provides some fundamental background for wireless transmission. We begin with an overview of antennas and then look at signal propagation.

5.1   ANTENNAS

An antenna can be defined as an electrical conductor or system of conductors used either for radiating electromagnetic energy into space or for collecting electromagnetic energy from space. For transmission of a signal, radio-frequency electrical energy from the transmitter is converted into electromagnetic energy by the antenna and radiated into the surrounding environment (atmosphere, space, water). For reception of a signal, electromagnetic energy impinging on the antenna is converted into radio-frequency electrical energy and fed into the receiver.

In two-way communication, the same antenna can be and often is used for both transmission and reception. This is possible because any antenna transfers energy from the surrounding environment to its input receiver terminals with the same efficiency that it transfers energy from the output transmitter terminals into the surrounding environment, assuming that the same frequency is used in both directions. Put another way, antenna characteristics are essentially the same whether an antenna is sending or receiving electromagnetic energy.

Radiation Patterns

An antenna will radiate power in all directions but, typically, does not perform equally well in all directions. A common way to characterize the performance of an antenna is the radiation pattern, which is a graphical representation of the radiation properties of an antenna as a function of space coordinates. The simplest pattern is produced by an idealized antenna known as the isotropic antenna. An **isotropic antenna** is a point in space that radiates power in all directions equally. The actual radiation pattern for the isotropic antenna is a sphere with the antenna at the center. However, radiation patterns are almost always depicted as a two-dimensional cross section of the three-dimensional pattern. The pattern for the isotropic antenna is shown in Figure 5.1a. The distance from the antenna to each point on the radiation pattern is proportional to the power radiated from the antenna in that direction. Figure 5.1b shows the radiation pattern of another idealized antenna. This is a directional antenna in which the preferred direction of radiation is along one axis.

The actual size of a radiation pattern is arbitrary. What is important is the relative distance from the antenna position in each direction. The relative distance determines the relative power. To determine the relative power in a given direction, a line is drawn from the antenna position at the appropriate angle, and the point of intercept with the radiation pattern is determined. Figure 5.1 shows a comparison of two transmission angles, A and B, drawn on the two radiation patterns. The isotropic antenna produces an omnidirectional radiation pattern of equal strength in all directions, so the A and B vectors are of equal length. For the Hertz antenna, the B vector is longer than the A vector, indicating that more power is radiated in

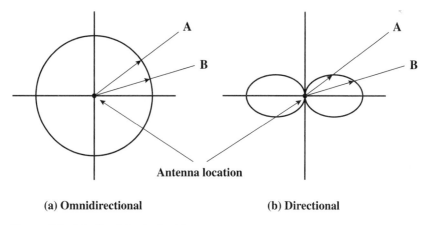

(a) Omnidirectional   (b) Directional

Figure 5.1 Idealized Radiation Patterns

the B direction than in the A direction, and the relative lengths of the two vectors are proportional to the amount of power radiated in the two directions.

The radiation pattern provides a convenient means of determining the **beam width** of an antenna, which is a common measure of the directivity of an antenna. The beam width, also referred to as the half-power beam width, is the angle within which the power radiated by the antenna is at least half of what it is in the most pre-ferred direction.

When an antenna is used for reception, the radiation pattern becomes a **reception pattern**. The longest sections of the pattern indicates the best direction for reception.

Antenna Types

Dipoles

Two of the simplest and most basic antennas are the half-wave dipole, or Hertz, antenna (Figure 5.2a) and the quarter-wave vertical, or Marconi, antenna (Figure 5.2b). The half-wave dipole consists of two straight collinear conductors of equal length, separated by a small feeding gap. The length of the antenna is one-half

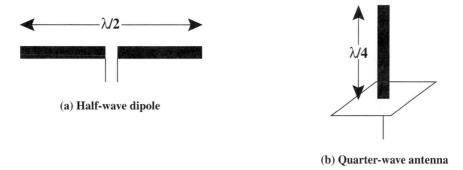

(a) Half-wave dipole

(b) Quarter-wave antenna

Figure 5.2 Simple Antennas

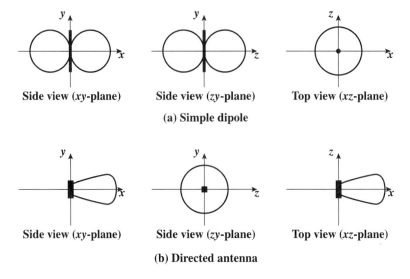

| Side view (*xy*-plane) | Side view (*zy*-plane) | Top view (*xz*-plane) |

(a) Simple dipole

| Side view (*xy*-plane) | Side view (*zy*-plane) | Top view (*xz*-plane) |

(b) Directed antenna

Figure 5.3   Radiation Patterns in Three Dimensions [SCHI00]

the wavelength of the signal that can be transmitted most efficiently. A vertical quarter-wave antenna is the type commonly used for automobile radios and portable radios.

A half-wave dipole has a uniform or omnidirectional radiation pattern in one dimension and a figure eight pattern in the other two dimensions (Figure 5.3a). More complex antenna configurations can be used to produce a directional beam. A typical directional radiation pattern is shown in Figure 5.3b. In this case the main strength of the antenna is in the x direction.

Parabolic Reflective Antenna

An important type of antenna is the **parabolic reflective antenna**, which is used in terrestrial microwave and satellite applications. You may recall from your pre-college geometry studies that a parabola is the locus of all points equidistant from a fixed line and a fixed point not on the line. The fixed point is called the *focus* and the fixed line is called the *directrix* (Figure 5.4a). If a parabola is revolved about its axis, the surface generated is called a *paraboloid*. A cross section through the paraboloid parallel to its axis forms a parabola and a cross section perpendicular to the axis forms a circle. Such surfaces are used in headlights, optical and radio telescopes, and microwave antennas because of the following property: If a source of electromagnetic energy (or sound) is placed at the focus of the paraboloid, and if the paraboloid is a reflecting surface, then the wave will bounce back in lines parallel to the axis of the paraboloid; Figure 5.4b shows this effect in cross section. In theory, this effect creates a parallel beam without dispersion. In practice, there will be some dispersion, because the source of energy must occupy more than one point. The converse is also true. If incoming waves are parallel to the axis of the reflecting paraboloid, the resulting signal will be concentrated at the focus.

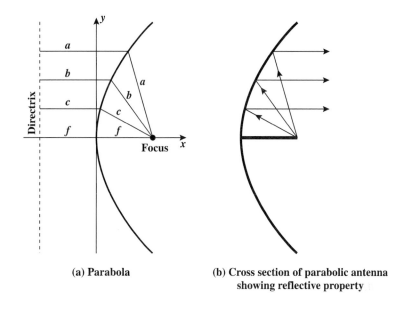

(a) Parabola

(b) Cross section of parabolic antenna
showing reflective property

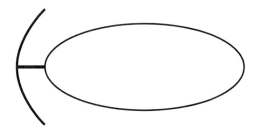

(c) Cross section of parabolic antenna
showing radiation pattern

Figure 5.4   Parabolic Reflective Antenna

Figure 5.4c shows a typical radiation pattern for the parabolic reflective antenna, and Table 5.1 lists beam widths for antennas of various sizes at a frequency of 12 GHz. Note that the larger the diameter of the antenna, the more tightly directional is the beam.

Antenna Gain

Antenna gain is a measure of the directionality of an antenna. Antenna gain is defined as the power output, in a particular direction, compared to that produced in any direction by a perfect omnidirectional antenna (isotropic antenna). For example, if an antenna has a gain of 3 dB, that antenna improves upon the isotropic antenna in that direction by 3 dB, or a factor of 2. The increased power radiated in

Table 5.1 Antenna Beamwidths for Various Diameter Parabolic Reflective Antennas at $f = 12$ GHz [FREE97]

Antenna Diameter (m)	Beam Width (degrees)
0.5	3.5
0.75	2.33
1.0	1.75
1.5	1.166
2.0	0.875
2.5	0.7
5.0	0.35

a given direction is at the expense of other directions. In effect, increased power is radiated in one direction by reducing the power radiated in other directions. It is important to note that antenna gain does not refer to obtaining more output power than input power but rather to directionality.

A concept related to that of antenna gain is the **effective area** of an antenna. The effective area of an antenna is related to the physical size of the antenna and to its shape. The relationship between antenna gain and effective area is

$$G = \frac{4\pi A_e}{\lambda^2} = \frac{4\pi f^2 A_e}{c^2} \tag{5.1}$$

where

$$
\begin{aligned}
G &= \text{antenna gain} \\
A_e &= \text{effective area} \\
f &= \text{carrier frequency} \\
c &= \text{speed of light } (\approx 3 \times 10^8 \text{ m/s}) \\
\lambda &= \text{carrier wavelength}
\end{aligned}
$$

Table 5.2 shows the antenna gain and effective area of some typical antenna shapes.

Table 5.2 Antenna Gains and Effective Areas [COUC01]

Type of Antenna	Effective Area A_e (m²)	Power Gain (relative to isotropic)
Isotropic	$\lambda^2/4\pi$	1
Infinitesimal dipole or loop	$1.5\ \lambda^2/4\pi$	1.5
Half-wave dipole	$1.64\ \lambda2/4\pi$	1.64
Horn, mouth area A	$0.81\ A$	$10\ A/\lambda^2$
Parabolic, face area A	$0.56\ A$	$7\ A/\lambda^2$
Turnstile (two crossed, perpendicular dipoles)	$1.15\ \lambda^2/4\pi$	1.15

> **Example.** For a parabolic reflective antenna with a diameter of 2 m, operating at 12 GHz, what is the effective area and the antenna gain? We have an area of $A = \pi r^2 = \pi$ and an effective area of $A_e = 0.56\pi$. The wavelength is $\lambda = c / f = (3 \times 10^8) / (12 \times 10^9) = 0.025$ m. Then
>
> $$G = (7A) / \lambda^2 = (7 \times \pi) / (0.025)^2 = 35,186$$
> $$G_{dB} = 45.46 \text{ dB}$$

5.2 PROPAGATION MODES

A signal radiated from an antenna travels along one of three routes: ground wave, sky wave, or line of sight (LOS). Table 5.3 shows in which frequency range each predominates. In this book, we are almost exclusively concerned with LOS communication, but a short overview of each mode is given in this section.

Ground Wave Propagation

Ground wave propagation (Figure 5.5a) more or less follows the contour of the earth and can propagate considerable distances, well over the visual horizon. This effect is found in frequencies up to about 2 MHz. Several factors account for the tendency of electromagnetic wave in this frequency band to follow the earth's curvature. One factor is that the electromagnetic wave induces a current in the earth's surface, the result of which is to slow the wavefront near the earth, causing the wavefront to tilt downward and hence follow the earth's curvature. Another factor is diffraction, which is a phenomenon having to do with the behavior of electromagnetic waves in the presence of obstacles.

Electromagnetic waves in this frequency range are scattered by the atmosphere in such a way that they do not penetrate the upper atmosphere.

The best-known example of ground wave communication is AM radio.

Sky Wave Propagation

Sky wave propagation is used for amateur radio, CB radio, and international broadcasts such as BBC and Voice of America. With sky wave propagation, a signal from an earth-based antenna is reflected from the ionized layer of the upper atmosphere (ionosphere) back down to earth. Although it appears the wave is reflected from the ionosphere as if the ionosphere were a hard reflecting surface, the effect is in fact caused by refraction. Refraction is described subsequently.

A sky wave signal can travel through a number of hops, bouncing back and forth between the ionosphere and the earth's surface (Figure 5.5b). With this propagation mode, a signal can be picked up thousands of kilometers from the transmitter.

Line-of-Sight Propagation

Above 30 MHz, neither ground wave nor sky wave propagation modes operate, and communication must be by line of sight (Figure 5.5c). For satellite communication,

Table 5.3 Frequency Bands

Band	Frequency Range	Free-Space Wavelength Range	Propagation Characteristics	Typical Use
ELF (extremely low frequency)	30 to 300 Hz	10,000 to 1,000 km	GW	Power line frequencies; used by some home control systems.
VF (voice frequency)	300 to 3000 Hz	1,000 to 100 km	GW	Used by the telephone system for analog subscriber lines.
VLF (very low frequency)	3 to 30 kHz	100 to 10 km	GW; low attenuation day and night; high atmospheric noise level	Long-range navigation; submarine communication
LF (low frequency)	30 to 300 kHz	10 to 1 km	GW; slightly less reliable than VLF; absorption in daytime	Long-range navigation; marine communication radio beacons
MF (medium frequency)	300 to 3000 kHz	1,000 to 100 m	GW and night SW; attenuation low at night, high in day; atmospheric noise	Maritime radio; direction finding; AM broadcasting.
HF (high frequency)	3 to 30 MHz	100 to 10 m	SW; quality varies with time of day, season, and frequency.	Amateur radio; international broadcasting, military communication; long-distance aircraft and ship communication
VHF (very high frequency)	30 to 300 MHz	10 to 1 m	LOS; scattering because of temperature inversion; cosmic noise	VHF television; FM broadcast and two-way radio, AM aircraft communication; aircraft navigational aids
UHF (ultra high frequency)	300 to 3000 MHz	100 to 10 cm	LOS; cosmic noise	UHF television; cellular telephone; radar; microwave links; personal communications systems
SHF (super high frequency)	3 to 30 GHz	10 to 1 cm	LOS; rainfall attenuation above 10 GHz;atmospheric attenuation due to oxygen and water vapor	Satellite communication; radar; terrestrial microwave links; wireless local loop
EHF (extremely high frequency)	30 to 300 GHz	10 to 1 mm	LOS; atmospheric attenuation due to oxygen and water vapor	Experimental; wireless local loop
Infrared	300 GHz to 400 THz	1 mm to 770 nm	LOS	Infrared LANs; consumer electronic applications
Visible light	400 THz to 900 THz	770 nm to 330 nm	LOS	Optical communication

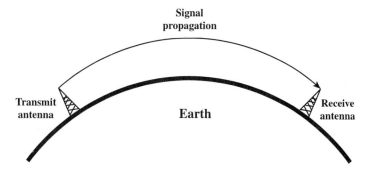

(a) Ground wave propagation (below 2 MHz)

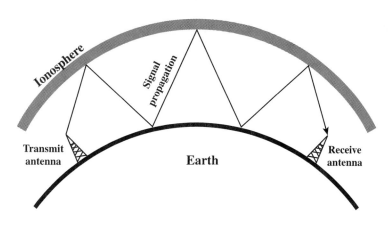

(b) Sky wave propagation (2 to 30 MHz)

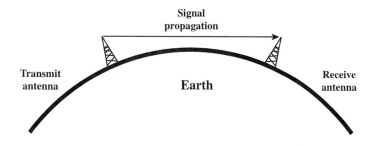

(c) Line-of-sight (LOS) propagation (above 30 MHz)

Figure 5.5   Wireless Propagation Modes

a signal above 30 MHz is not reflected by the ionosphere and therefore a signal can be transmitted between an earth station and a satellite overhead that is not beyond the horizon. For ground-based communication, the transmitting and receiving antennas must be within an *effective* line of sight of each other. The term *effective* is used because microwaves are bent or refracted by the atmosphere. The amount and even the direction of the bend depends on conditions, but generally microwaves are bent with the curvature of the earth and will therefore propagate farther than the optical line of sight.

Refraction

Before proceeding, a brief discussion of refraction is warranted. Refraction occurs because the velocity of an electromagnetic wave is a function of the density of the medium through which it travels. In a vacuum, an electromagnetic wave (such as light or a radio wave) travels at approximately 3×10^8 m/s. This is the constant, c, commonly referred to as the speed of light, but actually referring to the speed of light in a vacuum. In air, water, glass, and other transparent or partially transparent media, electromagnetic waves travel at speeds less than c.

When an electromagnetic wave moves from a medium of one density to a medium of another density, its speed changes. The effect is to cause a one-time bending of the direction of the wave at the boundary between the two media. This is illustrated in Figure 5.6. If moving from a less dense to a more dense medium, the wave will bend toward the more dense medium. This phenomenon is easily observed by partially immersing a stick in water. The result will look much like Figure 5.6, with the stick appearing shorter and bent.

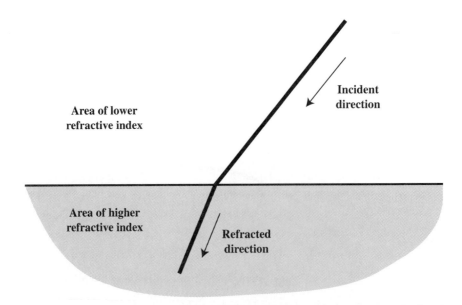

Figure 5.6   Refraction of an Electromagnetic Wave [POOL98]

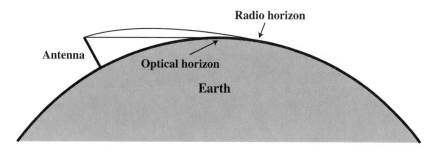

Figure 5.7 Optical and Radio Horizons

The index of refraction of one medium relative to another is the sine of the angle of incidence divided by the sine of the angle of refraction. The index of refraction is also equal to the ratio of the respective velocities in the two media. The absolute index of refraction of a medium is calculated in comparison with that of a vacuum. Refractive index varies with wavelength, so that refractive effects differ for signals with different wavelengths.

Although Figure 5.6 shows an abrupt, one-time change in direction as a signal moves from one medium to another, a continuous, gradual bending of a signal will occur if it is moving through a medium in which the index of refraction gradually changes. Under normal propagation conditions, the refractive index of the atmosphere decreases with height so that radio waves travel more slowly near the ground than at higher altitudes. The result is a slight bending of the radio waves toward the earth.

Optical and Radio Line of Sight

With no intervening obstacles, the optical line of sight can be expressed as

$$d = 3.57\sqrt{h}$$

where d is the distance between an antenna and the horizon in kilometers and h is the antenna height in meters. The effective, or radio, line of sight to the horizon is expressed as (Figure 5.7)

$$d = 3.57\sqrt{Kh}$$

where K is an adjustment factor to account for the refraction. A good rule of thumb is K = 4/3. Thus, the maximum distance between two antennas for LOS propagation is $3.57(\sqrt{Kh_1} + \sqrt{Kh_2})$, where h_1 and h_2 are the heights of the two antennas.

Example. The maximum distance between two antennas for LOS transmission if one antenna is 100 m high and the other is at ground level is

$$d = 3.57\sqrt{Kh} = 3.57\sqrt{133} = 41 \text{ km}$$

Now suppose that the receiving antenna is 10 m high. To achieve the same distance, how high must the transmitting antenna be? The result is

$$41 = 3.57(\sqrt{Kh_1} + \sqrt{13.3})$$
$$\sqrt{Kh_1} = \frac{41}{3.57} - \sqrt{13.3} = 7.84$$
$$h_1 = 7.84^2/1.33 = 46.2 \text{ m}$$

This is a savings of over 50 m in the height of the transmitting antenna. This example illustrates the benefit of raising receiving antennas above ground level to reduce the necessary height of the transmitter.

5.3 LINE-OF-SIGHT TRANSMISSION

With any communications system, the signal that is received will differ from the signal that is transmitted, due to various transmission impairments. For analog signals, these impairments introduce various random modifications that degrade the signal quality. For digital data, bit errors are introduced: A binary 1 is transformed into a binary 0, and vice versa. In this section we examine the various impairments and comment on their effect on the information-carrying capacity of a communications link. Our concern in this book is with LOS wireless transmission, and in this context, the most significant impairments are as follows:

- Attenuation and attenuation distortion
- Free space loss
- Noise
- Atmospheric absorption
- Multipath
- Refraction

Attenuation

The strength of a signal falls off with distance over any transmission medium. For guided media, this reduction in strength, or attenuation, is generally logarithmic and thus is typically expressed as a constant number of decibels per unit distance. For unguided media, attenuation is a more complex function of distance and the makeup of the atmosphere. Attenuation introduces three factors for the transmission engineer:

1. A received signal must have sufficient strength so that the electronic circuitry in the receiver can detect and interpret the signal.
2. The signal must maintain a level sufficiently higher than noise to be received without error.
3. Attenuation is greater at higher frequencies, causing distortion.

The first and second factors are dealt with by attention to signal strength and the use of amplifiers or repeaters. For a point-to-point link, the signal strength of the transmitter must be strong enough to be received intelligibly, but not so strong as to overload the circuitry of the transmitter or receiver, which would cause distortion. Beyond a certain distance, the attenuation becomes unacceptably great, and repeaters or amplifiers are used to boost the signal at regular intervals. These problems are more complex when there are multiple receivers, where the distance from transmitter to receiver is variable.

The third factor is known as attenuation distortion. Because the attenuation varies as a function of frequency, the received signal is distorted, reducing intelligibility. Specifically, the frequency components of the received signal have different relative strengths than the frequency components of the transmitted signal. To overcome this problem, techniques are available for equalizing attenuation across a band of frequencies. One approach is to use amplifiers that amplify high frequencies more than lower frequencies.

Free Space Loss

For any type of wireless communication the signal disperses with distance. Therefore, an antenna with a fixed area will receive less signal power the farther it is from the transmitting antenna. For satellite communication this is the primary mode of signal loss. Even if no other sources of attenuation or impairment are assumed, a transmitted signal attenuates over distance because the signal is being spread over a larger and larger area. This form of attenuation is known as **free space loss**, which can be express in terms of the ratio of the radiated power P_t to the power P_r received by the antenna or, in decibels, by taking 10 times the log of that ratio. For the ideal isotropic antenna, free space loss is

$$\frac{P_t}{P_r} = \frac{(4\pi d)^2}{\lambda^2} = \frac{(4\pi f d)^2}{c^2}$$

where

P_t = signal power at the transmitting antenna
P_r = signal power at the receiving antenna
λ = carrier wavelength
d = propagation distance between antennas
c = speed of light (3×10^8 m/s)

where d and λ are in the same units (e.g., meters).

This can be recast as

$$L_{dB} = 10 \log\frac{P_t}{P_r} = 20 \log\left(\frac{4\pi d}{\lambda}\right) = -20 \log(\lambda) + 20 \log(d) + 21.98 \text{ dB}$$

$$= 20 \log\left(\frac{4\pi f d}{c}\right) = 20 \log(f) + 20 \log(d) - 147.56 \text{ dB}$$

(5.2)

Figure 5.8 illustrates the free space loss equation.[1]

For other antennas, we must take into account the gain of the antenna, which yields the following free space loss equation:

$$\frac{P_t}{P_r} = \frac{(4\pi)^2(d)^2}{G_r G_t \lambda^2} = \frac{(\lambda d)^2}{A_r A_t} = \frac{(cd)^2}{f^2 A_r A_t}$$

where

G_t = gain of the transmitting antenna
G_r = gain of the receiving antenna
A_t = effective area of the transmitting antenna
A_r = effective area of the receiving antenna

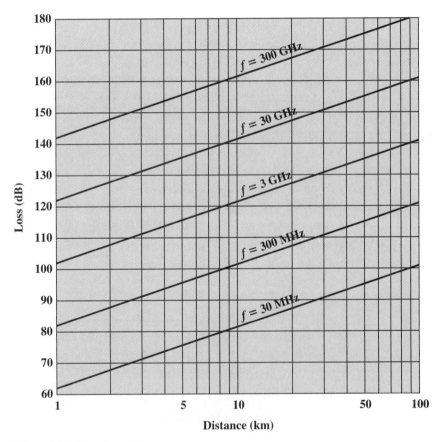

Figure 5.8   Free Space Loss

---

[1]As was mentioned in Appendix 2A, there is some inconsistency in the literature over the use of the terms *gain* and *loss*. Equation (5.2) follows the convention of Equation (2.2).

The third fraction is derived from the second fraction using the relationship between antenna gain and effective area defined in Equation (5.1). We can recast this equation as

$$L_{dB} = 20 \log (\lambda) + 20 \log (d) - 10 \log (A_rA_r)$$
$$= -20 \log (f) + 20 \log (d) - 10 \log (A_rA_t) + 169.54 \text{ dB} \qquad (5.3)$$

Thus, for the same antenna dimensions and separation, the longer the carrier wavelength (lower the carrier frequency f), the higher is the free space path loss. It is interesting to compare Equations (5.2) and (5.3). Equation (5.2) indicates that as the frequency increases, the free space loss also increases, which would suggest that at higher frequencies, losses become more burdensome. However, Equation (5.3) shows that we can easily compensate for this increased loss with antenna gains. In fact, there is a net gain at higher frequencies, other factors remaining constant. Equation (5.2) shows that at a fixed distance an increase in frequency results in an increased loss measured by $20 \log(f)$. However, if we take into account antenna gain, and fix antenna area, then the change in loss is measured by $-20 \log(f)$; that is, there is actually a decrease in loss at higher frequencies.

Example. Determine the isotropic free space loss at 4 GHz for the shortest path to a synchronous ssttelite from earth (35,863 km). At 4 GHz, the wavelength is $(3 \times 10^8) / (4 \times 10^9) = 0.075$ m. Then

$$L_{dB} = -20 \log (0.075) + 20 \log(35.853 \times 10^6) + 21.98 = 195.6 \text{ dB}$$

Now consider the antenna gain of both the satellite- and ground-based antennas. Typical values are 44 dB and 48 dB, respectively. The free space loss is

$$L_{dB} = 195.6 - 44 - 48 = 103.6 \text{ dB}$$

Now assume a transmit power of 250 W at the earth station. What is the power received at the satellite antenna? A power of 250 W translates into 24 dBW, so the power at the receiving antenna is $24 - 103.6 = -79.6$ dBW.

Noise

For any data transmission event, the received signal will consist of the transmitted signal, modified by the various distortions imposed by the transmission system, plus additional unwanted signals that are inserted somewhere between transmission and reception. These unwanted signals are referred to as noise. Noise is the major limiting factor in communications system performance.

Noise may be divided into four categories:

- Thermal noise
- Intermodulation noise
- Crosstalk
- Impulse noise

Thermal noise is due to thermal agitation of electrons. It is present in all electronic devices and transmission media and is a function of temperature. Thermal noise is uniformly distributed across the frequency spectrum and hence is often referred to as white noise. Thermal noise cannot be eliminated and therefore places an upper bound on communications system performance. Because of the weakness of the signal received by satellite earth stations, thermal noise is particularly significant for satellite communication.

The amount of thermal noise to be found in a bandwidth of 1 Hz in any device or conductor is

$$N_0 = kT \text{ (W/Hz)}$$

where[2]

N_0 =noise power density in watts per 1 Hz of bandwidth
k =Boltzmann's constant = 1.3803×10^{-23} J/K
T =temperature, in kelvins (absolute temperature)

Example. Room temperature is usually specified as $T = 17°C$, or 290 K. At this temperature, the thermal noise power density is

$$N_0 = (1.3803 \times 10^{-23}) \times 290 = 4 \times 10^{-21} \text{ W/Hz} = -204 \text{ dBW/Hz}$$

where dBW is the decibel-watt, defined in Appendix 2A.

The noise is assumed to be independent of frequency. Thus the thermal noise in watts present in a bandwidth of B Hertz can be expressed as

$$N = kTB$$

or, in decibel-watts,

$$N = 10 \log k + 10 \log T + 10 \log B$$
$$= -228.6 \text{ dBW} + 10 \log T + 10 \log B$$

Example. Given a receiver with an effective noise temperature of 294 K and a 10-MHz bandwidth, the thermal noise level at the receiver's output is

$$N = -228.6 \text{ dBW} + 10 \log(294) + 10 \log 10^7$$
$$= -228.6 + 24.7 + 70$$
$$= -133.9 \text{ dBW}$$

---

[2]A Joule (J) is the International System (SI) unit of electrical, mechanical, and thermal energy. A watt is the SI unit of power, equal to one joule per second. The kelvin (K) is the SI unit of thermodynamic temperature. For a temperature in degrees kelvin of T, the corresponding temperature in degrees Celsius is equal to T − 273.15.

When signals at different frequencies share the same transmission medium, the result may be **intermodulation noise**. Intermodulation noise produces signals at a frequency that is the sum or difference of the two original frequencies or multiples of those frequencies. For example, the mixing of signals at frequencies f_1 and f_2 might produce energy at the frequency $f_1 + f_2$. This derived signal could interfere with an intended signal at the frequency $f_1 + f_2$.

Intermodulation noise is produced when there is some nonlinearity in the transmitter, receiver, or intervening transmission system. Normally, these components behave as linear systems; that is, the output is equal to the input times a constant. In a nonlinear system, the output is a more complex function of the input. Such nonlinearity can be caused by component malfunction, the use of excessive signal strength, or just the nature of the amplifiers used. It is under these circumstances that the sum and difference frequency terms occur.

Crosstalk has been experienced by anyone who, while using the telephone, has been able to hear another conversation; it is an unwanted coupling between signal paths. It can occur by electrical coupling between nearby twisted pairs or, rarely, coax cable lines carrying multiple signals. Crosstalk can also occur when unwanted signals are picked up by microwave antennas; although highly directional antennas are used, microwave energy does spread during propagation. Typically, crosstalk is of the same order of magnitude as, or less than, thermal noise. However, in the unlicensed ISM bands, crosstalk often dominates.

All of the types of noise discussed so far have reasonably predictable and relatively constant magnitudes. Thus it is possible to engineer a transmission system to cope with them. **Impulse noise**, however, is noncontinuous, consisting of irregular pulses or noise spikes of short duration and of relatively high amplitude. It is generated from a variety of causes, including external electromagnetic disturbances, such as lightning, and faults and flaws in the communications system.

Impulse noise is generally only a minor annoyance for analog data. For example, voice transmission may be corrupted by short clicks and crackles with no loss of intelligibility. However, impulse noise is the primary source of error in digital data transmission. For example, a sharp spike of energy of 0.01 s duration would not destroy any voice data but would wash out about 560 bits of data being transmitted at 56 kbps.

The Expression E_b/N_0

Chapter 2 introduced the signal-to-noise ratio (SNR). There is a parameter related to SNR that is more convenient for determining digital data rates and error rates and that is the standard quality measure for digital communication system performance. The parameter is the ratio of signal energy per bit to noise power density per Hertz, E_b/N_0. Consider a signal, digital or analog, that contains binary digital data transmitted at a certain bit rate R. Recalling that 1 watt = 1 J/s, the energy per bit in a signal is given by $E_b = ST_b$, where S is the signal power and T_b is the time required to send one bit. The data rate R is just $R = 1/T_b$. Thus

$$\frac{E_b}{N_0} = \frac{S/R}{N_0} = \frac{S}{kTR}$$

or, in decibel notation,

$$\left(\frac{E_b}{N_0}\right)_{dB} = S_{dBW} - 10 \log R - 10 \log k - 10 \log T$$

$$= S_{dBW} - 10 \log R + 228.6 \text{ dBW} - 10 \log T$$

The ratio E_b/N_0 is important because the bit error rate for digital data is a (decreasing) function of this ratio. Given a value of E_b/N_0 needed to achieve a desired error rate, the parameters in the preceding formula may be selected. Note that as the bit rate R increases, the transmitted signal power, relative to noise, must increase to maintain the required E_b/N_0.

Let us try to grasp this result intuitively by considering again Figure 2.9. The signal here is digital, but the reasoning would be the same for an analog signal. In several instances, the noise is sufficient to alter the value of a bit. If the data rate were doubled, the bits would be more tightly packed together, and the same passage of noise might destroy two bits. Thus, for constant signal and noise strength, an increase in data rate increases the error rate.

The advantage of E_b/N_0 over SNR is that the latter quantity depends on the bandwidth.

Example. Suppose a signal encoding technique requires that $E_b/N_0 = 8.4$ dB for a bit error rate of 10^{-4} (one bit error out of every 10,000). If the effective noise temperature is 290°K (room temperature) and the data rate is 2400 bps, what received signal level is required to overcome thermal noise?

We have

$$8.4 = S_{dBW} - 10 \log 2400 + 228.6 \text{ dBW} - 10 \log 290$$
$$= S_{dBW} - (10)(3.38) + 228.6 - (10)(2.46)$$
$$S = -161.8 \text{ dBW}$$

We can relate E_b/N_0 to SNR as follows. We have

$$\frac{E_b}{N_0} = \frac{S}{N_0 R}$$

The parameter N_0 is the noise power density in watts/hertz. Hence, the noise in a signal with bandwidth B_T is $N = N_0 B_T$. Substituting, we have

$$\frac{E_b}{N_0} = \frac{S}{N} \frac{B_T}{R} \qquad (5.4)$$

Another formulation of interest relates to E_b/N_0 spectral efficiency. Recall, from Chapter 2, Shannon's result that the maximum channel capacity, in bits per second, obeys the equation

$$C = B \log_2 (1 + S/N)$$

where C is the capacity of the channel in bits per second and B is the bandwidth of the channel in Hertz. This can be rewritten as

$$\frac{S}{N} = 2^{C/B} - 1$$

Using Equation (5.4), and equating B_T with B and R with C, we have

$$\frac{E_b}{N_0} = \frac{B}{C} (2^{C/B} - 1)$$

This is a useful formula that relates the achievable spectral efficiency C/B to E_b/N_0.

Example. Suppose we want to find the minimum E_b/N_0 required to achieve a spectral efficiency of 6 bps/Hz. Then $E_b/N_0 = (1/6)(2^6 - 1) = 10.5 = 10.21$ dB.

Atmospheric Absorption

An additional loss between the transmitting and receiving antennas is atmospheric absorption. Water vapor and oxygen contribute most to attenuation. A peak attenuation occurs in the vicinity of 22 GHz due to water vapor. At frequencies below 15 GHz, the attenuation is less. The presence of oxygen results in an absorption peak in the vicinity of 60 GHz but contributes less at frequencies below 30 GHz. Rain and fog (suspended water droplets) cause scattering of radio waves that results in attenuation. This can be a major cause of signal loss. Thus, in areas of significant precipitation, either path lengths have to be kept short or lower-frequency bands should be used.

Multipath

For wireless facilities where there is a relatively free choice of where antennas are to be located, they can be placed so that if there are no nearby interfering obstacles, there is a direct line-of-sight path from transmitter to receiver. This is generally the case for many satellite facilities and for point-to-point microwave. In other cases, such as mobile telephony, there are obstacles in abundance. The signal can be reflected by such obstacles so that multiple copies of the signal with varying delays can be received. In fact, in extreme cases, there may be no direct signal. Depending on the differences in the path lengths of the direct and reflected waves, the composite signal can be either larger or smaller than the direct signal. Reinforcement and cancellation of the signal resulting from the signal following multiple paths can be controlled for communication between fixed, well-sited antennas, and between satellites and fixed ground stations. One exception is when the path goes across water, where the wind keeps the reflective surface of the water in motion. For mobile telephony and communication to antennas that are not well sited, multipath considerations can be paramount.

Figure 5.9 illustrates in general terms the types of multipath interference typical in terrestrial, fixed microwave and in mobile communications. For fixed

(a) Microwave line of sight

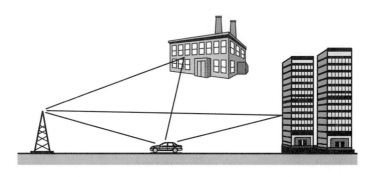

(b) Mobile radio

Figure 5.9   Examples of Multipath Interference

microwave, in addition to the direct line of sight, the signal may follow a curved path through the atmosphere due to refraction and the signal may also reflect from the ground. For mobile communications, structures and topographic features provide reflection surfaces.

Refraction

Radio waves are refracted (or bent) when they propagate through the atmosphere. The refraction is caused by changes in the speed of the signal with altitude or by other spatial changes in the atmospheric conditions. Normally, the speed of the signal increases with altitude, causing radio waves to bend downward. However, on occasion, weather conditions may lead to variations in speed with height that differ significantly from the typical variations. This may result in a situation in which only a fraction or no part of the line-of-sight wave reaches the receiving antenna.

5.4   FADING IN THE MOBILE ENVIRONMENT

Perhaps the most challenging technical problem facing communications systems engineers is fading in a mobile environment. The term *fading* refers to the time variation of received signal power caused by changes in the transmission medium or path(s). In a fixed environment, fading is affected by changes in atmospheric conditions, such as rainfall. But in a mobile environment, where one of the two antennas is moving relative to the other, the relative location of various obstacles changes over time, creating complex transmission effects.

Multipath Propagation

Three propagation mechanisms, illustrated in Figure 5.10, play a role. **Reflection** occurs when an electromagnetic signal encounters a surface that is large relative to the wavelength of the signal. For example, suppose a ground-reflected wave near the mobile unit is received. Because the ground-reflected wave has a 180° phase shift after reflection, the ground wave and the line-of-sight (LOS) wave may tend to cancel, resulting in high signal loss.[3] Further, because the mobile antenna is lower than most human-made structures in the area, multipath interference occurs. These reflected waves may interfere constructively or destructively at the receiver.

Diffraction occurs at the edge of an impenetrable body that is large compared to the wavelength of the radio wave. When a radio wave encounters such an edge, waves propagate in different directions with the edge as the source. Thus, signals can be received even when there is no unobstructed LOS from the transmitter.

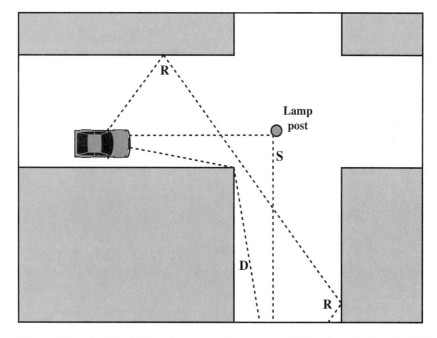

Figure 5.10 Sketch of Three Important Propagation Mechanisms: Reflection (R), Scattering (S), Diffraction (D) [ANDE95]

---

[3]On the other hand, the reflected signal has a longer path, which creates a phase shift due to delay relative to the unreflected signal. When this delay is equivalent to half a wavelength, the two signals are back in phase.

If the size of an obstacle is on the order of the wavelength of the signal or less, **scattering** occurs. An incoming signal is scattered into several weaker outgoing signals. At typical cellular microwave frequencies, there are numerous objects, such as lamp posts and traffic signs, that can cause scattering. Thus, scattering effects are difficult to predict.

These three propagation effects influence system performance in various ways depending on local conditions and as the mobile unit moves within a cell. If a mobile unit has a clear LOS to the transmitter, then diffraction and scattering are generally minor effects, although reflection may have a significant impact. If there is no clear LOS, such as in an urban area at street level, then diffraction and scattering are the primary means of signal reception.

The Effects of Multipath Propagation

As just noted, one unwanted effect of multipath propagation is that multiple copies of a signal may arrive at different phases. If these phases add destructively, the signal level relative to noise declines, making signal detection at the receiver more difficult.

A second phenomenon, of particular importance for digital transmission, is intersymbol interference (ISI). Consider that we are sending a narrow pulse at a given frequency across a link between a fixed antenna and a mobile unit. Figure 5.11 shows what the channel may deliver to the receiver if the impulse is sent at two different times. The upper line shows two pulses at the time of transmission. The lower line shows the resulting pulses at the receiver. In each case the first received pulse is the desired LOS signal. The magnitude of that pulse may change because of changes in atmospheric attenuation. Further, as the mobile unit moves farther away from the fixed antenna, the amount of LOS attenuation increases. But in addition to this primary pulse, there may be multiple secondary pulses due to reflection, diffraction,

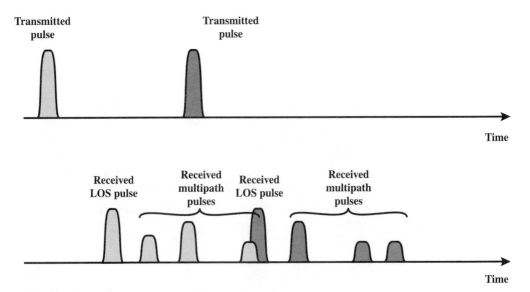

Figure 5.11   Two Pulses in Time-Variant Multipath

and scattering. Now suppose that this pulse encodes one or more bits of data. In that case, one or more delayed copies of a pulse may arrive at the same time as the primary pulse for a subsequent bit. These delayed pulses act as a form of noise to the subsequent primary pulse, making recovery of the bit information more difficult.

As the mobile antenna moves, the location of various obstacles changes; hence the number, magnitude, and timing of the secondary pulses change. This makes it difficult to design signal processing techniques that will filter out multipath effects so that the intended signal is recovered with fidelity.

Types of Fading

Fading effects in a mobile environment can be classified as either fast or slow. Referring to Figure 5.10, as the mobile unit moves down a street in an urban environment, rapid variations in signal strength occur over distances of about one-half a wavelength. At a frequency of 900 MHz, which is typical for mobile cellular applications, a wavelength is 0.33 m. The rapidly changing waveform in Figure 5.12 shows an example of the spatial variation of received signal amplitude at 900 MHz in an urban setting. Note that changes of amplitude can be as much as 20 or 30 dB over a short distance. This type of rapidly changing fading phenomenon, known as **fast fading**, affects not only mobile phones in automobiles, but even a mobile phone user walking down an urban street.

As the mobile user covers distances well in excess of a wavelength, the urban environment changes, as the user passes buildings of different heights, vacant lots, intersections, and so forth. Over these longer distances, there is a change in the average received power level about which the rapid fluctuations occur. This is indicated by the slowly changing waveform in Figure 5.12 and is referred to as **slow fading**.

Fading effects can also be classified as flat or selective. **Flat fading**, or nonselective fading, is that type of fading in which all frequency components of the received signal fluctuate in the same proportions simultaneously. **Selective fading** affects unequally the different spectral components of a radio signal. The term *selec-*

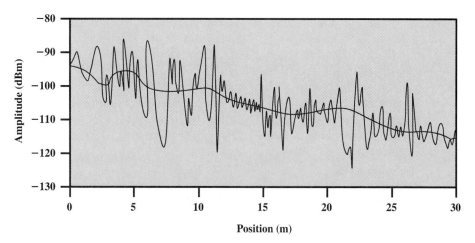

Figure 5.12 Typical Slow and Fast Fading in an Urban Mobile Environment

tive fading is usually significant only relative to the bandwidth of the overall communications channel. If attenuation occurs over a portion of the bandwidth of the signal, the fading is considered to be selective; nonselective fading implies that the signal bandwidth of interest is narrower than, and completely covered by, the spectrum affected by the fading.

The Fading Channel

In designing a communications system, the communications engineer needs to estimate the effects of multipath fading and noise on the mobile channel. The simplest channel model, from the point of view of analysis, is the **additive white Gaussian noise (AWGN)** channel. In this channel, the desired signal is degraded by thermal noise associated with the physical channel itself as well as electronics at the transmitter and receiver (and any intermediate amplifiers or repeaters). This model is fairly accurate in some cases, such as space communications and some wire transmissions, such as coaxial cable. For terrestrial wireless transmission, particularly in the mobile situation, AWGN is not a good guide for the designer.

Rayleigh fading occurs when there are multiple indirect paths between transmitter and receiver and no distinct dominant path, such as an LOS path. This represents a worst-case scenario. Fortunately, Rayleigh fading can be dealt with analytically, providing insights into performance characteristics that can be used in difficult environments, such as downtown urban settings.

Rician fading best characterizes a situation where there is a direct LOS path in addition to a number of indirect multipath signals. The Rician model is often applicable in an indoor environment whereas the Rayleigh model characterizes outdoor settings. The Rician model also becomes more applicable in smaller cells or in more open outdoor environments. The channels can be characterized by a parameter K, defined as follows:

$$K = \frac{\text{power in the dominant path}}{\text{power in the scattered paths}}$$

When $K = 0$ the channel is Rayleigh (i.e., numerator is zero) and when $K = \infty$, the channel is AWGN (i.e., denominator is zero). Figure 5.13, based on [FREE98a] and [SKLA01], shows system performance in the presence of noise. Here bit error rate is plotted as a function of the ratio E_b/N_0. Of course, as that ratio increases, the bit error rate drops. The figure shows that with a reasonably strong signal, relative to noise, an AWGN exhibit provides fairly good performance, as do Rician channels with larger values of K, roughly corresponding to microcells or an open country environment. The performance would be adequate for a digitized voice application, but for digital data transfer efforts to compensate would be needed. The Rayleigh channel provides relatively poor performance; this is likely to be seen for flat fading and for slow fading; in these cases, error compensation mechanisms become more desirable. Finally, some environments produce fading effects worse than the so-called worst case of Rayleigh. Examples are fast fading in an urban environment and the fading within the affected band of a selective fading channel. In these cases, no level of E_b/N_0 will help achieve the desired performance, and

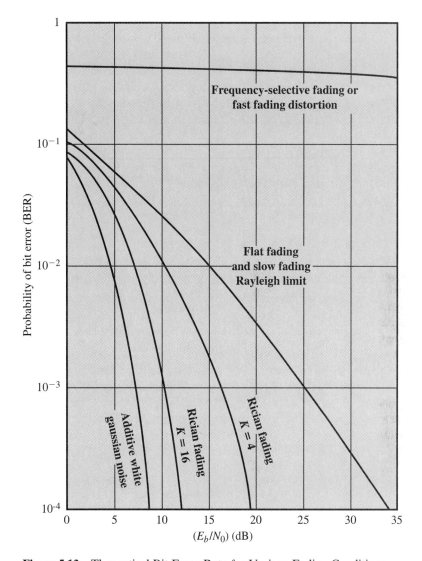

Figure 5.13   Theoretical Bit Error Rate for Various Fading Conditions

compensation mechanisms are mandatory. We turn to a discussion of those mechanisms next.

Error Compensation Mechanisms

The efforts to compensate for the errors and distortions introduced by multipath fading fall into three general categories: forward error correction, adaptive equalization, and diversity techniques. In the typical mobile wireless environment, techniques from all three categories are combined to combat the error rates encountered.

Forward Error Correction

Forward error correction is applicable in digital transmission applications: those in which the transmitted signal carries digital data or digitized voice or video data. The term *forward* refers to procedures whereby a receiver, using only information contained in the incoming digital transmission, corrects bit errors in the data. This is in contrast to backward error correction, in which the receiver merely detects the presence of errors and then sends a request back to the transmitter to retransmit the data in error. Backward error correction is not practical in many wireless applications. For example, in satellite communications, the amount of delay involved makes retransmission undesirable. In mobile communications, the error rates are often so high that there is a high probability that the retransmitted block of bits will also contain errors. In these applications, forward error correction is required. In essence, forward error correction is achieved as follows:

1. The transmitter adds a number of additional, redundant bits to each transmitted block of data. These bits form an **error-correcting code** and are calculated as a function of the data bits.

2. For each incoming block of bits (data plus error-correcting code), the receiver calculates a new error-correcting code from the incoming data bits. If the calculated code matches the incoming code, then the receiver assumes that no error has occurred in this block of bits.

3. If the incoming and calculated codes do not match, then one or more bits are in error. If the number of bit errors is below a threshold that depends on the length of the code and the nature of the algorithm, it is possible for the receiver to determine the bit positions in error and correct all errors.

Typically in mobile wireless applications, the ratio of total bits sent to data bits sent is between 2 and 3. This may seem an extravagant amount of overhead, in that the capacity of the system is cut to one-half or one-third of its potential, but the mobile wireless environment is so difficult that such levels of redundancy are necessary.

Chapter 8 examines forward error correction techniques in detail.

Adaptive Equalization

Adaptive equalization can be applied to transmissions that carry analog information (e.g., analog voice or video) or digital information (e.g., digital data, digitized voice or video) and is used to combat intersymbol interference. The process of equalization involves some method of gathering the dispersed symbol energy back together into its original time interval. Equalization is a broad topic; techniques include the use of so-called lumped analog circuits as well as sophisticated digital signal processing algorithms. Here we give a flavor of the digital signal processing approach.

Figure 5.14 illustrates a common approach using a linear equalizer circuit. In this specific example, for each output symbol, the input signal is sampled at five uniformly spaced intervals of time, separated by a delay τ. These samples are individually weighted by the coefficients C_i and then summed to produce the output. The circuit is referred to as adaptive because the coefficients are dynamically adjusted.

Unequalized
input

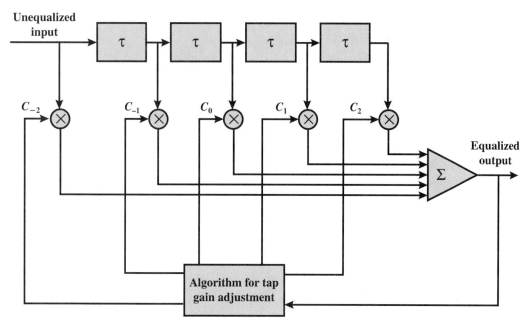

Equalized
output

Figure 5.14   Linear Equalizer Circuit [PROA94]

Typically, the coefficients are set using a *training sequence*, which is a known sequence of bits. The training sequence is transmitted. The receiver compares the received training sequence with the expected training sequence and on the basis of the comparison calculates suitable values for the coefficients. Periodically, a new training sequence is sent to account for changes in the transmission environment.

For Rayleigh channels, or worse, it may be necessary to include a new training sequence with every single block of data. Again, this represents considerable overhead but is justified by the error rates encountered in a mobile wireless environment.

Diversity Techniques

Diversity is based on the fact that individual channels experience independent fading events. We can therefore compensate for error effects by providing multiple logical channels in some sense between transmitter and receiver and sending part of the signal over each channel. This technique does not eliminate errors but it does reduce the error rate, since we have spread the transmission out to avoid being subjected to the highest error rate that might occur. The other techniques (equalization, forward error correction) can then cope with the reduced error rate.

Some diversity techniques involve the physical transmission path and are referred to as **space diversity**. For example, multiple nearby antennas may be used to receive the message, with the signals combined in some fashion to reconstruct the most likely transmitted signal. Another example is the use of collocated multiple directional antennas, each oriented to a different reception angle with the incoming signals again combined to reconstitute the transmitted signal.

More commonly, the term *diversity* refers to frequency diversity or time diversity techniques. With **frequency diversity**, the signal is spread out over a larger frequency bandwidth or carried on multiple frequency carriers. The most important example of this approach is spread spectrum, which is examined in Chapter 7.

Time diversity techniques aim to spread the data out over time so that a noise burst affects fewer bits. Time diversity can be quite effective in a region of slow fading. If a mobile unit is moving slowly, it may remain in a region of a high level of fading for a relatively long interval. The result will be a long burst of errors even though the local mean signal level is much higher than the interference. Even powerful error correction codes may be unable to cope with an extended error burst. If digital data is transmitted in a time division multiplex (TDM) structure, in which multiple users share the same physical channel by the use of time slots (see Figure 2.13b), then block interleaving can be used to provide time diversity. Figure 5.15a,

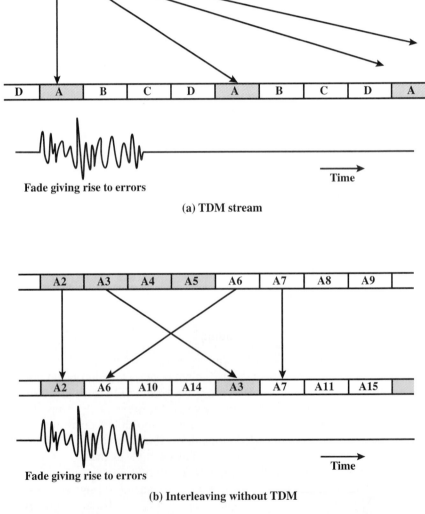

(a) TDM stream

(b) Interleaving without TDM

Figure 5.15 Interleaving Data Blocks to Spread the Effects of Error Bursts based on one in [JONE93], illustrates the concept. Note that the same number of bits are still affected by the noise surge, but they are spread out over a number of logical channels. If each channel is protected by forward error correction, the error-correcting code may be able to cope with the fewer number of bits that are in error in a particular logical channel. If TDM is not used, time diversity can still be applied by viewing the stream of bits from the source as a sequence of blocks and then shuffling the blocks. In Figure 5.15b, blocks are shuffled in groups of four. Again, the same number of bits is in error, but the error-correcting code is applied to sets of bits that are spread out in time. Even greater diversity is achieved by combining TDM interleaving with block shuffling.

The tradeoff with time diversity is delay. The greater the degree of interleaving and shuffling used, the longer the delay in reconstructing the original bit sequence at the receiver.

5.5 RECOMMENDED READING

[FREE97] provides good coverage of all of the topics in this chapter. A rigorous treatment of antennas and propagation is found in [BERT00]. [THUR00] provides an exceptionally clear discussion of antennas.

BERT00 Bertoni, H. *Radio Propagation for Modern Wireless Systems.* Upper Saddle River, NJ: Prentice Hall, 2000.

FREE97 Freeman, R. *Radio System Design for Telecommunications.* New York: Wiley, 1997.

THUR00 Thurwachter, C. *Data and Telecommunications: Systems and Applications.* Upper Saddle River, NJ: Prentice Hall, 2000.

5.6 KEY TERMS, REVIEW QUESTIONS, AND PROBLEMS

Key Terms

adaptive equalization	flat fading	optical LOS
antenna	forward error correction	parabolic reflective antenna
antenna gain	(FEC)	radiation pattern
atmospheric absorption	free space loss	radio LOS
attenuation	ground wave propagation	reception pattern
beam width	Hertz antenna	reflection
crosstalk	impulse noise	refraction
diffraction	intermodulation noise	scattering
dipole	isotropic antenna	selective fading
diversity	line of sight (LOS)	sky wave propagation
fading	multipath	slow fading
fast fading	noise	thermal noise

Review Questions

1 What two functions are performed by an antenna?
2 What is an isotropic antenna?
3 What information is available from a radiation pattern?
4 What is the advantage of a parabolic reflective antenna?
5 What factors determine antenna gain?
6 What is the primary cause of signal loss in satellite communications?
7 Name and briefly define four types of noise.
8 What is refraction?
9 What is fading?
10 What is the difference between diffraction and scattering?
11 What is the difference between fast and slow fading?
12 What is the difference between flat and selective fading?
13 Name and briefly define three diversity techniques.

Problems

1 For radio transmission in free space, signal power is reduced in proportion to the square of the distance form the source, whereas in wire transmission, the attenuation is a fixed number of dB per kilometer. The following table is used to show the dB reduction relative to some reference for free space radio and uniform wire. Fill in the missing numbers to complete the table.
2 Find the optimum wavelength and frequency for a half-wave dipole of length 10 m.
3 It turns out that the depth in the ocean to which airborne electromagnetic signals can be detected grows with the wavelength. Therefore, the military got the idea of using very long wavelengths corresponding to about 30 Hz to communicate with submarines

Distance (km)	Radio (dB)	Wire (dB)
1	−6	−3
2		
4		
8		
16		

throughout the world. If we want to have an antenna that is about one-half wavelength long, how long would that be?
4 The audio power of the human voice is concentrated at about 300 Hz. Antennas of the appropriate size for this frequency are impracticably large, so that to send voice by radio the voice signal must be used to modulate a higher (carrier) frequency for which the natural antenna size is smaller.
   a. What is the length of an antenna one-half wavelength long for sending radio at 300 Hz?
   b. An alternative is to use a modulation scheme, as described in Chapter 6, for transmitting the voice signal by modulating a carrier frequency, so that the bandwidth of the signal is a narrow band centered on the carrier frequency. Suppose we would like a half-wave antenna to have a length of 1 m. What carrier frequency would we use?
5 Stories abound of people who receive radio signals in fillings in their teeth. Suppose you have one filling that is 2.5 mm (0.0025 m) long that acts as a radio antenna. That is, it is equal in length to one-half the wavelength. What frequency do you receive?

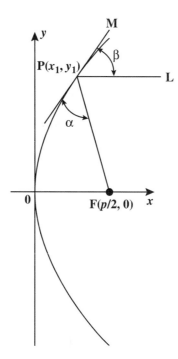

Figure 5.16   Parabolic Reflection

6 Section 5.1 stated that if a source of electromagnetic energy is placed at the focus of the paraboloid, and if the paraboloid is a reflecting surface, then the wave will bounce back in lines parallel to the axis of the paraboloid. To demonstrate this, consider the parabola $y^2 = 2px$ shown in Figure 5.16. Let $P(x_1, y_1)$ be a point on the parabola, and PF be the line from P to the focus. Construct the line L through P parallel to the *x*-axis and the line M tangent to the parabola at P. The angle between L and M is β, and the angle between PF and M is α. The angle α is the angle at which a ray from F strikes the parabola at P. Because the angle of incidence equals the angle of reflection, the ray reflected from P must be at an angle α to M. Thus, if we can show that $\alpha = \beta$, we have demonstrated that rays reflected from the parabola starting at F will be parallel to the *x* axis.

   a. First show that $\tan \beta = (p/y_1)$. *Hint:* Recall from trigonometry that the slope of a line is equal to the tangent of the angle the line makes with the positive *x* direction. Also recall that the slope of the line tangent to a curve at a given point is equal to the derivative of the curve at that point.

   b. Now show that $\tan \alpha = (p/y_1)$, which demonstrates that $\alpha = \beta$. *Hint:* Recall from trigonometry that the formula for the tangent of the difference between two angles α_1 and α_2 is $\tan(\alpha_2 - \alpha_1) = (\tan \alpha_2 - \tan \alpha_1) / (1 + \tan \alpha_2 \times \tan \alpha_1)$.

7 For each of the antenna types listed in Table 5.2, what is the effective area and gain at a wavelength of 30 cm? Repeat for a wavelength of 3 mm. Assume that the actual area for the horn and parabolic antennas is π.

8 It is often more convenient to express distance in km rather than m and frequency in MHz rather than Hz. Rewrite Equation (5.2) using these dimensions.

9 Assume that two antennas are half-wave dipoles and each has a directive gain of 3 dB. If the transmitted power is 1 W and the two antennas are separated by a distance of

10 km, what is the received power? Assume that the antennas are aligned so that the directive gain numbers are correct and that the frequency used is 100 MHz.

10 Suppose a transmitter produces 50 W of power.

    a. Express the transmit power in units of dBm and dBW.

    b. If the transmitter's power is applied to a unity gain antenna with a 900-MHz carrier frequency, what is the received power in dBm at a free space distance of 100 m?

    c. Repeat (b) for a distance of 10 km.

    d. Repeat (c) but assume a receiver antenna gain of 2.

11 A microwave transmitter has an output of 0.1 W at 2 GHz. Assume that this transmitter is used in a microwave communication system where the transmitting and receiving antennas are parabolas, each 1.2 m in diameter.

    a. What is the gain of each antenna in decibels?

    b. Taking into account antenna gain, what is the effective radiated power of the transmitted signal?

    c. If the receiving antenna is located 24 km from the transmitting antenna over a free space path, find the available signal power out of the receiving antenna in dBm units.

12 Section 5.2 states that with no intervening obstacles, the optical line of sight can be expressed as $d = 3.57\sqrt{h}$, where d is the distance between an antenna and the horizon in kilometers and h is the antenna height in meters. Using a value for the earth's radius of 6370 km, derive this equation. *Hint:* Assume that the antenna is perpendicular to the earth's surface, and note that the line from the top of the antenna to the horizon forms a tangent to the earth's surface at the horizon. Draw a picture showing the antenna, the line of sight, and the earth's radius to help visualize the problem.

13 Determine the height of an antenna for a TV station that must be able to reach customers up to 80 km away.

14 What is the thermal noise level of a channel with a bandwidth of 10 kHz carrying 1000 watts of power operating at 50°C? Compare the noise level to the operating power.

15 The square wave of Figure 2.5c, with $T = 1$ ms, is passed through a low-pass filter that passes frequencies up to 8 kHz with no attenuation.

    a. Find the power in the output waveform.

    b. Assuming that at the filter input there is a thermal noise voltage with $N_0 = 0.1$ μW/Hz, find the output signal to noise ratio in dB.

16 If the received signal level for a particular digital system is −151 dBW and the receiver system effective noise temperature is 1500°K, what is E_b/N_0 for a link transmitting 2400 bps?

17 Suppose a ray of visible light passes from the atmosphere into water at an angle to the horizontal of 30°. What is the angle of the ray in the water? *Note:* At standard atmospheric conditions at the earth's surface, a reasonable value for refractive index is 1.0003. A typical value of refractive index for water is 4/3.

CHAPTER **6**

SIGNAL ENCODING TECHNIQUES

n Chapter 2 a distinction was made between analog and digital data and analog and digital signals. Figure 2.8 suggested that either form of data could be encoded into either form of signal.

Figure 6.1 is another depiction that emphasizes the process involved. For **digital signaling**, a data source $g(t)$, which may be either digital or analog, is encoded into a digital signal $x(t)$. The actual form of $x(t)$ depends on the encoding technique and is chosen to optimize use of the transmission medium. For example, the encoding may be chosen to conserve bandwidth or to minimize errors.

The basis for **analog signaling** is a continuous constant-frequency signal known as the carrier signal. The frequency of the carrier signal is chosen to be compatible with the transmission medium being used. Data may be transmitted using a carrier signal by modulation. Modulation is the process of encoding source data onto a carrier signal with frequency f_c. All modulation techniques involve operation on one or more of the three fundamental frequency domain parameters: amplitude, frequency, and phase.

The input signal $m(t)$ may be analog or digital and is called the modulating signal or baseband signal. The result of modulating the carrier signal is called the modulated signal $s(t)$. As Figure 6.1b indicates, $s(t)$ is a bandlimited (bandpass) signal. The location of the bandwidth on the spectrum is related to f_c and is often centered on f_c. Again, the actual form of the encoding is chosen to optimize some characteristic of the transmission.

Figure 6.1 suggests four different mappings, or encodings, as was discussed in Chapter 2: digital-to-digital, digital-to-analog, analog-to-analog, and analog-to-digital.

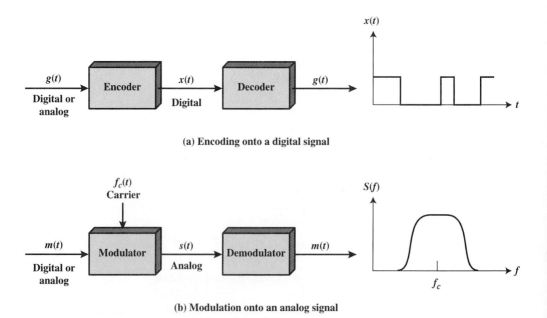

(a) Encoding onto a digital signal

(b) Modulation onto an analog signal

Figure 6.1   Encoding and Modulation Techniques

The latter three techniques are all relevant in the context of wireless communication, and in widespread use in that context:

- **digital-to-analog:** Digital data and digital signals must be converted to analog signals for wireless transmission.
- **analog-to-analog:** Typically, a baseband analog signal, such as voice or video, must be modulated onto a higher-frequency carrier for transmission.
- **analog-to-digital:** It is common to digitize voice signals prior to transmission over either guided or unguided media to improve quality and to take advantage of TDM schemes. For wireless transmission, the resulting digital data must be modulated onto an analog carrier.

The three techniques are examined in this chapter. First we look at some criteria that can be used in evaluating various approaches in each category. Chapter 7 examines spread spectrum, which combines techniques from several categories.

6.1 SIGNAL ENCODING CRITERIA

To begin, we need to define some terms. Recall that a digital signal is a sequence of discrete, discontinuous voltage pulses. Each pulse is a signal element. Binary data are transmitted by encoding each data bit into signal elements. In the simplest case, there is a one-to-one correspondence between bits and signal elements. An example is shown in Figure 2.9, in which binary 0 is represented by a lower voltage level and binary 1 by a higher voltage level. Similarly, a digital bit stream can be encoded onto an analog signal as a sequence of signal elements, with each signal element being a pulse of constant frequency, phase, and amplitude. There may be a one-to-one correspondence between data elements (bits) and analog signal elements. For both analog and digital signals, there may be a one-to-multiple or multiple-to-one correspondence between data elements and signal elements, as will be shown.

The data signaling rate, or just data rate, of a signal is the rate, in bits per second, that data are transmitted. The duration or length of a bit is the amount of time it takes for the transmitter to emit the bit; for a data rate R, the bit duration is $1/R$. The modulation rate, in contrast, is the rate at which the signal level is changed. This will depend on the nature of the encoding, as explained later. The modulation rate is expressed in baud, which means signal elements per second. Table 6.1 summarizes key terms; these should be clearer when we see an example later in this section.

The tasks involved in interpreting digital signals at the receiver can be summarized by again referring to Figure 2.9. First, the receiver must know the timing of each bit. That is, the receiver must know with some accuracy when a bit begins and ends. Second, the receiver must determine whether the signal level for each bit position is high (1) or low (0). In Figure 2.9, these tasks are performed by sampling each bit position in the middle of the interval and comparing the value to a threshold. Because of noise and other impairments, there will be errors, as shown.

Table 6.1 Key Data Transmission Terms

Term	Units	Definition
Data element	Bits	A single binary one or zero
Data rate	Bits per second (bps)	The rate at which data elements are transmitted
Signal element	Digital: a voltage pulse of constant amplitude Analog: a pulse of constant frequency, phase, and amplitude	That part of a signal that occupies the shortest interval of a signaling code
Signaling rate or modulation rate	Signal elements per second (baud)	The rate at which signal elements are transmitted

What factors determine how successful the receiver will be in interpreting the incoming signal? We saw in Chapter 2 that three factors are important: the signal-to-noise ratio (or, better, E_b/N_0), the data rate, and the bandwidth. With other factors held constant, the following statements are true:

- An increase in data rate increases bit error rate (BER).[1]
- An increase in SNR decreases bit error rate.
- An increase in bandwidth allows an increase in data rate.

There is another factor that can be used to improve performance, and that is the encoding scheme. The encoding scheme is simply the mapping from data bits to signal elements. A variety of approaches are in use. Before describing these techniques, let us consider the following ways of evaluating or comparing the various techniques.

- **Signal spectrum:** Several aspects of the signal spectrum are important. A lack of high-frequency components means that less bandwidth is required for transmission. In addition, lack of a direct current (dc) component is also desirable. With a dc component to the signal, there must be direct physical attachment of transmission components. With no dc component, alternating current (ac) coupling via transformer is possible; this provides excellent electrical isolation, reducing interference. Finally, the magnitude of the effects of signal distortion and interference depend on the spectral properties of the transmitted signal. In practice, it usually happens that the transfer function of a channel is worse near the band edges. Therefore, a good signal design should concentrate the transmitted power in the middle of the transmission bandwidth. In such a case,

---

[1]The BER is the most common measure of error performance on a data circuit and is defined as the probability that a bit is received in error. It is also called the *bit error ratio*. This latter term is clearer, because the term *rate* typically refers to some quantity that varies with time. Unfortunately, most books and standards documents refer to the R in BER as *rate*.

less distortion should be present in the received signal. To meet this objective, codes can be designed with the aim of shaping the spectrum of the transmitted signal.

- **Clocking:** The receiver must determine the beginning and end of each bit position. This is no easy task. One rather expensive approach is to provide a separate clock channel to synchronize the transmitter and receiver. The alternative is to provide some synchronization mechanism that is based on the transmitted signal. This can be achieved with suitable encoding.

- **Signal interference and noise immunity:** Certain codes exhibit superior performance in the presence of noise. This is usually expressed in terms of a BER.

- **Cost and complexity:** Although digital logic continues to drop in price, this factor should not be ignored. In particular, the higher the signaling rate to achieve a given data rate, the greater the cost. We will see that some codes require a signaling rate that is in fact greater than the actual data rate.

We now turn to a discussion of various techniques.

6.2 DIGITAL DATA, ANALOG SIGNALS

We start with the case of transmitting digital data using analog signals. The most familiar use of this transformation is for transmitting digital data through the public telephone network. The telephone network was designed to receive, switch, and transmit analog signals in the voice-frequency range of about 300 to 3400 Hz. It is not at present suitable for handling digital signals from the subscriber locations (although this is beginning to change). Thus digital devices are attached to the network via a modem (modulator-demodulator), which converts digital data to analog signals, and vice versa.

For the telephone network, modems are used that produce signals in the voice-frequency range. The same basic techniques are used for modems that produce signals at higher frequencies (e.g., microwave). This section introduces these techniques and provides a brief discussion of the performance characteristics of the alternative approaches.

We mentioned that modulation involves operation on one or more of the three characteristics of a carrier signal: amplitude, frequency, and phase. Accordingly, there are three basic encoding or modulation techniques for transforming digital data into analog signals, as illustrated in Figure 6.2: amplitude-shift keying (ASK), frequency-shift keying (FSK), and phase-shift keying (PSK). In all these cases, the resulting signal occupies a bandwidth centered on the carrier frequency.

Amplitude-Shift Keying

In ASK, the two binary values are represented by two different amplitudes of the carrier frequency. Commonly, one of the amplitudes is zero; that is, one binary digit is represented by the presence, at constant amplitude, of the carrier, the other by the absence of the carrier (Figure 6.2a). The resulting transmitted signal for one bit time is

ASK
$$s(t) = \begin{cases} A\cos(2\pi f_c t) & \text{binary 1} \\ 0 & \text{binary 0} \end{cases}$$
(6.1)

where the carrier signal is $A\cos(2\pi f_c t)$. ASK is susceptible to sudden gain changes and is a rather inefficient modulation technique. On voice-grade lines, it is typically used only up to 1200 bps.

The ASK technique is used to transmit digital data over optical fiber. For LED (light-emitting diode) transmitters, Equation (6.1) is valid. That is, one signal element is represented by a light pulse while the other signal element is represented by the absence of light. Laser transmitters normally have a fixed "bias" current that causes the device to emit a low light level. This low level represents one signal element, while a higher-amplitude lightwave represents another signal element.

Frequency-Shift Keying

The most common form of FSK is binary FSK (BFSK), in which the two binary values are represented by two different frequencies near the carrier frequency (Figure 6.2b). The resulting transmitted signal for one bit time is

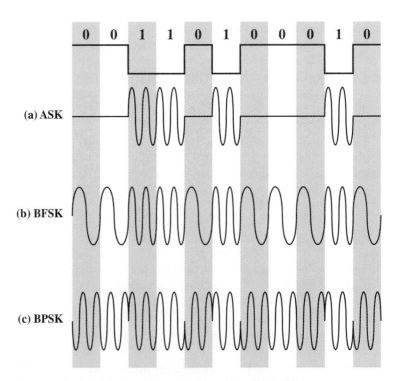

Figure 6.2   Modulation of Analog Signals for Digital Data

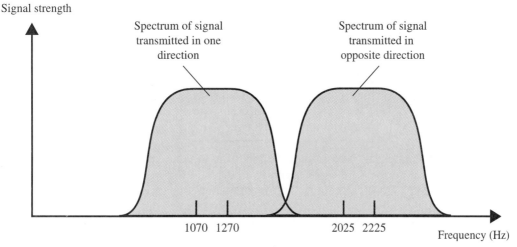

Figure 6.3   Full-Duplex FSK Transmission on a Voice-Grade Line

$$\textbf{BFSK} \qquad s(t) = \begin{cases} A\cos(2\pi f_1 t) & \text{binary 1} \\ A\cos(2\pi f_2 t) & \text{binary 0} \end{cases} \qquad\qquad (6.2)$$

where f_1 and f_2 are typically offset from the carrier frequency f_c by equal but opposite amounts.

Figure 6.3 shows an example of the use of FSK for full-duplex operation over a voice-grade line. The figure is a specification for the Bell System 108 series modems. A voice-grade line will pass frequencies in the approximate range 300 to 3400 Hz. *Full duplex* means that signals are transmitted in both directions at the same time. To achieve full-duplex transmission, this bandwidth is split. In one direction (transmit or receive), the frequencies used to represent 1 and 0 are centered on 1170 Hz, with a shift of 100 Hz on either side. The effect of alternating between those two frequencies is to produce a signal whose spectrum is indicated as the shaded area on the left in Figure 6.3. Similarly, for the other direction (receive or transmit) the modem uses frequencies shifted 100 Hz to each side of a center frequency of 2125 Hz. This signal is indicated by the shaded area on the right in Figure 6.3. Note that there is little overlap and thus little interference.

BFSK is less susceptible to error than ASK. On voice-grade lines, it is typically used up to 1200 bps. It is also commonly used for high-frequency (3 to 30 MHz) radio transmission. It can also be used at even higher frequencies on local area networks that use coaxial cable.

A signal that is more bandwidth efficient, but also more susceptible to error, is multiple FSK (MFSK), in which more than two frequencies are used. In this case each signaling element represents more than one bit. The transmitted MFSK signal for one signal element time can be defined as follows:

MFSK
$$s_i(t) = A \cos 2\pi f_i t, \qquad 1 \leq i \leq M \qquad (6.3)$$

where

$f_i = f_c + (2i - 1 - M)f_d$
f_c = the carrier frequency
f_d = the difference frequency
M = number of different signal elements = 2^L
L = number of bits per signal element

To match the data rate of the input bit stream, each output signal element is held for a period of $T_s = LT$ seconds, where T is the bit period (data rate = $1/T$). Thus, one signal element, which is a constant-frequency tone, encodes L bits. The total bandwidth required is $2Mf_d$. It can be shown that the minimum frequency separation required is $2f_d = 1/T_s$. Therefore, the modulator requires a bandwidth of $W_d = 2Mf_d = M/T_s$.

Example. With f_c = 250 kHz, f_d = 25 kHz, and M = 8 (L = 3 bits), we have the following frequency assignments for each of the 8 possible 3-bit data combinations:

f_1 = 75 kHz 000 f_2 = 125 kHz 001 f_3 = 175 kHz 010 f_4 = 225 kHz 011
f_5 = 275 kHz 100 f_6 = 325 kHz 101 f_7 = 375 kHz 110 f_8 = 425 kHz 111

This scheme can support a data rate of $2f_d = 1/T_s$ = 50 kbps.

Figure 6.4 shows an example of MFSK with M = 4. An input bit stream is encoded 2 bits at a time, with each of the four possible 2-bit combinations transmitted as a different frequency.

Phase-Shift Keying

In PSK, the phase of the carrier signal is shifted to represent data.

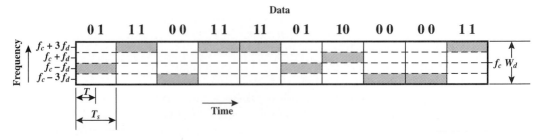

Figure 6.4   MFSK Frequency Use (M = 4)

Two-Level PSK

The simplest scheme uses two phases to represent the two binary digits (Figure 6.2c) and is known as binary phase-shift keying. The resulting transmitted signal for one bit time is

$$\text{BPSK} \qquad s(t) = \begin{cases} A \cos(2\pi f_c t) \\ A \cos(2\pi f_c t + \pi) \end{cases} = \begin{cases} A \cos(2\pi f_c t) & \text{binary 1} \\ -A \cos(2\pi f_c t) & \text{binary 0} \end{cases} \qquad (6.4)$$

Because a phase shift of 180° (π) is equivalent to flipping the sine wave or multiplying it by -1, the rightmost expressions in Equation (6.4) can be used. This leads to a convenient formulation. If we have a bit stream, and we define $d(t)$ as the discrete function that takes on the value of $+1$ for one bit time if the corresponding bit in the bit stream is 1 and the value of -1 for one bit time if the corresponding bit in the bit stream is 0, then we can define the transmitted signal as

$$\text{BPSK} \qquad s_d(t) = A\, d(t) \cos (2\pi f_c t) \qquad (6.5)$$

An alternative form of two-level PSK is differential PSK (DPSK). Figure 6.5 shows an example. In this scheme, a binary 0 is represented by sending a signal burst of the same phase as the previous signal burst sent. A binary 1 is represented by sending a signal burst of opposite phase to the preceding one. This term *differential* refers to the fact that the phase shift is with reference to the previous bit transmitted rather than to some constant reference signal. In differential encoding, the information to be transmitted is represented in terms of the changes between successive data symbols rather than the signal elements themselves. DPSK avoids the requirement for an accurate local oscillator phase at the receiver that is matched with the transmitter. As long as the preceding phase is received correctly, the phase reference is accurate.

Four-Level PSK

More efficient use of bandwidth can be achieved if each signaling element represents more than one bit. For example, instead of a phase shift of 180°, as allowed in PSK, a common encoding technique, known as quadrature phase-shift keying (QPSK), uses phase shifts of multiples of $\pi/2$ (90°).

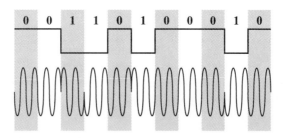

Figure 6.5 Differential Phase Shift Keying (DPSK)

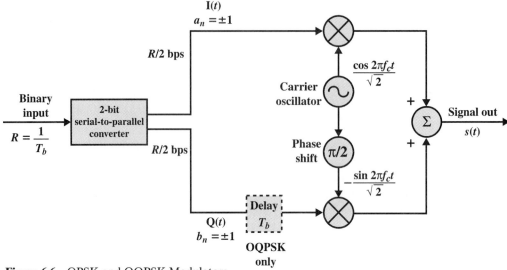

Figure 6.6 QPSK and OQPSK Modulators

$$
\text{QPSK} \qquad s(t) = \begin{cases} A \cos\left(2\pi f_c t + \dfrac{\pi}{4}\right) & 11 \\[2mm] A \cos\left(2\pi f_c t + \dfrac{3\pi}{4}\right) & 01 \\[2mm] A \cos\left(2\pi f_c t - \dfrac{3\pi}{4}\right) & 00 \\[2mm] A \cos\left(2\pi f_c t - \dfrac{\pi}{4}\right) & 10 \end{cases} \qquad (6.6)
$$

Thus each signal element represents two bits rather than one.

Figure 6.6 shows the QPSK modulation scheme in general terms. The input is a stream of binary digits with a data rate of $R = 1/t_B$, where t_B is the width of each bit. This stream is converted into two separate bit streams of $R/2$ bps each, by taking alternate bits for the two streams. The two data streams are referred to as the I (in-phase) and Q (quadrature phase) streams. In the diagram, the upper stream is modulated on a carrier of frequency f_c by multiplying the bit stream by the carrier. For convenience of modulator structure we map binary 1 to $\sqrt{1/2}$ and binary 0 to $-\sqrt{1/2}$. Thus, a binary 1 is represented by a scaled version of the carrier wave and a binary 0 is represented by a scaled version of the negative of the carrier wave, both at a constant amplitude. This same carrier wave is shifted by 90° and used for modulation of the lower binary stream. The two modulated signals are then added together and transmitted. The transmitted signal can be expressed as follows:

$$
\text{QPSK} \qquad s(t) = \frac{1}{\sqrt{2}} I(t)\cos 2\pi f_c t - \frac{1}{\sqrt{2}} Q(t)\sin 2\pi f_c t
$$

Figure 6.7 shows an example of QPSK coding. Each of the two modulated streams is a BPSK signal at half the data rate of the original bit stream. Thus, the combined signals have a symbol rate that is half the input bit rate. Note that from one symbol time to the next, a phase change of as much as 180° (π) is possible.

Figure 6.6 also shows a variation of QPSK known as offset QPSK (OQPSK), or orthogonal QPSK. The difference is that a delay of one bit time is introduced in the Q stream, resulting in the following signal:

$$s(t) = \frac{1}{\sqrt{2}} I(t)\cos 2\pi f_c t - \frac{1}{\sqrt{2}} Q(t - T_b)\sin 2\pi f_c t$$

Because OQPSK differs from QPSK only by the delay in the Q stream, its spectral characteristics and bit error performance are the same as that of QPSK. From Figure 6.7, we can observe that only one of two bits in the pair can change sign at any time and thus the phase change in the combined signal never exceeds 90° ($\pi/2$). This can be an advantage because physical limitations on phase modulators make large phase shifts at high transition rates difficult to perform. OQPSK also provides superior performance when the transmission channel (including transmitter and receiver) have significant nonlinear components. The effect of nonlinearities is a spreading of the signal bandwidth, which may result in adjacent channel interference. It is easier to control this spreading if the phase changes are smaller, hence the advantage of OQPSK over QPSK.

Multilevel PSK

The use of multiple levels can be extended beyond taking bits two at a time. It is possible to transmit bits three at a time using eight different phase angles.

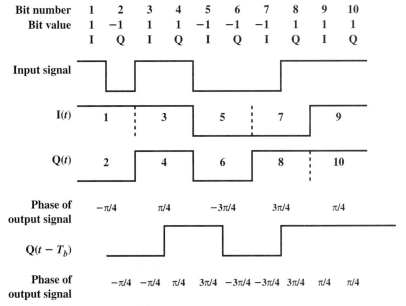

Figure 6.7 Example of QPSK and OQPSK Waveforms

Further, each angle can have more than one amplitude. For example, a standard 9600 bps modem uses 12 phase angles, four of which have two amplitude values, for a total of 16 different signal elements.

This latter example points out very well the difference between the data rate R (in bps) and the modulation rate D (in baud) of a signal. Let us assume that this scheme is being employed with digital input in which each bit is represented by a constant voltage pulse, one level for binary one and one level for binary zero. The data rate is $R = 1/t_B$. However, the encoded signal contains $L = 4$ bits in each signal element using $M = 16$ different combinations of amplitude and phase. The modulation rate can be seen to be $R/4$, because each change of signal element communicates four bits. Thus the line signaling speed is 2400 baud, but the data rate is 9600 bps. This is the reason that higher bit rates can be achieved over voice-grade lines by employing more complex modulation schemes.

In general,

$$d = \frac{R}{L} = \frac{R}{\log_2 M}$$ (6.7)

where

$$
\begin{aligned}
D &= \text{modulation rate, baud} \\
R &= \text{data rate, bps} \\
M &= \text{number of different signal elements} = 2^L \\
L &= \text{number of bits per signal element}
\end{aligned}
$$

Performance

In looking at the performance of various digital-to-analog modulation schemes, the first parameter of interest is the bandwidth of the modulated signal. This depends on a variety of factors, including the definition of bandwidth used and the filtering technique used to create the bandpass signal. We will use some straightforward results from [COUC01].

The transmission bandwidth B_T for ASK is of the form

ASK $\qquad\qquad B_T = (1 + r)R$ (6.8)

where R is the bit rate and r is related to the technique by which the signal is filtered to establish a bandwidth for transmission; typically $0 < r < 1$. Thus the bandwidth is directly related to the bit rate. The preceding formula is also valid for PSK.

For FSK, the bandwidth can be expressed as

FSK $\qquad\qquad B_T = 2\Delta F + (1 + r)R$ (6.9)

where $\Delta F = f_2 - f_c = f_c - f_1$ is the offset of the modulated frequency from the carrier frequency. When very high frequencies are used, the ΔF term dominates. For example, one of the standards for FSK signaling on a coaxial cable multipoint local network uses $\Delta F = 1.25$ MHz, $f_c = 5$ MHz, and $R = 1$ Mbps; in this case the $2\Delta F = 2.5$ MHz term dominates. In the example of the preceding section for the Bell 108 modem, $\Delta F = 100$ Hz, $f_c = 1170$ Hz (in one direction), and $R = 300$ bps; in this case the $(1 + r)R$ term dominates.

With multilevel PSK (MPSK), significant improvements in bandwidth can be achieved. In general,

$$\textbf{MPSK} \qquad B_r = \left(\frac{1 + r}{L}\right)R = \left(\frac{1 + r}{\log_2 M}\right)R \qquad (6.10)$$

where L is the number of bits encoded per signal element and M is the number of different signal elements.

For multilevel FSK (MFSK), we have

$$\textbf{MFSK} \qquad B_r = \left(\frac{(1 + r)M}{\log_2 M}\right)R \qquad (6.11)$$

Table 6.2 shows the ratio of data rate, R, to transmission bandwidth for various schemes. This ratio is also referred to as the bandwidth efficiency. As the name suggests, this parameter measures the efficiency with which bandwidth can be used to transmit data. The advantage of multilevel signaling methods now becomes clear.

Of course, the preceding discussion refers to the spectrum of the input signal to a communications line. Nothing has yet been said of performance in the presence of noise. Figure 6.8 summarizes some results based on reasonable assumptions concerning the transmission system [COUC01]. Here bit error rate is plotted as a function of the ratio E_b/N_0 defined in Chapter 5. Of course, as that ratio increases, the bit error rate drops. Further, DPSK and BPSK are about 3 dB superior to ASK and BFSK.

Figure 6.9 shows the same information for various levels of M for MFSK and MSPK. There is an important difference. For MFSK, the error probability for a given value E_b/N_0 of decreases as M increases, while the opposite is true for MPSK. On the other hand, comparing Equations (6.10) and (6.11), the bandwidth efficiency of MFSK decreases as M increases, while the opposite is true of MPSK.

Table 6.2   Data Rate to Transmission Bandwidth Ratio for Various Digital-to-Analog Encoding Schemes

	$r = 0$	$r = 0.5$	$r = 1$
ASK	1.0	0.67	0.5
BFSK			
Wideband ($\Delta F \gg R$)	~0	~0	~0
Narrowband ($\Delta F \approx f_c$)	1.0	0.67	0.5
PSK	1.0	0.67	0.5
Multilevel PSK			
$M = 4, L = 2$	2.00	1.33	1.00
$M = 8, L = 3$	3.00	2.00	1.50
$M = 16, L = 4$	4.00	2.67	2.00
$M = 32, L = 5$	5.00	3.33	2.50

Example. What is the bandwidth efficiency for FSK, ASK, PSK, and QPSK for a bit error rate of 10^{-7} on a channel with an SNR of 12 dB?

Using Equation (5.4), we have

$$\frac{E_b}{N_0} = 12 \text{ dB} - \left(\frac{R}{B_T}\right)_{\text{dB}}$$

For FSK and ASK, from Figure 6.8,

$$\frac{E_b}{N_0} = 14.2 \text{ dB}$$

$$\left(\frac{R}{B_T}\right)_{\text{dB}} = -2.2 \text{ dB}$$

$$\frac{R}{B_T} = 0.6$$

For PSK, from Figure 6.8,

$$\frac{E_b}{N_0} = 11.2 \text{ dB}$$

$$\left(\frac{R}{B_T}\right)_{\text{dB}} = 0.8 \text{ dB}$$

$$\frac{R}{B_T} = 1.2$$

The result for QPSK must take into account that the baud rate $D = R/2$. Thus

$$\frac{R}{B_T} = 2.4$$

Figure 6.8 Theoretical Bit Error Rate for Various Encoding Schemes

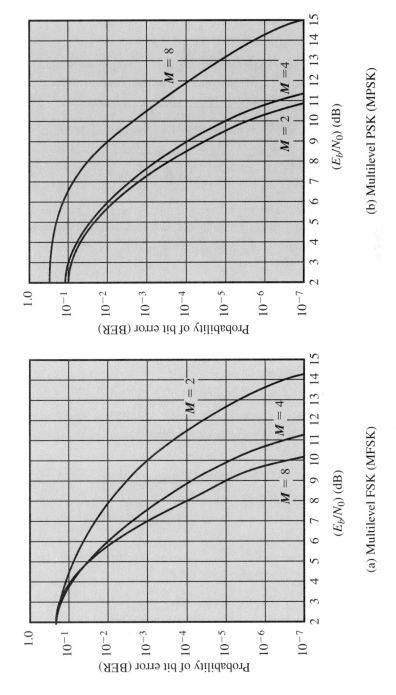

(a) Multilevel FSK (MFSK)

(b) Multilevel PSK (MPSK)

Figure 6.9 Theoretical Bit Error Rate for Multilevel FSK and PSK

145

As the preceding example shows, ASK and FSK exhibit the same bandwidth efficiency, PSK is better, and even greater improvement can be achieved with multilevel signaling.

Quadrature Amplitude Modulation

Quadrature Amplitude Modulation (QAM) is a popular analog signaling technique that is used in some wireless standards. This modulation technique is a combination of ASK and PSK. QAM can also be considered a logical extension of QPSK. QAM takes advantage of the fact that it is possible to send two different signals simultaneously on the same carrier frequency, by using two copies of the carrier frequency, one shifted by 90° with respect to the other. For QAM, each carrier is ASK modulated. The two independent signals are simultaneously transmitted over the same medium. At the receiver, the two signals are demodulated and the results combined to produce the original binary input.

Figure 6.10 shows the QAM modulation scheme in general terms. The input is a stream of binary digits arriving at a rate of R bps. This stream is converted into two separate bit streams of $R/2$ bps each, by taking alternate bits for the two streams. In the diagram, the upper stream is ASK modulated on a carrier of frequency f_c by multiplying the bit stream by the carrier. Thus, a binary zero is represented by the absence of the carrier wave and a binary one is represented by the presence of the carrier wave at a constant amplitude. This same carrier wave is shifted by 90° and used for ASK modulation of the lower binary stream. The two modulated signals are then added together and transmitted. The transmitted signal can be expressed as follows:

$$\textbf{QAM} \qquad s(t) = d_1(t)\cos 2\pi f_c t + d_2(t)\sin 2\pi f_c t$$

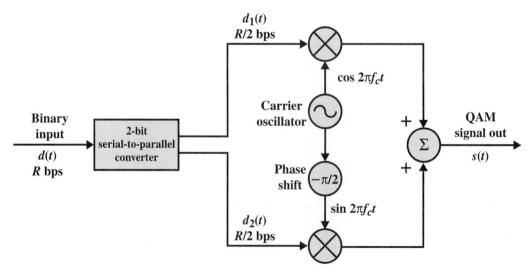

Figure 6.10 QAM Modulator

If two-level ASK is used, then each of the two streams can be in one of two states and the combined stream can be in one of $4 = 2 \times 2$ states. This is essentially QPSK. If four-level ASK is used (i.e., four different amplitude levels), then the combined stream can be in one of $16 = 4 \times 4$ states. Systems using 64 and even 256 states have been implemented. The greater the number of states, the higher the data rate that is possible within a given bandwidth. Of course, as discussed previously, the greater the number of states, the higher the potential error rate due to noise and attenuation.

6.3   ANALOG DATA, ANALOG SIGNALS

Modulation has been defined as the process of combining an input signal $m(t)$ and a carrier at frequency f_c to produce a signal $s(t)$ whose bandwidth is (usually) centered on f_c. For digital data, the motivation for modulation should be clear: When only analog transmission facilities are available, modulation is required to convert the digital data to analog form. The motivation when the data are already analog is less clear. After all, voice signals are transmitted over telephone lines at their original spectrum (referred to as baseband transmission). There are two principal reasons for analog modulation of analog signals:

- A higher frequency may be needed for effective transmission. For unguided transmission, it is virtually impossible to transmit baseband signals; the required antennas would be many kilometers in diameter.
- Modulation permits frequency division multiplexing, an important technique that was discussed in Chapter 2.

In this section we look at the principal techniques for modulation using analog data: amplitude modulation (AM), frequency modulation (FM), and phase modulation (PM). As before, the three basic characteristics of a signal are used for modulation.

Amplitude Modulation

Amplitude modulation (AM), the simplest form of modulation, is depicted in Figure 6.11. Mathematically, the process can be expressed as

$$\textbf{AM} \qquad\qquad s(t) = [1 + n_a x(t)]\cos 2\pi f_c t \qquad\qquad (6.12)$$

where $\cos 2\pi f_c t$ is the carrier and $x(t)$ is the input signal (carrying data), both normalized to unity amplitude. The parameter n_a, known as the modulation index, is the ratio of the amplitude of the input signal to the carrier. Corresponding to our previous notation, the input signal is $m(t) = n_a x(t)$. The "1" in Equation (6.12) is a dc component that prevents loss of information, as explained subsequently. This scheme is also known as double sideband transmitted carrier (DSBTC).

Example. Derive an expression for $s(t)$ if $x(t)$ is the amplitude-modulating signal $\cos 2\pi f_m t$.
We have

$$s(t) = [1 + n_a \cos 2\pi f_m t] \cos 2\pi f_c t$$

By trigonometric identity, this may be expanded to

$$s(t) = \cos 2\pi f_c t + \frac{n_a}{2} \cos 2\pi (f_c - f_m)t + \frac{n_a}{2} \cos 2\pi (f_c - f_m)t$$

The resulting signal has a component at the original carrier frequency plus a pair of components each spaced f_m hertz from the carrier.

From Equation (6.12) and Figure (6.11), it can be seen that AM involves the multiplication of the input signal by the carrier. The envelope of the resulting signal is $[1 + n_a x(t)]$ and, as long as $n_a < 1$, the envelope is an exact reproduction of the original signal. If $n_a > 1$, the envelope will cross the time axis and information is lost.

It is instructive to look at the spectrum of the AM signal. An example is shown in Figure 6.12. The spectrum consists of the original carrier plus the spectrum of the

(a) Sinusoidal modulating wave

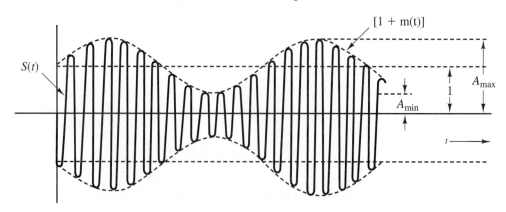

(b) Resulting AM signal

Figure 6.11   Amplitude Modulation

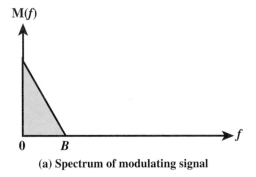

(a) Spectrum of modulating signal

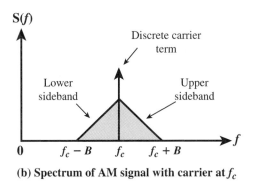

(b) Spectrum of AM signal with carrier at f_c

Figure 6.12   Spectrum of an AM Signal

input signal translated to f_c. The portion of the spectrum for $|f| > |f_c|$ is the *upper sideband*, and the portion of the spectrum for $|f| < |f_c|$ is *lower sideband*. Both the upper and lower sidebands are replicas of the original spectrum $M(f)$, with the lower sideband being frequency reversed. As an example, consider a voice signal with a bandwidth that extends from 300 to 3000 Hz being modulated on a 60-kHz carrier. The resulting signal contains an upper sideband of 60.3 to 63 kHz, a lower sideband of 57 to 59.7 kHz, and the 60-kHz carrier. An important relationship is

$$P_t = P_c\left(1 + \frac{n_a^2}{2}\right)$$

where P_t is the total transmitted power in $s(t)$ and P_c is the transmitted power in the carrier. We would like n_a as large as possible so that most of the signal power is used to carry information. However, n_a must remain below 1.

It should be clear that $s(t)$ contains unnecessary components, because each of the sidebands contains the complete spectrum of $m(t)$. A popular variant of AM, known as single sideband (SSB), takes advantage of this fact by sending only one of the sidebands, eliminating the other sideband and the carrier. The principal advantages of this approach are as follows:

- Only half the bandwidth is required, that is, $B_T = B$, where B is the bandwidth of the original signal. For DSBTC, $B_T = 2B$.
- Less power is required because no power is used to transmit the carrier or the other sideband. Another variant is double sideband suppressed carrier (DSBSC), which filters out the carrier frequency and sends both sidebands. This saves some power but uses as much bandwidth as DSBTC.

The disadvantage of suppressing the carrier is that the carrier can be used for synchronization purposes. For example, suppose that the original analog signal is an ASK waveform encoding digital data. The receiver needs to know the starting point of each bit time to interpret the data correctly. A constant carrier provides a clocking mechanism by which to time the arrival of bits. A compromise approach is vestigial sideband (VSB), which uses one sideband and a reduced-power carrier.

Angle Modulation

Frequency modulation (FM) and phase modulation (PM) are special cases of angle modulation. The modulated signal is expressed as

$$\textbf{Angle Modulation} \qquad s(t) = A_c \cos[2\pi f_c t + \phi(t)] \tag{6.13}$$

For phase modulation, the phase is proportional to the modulating signal:

$$\textbf{PM} \qquad \qquad \phi(t) = n_p m(t) \tag{6.14}$$

where n_p is the phase modulation index.

For frequency modulation, the derivative of the phase is proportional to the modulating signal:

$$\textbf{AM} \qquad \qquad \phi'(t) = n_f m(t) \tag{6.15}$$

where n_f is the frequency modulation index.

For those who wish a more detailed mathematical explanation of the preceding, consider the following. The phase of $s(t)$ at any instant is just $2\pi f_c t + \phi(t)$. The instantaneous phase deviation from the carrier signal is $\phi(t)$. In PM, this instantaneous phase deviation is proportional to $m(t)$. Because frequency can be defined as the rate of change of phase of a signal, the instantaneous frequency of $s(t)$ is

$$2\pi f_i(t) = \frac{d}{dt}[2\pi f_c t + \phi(t)]$$

$$f_i(t) = f_c + \frac{1}{2\pi}\phi'(t)$$

and the instantaneous frequency deviation from the carrier frequency is $\phi'(t)$, which in FM is proportional to $m(t)$.

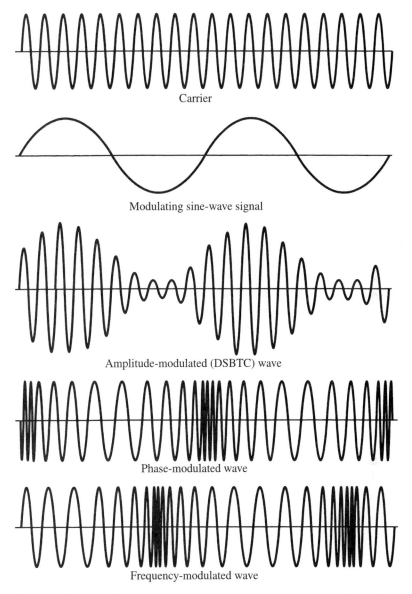

Figure 6.13 Amplitude, Phase, and Frequency Modulation of a Sine-Wave Carrier by a Sine-Wave Signal

Figure 6.13 illustrates amplitude, phase, and frequency modulation by a sine wave. The shapes of the FM and PM signals are very similar. Indeed, it is impossible to tell them apart without knowledge of the modulation function.

Several observations about the FM process are in order. The peak deviation ΔF can be seen to be

$$\Delta F = \frac{1}{2\pi} n_f A_m \text{ Hz}$$

where A_m is the maximum value of $m(t)$. Thus an increase in the magnitude of $m(t)$ will increase ΔF, which, intuitively, should increase the transmitted bandwidth B_T. However, as should be apparent from Figure 6.13, this will not increase the average power level of the FM signal, which is $A_c^2/2$. This is distinctly different from AM, where the level of modulation affects the power in the AM signal but does not affect its bandwidth.

Example. Derive an expression for $s(t)$ if $\phi(t)$ is the phase-modulating signal $n_p \cos 2\pi f_m t$. Assume that $A_c = 1$. This can be seen directly to be

$$s(t) = \cos[2\pi f_c t + n_p \cos 2\pi f_m t]$$

The instantaneous phase deviation from the carrier signal is $n_p \cos \pi f_m t$. The phase angle of the signal varies from its unmodulated value in a simple sinusoidal fashion, with the peak phase deviation equal to n_p.

The preceding expression can be expanded using Bessel's trigonometric identities:

$$s(t) = \sum_{n=-\infty}^{\infty} J_n(n_p)\cos\left(2\pi f_c t + 2\pi f_m t + \frac{n\pi}{2}\right)$$

where $J_n(n_p)$ is the nth-order Bessel function of the first kind. Using the property

$$J_{-n}(x) = (-1)^n J_n(x)$$

this can be rewritten as

$$s(t) = J_0(n_p)\cos 2\pi f_c t +$$
$$\sum_{n=-\infty}^{\infty} J_n(n_p)\left[\cos\left(2\pi(f_c + nf_m)t + \frac{n\pi}{2}\right) + \cos\left(2\pi(f_c + nf_m)t + \frac{(n+2)\pi}{2}\right)\right]$$

The resulting signal has a component at the original carrier frequency plus a set of sidebands displaced from f_c by all possible multiples of f_m. For $n_p \ll 1$, the higher-order terms fall off rapidly.

Example. Derive an expression for $s(t)$ if $\phi'(t)$ is the frequency-modulating signal $-n_f \sin 2\pi f_m t$. The form of $\phi'(t)$ was chosen for convenience. We have

$$\phi(t) = -\int f n_f \sin 2\pi f_m t \, dt = \frac{n_f}{2\pi f_m}\cos 2\pi f_m t$$

Thus

$$s(t) = \cos\left[2\pi f_c t + \frac{n_f}{2\pi f_m}\cos 2\pi f_m t\right]$$
$$= \cos\left[2\pi f_c t + \frac{\Delta F}{f_m}\cos 2\pi f_m t\right]$$

> The instantaneous frequency deviation from the carrier signal is $-n_f \sin 2\pi f_m t$. The frequency of the signal varies from its unmodulated value in a simple sinusoidal fashion, with the peak frequency deviation equal to n_f radians/second.
>
> The equation for the FM signal has the identical form as for the PM signal, with $\Delta F/f_m$ substituted for n_p. Thus the Bessel expansion is the same.

As with AM, both FM and PM result in a signal whose bandwidth is centered at f_c. However, we can now see that the magnitude of that bandwidth is very different. Amplitude modulation is a linear process and produces frequencies that are the sum and difference of the carrier signal and the components of the modulating signal. Hence, for AM,

$$B_T = 2B$$

However, angle modulation includes a term of the form $\cos(\phi(t))$, which is non-linear and will produce a wide range of frequencies. In essence, for a modulating sinusoid of frequency f_m, $s(t)$ will contain components at $f_c + f_m, f_c + 2f_m$, and so on. In the most general case, infinite bandwidth is required to transmit an FM or PM signal. As a practical matter, a very good rule of thumb, known as Carson's rule [COUC01], is

$$B_T = 2(\beta + 1)B$$

where

$$\beta = \begin{cases} n_p A_m & \text{for PM} \\ \dfrac{\Delta F}{B} = \dfrac{n_f A_m}{2\pi B} & \text{for FM} \end{cases}$$

We can rewrite the formula for FM as

$$B_T = 2\Delta F + 2B \tag{6.16}$$

Thus both FM and PM require greater bandwidth than AM.

6.4 ANALOG DATA, DIGITAL SIGNALS

In this section we examine the process of transforming analog data into digital signals. Strictly speaking, it might be more correct to refer to this as a process of converting analog data into digital data; this process is known as digitization. Once analog data have been converted into digital data, a number of things can happen. The three most common are as follows:

Figure 6.14 Digitizing Analog Data

1. The digital data can be transmitted using NRZ-L.[2] In this case, we have in fact gone directly from analog data to a digital signal.
2. The digital data can be encoded as a digital signal using a code other than NRZ-L. Thus an extra step is required.
3. The digital data can be converted into an analog signal, using one of the modulation techniques discussed in Section 6.2.

This last, seemingly curious, procedure is illustrated in Figure 6.14, which shows voice data that are digitized and then converted to an analog ASK signal. This allows digital transmission in the sense defined in Chapter 2. The voice data, because they have been digitized, can be treated as digital data, even though transmission requirements (e.g., use of microwave) dictate that an analog signal be used.

The device used for converting analog data into digital form for transmission, and subsequently recovering the original analog data from the digital, is known as a codec (coder-decoder). In this section we examine the two principal techniques used in codecs, pulse code modulation and delta modulation. The section closes with a discussion of comparative performance.

Pulse Code Modulation

Pulse code modulation (PCM) is based on the sampling theorem, which states as follows:

> If a signal $f(t)$ is sampled at regular intervals of time and at a rate higher than twice the highest signal frequency, then the samples contain all the information of the original signal. The function $f(t)$ may be reconstructed from these samples by the use of a low-pass filter.

For the interested reader, a proof is provided in Appendix 6A. If voice data are limited to frequencies below 4000 Hz, a conservative procedure for intelligibility, 8000 samples per second would be sufficient to characterize the voice signal completely. Note, however, that these are analog samples, called pulse amplitude modulation (PAM) samples. To convert to digital, each of these analog samples must be assigned a binary code. Figure 6.15 shows an example in which each sample is approximated by being "quantized" into one of 16 different levels. Each

---

[2]NRZ-L (nonreturn to zero, level) is the most common, and easiest, way to transmit digital signals. It uses two different voltage levels for the two binary digits: A negative voltage represents binary 1 and a positive voltage represents binary 0. NRZ-L is generally the code used to generate or interpret digital data by terminals and other devices. If a different code is to be used for transmission, it is typically generated from an NRZ-L signal by the transmission system.

sample can then be represented by 4 bits. But because the quantized values are only approximations, it is impossible to recover the original signal exactly. By using an 8-bit sample, which allows 256 quantizing levels, the quality of the recovered voice signal is comparable with that achieved via analog transmission. Note that this implies that a data rate of 8000 samples per second $\times$ 8 bits per sample = 64 kbps is needed for a single voice signal.

Thus, PCM starts with a continuous-time, continuous-amplitude (analog) signal, from which a digital signal is produced. The digital signal consists of blocks of n bits, where each n-bit number is the amplitude of a PCM pulse. On reception, the process is reversed to reproduce the analog signal. Notice, however, that this process violates the terms of the sampling theorem. By quantizing the PAM pulse, the original signal is now only approximated and cannot be recovered exactly. This effect is known as quantizing error or quantizing noise. The signal-to-noise ratio for quantizing noise can be expressed as [GIBS93]

$$\text{SNR}_{\text{dB}} = 20 \log 2^n + 1.76 \text{ dB} = 6.02n + 1.76 \text{ dB}$$

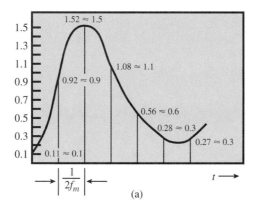

(a)

Digit	Binary equivalent	PCM waveform	Digit	Binary equivalent	PCM waveform
0	0000		8	1000	
1	0001		9	1001	
2	0010		10	1010	
3	0011		11	1011	
4	0100		12	1100	
5	0101		13	1101	
6	0110		14	1110	
7	0111		15	1111	

(b)

Figure 6.15 Pulse Code Modulation

Thus each additional bit used for quantizing increases SNR by about 6 dB, which is a factor of 4.

Typically, the PCM scheme is refined using a technique known as nonlinear encoding, which means, in effect, that the quantization levels are not equally spaced. The problem with equal spacing is that the mean absolute error for each sample is the same, regardless of signal level. Consequently, lower amplitude values are relatively more distorted. By using a greater number of quantizing steps for signals of low amplitude and a smaller number of quantizing steps for signals of large amplitude, a marked reduction in overall signal distortion is achieved (e.g., see Figure 6.16).

The same effect can be achieved by using uniform quantizing but companding (compressing-expanding) the input analog signal. Companding is a process that compresses the intensity range of a signal by imparting more gain to weak signals than to strong signals on input. At output, the reverse operation is performed. Figure 6.17 shows typical companding functions. Note that the effect on the input side is to compress the sample so that the higher values are reduced with respect to the lower values. Thus, with a fixed number of quantizing levels, more levels are available for lower-level signals. On the output side, the compander expands the samples so the compressed values are restored to their original values.

Nonlinear encoding can significantly improve the PCM SNR ratio. For voice signals, improvements of 24 to 30 dB have been achieved.

Delta Modulation

A variety of techniques have been used to improve the performance of PCM or to reduce its complexity. One of the most popular alternatives to PCM is delta modulation (DM).

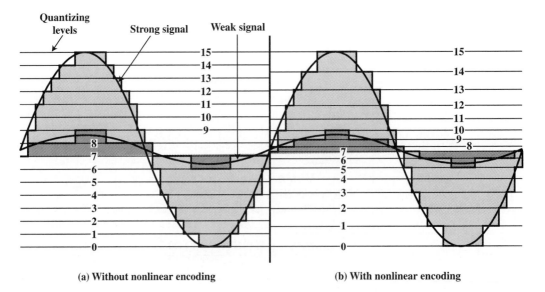

Figure 6.16   Effect of Nonlinear Coding

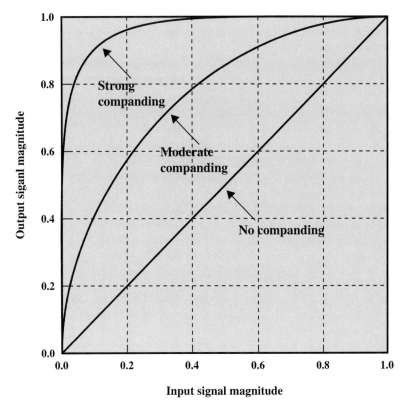

Figure 6.17 Typical Companding Functions

With delta modulation, an analog input is approximated by a staircase function that moves up or down by one quantization level (δ) at each sampling interval (T_s). An example is shown in Figure 6.18, where the staircase function is overlaid on the original analog waveform. The important characteristic of this staircase function is that its behavior is binary: At each sampling time, the function moves up or down a constant amount δ. Thus, the output of the delta modulation process can be represented as a single binary digit for each sample. In essence, a bit stream is produced by approximating the derivative of an analog signal rather than its amplitude: A 1 is generated if the staircase function is to go up during the next interval; a 0 is generated otherwise.

The transition (up or down) that occurs at each sampling interval is chosen so that the staircase function tracks the original analog waveform as closely as possible. Figure 6.19 illustrates the logic of the process, which is essentially a feedback mechanism. For transmission, the following occurs: At each sampling time, the analog input is compared to the most recent value of the approximating staircase function. If the value of the sampled waveform exceeds that of the staircase function, a 1 is generated; otherwise, a 0 is generated. Thus, the staircase is always changed in the direction of the input signal. The output of the DM process is therefore a binary sequence that can be used at the receiver to reconstruct the staircase function. The staircase function can then be smoothed by some type of integration process or by passing it through a low-pass filter to produce an analog approximation of the analog input signal.

There are two important parameters in a DM scheme: the size of the step assigned to each binary digit, δ, and the sampling rate. As Figure 6.18 illustrates, δ must be chosen to produce a balance between two types of errors or noise. When the analog waveform is changing very slowly, there will be quantizing noise. This noise increases as δ is increased. On the other hand, when the analog waveform is changing more rapidly than the staircase can follow, there is slope overload noise. This noise increases as δ is decreased.

It should be clear that the accuracy of the scheme can be improved by increasing the sampling rate. However, this increases the data rate of the output signal.

The principal advantage of DM over PCM is the simplicity of its implementation. In general, PCM exhibits better SNR characteristics at the same data rate.

Performance

Good voice reproduction via PCM can be achieved with 128 quantization levels, or 7-bit coding ($2^7 = 128$). A voice signal, conservatively, occupies a bandwidth of 4 kHz. Thus, according to the sampling theorem, samples should be taken at a rate

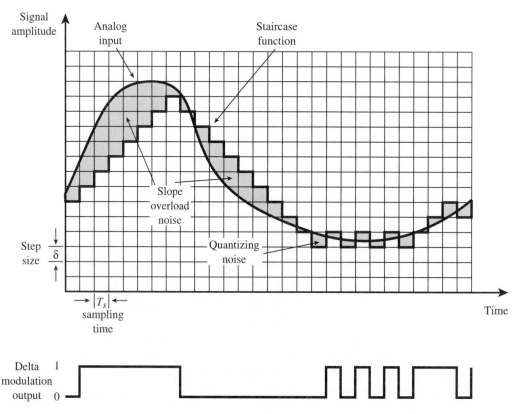

Figure 6.18 Example of Delta Modulation

(a) Transmission

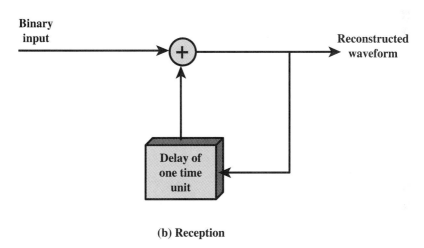

(b) Reception

Figure 6.19   Delta Modulation

of 8000 samples per second. This implies a data rate of $8000 \times 7 = 56$ kbps for the PCM-encoded digital data.

Consider what this means from the point of view of bandwidth requirement. An analog voice signal occupies 4 kHz. Using PCM this 4-kHz analog signal can be converted into a 56-kbps digital signal. But using the Nyquist criterion from Chapter 2, this digital signal could require on the order of 28 kHz of bandwidth. Even more severe differences are seen with higher bandwidth signals. For example, a common PCM scheme for color television uses 10-bit codes, which works out to 92 Mbps for a 6.6-MHz bandwidth signal. In spite of these numbers, digital techniques continue to grow in popularity for transmitting analog data. The principal reasons for this are as follows:

- Because repeaters are used instead of amplifiers, there is no additive noise.
- As we shall see, time division multiplexing (TDM) is used for digital signals instead of the frequency division multiplexing (FDM) used for analog signals. With TDM, there is no intermodulation noise, whereas we have seen that this is a concern for FDM.
- The conversion to digital signaling allows the use of the more efficient digital switching techniques.

Furthermore, techniques have been developed to provide more efficient codes. In the case of voice, a reasonable goal appears to be in the neighborhood of 4 kbps. With video, advantage can be taken of the fact that from frame to frame, most picture elements will not change. Interframe coding techniques should allow the video requirement to be reduced to about 15 Mbps, and for slowly changing scenes, such as found in a video teleconference, down to 64 kbps or less.

As a final point, we mention that in many instances, the use of a telecommunications system will result in both digital-to-analog and analog-to-digital processing. The overwhelming majority of local terminations into the telecommunications network is analog, and the network itself uses a mixture of analog and digital techniques. Thus digital data at a user's terminal may be converted to analog by a modem, subsequently digitized by a codec, and perhaps suffer repeated conversions before reaching its destination.

Thus, telecommunication facilities handle analog signals that represent both voice and digital data. The characteristics of the waveforms are quite different. Whereas voice signals tend to be skewed to the lower portion of the bandwidth (Figure 3.9), analog encoding of digital signals has a more uniform spectral content over the bandwidth and therefore contains more high-frequency components. Studies have shown that, because of the presence of these higher frequencies, PCM-related techniques are preferable to DM-related techniques for digitizing analog signals that represent digital data.

6.5 RECOMMENDED READING

There are many good references on analog modulation schemes for digital data. Good choices are [COUC01], [XION00], and [GLOV98]; these three also provide comprehensive treatment of digital and analog modulation schemes for analog data.

An exceptionally clear exposition that covers digital-to-analog, analog-to-digital, and analog-to-analog techniques is [PEAR92]. Another comprehensive treatment of the topics in this chapter is [SKLA01].

An instructive treatment of the concepts of bit rate, baud, and bandwidth is [FREE98]. A recommended tutorial that expands on the concepts treated in this chapter relating to bandwidth efficiency and encoding schemes is [SKLA93].

COUC01 Couch, L. *Digital and Analog Communication Systems.* Upper Saddle River, NJ: Prentice Hall, 2001.

FREE98 Freeman, R. "Bits, Symbols, Baud, and Bandwidth." *IEEE Communications Magazine*, April 1998.

GLOV98 Glover, I., and Grant, P. *Digital Communications.* Upper Saddle River, NJ: Prentice Hall, 1998.

PEAR92 Pearson, J. *Basic Communication Theory.* Englewood Cliffs, NJ: Prentice Hall, 1992.

SKLA93 Sklar, B. "Defining, Designing, and Evaluating Digital Communication Systems." *IEEE Communications Magazine*, November 1993.

SKLA01 Sklar, B. *Digital Communications: Fundamentals and Applications.* Upper Saddle River, NJ: Prentice Hall, 2001.

XION00 Xiong, F. *Digital Modulation Techniques.* Boston: Artech House, 2000.

6.6 KEY TERMS, REVIEW QUESTIONS, AND PROBLEMS

Key Terms

amplitude modulation (AM)	delta modulation (DM)	phase modulation (PM)
amplitude shift keying (ASK)	differential PSK (DPSK)	phase shift keying (PSK)
angle modulation	frequency modulation (FM)	pulse code modulation (PCM)
bit error rate (BER)	frequency shift keying (FSK)	quadrature amplitude modulation (QAM)
carrier frequency	modulation	quadrature PSK (QPSK)

Review Questions

1 What is differential encoding?

2 What function does a modem perform?

3 Indicate three major advantages of digital transmission over analog transmission.

4 How are binary values represented in amplitude shift keying, and what is the limitation of this approach?

5 What is NRZ-L? What is a major disadvantage of this data encoding approach?

Problems

1 Figure 6.20 shows the QAM demodulator corresponding to the QAM modulator of Figure 6.10. Show that this arrangement does recover the two signals $d_1(t)$ and $d_2(t)$, which can be combined to recover the original input.

2 A sine wave is to be used for two different signaling schemes: (a) PSK; (b) QPSK. The duration of a signal element is 10^{-5} s. If the received signal is of the following form,

$$s(t) = 0.005 \sin(2\pi\, 10^6 t + \theta) \text{ volts}$$

and if the measured noise power at the receiver is 2.5×10^{-8} watts, determine the E_b/N_0 (in dB) for each case.

3 What SNR ratio is required to achieve a bandwidth efficiency of 1.0 for ASK, FSK, PSK, and QPSK? Assume that the required bit error rate is 10^{-6}.

4 An NRZ-L signal is passed through a filter with $r = 0.5$ and then modulated onto a carrier. The data rate is 2400 bps. Evaluate the bandwidth for ASK and FSK. For FSK assume that the two frequencies used are 50 kHz and 55 kHz.

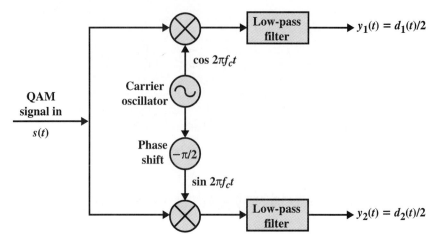

Figure 6.20 QAM Demodulator

5 Assume that a telephone line channel is equalized to allow bandpass data transmission over a frequency range of 600 to 3000 Hz. The available bandwidth is 2400 Hz. For $r = 1$, evaluate the required bandwidth for 2400 bps QPSK and 4800-bps, eight-level multilevel signaling. Is the bandwidth adequate?

6 Why should PCM be preferable to DM for encoding analog signals that represent digital data?

7 Are the modem and the codec functional inverses (i.e., could an inverted modem function as a codec, or vice versa)?

8 A signal is quantized using 10-bit PCM. Find the signal-to-quantization noise ratio.

9 Consider an audio signal with spectral components in the range 300 to 3000 Hz. Assume that a sampling rate of 7000 samples per second will be used to generate a PCM signal.
    a. For SNR = 30 dB, what is the number of uniform quantization levels needed?
    b. What data rate is required?

10 Find the step size δ required to prevent slope overload noise as a function of the frequency of the highest-frequency component of the signal. Assume that all components have amplitude A.

11 A PCM encoder accepts a signal with a full-scale voltage of 10 V and generates 8-bit codes using uniform quantization. The maximum normalized quantized voltage is $1 - 2^{-8}$. Determine (a) normalized step size, (b) actual step size in volts, (c) actual maximum quantized level in volts, (d) normalized resolution, (e) actual resolution, and (f) percentage resolution.

12 The analog waveform shown in Figure 6.21 is to be delta modulated. The sampling period and the step size are indicated by the grid on the figure. The first DM output and the staircase function for this period are also shown. Show the rest of the staircase function and give the DM output. Indicate regions where slope overload distortion exists.

13 Consider the angle-modulated signal
$$s(t) = 10 \cos[(10^8)\pi t + 5 \sin 2\pi(10^3)t]$$
Find the maximum phase deviation and the maximum frequency deviation.

Figure 6.21 Delta Modulation Example

14 Consider the angle-modulated signal

$$s(t) = 10 \cos [2\pi(10^6)t + 0.1 \sin (10^3)\pi t]$$

a. Express $s(t)$ as a PM signal with $n_p = 10$.

b. Express $s(t)$ as an FM signal with $n_f = 10\,\pi$.

15 Let $m_1(t)$ and $m_2(t)$ be message signals and let $s_1(t)$ and $s_2(t)$ be the corresponding modulated signals using a carrier frequency of f_c.

a. Show that if simple AM modulation is used, then $m_1(t) + m_2(t)$ produces a modulated signal equal that is a linear combination of $s_1(t)$ and $s_2(t)$. This is why AM is sometimes referred to as linear modulation.

b. Show that if simple PM modulation is used, then $m_1(t) + m_2(t)$ produces a modulated signal that is not a linear combination of $s_1(t)$ and $s_2(t)$. This is why angle modulation is sometimes referred to as nonlinear modulation.

APPENDIX 6A PROOF OF THE SAMPLING THEOREM

The sampling theorem can be restated as follows. Given:

- $x(t)$ is a bandlimited signal with bandwidth f_h.
- $p(t)$ is a sampling signal consisting of pulses at intervals $T_s = 1/f_s$, where f_s is the sampling frequency.
- $x_s(t) = x(t)p(t)$ is the sampled signal.

Then $x(t)$ can be recovered exactly from $x_s(t)$ if and only if $f_s \geq 2f_h$.

Proof

Because $p(t)$ consists of a uniform series of pulses, it is a periodic signal and can be represented by a Fourier series:

$$p(t) = \sum_{n=-\infty}^{\infty} P_n e^{j2\pi nf_s t}$$

We have

$$x_s(t) = x(t)p(t) = \sum_{n=-\infty}^{\infty} P_n x(t) e^{j2\pi nf_s t}$$

Now consider the Fourier transform of $x_s(t)$:

$$X_s(f) = \int_{-\infty}^{\infty} x_s(t) e^{-j2\pi ft}\, dt$$

Substituting for $x_s(t)$, we have

$$X_s(f) = \int_{-\infty}^{\infty} \sum_{n=-\infty}^{\infty} P_n x(t) e^{j2\pi nf_s t} e^{-j2\pi ft}\, dt$$

Rearranging yields

$$X_s(f) = \sum_{n=-\infty}^{\infty} P_n \int_{-\infty}^{\infty} x(t) e^{-j2\pi(f-nf_s)t}\, dt$$

From the definition of the Fourier transform, we can write

$$X(f - nf_s) = \int_{-\infty}^{\infty} x(t) e^{-j2\pi(f-nf_s)t}\, dt$$

where $X(f)$ is the Fourier transform of $x(t)$. Substituting this into the preceding equation, we have

$$X_s(f) = \sum_{n=-\infty}^{\infty} P_n X(f - nf_s)$$

This last equation has an interesting interpretation, which is illustrated in Figure 6.22, where we assume without loss of generality that the bandwidth of $x(t)$ is in the range 0 to f_h. The spectrum of $x_s(t)$ is composed of the spectrum of $x(t)$ plus the spectrum of $x(t)$ translated to each harmonic of the sampling frequency. Each of the

(a) Spectrum of $x(t)$

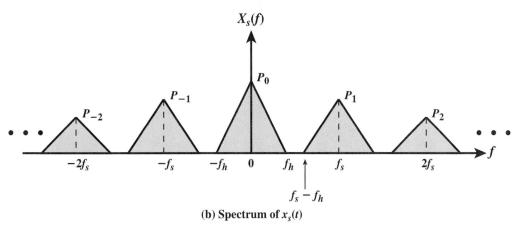

(b) Spectrum of $x_s(t)$

Figure 6.22   Demonstration of Sampling Theorem

translated spectra is multiplied by the corresponding coefficient of the Fourier series of $p(t)$. If $f_s \geq 2f_h$, these various translations do not overlap, and the spectrum of $x(t)$, multiplied by P_0, appears in $X_s(f)$. By passing $X_s(f)$ through a bandpass filter with $f \leq f_s$, the spectrum of $x(t)$ is recovered. In equation form,

$$X_s(f) = P_0 X(f) \qquad \frac{-f_s}{2} \leq f \leq \frac{f_s}{2}$$

CHAPTER 7

SPREAD SPECTRUM

An increasingly important form of communications is known as spread spectrum. This technique does not fit neatly into the categories defined in the preceding chapter, as it can be used to transmit either analog or digital data, using an analog signal.

The spread spectrum technique was developed initially for military and intelligence requirements. The essential idea is to spread the information signal over a wider bandwidth to make jamming and interception more difficult. The first type of spread spectrum developed is known as frequency hopping.[1] A more recent type of spread spectrum is direct sequence. Both of these techniques are used in various wireless communications standards and products.

After a brief overview, we look at these two spread spectrum techniques. We then examine a multiple access technique based on spread spectrum.

7.1 THE CONCEPT OF SPREAD SPECTRUM

Figure 7.1 highlights the key characteristics of any spread spectrum system. Input is fed into a channel encoder that produces an analog signal with a relatively narrow bandwidth around some center frequency. This signal is further modulated using a sequence of digits known as a spreading code or spreading sequence. Typically, but not always, the spreading code is generated by a pseudonoise, or pseudorandom number, generator. The effect of this modulation is to increase significantly the bandwidth (spread the spectrum) of the signal to be transmitted. On the receiving end, the same digit sequence is used to demodulate the spread spectrum signal. Finally, the signal is fed into a channel decoder to recover the data.

Several things can be gained from this apparent waste of spectrum:

- We can gain immunity from various kinds of noise and multipath distortion. The earliest applications of spread spectrum were military, where it was used for its immunity to jamming.

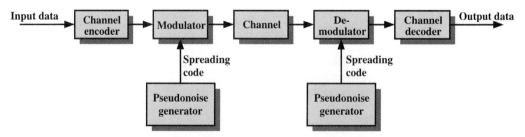

Figure 7.1 General Model of Spread Spectrum Digital Communication System

---

[1]Spread spectrum (using frequency hopping) was invented, believe it or not, by Hollywood screen siren Hedy Lamarr in 1940 at the age of 26. She and a partner who later joined her effort were granted a patent in 1942 (U.S. Patent 2,292,387; 11 August 1942). Lamarr considered this her contribution to the war effort and never profited from her invention.

- It can also be used for hiding and encrypting signals. Only a recipient who knows the spreading code can recover the encoded information.
- Several users can independently use the same higher bandwidth with very little interference. This property is used in cellular telephony applications, with a technique know as code division multiplexing (CDM) or code division multiple access (CDMA).

7.2 FREQUENCY-HOPPING SPREAD SPECTRUM

With frequency-hopping spread spectrum (FHSS), the signal is broadcast over a seemingly random series of radio frequencies, hopping from frequency to frequency at fixed intervals. A receiver, hopping between frequencies in synchronization with the transmitter, picks up the message. Would-be eavesdroppers hear only unintelligible blips. Attempts to jam the signal on one frequency succeed only at knocking out a few bits of it.

Basic Approach

Figure 7.2 shows an example of a frequency-hopping signal. A number of channels are allocated for the FH signal. Typically, there are 2^k carrier frequencies forming 2^k channels. The spacing between carrier frequencies and hence the width of each channel usually corresponds to the bandwidth of the input signal. The transmitter operates in one channel at a time for a fixed interval; for example, the IEEE 802.11 standard uses a 300-ms interval. During that interval, some number of bits (possibly a fraction of a bit, as discussed subsequently) are transmitted using some encoding scheme. The sequence of channels used is dictated by a spreading code. Both transmitter and receiver use the same code to tune into a sequence of channels in synchronization.

Figure 7.2 Frequency-Hopping Example

(a) Transmitter

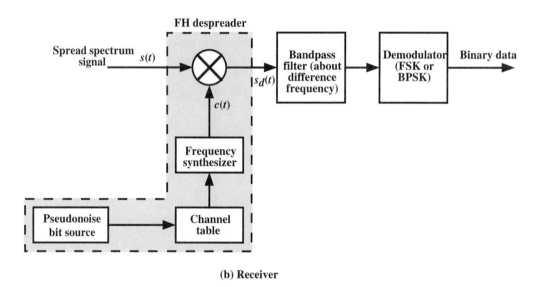

(b) Receiver

Figure 7.3 Frequency-Hopping Spread Spectrum System

A typical block diagram for a frequency-hopping system is shown in Figure 7.3. For transmission, binary data are fed into a modulator using some digital-to-analog encoding scheme, such as frequency-shift keying (FSK) or binary phase shift keying (BPSK). The resulting signal is centered around some base frequency. A pseudonoise (PN), or pseudorandom number, source serves as an index into a table of frequencies; this is the spreading code referred to previously. Each k bits of the PN source specifies one of the 2^k carrier frequencies. At each successive interval (each k PN bits), a new carrier frequency is selected. This frequency is then modulated by the signal produced from the initial modulator to produce a new signal with the same shape but now centered on the selected carrier frequency. On reception, the spread spectrum signal is demodulated using the same sequence of PN-derived frequencies and then demodulated to produce the output data.

Figure 7.3 indicates that the two signals are multiplied. Let us give an example of how this works, using BFSK as the data modulation scheme. We can define the FSK input to the FHSS system as [compare to Equation (6.2)]

$$s_d(t) = A\,\cos(2\pi(f_0 + 0.5(b_i + 1)\Delta f)t) \qquad \text{for } iT < t < (i + 1)T \qquad (7.1)$$

where

A = amplitude of signal
f_0 = base frequency
b_i = value of the ith bit of data ($+1$ for binary 1, -1 for binary 0)
Δf = frequency separation
T = bit duration; data rate = $1/T$

Thus, during the ith bit interval, the frequency of the data signal is f_0 if the data bit is -1 and $f_0 + \Delta f$ if the data bit is $+1$.

The frequency synthesizer generates a constant-frequency tone whose frequency hops among a set of 2^k frequencies, with the hopping pattern determined by k bits from the PN sequence. For simplicity, assume the duration of one hop is the same as the duration of one bit and we ignore phase differences between the data signal $s_d(t)$ and the spreading signal, also called a chipping signal, $c(t)$. Then the product signal during the ith hop (during the ith bit) is

$$p(t) = s_d(t)c(t) = A\,\cos(2\pi(f_0 + 0.5(b_i + 1)\Delta f)t)\cos(2\pi f_i t)$$

where f_i is the frequency of the signal generated by the frequency synthesizer during the ith hop. Using the trigonometric identity[2] $\cos(x)\cos(y) = (1/2)(\cos(x + y) + \cos(x - y))$, we have

$$p(t) = 0.5A[\cos(2\pi(f_0 + 0.5(b_i + 1)\Delta f + f_i)t) + \cos(2\pi(f_0 + 0.5(b_i + 1)\Delta f - f_i)t)]$$

A bandpass filter (Figure 7.3) is used to block the difference frequency and pass the sum frequency, yielding an FHSS signal of

$$s(t) = 0.5A\,\cos(2\pi(f_0 + 0.5(b_i + 1)\Delta f + f_i)t) \qquad (7.2)$$

Thus, during the ith bit interval, the frequency of the data signal is $f_0 + f_i$ if the data bit is -1 and $f_0 + f_i + \Delta f$ if the data bit is $+1$.

At the receiver, a signal of the form $s(t)$ just defined will be received. This is multiplied by a replica of the spreading signal to yield a product signal of the form

---

[2]See the math refresher document at WilliamStallings.com/StudentSupport.html for a summary of trigonometric identities.

$$p(t) = s(t)c(t) = 0.5A \cos(2\pi(f_0 + 0.5(b_i + 1)\Delta f + f_i)t)\cos(2\pi f_i t)$$

Again using the trigonometric identity, we have

$$p(t) = s(t)c(t)$$
$$= 0.25A \left[\cos(2\pi(f_0 + 0.5(b_i + 1)\Delta f + f_i + f_i)t) + \cos(2\pi(f_0 + 0.5(b_i + 1)\Delta f)t)\right]$$

A bandpass filter (Figure 7.3) is used to block the sum frequency and pass the difference frequency, yielding an signal of the form of $s_d(t)$, defined in Equation (7.1):

$$0.25A \cos(2\pi(f_0 + 0.5(b_i + 1)\Delta f)t)$$

FHSS Using MFSK

A common modulation technique used in conjunction with FHSS is multiple FSK (MFSK). Recall from Chapter 6 that MFSK uses $M = 2^L$ different frequencies to encode the digital input L bits at a time. The transmitted signal is of the form [Equation (6.3)]:

$$s_i(t) = A \cos 2\pi f_i t, \qquad\qquad 1 \le i \le M$$

where

$$f_i = f_c + (2i - 1 - M)f_d$$
$$f_c = \text{denotes the carrier frequency}$$
$$f_d = \text{denotes the difference frequency}$$
$$M = \text{number of different signal elements} = 2^L$$
$$L = \text{number of bits per signal element}$$

For FHSS, the MFSK signal is translated to a new frequency every T_c seconds by modulating the MFSK signal with the FHSS carrier signal. The effect is to translate the MFSK signal into the appropriate FHSS channel. For a data rate of R, the duration of a bit is $T = 1/R$ seconds and the duration of a signal element is $T_s = LT$ seconds. If T_c is greater than or equal to T_s, the spreading modulation is referred to as slow-frequency-hop spread spectrum; otherwise it is known as fast-frequency-hop spread spectrum.[3] To summarize,

Slow-frequency-hop spread spectrum	$T_c \ge T_s$
Fast-frequency-hop spread spectrum	$T_c < T_s$

Figure 7.4 shows an example of slow FHSS, using the MFSK example from Figure 6.4. Here we have $M = 4$, which means that four different frequencies are used to encode the data input 2 bits at a time. Each signal element is a discrete

---

[3]Some authors use a somewhat different definition (e.g., [PICK82]) of multiple hops per bit for fast frequency hop, multiple bits per hop for slow frequency hop, and one hop per bit if neither fast nor slow. The more common definition, which we use, relates hops to signal elements rather than bits.

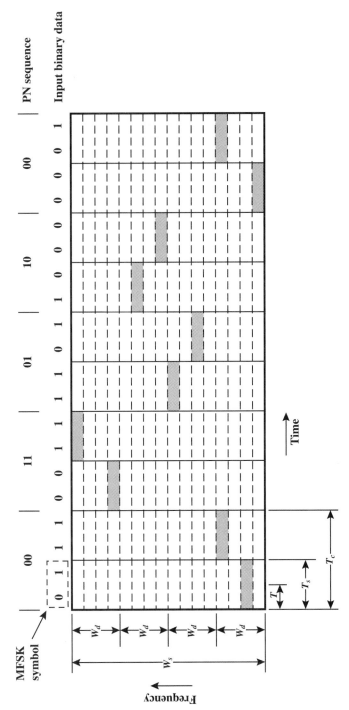

Figure 7.4 Slow Frequency Hop Spread Spectrum Using MFSK ($M=4$, $k=2$)

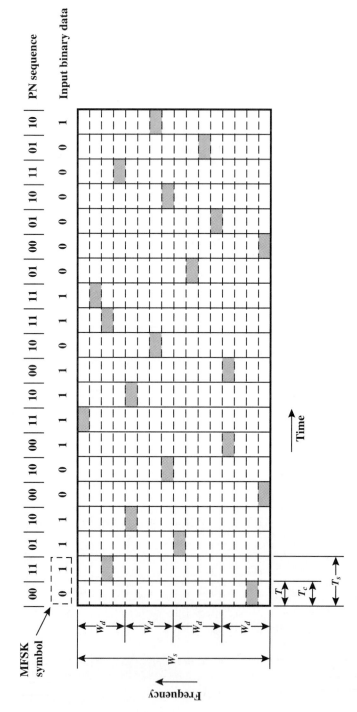

Figure 7.5 Fast Frequency Hop Spread Spectrum Using MFSK ($M=4$, $k=2$)

frequency tone, and the total MFSK bandwidth is $W_d = Mf_d$. We use an FHSS scheme with $k = 2$. That is, there are $4 = 2^k$ different channels, each of width W_d. The total FHSS bandwidth is $W_s = 2^k W_d$. Each 2 bits of the PN sequence is used to select one of the four channels. That channel is held for a duration of two signal elements, or four bits ($T_c = 2T_s = 4T$).

Figure 7.5 shows an example of fast FHSS, using the same MFSK example. Again, $M = 4$ and $k = 2$. In this case, however, each signal element is represented by two frequency tones. Again, $W_d = Mf_d$ and $W_s = 2^k W_d$. In this example $T_s = 2T_c = 2T$. In general, fast FHSS provides improved performance compared to slow FHSS in the face of noise or jamming. For example, if three or more frequencies (chips) are used for each signal element, the receiver can decide which signal element was sent on the basis of a majority of the chips being correct.

FHSS Performance Considerations

Typically, a large number of frequencies are used in FHSS so that W_s is much larger than W_d. One benefit of this is that a large value of k results in a system that is quite resistant to jamming. For example, suppose we have an MFSK transmitter with bandwidth W_d and noise jammer of the same bandwidth and fixed power S_j on the signal carrier frequency. Then we have a ratio of signal energy per bit to noise power density per hertz of

$$\frac{E_b}{N_j} = \frac{E_b W_d}{S_j}$$

If frequency hopping is used, the jammer must jam all 2^k frequencies. With a fixed power, this reduces the jamming power in any one frequency band to $S_j/2^k$. The gain in signal-to-noise ratio, or processing gain, is

$$G_P = 2^k = \frac{W_s}{W_d} \tag{7.3}$$

7.3   DIRECT SEQUENCE SPREAD SPECTRUM

With direct sequence spread spectrum (DSSS), each bit in the original signal is represented by multiple bits in the transmitted signal, using a spreading code. The spreading code spreads the signal across a wider frequency band in direct proportion to the number of bits used. Therefore, a 10-bit spreading code spreads the signal across a frequency band that is 10 times greater than a 1-bit spreading code.

One technique with direct sequence spread spectrum is to combine the digital information stream with the spreading code bit stream using an exclusive-OR (XOR). The XOR obeys the following rules:

$$0 \oplus 0 = 0 \qquad 0 \oplus 1 = 1 \qquad 1 \oplus 0 = 1 \qquad 1 \oplus 1 = 0$$

Figure 7.6 shows an example. Note that an information bit of one inverts the spreading code bits in the combination, while an information bit of zero causes the spreading code bits to be transmitted without inversion. The combination bit stream has the data rate of the original spreading code sequence, so it has a wider bandwidth than the information stream. In this example, the spreading code bit stream is clocked at four times the information rate.

DSSS Using BPSK

To see how this technique works out in practice, assume that a BPSK modulation scheme is to be used. Rather than represent binary data with 1 and 0, it is more convenient for our purposes to use +1 and −1 to represent the two binary digits. In that case, a BPSK signal can be represented as was shown in Equation (6.5):

$$s_d(t) = A\, d(t)\, \cos(2\pi f_c t) \tag{7.4}$$

where

A = amplitude of signal
f_c = carrier frequency
$d(t)$ = the discrete function that takes on the value of +1 for one bit time
     if the corresponding bit in the bit stream is 1 and the value of −1
     for one bit time if the corresponding bit in the bit stream is 0

To produce the DSSS signal, we multiply the above by c(t), which is the PN sequence taking on values of +1 and −1:

$$s(t) = A\, d(t)c(t)\cos(2\pi f_c t) \tag{7.5}$$

Figure 7.6 Example of Direct Sequence Spread Spectrum

At the receiver, the incoming signal is multiplied again by $c(t)$. But $c(t) \times c(t) = 1$ and therefore the original signal is recovered:

$$s(t)c(t) = A \ d(t)c(t)c(t)\cos(2\pi f_c t) = s_d(t)$$

Equation (7.5) can be interpreted in two ways, leading to two different implementations. The first interpretation is to first multiply $d(t)$ and $c(t)$ together and then perform the BPSK modulation. That is the interpretation we have been discussing. Alternatively, we can first perform the BPSK modulation on the data stream $d(t)$ to generate the data signal $s_d(t)$. This signal can then be multiplied by $c(t)$.

An implementation using the second interpretation is shown in Figure 7.7. Figure 7.8 is an example of this approach.

DSSS Performance Considerations

The spectrum spreading achieved by the direct sequence technique is easily determined (Figure 7.9). In our example, the information signal has a bit width of T,

(a) Transmitter

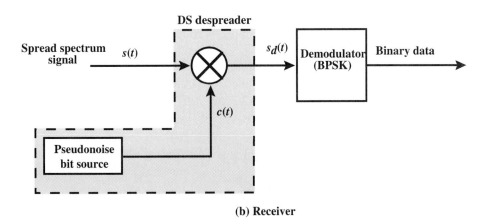

(b) Receiver

Figure 7.7   Direct Sequence Spread Spectrum System

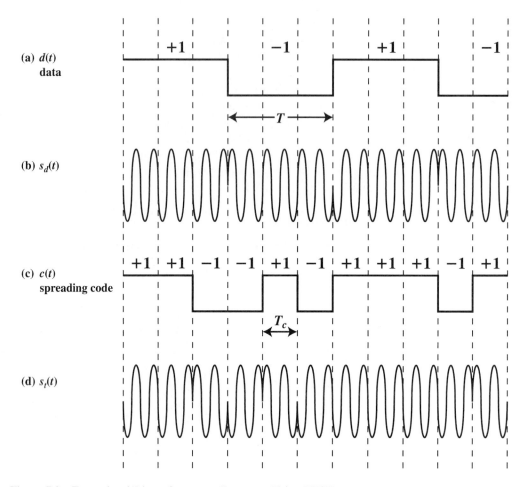

Figure 7.8 Example of Direct Sequence Spectrum Using BPSK

which is equivalent to a data rate of $1/T$. In that case, the spectrum of the signal, depending on the encoding technique, is roughly $2/T$. Similarly, the spectrum of the PN signal is $2/T_c$. Figure 7.9c shows the resulting spectrum spreading. The amount of spreading that is achieved is a direct result of the data rate of the PN stream.

As with FHSS, we can get some insight into the performance of DSSS by looking at its effectiveness against jamming. Let us assume a simple jamming signal at the center frequency of the DSSS system. The jamming signal has the form

$$s_j(t) = \sqrt{2S_j}\,\cos(2\pi f_c t)$$

and the received signal is

$$s_r(t) = s(t) + s_j(t) + n(t)$$

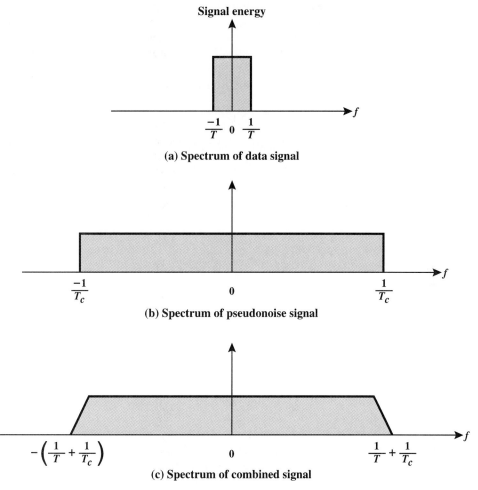

Figure 7.9 Approximate Spectrum of Direct Sequence Spread Spectrum Signal

where

$$s(t) = \text{transmitted signal}$$
$$s_j(t) = \text{jamming signal}$$
$$n(t) = \text{additive white noise}$$
$$S_j = \text{jammer signal power}$$

The despreader at the receiver multiplies $s_r(t)$ by $c(t)$, so the signal component due to the jamming signal is

$$y_j(t) = \sqrt{2S_j}\, c(t)\cos(2\pi f_c t)$$

This is simply a BPSK modulation of the carrier tone. Thus, the carrier power S_j is spread over a bandwidth of approximately $2/T_c$. However, the BPSK demodulator (Figure 7.7) following the DSSS despreader includes a bandpass filter matched to the BPSK data, with bandwidth of $2/T$. Thus, most of the jamming power is filtered. Although a number of factors come into play, as an approximation, we can say that the jamming power passed by the filter is

$$S_j F = S_j(2/T)/(2/T_c) = S_j(T_c/T)$$

The jamming power has been reduced by a factor of (T_c/T) through the use of spread spectrum. The inverse of this factor is the gain in signal-to-noise ratio:

$$G_p = \frac{T}{T_c} = \frac{R_c}{R} \approx \frac{W_s}{W_d} \tag{7.6}$$

where R_c is the spreading bit rate, R is the data rate, W_d is the signal bandwidth, and W_s is the spread spectrum signal bandwidth. The result is similar to the result for FHSS [Equation (7.3)].

7.4 CODE DIVISION MULTIPLE ACCESS

Basic Principles

CDMA is a multiplexing technique used with spread spectrum. The scheme works in the following manner. We start with a data signal with rate D, which we call the bit data rate. We break each bit into k *chips* according to a fixed pattern that is specific to each user, called the user's code. The new channel has a chip data rate of kD chips per second. As an illustration we consider a simple example[4] with $k = 6$. It is simplest to characterize a code as a sequence of 1s and -1s. Figure 7.10 shows the codes for three users, A, B, and C, each of which is communicating with the same base station receiver, R. Thus, the code for user A is $c_A = <1, -1, -1, 1, -1, 1>$. Similarly, user B has code $c_B = <1, 1, -1, -1, 1, 1>$, and user C has code $c_C = <1, 1, -1, 1, 1, -1>$.

We now consider the case of user A communicating with the base station. The base station is assumed to know A's code. For simplicity, we assume that communication is already synchronized so that the base station knows when to look for codes. If A wants to send a 1 bit, A transmits its code as a chip pattern $<1, -1, -1, 1, -1, 1>$. If a 0 bit is to be sent, A transmits the complement (1s and -1s reversed) of its code, $<-1, 1, 1, -1, 1, -1>$. At the base station the receiver decodes the chip patterns. In our simple version, if the receiver R receives a chip pattern $d = <d1, d2, d3, d4, d5, d6>$, and the receiver is seeking to communicate with a user u so that it

---

[4]This example was provided by Prof. Richard Van Slyke of the Polytechnic University of Brooklyn.

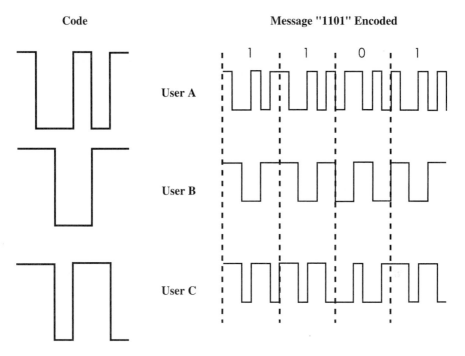

Figure 7.10 CDMA Example

has at hand u's code, $<c1, c2, c3, c4, c5, c6>$, the receiver performs electronically the following decoding function:

$$S_u(d) = d1 \times c1 + d2 \times c2 + d3 \times c3 + d4 \times c4 + d5 \times c5 + d6 \times c6$$

The subscript u on S simply indicates that u is the user that we are interested in. Let's suppose the user u is actually A and see what happens. If A sends a 1 bit, then d is $<1, -1, -1, 1, -1, 1>$ and the preceding computation using S_A becomes

$$S_A(1, -1, -1, 1, -1, 1) = 1 \times 1 + (-1) \times (-1) + (-1) \times (-1) +$$
$$1 \times 1 + (-1) \times (-1) + 1 \times 1 = 6$$

If A sends a 0 bit that corresponds to $d = <-1, 1, 1, -1, 1, -1>$, we get

$$S_A(-1, 1, 1, -1, 1, -1) = -1 \times 1 + 1 \times (-1) + 1 \times (-1) +$$
$$(-1) \times 1 + 1 \times (-1) + (-1) \times 1 = -6$$

Please note that it is always the case that $-6 \le S_A(d) \le 6$ no matter what sequence of -1s and 1s that d is, and that the only d's resulting in the extreme values of 6 and -6 are A's code and its complement, respectively. So if S_A produces a $+6$, we say that we have received a 1 bit from A; if S_A produces a -6, we say that we have received a 0 bit from user A; otherwise, we assume that someone else is sending information or there is an error. So why go through all this? The reason becomes clear if we see what happens if user B is sending and we try to receive it with S_A, that is, we are decoding with the wrong code, A's. If B sends a 1 bit, then $d = \langle 1, 1, -1, -1, 1, 1\rangle$. Then

$$S_A(1, 1, -1, -1, 1, 1) = (-1) \times 1 + (-1) \times (-1) + 1 \times (-1)$$
$$+ 1 \times 1 + (-1) \times (-1) + (-1) \times 1 = 0$$

Table 7.1 CDMA Example

(a) User's codes

User A	1	−1	−1	1	−1	1
User B	1	1	−1	−1	1	1
User C	1	1	−1	1	1	−1

(b) Transmission from A

Transmit (data bit = 1)	1	−1	−1	1	−1	1	
Receiver codeword	1	−1	−1	1	−1	1	
Multiplication	1	1	1	1	1	1	= 6

Transmit (data bit = 0)	−1	1	1	−1	1	−1	
Receiver codeword	1	−1	−1	1	−1	1	
Multiplication	−1	−1	−1	−1	−1	−1	= −6

(c) Transmission from B, receiver attempts to recover A's transmission

Transmit (data bit = 1)	1	1	−1	−1	1	1	
Receiver codeword	1	−1	−1	1	−1	1	
Multiplication	1	−1	1	−1	−1	1	= 0

(d) Transmission from C, receiver attempts to recover B's transmission

Transmit (data bit = 1)	1	1	−1	1	1	−1	
Receiver codeword	1	1	−1	−1	1	1	
Multiplication	1	1	1	−1	1	−1	= 2

(e) Transmission from B and C, receiver attempts to recover B's transmission

B (data bit = 1)	1	1	−1	−1	1	1	
C (data bit = 1)	1	1	−1	1	1	−1	
Combined signal	2	2	−2	0	2	0	
Receiver codeword	1	1	−1	−1	1	1	
Multiplication	2	2	2	0	2	0	= 8

Thus, the unwanted signal (from B) does not show up at all. You can easily verify that if B had sent a 0 bit, the decoder would produce a value of 0 for S_A again. This means that if the decoder is linear and if A and B transmit signals s_A and s_B, respectively, at the same time, then $S_A(s_A + s_B) = S_A(s_A) + S_A(s_B) = S_A(s_A)$ since the decoder ignores B when it is using A's code. The codes of A and B that have the property that $S_A(c_B) = S_B(c_A) = 0$ are called *orthogonal*. Such codes are very nice to have but there are not all that many of them. More common is the case when $S_X(c_Y)$ is small in absolute value when $X \neq Y$. Then it is easy to distinguish between the two cases when $X = Y$ and when $X \neq Y$. In our example $S_A(c_C) = S_C(c_A) = 0$, but $S_B(c_C) = S_C(c_B) = 2$. In the latter case the C signal would make a small contribution to the decoded signal instead of 0. Using the decoder, S_u, the receiver can sort out transmission from u even when there may be other users broadcasting in the same cell.

Table 7.1 summarizes the example from the preceding discussion.

In practice, the CDMA receiver can filter out the contribution from unwanted users or they appear as low-level noise. However, if there are many users competing for the channel with the user the receiver is trying to listen to, or if the signal power of one or more competing signals is too high, perhaps because it is very near the receiver (the "near/far" problem), the system breaks down.

CDMA for Direct Sequence Spread Spectrum

Let us now look at CDMA from the viewpoint of a DSSS system using BPSK. Figure 7.11 depicts a configuration in which there are n users, each transmitting using a

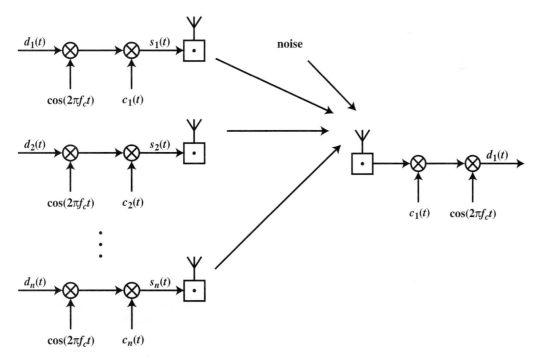

Figure 7.11 CDMA in a DSSS Environment

different, orthogonal, PN sequence (compare Figure 7.7). For each user, the data stream to be transmitted, $d_i(t)$, is BPSK modulated to produce a signal with a bandwidth of W_s and then multiplied by the spreading code for that user, $c_i(t)$. All of the signals, plus noise, are received at the receiver's antenna. Suppose that the receiver is attempting to recover the data of user 1. The incoming signal is multiplied by the spreading code of user 1 and then demodulated. The effect of this is to narrow the bandwidth of that portion of the incoming signal corresponding to user 1 to the original bandwidth of the unspread signal, which is proportional to the data rate. Because the remainder of the incoming signal is orthogonal to the spreading code of user 1, that remainder still has the bandwidth W_s. Thus the unwanted signal energy remains spread over a large bandwidth and the wanted signal is concentrated in a narrow bandwidth. The bandpass filter at the demodulator can therefore recover the desired signal.

7.5 GENERATION OF SPREADING SEQUENCES

As was mentioned the spreading sequence, $c(t)$, is a sequence of binary digits shared by transmitter and receiver. Spreading consists of multiplying (XOR) the input data by the spreading sequence, where the bit rate of the spreading sequence is higher than that of the input data. When the signal is received, the spreading is removed by multiplying with the same spreading code, exactly synchronized with the received signal.

The resulting data rate is consequently that of the spreading sequence. This increases the transmitted data rate and therefore increases the required bandwidth. The redundancy of the system is also increased. The spreading codes are chosen so that the resulting signal is noiselike; therefore, there should be an approximately equal number of ones and zeros in the spreading code and few or no repeated patterns. When spreading codes are used in a CDMA application, then there is the further requirement of lack of correlation. When multiple signals are received, each spread with a different spreading code, the receiver should be able to pick out any individual signal using that signal's spreading code. The spread signals should behave as if they were uncorrelated with each other, so that other signals will appear as noise and not interfere with the despreading of a particular signal. Because of the high degree of redundancy provided by the spreading operation, the despreading operation is able to cope with the interference of other signals in the same bandwidth.

Two general categories of spreading sequences have been used: PN sequences and orthogonal codes. PN sequences are the most common ones used in FHSS systems and in DSSS systems not employing CDMA. In DSSS CDMA systems, both PN and orthogonal codes have been used. We examine each of these approaches in turn.

PN Sequences

An ideal spreading sequence would be a random sequence of binary ones and zeros. However, because it is required that transmitter and receiver must have a copy of the random bit stream, a predictable way is needed to generate the same bit stream at transmitter and receiver and yet retain the desirable properties of a random bit stream. This requirement is met by a PN generator. A PN generator will produce a periodic sequence that eventually repeats but that appears to be random.

PN sequences are generated by an algorithm using some initial value called the seed. The algorithm is deterministic and therefore produces sequences of numbers that are not statistically random. However, if the algorithm is good, the resulting sequences will pass many reasonable tests of randomness. Such numbers are often referred to as pseudorandom numbers, or pseudonoise sequences. The important point is that unless you know the algorithm and the seed, it is impractical to predict the sequence. Hence, only a receiver that shares this information with a transmitter will be able to decode the signal successfully.

PN sequences find a number of uses in computers and communications, and the principles involved are well developed. We begin with a general description of desirable properties of PNs and then look at the generation method typically used for spread spectrum applications.

PN Properties

Two important properties for PNs are randomness and unpredictability.

Traditionally, the concern in the generation of a sequence of allegedly random numbers has been that the sequence of numbers be random in some well-defined statistical sense. The following two criteria are used to validate that a sequence of numbers is random:

- **Uniform distribution:** The distribution of numbers in the sequence should be uniform; that is, the frequency of occurrence of each of the numbers should be approximately the same. For a stream of binary digits, we need to expand on this definition because we are dealing with only 2 numbers (0 and 1). Generally, we desire the following two properties:

  —**Balance property:** In a long sequence the fraction of binary ones should approach 1/2.

  —**Run property:** A run is defined as a sequence of all 1s or a sequence of all 0s. The appearance of the alternate digit signals the beginning of a new run. About one-half of the runs of each type should be of length 1, one-fourth of length 2, one-eighth of length 3, and so on.

- **Independence:** No one value in the sequence can be inferred from the others.

Although there are well-defined tests for determining that a sequence of numbers matches a particular distribution, such as the uniform distribution, there is no such test to "prove" independence. Rather, a number of tests can be applied to demonstrate that a sequence does not exhibit independence. The general strategy is to apply a number of such tests until the confidence that independence exists is sufficiently strong.

In applications such as spread spectrum, there is also the following requirement:

- **Correlation property:** If a period of the sequence is compared term by term with any cycle shift of itself, the number of terms that are the same differs from those that are different by at most 1.

Linear Feedback Shift Register Implementation

The PN generator for spread spectrum is usually implemented as a circuit consisting of XOR gates and a shift register, called a linear feedback shift register (LFSR). The LFSR is a string of 1-bit storage devices. Each device has an output line, which indicates the value currently stored, and an input line. At discrete time instants, known as clock times, the value in the storage device is replaced by the value indicated by its input line. The entire LFSR is clocked simultaneously, causing a 1-bit shift along the entire register.

The circuit is implemented as follows:

1. The LFSR contains n bits.
2. There are from 1 to $(n - 1)$ XOR gates.
3. The presence or absence of a gate corresponds to the presence or absence of a term in the generator polynomial (explained subsequently), $P(X)$, excluding the X^n term.

Two equivalent ways of characterizing the PN LFSR are used. We can think of the generator as implementing a sum of XOR terms:

$$B_n = A_0B_0 \oplus A_1B_1 \oplus A_2B_2 \oplus \ldots \oplus A_{n-1}B_{n-1} \qquad (7.7)$$

Figure 7.12 illustrates this equation. An actual implementation would not have the multiply circuits; instead, for $A_i = 0$, the corresponding XOR circuit is eliminated. Figure 7.13a is an example of a 4-bit LFSR that implements the equation:

$$B_3 = B_0 \oplus B_1 \qquad (7.8)$$

The shift register technique has several important advantages. The sequences generated by an LFSR can be nearly random with long periods, which aids in making the spread signal appear noiselike. In addition, LFSRs are easy to implement in

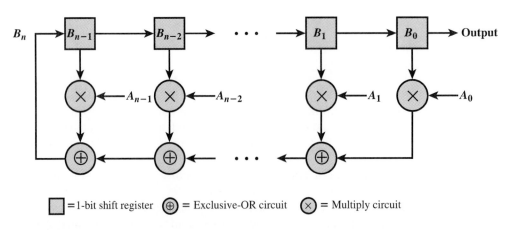

Figure 7.12   Binary Linear Feedback Shift Register Sequence Generator

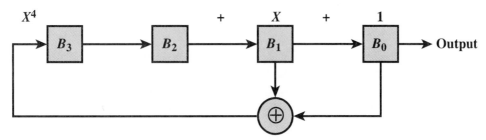

(a) Shift register implementation

State	B_3	B_2	B_1	B_0	$B_0 \oplus B_1$	Output
Initial = 0	1	0	0	0	0	0
1	0	1	0	0	0	0
2	0	0	1	0	1	0
3	1	0	0	1	1	1
4	1	1	0	0	0	0
5	0	1	1	0	1	0
6	1	0	1	1	0	1
7	0	1	0	1	1	1
8	1	0	1	0	1	0
9	1	1	0	1	1	1
10	1	1	1	0	1	0
11	1	1	1	1	0	1
12	0	1	1	1	0	1
13	0	0	1	1	0	1
14	0	0	0	1	1	1
15 = 0	1	0	0	0	0	0

(b) Example with initial state of 1000

Figure 7.13   Circuit with Shift Registers for Generating PN Sequence

hardware and can run at high speeds; this is important because the spreading rate is higher than the data rate.

It can be shown that the output of an LFSR is periodic with maximum period $N = 2^n - 1$. The all-zeros sequence occurs only if either the initial contents of the LFSR are all zero or the coefficients in Equation (7.7) are all zero (no feedback). A feedback configuration can always be found that gives a period of N; the resulting sequences are called *maximal-length sequences*, or *m-sequences*. The m-sequences are important in enabling synchronization by the receiver and in use in multiple access techniques, such as CDMA, as will be explained.

Figure 7.13b shows the generation of an m-sequence for the LFSR of Figure 7.13a. The LFSR implements Equation (7.8) with an initial state of 1000

$(B_3 = 1, B_2 = 0, B_1 = 0, B_0 = 0)$. Figure 7.13b is a table that shows the step-by-step operation as the LFSR is clocked one bit at a time. Each row of the table shows the values currently stored in the four shift register elements. In addition, the row shows the values that appear at the output of the exclusive-OR circuit. Finally, the row shows the value of the output bit, which is just B_0. Note that the output repeats after 15 bits. That is, the period of the sequence, or the length of the m-sequence, is $15 = 2^4 - 1$. This same periodic m-sequence is generated regardless of the initial state of the LFSR (except for 0000), as shown in Table 7.2. With each different initial state, the m-sequence begins at a different point in its cycle, but it is the same sequence.

For any given size of LFSR, a number of different unique m-sequences can be generated by using different values for the A_i in Equation (7.7). Table 7.3 shows the sequence length and number of unique m-sequences that can be generated for LFSRs of various sizes.

An equivalent definition of an LFSR configuration is a generator polynomial. The generator polynomial $P(X)$ that corresponds to Equation (7.7) has the form

$$P(X) = A_0 + A_1X + A_2X^2 + \ldots + A_{n-1}X^{n-1} \tag{7.9}$$

One useful attribute of the generator polynomial is that it can be used to find the sequence generated by the corresponding LFSR, by taking the reciprocal of the polynomial. For example, for the three bit LSFR with $P(X) = 1 + X + X^3$, we perform the division $1/(1 + X + X^3)$. Figure 7.14 depicts the long division. The result is

$$1 + X + X^2 + (0 \times X^3) + X^4 + (0 \times X^5) + (0 \times X^6)$$

after which the pattern repeats. This means that the shift register output is

$$1110100$$

Table 7.2   The 15 PRN Sequences Obtained From Figure 7.13a

Initial State	Output Sequence
1000	000100110101111
0100	001001101011110
0010	010011010111100
1001	100110101111000
1100	001101011110001
0110	011010111100010
1011	110101111000100
0101	101011110001001
1010	010111100010011
1101	101111000100110
1110	011110001001101
1111	111100010011010
0111	111000100110101
0011	110001001101011
0001	100010011010111

Table 7.3   Maximal-Length Shift Register Sequences

Number of shift register stages N	Sequence length $L = 2^N - 1$	Number of m-sequences	Example generating polynomial	B_n in Figure 7.12 for example polynomial
2	3	1	$X2 + X + 1$	$B_1 \oplus B_0$
3	7	2	$X^3 + X + 1$	$B_1 \oplus B_0$
4	15	2	$X^4 + X + 1$	$B_1 \oplus B_0$
5	31	6	$X^5 + X^2 + 1$	$B_2 \oplus B_0$
6	63	6	$X^6 + X + 1$	$B_1 \oplus B_0$
7	127	18	$X^7 + X + 1$	$B_1 \oplus B_0$
8	255	16	$X^8 + X^6 + X^5 + X + 1$	$B_6 \oplus B_5 \oplus B_1 \oplus B_0$
9	511	48	$X^9 + X^4 + 1$	$B_4 \oplus B_0$
10	1023	60	$X^{10} + X^3 + 1$	$B_3 \oplus B_0$
11	2047	176	$X^{11} + X^2 + 1$	$B_2 \oplus B_0$
12	4095	144	$X^{12} + X^7 + X^4 + X^3 + 1$	$B_7 \oplus B_4 \oplus B_3 \oplus B_0$
13	8191	630	$X^{13} + X^4 + X^3 + X + 1$	$B_4 \oplus B_3 \oplus B_1 \oplus B_0$
14	16,383	756	$X^{14} + X^{12} + X^{11} + X + 1$	$B_{12} \oplus B_{11} \oplus B_1 \oplus B_0$
15	32,767	1800	$X^{15} + X + 1$	$B_1 \oplus B_0$
20	1,048,575	2400	$X^{20} + X^3 + 1$	$B_3 \oplus B_0$

$$
\begin{array}{r}
1 + X + X^2 + X^4 + X^7 + X^8 + \cdots \\
\hline
1 + X + X^3 \, \big) \, 1
\end{array}
$$

$$\frac{1 + X + X^3}{XX^3}$$

$$\frac{X + X^2 + X^4}{X^2 + X^3 + X^4}$$

$$\frac{X^2 + X^3 + X^5}{X^4 + X^5}$$

$$\frac{X^4 + X^5 + X^7}{X^7}$$

$$\frac{X^7 + X^8 + X^{10}}{X^8 + X^{10}}$$

$$X^8 + X^9 + \phantom{X^{10}}X^{11}$$

Figure 7.14 $1/(1 + X + X^3)$

Because the period of this sequence is $7 = 2^3 - 1$, this is an m-sequence. Notice that we are doing division somewhat differently from the normal method. This is because the subtractions are done modulo 2, or using the XOR function, and in this system, subtraction produces the same result as addition.

Table 7.3 lists a generator polynomial that produces an m-sequence for LFSRs of various sizes.

Properties of M-Sequences

M-sequences have several properties that make them attractive for spread spectrum applications:

Property 1. An m-sequence has 2^{n-1} ones and $2^{n-1} - 1$ zeros.

Property 2. If we slide a window of length n along the output sequence for N shifts, where $N = 2^{n-1}$, each n-tuple, except the all-zeros sequence, appears exactly once.

Property 3. There is one run of ones of length n; one run of zeros of length $n - 1$; one run of ones and one run of zeros of length $n - 2$; two runs of ones and two runs of zeros of length $n - 3$; and, in general, 2^{n-3} runs of ones and 2^{n-3} runs of zeros of length 1.

For many communications applications, the 0, 1 sequence is changed to a ± 1 sequence by representing a binary 1 with 1 and a binary 0 with -1.[5] We define the periodic autocorrelation of the resulting sequence as

$$R(\tau) = \frac{1}{N} \sum_{k=1}^{N} B_k B_{k-\tau} \tag{7.10}$$

Then,

Property 4. The periodic autocorrelation of a ± 1 m-sequence is

$$R(\tau) = \begin{cases} 1 & \tau = 0, N, 2N, \ldots \\ -\dfrac{1}{N} & \text{otherwise} \end{cases}$$

Figure 7.15 shows the general autocorrelation case for m-sequences and the autocorrelation function for m-sequences generated by a 4-bit LFSR.

In essence, correlation is the concept of determining how much similarity one set of data has with another. Correlation is defined with a range between -1 and 1 with the following meanings:

Correlation Value	Interpretation
1	The second sequence matches the first sequence exactly.
0	There is no relation at all between the two sequences.
-1	The two sequences are mirror images of each other.

---

[5]In some of the literature, the opposite convention is used, representing binary 0 by 1 and binary 1 by -1. It makes no difference so long as the convention is consistently followed.

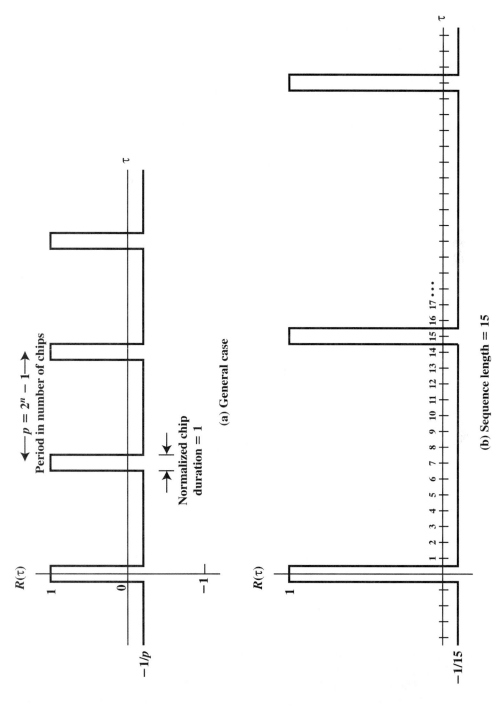

Figure 7.15 PN Autocorrelation Function

191

Other values indicate a partial degree of correlation. Autocorrelation, which is defined in Equation (7.10), is the correlation of a sequence with all phase shifts of itself. Pure random data should have a correlation value close to 0 for all auto-correlations with a phase shift other than 0. The m-sequences have this property. It can be shown that the autocorrelation function of an m-sequence, with its single sharp peak, is a powerful aid to synchronization by the receiver.

A related function, also important in the spread spectrum context, is the cross correlation function. In this case, the comparison is made between two sequences from different sources rather than a shifted copy of a sequence with itself. The cross correlation between two sources, A and B, is defined as

$$R_{A,B}(\tau) = \frac{1}{N} \sum_{k=1}^{N} A_k B_{k-\tau} \qquad (7.11)$$

In general, the cross correlation value produced by matching a sequence with a random sequence is low, which has two advantages:

1. The cross correlation between an m-sequence and noise is low, and this property is useful to the receiver in filtering out noise.
2. The cross correlation between two different m-sequences is low, and this property is useful for CDMA applications because it enables a receiver to discriminate among spread spectrum signals generated by different m-sequences.

Gold Sequences

M-sequences are easy to generate and are very useful for FHSS and DSSS systems not used for CDMA. However, for CDMA DSSS, m-sequences are not optimal. For CDMA, we need to construct a family of spreading sequences, one for each user, in which the codes have well-defined cross-correlation properties. In general, m-sequences do not satisfy this criterion. One popular set of sequences that does are the Gold sequences. Gold sequences are attractive because only simple circuitry is needed to generate a large number of unique codes.

A Gold sequence is constructed by the XOR of two m-sequences with the same clocking. Figure 7.16a shows an example; in this example the two shift registers generate the two m-sequences and these are then bitwise XORed. In general, the length of the resulting sequence is not maximal. Further, the desired Gold sequences can only be generated by **preferred pairs** of m-sequences. These preferred pairs can be selected from tables of pairs or generated by an algorithm. [DIXO94] lists sets of preferred pairs and describes the algorithm. Here, we summarize the mathematical conditions that lead to a Gold code.

Suppose we take an m-sequence represented by a binary vector **a** of length N, and generate a new sequence **a′** by sampling every qth symbol of **a**. We use multiple copies of **a** until we have enough samples to produce a sequence of **a′** of length N. The sequence **a′** is said to be a decimation of the sequence **a** and is written as **a′** = **a**[q]. The sequence **a′** does not necessarily have a period N and is therefore not necessarily an m-sequence. It can be shown that **a′** will be an m-sequence, with period N, if and only if gcd(n, q) = 1, where gcd stands for greatest common divi-

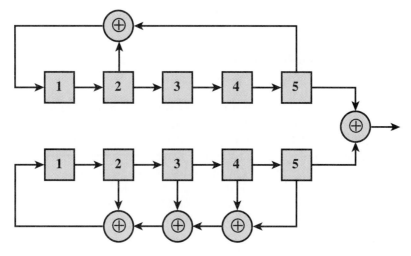

(a) Shift register implementation

Sequence 1:   111110001101110101000100101100
Sequence 2:   111110010011000010110101010001110
0 shift XOR: 000000011110110111111011110100010
1 shift XOR: 000010101011110000101000110001

•

•

30 shift XOR: 100001000100010100011000110001101011

(b) Resulting Gold sequences

Figure 7.16   Example of Generating a Set of Gold Sequences [DINA98]

sor; in other words, n and q have no common factor except 1. For Gold sequences, we need to start with a preferred pair **a** and $\mathbf{a}' = \mathbf{a}[q]$ that are both m-sequences and that meet the following conditions:

1. $n/4 \neq 0$; that is, all n except 0, 4, 8, 12, . . .
2. q is odd and $q = (2^k + 1)$ or $q = (2^{2k} - 2^k + 1)$ for some k
3. $\gcd(n,k) = \begin{cases} 1 & \text{for } n \text{ odd} \\ 2 & \text{for } n = 2 \bmod 4 \end{cases}$

For shift registers of length n, the cross correlation of the Gold sequences produced by a preferred pair is bounded by $|R| \leq 2^{(n+1)/2} + 1$ for n odd and $|R| \leq 2^{(n+2)/2} + 1$ for n even.

Starting with a preferred pair, a set of Gold codes consists of the sequences $\{\mathbf{a}, \mathbf{a}', \mathbf{a} \oplus \mathbf{a}', \mathbf{a} \oplus D\mathbf{a}', \mathbf{a} \oplus D^2\mathbf{a}', \ldots, \mathbf{a} \oplus D^{N-1}\mathbf{a}'\}$, where D is the delay element; that is, D represents a one-bit shift of $\mathbf{a}'$ relative to $\mathbf{a}$. To generate the Gold codes from shift registers, we start with the all-ones vector set in both registers as an initial condition. The resulting sequences are XORed to produce one Gold sequence. This yields the first three sequences in the set. To generate the remaining sequences, the second of the first two sequences is shifted by one bit and the XOR operation performed again. This process continues through all possible shifts, with each additional one-bit shift followed by an XOR producing a new sequence in the set. For a preferred pair of 5-bit shift registers, it can be shown that for any shift in the initial condition from 0 to 30, a new Gold sequence is generated (a 31-bit shift is the same as a 0 shift). The Gold sequences are the two initial m-sequences plus the generated sequences for a total of 33 sequences. This is illustrated in Figure 7.16b.

In general, the period of any code in a Gold set generated with 2 n-bit shift registers is $N = 2^n - 1$, which is the same as the period of the m-sequences. There are a total of $N + 2$ codes in any family of Gold codes. As an example of the effectiveness of Gold codes, for $n = 13$ ($N = 2^{13} - 1 = 8191$), there are 630 m-sequences (Table 7.3) and there exist pairs of these sequences whose correlation values are at $R = 703$, while Gold sequence guarantee the selection of pairs such that $R \leq (2^{(n+1)/2} + 1) = 129$.

Kasami Sequences

Another important set of PN sequences are the Kasami sequences, which are likely to find use in third-generation wireless schemes. Kasami sequences are defined by a procedure similar to that for Gold codes. There are two sorts of sequences, small sets and large sets.

For n even, we can generate a **small set** of Kasami sequences containing $M = 2^{n/2}$ distinct sequences each with period $N = 2^n - 1$. A set is defined by starting with an m-sequence **a** with period N and decimating the sequence by $q = 2^{n/2} + 1$. It can be shown that the resulting sequence **a'** has a period $2^{n/2} - 1$. Now we replicate a single period of **a'** q times to produce a sequence of length $(2^{n/2} - 1)(2^{n/2} + 1) = N$. For example, for $n = 10$, the period of **a** is $2^{10} - 1 = 1023$ and the period of **a'** is $2^5 - 1 = 31$. If we observe 1023 bits of sequence **a'**, we see 33 repetitions of the 31-bit sequence. Finally, we generate the Kasami set by taking N bits of **a** and N bits of **a'** and forming a new set of sequences by XORing the bits from **a** and the bits from **a'** as well as all $2^{n/2} - 1$ cyclic shifts of the bits from **a'**.

It can be shown that the maximum cross correlation value for the set is $2^{n/2} - 1$. This is smaller than for Gold sequences and in fact is optimal.

The **large set** of Kasami sequences also consists of certain sequences, each with period $N = 2^n - 1$ for n even, and contains both Gold sequences and the small set of Kasami sequences as subsets. A set is defined by starting with an m-sequence **a** with period N and decimating the sequence by $q = 2^{n/2} + 1$ to form **a'** and decimating the sequence by $q = 2^{(n+2)/2} + 1$ to form **a''**. A set is then formed by taking the XOR of **a**, **a'**, and **a''** with different shifts of **a'** and **a''**. It can be shown that the maximum cross correlation value for a large set is $2^{(n+2)/2}$.

Orthogonal Codes

Unlike PN sequences, an orthogonal codes is a set of sequences in which all pairwise cross correlations are zero. An orthogonal set of sequences is characterized by the following equality:

$$\sum_{k=0}^{M-1} \phi_i(k\tau)\phi_j(k\tau) = 0, \qquad i \neq j$$

where M is the length of each of the sequences in the set, ϕ_i and ϕ_j are the ith and jth members of the set, and t is the bit duration.

Both fixed- and variable-length orthogonal codes have been used in CDMA systems. For the CDMA application, each mobile user uses one of the sequences in the set as a spreading code, providing zero cross correlation among all users.

Walsh Codes

Walsh codes are the most common orthogonal codes used in CDMA applications. A set of Walsh codes of length n consists of the n rows of an $n \times n$ Walsh matrix. The matrix is defined recursively as follows:

$$W_1 = (0) \qquad W_{2n} = \begin{pmatrix} W_n & W_n \\ W_n & \overline{W_n} \end{pmatrix}$$

where n is the dimension of the matrix and the overscore denotes the logical NOT of the bits in the matrix. The Walsh matrix has the property that every row is orthogonal to every other row and to the logical NOT of every other row.

Figure 7.17 shows the Walsh matrices of dimensions 2, 4, and 8. Recall that to compute the cross correlation, we replace 1 with +1 and 0 with −1.

Orthogonal spreading codes such as the Walsh sequences can only be used if all of the users in the same CDMA channel are synchronized to the accuracy of a small fraction of one chip. Because the cross correlation between different shifts of

$$W_2 = \begin{pmatrix} 0 & 0 \\ 0 & 1 \end{pmatrix}$$

$$W_4 = \begin{pmatrix} 0 & 0 & 0 & 0 \\ 0 & 1 & 0 & 1 \\ 0 & 0 & 1 & 1 \\ 0 & 1 & 1 & 0 \end{pmatrix}$$

$$W_8 = \begin{pmatrix} 0 & 0 & 0 & 0 & 0 & 0 & 0 & 0 \\ 0 & 1 & 0 & 1 & 0 & 1 & 0 & 1 \\ 0 & 0 & 1 & 1 & 0 & 0 & 1 & 1 \\ 0 & 1 & 1 & 0 & 0 & 1 & 1 & 0 \\ 0 & 0 & 0 & 0 & 1 & 1 & 1 & 1 \\ 0 & 1 & 0 & 1 & 1 & 0 & 1 & 0 \\ 0 & 0 & 1 & 1 & 1 & 1 & 0 & 0 \\ 0 & 1 & 1 & 0 & 1 & 0 & 0 & 1 \end{pmatrix}$$

(a) 2 × 2   (b) 4 × 4   (c) 8 × 8

Figure 7.17 Walsh Matrices

Walsh sequences is not zero, if tight synchronization is not provided, PN sequences are needed.

Variable-Length Orthogonal Codes

Third-generation mobile CDMA systems are designed to support users at a number of different data rates. Thus, effective support can be provided by using spreading codes at different rates while maintaining orthogonality. Suppose that the minimum data rate to be supported is R_{min} and that all other data rates are related by powers of 2. If a spreading sequence of length N is used for the R_{min} data rate, such that each bit of data is spread by $N = 2^n$ bits of the spreading sequence (transmit the sequence for data bit 0; transmit the complement of the sequence for data bit 1), then the transmitted data rate is NR_{min}. For a data rate of $2 R_{min}$, a spreading sequence of length $N/2 = 2^{n-1}$ will produce the same output rate of $N \times R_{min}$. In general, a code length of 2^{n-k} is needed for a bit rate of $2^k R_{min}$.

A set of variable-length orthogonal sequences is readily generated from Walsh matrices of different dimensions. For example, see [DINA98] for a description.

Multiple Spreading

When sufficient bandwidth is available, a multiple spreading technique can prove highly effective. A typical approach is to spread the data rate by an orthogonal code to provide mutual orthogonality among all users in the same cell and to further spread the result by a PN sequence to provide mutual randomness (low cross correlation) between users in different cells. In such a two-stage spreading, the orthogonal codes are referred to as **channelization codes**, and the PN codes are referred to as **scrambling codes**. We show an example of this technique in Chapter 10, with the IS-95 standard.

7.6 RECOMMENDED READING

Both [PETE95] and [DIXO94] provide comprehensive treatment of spread spectrum. [TANT98] contains reprints of many important papers in the field, including [PICK82], which provides an excellent introduction to spread spectrum.

A good survey of PN sequences for spread spectrum is [MACW76], and a good survey of CDMA is [PRAS98].

DIXO94   Dixon, R. *Spread Spectrum Systems with Commercial Applications*. New York: Wiley, 1994.

MACW76   Macwilliams, F., and Sloane, N. "Pseudo-Random Sequences and Arrays." *Proceedings of the IEEE*, December 1976. Reprinted in [TANT98].

PETE95   Peterson, R.; Ziemer, R.; and Borth, D. *Introduction to Spread Spectrum Communications*. Englewood Cliffs, NJ: Prentice Hall, 1995.

PICK82   Pickholtz, R.; Schilling, D.; and Milstein, L. "Theory of Spread Spectrum Communications-A Tutorial." *IEEE Transactions on Communications*, May 1982. Reprinted in [TANT98].

PRAS98   Prasad, R., and Ojanpera, T. "An Overview of CDMA Evolution: Toward Wideband CDMA." *IEEE Communications Surveys*, Fourth Quarter 1998. Available at www.comsoc.org.

TANT98   Tantaratana, S, and Ahmed, K., eds. *Wireless Applications of Spread Spectrum Systems: Selected Readings*. Piscataway, NJ: IEEE Press, 1998.

7.7 KEY TERMS, REVIEW QUESTIONS, AND PROBLEMS

Key Terms

autocorrelation	fast FHSS	orthogonal
chip	frequency-hopping spread	pseudonoise (PN)
code division multiple	spectrum(FHSS)	slow FHSS
access (CDMA)	linear feedback shift	spread spectrum
correlation	register (LFSR)	spreading code
cross correlation	m-sequence	spreading sequence
direct sequence spread		
spectrum (DSSS)		

Review Questions

1 What is the relationship between the bandwidth of a signal before and after it has been encoded using spread spectrum?

2 List three benefits of spread spectrum.

3 What is frequency-hopping spread spectrum?

4 Explain the difference between slow FHSS and fast FHSS.

5 What is direct sequence spread spectrum?

6 What is the relationship between the bit rate of a signal before and after it has been encoded using DSSS?

7 What is CDMA?

8 Explain the difference between autocorrelation and cross correlation.

Problems

1 Assume we wish to transmit a 56-kbps data stream using spread spectrum.

   a. Find the channel bandwidth required when SNR = 0.1, 0.01, and 0.001.

   b. In an ordinary (not spread spectrum) system, a reasonable goal for bandwidth efficiency might be 1 bps/Hz. That is, to transmit a data stream of 56 kbps, a bandwidth of 56-kHz is used. In this case, what is the maximum SNR that can be endured for transmission without appreciable errors? Compare to the spread spectrum case.

   Hint: Review the discussion of channel capacity in Section 2.3.

2 An FHSS system employs a total bandwidth of $W_s = 400$ MHz and an individual channel bandwidth of 100 Hz. What is the minimum number of PN bits required for each frequency hop?

3 An FHSS system using MFSK with $M = 4$ employs 1000 different frequencies. What is the processing gain?

4 The following table illustrates the operation of an FHSS system for one complete period of the PN sequence.

Time	0	1	2	3	4	5	6	7	8	9	10	11
Input data	0	1	1	1	1	1	1	0	0	0	1	0
Frequency	f_1		f_3		f_{27}		f_{26}		f_8		f_{10}	
PN sequence	001				110				011			

Time	12	13	14	15	16	17	18	19
Input data	0	1	1	1	1	0	1	0
Frequency	f_1		f_3		f_2		f_2	
PN sequence	001				001			

a. What is the period of the PN sequence?
b. The system makes use of a form of FSK. What form of FSK is it?
c. What is the number of bits per symbol?
d. What is the number of FSK frequencies?
e. What is the length of a PN sequence per hop?
f. Is this a slow or fast FH system?
g. What is the total number of possible hops?
h. Show the variation of the dehopped frequency with time.

5 The following table illustrates the operation of a FHSS system using the same PN sequence as Problem 4.

Time	0	1	2	3	4	5	6	7	8	9	10	11
Input data	0	1	1	1	1	1	1	0	0	0	1	0
Frequency	f_1	f_{21}	f_{11}	f_3	f_3	f_3	f_{22}	f_{10}	f_0	f_0	f_1	f_{22}
PN sequence	001	110	011	001	001	001	110	011	001	001	001	110

Time	12	13	14	15	16	17	18	19
Input data	0	1	1	1	1	0	1	0
Frequency	f_9	f_1	f_3	f_3	f_{22}	f_{11}	f_3	f_3
PN sequence	011	001	001	001	110	011	001	001

a. What is the period of the PN sequence?
b. The system makes use of a form of FSK. What form of FSK is it?
c. What is the number of bits per symbol?
d. What is the number of FSK frequencies?
e. What is the length of a PN sequence per hop?

    f. Is this a slow or fast FH system?

    g. What is the total number of possible hops?

    h. Show the variation of the dehopped frequency with time.

6 Consider an MFSK scheme with $f_c = 250$ kHz, $f_d = 25$ kHz, and $M = 8$ ($L = 3$ bits)

    a. Make a frequency assignment for each of the eight possible 3-bit data combinations.

    b. We wish to apply FHSS to this MFSK scheme with $k = 2$; that is, the system will hop among four different carrier frequencies. Expand the results of part (a) to show the $4 \times 8 = 32$ frequency assignments.

7 Figure 7.18, based on one in [BELL00], depicts a simplified scheme for CDMA encoding and decoding. There are seven logical channels, all using DSSS with a spreading code of 7 bits. Assume that all sources are synchronized. If all seven sources transmit a data bit, in the form of a 7-bit sequence, the signals from all sources combine at the receiver so that two positive or two negative values reinforce and a positive and negative value cancel. To decode a given channel, the receiver multiplies the incoming composite signal by the spreading code for that channel, sums the result, and assigns binary 1 for a positive value and binary 0 for a negative value.

    a. What are the spreading codes for the seven channels?

    b. Determine the receiver output measurement for channel 1 and the bit value assigned.

    c. Repeat part b for channel 2.

8 For the spreading codes of the preceding problem, determine the cross correlation between channel 0 and each of the other 6 channels.

9 By far, the most widely used technique for pseudorandom number generation is the linear congruential method. The algorithm is parameterized with four numbers, as follows:

$$
\begin{array}{lll}
m & \text{the modulus} & m > 0 \\
a & \text{the multiplier} & 0 \le a < m \\
c & \text{the increment} & 0 \le c < m \\
X_0 & \text{the starting value, or seed} & 0 \le X_0 < m
\end{array}
$$

The sequence of pseudorandom numbers $\{X_n\}$ is obtained via the following iterative equation:

$$X_{n+1} = (aX_n + c)\bmod m$$

If m, a, c, and X_0 are integers, then this technique will produce a sequence of integers with each integer in the range $0 \le X_n < m$. An essential characteristic of a pseudorandom number generator is that the generated sequence should appear random. Although the sequence is not random, because it is generated deterministically, there is a variety of statistical tests that can be used to assess the degree to which a sequence exhibits randomness. Another desirable characteristic is that the function should be a full-period generating function. That is, the function should generate all the numbers between 0 and m before repeating.

With the linear congruential algorithm, a choice of parameters that provides a full period does not necessarily provide a good randomization. For example, consider the two generators:

$$X_{n+1} = (6X_n)\bmod 13$$
$$X_{n+1} = (7X_n)\bmod 13$$

Write out the two sequences to show that both are full period. Which one appears more random to you?

10 We would like m to be very large so that there is the potential for producing a long series of distinct random numbers. A common criterion is that m be nearly equal to the maximum representable nonnegative integer for a given computer. Thus, a value of m near to or equal to 2^{31} is typically chosen. Many experts recommend a value of $2^{31} - 1$. You may wonder why one should not simply use 2^{31}, because this latter number can be represented with no additional bits, and the mod operation should be easier to perform. In general, the modulus $2^k - 1$ is preferable to 2^k. Why is this so?

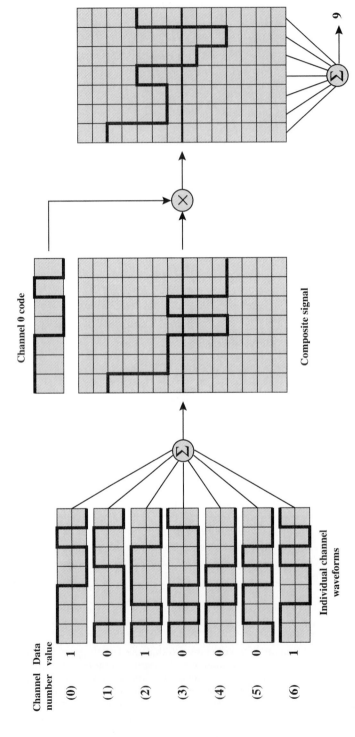

Figure 7.18 Example Seven-Channel CDMA Encoding and Decoding

11 In any use of pseudorandom numbers, whether for encryption, simulation, or statistical design, it is dangerous to trust blindly the random number generator that happens to be available in your computer's system library. [PARK88] found that many contemporary textbooks and programming packages make use of flawed algorithms for pseudorandom number generation. This exercise will enable you to test your system.

The test is based on a theorem attributed to Ernesto Cesaro (see [KNUT98] for a proof), which states that the probability is equal to $\frac{6}{\pi^2}$ that the greatest common divisor of two randomly chosen integers is 1. Use this theorem in a program to determine statistically the value of π. The main program should call three subprograms: the random number generator from the system library to generate the random integers; a subprogram to calculate the greatest common divisor of two integers using Euclid's algorithm; and a subprogram that calculates square roots. If these latter two programs are not available, you will have to write them as well. The main program should loop through a large number of random numbers to give an estimate of the aforementioned probability. From this, it is a simple matter to solve for your estimate of π.

If the result is close to 3.14, congratulations! If not, then the result is probably low, usually a value of around 2.7. Why would such an inferior result be obtained?

12 This problem demonstrates that different LFSRs can be used to generate an m-sequence.
   a. Assume an initial state of 10000 in the LFSR of Figure 7.19a. In a manner similar to Figure 7.13b, shows the generation of an m-sequence.
   b. Now assume the configuration of Figure 7.19b, with the same initial state, and repeat part a. Show that this configuration also produces an m-sequence, but that it is a different sequence from that produced by the first LFSR.

13 Demonstrate that the codes in an 8×8 Walsh matrix are orthogonal to each other by showing that multiplying any code by any other code produces a result of zero.

14 Consider a CDMA system in which users A and B have the Walsh codes $(-1\ 1\ -1\ 1\ -1\ 1\ -1\ 1)$ and $(-1\ -1\ 1\ 1\ -1\ -1\ 1\ 1)$; respectively.
   a. Show the output at the receiver if A transmits a data bit 1 and B does not transmit.
   b. Show the output at the receiver if A transmits a data bit 0 and B does not transmit.
   c. Show the output at the receiver if A transmits a data bit 1 and B transmits a data bit 1. Assume the received power from both A and B is the same.

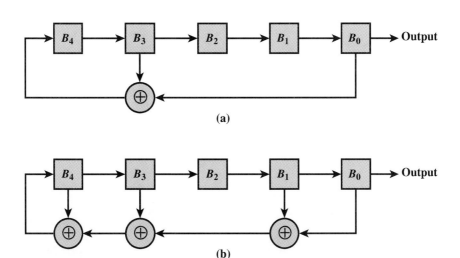

(a)

(b)

Figure 7.19 Two Different Configurations of LFSRs of Length 5

d. Show the output at the receiver if A transmits a data bit 0 and B transmits a data bit 1. Assume the received power from both A and B is the same.

e. Show the output at the receiver if A transmits a data bit 1 and B transmits a data bit 0. Assume the received power from both A and B is the same.

f. Show the output at the receiver if A transmits a data bit 0 and B transmits a data bit 0. Assume the received power from both A and B is the same.

g. Show the output at the receiver if A transmits a data bit 1 and B transmits a data bit 1. Assume the received power from B is twice the received power from A. This can be represented by showing the received signal component from A as consisting of elements of magnitude 1 ($+1$, -1) and the received signal component from B as consisting of elements of magnitude 2 ($+2$, -2).

h. Show the output at the receiver if A transmits a data bit 0 and B transmits a data bit 1. Assume the received power from B is twice the received power from A.

CHAPTER 8

CODING AND ERROR CONTROL

In earlier chapters, we talked about transmission impairments and the effect of data rate and signal-to-noise ratio on bit error rate. Regardless of the design of the transmission system, there will be errors, resulting in the change of one or more bits in a transmitted frame.

Three approaches are in common use for coping with data transmission errors:

- Error detection codes
- Error correction codes, also called forward error correction (FEC) codes
- Automatic repeat request (ARQ) protocols

An error detection code simply detects the presence of an error. Typically, such codes are used in conjunction with a protocol at the data link or transport level (see Figure 4.4) that uses an ARQ scheme. With an ARQ scheme, a receiver discards a block of data in which an error is detected and the transmitter retransmits that block of data. FEC codes are designed not just to detect but correct errors, avoiding the need for retransmission. FEC schemes are frequently used in wireless transmission, where retransmission schemes are highly inefficient and error rates may be high.

This chapter looks at all three approaches in turn.

8.1 ERROR DETECTION

In what follows, we assume that data are transmitted as one or more contiguous sequences of bits, called frames. Let us define these probabilities with respect to errors in transmitted frames:

P_b: Probability of a single bit error; also known as the bit error rate (BER)
P_1: Probability that a frame arrives with no bit errors
P_2: Probability that, with an error detection algorithm in use, a frame arrives with one or more undetected errors
P_3: Probability that, with an error detection algorithm in use, a frame arrives with one or more detected bit errors but no undetected bit errors

First consider the case when no means are taken to detect errors. Then the probability of detected errors (P_3) is zero. To express the remaining probabilities, assume the probability that any bit is in error (P_b) is constant and independent for each bit. Then we have

$$P_1 = (1 - P_b)^F$$
$$P_2 = 1 - P_1$$

where F is the number of bits per frame. In words, the probability that a frame arrives with no bit errors decreases when the probability of a single bit error in-

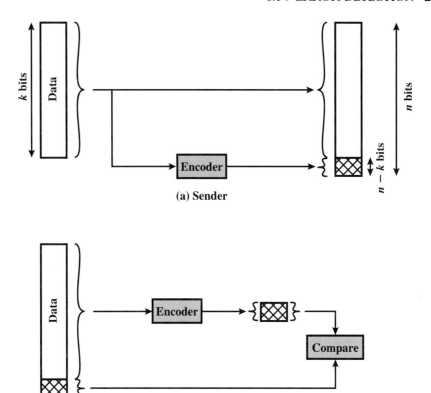

Figure 8.1   Error Detection Process

creases, as you would expect. Also, the probability that a frame arrives with no bit errors decreases with increasing frame length; the longer the frame, the more bits it has and the higher the probability that one of these is in error.

Let us take a simple example to illustrate these relationships. A defined objective for ISDN (Integrated Services Digital Network) connections is that the BER on a 64-kbps channel should be less than 10^{-6} on at least 90% of observed 1-minute intervals. Suppose now that we have the rather modest user requirement that on average one frame with an undetected bit error should occur per day on a continuously used 64-kbps channel, and let us assume a frame length of 1000 bits. The number of frames that can be transmitted in a day comes out to 5.529×10^{6}, which yields a desired maximum frame error rate of $P_2 = 1/(5.529 \times 10^6) = 0.18 \times 10^{-6}$. But if we assume a value of P_b of 10^{-6}, then $P_1 = (0.999999)^{1000} = 0.999$ and therefore $P_2 = 10^{-3}$, which is about three orders of magnitude too large to meet our requirement.

This is the kind of result that motivates the use of error detection techniques. All of these techniques operate on the following principle (Figure 8.1). For a given frame of bits, additional bits that constitute an error-detecting code are added by the transmitter. This code is calculated as a function of the other transmitted bits.

Typically, for a data block of k bits, the error detection algorithm yields an error detection code of $n - k$ bits, where $(n - k) < k$. The error detection code, also referred to as the **check bits**, is appended to the data block to produce a frame of n bits, which is then transmitted. The receiver separates the incoming frame into the k bits of data and $(n - k)$ bits of the error detection code. The receiver performs the same error detection calculation on the data bits and compares this value with the value of the incoming error detection code. A detected error occurs if and only if there is a mismatch. Thus P_3 is the probability that a frame contains errors and that the error detection scheme will detect that fact. P_2 is known as the residual error rate and is the probability that an error will be undetected despite the use of an error detection scheme.

Parity Check

The simplest error detection scheme is to append a parity bit to the end of a block of data. A typical example is character transmission, in which a parity bit is attached to each 7-bit character. The value of this bit is selected so that the character has an even number of 1s (even parity) or an odd number of 1s (odd parity). So, for example, if the transmitter is transmitting 1110001 and using odd parity, it will append a 1 and transmit 11100011. The receiver examines the received character and, if the total number of 1s is odd, assumes that no error has occurred. If one bit (or any odd number of bits) is erroneously inverted during transmission (for example, 11000011), then the receiver will detect an error. Note, however, that if two (or any even number) of bits are inverted due to error, an undetected error occurs. Typically, even parity is used for synchronous transmission and odd parity for asynchronous transmission.

The use of the parity bit is not foolproof, as noise impulses are often long enough to destroy more than one bit, particularly at high data rates.

Cyclic Redundancy Check

One of the most common, and one of the most powerful, error-detecting codes is the cyclic redundancy check (CRC), which can be described as follows. Given a k-bit block of bits, or message, the transmitter generates an $(n - k)$-bit sequence, known as a frame check sequence (FCS), such that the resulting frame, consisting of n bits, is exactly divisible by some predetermined number. The receiver then divides the incoming frame by that number and, if there is no remainder, assumes there was no error.[1]

To clarify this, we present the procedure in three ways: modulo 2 arithmetic, polynomials, and digital logic.

---

[1]This procedure is slightly different from that of Figure 8.1. As shall be seen, the CRC process could be implemented as follows. The receiver could perform a division operation on the incoming k data bits and compare the result to the incoming $(n - k)$ check bits.

Modulo 2 Arithmetic

Modulo 2 arithmetic uses binary addition with no carries, which is just the exclusive-OR (XOR) operation. Binary subtraction with no carries is also interpreted as the XOR operation: For example,

$$
\begin{array}{ccc}
\begin{array}{r} 1111 \\ + \ 1010 \\ \hline 0101 \end{array} &
\begin{array}{r} 1111 \\ - \ 0101 \\ \hline 1010 \end{array} &
\begin{array}{r} 11001 \\ \times \ 11 \\ \hline 11001 \\ 11001 \ \ \\ \hline 101011 \end{array}
\end{array}
$$

Now define

$T = n$-bit frame to be transmitted
$D = k$-bit block of data, or message, the first k bits of T
$F = (n - k)$-bit FCS, the last $(n - k)$ bits of T
$P = $ pattern of $n - k + 1$ bits; this is the predetermined divisor

We would like T/P to have no remainder. It should be clear that

$$ T = 2^{n-k}D + F $$

That is, by multiplying D by 2^{n-k}, we have in effect shifted it to the left by $n - k$ bits and padded out the result with zeroes. Adding F yields the concatenation of D and F, which is T. We want T to be exactly divisible by P. Suppose that we divide $2^{n-k}D$ by P:

$$ \frac{2^{n-k}D}{P} = Q + \frac{R}{P} \tag{8.1} $$

There is a quotient and a remainder. Because division is modulo 2, the remainder is always at least one bit shorter than the divisor. We will use this remainder as our FCS. Then

$$ T = 2^{n-k}D + R \tag{8.2} $$

Does this R satisfy our condition that T/P have no remainder? To see that it does, consider

$$ \frac{T}{P} = \frac{2^{n-k}D + R}{P} = \frac{2^{n-k}D}{P} + \frac{R}{P} $$

Substituting Equation (8.1), we have

$$\frac{T}{P} = Q + \frac{R}{P} + \frac{R}{P}$$

However, any binary number added to itself modulo 2 yields zero. Thus

$$\frac{T}{P} = Q + \frac{R + R}{P} = Q$$

There is no remainder, and therefore T is exactly divisible by P. Thus, the FCS is easily generated: Simply divide $2^{n-k}D$ by P and use the $(n - k)$-bit remainder as the FCS. On reception, the receiver will divide T by P and will get no remainder if there have been no errors.

Let us now consider a simple example.

Example.

1. Given

$$\text{Message } D = 1010001101 \text{ (10 bits)}$$
$$\text{Pattern } P = 110101 \text{ (6 bits)}$$
$$\text{FCS } R = \text{to be calculated (5 bits)}$$

Thus, $n = 15$, $k = 10$, and $(n - k) = 5$.

2. The message is multiplied by 2^5, yielding 101000110100000.

3. This product is divided by P:

```
                              1 1 0 1 0 1 0 1 1 0 ← Q
P→1 1 0 1 0 1 / 1 0 1 0 0 0 1 1 0 1 0 0 0 0 0 ← 2^{n-k}D
              1 1 0 1 0 1
              1 1 1 0 1 1
              1 1 0 1 0 1
                1 1 1 0 1 0
                1 1 0 1 0 1
                  1 1 1 1 1 0
                  1 1 0 1 0 1
                    1 0 1 1 0 0
                    1 1 0 1 0 1
                      1 1 0 0 1 0
                      1 1 0 1 0 1
                        0 1 1 1 0 ← R
```

4. The remainder is added to 2^5D to give $T = 101000110101110$, which is transmitted.

5. If there are no errors, the receiver receives T intact. The received frame is divided by P:

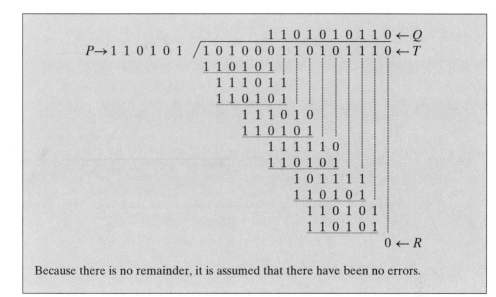

Because there is no remainder, it is assumed that there have been no errors.

The pattern P is chosen to be one bit longer than the desired FCS, and the exact bit pattern chosen depends on the type of errors expected. At minimum, both the high- and low-order bits of P must be 1.

There is a concise method for specifying the occurrence of one or more errors. An error results in the reversal of a bit. This is equivalent to taking the XOR of the bit and 1 (modulo 2 addition of 1 to the bit): $0 + 1 = 1; 1 + 1 = 0$. Thus, the errors in an n-bit frame can be represented by an n-bit field with 1s in each error position. The resulting frame T_r can be expressed as

$$T_r = T \oplus E.$$

where

$T =$ transmitted frame
$E =$ error pattern with 1s in positions where errors occur
$T_r =$ received frame

If there is an error ($E \neq 0$), the receiver will fail to detect the error if and only if T_r is divisible by P, which is equivalent to E divisible by P. Intuitively, this seems an unlikely occurrence.

Polynomials

A second way of viewing the CRC process is to express all values as polynomials in a dummy variable X, with binary coefficients. The coefficients correspond to the bits in the binary number. Arithmetic operations are again modulo 2. The CRC process can now be described as

$$\frac{X^{n-k}D(X)}{P(X)} = Q(X) + \frac{R(X)}{P(X)}$$

$$T(X) = X^{n-k}D(X) + R(X)$$

Compare these equations with Equations (8.1) and (8.2).

Example. Using the preceding example, for $D = 1010001101$, we have $D(X) = X^9 + X^7 + X^3 + X^2 + 1$, and for $P = 110101$, we have $P(X) = X^5 + X^4 + X^2 + 1$. We should end up with $R = 01110$, which corresponds to $R(X) = X^3 + X^2 + X$. Figure 8.2 shows the polynomial division that corresponds to the binary division in the preceding example.

An error $E(X)$ will only be undetectable if it is divisible by $P(X)$. It can be shown [PETE 61, RAMA88] that all of the following errors are not divisible by a suitably chosen $P(X)$ and hence are detectable:

- All single-bit errors, if $P(X)$ has more than one nonzero term
- All double-bit errors, as long as $P(X)$ has a factor with three terms
- Any odd number of errors, as long as $P(X)$ contains a factor $(X + 1)$
- Any burst error[2] for which the length of the burst is less than or equal to $n - k$; that is, less than or equal to the length of the FCS

Figure 8.2 Example of Polynomial Divison

---

[2]A burst error of length B is a contiguous sequence of B bits in which the first and last bits and any number of intermediate bits are received in error.

- A fraction of error bursts of length $n - k + 1$; the fraction equals $1 - 2^{-(n-k-1)}$
- A fraction of error bursts of length greater than $n - k + 1$; the fraction equals $1 - 2^{-(n-k)}$

In addition, it can be shown that if all error patterns are considered equally likely, then for a burst error of length $r + 1$, the probability of an undetected error [i.e., $E(X)$ is divisible by $P(X)$] is $1/2^{r-1}$, and for a longer burst, the probability is $1/2^r$, where r is the length of the FCS.

Four versions of $P(X)$ have been widely used:

$$
\begin{aligned}
\text{CRC-12} \quad &= X^{12} + X^{11} + X^3 + X^2 + X + 1 \\
\text{CRC-16} \quad &= X^{16} + X^{15} + X^2 + 1 \\
\text{CRC-CCITT} &= X^{16} + X^{12} + X^5 + 1 \\
\text{CRC-32} \quad &= X^{32} + X^{26} + X^{23} + X^{22} + X^{16} + X^{12} + X^{11} \\
&\quad + X^{10} + X^8 + X^7 + X^5 + X^4 + X^2 + X + 1
\end{aligned}
$$

The CRC-12 system is used for transmission of streams of 6-bit characters and generates a 12-bit FCS. Both CRC-16 and CRC-CCITT are popular for 8-bit characters, in the United States and Europe, respectively, and both result in a 16-bit FCS. This would seem adequate for most applications, although CRC-32 is specified as an option in some point-to-point synchronous transmission standards.

Digital Logic

The CRC process can be represented by, and indeed implemented as, a dividing circuit consisting of XOR gates and a shift register. The shift register is a string of 1-bit storage devices. Each device has an output line, which indicates the value currently stored, and an input line. At discrete time instants, known as clock times, the value in the storage device is replaced by the value indicated by its input line. The entire register is clocked simultaneously, causing a 1-bit shift along the entire register.

The circuit is implemented as follows:

1. The register contains $n - k$ bits, equal to the length of the FCS.

2. There are up to $n - k$ XOR gates.

3. The presence or absence of a gate corresponds to the presence or absence of a term in the divisor polynomial, $P(X)$, excluding the terms 1 and X^{n-k}.

Example. The architecture of this circuit is best explained by first considering an example, which is illustrated in Figure 8.3. In this example, we use:

Data $D = 1010001101$;	$D(X) = X^9 + X^7 + X^3 + X^2 + 1$
Divisor $P = 110101$;	$P(X) = X^5 + X^4 + X^2 + 1$

which were used earlier in the discussion.

Figure 8.3a shows the shift register implementation. The process begins with the shift register cleared (all zeros). The message, or dividend, is then entered, one bit at a time, starting with the most significant bit. Figure 8.3b is a table that shows the step-by-step operation as the input is applied one bit at a time. Each row of the table shows the values currently stored in the five shift-register elements. In addition, the row shows the values that appear at the outputs of the three XOR circuits. Finally, the row shows the value of the next input bit, which is available for the operation of the next step.

Note that the XOR operation affects C_4, C_2, and C_0 on the next shift. This is identical to the binary long division process illustrated earlier. The process continues through all the bits of the message. To produce the proper output, two switches are used. The input data bits are fed in with both switches in the A position. As a result, for the first 10 steps, the input bits are fed into the shift register and also used as output bits. After the last data bit is processed, the shift register contains the remainder (FCS) (shown shaded). As soon as the last data bit is provided to the shift register, both switches are set to the B position. This has two effects: (1) All of the XOR gates become simple pass-throughs; no bits are changed, and (2) as the shifting process continues, the 5 CRC bits are output.

At the receiver, the same logic is used. As each bit of M arrives, it is inserted into the shift register. If there have been no errors, the shift register should contain the bit pattern for R at the conclusion of M. The transmitted bits of R now begin to arrive, and the effect is to zero out the register so that, at the conclusion of reception, the register contains all 0s.

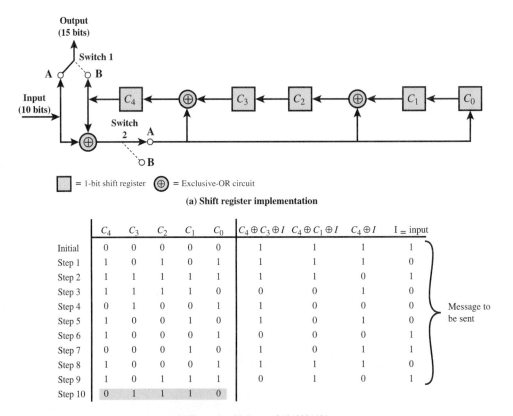

	C_4	C_3	C_2	C_1	C_0	$C_4 \oplus C_3 \oplus I$	$C_4 \oplus C_1 \oplus I$	$C_4 \oplus I$	$I =$ input	
Initial	0	0	0	0	0	1	1	1	1	
Step 1	1	0	1	0	1	1	1	1	0	
Step 2	1	1	1	1	1	1	1	0	1	
Step 3	1	1	1	1	0	0	0	1	0	
Step 4	0	1	0	0	1	1	0	0	0	Message to
Step 5	1	0	0	1	0	1	0	1	0	be sent
Step 6	1	0	0	0	1	0	0	0	1	
Step 7	0	0	0	1	0	1	0	1	1	
Step 8	1	0	0	0	1	1	1	1	0	
Step 9	1	0	1	1	1	0	1	0	1	
Step 10	0	1	1	1	0					

(b) Example with input of 1010001101

Figure 8.3 Circuit with Shift Registers for Dividing by the Polynomial
$X^5 + X^4 + X^2 + 1$

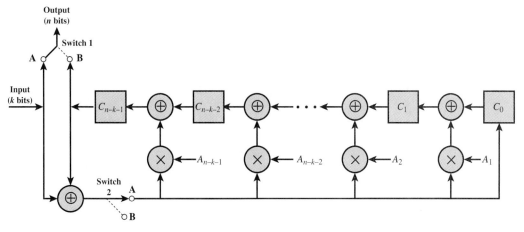

Figure 8.4   General CRC Architecture to Implement Divisor
$$1 + A_1X + A_2X^2 + \ldots + A_{n-1}X^{n-k-1} + X^{n-k}$$

Figure 8.4 indicates the general architecture of the shift register implementation of a CRC for the polynomial $P(X) = \sum_{i=0}^{n-k} A_iX^i$, where $A_0 = A_{n-k} = 1$ and all other A_i equal either 0 or 1.[3]

8.2   BLOCK ERROR CORRECTION CODES

Error detection is a useful technique, found in data link control protocols, such as HDLC, and in transport protocols, such as TCP. However, correction of errors using an error detection code requires that block of data be retransmitted, using the ARQ discipline explained in Section 8.4. For wireless applications this approach is inadequate for two reasons.

1. The bit error rate on a wireless link can be quite high, which would result in a large number of retransmissions.

2. In some cases, especially satellite links, the propagation delay is very long compared to the transmission time of a single frame. The result is a very inefficient system. As is discussed in Section 8.4, the common approach to retransmission is to retransmit the frame in error plus all subsequent frames. With a long data link, an error in a single frame necessitates retransmitting many frames.

Instead, it would be desirable to enable the receiver to correct errors in an incoming transmission on the basis of the bits in that transmission. Figure 8.5 shows in gen-

---

[3]It is common for the CRC register to be shown shifting to the right, which is the reverse of the analogy to binary division. Because binary numbers are usually shown with the most significant bit on the left, a left-shifting register is more appropriate.

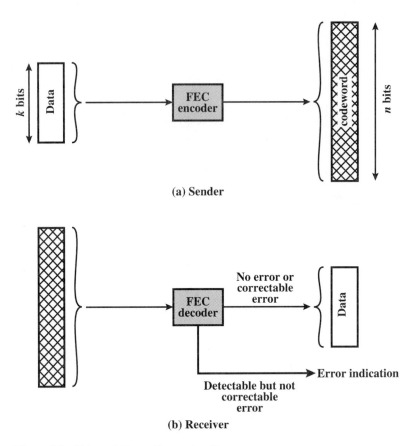

Figure 8.5   Forward Error Correction Process

eral how this is done. On the transmission end, each k-bit block of data is mapped into an n-bit block $(n > k)$ called a **codeword**, using an FEC (forward error correction) encoder. The codeword is then transmitted; in the case of wireless transmission a modulator produces an analog signal for transmission. During transmission, the signal is subject to noise, which may produce bit errors in the signal. At the receiver, the incoming signal is demodulated to produce a bit string that is similar to the original codeword but may contain errors. This block is passed through an FEC decoder, with one of four possible outcomes:

1. If there are not bit errors, the input to the FEC decoder is identical to the original codeword, and the decoder produces the original data block as output.
2. For certain error patterns, it is possible for the decoder to detect and correct those errors. Thus, even though the incoming data block differs from the transmitted codeword, the FEC decoder is able to map this block into the original data block.
3. For certain error patterns, the decoder can detect but not correct the errors. In this case, the decode simply reports an uncorrectable error.

4. For certain, typically rare, error patterns, the decoder does not detect that any errors have occurred and maps the incoming n-bit data block into a k-bit block that differs from the original k-bit block.

How is it possible for the decoder to correct bit errors? In essence, error correction works by adding redundancy to the transmitted message. The redundancy makes it possible for the receiver to deduce what the original message was, even in the face of a certain level of error rate. In this section we look at a widely used form of error correction code known as a block error correction code. We begin with a discussion of general principles and then look at some specific codes.

Before proceeding, we note that in many cases, the error correction code follows the same general layout as shown for error detection codes in Figure 8.1. That is, the FEC algorithm takes as input a k-bit block and adds $(n - k)$ check bits to that block to produce an n-bit block; all of the bits in the original k-bit block show up in the n-bit block. For some FEC algorithms, such as the convolutional code discussed in Section 8.3, the FEC algorithm maps the k-bit input into an n-bit codeword in such a way that the original k bits do not appear in the codeword.

Block Code Principles

To begin, we define a term that shall be of use to us. The **Hamming distance** $d(\mathbf{v}_1, \mathbf{v}_2)$ between two n-bit binary sequences $\mathbf{v}_1$ and $\mathbf{v}_2$ is the number of bits in which $\mathbf{v}_1$ and $\mathbf{v}_2$ disagree. For example, if

$$\mathbf{v}_1 = 011011, \qquad \mathbf{v}_2 = 110001$$

then

$$d(\mathbf{v}_1, \mathbf{v}_2) = 3$$

Now let us consider the block code technique for error correction. Suppose we wish to transmit blocks of data of length k bits. Instead of transmitting each block as k bits, we map each k-bit sequence into a unique n-bit codeword.

Example. For $k = 2$ and $n = 5$, we can make the following assignment:

Data block	Codeword
00	00000
01	00111
10	11001
11	11110

Now, suppose that a codeword block is received with the bit pattern 00100. This is not a valid codeword and so the receiver has detected an error. Can the error be corrected? We can not be sure which data block was sent because 1, 2, 3, 4, or even all 5 of the bits that were transmitted may have been corrupted by noise. However, notice that it would require only a single bit change to transform the valid codeword 00000 into 00100. It would take two bit changes to transform 00111 to 00100, three bit changes to transform 11110 to 00100, and it would take four bit changes to transform 11001 into 00100. Thus, we can deduce that the most likely codeword that was sent was 00000 and that therefore the desired data block is 00. This is error correction. In terms of Hamming distances, we have

$d(00000, 00100) = 1; d(00111, 00100) = 2; \quad d(11001, 00100) = 4; \quad d(11110, 00100) = 3$

So the rule we would like to impose is that if an invalid codeword is received, then the valid codeword that is closest to it (minimum distance) is selected. This will only work if there is a unique valid codeword at a minimum distance from each invalid codeword.

For our example, it is not true that for every invalid codeword there is one and only one valid codeword at a minimum distance. There are $2^5 = 32$ possible codewords of which 4 are valid, leaving 28 invalid codewords. For the invalid codewords, we have the following:

Invalid codeword	Minimum distance	Valid codeword	Invalid codeword	Minimum distance	Valid codeword
00001	1	00000	10000	1	00000
00010	1	00000	10001	1	11001
00011	1	00111	10010	2	00000 or 11110
00100	1	00000	10011	2	00111 or 11001
00101	1	00111	10100	2	00000 or 11110
00110	1	00111	10101	2	00111 or 11001
01000	1	00000	10110	1	11110
01001	1	11001	10111	1	00111
01010	2	00000 or 11110	11000	1	11001
01011	2	00111 or 11001	11010	1	11110
01100	2	00000 or 11110	11011	1	11001
01101	2	00111 or 11001	11100	1	11110
01110	1	11110	11101	1	11001
01111	1	00111	11111	1	11110

There are eight cases in which an invalid codeword is at a distance 2 from two different valid codewords. Thus, if one such invalid codeword is received, an error in 2 bits could have caused it and the receiver has no way to choose between the two alternatives. An error is detected but cannot be corrected. However, in every case in which a single bit error occurs, the resulting codeword is of distance 1 from only one valid codeword and the decision can be made. This code is therefore capable of correcting all single-bit errors but cannot correct double bit errors. Another way to see this is to look at the pairwise distances between valid codewords:

$$d(00000, 00111) = 3; \quad d(00000, 11001) = 3; \quad d(00000, 11110) = 4;$$
$$d(00111, 11001) = 4; \quad d(00111, 11110) = 3; \quad d(11001, 11110) = 3;$$

The minimum distance between valid codewords is 3. Therefore, a single bit error will result in an invalid codeword that is a distance 1 from the original valid codeword but a distance at least 2 from all other valid codewords. As a result, the code can always correct a single-bit error. Note that the code also will always detect a double-bit error.

The preceding examples illustrates the essential properties of a block error-correcting code. An (n, k) block code encodes k data bits into n-bit codewords. Typically, each valid codeword reproduces the original k data bits and adds to them $(n - k)$ check bits to form the n-bit codeword. Thus the design of a block code is equivalent to the design of a function of the form $\mathbf{v_c} = f(\mathbf{v_d})$, where $\mathbf{v_d}$ is a vector of k data bits and $\mathbf{v_c}$ is a vector of n codeword bits.

With an (n, k) block code, there are 2^k valid codewords out of a total of 2^n possible codewords. The ratio of redundant bits to data bits, $(n - k)/k$, is called the **redundancy** of the code, and the ratio of data bits to total bits, k/n, is called the **code rate**. The code rate is a measure of how much additional bandwidth is required to carry data at the same data rate as without the code. For example, a code rate of 1/2 requires double the bandwidth of an uncoded system to maintain the same data rate. Our example has a code rate of 2/5 and so requires a bandwidth 2.5 times the bandwidth for an uncoded system. For example, if the data rate input to the encoder is 1 Mbps, then the output from the encoder must be at a rate of 2.5 Mbps to keep up.

For a code consisting of the codewords $\mathbf{w}_1, \mathbf{w}_2, \ldots, \mathbf{w}_s$, where $s = 2^n$, the minimum distance $d_{\min}$ of the code is defined as

$$d_{min} = \frac{\min}{i \neq j}[d(\mathbf{w}_i, \mathbf{w_j})]$$

It can be shown that the following conditions hold. For a given positive integer t, if a code satisfies $d_{\min} \geq 2t + 1$, then the code can correct all bit errors up to and including errors of t bits. If $d_{\min} \geq 2t$, then all errors $\leq t - 1$ bits can be corrected and errors of t bits can be detected but not, in general, corrected. Conversely, any code for which all errors of magnitude $\leq t$ are corrected must satisfy $d_{\min} \geq 2t + 1$, and any code for which all errors of magnitude $\leq t - 1$ are corrected and all errors of magnitude t are detected must satisfy $d_{\min} \geq 2t$.

Another way of putting the relationship between $d_{\min}$ and t is to say that the maximum number of guaranteed correctable errors per codeword satisfies

$$t = \left\lfloor \frac{d_{min} - 1}{2} \right\rfloor$$

where $\lfloor x \rfloor$ means the largest integer not to exceed x (e.g., $\lfloor 6.3 \rfloor = 6$). Furthermore, if we are concerned only with error detection and not error correction, then the number of errors, t, that can be detected satisfies

$$t = d_{\min} - 1$$

To see this, consider that if $d_{\min}$ errors occur, this could change one valid codeword into another. Any number of errors less than $d_{\min}$ cannot result in another valid codeword.

The design of a block code involves a number of considerations.

1. For given values of n and k, we would like the largest possible value of $d_{\min}$.
2. The code should be relatively easy to encode and decode, requiring minimal memory and processing time.
3. We would like the number of extra bits, $(n - k)$, to be small, to reduce bandwidth.
4. We would like the number of extra bits, $(n - k)$, to be large, to reduce error rate.

Clearly, the last two objectives are in conflict, and tradeoffs must be made.

Before looking at specific codes, it will be useful to examine Figure 8.6, based on one in [LEBO98]. The literature on error-correcting codes frequently includes

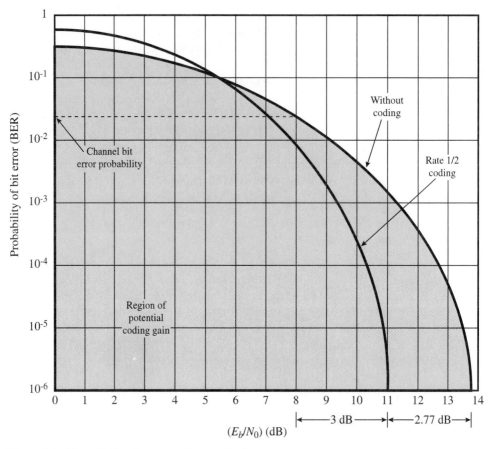

Figure 8.6   How Coding Improves System Performance

graphs of this sort to demonstrate the effectiveness of various encoding schemes. Recall from Chapter 6 that coding can be used to reduce the required $E_b/N0$ value to achieve a given bit error rate.[4] The coding discussed in Chapter 6 has to do with the definition of signal elements to represent bits. The coding discussed in this chapter also has an effect on E_b/N_0. In Figure 8.6, the curve on the right is for an uncoded modulation system; the shaded region represents the area in which improvement can be achieved. In this region, a smaller BER (bit error rate) is achieved for a given E_b/N_0, and conversely, for a given BER, a smaller E_b/N_0 is required. The other curve is a typical result of a code rate of one-half (equal number of data and check bits). Note that at an error rate of 10^{-5}, the use of coding allows a reduction in E_b/N_0 of 2.77 dB. This reduction is referred to as the **coding gain**, which is defined as the reduction, in decibels, in the required E_b/N_0 to achieve a specified BER of an error-correcting coded system compared to an uncoded system using the same modulation.

---

[4]E_b/N_0 is the ratio of signal energy per bit to noise power density per Hertz; it is defined and discussed in Chapter 5.

It is important to realize that the BER for the second rate 1/2 curve refers to the rate of uncorrected errors and that the E_b value refers to the energy per data bit. Because the rate is 1/2, there are two bits on the channel for each data bit, and the energy per coded bit is half that of the energy per data bit, or a reduction of 3 dB. If we look at the energy per coded bit for this system, then we see that the channel bit error rate is about 2.4×10^{-2}, or 0.024.

Finally, note that below a certain threshold of E_b/N_0, the coding scheme actually degrades performance. In our example of Figure 8.6, the threshold occurs at about 5.4 dB. Below the threshold, the extra check bits add overhead to the system that reduces the energy per data bit causing increased errors. Above the threshold, the error-correcting power of the code more than compensates for the reduced E_b, resulting in a coding gain.

We now turn to a look at some specific block error correction codes.

Hamming Code

Hamming codes are a family of (n, k) block error-correcting codes that have the following parameters:

$$
\begin{array}{ll}
\textbf{Block length:} & n = 2^m - 1 \\
\textbf{Number of data bits:} & k = 2^m - m - 1 \\
\textbf{Number of check bits:} & n - k = m \\
\textbf{Minimum distance:} & d_{\min} = 3
\end{array}
$$

where $m \geq 3$. Hamming codes are straightforward and easy to analyze but are rarely used. We begin with these codes because they illustrate some of the fundamental principles of block codes.

Hamming codes are designed to correct single bit errors. To start, let us determine how long the code must be. The Hamming code process has the same structure as the error detection logic shown in Figure 8.1; that is, the encoding process preserves the k data bits and adds $(n - k)$ check bits. For decoding, the comparison logic receives as input two $(n - k)$-bit values, one from the incoming codeword and one from a calculation performed on the incoming data bits. A bit-by-bit comparison is done by taking the XOR of the two inputs. The result is called the **syndrome word**. Thus, each bit of the syndrome is 0 or 1 according to whether there is or is not a match in that bit position for the two inputs.

The syndrome word is therefore $(n - k)$ bits wide and has a range between 0 and $2^{(n-k)} - 1$. The value 0 indicates that no error was detected, leaving $2^{(n-k)} - 1$ values to indicate, if there is an error, which bit was in error. Now, because an error could occur on any of the k data bits or $(n - k)$ check bits, we must have

$$
2^{(n-k)} - 1 \geq k + (n - k) = n
$$

This equation gives the number of bits needed to correct a single bit error in a word containing k data bits. Table 8.1 lists the number of check bits required for various data lengths.

Table 8.1 Hamming Code Requirements

Data Bits	Single-Error Correction		Single-Error Correction/ Double-Error Detection	
	Check Bits	% Increase	Check Bits	% Increase
8	4	50	5	62.5
16	5	31.25	6	37.5
32	6	18.75	7	21.875
64	7	10.94	8	12.5
128	8	6.25	9	7.03
256	9	3.52	10	3.91

For convenience, we would like to generate a syndrome with the following characteristics:

- If the syndrome contains all 0s, no error has been detected.
- If the syndrome contains one and only one bit set to 1, then an error has occurred in one of the check bits. No correction is needed.
- If the syndrome contains more than one bit set to 1, then the numerical value of the syndrome indicates the position of the data bit in error. This data bit is inverted for correction.

To achieve these characteristics, the data and check bits are arranged into an n-bit block as follows. Counting from the least-significant (rightmost) position, the Hamming check bits are inserted at positions that are a power of 2 [i.e., positions 1, 2, 4, ..., $2^{(n-k)}$]. The remaining bits are data bits. To calculate the check bits, each data position which has a value 1 is represented by a binary value equal to its position; thus if the 9th bit is 1, the corresponding value is 1001. All of the position values are then XORed together to produce the bits of the Hamming code. At the receiver all bit position values where there is 1 are XORed. In this case, the XOR includes both data bits and check bits. Because the check bits occur at bit positions that are a power of 2, we can simply XOR all data bit positions with a value of 1, plus the Hamming code formed by the check bits. If the result of the XOR is zero, no error is detected. If the result is nonzero, then the result is the syndrome, and its value equals the bit position that is in error.

Example. An (8.4) Hamming code has the assignment shown in Table 8.2. The 8-bit data block is 00111001. Four of the data bits have a value 1 (shaded in the table), and their bit position values are XORed to produce the Hamming code 0111, which forms the four check digits. The entire block that is transmitted is 001101001111. Suppose now that data bit 3, in bit position 6, sustains an error and is changed from 0 to 1. Then the received block is 001101101111. The received Hamming code is still 0111. The receiver performs an XOR of the Hamming code and all of the bit position values for nonzero data bits, with a result of 0110. The nonzero result detects and error and indicates that the error is in bit position 6.

Table 8.2 Layout of Data Bits and Check Bits

(a) Transmitted block

Bit Position	12	11	10	9	8	7	6	5	4	3	2	1
Position Number	1100	1011	1010	1001	1000	0111	0110	0101	0100	0011	0010	0001
Data Bit	D8	D7	D6	D5		D4	D3	D2		D1		
Check Bit					C8				C4		C2	C1
Transmitted Block	0	0	1	1	0	1	0	0	1	1	1	1
Codes			1010	1001		0111				0011		

(b) Check bit calculation prior to transmission

Position	Code
10	1010
9	1001
7	0111
3	0011
XOR = C8 C4 C2 C1	0111

Table 8.2 Layout of Data Bits and Check Bits (*continued*)

(c) Received block

Bit Position	12	11	10	9	8	7	6	5	4	3	2	1
Position Number	1100	1011	1010	1001	1000	0111	0110	0101	0100	0011	0010	0001
Data Bit	D8	D7	D6	D5		D4	D3	D2		D1		
Check Bit					C8				C4		C2	C1
Transmitted Block	0	0	1	1	0	1	1	0	1	1	1	1
Codes			1010	1001		0111	0110			0011		

(d) Check bit calculation after reception

Position	Code
Hamming	0111
10	1010
9	1001
7	0111
6	0110
3	0011
XOR = syndrome	0111

The code just described is known as a *single-error-correcting* (SEC) code. A variation is a single-error-correcting, double-error-detecting (SEC-DED) code. As Table 8.1 shows, such codes require one additional bit compared with SEC codes. The extra bit is a parity bit over the entire code block.

Cyclic Codes

Most of the error-correcting block codes that are in use are in a category called cyclic codes. For such codes, if the n-bit sequence $\mathbf{c} = (c_0, c_1, \ldots, c_{n-1})$ is a valid codeword, then $(c_{n-1}, c_0, c_1, \ldots, c_{n-2})$, which is formed by cyclically shifting $\mathbf{c}$ one place to the right, is also a valid codeword. This class of codes can be easily encoded and decoded using linear feedback shift registers (LFSRs). Examples of cyclic codes include the Bose-Chaudhuri-Hocquenhem (BCH) and Reed-Solomon codes.

The LFSR implementation of a cyclic error-correcting encoder is the same as that of the CRC error-detecting code, illustrated in Figure 8.4. The key difference is that the CRC code takes an input of arbitrary length and produces a fixed-length CRC check code, while a cyclic error-correcting code takes a fixed-length input (k bits) and produces a fixed-length check code ($n - k$ bits).

Figure 8.7 shows the LFSR implementation of the decoder for a cyclic block code. Compare this to the encoder logic in Figure 8.4. Note that for the encoder, the k data bits are treated as input to produce an $(n - k)$ code of check bits in the shift register. For the decoder, the input is the received bit stream of n bits, consisting of k data bits followed by $(n - k)$ check bits. If there have been no errors, after the first k steps, the shift register contains the pattern of check bits that were transmitted. After the remaining $(n - k)$ steps, the shift register contains a syndrome code.

For decoding of a cyclic code, the following procedure is used:

1. Process received bits to compute the syndrome code in exactly the same fashion as the encoder processes the data bits to produce the check code.
2. If the syndrome bits are all zero, no error has been detected.
3. If the syndrome is nonzero, perform additional processing on the syndrome for error correction.

To understand the significance of the syndrome, let us examine the block code using polynomials. As in the case of the CRC, a particular cyclic code can be represented by a polynomial divisor, called the generator polynomial. For an (n, k) code, the generator polynomial has the form

$$P(X) = 1 + \sum_{i=1}^{n-k-1} A_i X^i + X^{n-k}$$

where each coefficient A_i is either 0 or 1, corresponding to one bit position in the divisor. For example, for $P = 11001$, we have $P(X) = X^4 + X^3 + 1$. Similarly, the set of data bits is represented by the polynomial $D(X)$ and the check code by the polynomial $C(X)$. Recall from the CRC discussion that a check code is determined in the following way:

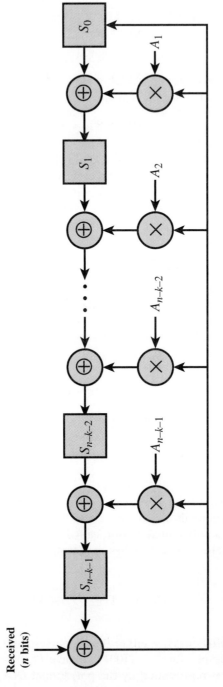

Figure 8.7 Block Syndrome Generator for Divisor $1 + A_1X + A_2X^2 + \ldots + A_{n-1}X^{m-k-1} + X^{n-k}$

$$\frac{X^{n-k}D(X)}{P(X)} = Q(X) + \frac{C(X)}{P(X)}$$

That is, the data block $D(X)$ is shifted to the left by $(n - k)$ bits and divided by $P(X)$. This produces a quotient $Q(X)$ and a remainder $C(X)$ of length $(n - k)$ bits. The transmitted block is formed by concatenating $D(X)$ and $C(X)$:

$$T(X) = X^{n-k}D(X) + C(X) \tag{8.3}$$

If there is no error on reception, $T(X)$ will be exactly divisible by $P(X)$ with no remainder. This is easily demonstrated:

$$\begin{aligned}\frac{T(X)}{P(X)} &= \frac{X^{n-k}D(X)}{P(X)} + \frac{C(X)}{P(X)} \\ &= \left(Q(X) + \frac{C(X)}{P(X)}\right) + \frac{C(X)}{P(X)} = Q(X)\end{aligned} \tag{8.4}$$

The last equality is valid because of the rules of modulo 2 arithmetic ($a + a = 0$, whether $a = 1$ or $a = 0$). Thus, if there are no errors the division of $T(X)$ by $P(X)$ produces no remainder.

If one or more bit errors occur, then the received block $Z(X)$ will be of the form

$$Z(X) = T(X) + E(X)$$

where $E(X)$ is an n-bit error polynomial with a value of 1 in each bit position that is in error in $Z(X)$. If we pass $Z(X)$ through the LFSR of Figure 8.7, we are performing the division $Z(X)/P(X)$, which produces the $(n - k)$ bit syndrome $S(X)$:

$$\frac{Z(X)}{P(X)} = B(X) + \frac{S(X)}{P(X)} \tag{8.5}$$

where $B(X)$ is the quotient and $S(X)$ is the remainder. Thus, $S(X)$ is a function of $Z(X)$. But how does this help us perform error correction? To see this, let us expand Equation (8.5).

$$\frac{Z(X)}{P(X)} = B(X) + \frac{S(X)}{P(X)}$$

$$\frac{T(X) + E(X)}{P(X)} = B(X) + \frac{S(X)}{P(X)} \tag{8.6}$$

$$Q(X) + \frac{E(X)}{P(X)} = B(X) + \frac{S(X)}{P(X)}$$

$$\frac{E(X)}{P(X)} = [Q(X) + B(X)] + \frac{S(X)}{P(X)}$$

What we see is that $E(X)/P(X)$ produces the same remainder as $Z(X)/P(X)$. Therefore, regardless of the initial pattern of bits (transmitted value of $T(X)$), the syndrome value $S(X)$ depends only on the error bits. If we can recover the error bits, $E(X)$, from $S(X)$, then we can correct the errors in $Z(X)$ by simple addition:

$$Z(X) + E(X) = T(X) + E(X) + E(X) = T(X)$$

Because $S(X)$ depends only on $E(X)$, we can easily determine the power of a cyclic block code. The syndrome pattern consists of $n - k$ bits and therefore takes on 2^{n-k} possible values. A value of all zeros indicates no errors. Therefore, a total of $2^{n-k} - 1$ different error patterns can be corrected. To be able to correct all possible single bit errors with an (n, k) code, we must have $n \le (2^{n-k} - 1)$. To be able to correct all single and double bit errors, the relationship is

$$\left(n + \frac{n(n - 1)}{2}\right) \le (2^{n-k} - 1).$$

The way in which $E(X)$ is recovered from $S(X)$ may depend on the specific code involved. The most straightforward approach is to develop a table of all possible values of $E(X)$ with the corresponding value of $S(X)$ of each. Then a simple table lookup is required.

Example.[5] Consider a (7, 4) code with the generator polynomial $P(X) = X^3 + X^2 + 1$. We have $7 = 2^3 - 1$, so this code is capable of correcting all single-bit errors. Table 8.3a lists all of the valid codewords; note that d_{min} is 3, confirming that this is a single-error-correcting code. For example, for the data block 1010, we have $D(X) = X^3 + X$ and $X^{n-k}D(X) = X^6 + X^4$. Dividing as in Equation (8.4),

$$
\begin{array}{r}
X^3 + X^2 + 1 \qquad\qquad\qquad\qquad \leftarrow Q(X) \\
P(X)\rightarrow X^3 + X^2 + 1 \,\big/\, \overline{X^6 \qquad\quad X^4 \qquad\qquad\qquad} \quad \leftarrow 2^3D(X) \\
\underline{X^6 + X^5 + \qquad\quad X^3} \\
X^5 + X^4 + X^3 \\
\underline{X^5 + X^4 + \qquad\quad X^2} \\
X^3 + X^2 \\
\underline{X^3 + X^2 + \qquad 1} \\
1 \leftarrow C(X)
\end{array}
$$

---

[5]This example is taken from [LATH98].

Table 8.3 A Single-Error-Correcting (7,4) Cyclic Code

(a) Table of valid codewords

Data Block	Codeword
0000	0000000
0001	0001101
0010	0010111
0011	0011010
0100	0100011
0101	0101110
0110	0110100
0111	0111001
1000	1000110
1001	1001011
1010	1010001
1011	1011100
1100	1100101
1101	1101000
1110	1110010
1111	1111111

(b) Table of syndromes for single-bit errors

Error pattern E	Syndrome S
0000001	001
0000010	010
0000100	100
0001000	101
0010000	111
0100000	011
1000000	110

Then, using Equation (8.3), we have $T(X) = X^6 + X^4 + 1$, which is the code word 1010001.

For error correction, we need to construct the syndrome table shown in Table 8.3b. For example, for an error pattern of 1000000, $E(X) = X^6$. Using the last line of Equation (8.6), we calculate

$$
\begin{array}{r}
X^3 + X^2 + X \quad \leftarrow Q(X) + B(X) \\
P(X) \rightarrow X^3 + X^2 + 1\ \overline{)\ X^6} \qquad\qquad \leftarrow Z(X) \\
\underline{X^6 + X^5 + \qquad X^3} \\
X^5 + \qquad X^3 \\
\underline{X^5 + X^4 + \qquad X^2} \\
X^4 + X^3 + X^2 \\
\underline{X^4 + X^3 + \qquad X} \\
X^2 + X \ \leftarrow S(X)
\end{array}
$$

Therefore, $S = 110$. The remaining entries in Table 8.3b are calculated similarly. Now suppose the received block is 1101101, or $Z(X) = X^6 + X^6 + X^3 + X^2 + 1$. Using Equation (8.5),

$$
\begin{array}{r}
X^3 \qquad\qquad\qquad\qquad \leftarrow B(X) \\
P(X) \rightarrow X^3 + X^2 + 1\ \overline{)\ X^6 + X^5 + \qquad X^3 + X^2 + 1} \ \leftarrow Z(X) \\
\underline{X^6 + X^5 + \qquad X^3} \\
X^2 + 1 \ \leftarrow S(X)
\end{array}
$$

Thus $S = 101$. Using Table 8.3b, this yields $E = 0001000$. Then

$$T = 1101101 \oplus 0001000 = 1100101$$

Then, from Table 8.3a the transmitted data block is 1100.

BCH Codes

BCH codes are among the most powerful cyclic block codes and are widely used in wireless applications. For any positive pair of integers m and t, there is a binary (n, k) BCH codes with the following parameters:

Block length:	$n = 2^m - 1$
Number of check bits:	$n - k \leq mt$
Minimum distance:	$d_{min} \geq 2t + 1$

This code can correct all combinations of t or fewer errors. The generator polynomial for this code can be constructed from the factors of $(X^{2m-1} + 1)$. The BCH codes provide flexibility in the choice of parameters (block length, code rate). Table 8.4 lists the BCH parameters for code lengths up to $2^8 - 1$. Table 8.5 lists some of the BCH generator polynomials.

Table 8.4 BCH Code Parameters

n	k	t
7	4	1
15	11	1
	7	2
	5	3
31	26	1
	21	2
	16	3
	11	5
	6	7
63	57	1
	51	2
	45	3
	39	4
	36	5

n	k	t
63	30	6
	24	7
	18	10
	16	11
	10	13
	7	15
127	120	1
	113	2
	106	3
	99	4
	92	5
	85	6
	78	7
	71	9

n	k	t
127	64	10
	57	11
	50	13
	43	14
	36	15
	29	21
	22	23
	15	27
	8	31
255	247	1
	239	2
	231	3
	223	4
	215	5

n	k	t
255	207	6
	199	7
	191	8
	187	9
	179	10
	171	11
	163	12
	155	13
	147	14
	139	15
	131	18
	123	19
	115	21
	107	22

n	k	t
255	99	23
	91	25
	87	26
	79	27
	71	29
	63	30
	55	31
	47	42
	45	43
	37	45
	29	47
	21	55
	13	59
	9	63

Table 8.5 BCH Polynomial Generators

n	k	t	$P(X)$
7	4	1	$X^3 + X + 1$
15	11	1	$X^4 + X + 1$
15	7	2	$X^8 + X^7 + X^6 + X^4 + 1$
15	5	3	$X^{10} + X^8 + X^5 + X^4 + X^2 + X + 1$
31	26	1	$X^5 + X^2 + 1$
31	21	2	$X^{10} + X^9 + X^8 + X^6 + X^5 + X^3 + 1$

A number of techniques have been designed for BCH decoding that require less memory than a simple table lookup. One of the simplest was proposed by Berlekamp [BERL80]. The central idea is to compute an error-locator polynomial and solve for its roots. The complexity of the algorithm increases only as the square of the number of errors to be corrected.

Reed–Solomon Codes

Reed-Solomon (RS) codes are a widely used subclass of nonbinary BCH codes. With RS codes, data are processed in chunks of m bits, called symbols. An (n, k) RS code has the following parameters:

Symbol length:	m bits per symbol
Block length:	$n = 2^m - 1$ symbols $= m(2^m - 1)$ bits
Data length:	k symbols
Size of check code:	$n - k = 2t$ symbols $= m(2t)$ bits
Minimum distance:	$d_{min} = 2t + 1$ symbols

Thus, the encoding algorithm expands a block of k symbols to n symbols by adding $n - k$ redundant check symbols. Typically, m is a power of 2; a popular value of m is 8.

Example. Let $t = 1$ and $m = 2$. Denoting the symbols as 0, 1, 2, 3 we can write their binary equivalents as $0 = 00$; $1 = 01$; $2 = 10$; $3 = 11$. The code has the following parameters:

$$n = 2^2 - 1 = 3 \text{ symbols} = 6 \text{ bits}$$
$$(n - k) = 2 \text{ symbols} = 4 \text{ bits}$$

This code can correct any burst error that spans a symbol of 2 bits.

RS codes are well suited for burst error correction. They make highly efficient use of redundancy, and block lengths and symbol sizes can be easily adjusted to accommodate a wide range of message sizes. In addition, efficient coding techniques are available for RS codes.

Block Interleaving

Block interleaving is a common technique used with block codes in wireless systems; we saw an example of this in Figure 5.15. The advantage of interleaving is that a burst error that affects a sequence of bits is spread out over a number of separate blocks at the receiver so that error correction is possible. Interleaving is accomplished by reading and writing data from memory in different orders. Figure 8.8 illustrates a simple and common interleaving technique. In this case, the data to be transmitted are stored in a rectangular array in which each row consists of n bits, equal to the block size. Data are then read out one column at a time. The result is that the k data bits and their corresponding $(n - k)$ check bits, which form a single n-bit block, are spread out and interspersed with bits from other blocks. At the receiver, the data are deinterleaved to recover the original order. If, during transmission, a burst of noise affects a consecutive sequence of bits, those bits belong to different blocks and hence only a fraction of the bits in error need to be corrected by any one set of check bits. Specifically, a burst of length $l = mb$ is broken up into m bursts of length b. Some thought should convince you of the following assertion: Suppose we have an (n, k) code that can correct all combinations of t or fewer errors, where $t = \lfloor (n - k)/2 \rfloor$. If we use an interleaver of degree m, then the result is an (mn, mk) code that can correct burst errors of up to mt bits.

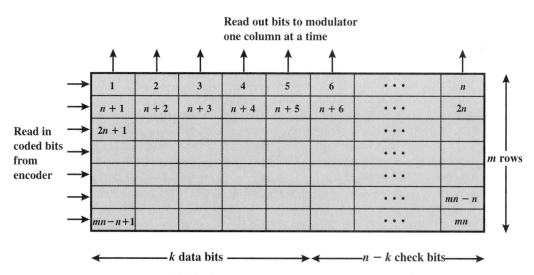

Note: The numbers in the matrix indicate the order in which bits are read in.
  Interleaver output sequence: $1, n + 1, 2n + 1, \ldots$

Figure 8.8   Block Interleaving

8.3 CONVOLUTIONAL CODES

Block codes are one of the two widely used categories of error correcting codes for wireless transmission; the other is convolutional codes. An (n, k) block code process data in blocks of k bits at a time, producing a block of n bits $(n > k)$ as output for every block of k bits as input. If data are transmitted and received in a more or less continuous stream, a block code, particularly one with a large value of n, may not be as convenient as a code that generates redundant bits continuously so that error checking and correcting are carried out continuously. This is the function of convolution codes.

A convolutional code is defined by three parameters: n, k, and K. An (n, k, K) code processes input data k bits at a time and produces an output of n bits for each incoming k bits. So far this is the same as the block code. In the case of a convolutional code, n and k are generally quite small numbers. The difference is that convolutional codes have memory, which is characterized by the *constraint factor K*. In essence, the current n-bit output of an (n, k, K) code depends not only on the value of the current block of k input bits but also on the previous $K - 1$ blocks of k input bits. Hence, the current output of n bits is a function of the last $K \times k$ input bits.

Convolutional codes are best understood by looking at a specific example. We use the example shown in Figure 8.9. There are two alternative representations of the code shown in the figure. Figure 8.9a is a shift register, which is most convenient for describing and implementing the encoding process. Figure 8.9b is an equivalent representation that is useful in discussing the decoding process.

For an (n, k, K) code, the shift register contains the most recent $K \times k$ input bits; the register is initialized to all zeros.[6] The encoder produces n output bits, after which the oldest k bits from the register are discarded and k new bits are shifted in. Thus, although the output of n bits depends on $K \times k$ input bits, the rate of encoding is n output bits per k input bits. As in a block code, the code rate is therefore k/n. The most commonly used binary encoders have $k = 1$ and hence a shift register length of K. Our example is of a $(2, 1, 3)$ code (Figure 8.9a). In this example, the encoder converts an input bit u_n into two output bits v_{n1} and v_{n2}, using the three most recent bits. The first output bit produced is from the upper logic circuit ($v_{n1} = u_n \oplus u_{n-1} \oplus u_{n-2}$), and the second output bit from the lower logic circuit ($v_{n2} = u_n \oplus u_{n-2}$).

For any given input of k bits, there are $2^{k(K-1)}$ different functions that map the k input bits into n output bits. Which function is used depends on the history of the last $(K - 1)$ input blocks of k bits each. We can therefore represent a convolutional code using a finite-state machine. The machine has $2^{k(K-1)}$ states, and the transition from one state to another is determined by the most recent k bits of inputs and produces n output bits. The initial state of the machine corresponds to the all-zeros state. For our example (Figure 8.9b) there are 4 states, one for each possible pair of values for the last two bits. The next input bit causes a transition and produces an output of two bits. For example, if the last two bits were 10 ($u_{n-1} = 1, u_{n-2} = 0$) and

---

[6]In some of the literature, the shift register is shown with one less storage cell and with the input bits feeding the XOR circuits as well as a storage cell; the depictions are equivalent.

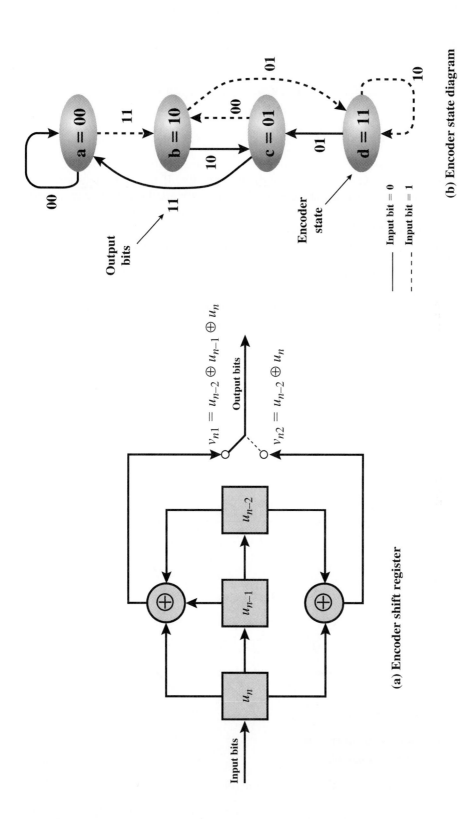

(b) Encoder state diagram

(a) Encoder shift register

Figure 8.9 Convolutional Encoder with $(n, k, K) = (2, 1, 3)$

233

the next bit is 1 ($u_n = 1$), then the current state is state b(10) and the next state is d(11). The output is

$$v_{n1} = u_{n-2} \oplus u_{n-1} \oplus u_n = 0 \oplus 1 \oplus 1 = 0$$
$$v_{n2} = 0 \oplus 1 = 1$$

Decoding

To understand the decoding process, it simplifies matters to expand the state diagram to show the time sequence of the encoder. If the state diagram is laid out vertically, as shown in Figure 8.9b, then the expanded diagram, called a **trellis**, is constructed by reproducing the states horizontally and showing the state transitions going from left to right corresponding to time, or data input (Figure 8.10). If the constraint length K is large, then the trellis diagram becomes unwieldy. In that case, 2^{K-2} simplified trellis fragments can be used to depict the transitions. Figure 8.11 demonstrates this for a (2, 1, 7) code. Each of the states of the encoder is shown, along with the branch definition.

Any valid output is defined by a path through the trellis. In our example, the path a-b-c-b-d-c-a-a produces the output 11 10 00 01 01 11 00 and was generated by the input 1011000. If an invalid path occurs, such as a-c, then the decoder attempts error correction. In essence, the decoder must determine what data input was most likely to have produced the invalid output.

A number of error correction algorithms have been developed for convolutional codes. Perhaps the most important is the Viterbi code. In essence, the Viterbi technique compares the received sequence with all possible transmitted sequences. The algorithm chooses a path through the trellis whose coded sequence differs from

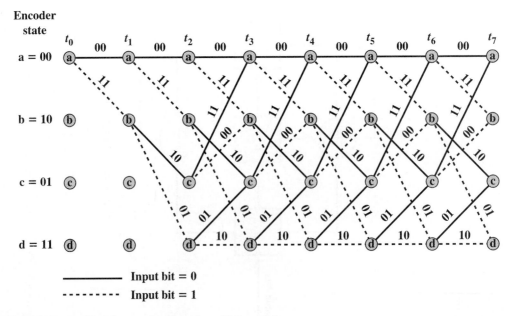

Figure 8.10 Trellis Diagram for Encoder of Figure 8.9

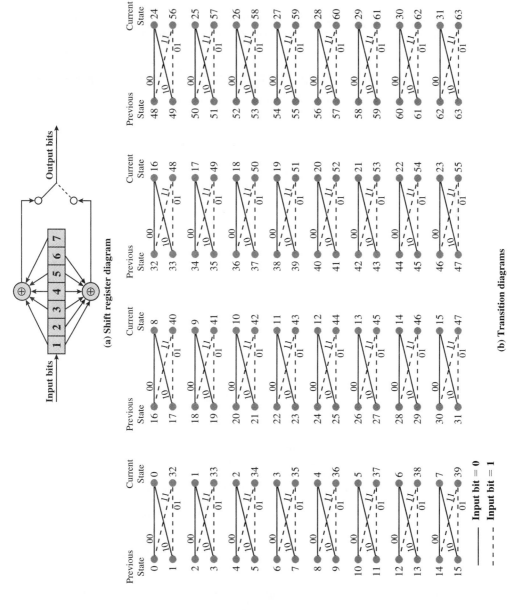

(a) Shift register diagram

(b) Transition diagrams

—— Input bit = 0

- - - - Input bit = 1

Figure 8.11 Trellis Diagrams for Encoder with $(n, k, K) = (2, 1, 7)$ [JAIN90]

235

the received sequence in the fewest number of places. Once a valid path is selected as the correct path, the decoder can recover the input data bits from the output code bits.

There are several variations on the Viterbi algorithm, depending on which metric is used to measure differences between received sequences and valid sequences. To give an idea of the operation of the algorithm, we use the common metric of Hamming distance. We represent a received coded sequence as the word $\mathbf{w} = w_0 w_1 w_2, \ldots$, and attempt to find the most likely valid path through the trellis. At each time i and for each state we list the *active path* (or paths) through the trellis to the state. An active path is a valid path through the trellis whose Hamming distance from the received word up to time i is minimal. We label each state at time i by the distance of its active path from the received word. The following relationship is used:

distance of a path = distance of the last edge + distance of the last-but-one state (8.7)

The algorithm proceeds in $b + 1$ steps, where b is a prechosen window size. For an (n, k, K) code, the first output block of n bits, $w_0 w_1 w_2 \ldots w_{n-1}$, is decoded in the following steps.

Step 0:   The initial state of the trellis at time 0 is labeled 0, because there is so far no discrepancy.

Step $i + 1$: For each state S at time $i + 1$, find all active paths leading to S [using Equation (8.7)]. Label S by the distance of that path or paths.

Step b: The algorithm terminates at time b. If all the active paths at that time have the same first edge and the label of that edge is $x_0 x_1 x_2 \ldots x_{n-1}$, then the first code block $w_0 w_1 w_2 \ldots w_{n-1}$ is corrected to $x_0 x_1 x_2 \ldots x_{n-1}$. If the are two active first edges, the error is not correctable.

After accepting and, if necessary, correcting, the first code block, the decoding window is moved n bits to the right and the decoding of the next block is performed.

Example.[7] Using the encoder defined in Figures 8.9 and 8.10, Figure 8.12 shows the application of the Viterbi algorithm to the sequence 10010100101100, . . . , with a decoding window of length $b = 7$. The lines in the figure represent valid paths through the trellis. The bold lines indicate the current active paths. At step 1, we have a received sequence of $w_0 w_1 = 10$. The two valid sequences are 00 and 11. For both of these sequences, there is a distance of 1 from the received sequence. Two active paths are defined, each with a state label of 1. For the next step, we have $w_2 w_3 = 01$. Using Equation (8.7), we compute the differences for the four possible valid states (from top to bottom) as 2, 2, 3, and 1. So far, all possible valid paths are included as active paths. In Step 3, we see that some valid paths do not survive as active paths. This is because each such path terminates on a state for which there is another valid path that has a smaller distance. For example, the state sequence a-a-a-a has a discrepancy of 3, while the state sequence a-b-c-a has the discrepancy of 4. At the conclusion of step 7, all active paths pass through the first edge a-b, which has the output 11. The algorithm corrects $w_0 w_1$ to 11 and continues with the next block $w_2 w_3$. Note that if the window size b was 5, the error would not have been correctable.

---

[7]This example is based on one in [ADAM91].

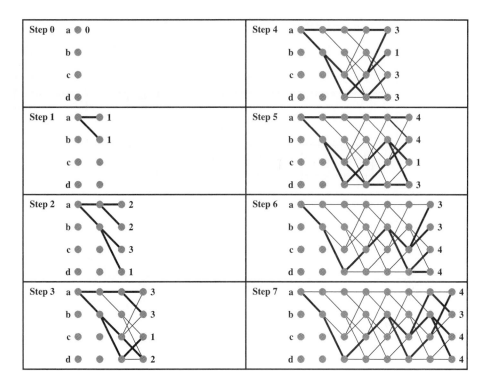

Figure 8.12 Viterbi Algorithm for $w = 10010100101100\dots$ with decoding window $b = 7$

Convolutional codes provide good performance in noisy channels where a high proportion of the bits are in error. Thus, they have found increasing use in wireless applications.

Turbo Coding

As higher and higher speeds are used in wireless applications, error correction continues to pose a major design challenge. Recently, a new class of codes, called turbo codes, has emerged as a popular choice for third-generation wireless systems. Turbo codes exhibit performance, in terms of bit error probability, that is very close to the Shannon limit and can be efficiently implemented for high-speed use. A number of different turbo encoders and decoders have been introduced, most of which are based on convolutional encoding. In this subsection, we give a general overview.

Figure 8.13a depicts a turbo encoder. In this scheme, the encoder is replicated. One copy of the encoder receives a stream of input bits and produces a single output check bit C_1 for each input bit. The input to the other encoder is an interleaved version of the input bit stream, producing a sequence of C_2 check bits. The initial input bit plus the two check bits are then multiplexed to produce the sequence $I_1C_{11}C_{21}I_2C_{12}C_{22}, \dots$, that is, the first input bit followed by the first bit from encoder one, followed by the first bit from encoder 2, and so on. The resulting sequence has

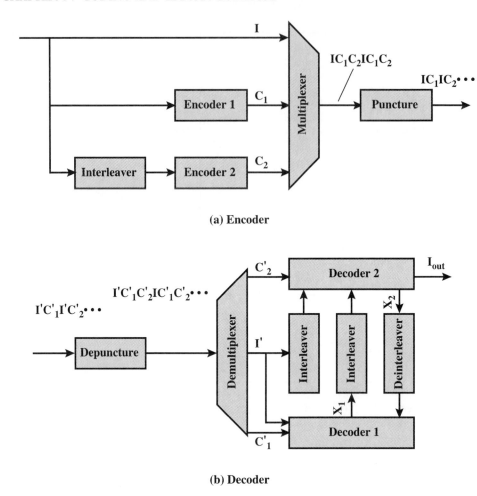

(a) Encoder

(b) Decoder

Figure 8.13 Turbo Encoding and Decoding [COTT00]

a code rate of 1/3. A code rate of 1/2 can be achieved by taking only half of the check bits, alternating between outputs from the two encoders; this process is called *puncturing*. Rates of 1/3 and 1/2 are both found in third-generation systems.

Note that each encoder only produces a single check bit for each input bit and that the input bit is preserved. In the convolutional encoders we have discussed so far (e.g., Figure 8.9a), the input bits are not preserved, and there are multiple output bits (n output check bits for k input bits). For turbo coding, a variation of the convolutional code, known as a recursive systematic convolutional code (RSC), is used. In a $(2, 1, K)$ RSC encoder, which is typical, one of the two check bit calculations is fed back to the shift register, and the other check bit calculation produces an output bit (Figure 8.14). The output of the encoder consists of alternating input and check bits. The RSC encoder has the same trellis structure as a conventional convolutional encoder and similar statistical properties.

Figure 8.15 shows how a turbo encoder can be implemented using two RSC coders, where the switch is used to puncture the code, producing a code rate of 1/3. Without the switch, the code rate is 1/2.

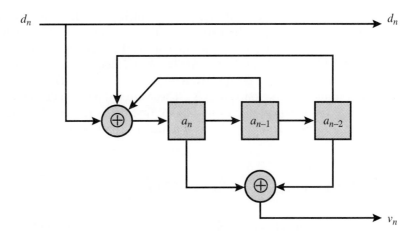

Figure 8.14   Recursive Systematic Concolutional (RSC) Encoder

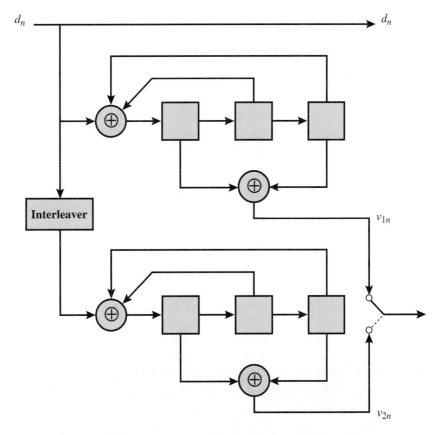

Figure 8.15   Parallel Concatenation of Two RSC Encoders [SKLA97b]

Figure 8.13b is a general diagram of a turbo decoder. The received data are depunctured, if necessary, by estimating the missing check bits or by setting the missing bits to 0. Decoder 1 operates first, using the I' and P'_1 values to produce correction (X_1) bits. The I' and X_1 bits are fed into decoder 2, together with the P'_2 values. Interleaving must be performed to align bits properly. Decoder 2 uses all of its input to produce correction values X_2. These are fed back to decoder 1 for a second iteration of the decoding algorithm, being first deinterleaved for alignment. After sufficient iterations, an output bit is generated from I' and X_2.

8.4 AUTOMATIC REPEAT REQUEST

Automatic repeat request (ARQ) is a mechanism used in data link control and transport protocols and relies on the use of an error detection code, such as the cyclic redundancy check (CRC) described in Section 8.1. The ARQ error control mechanism is closely related to a flow control mechanism that is also a part of these protocols. We first examine flow control and then go on to look at ARQ. In what follows, we refer to the block of data that is transmitted from one protocol entity to another as a protocol data unit (PDU); this term was introduced in Chapter 4.

Flow Control

Flow control is a technique for assuring that a transmitting entity does not overwhelm a receiving entity with data. The receiving entity typically allocates a data buffer of some maximum length for a transfer. When data are received, the receiver must do a certain amount of processing (e.g., examine the header and strip it off the PDU) before passing the data to the higher-level software. In the absence of flow control, the receiver's buffer may fill up and overflow while it is processing old data.

To begin, we examine mechanisms for flow control in the absence of errors. The model we will use is depicted in Figure 8.16a, which is a vertical-time sequence diagram. It has the advantages of showing time dependencies and illustrating the correct send-receive relationship. Each arrow represents a single PDU traversing a data link between two stations. The data are sent in a sequence of PDUs, with each PDU containing a portion of the data and some control information. For now, we assume that all PDUs that are transmitted are successfully received; no PDUs are lost and none arrive with errors. Furthermore, PDUs arrive in the same order in which they are sent. However, each transmitted PDU suffers an arbitrary and variable amount of delay before reception.

Typically, when a source has a block or stream of data to transmit, the source will break up the block of data into smaller blocks and transmit the data in many PDUs. This is done for the following reasons:

- The buffer size of the receiver may be limited.
- The longer the transmission, the more likely that there will be an error, necessitating retransmission of the entire PDU. With smaller PDUs, errors are detected sooner, and a smaller amount of data needs to be retransmitted.

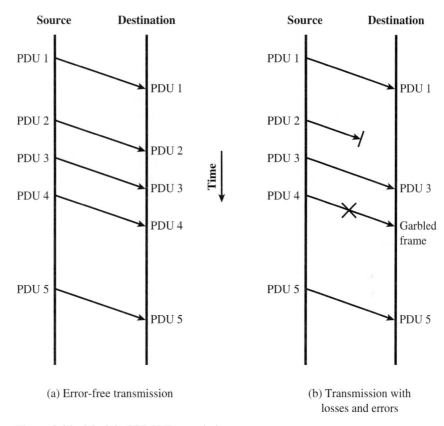

(a) Error-free transmission

(b) Transmission with
losses and errors

Figure 8.16   Model of PDU Transmission

- On a shared medium, such as a LAN, it is usually desirable not to permit one
  station to occupy the medium for an extended period, thus causing long delays
  at the other sending stations.

Typically, protocols that have a flow control mechanism allow multiple PDUs
to be in transit at the same time. Let us examine how this might work for two stations, A and B, connected via a full-duplex link. Station B allocates buffer space
for W PDUs. Thus B can accept W PDUs, and A is allowed to send W PDUs without waiting for any acknowledgments. To keep track of which PDUs have been
acknowledged, each is labeled with a sequence number. B acknowledges a PDU by
sending an acknowledgment that includes the sequence number of the next PDU
expected. This acknowledgment also implicitly announces that B is prepared to
receive the next W PDUs, beginning with the number specified. This scheme can
also be used to acknowledge multiple PDUs. For example, B could receive PDUs
2, 3, and 4 but withhold acknowledgment until PDU 4 has arrived. By then returning an acknowledgment with sequence number 5, B acknowledges PDUs 2, 3, and
4 at one time. A maintains a list of sequence numbers that it is allowed to send,
and B maintains a list of sequence numbers that it is prepared to receive. Each of

these lists can be thought of as a *window* of PDUs. The operation is referred to as **sliding-window flow control**.

Several additional comments need to be made. Because the sequence number to be used occupies a field in the PDU, it is clearly of bounded size. For example, for a 3-bit field, the sequence number can range from 0 to 7. Accordingly, PDUs are numbered modulo 8; that is, after sequence number 7, the next number is 0. In general, for a k-bit field the range of sequence numbers is 0 through $2^k - 1$, and PDUs are numbered modulo 2^k.

Figure 8.17 is a useful way of depicting the sliding-window process. It assumes the use of a 3-bit sequence number, so that PDUs are numbered sequentially from 0 through 7, and then the same numbers are reused for subsequent PDUs. The shaded rectangle indicates the PDUs that may be sent; in this figure, the sender may transmit five PDUs, beginning with PDU 0. Each time a PDU is sent, the shaded window shrinks; each time an acknowledgment is received, the shaded window grows. PDUs between the vertical bar and the shaded window have been sent but not yet acknowledged. As we shall see, the sender must buffer these PDUs in case they need to be retransmitted.

The window size need not be the maximum possible size for a given sequence number length. For example, using a 3-bit sequence number, a window size of 4 could be configured for the stations using the sliding-window flow control protocol.

> **Example.** An example is shown in Figure 8.18. The example assumes a 3-bit sequence number field and a maximum window size of seven PDUs. Initially, A and B have windows indicating that A may transmit seven PDUs, beginning with PDU 0 (P0). After transmitting three PDUs (P0, P1, P2) without acknowledgment, A has shrunk its window to four PDUs and maintains a copy of the three transmitted PDUs. The window indicates that A may transmit four PDUs, beginning with PDU number 3. B then transmits an RR (Receive Ready) 3, which means "I have received all PDUs up through PDU number 2 and am ready to receive PDU number 3; in fact, I am prepared to receive seven PDUs, beginning with PDU number 3." With this acknowledgment, A is back up to permission to transmit seven PDUs, still beginning with PDU 3; also A may discard the buffered PDUs that have now been acknowledged. A proceeds to transmit PDUs 3, 4, 5, and 8. B returns RR 4, which acknowledges P3, and allows transmission of P4 through the next instance of P2. By the time this RR reaches A, it has already transmitted P4, P5, and P6, and therefore A may only open its window to permit sending four PDUs beginning with P7.

The mechanism so far described does indeed provide a form of flow control: The receiver must only be able to accommodate seven PDUs beyond the one it has last acknowledged. Most protocols also allow a station to cut off the flow of PDUs from the other side by sending a Receive Not Ready (RNR) message, which acknowledges former PDUs but forbids transfer of future PDUs. Thus, RNR 5 means "I have received all PDUs up through number 4 but am unable to accept any more." At some subsequent point, the station must send a normal acknowledgment to reopen the window.

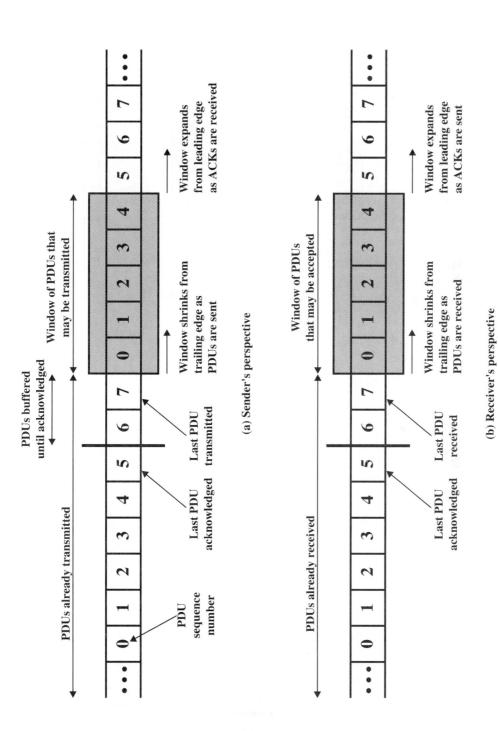

Figure 8.17 Sliding-Window Depiction

243

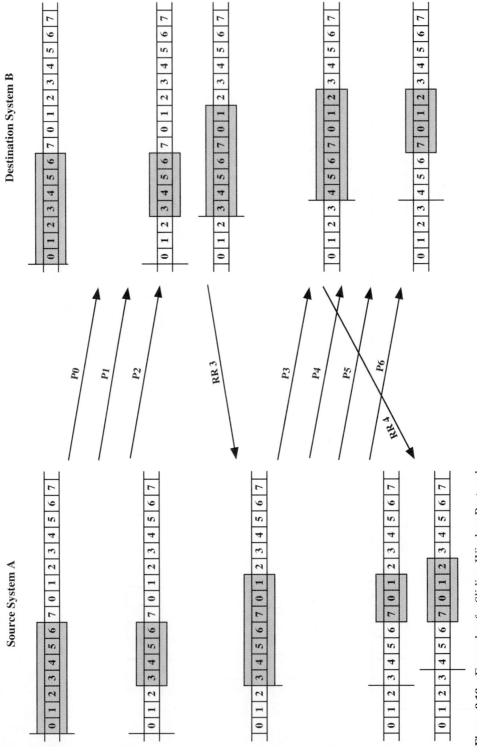

Figure 8.18 Example of a Sliding-Window Protocol

So far, we have discussed transmission in one direction only. If two stations exchange data, each needs to maintain two windows, one for transmit and one for receive, and each side needs to send the data and acknowledgments to the other. To provide efficient support for this requirement, a feature known as *piggybacking* is typically provided. Each *data PDU* includes a field that holds the sequence number of that PDU plus a field that holds the sequence number used for acknowledgment. Thus, if a station has data to send and an acknowledgment to send, it sends both together in one PDU, saving communication capacity. Of course, if a station has an acknowledgment but no data to send, it sends a separate *acknowledgment PDU*. If a station has data to send but no new acknowledgment to send, it must repeat the last acknowledgment that it sent. This is because the data PDU includes a field for the acknowledgment number, and some value must be put into that field. When a station receives a duplicate acknowledgment, it simply ignores it.

Error Control

Error control refers to mechanisms to detect and correct errors that occur in the transmission of PDUs. The model that we will use, which covers the typical case, is illustrated in Figure 8.16b. As before, data are sent as a sequence of PDUs; PDUs arrive in the same order in which they are sent; and each transmitted PDU suffers an arbitrary and variable amount of delay before reception. In addition, we admit the possibility of two types of errors:

- **Lost PDU:** A PDU fails to arrive at the other side. For example, a noise burst may damage a PDU to the extent that the receiver is not aware that a PDU has been transmitted.
- **Damaged PDU:** A recognizable PDU does arrive, but some of the bits are in error (have been altered during transmission).

The most common techniques for error control are based on some or all of the following ingredients:

- **Error detection:** The receiver detects errors and discards PDUs that are in error.

- **Positive acknowledgment:** The destination returns a positive acknowledgment to successfully received, error-free PDUs.
- **Retransmission after timeout:** The source retransmits a PDU that has not been acknowledged after a predetermined amount of time.
- **Negative acknowledgment and retransmission:** The destination returns a negative acknowledgment to PDUs in which an error is detected. The source retransmits such PDUs.

Collectively, these mechanisms are all referred to as **automatic repeat request** (ARQ); the effect of ARQ is to turn an unreliable data link into a reliable one. The most commonly used versions of ARQ is known as go-back-N ARQ. Go-back-N ARQ is based on the sliding-window flow control mechanism just discussed.

In go-back-N ARQ, a station may send a series of PDUs sequentially numbered modulo some maximum value. The number of unacknowledged PDUs outstanding is determined by window size, using the sliding-window flow control technique. While no errors occur, the destination will acknowledge incoming PDUs as usual (RR = receive ready, or piggybacked acknowledgment). If the destination station detects an error in a PDU, it sends a negative acknowledgment (REJ = reject) for that PDU. The destination station will discard that PDU and all future incoming PDUs until the PDU in error is correctly received. Thus the source station, when it receives a REJ, must retransmit the PDU in error plus all succeeding PDUs that had been transmitted in the interim.

Consider that station A is sending PDUs to station B. After each transmission, A sets an acknowledgment timer for the PDU just transmitted. Suppose that B has previously successfully received PDU $(i - 1)$ and A has just transmitted PDU i. The go-back-N technique takes into account the following contingencies:

1. **Damaged PDU.** If the received PDU is invalid (i.e., B detects an error), B discards the PDU and takes no further action as the result of that PDU. There are two subcases:
   a. Within a reasonable period of time, A subsequently sends PDU $(i + 1)$. B receives PDU $(i + 1)$ out of order and sends a REJ i. A must retransmit PDU i and all subsequent PDUs.
   b. A does not soon send additional PDUs. B receives nothing and returns neither an RR nor a REJ. When A's timer expires, it transmits an RR PDU that includes a bit known as the P bit, which is set to 1. B interprets the RR PDU with a P bit of 1 as a command that must be acknowledged by sending an RR indicating the next PDU that it expects, which is PDU i. When A receives the RR, it retransmits PDU i.

2. **Damaged RR.** There are two subcases:
   a. B receives PDU i and sends RR $(i + 1)$, which suffers an error in transit. Because acknowledgments are cumulative (e.g., RR 6 means that all PDUs through 5 are acknowledged), it may be that A will receive a subsequent RR to a subsequent PDU and that it will arrive before the timer associated with PDU i expires.
   b. If A's timer expires, it transmits an RR command as in Case 1b. It sets another timer, called the P-bit timer. If B fails to respond to the RR command, or if its response suffers an error in transit, then A's P-bit timer will expire. At this point, A will try again by issuing a new RR command and restarting the P-bit timer. This procedure is tried for a number of iterations. If A fails to obtain an acknowledgment after some maximum number of attempts, it initiates a reset procedure.

3. **Damaged REJ.** If a REJ is lost, this is equivalent to Case 1b.

Figure 8.19 is an example of the PDU flow for go-back-N ARQ. Because of the propagation delay on the line, by the time that an acknowledgment (positive or negative) arrives back at the sending station, it has already sent two additional PDUs beyond the one being acknowledged. Thus, when a REJ is received to PDU 5, not only PDU 5 but PDUs 6 and 7 must be retransmitted. Thus, the transmitter must keep a copy of all unacknowledged PDUs.

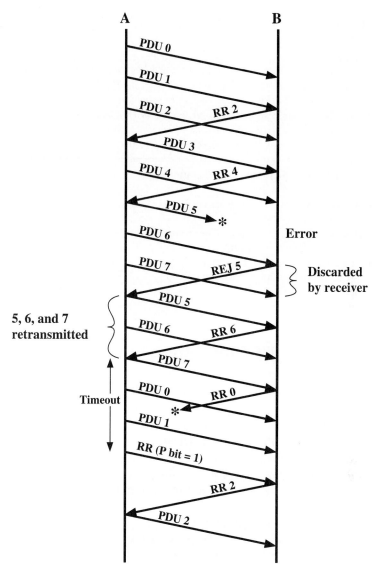

Figure 8.19 Go-back-N ARQ

8.5 RECOMMENDED READING

The classic treatment of error detecting codes and CRC is [PETE61]. [RAMA88] is an excellent tutorial on CRC.

[ADAM91] provides comprehensive treatment of error-correcting codes. [SKLA01] contains a clear, well-written section on the subject. Two useful survey articles are [BERL87] and [BHAR83]. A quite readable theoretical and mathematical treatment of error-correcting codes is [ASH90].

Two good treatments of turbo codes are [SKLA97] and [BERR96]. A more detailed analysis is [VUCE00].

ADAM91 Adamek, J. *Foundations of Coding.* New York: Wiley, 1991.

ASH90 Ash, R. *Information Theory.* New York: Dover, 1990.

BERL87 Berlekamp, E.; Peile, R.; and Pope, S. "The Application of Error Control to Communications." *IEEE Communications Magazine*, April 1987.

BERR96 Berrou, C., and Glavieux, A. "Near Optimum Error Correcting Codes and Decoding: Turbo Codes." *IEEE Transactions on Communications*, October 1996.

BHAR83 Bhargava, V. "Forward Error Correction Schemes for Digital Communications." *IEEE Communications Magazine*, January 1983.

PETE61 Peterson, W., and Brown, D. "Cyclic Codes for Error Detection." *Proceedings of the IEEE*, January 1961.

RAMA88 Ramabadran, T., and Gaitonde, S. "A Tutorial on CRC Computations." *IEEE Micro*, August 1988.

SKLA97 Sklar, B. "A Primer on Turbo Code Concepts." *IEEE Communications Magazine*, December 1997.

SKLA01 Sklar, B. *Digital Communications: Fundamentals and Applications.* Upper Saddle River, NJ: Prentice Hall, 2001.

VUCE00 Vucetic, B., and Yuan, J. *Turbo Codes: Principles and Applications.* Boston: Kluwer Academic Publishers, 2000.

8.6 KEY TERMS, REVIEW QUESTIONS, AND PROBLEMS

Key Terms

automatic repeat request (ARQ)	error control	go-back-N ARQ
	error correction	Hamming code
block ECC	error correction code (ECC)	Hamming distance
block interleaving	error detection	parity bit
check bits	error detection code	parity check
codeword	flow control	protocol data unit (PDU)
convolutional code	forward error	sliding-window flow
cyclic code	correction(FEC)	control
cyclic redundancy	frame check sequence	trellis
check(CRC)	(FCS)	turbo code

Review Questions

1 What is a parity bit?
2 What is the CRC?
3 Why would you expect a CRC to detect more errors than a parity bit?
4 List three different ways in which the CRC algorithm can be described.
5 Is it possible to design an ECC that will correct some double bit errors but not all double bit errors? Why or why not?
6 In an (n, k) block ECC, what do n and k represent?
7 In an (n, k, K) convolutional code, what to n, k, and K represent?

8 What is a trellis in the context of a convolutional code?

9 What two key elements comprise error control?

10 Explain how Go-back-N ARQ works.

Problems

1 What is the purpose of using modulo 2 arithmetic rather than binary arithmetic in computing an FCS?

2 Consider a frame consisting of two characters of four bits each. Assume that the probability of bit error is 10^{-3} and that it is independent for each bit.

  a. What is the probability that the received frame contains at least one error?

  b. Now add a parity bit to each character. What is the probability?

3 Using the CRC-CCITT polynomial, generate the 16-bit CRC code for a message consisting of a 1 followed by 15 0s.

  a. Use long division.

  b. Use the shift register mechanism shown in Figure 8.3.

4 Explain in words why the shift register implementation of CRC will result in all 0s at the receiver if there are no errors. Demonstrate by example.

5 For $P = 110011$ and $M = 11100011$, find the CRC.

6 A CRC is constructed to generate a 4-bit FCS for an 11-bit message. The generator polynomial is $X^4 + X^3 + 1$.

  a. Draw the shift register circuit that would perform this task (see Figure 8.4).

  b. Encode the data bit sequence 10011011100 (leftmost bit is the least significant) using the generator polynomial and give the code word.

  c. Now assume that bit 7 (counting from the LSB) in the code word is in error and show that the detection algorithm detects the error.

7 A modified CRC procedure is commonly used in communications standards such as HDLC. It is defined as follows:

$$\frac{X^{16}M(X) + X^kL(X)}{P(X)} = Q + \frac{R(X)}{P(X)}$$

$$FCS = L(X) + R(X)$$

where

$$L(X) = X^{15} + X^{14} + X^{13} + \ldots + X + 1$$

and k is the number of bits being checked (address, control, and information fields).

  a. Describe in words the effect of this procedure.

  b. Explain the potential benefits.

  c. Show a shift register implementation for $P(X) = X^{16} + X^{12} + X^5 + 1$.

8 Figure 8.20 shows a polynomial division circuit that produces a result equivalent to that of the circuit in Figure 8.4.

  a. Using this alternative structure, draw a LFSR for dividing by $X^5 + X^5 + X^2 + 1$ that is equivalent to that of Figure 8.3a.

  b. Show the sequence of steps that produces the resulting CRC, following the method of Figure 8.3. You should end up with the same pattern, 01110, in the shift register at the end of the operation. *Hint:* Note that there is a delay in outputting the input bits of $(n - k)$ bits, so you need to perform $(n - k)$ additional shifts to produce the final result.

  c. An advantage of the structure in Figure 8.20, compared to that in Figure 8.4, is that it shows the correspondence with the long division process more clearly. Explain.

  d. What is a disadvantage of the structure in Figure 8.20?

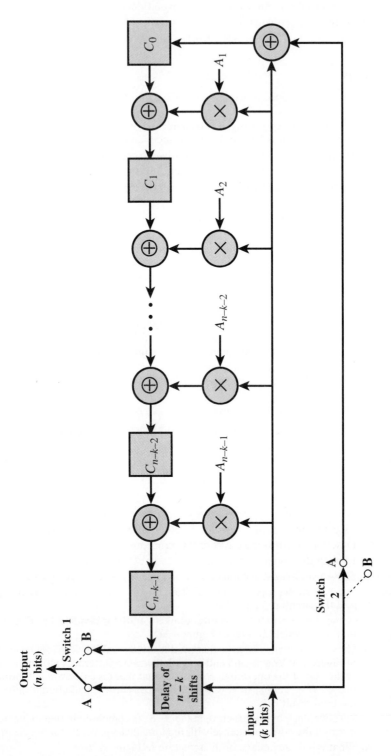

Figure 8.20 Another CRC Architecture to Implement Divisor
$1 + A_1X + A_2X^2 + \ldots + A_{n-1}X^{m-k-1} + X^{m-k}$

250

9 Calculate the Hamming pairwise distances among the following codewords:
a. 00000, 10101, 01010
b. 000000, 010101, 101010, 110110

10 Section 8.2 discusses block error correction codes that make a decision on the basis of minimum distance. That is, given a code consisting of s equally likely code words of length n, for each received sequence $\mathbf{v}$, the receiver selects the codeword $\mathbf{w}$ for which the distance $d(\mathbf{w}, \mathbf{v})$ is a minimum. We would like to prove that this scheme is "ideal" in the sense that the receiver always selects the codeword for which the probability of $\mathbf{w}$ given $\mathbf{v}$, $p(\mathbf{w} \mid \mathbf{v})$, is a maximum. Because all codewords are assumed equally likely, the codeword that maximizes $p(\mathbf{w} \mid \mathbf{v})$ is the same as the codeword that maximizes $p(\mathbf{v} \mid \mathbf{w})$.
a. In order that $\mathbf{w}$ be received as $\mathbf{v}$, there must be exactly $d(\mathbf{w}, \mathbf{v})$ errors in transmission, and these errors must occur in those bits where $\mathbf{w}$ and $\mathbf{v}$ disagree. Let β be the probability that a given bit is transmitted incorrectly and n be the length of a codeword. Write an expression for $p(\mathbf{v} \mid \mathbf{w})$ as a function of β, $d(\mathbf{w}, \mathbf{v})$, and n. *Hint:* The number of bits in error is $d(\mathbf{w}, \mathbf{v})$ and the number of bits not in error is $n - d(\mathbf{w}, \mathbf{v})$.
b. Now compare $p(\mathbf{v} \mid \mathbf{w}_1)$ and $p(\mathbf{v} \mid \mathbf{w}_2)$ for two different codewords $\mathbf{w}_1$ and $\mathbf{w}_1$ by calculating $p(\mathbf{v} \mid \mathbf{w}_1)/p(\mathbf{v} \mid \mathbf{w}_2)$.
c. Assume that $0 < \beta < 0.5$ and show that $p(\mathbf{v} \mid \mathbf{w}_1) > p(\mathbf{v} \mid \mathbf{w}_2)$ if and only if $d(\mathbf{v}, \mathbf{w}_1) < d(\mathbf{v}, \mathbf{w}_1)$. This proves that the codeword $\mathbf{w}$ that gives the largest value of $p(\mathbf{v} \mid \mathbf{w})$ is that word whose distance from $\mathbf{v}$ is a minimum.

11 Section 8.2 states that for a given positive integer t, if a code satisfies $d_{min} \geq 2t + 1$, then the code can correct all bit errors up to and including errors of t bits. Prove this assertion. *Hint:* Start by observing that for a codeword $\mathbf{w}$ to be decoded as another codeword $\mathbf{w}'$, the received sequence must be at least as close to $\mathbf{w}'$ as to $\mathbf{w}$.

12 For the Hamming code shown in Table 8.2, show the formulas used to calculate the check bits as functions of the data bits.

13 For the Hamming code shown in Table 8.2, show what happens when a check bit rather than a data bit is received in error.

14 Suppose an 8-bit data word stored in memory is 11000010. Using the Hamming algorithm, determine what check bits would be stored in memory with the data word. Show how you got your answer.

15 For the 8 bit word 00111001, the check bits stored with it would be 0111. Suppose when the word is read from memory, the check bits are calculated to be 1101. What is the data word that was read from memory?

16 How many check bits are needed if the Hamming error correction code is used to detect single bit errors in a 1024-bit data word?

17 Divide $f(X) = X^6 + 1$ by $g(X) = X^4 + X^3 + X + 1$. Verify the result by multiplying the quotient by $g(X)$ to recover $f(X)$.

18 For the example related to Table 8.3,
a. Draw the LFSR.
b. Using a layout similar to Figure 8.3b, show that the check bits for the data block 1010 are 001.

19 Using an interleaving structure of $n = 4$, $m = 6$ (Figure 8.8), demonstrate each of the following block interleaving characteristics:
a. Any burst of m contiguous channel bit errors results in isolated errors at the deinterleaver output that are separated from each other by at least n bits.
b. Any bm bursts of errors ($b > 1$) results in output bursts from the deinterleaver of no more than $\lceil b \rceil$ errors. Each output burst is separated from the other bursts by no less than $\lfloor b \rfloor$ bits. The notation $\lceil b \rceil$ means the smallest integer no less than b, and $\lfloor b \rfloor$ means the largest integer no greater than b.
c. A periodic sequence of single bit errors spaced m bits apart results in a single burst of errors of length n at the deinterleaver output.

    d. Not including channel propagation delay, the interleaver end-to-end delay is $2(n(m-1)+1)$. Only $(n(m-1)+1)$ cells need to be filled before transmission can begin and a corresponding number needs to be filled at the receiver before deinterleaving can begin.

20 Consider a convolutional encoder defined by $(v_{n1} = u_n \oplus u_{n-2})$ and $(v_{n2} = u_{n-1} \oplus u_{n-2})$.

    a. Draw a shift register implementation for this encoder similar to Figure 8.9a.

    b. Draw an state diagram for this encoder similar to Figure 8.9b.

    c. Draw a trellis diagram for this encoder similar to Figure 8.10.

21 For the encoder of Problem 20, assume that the shift register is initialized to all zeros and that after the transmission of the last information bit, two zero bits are transmitted.

    a. Why are the two extra bits needed?

    b. What is the encoded sequence corresponding to the information sequence 1101011, where the leftmost bit is the first bit presented to the encoder.?

22 The simplest form of flow control, known as **stop-and-wait flow control**, works as follows. A source entity transmits a frame. After the destination entity receives the frame, it indicates its willingness to accept another frame by sending back an acknowledgment to the frame just received. The source must wait until it receives the acknowledgment before sending the next frame. The destination can thus stop the flow of data simply by withholding acknowledgment. Consider a half-duplex point-to-point link using a stop-and-wait scheme, in which a series of messages is sent, with each message segmented into a number of frames. Ignore errors and frame overhead.

    a. What is the effect on line utilization of increasing the message size so that fewer messages will be required? Other factors remain constant.

    b. What is the effect on line utilization of increasing the number of frames for a constant message size?

    c. What is the effect on line utilization of increasing frame size?

23 In Figure 8.21, frames are generated at node A and sent to node C through node B. Determine the minimum data rate required between nodes B and C so that the buffers of node B are not flooded, based on the following:

- The data rate between A and B is 100 kbps.
- The propagation delay is 5 μs/km for both lines.
- There are full-duplex lines between the nodes.
- All data frames are 1000 bits long; ACK frames are separate frames of negligible length.
- Between A and B, a sliding-window protocol with a window size of 3 is used.
- Between B and C, stop-and-wait is used.
- There are no errors.

Hint: In order not to flood the buffers of B, the average number of frames entering and leaving B must be the same over a long interval.

24 A channel has a data rate of R bps and a propagation delay of t seconds per kilometer. The distance between the sending and receiving nodes is L kilometers. Nodes exchange fixed-size frames of B bits. Find a formula that gives the minimum sequence field size of the frame as a function of R, t, B, and L (considering maximum utilization). Assume that ACK frames are negligible in size and the processing at the nodes is instantaneous.

Figure 8.21 Configuration for Problem 22

25 Two neighboring nodes (A and B) use a sliding-window protocol with a 3-bit sequence number. As the ARQ mechanism, Go-back-N is used with a window size of 4. Assuming A is transmitting and B is receiving, show the window positions for the following succession of events:

a. Before A sends any frames

b. After A sends frames 0, 1, 2 and receives acknowledgment from B for 0 and 1

c. After A sends frames 3, 4, and 5 and B acknowledges 4 and the ACK is received by A

26 Two stations communicate via a 1-Mbps satellite link with a propagation delay of 270 ms. The satellite serves merely to retransmit data received from one station to another, with negligible switching delay. Using frames of 1024 bits with 3-bit sequence numbers, what is the maximum possible data throughput; that is, what is the throughput of data bits carried in frames?

PART THREE

Wireless Networking

CHAPTER 9

SATELLITE COMMUNICATIONS

S atellite communications is comparable in importance to optical fiber in the evolution of telecommunications and data communications. The first section of this chapter provides an introduction to key concerns and parameters related to the use of satellite antennas in wireless communications. The remainder of the chapter is devoted to a study of capacity allocation.

9.1 SATELLITE PARAMETERS AND CONFIGURATIONS

The heart of a satellite communications system is a satellite-based antenna in a stable orbit above the earth. In a satellite communications system, two or more stations on or near the earth communicate via one or more satellites that serve as relay stations in space. The antenna systems on or near the earth are referred to as **earth stations**. A transmission from an earth station to the satellite is referred to as **uplink**, whereas transmissions from the satellite to the earth station are **downlink**. The electronics in the satellite that takes an uplink signal and converts it to a downlink signal is called a **transponder**.

There are a number of different ways of categorizing communications satellites:

- **Coverage area:** global, regional, or national. The larger the area of coverage, the more satellites must be involved in a single networked system.
- **Service type:** fixed service satellite (FSS), broadcast service satellite (BSS), and mobile service satellite (MSS). This chapter is concerned with FSS and BSS types.
- **General usage:** commercial, military, amateur, experimental.

There are a number of differences between satellite-based and terrestrial wireless communications that affect design:

- The area of coverage of a satellite system far exceeds that of a terrestrial system. In the case of a geostationary satellite, a single antenna is visible to about one-fourth of the earth's surface.
- Spacecraft power and allocated bandwidth are limited resources that call for careful tradeoffs in earth station/satellite design parameters.
- Conditions between communicating satellites are more time invariant than those between satellite and earth station or between two terrestrial wireless antennas. Thus, satellite-to-satellite communication links can be designed with great precision.
- Transmission cost is independent of distance, within the satellite's area of coverage.
- Broadcast, multicast, and point-to-point applications are readily accommodated.
- Very high bandwidths or data rates are available to the user.
- Although satellite links are subject to short-term outages or degradations, the quality of transmission is normally extremely high.
- For a geostationary satellite, there is an earth-satellite-earth propagation delay of about one-fourth of a second.

- A transmitting earth station can in many cases receive its own transmission.

Satellite Orbits

Satellite orbits may be classified in a number of ways:

1. The orbit may be circular, with the center of the circle at the center of the earth, or elliptical, with the earth's center at one of the two foci of the ellipse.
2. A satellite may orbit around the earth in different planes. An **equatorial orbit** is directly above the earth's equator. A **polar orbit** passes over both poles. Other orbits are referred to as **inclined orbits**.
3. The altitude of communications satellites is classified as geostationary orbit (GEO), medium earth orbit (MEO), and low earth orbit (LEO), as explained subsequently.

Distance

Figure 9.1 illustrates the geometry that dictates satellite coverage. A key factor is the **elevation angle** θ of the earth station, which is the angle from the horizontal (i.e., a line tangent to the surface of the earth at the antenna's location) to the point on the center of the main beam of the antenna when the antenna is pointed directly at the satellite. To obtain maximum satellite coverage, we would like to use an elevation angle of $0°$, which would enable the satellite's coverage to extend to the optical horizon from the satellite in all directions. However, three problems dictate that the **minimum elevation angle** of the earth station's antenna be somewhat greater than $0°$ [INGL97]:

1. Buildings, trees, and other terrestrial objects that would block the line of sight. These may result in attenuation of the signal by absorption or in distortions due to multipath reflection.
2. Atmospheric attenuation is greater at low elevation angles because the signal traverses the atmosphere for longer distances the smaller the elevation angle.
3. Electrical noise generated by the earth's heat near its surface adversely affects reception.

For downlinks, current design practice is to use a minimum elevation angle of from $5°$ to $20°$ depending on frequency. For uplinks, the FCC requires a minimum elevation angle of $5°$.

The **coverage angle** β is a measure of the portion of the earth's surface visible to the satellite taking into account the minimum elevation angle; β defines a circle on the earth's surface centered on the point directly below the satellite. The following equation holds:[1]

---

[1]The first equation uses the law of sines, which states that in any triangle the sides are proportional to the sines of the opposite angles. The second equation uses that fact that the sum of the angles of a triangle equals π. The third equation uses the trigonometric identity $\sin(x) = \cos(x - \pi/2)$.

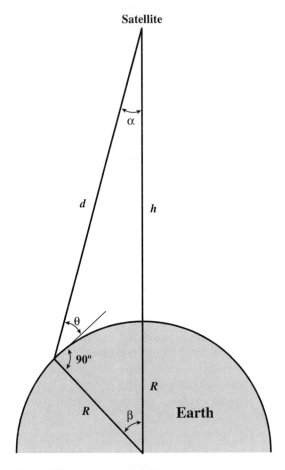

Figure 9.1   Coverage and Elevation Angles

$$\frac{R}{R + h} = \frac{\sin(\alpha)}{\sin\left(\theta + \dfrac{\pi}{2}\right)} = \frac{\sin\left(\dfrac{\pi}{2} - \beta - \theta\right)}{\sin\left(\theta + \dfrac{\pi}{2}\right)} = \frac{\cos(\beta + \theta)}{\cos(\theta)}$$

where

      R = earth's radius, 6370 km
      h = orbit height (altitude from point on earth directly below satellite)
      β = coverage angle
      θ = minimum elevation angle

The distance from the satellite to the furthest point of coverage is calculated as follows:

$$\frac{d}{R+h} = \frac{\sin(\beta)}{\sin\left(\theta + \dfrac{\pi}{2}\right)} = \frac{\sin\beta}{\cos(\theta)}$$

$$d = \frac{(R+h)\sin\beta}{\cos\theta} = \frac{R\sin\beta}{\sin\alpha}$$

(9.1)

The round-trip transmission delay is therefore in the range:

$$\frac{2h}{c} \le t \le \frac{2(R+h)\sin\beta}{c(\cos\theta)}$$

where c is the speed of light, approximately 3×10^8 m/s.

The coverage of a satellite is typically expressed as the diameter of the area covered, which is just $2\beta R$, with β expressed in radians.

Figure 9.2 shows the satellite period of rotation, coverage (in terms of terrestrial radius of coverage), and the maximum round-trip propagation delay.

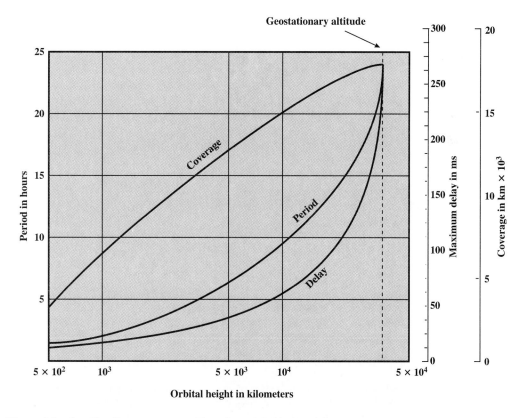

Figure 9.2 Satellite Parameters as a Function of Orbital Height

Geostationary Satellites

The most common type of communications satellite today is the geostationary (GEO) satellite, first proposed by the science fiction author Arthur C. Clarke, in a 1945 article in *Wireless World*. If the satellite is in a circular orbit 35,863 km above the earth's surface and rotates in the equatorial plane of the earth, it will rotate at exactly the same angular speed as the earth and will remain above the same spot on the equator as the earth rotates.[2] Figure 9.3 depicts the GEO orbit in scale with the

Orbit: 35,863 km
at the equator

◯ = Satellite

Figure 9.3   Geostationary Earth Orbit (GEO)

---

[2]The term *geosynchronous* is often used in place of *geostationary*. For purists, the difference is that a geosynchronous orbit is any circular orbit at an altitude of 35,863 km, and a geostationary orbit is a geosynchronous orbit with zero inclination, so the satellite hovers over one spot on the earth's equator.

size of the earth; the satellite symbols are intended to suggest that there are many satellites in GEO orbit, some of which are quite close together.

The GEO orbit has several advantages to recommend it:

- Because the satellite is stationary relative to the earth, there is no problem with frequency changes due to the relative motion of the satellite and antennas on earth (Doppler effect).
- Tracking of the satellite by its earth stations is simplified.
- At 35,863 km above the earth the satellite can communicate with roughly a fourth of the earth; three satellites in geostationary orbit separated by 120° cover most of the inhabited portions of the entire earth excluding only the areas near the north and south poles.

On the other hand, there are problems:

- The signal can get quite weak after traveling over 35,000 km.
- The polar regions and the far northern and southern hemispheres are poorly served by geostationary satellites.
- Even at the speed of light, about 300,000 km/s, the delay in sending a signal from a point on the equator beneath the satellite to the satellite and back is substantial.

The delay of communication between two locations on earth directly under the satellite is in fact $(2 \times 35,863)/300,000 \approx 0.24$ s. For other locations not directly under the satellite, the delay is even longer. If the satellite link is used for telephone communication, the added delay between when one person speaks and the other responds is increased twofold, to almost 0.5 s. This is definitely noticeable. Another feature of geostationary satellites is that they use their assigned frequencies over a very large area. For point-to-multipoint applications such as broadcasting TV programs, this can be desirable, but for point-to-point communications it is very wasteful of spectrum. Special spot and steered beam antennas, which restrict the area covered by the satellite's signal, can be used to control the "footprint" or signaling area. To solve some of these problems, orbits other than geostationary have been designed for satellites. *Low-earth-orbiting satellites (LEOS)* and *medium-earth-orbiting satellites (MEOS)* are important for third-generation personal communications.

LEO Satellites

LEOs (Figure 9.4a) have the following characteristics:

- Circular or slightly elliptical orbit at under 2000 km. Proposed and actual systems are in the range 500 to 1500 km.
- The orbit period is in the range of 1.5 to 2 hours.
- The diameter of coverage is about 8000 km.
- Round-trip signal propagation delay is less than 20 ms.

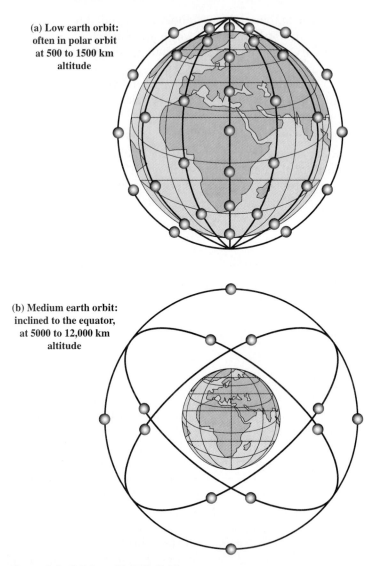

Figure 9.4 LEO and MEO Orbits

- The maximum time that the satellite is visible from a fixed point on earth (above the radio horizon) is up to 20 minutes.
- Because the motion of the satellite relative to a fixed point on earth is high, the system must be able to cope with large Doppler shifts, which change the frequency of the signal.
- The atmospheric drag on a LEO satellite is significant, resulting in gradual orbital deterioration.

Practical use of this system requires the multiple orbital planes be used, each with multiple satellites in orbit. Communication between two earth stations typically will involve handing off the signal from one satellite to another.

LEO satellites have a number of advantages over GEO satellites. In addition to the reduced propagation delay mentioned previously, a received LEO signal is much stronger than that of GEO signals for the same transmission power. LEO coverage can be better localized so that spectrum can be better conserved. For this reason, this technology is currently being proposed for communicating with mobile terminals and with personal terminals that need stronger signals to function. On the other hand, to provide broad coverage over 24 hours, many satellites are needed.

A number of commercial proposals have been made to use clusters of LEOs to provide communications services. These proposals can be divided into two categories:

- **Little LEOs:** Intended to work at communication frequencies below 1 GHz using no more than 5 MHz of bandwidth and supporting data rates up to 10 kbps. These systems are aimed at paging, tracking, and low-rate messaging. Orbcomm is an example of such a satellite system. It was the first (little) LEO in operation; its first two satellites were launched in April of 1995. It is designed for paging and burst communication and is optimized for handling small bursts of data from 6 to 250 bytes in length. It is used by businesses to track trailers, railcars, heavy equipment, and other remote and mobile assets. It can also be used to monitor remote utility meters and oil and gas storage tanks, wells, and pipelines. It can be used to stay in touch with remote workers anywhere in the world as well. It uses the frequencies 148.00 to 150.05 MHz to the satellites, and 137.00 to 138.00 from the satellites. It has well over 30 satellites in low earth orbit. It supports subscriber data rates of 2.4 kbps to the satellite and 4.8 kbps down.

- **Big LEOs:** Work at frequencies above 1 GHz and support data rates up to a few megabits per second. These systems tend to offer the same services as those of small LEOs, with the addition of voice and positioning services. Globalstar is one example of a Big LEO system. Its satellites are fairly rudimentary. Unlike some of the little LEO systems, it has no onboard processing or communications between satellites. Most processing is done by the system's earth stations. It uses CDMA as in the CDMA cellular standard. It uses the S-Band (about 2 GHz) for the downlink to mobile users. Globalstar is tightly integrated with traditional voice carriers. All calls must be processed through earth stations. The satellite constellation consists of 48 operating satellites and 8 spares. They are in 1413-km-high orbits.

MEO Satellites

MEOs (Figure 9.4b) have the following characteristics:

- Circular orbit at an altitude in the range 5000 to 12,000 km.
- The orbit period is about 6 hours.
- The diameter of coverage is from 10,000 to 15,000 km.
- Round-trip signal propagation delay is less than 50 ms.
- The maximum time that the satellite is visible from a fixed point on earth (above the radio horizon) is a few hours.

MEO satellites require much fewer handoffs than LEO satellites. While propagation delay to earth from such satellites and the power required are greater than for LEOs, they are still substantially less than for GEO satellites. New ICO, established in January 1995, proposed a MEO system. Launches began in 2000. Twelve satellites, including two spares, are planned in 10,400-km-high orbits. The satellites will be divided equally between two planes tilted 45° to the equator. Proposed applications are digital voice, data, facsimile, high-penetration notification, and messaging services.

Frequency Bands

Table 9.1 lists the frequency bands available for satellite communications. Note that increasing bandwidth is available in the higher-frequency bands. However, in general, the higher the frequency, the greater the effect of transmission impairments. The mobile satellite service (MSS) is allocated frequencies in the L- and S-bands. In these bands, compared to higher frequencies, there is a greater degree of refraction and greater penetration of physical obstacles, such as foliage and nonmetallic structures. These characteristics are desirable for mobile service. However, the L- and S-bands are also heavily used for terrestrial applications. Thus, there is intense competition among the various microwave services for L- and S-band capacity.

For any given frequency allocation for a service, there is an allocation of an uplink band and a downlink band, with the uplink band always of higher frequency. The higher frequency suffers greater spreading, or free space loss, than its lower-frequency counterpart. The earth station is capable of higher power, which helps to compensate for the poorer performance at higher frequency.

Transmission Impairments

The performance of a satellite link depends on three factors:

- Distance between earth station antenna and satellite antenna

Table 9.1 Frequency Bands for Satellite Communications

Band	Frequency Range	Total Bandwidth	General Application
L	1 to 2 GHz	1 GHz	Mobile satellite service (MSS)
S	2 to 4 GHz	2 GHz	MSS, NASA, deep space research
C	4 to 8 GHz	4 GHz	Fixed satellite service (FSS)
X	8 to 12.5 GHz	4.5 GHz	FSS military, terrestrial earth exploration, and meteorological satellites
Ku	12.5 to 18 GHz	5.5 GHz	FSS, broadcast satellite service (BSS)
K	18 to 26.5 GHz	8.5 GHz	BSS, FSS
Ka	26.5 to 40 GHz	13.5 GHz	FSS

- In the case of the downlink, terrestrial distance between earth station antenna and the "aim point" of the satellite
- Atmospheric attenuation

We look at each of these factors in turn.

Distance

Recall from Equation (5.2) that free space loss can be expressed as:

$$L_{dB} = 10 \log \frac{P_t}{P_r} = 20 \log \left(\frac{4\pi d}{\lambda} \right) = -20 \log(\lambda) + 20 \log(d) + 21.98 \text{ dB} \quad (9.2)$$

where

P_t = signal power at the transmitting antenna
P_r = signal power at the receiving antenna
λ = carrier wavelength
d = propagation distance between antennas

and d and λ are in the same units (e.g., meters).

The higher the frequency (shorter the wavelength), the greater the loss. For a GEO satellite, the free space loss at the equator is

$$L_{db} = -20 \log(\lambda) + 20 \log(35.863 \times 10^6) + 21.98 \text{ dB} = -20 \log(\lambda) + 173.07$$

Losses at points on the surface of the earth away from the equator but still visible from the satellite will be somewhat higher. The maximum distance (from the satellite to the horizon) for a GEO satellite is 42,711 km. At this distance, the free space loss is

$$L_{db} = -20 \log(\lambda) + 174.59$$

Figure 9.5 plots the attenuation as a function of frequency and orbital height.

Satellite Footprint

At microwave frequencies, which are used in satellite communications, highly directional antennas are used. Thus, the signal from a satellite is not isotropically broadcast but is aimed at a specific point on the earth, depending on which area of coverage is desired. The center point of that area will receive the highest radiated power, and the power drops off as you move away from the center point in any direction. This effect is typically displayed in a pattern known as a satellite footprint; an example is shown in Figure 9.6. The satellite footprint displays the effective radiated power of the antenna at each point, taking into account the signal power fed into the antenna and the directionality of the antenna. In the example figure, the power for Arkansas is +36 dBW and for Massachusetts is +32 dBW. The actual power received at any point on the footprint is found by subtracting the free space loss from the effective power figure.

Figure 9.5 Minimum Free Space Loss as a Function of Orbital Height

Atmospheric Attenuation

The primary causes of atmospheric attenuation are oxygen, which is of course always present, and water. Attenuation due to water is present in humid air and is more pronounced with fog and rain. Another factor that affects attenuation is the angle of elevation of the satellite from the earth station (angle θ in Figure 9.1). The smaller the angle of elevation, the more of the atmosphere that the signal must travel through. Finally, atmospheric attenuation depends on frequency. In general, the higher the frequency, the greater the effect. Figure 9.7 shows the typical amount of attenuation as a function of angle of elevation for frequencies in the C-band. Of

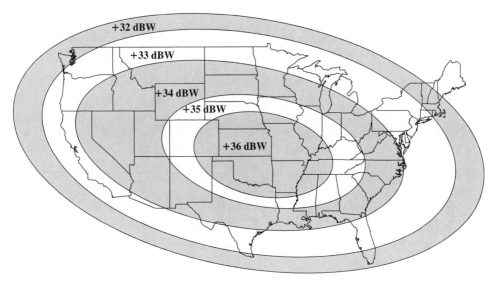

Figure 9.6 Typical Satellite Footprint

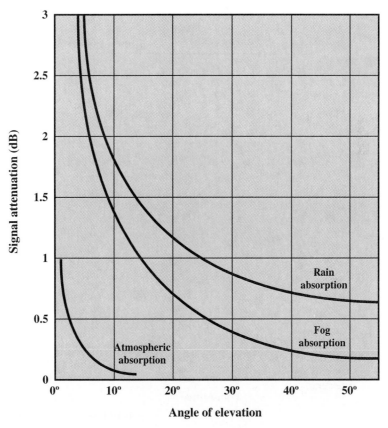

Figure 9.7 Signal Attenuation Due to Atmospheric Absorption (C-Band)

course, the attenuation due to fog and rain only occurs when those elements are present in the atmosphere.

Satellite Network Configurations

Figure 9.8 depicts in a general way two common configurations for satellite communication. In the first, the satellite is being used to provide a point-to-point link between two distant ground-based antennas. In the second, the satellite provides communications between one ground-based transmitter and a number of ground-based receivers.

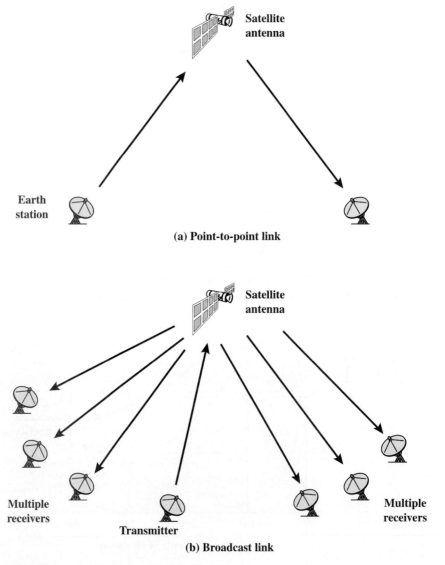

Figure 9.8 Satellite Communication Configurations

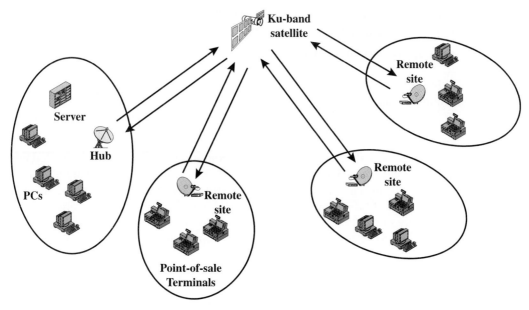

Figure 9.9 Typical VSAT Configuration

A variation on the second configuration is one in which there is two-way communication among earth stations, with one central hub and many remote stations. This type of configuration, depicted in Figure 9.9, is used with the very small aperture terminal (VSAT) system. A number of subscriber stations are equipped with low-cost VSAT antennas. Using some discipline, these stations share a satellite transmission capacity for transmission to a hub station. The hub station can exchange messages with each of the subscribers and can relay messages between subscribers.

9.2 CAPACITY ALLOCATION—FREQUENCY DIVISION

Typically, a single GEO satellite will handle a rather large bandwidth (e.g., 500 MHz) and divide it into a number of channels of smaller bandwidth (e.g. 40 MHz). Within each of these channels, there is a capacity allocation task to be performed. In some instances, such as TV broadcasting or a single 50-Mbps digital data stream, the entire channel is dedicated to a single user or application. With these exceptions, however, the cost-effective use of the satellite requires that each channel be shared by many users. Hence, the task is fundamentally one of multiplexing, which is a concept introduced in Chapter 2. In so.me cases, the allocation is carried out by a centralized control, usually by the satellite; but in other cases, the allocation is a distributed function carried out by the earth stations. We will see examples of both.

All of the allocation strategies fall into one of three categories:

- Frequency division multiple access (FDMA)
- Time division multiple access (TDMA)
- Code division multiple access (CDMA)

In this section and the next, we examine FDMA and TDMA. CDMA was discussed in Chapter 7.

Frequency Division Multiplexing

As was mentioned, the overall capacity of a communications satellite is divided into a number of channels. This is a top level of FDM, with further capacity allocation carried out within each channel. Figure 9.10 is an example of an FDM scheme, which is typical of GEO communications satellites; this particular allocation is used in the Galaxy satellites from PanAmSat.[3] The satellite uses C-band frequencies and provides a 500-MHz bandwidth, which is broken up into 24 40-MHz channels. The satellite is able to squeeze 24 channels into the 500 MHz by means of **frequency reuse:** Each frequency assignment is used by two carriers with orthogonal polarization. Each 40-MHz channel includes a 4-MHz guardband, so each channel is actually 36 MHz wide. When used in a point-to-point configuration (Figure 9.8a), each channel could be used for one of a number of alternative purposes. Examples include the following:

Figure 9.10   Typical Satellite Transponder Frequency Plan for the Downlink Channels (for the uplink plan, add 2225 MHz to the numbers given above)

---

[3]PanAmSat is the largest satellite operator in the world. It is a private corporation providing satellite communications capacity worldwide.

- 1200 voice-frequency (VF) voice channels
- One 50-Mbps data stream
- 16 channels of 1.544 Mbps each
- 400 channels of 64 kbps each
- 600 channels of 40 kbps each
- One analog video signal
- Six to nine digital video signals

The bandwidth for an analog video signal may seem surprisingly high. To determine it, we need to use Carson's rule [(Equation (6.16)], discussed in Chapter 6. The bandwidth of the video signal combined with the audio signal is approximately 6.8 MHz. This is then translated to a carrier at 6 GHz using frequency modulation (FM). The peak deviation of the signal using this process turns out to be $\Delta F = 12.5$ MHz. The transmission bandwidth is

$$B_T = 2\Delta F + 2B = 2(12.5 + 6.8) = 38.6 \text{ MHz}$$

which is accepted by the 36-MHz transponder.

For digital video, the use of compression can result in a data rate for a single channel in the range of 3 to 5 Mbps, depending on the amount of motion in the video.

Frequency Division Multiple Access

The discussion in the preceding subsection suggests that the satellite is used as in intermediate device providing, in effect, a point-to-point link between two earth stations. Because of the wide area coverage of the satellite, this is not necessarily the case. For example, the INTELSAT[4] series satellites allow a single 36-MHz channel to be divided using FDM into a number of smaller channels, each of which uses FM. Each of the smaller channels in turn carries a number of voice frequency (VF) signals using FDM. The ability of multiple earth stations to access the same channel is referred to as FDMA (frequency division multiple access).

The number of subchannels provided within a satellite channel via FDMA is limited by three factors:

- Thermal noise
- Intermodulation noise
- Crosstalk

These terms are defined and discussed in Chapter 5. The first two factors work in opposite directions. With too little signal strength, the transmitted signal will be

---

[4]INTELSAT (International Telecommunications Satellite Organization) is a consortium of national satellite providers established under international treaty. INTELSAT purchases spacecraft based on the global demand for telephone and TV services; it operates as a wholesaler, providing space segment services to end users who operate their own earth stations. COMSAT is the U.S. member. INTELSAT is currently in the process of privatization.

corrupted by background noise. With too much signal strength, nonlinear effects in the satellite's amplifiers result in high intermodulation noise. Crosstalk stems from a desire to increase capacity by reusing frequencies and limits but does not eliminate that practice. A frequency band can be reused if antennas that can radiate two polarized signals of the same frequency (cochannels) in orthogonal planes are employed. Again if signal strength is too high, cochannel interference becomes significant.

Two forms of FDMA are possible:

- **Fixed-assignment multiple access (FAMA):** The assignment of capacity within the overall satellite channel is distributed in a fixed manner among multiple stations. This often results in significant underuse of the capacity, as demand may fluctuate.
- **Demand-assignment multiple access (DAMA):** The capacity assignment is changed as needed to respond optimally to demand changes among the multiple stations.

FAMA-FDMA

Figure 9.11 is a specific example of FAMA-FDMA, with seven earth stations sharing the 36-MHz uplink capacity; a similar downlink diagram can be drawn. Station A is assigned the 5-MHz bandwidth from 6237.5 to 6242.5 MHz, in which it can transmit 60 VF channels using FDM-FM. That is, FDM is used to carry the 60 channels, and FM is used to modulate the channels onto the carrier frequency of 6240 MHz. The figure indicate that station A has traffic for other station as follows: 24 channels to B, 24 channels to D, and 12 channels to E. The remaining spectrum of the 36-MHz channel is divided among the other earth stations according to their traffic needs. This example brings up several instructive points:

- The scheme illustrates both FAMA and FDMA. The term *FAMA* refers to the fact that the logical links between stations are preassigned. Thus in Figure 9.11, it appears to station A that it has three direct point-to-point links, one each to B (24 channels), D (24 channels), and E (12 channels). The term *FDMA* refers to the fact that multiple stations are accessing the satellite link by using different frequency bands.
- Although an earth station may transmit only one carrier up to the satellite (e.g., station A transmits at 6.24 GHz with a bandwidth of 5 MHz), it must be able to receive at least one carrier for each remote location with which it wishes to communicate (e.g., A must receive three carriers, parts of the transmission of B, D, and E).
- The satellite performs no switching function. Although it is receiving portions of the 36-MHz channel from various sources, it simply accepts signals across that spectrum, translates them to the 4-Ghz band, and retransmits them.
- Considerable bandwidth is used. For example, station A has 60 VF channels to transmit, which occupy only 240 kHz (one VF channel = 4 kHz). Yet the satellite bandwidth allocation is 5 MHz. This is due to the use of FM (rather than AM) to maintain signal over the long distance of the satellite link and to minimize satellite power requirements.

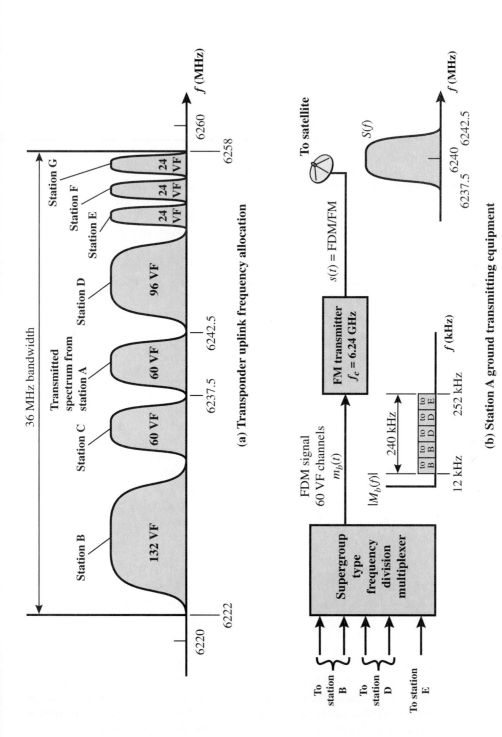

(a) Transponder uplink frequency allocation

(b) Station A ground transmitting equipment

Figure 9.11 Fixed-Assignment FDMA Format for Satellite Communication [COUC01]

273

DAMA-FDMA

The FAMA-FDMA scheme just described is not efficient. Typically, in the C-band, each channel has a usable bandwidth of 36 MHz. One INTELSAT FDMA scheme divides this into 7 5-MHz blocks, each of which carries a group of 60 VF channels, for a total of 420 channels. Our example (Figure 9.11) also carries 420 channels. When the bandwidth is divided into 14 2.5-MHz subchannels, two groups of 48 VF channels can be carried in each channel for a total of 336 channels. It turns out to be more efficient to avoid groupings altogether and simply to divide the 36-MHz bandwidth into individual VF channels. This technique is known as **single channel per carrier** (SCPC).

SCPC is currently provided in the C-band. A single 36-MHz channel is subdivided into 800 45-kHz analog channels, each dedicated to a simplex VF link, using FM. There is also digital SCPC, using QPSK which provides 64-kbps service in the same 45-kHz bandwidth, enough for digitized voice. With FAMA, pairs of channels (for full duplex) are assigned to pairs of earth stations. Typically, each earth station is multiplexed, supporting a small number of user stations. With multiple user stations per earth station, a high degree of connectivity is achieved even with FAMA. As with conventional FDMA, the satellite accepts frequencies across the entire 36-MHz channel, translates them to the 4-GHz band, and broadcasts the channel to all stations.

SCPC is attractive for remote areas where there are few user stations near each site. Whereas FDMA is used as a trunk facility in the long-haul telecommunication system, SCPC provides direct end-user service. Although SCPC is more efficient of bandwidth than FDMA, it does suffer from the inefficiency of fixed assignment. This is especially unsuitable in very remote areas where it is typical that each earth station serves one or a very few user stations. To achieve greater efficiency, DAMA is used. With DAMA, the set of subchannels in a channel is treated as a pool of available links. To establish a full-duplex link between two earth stations, a pair of subchannels is dynamically assigned on demand.

The first commercially available DAMA SCPC system was SPADE (**s**ingle channel per carrier, **p**ulse code modulation, multiple-**a**ccess, **d**emand-assignment **e**quipment), introduced in the early 1970s and currently available on INTELSAT satellites. Each subchannel carries a 64-kbps QPSK signal, which occupies 38 kHz, plus a 7-kHz guardband. Typically, the signal is used to carry PCM voice traffic. With control overhead, explained later, a total of 794 subchannels are available (Figure 9.12a). These subchannels are paired such that two channels 18.045 MHz apart are always used to form a full-duplex circuit (e.g., 3 and 404, 4 and 405, 399 and 800). In addition, there is a 160-kHz common-signaling channel (CSC) that carries a 128-kbps PSK signal.

Demand assignment is performed in a distributed fashion, by the earth station, using the CSC. The CSC is used to transmit a repetitive TDM frame as shown in Figure 9.12c (compare Figure 2.13). A frame consists of 50 slots, the first of which is devoted to a preamble pattern for synchronization. The remaining slots are permanently assigned to 49 stations. These stations have the privilege of forming full-duplex circuits on demand. This is accomplished as follows. Assume that station S_i wishes to establish a circuit with S_j. S_i selects a subchannel randomly from the available idle channels and transmits the subchannel identifier plus the address of station S_j in the S_i time slot. S_j will hear this request on the downlink about 0.25 s later. Assuming that the subchannel is still available and S_j is available, S_j transmits an

(a) Frequency allocation

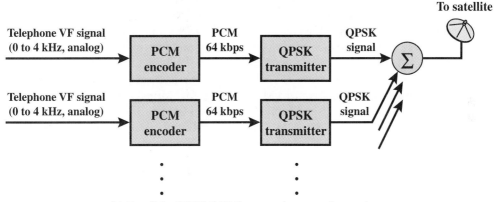

(b) Possible QPSK SCPC transmitter configuration

(c) TDMA CSC frame format

Figure 9.12 SPADE Satellite Communication System for Switched SCPC Service [COUC01]

acknowledgment in its own time slot, which is heard by S_i another quarter second later. When the call is complete, disconnect information is transmitted in the time slot of one of the stations to inform the others that the subchannel is again idle.

Because only 49 stations can participate in this scheme, most of the subchannels are not required for demand assignment. These are used for ordinary FAMA SCPC.

9.3 CAPACITY ALLOCATION—TIME DIVISION

Although FDM techniques are still quite common in satellite transmission, TDM techniques are in increasingly widespread use. The reasons include the following:

- The continuing drop in the cost of digital components
- The advantages of digital techniques, including the use of error correction
- The increased efficiency of TDM due to the lack of intermodulation noise

As with FDM, all of the techniques to be discussed provide for multiple access and include FAMA-TDMA and DAMA-TDMA. FAMA-TDMA is in essence the same as synchronous TDM (Section 2.5). Transmission is in the form of a repetitive sequence of frames, each of which is divided into a number of time slots. Each slot position across the sequence of frames is dedicated to a particular transmitter. Frame periods range from 100 μs to over 2 ms and consist of from 3 to over 100 slots. Data rates range from 10 Mbps to over 100 Mbps.

Figure 9.13 depicts a typical frame format (compare Figure 2.13b). Typically, a frame begins with two reference bursts to define the beginning of the frame. Two bursts are used, provided by two different earth stations, so that the system can continue to function even if one reference station is lost due to malfunction. Each reference burst begins with a carrier and bit timing recovery pattern, which is a unique pattern that allows all stations to synchronize to a master clock. Each of the N stations is assigned one or more slots in the frame. The station uses an assigned slot to transmit a burst of data, consisting of a preamble and user information. The preamble contains control and timing information, plus the identification of the destination station. The individual bursts are separated by guard times to ensure that there is no overlap.

Figure 9.14 depicts the operation of FAMA-TDMA. Individual earth stations take turns using the uplink channel and may put a burst of data in the assigned time slot. The satellite repeats all incoming transmissions, which are broadcast to all stations. Thus, all stations must know not only which time slot to use for transmission, but which time slot to use for reception. The satellite also repeats the reference burst, and all stations synchronize on the reception of that burst.

Each of the repetitive time slots is a channel and is independent of the other channels. Hence it can be used in any way that is required by the transmitting station. For example, a form of switching can be achieved by including an address field in each time slot. In such a case, although the transmitting slot is dedicated, a number of stations could read the data in each downlink slot looking for data addressed to them. Another technique is for a transmitting earth station to divide its time slots into subslots so that multiple subchannels of data can be sent in one TDMA channel.

Ordinary TDMA is more efficient than ordinary FDMA because the guard times and control bits of TDMA utilize less capacity than the guard bands of FDMA. This is illustrated in Figure 9.15. Note the dramatic drop in capacity of FDMA as the number of channels increase. By contrast, TDMA drops much more slowly as the number of time slots (channels) increase. The use of a long frame time also increase efficiency. For comparison, an SCPC system provides a constant capacity of 800 channels whether its bandwidth is divided among many or a few earth stations.

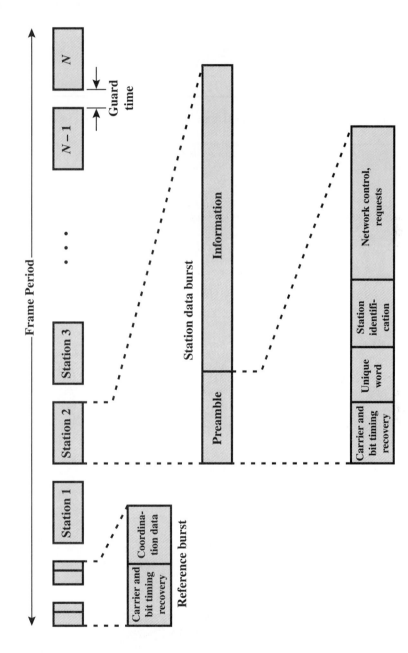

Figure 9.13 Example of TDMA Frame Format

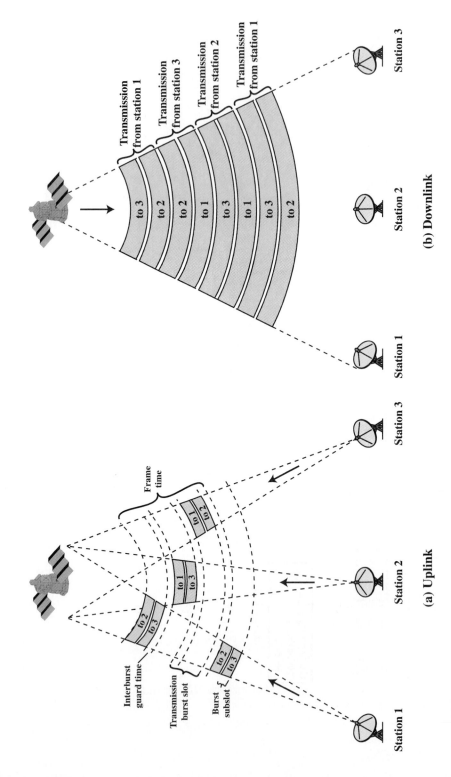

Figure 9.14 FAMA-TDMA Operation

(a) Uplink

(b) Downlink

Station 1

Station 2

Station 3

Frame time

Interburst guard time

Transmission burst slot

Burst subslot

to 1
to 2

to 1
to 3

to 2
to 3

to 2
to 3

Transmission from station 1

Transmission from station 3

Transmission from station 2

Transmission from station 1

to 3
to 2
to 2
to 1
to 3
to 1
to 3
to 2

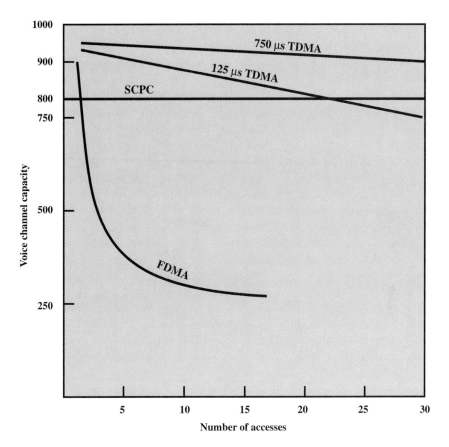

Figure 9.15 Relative Efficiency for Various Satellite Capacity Allocation Schemes [EDEL82]

Even greater efficiencies can be achieved at the higher frequency bands (Ku- and K-bands). At these frequencies, satellite transmission beams can be quite narrowly focused, allowing multiple beams on the same frequency transmitted to different areas. Thus a satellite can service a number of areas, each containing a number of earth stations. Communication among the stations within a single area is accomplished with ordinary FAMA-TDMA. Moreover, communication among stations in different areas can be achieved if the satellite has the ability to switch time slots from one beam to another. This is known as satellite-switched TDMA (SS/TDMA).

Figure 9.16 shows a simple SS/TDMA system serving two areas, each with two stations. As with ordinary TDMA, only one station at a time may transmit within an area. Thus, within area A, either station 1 or 2 may transmit in any given time slot. Similarly, either station 3 or station 4 may transmit in area B at any one time. Stations from the two areas do not interfere either through the use of polarized signals or different frequencies. At the satellite, data that are received are immediately retransmitted on a downlink frequency. Two separate downlink beams are used. The satellite contains a switch for interconnecting input beams and output beams. The connections through the switch may change over time. In the figure, downlink beam

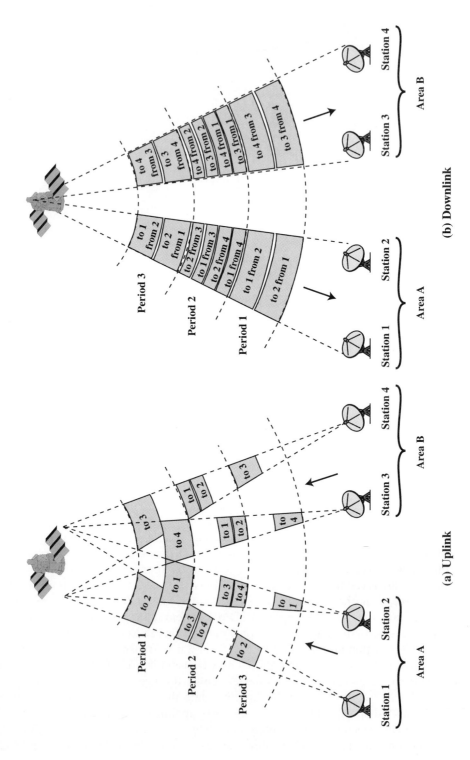

Figure 9.16 SS/TDMA Operation

Table 9.2 SS-TDMA Modes (three beams)

	Output					
Input	**Mode 1**	**Mode 2**	**Mode 3**	**Mode 4**	**Mode 5**	**Mode 6**
A	A	A	B	C	B	C
B	B	C	C	A	C	B
C	C	B	A	B	A	A

A repeats uplink beam A during periods 1 and 3 and repeats uplink beam B during period 2. Thus any station in any area can send data to any other station in any area.

For a satellite serving N areas, there are N TDM input streams. At any given time, the switch is configured to route these uplink beams in a particular fashion to the N downlink beams. Each configuration is referred to as a *mode* and $N!$ different modes are required for full connectivity. Table 9.2 Shows the modes for a three-area system. For example, stations in area A can communicate with each other during modes 1 and 2, communicate with stations in area B during modes 3 and 5, and so on. The satellite will change from mode to mode periodically. At most, a mode change would occur once per slot time. The mode pattern and duration are normally adjustable by ground command to meet changing traffic requirements.

Finally, DAMA techniques are employed with TDMA satellite schemes. The SS/TDMA system is to some extent a DAMA system if the mode pattern can be changed by ground command. More commonly DAMA in the TDM context refers to multiple-access techniques for sharing a single channel. With such techniques, the ground stations typically cooperate to use the channel.

9.4 RECOMMENDED READING AND WEB SITES

A readable, relatively nontechnical overview of satellite communications is [INGL97]. [ELBE99] provides more technical detail. An excellent technical treatment is provided in [FREE97].

ELBE99 Elbert, B. *Introduction to Satellite Communication*. Boston: Artech House, 1999.
FREE97 Freeman, R. *Radio System Design for Telecommunications*. New York: Wiley, 1997.
INGL97 Inglis, A., and Luther, A. *Satellite Technology: An Introduction*. Boston: Focal Press, 1997.

 Recommended Web sites:

- **Lloyd Wood's satellite Web page:** An excellent overview of satellite communications, with lots of links.
- **Satellite Industry Association:** Trade organization representing U.S. space and communications companies in the commercial satellite arena. Lots of links.

9.5 KEY TERMS, REVIEW QUESTIONS, AND PROBLEMS

Key Terms

broadcast service satellite (BSS) communications satellite demand assignment multiple access (DAMA) downlink earth station fixed assignment multiple access (FAMA)	fixed service satellite (FSS) frequency division multiple access (FDMA) frequency reuse geostationary (GEO) geosynchronous (GEO) low earth orbit (LEO) medium earth orbit (MEO) mobile service satellite (MSS) polarization	satellite satellite footprint satellite orbit satellite-switched TDMA (SS/TDMA) single channel per carrier (SCPC) time division multiple access (TDMA) transponder uplink

Review Questions

1 List three different ways of categorizing communications satellites.

2 What are some key differences between satellite-based and terrestrial wireless communications?

3 List three different ways of classifying satellite orbits.

4 Explain what GEO, LEO, and MEO satellites are (including what the acronyms stand for). Compare the three types with respect to factors such as size and shape of orbits, signal power, frequency reuse, propagation delay, number of satellites for global coverage, and handoff frequency.

5 Under what circumstances would you use GEO, LEO, and MEO satellites, respectively?

6 What are three key factors related to satellite communications performance?

7 What are the primary causes of atmospheric attenuation for satellite communications?

8 What are three factors that limit the number of subchannels that can be provided within a satellite channel via FDMA?

Problems

1 For the transponder scheme of Figure 9.10, what is the percentage bandwidth used for the guardbands?

2 For the TDMA frame of Figure 9.13, assume the following parameters. The frame length is 2 ms. Data are encoded using QPSK with a signal element rate of 60.136 Mbaud. All traffic bursts are of equal length of 16,512 bits. The reference burst has length 576 bits, the preamble is 560 bits, and the guard interval is 24 bits. Assume that there are two participating reference stations, so that two reference bursts are required.

   a. Determine the maximum number of earth stations the system can serve.

   b. What is the frame efficiency (fraction of frame carrying user data rather than overhead bits)?

CHAPTER 10

CELLULAR WIRELESS NETWORKS

O f all the tremendous advances in data communications and telecommunications, perhaps the most revolutionary is the development of cellular networks. Cellular technology is the foundation of mobile wireless communications and supports users in locations that are not easily served by wired networks. Cellular technology is the underlying technology for mobile telephones, personal communications systems, wireless Internet and wireless Web applications, and much more.

We begin this chapter with a look at the basic principles used in all cellular networks. Then we look at specific cellular technologies and standards, which are conveniently grouped into three generations. The first-generation is analog based and, while still widely used, is passing from the scene. The dominant technology today is the digital second-generation systems. Finally, third-generation high-speed digital systems have begun to emerge.

10.1 PRINCIPLES OF CELLULAR NETWORKS

Cellular radio is a technique that was developed to increase the capacity available for mobile radio telephone service. Prior to the introduction of cellular radio, mobile radio telephone service was only provided by a high-power transmitter/receiver. A typical system would support about 25 channels with an effective radius of about 80 km. The way to increase the capacity of the system is to use lower-power systems with shorter radius and to use numerous transmitters/receivers. We begin this section with a look at the organization of cellular systems and then examine some of the details of their implementation.

Cellular Network Organization

The essence of a cellular network is the use of multiple low-power transmitters, on the order of 100 W or less. Because the range of such a transmitter is small, an area can be divided into cells, each one served by its own antenna. Each cell is allocated a band of frequencies and is served by a **base station**, consisting of transmitter, receiver, and control unit. Adjacent cells are assigned different frequencies to avoid interference or crosstalk. However, cells sufficiently distant from each other can use the same frequency band.

The first design decision to make is the shape of cells to cover an area. A matrix of square cells would be the simplest layout to define (Figure 10.1a). However, this geometry is not ideal. If the width of a square cell is d, then a cell has four neighbors at a distance d and four neighbors at a distance $\sqrt{2}d$. As a mobile user within a cell moves toward the cell's boundaries, it is best if all of the adjacent antennas are equidistant. This simplifies the task of determining when to switch the user to an adjacent antenna and which antenna to choose. A hexagonal pattern provides for equidistant antennas (Figure 10.1b). The radius of a hexagon is defined to be the radius of the circle that circumscribes it (equivalently, the distance from the center to each vertex; also equal to the length of a side of a hexagon). For a cell radius R, the distance between the cell center and each adjacent cell center is $d = \sqrt{3}R$

In practice, a precise hexagonal pattern is not used. Variations from the ideal are due to topographical limitations, local signal propagation conditions, and practical limitation on siting antennas.

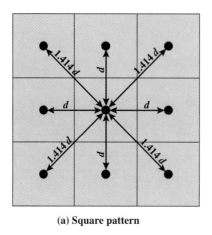

(a) Square pattern   (b) Hexagonal pattern

Figure 10.1   Cellular Geometries

With a wireless cellular system, you are limited in how often you can use the same frequency for different communications because the signals, not being constrained, can interfere with one another even if geographically separated. Systems supporting a large number of communications simultaneously need mechanisms to conserve spectrum.

Frequency Reuse

In a cellular system, each cell has a base transceiver. The transmission power is carefully controlled (to the extent that it is possible in the highly variable mobile communication environment) to allow communication within the cell using a given frequency while limiting the power at that frequency that escapes the cell into adjacent ones. The objective is to use the same frequency in other nearby cells, thus allowing the frequency to be used for multiple simultaneous conversations. Generally, 10 to 50 frequencies are assigned to each cell, depending on the traffic expected.

The essential issue, of course, is to determine how many cells must intervene between two cells using the same frequency so that the two cells do not interfere with each other. Various patterns of frequency reuse are possible. Figure 10.2 shows some examples. If the pattern consists of N cells and each cell is assigned the same number of frequencies, each cell can have K/N frequencies, where K is the total number of frequencies allotted to the system. For AMPS, $K = 395$, and $N = 7$ is the smallest pattern that can provide sufficient isolation between two uses of the same frequency. This implies that there can be at most 57 frequencies per cell on average.

In characterizing frequency reuse, the following parameters are commonly used:

D = minimum distance between centers of cells that use the same band of frequencies (called cochannels)

R = radius of a cell

d = distance between centers of adjacent cells ($d = \sqrt{3}R$)

N = number of cells in a repetitious pattern (each cell in the pattern uses a unique band of frequencies), termed the **reuse factor**

Circle with radius D

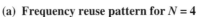

(a) **Frequency reuse pattern for $N = 4$**   (b) **Frequency reuse pattern for $N = 7$**

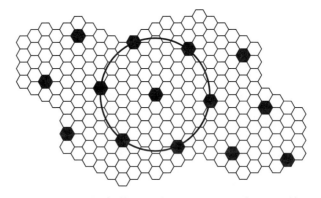

(c) **Black cells indicate a frequency reuse for $N = 19$**

Figure 10.2   Frequency Reuse Patterns

In a hexagonal cell pattern, only the following values of N are possible:

$$N = I^2 + J^2 + (I \times J), \quad I, J = 0, 1, 2, 3, \ldots$$

Hence, possible values of N are 1, 3, 4, 7, 9, 12, 13, 16, 19, 21, etc. The following relationship holds:

$$\frac{D}{R} = \sqrt{3N}$$

This can also be expressed as $D/d = \sqrt{N}$.

Increasing Capacity

In time, as more customers use the system, traffic may build up so that there are not enough frequencies assigned to a cell to handle its calls. A number of approaches have been used to cope with this situation, including the following:

- **Adding new channels:** Typically, when a system is set up in a region, not all of the channels are used, and growth and expansion can be managed in an orderly fashion by adding new channels.
- **Frequency borrowing:** In the simplest case, frequencies are taken from adjacent cells by congested cells. The frequencies can also be assigned to cells dynamically.
- **Cell splitting:** In practice, the distribution of traffic and topographic features is not uniform, and this presents opportunities of capacity increase. Cells in areas of high usage can be split into smaller cells. Generally, the original cells are about 6.5 to 13 km in size. The smaller cells can themselves be split; however, 1.5-km cells are close to the practical minimum size as a general solution (but see the subsequent discussion of microcells). To use a smaller cell, the power level used must be reduced to keep the signal within the cell. Also, as the mobile units move, they pass from cell to cell, which requires transferring of the call from one base transceiver to another. This process is called a *handoff*. As the cells get smaller, these handoffs become much more frequent. Figure 10.3 indicates schematically how cells can be divided to provide more capacity. A radius reduction by a factor of F reduces the coverage area and increases the required number of base stations by a factor of F^2.
- **Cell sectoring:** With cell sectoring, a cell is divided into a number of wedge-shaped sectors, each with its own set of channels, typically 3 or 6 sectors per cell. Each sector is assigned a separate subset of the cell's channels, and directional antennas at the base station are used to focus on each sector.
- **Microcells:** As cells become smaller, antennas move from the tops of tall buildings or hills, to the tops of small buildings or the sides of large buildings, and finally to lamp posts, where they form microcells. Each decrease in cell size is accompanied by a reduction in the radiated power levels from the base stations and the mobile units. Microcells are useful in city streets in congested areas, along highways, and inside large public buildings.

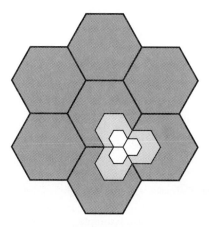

Figure 10.3   Cell Splitting

Table 10.1   Typical Parameters for Macrocells and Microcells [ANDE95]

	Macrocell	**Microcell**
Cell radius	1 to 20 km	0.1 to 1 km
Transmission power	1 to 10 W	0.1 to 1 W
Average delay spread	0.1 to 10 μs	10 to 100 ns
Maximum bit rate	0.3 Mbps	1 Mbps

Table 10.1 suggests typical parameters for traditional cells, called macrocells, and microcells with current technology. The average delay spread refers to multi-path delay spread (i.e., the same signal follows different paths and there is a time delay between the earliest and latest arrival of the signal at the receiver). As indicated, the use of smaller cells enables the use of lower power and provides superior propagation conditions.

Example. [HAAS00]. Assume a system of 32 cells with a cell radius of 1.6 km, a total of 32 cells, a total frequency bandwidth that supports 336 traffic channels, and a reuse factor of $N = 7$. If there are 32 total cells, what geographic area is covered, how many channels are there per cell, and what is the total number of concurrent calls that can be handled? Repeat for a cell radius of 0.8 km and 128 cells.

Figure 10.4a shows an approximately square pattern. The area of a hexagon of radius R is $1.5R^2\sqrt{3}$. A hexagon of radius 1.6 km has an area of 6.65 km^2, and the total area covered is $6.65 \times 32 = 213$ km^2. For $N = 7$, the number of channels per cell is $336/7 = 48$, for a total channel capacity of $48 \times 32 = 1536$ channels. For the layout of Figure 10.4b, the area covered is $1.66 \times 128 = 213$ km^2. The number of channels per cell is $336/7 = 48$, for a total channel capacity of $48 \times 128 = 6144$ channels.

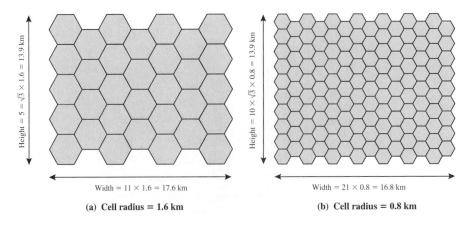

(a) Cell radius = 1.6 km   (b) Cell radius = 0.8 km

Figure 10.4   Frequency Reuse Example

Operation of Cellular Systems

Figure 10.5 shows the principal elements of a cellular system. In the approximate center of each cell is a base station (BS). The BS includes an antenna, a controller, and a number of transceivers, for communicating on the channels assigned to that cell. The controller is used to handle the call process between the mobile unit and the rest of the network. At any time, a number of mobile user units may be active and moving about within a cell, communicating with the BS. Each BS is connected to a mobile telecommunications switching office (MTSO), with one MTSO serving multiple BSs. Typically, the link between an MTSO and a BS is by a wire line, although a wireless link is also possible. The MTSO connects calls between mobile units. The MTSO is also connected to the public telephone or telecommunications network and can make a connection between a fixed subscriber to the public network and a mobile subscriber to the cellular network. The MTSO assigns the voice channel to each call, performs handoffs (discussed subsequently), and monitors the call for billing information.

The use of a cellular system is fully automated and requires no action on the part of the user other than placing or answering a call. Two types of channels are available between the mobile unit and the base station (BS): control channels and traffic channels. **Control channels** are used to exchange information having to do with setting up and maintaining calls and with establishing a relationship between a mobile unit and the nearest BS. **Traffic channels** carry a voice or data connection between users. Figure 10.6 illustrates the steps in a typical call between two mobile users within an area controlled by a single MTSO:

- **Mobile unit initialization:** When the mobile unit is turned on, it scans and selects the strongest setup control channel used for this system (Figure 10.6a). Cells with different frequency bands repetitively broadcast on different setup channels. The receiver selects the strongest setup channel and monitors that

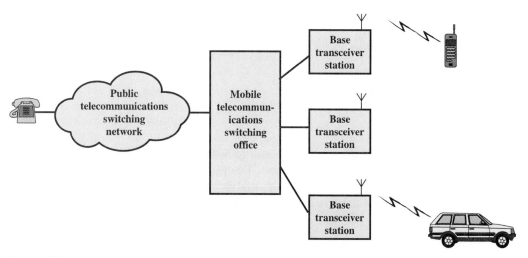

Figure 10.5   Overview of Cellular System

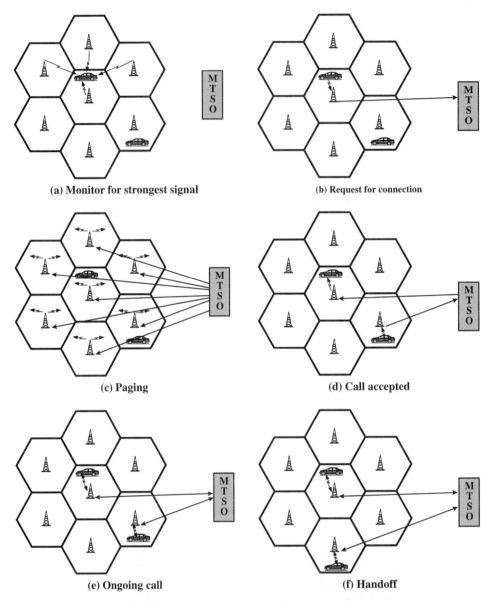

(a) Monitor for strongest signal

(b) Request for connection

(c) Paging

(d) Call accepted

(e) Ongoing call

(f) Handoff

Figure 10.6 Example of Mobile Cellular Call

channel. The effect of this procedure is that the mobile unit has automatically selected the BS antenna of the cell within which it will operate.[1] Then a handshake takes place between the mobile unit and the MTSO controlling this cell, through the BS in this cell. The handshake is used to identify the user and

---

[1]Usually, but not always, the antenna and therefore the base station selected is the closest one to the mobile unit. However, because of propagation anomalies, this is not always the case.

register its location. As long as the mobile unit is on, this scanning procedure is repeated periodically to account for the motion of the unit. If the unit enters a new cell, then a new BS is selected. In addition, the mobile unit is monitoring for pages, discussed subsequently.

- **Mobile-originated call:** A mobile unit originates a call by sending the number of the called unit on the preselected setup channel (Figure 10.6b). The receiver at the mobile unit first checks that the setup channel is idle by examining information in the forward (from the BS) channel. When an idle is detected, the mobile may transmit on the corresponding reverse (to BS) channel. The BS sends the request to the MTSO.

- **Paging:** The MTSO then attempts to complete the connection to the called unit. The MTSO sends a paging message to certain BSs depending on the called mobile number (Figure 10.6c). Each BS transmits the paging signal on its own assigned setup channel.

- **Call accepted:** The called mobile unit recognizes its number on the setup channel being monitored and responds to that BS, which sends the response to the MTSO. The MTSO sets up a circuit between the calling and called BSs. At the same time, the MTSO selects an available traffic channel within each BS's cell and notifies each BS, which in turn notifies its mobile unit (Figure 10.6d). The two mobile units tune to their respective assigned channels.

- **Ongoing call:** While the connection is maintained, the two mobile units exchange voice or data signals, going through their respective BSs and the MTSO (Figure 10.6e).

- **Handoff:** If a mobile unit moves out of range of one cell and into the range of another during a connection, the traffic channel has to change to one assigned to the BS in the new cell (Figure 10.6f). The system makes this change without either interrupting the call or alerting the user.

Other functions performed by the system but not illustrated in Figure 10.6 include the following:

- **Call blocking:** During the mobile-initiated call stage, if all the traffic channels assigned to the nearest BS are busy, then the mobile unit makes a preconfigured number of repeated attempts. After a certain number of failed tries, a busy tone is returned to the user.

- **Call termination:** When one of the two users hangs up, the MTSO is informed and the traffic channels at the two BSs are released.

- **Call drop:** During a connection, because of interference or weak signal spots in certain areas, if the BS cannot maintain the minimum required signal strength for a certain period of time, the traffic channel to the user is dropped and the MTSO is informed.

- **Calls to/from fixed and remote mobile subscriber:** The MTSO connects to the public switched telephone network. Thus, the MTSO can set up a connection between a mobile user in its area and a fixed subscriber via the telephone network. Further, the MTSO can connect to a remote MTSO via the telephone network or via dedicated lines and set up a connection between a mobile user in its area and a remote mobile user.

Mobile Radio Propagation Effects

Mobile radio communication introduces complexities not found in wire communication or in fixed wireless communication. Two general areas of concern are signal strength and signal propagation effects.

- **Signal strength:** The strength of the signal between the base station and the mobile unit must be strong enough to maintain signal quality at the receiver but no so strong as to create too much cochannel interference with channels in another cell using the same frequency band. Several complicating factors exist. Human-made noise varies considerably, resulting in a variable noise level. For example, automobile ignition noise in the cellular frequency range is greater in the city than in a suburban area. Other signal sources vary from place to place. The signal strength varies as a function of distance from the BS to a point within its cell. Moreover, the signal strength varies dynamically as the mobile unit moves.
- **Fading:** Even if signal strength is within an effective range, signal propagation effects may disrupt the signal and cause errors. Section 5.4 discussed fading and various countermeasures.

In designing a cellular layout, the communications engineer must take account of these various propagation effects, the desired maximum transmit power level at the base station and the mobile units, the typical height of the mobile unit antenna, and the available height of the BS antenna. These factors will determine the size of the individual cell. Unfortunately, as just described, the propagation effects are dynamic and difficult to predict. The best that can be done is to come up with a model based on empirical data and to apply that model to a given environment to develop guidelines for cell size. One of the most widely used models was developed by Okumura et al. [OKUM68] and subsequently refined by Hata [HATA80]. The original was a detailed analysis of the Tokyo area and produced path loss information for an urban environment. Hata's model is an empirical formulation that takes into account a variety of environments and conditions. For an urban environment, predicted path loss is

$$L_{dB} = 69.55 + 26.16 \log f_c - 13.82 \log h_t - A(h_r) + (44.9 - 6.55 \log h_t)\log d \quad (10.1)$$

where

$$
\begin{aligned}
f_c &= \text{carrier frequency in MHz from 150 to 1500 MHz} \\
h_t &= \text{height of transmitting antenna (base station) in m, from 30 to 300 m} \\
h_r &= \text{height of receiving antenna (mobile station) in m, from 1 to 10 m} \\
d &= \text{propagation distance between antennas in km, from 1 to 20 km} \\
A(h_r) &= \text{correction factor for mobile antenna height}
\end{aligned}
$$

For a small or medium-sized city, the correction factor is given by

$$A(h_r) = (1.1 \log f_c - 0.7) h_r - (1.56 \log f_c - 0.8) \text{ dB}$$

and for a large city it is given by

$$A(h_r) = 8.29[\log(1.54 \, h_r)]^2 - 1.1 \text{ dB} \quad \text{for } f_c \le 300 \text{ MHz}$$
$$A(h_r) = 3.2[\log(11.75 \, h_r)]^2 - 4.97 \text{ dB} \quad \text{for } f_c \ge 300 \text{ MHz}$$

To estimate the path loss in a suburban area, the formula for urban path loss in Equation (10.1) is modified as

$$L_{dB}(\text{suburban}) = L_{dB}(\text{urban}) - 2[\log(f_c/28)]^2 - 5.4$$

For the path loss in open areas, the formula is modified as

$$L_{dB}(\text{open}) = L_{dB}(\text{urban}) - 4.78(\log f_c)^2 - 18.733(\log f_c) - 40.98$$

The Okumura/Hata model is considered to be among the best in terms of accuracy in path loss prediction and provides a practical means of estimating path loss in a wide variety of situations [FREE97, RAPP97].

Example. [FREE97]. Let f_c = 900 MHz, h_t = 40 m, h_r = 5 m, and d = 10 km. Estimate the path loss for a medium-size city.

$$
\begin{aligned}
A(h_r) &= (1.1 \log 900 - 0.7) \, 5 - (1.56 \log 900 - 0.8) \text{ dB} \\
&= 12.75 - 3.8 = 8.95 \text{ dB}
\end{aligned}
$$

$$
\begin{aligned}
L_{db} &= 69.55 + 26.16 \log 900 - 13.82 \log 40 - 8.95 + (44.9 - 6.55 \log 40)\log 10 \\
&= 69.55 + 77.28 - 22.14 - 8.95 + 34.4 = 150.14 \text{ dB}
\end{aligned}
$$

Handoff

Handoff[2] is the procedure changing the assignment of a mobile unit from one BS to another as the mobile moves from one cell to another. Handoff is handled in different ways in different systems and involves a number of factors. Here we give a brief overview.

Handoff may be network initiated, in which the decision is made solely by the network measurements of received signals from the mobile unit. Alternatively, mobile-assisted handoff schemes enable the mobile unit to participate in the handoff decision by providing feedback to the network concerning signals received at the mobile unit. In either case, a number of different performance metrics may be used to make the decision. [HAAS00] lists the following:

- **Cell blocking probability:** The probability of a new call being blocked, due to heavy load on the BS traffic capacity. In this case, the mobile unit is handed off to a neighboring cell based not on signal quality but on traffic capacity.

---

[2]The term *handoff* is used in U.S. cellular standards documents. ITU documents use the term *handover*, and both terms appear in the technical literature. The meanings are the same.

- **Call dropping probability:** The probability that, due to a handoff, a call is terminated.
- **Call completion probability:** The probability that an admitted call is not dropped before it terminates.
- **Probability of unsuccessful handoff:** The probability that a handoff is executed while the reception conditions are inadequate.
- **Handoff blocking probability:** The probability that a handoff cannot be successfully completed.
- **Handoff probability:** The probability that a handoff occurs before call termination.
- **Rate of handoff:** The number of handoffs per unit time.
- **Interruption duration:** The duration of time during a handoff in which a mobile is not connected to either base station.
- **Handoff delay:** The distance the mobile moves from the point at which the handoff should occur to the point at which it does occur.

The principal parameter used to make the handoff decision is measured signal strength from the mobile at the BS. Typically, the BS averages the signal over a moving window of time to remove the rapid fluctuations due to multipath effects. Figure 10.7a, based on one in [POLL96], shows the average received power level at two adjacent base stations as a mobile unit moves from BS A, at L_A, to BS B, at L_B. This figure is useful in explaining various handoff strategies that have been used to determine the instant of handoff:

- **Relative signal strength:** The mobile unit is handed off from BS A to BS B when the signal strength at B first exceeds that at A. If the signal strength at B subsequently falls below that of A, the mobile unit is handed back to A. In Figure 10.7a, handoff occurs at point L_1. At this point, signal strength to BS A is still adequate but is declining. Because signal strength fluctuates due to multipath effects, even with power averaging, this approach can lead to a ping-pong effect in which the unit is repeatedly passed back and forth between two BSs.
- **Relative signal strength with threshold:** Handoff only occurs if (1) the signal at the current BS is sufficiently weak (less than a predefined threshold) and (2) the other signal is the stronger of the two. The intention is that so long as the signal at the current BS is adequate, handoff is unnecessary. If a high threshold is used, such as Th_1, this scheme performs the same as the relative signal strength scheme. With a threshold of Th_2, handoff occurs at L_2. If the threshold is set quite low compared to the crossover signal strength (signal strength at L_1), such as Th_3, the mobile may move far into the new cell (L_4) before handoff. This reduces the quality of the communication link and may result in a dropped call. A threshold should not be used alone because its effectiveness depends on prior knowledge of the crossover signal strength between the current and candidate base stations.
- **Relative signal strength with hysteresis:** Handoff occurs only if the new base station is sufficiently stronger (by a margin H in Figure 10.7a) than the current one. In this case, handoff occurs at L_3. This scheme prevents the ping-pong

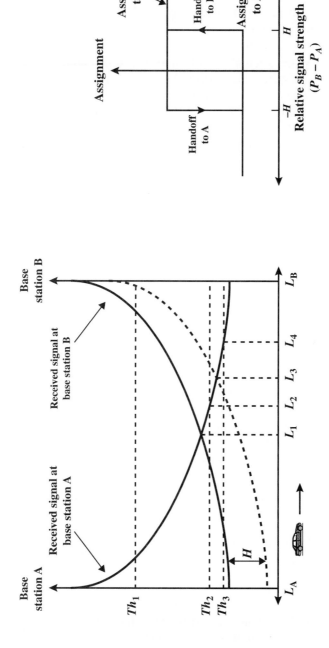

(a) Handoff decision as a function of handoff scheme

(b) Hysteresis mechanism

Figure 10.7 Handoff between Two Cells

295

effect, because once handoff occurs, the effect of the margin H is reversed. The term *hysteresis* refers to a phenomenon known as relay hysteresis and can be appreciated with the aid of Figure 10.7b. We can think of the handoff mechanism as having two states. While the mobile is assigned to BS A, the mechanism will generate a handoff when the relative signal strength reaches or exceeds the H. Once the mobile is assigned to B, it remains so until the relative signal strength falls below $-H$, at which point it is handed back to A. The only disadvantage of this scheme is that the first handoff may still be unnecessary if BS A still has sufficient signal strength.

- **Relative signal strength with hysteresis and threshold:** Handoff occurs only if (1) the current signal level drops below a threshold, and (2) the target base station is stronger than the current one by a hysteresis margin H. In our example, handoff occurs at L_3 if the threshold is either Th_1 or Th_2 and at L_4 if the threshold is at Th_3.

- **Prediction techniques:** The handoff decision is based on the expected future value of the received signal strength.

The handoff decision is complicated by the use of power control techniques, which enable the BS dynamically to adjust the power transmitted by the mobile. This topic is discussed next.

Power Control

A number of design issues make it desirable to include a dynamic power control capability in a cellular system:

1. The received power must be sufficiently above the background noise for effective communication, which dictates the required transmitted power. As the mobile unit moves away from the transmitter, the received power declines due to normal attenuation. In addition, the effects of reflection, diffraction, and scattering can cause rapid changes in received power levels over small distances. This is because the power level is the sum from signals coming from a number of different paths and the phases of those paths are random, sometimes adding and sometimes subtracting. As the mobile unit moves, the contributions along various paths change.

2. At the same time, it is desirable to minimize the power in the transmitted signal from the mobile, to reduce cochannel interference (interference with channels on the same frequency in remote cells), alleviate health concerns, and save battery power.

3. In spread spectrum (SS) systems using code division multiple access (CDMA), it is desirable to equalize the received power level from all mobile units at the BS. This is crucial to system performance because all users have the same frequency allocation.

Figure 10.8, based on one in [PICH97], illustrates the two kinds of power control. **Open-loop power control** depends solely on the mobile unit, with no feedback

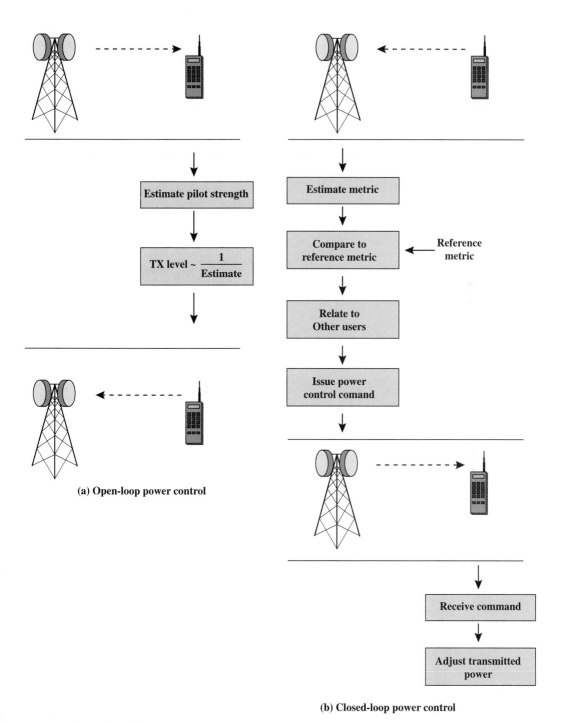

Figure 10.8 Reverse Link Power Control

from the BS, and is used in some SS systems. In SS systems, the BS continuously transmits an unmodulated signal, known as a pilot. The pilot allows a mobile unit to acquire the timing of the forward (BS to mobile) CDMA channel and provides a phase reference for demodulation. It can also be used for power control. The mobile monitors the received power level of the pilot and sets the transmitted power in the reverse (mobile to BS) channel inversely proportional to it. This approach assumes that the forward and reverse link signal strengths are closely correlated, which is generally the case. The open-loop approach is not as accurate as the closed-loop approach. However, the open-loop scheme can react more quickly to rapid fluctuations in signal strength, such as when a mobile emerges from behind a large building. This fast action is required in the reverse link of a CDMA system where the sudden increase in received strength at the BS may suppress all other signals.

Closed-loop power control adjusts signal strength in the reverse (mobile to BS) channel based on some metric of performance in that reverse channel, such as received signal power level, received signal-to-noise ratio, or received bit error rate. The BS makes the power adjustment decision and communicates a power adjustment command to the mobile on a control channel. Closed-loop power control is also used to adjust power in the forward channel. In this case, the mobile provides information about received signal quality to the BS, which then adjusts transmitted power.

Table 10.2 shows the power classes used in the GSM standard, which is a TDMA standard and is discussed in Section 10.3. GSM defines eight classes of base station channels and five classes of mobile stations, according to their power output. Adjustments in both directions are made using closed-loop power control.

Traffic Engineering

For an FDMA system, the capacity of a cell is equal to the number of frequency channels allocated to it. Ideally, the number of available channels in a cell would

Table 10.2 GSM Transmitter Classes

Power Class	Base station power (watts)	Mobile station power (watts)
1	320	20
2	160	8
3	80	5
4	40	2
5	20	0.8
6	10	
7	5	
8	2.5	

equal the total number of subscribers who could be active at any time. In practice, it is not feasible to have the capacity to handle any possible load at all times. Fortunately, not all subscribers place calls at the same time and so it is reasonable to size the network to be able to handle some expected level of load. This is the discipline of traffic engineering.

Traffic engineering concepts were developed in the design of telephone switches and circuit-switching telephone networks, but the concepts equally apply to cellular networks. Consider a cell able to handle N simultaneous users (capacity of N channels) that has L potential subscribers (L mobile units). If $L < N$, the system is referred to as *nonblocking*; all calls can be handled all the time. If $L > N$, the system is *blocking*; a subscriber may attempt a call and find the capacity fully in use and therefore be blocked. For a blocking system, the fundamental performance questions we wish to answer are as follows:

1. What is the degree of blocking; that is, what is the probability that a call request will be blocked? Alternatively, what capacity (N) is needed to achieve a certain upper bound on the probability of blocking?
2. If blocked calls are queued for service, what is the average delay? Alternatively, what capacity is needed to achieve a certain average delay?

In this subsection, we briefly introduce the relevant traffic engineering concepts and give an example of their use. Appendix B examines the subject in more detail.

Two parameters determine the amount of load presented to a system:

λ = the mean rate of calls (connection requests) attempted per unit time
h = the mean holding time per successful call

The basic measure of traffic is the **traffic intensity**, expressed in a dimensionless unit, the erlang:

$$A = \lambda h$$

A can be interpreted in several ways. It is a normalized version of λ: A equals the average number of calls arriving during the average holding period. We can also view the cell as a multiserver queuing system where the number of servers is equal to the channel capacity N. The average service time at a server is h. A basic relationship in a multiserver queue is $\lambda h = \rho N$, where ρ is server utilization, or the fraction of time that a server is busy. Therefore $A = \rho N$ and is a measure of the average number of channels required.

Example. If the calling rate averages 20 calls per minute and the average holding time is 3 minutes, then $A = 60$. We would expect a cell with a capacity of 120 channels to be about half utilized at any given time. A switch of capacity 50 would clearly be inadequate. A capacity of 60 would meet the average demand but, because of fluctuations around the mean rate A, this capacity would at times be inadequate.

Example. To clarify these concepts, consider Figure 10.9, which shows the pattern of activity in a cell of capacity 10 channels over a period of 1 hour. The rate of calls per minute is 97/60. The average holding time per call, in minutes, is 294/97. Thus $A = (97/60) \times (294/97) = 4.9$ erlangs. Another way of viewing the parameter A is that it is the mean number of calls in progress. Thus, on average, 4.9 channels are engaged. The latter interpretation, however, is true only in the nonblocking case. The parameter λ was defined as the rate of calls attempted, not carried traffic.

Typically, a blocking system is sized to deal with some upper limit of traffic intensity. It is generally thought unreasonable to size for the highest surge of traffic anticipated; rather, the common practice is to size the system to meet the average rate encountered during a busy hour. The busy hour is the 60-minute period during the day when the traffic is highest, in the long run. ITU-T recommends taking the average of the busy hour traffic on the 30 busiest days of the year, called the "mean busy-hour traffic," and using that quantity to size the system. The North American practice is to take the average over the 10 busiest days. These are typically measurements of carried rather than offered traffic and can only be used to estimate the true load.

The parameter A, as a measure of busy-hour traffic, serves as input to a traffic model. The model is then used to answer questions such as those posed in the beginning of this subsection. There are two key factors that determine the nature of the model:

- The manner in which blocked calls are handled
- The number of traffic sources

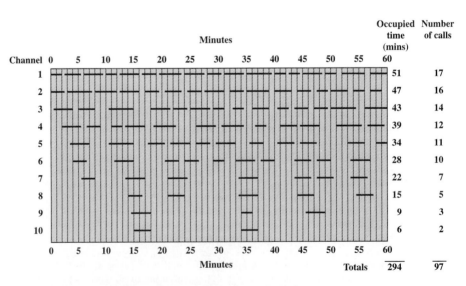

Note: Horizontal lines indicate occupied periods to the nearest 1/2 minute

Figure 10.9 Example Distribution of Traffic in a Cell with Capacity 10

Blocked calls may be handled in one of two ways. First, blocked calls can be put in a queue awaiting a free channel; this is referred to as **lost calls delayed** (LCD), although in fact the call is not lost, merely delayed. Second, a blocked call can be rejected and dropped. This in turn leads to two assumptions about the action of the user. If the user hangs up and waits some random time interval before another call attempt, this is known as **lost calls cleared** (LCC). If the user repeatedly attempts calling, it is known as **lost calls held** (LCH). For each of these blocking options, formulas have been developed that characterize the performance of the system. For cellular systems, the LCC model is generally used and is generally the most accurate.

The second key element of a traffic model is whether the number of users is assumed to be finite or infinite. For an infinite source model, there is assumed to be a fixed arrival rate. For the finite source case, the arrival rate will depend on the number of sources already engaged. In particular, if the total pool of users is L, each of which generates calls at an average rate of λ/L, then, when the cell is totally idle, the arrival rate is λ. However, if there are K users occupied at time t, then the instantaneous arrival rate at that time is $\lambda(L - K)/L$. Infinite source models are analytically easier to deal with. The infinite source assumption is reasonable when the number of sources is at least 5 to 10 times the capacity of the system.

Infinite Sources, Lost Calls Cleared

For an infinite source LCC model, the key parameter of interest is the probability of loss, or **grade of service**. Thus a grade of service of 0.01 means that, during a busy hour, the probability that an attempted call is blocked is 0.01. Values in the range 0.01 to 0.001 are generally considered quite good.

The equation of infinite source LCC, known as Erlang B, has the following form:

$$P = \frac{\dfrac{A^N}{N!}}{\displaystyle\sum_{x=0}^{N} \dfrac{A^x}{x!}}$$

where

$A =$ offered traffic, erlangs
$N =$ number of servers
$P =$ probability of blocking (grade of service)

This equation is easily programmed, and tables of values are readily available. Table 10.3 is an extract from such a table. Given the offered load and number of servers, the grade of service can be calculated or determined from a table. More often, the inverse problem is of interest: determining the amount of traffic that can be handled by a given capacity to produce a given grade of service. Another problem is to determine the capacity required to handle a given amount of traffic at a given grade of service. For both these problems, tables or suitable trial-and-error programs are needed.

Two important points can be deduced from Table 10.3:

Table 10.3 Erlang B Table

Number of servers (N)	Capacity (erlangs) for grade of service of				
	P = 0.02 (1/50)	P = 0.01 1/100)	P = 0.005 (1/200)	P = 0.002 (1/500)	P = 0.001 (1/1000)
1	0.02	0.01	0.005	0.002	0.001
4	1.09	0.87	0.7	0.53	0.43
5	1.66	1.36	1.13	0.9	0.76
10	5.08	4.46	3.96	3.43	3.09
20	13.19	12.03	11.10	10.07	9.41
24	16.64	15.27	14.21	13.01	12.24
40	31.0	29.0	27.3	25.7	24.5
70	59.13	56.1	53.7	51.0	49.2
100	87.97	84.1	80.9	77.4	75.2

1. A larger-capacity system is more efficient than a smaller-capacity one for a given grade of service.
2. A larger-capacity system is more susceptible to reduction of the grade of service.

Example. To illustrate the first point, consider two cells, each with a capacity of 10 channels. They have a joint capacity of 20 channels and can handle a combined offered traffic intensity of 6.86 for a grade of service of 0.002. However, a single cell of capacity 20 channels will handle 10.07 erlangs at a grade of service of 0.002. To illustrate the second point, consider a cell of 10 channels giving a grade of service of 0.002 for a load of 3.43 erlangs. A 30% increase in traffic reduces the grade of service to 0.01. However, for a cell of capacity 70 channels, only a 10% increase in traffic reduces the grade of service from 0.002 to 0.01.

All of the preceding discussion deals with offered traffic. If sizing is done on the basis of system measurement, all that we are likely to have is carried traffic. A program can readily be developed that accepts carried traffic as input and then performs a seeking algorithm to work backward to offered traffic. The relationship between carried traffic C and offered traffic A is:

$$C = A(1 - P)$$

For small value of P, A is a good approximation of C.

Effect of Handoff

One complication in cellular traffic models not found in other such models is the effect of handoff. This is illustrated in Figure 10.10. The arrival rate of calls at a cell has two components: new calls placed by mobile units in the cell (λ_1), and calls

Figure 10.10 Cell Traffic Model

handed off to the cell for mobile units entering the cell while connected (λ_2). The total arrival rate is $\lambda = \lambda_1 + \lambda_2$. Similarly, the completion rate consists of calls being terminated and calls being handed off. The model must be adjusted accordingly to obtain overall arrival rates and holding times.

10.2 FIRST-GENERATION ANALOG

The original cellular telephone networks provided analog traffic channels; these are now referred to as first-generation systems. Since the early 1980s the most common first-generation system in North America has been the **Advanced Mobile Phone Service (AMPS)** developed by AT&T. This approach is also common in South America, Australia, and China. Although gradually being replaced by second-generation systems, AMPS is still in common use. In this section, we provide an overview of AMPS.

Spectral Allocation

In North America, two 25-MHz bands are allocated to AMPS (Table 10.4), one for transmission from the base station to the mobile unit (869–894 MHz), the other for transmission from the mobile to the base station (824–849 MHz). Each of these bands is split in two to encourage competition (i.e., so that in each market two operators can be accommodated). An operator is allocated only 12.5 MHz in each direction for its system. The channels are spaced 30 kHz apart, which allows a total of 416 channels per operator. Twenty-one channels are allocated for control, leaving 395 to carry calls. The control channels are data channels operating at 10 kbps. The conversation channels carry the conversations in analog using frequency modulation. Control information is also sent on the conversation channels in bursts as data. This number of channels is inadequate for most major markets, so some way must be found either to use less bandwidth per conversation or to reuse frequencies. Both approaches have been taken in the various approaches to mobile telephony. For AMPS, frequency reuse is exploited.

Operation

Each AMPS-capable cellular telephone includes a *numeric assignment module* (NAM) in read-only memory. The NAM contains the telephone number of the phone, which is assigned by the service provider, and the serial number of the phone,

Table 10.4 AMPS Parameters

Base station transmission band	869 to 894 MHz
Mobile unit transmission band	824 to 849 MHz
Spacing between forward and reverse channels	45 MHz
Channel bandwidth	30 kHz
Number of full-duplex voice channels	790
Number of full-duplex control channels	42
Mobile unit maximum power	3 watts
Cell size, radius	2 to 20 km
Modulation, voice channel	FM, 12-kHz peak deviation
Modulation, control channel	FSK, 8-kHz peak deviation
Data transmission rate	10 kbps
Error control coding	BCH (48, 36,5) and (40, 28,5)

which is assigned by the manufacturer. When the phone is turned on, it transmits its serial number and phone number to the MTSO (Figure 10.5); the MTSO maintains a database with information about mobile units that have been reported stolen and uses serial number to lock out stolen units. The MTSO uses the phone number for billing purposes. If the phone is used in a remote city, the service is still billed to the user's local service provider.

When a call is placed, the following sequence of events occurs [COUC01]:

1. The subscriber initiates a call by keying in the telephone number of the called party and presses the send key.
2. The MTSO verifies that the telephone number is valid and that the user is authorized to place the call; some service providers require the user to enter a PIN (personal identification number) as well as the called number to counter theft.
3. The MTSO issues a message to the user's cell phone indicating which traffic channels to use for sending and receiving.
4. The MTSO sends out a ringing signal to the called party. All of these operations (steps 2 through 4) occur within 10 s of initiating the call.
5. When the called party answers, the MTSO establishes a circuit between the two parties and initiates billing information.
6. When one party hangs up, the MTSO releases the circuit, frees the radio channels, and completes the billing information.

AMPS Control Channels

Each AMPS service includes 21 full-duplex 30-kHz control channels, consisting of 21 reverse control channels (RCCs) from subscriber to base station, and 21 forward channels base station to subscriber. These channels transmit digital data using FSK. In both channels, data are transmitted in frames.

Figure 10.11a shows the RCC frame structure. The frame begins with a 48-bit precursor, consisting of a 30-bit bit sync field of alternating ones and zeros, an 11 bit word sync field (11100010010), and a 7-bit digital color code (DCC). The DCC is used to distinguish transmissions in cochannel cells; it is a unique identifier of a base station and acts as a destination address for an RCC frame. Following the precursor, the frame contains from one to 6 words of data. Each word contains 36 data bits and is encoded using a shortened version of an $(n, k, t) = (63, 51, 5)$ BCH block code (see Table 8.4). In this shortened version, 12 check bits are added to the 36 data bits to form a 48-bit word. To further increase reliability, each word is transmitted five times in the same frame, and a majority logic is used to recover the word at the base station. When all the overhead is taken into account, the data rate is on the order of a few hundred bits per second. Examples of RCC messages include origination, page response, and order confirmation.

The FCC frame structure (Figure 10.11b) starts with a 10-bit bit sync and an 11-bit word sync. Each frame contains two words of data. Each word is encoded using BCH and contains 28 data bits and 12 check bits. Again, for reliability, each word is repeated five times. In addition, each FCC frame provides information about the status (idle or busy) of the corresponding RCC frame through the busy/idle bits that are inserted every tenth bit in the frame. This brings the total frame size to 463 bits. At the 10-kbps signaling rate, the data rate (excluding overhead) is about 1.2 kbps. FCC messages include paging messages and frequency assignment messages.

Finally, control information can be transmitted over a voice channel during a conversation. The mobile unit or the base station can insert a burst of data by turning off the voice FM transmission for about 100 ms and replacing it with an FSK-encoded message. These messages are used to exchange urgent messages, such as change power level and handoff.

10.3 SECOND-GENERATION TDMA

This section begins our study of second-generation cellular systems. We begin with an overview and then look in detail at one type of second-generation cellular system.

First- and Second-Generation Cellular Systems

First-generation cellular networks, such as AMPS, quickly became highly popular, threatening to swamp available capacity. Second-generation systems have been developed to provide higher-quality signals, higher data rates for support of digital services, and greater capacity. [BLAC99] lists the following as the key differences between the two generations:

- **Digital traffic channels:** The most notable difference between the two generations is that first-generation systems are almost purely analog, whereas second-generation systems are digital. In particular, the first-generation systems are

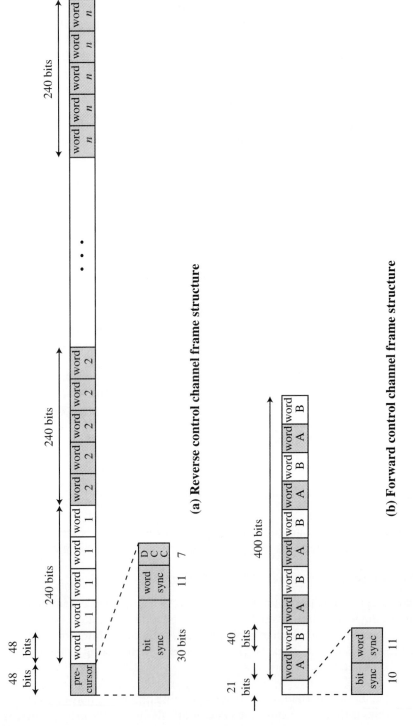

(a) Reverse control channel frame structure

(b) Forward control channel frame structure

Figure 10.11 AMPS Control Channel Frame Formats

306

designed to support voice channels using FM; digital traffic is supported only by the use of a modem that converts the digital data into analog form. Second-generation systems provide digital traffic channels. These readily support digital data; voice traffic is first encoded in digital form before transmitting. Of course, for second-generation systems, the user traffic (data or digitized voice) must be converted to an analog signal for transmission between the mobile unit and the base station (e.g., see Figure 6.14).

- **Encryption:** Because all of the user traffic, as well as control traffic, is digitized in second-generation systems, it is a relatively simple matter to encrypt all of the traffic to prevent eavesdropping. All second-generation systems provide this capability, whereas first-generation systems send user traffic in the clear, providing no security.

- **Error detection and correction:** The digital traffic stream of second-generation systems also lends itself to the use of error detection and correction techniques, such as those discussed in Chapter 8. The result can be very clear voice reception.

- **Channel access:** In first-generation systems, each cell supports a number of channels. At any given time a channel is allocated to only one user. Second-generation systems also provide multiple channels per cell, but each channel is dynamically shared by a number of users using time division multiple access (TDMA) or code division multiple access (CDMA). We look at TDMA-based systems in this section and CDMA-based systems in Section 10.4.

Beginning around 1990, a number of different second-generation systems have been deployed. Table 10.5 lists some key characteristics of three of the most important of these systems.

Time Division Multiple Access

First-generation cellular systems provide for the support of multiple users with frequency division multiple access (FDMA). FDMA was introduced in our discussion of satellite communications and the principle is the same here. FDMA for cellular systems can be described as follows. Each cell is allocated a total of $2M$ channels of bandwidth δ Hz each. Half the channels (the reverse channels) are used for transmission from the mobile unit to the base station: $f_c, f_c + \delta, f_c + 2\delta, \ldots, f_c + (M-1)\delta$, where f_c is the center frequency of the lowest-frequency channel. The other half of the channels (the forward channels) are used for transmission from the base station to the mobile unit: $f_c, f_c + \delta + \Delta, f_c + 2\delta + \Delta, \ldots, f_c + (M-1)\delta + \Delta$, where Δ is the spacing between the reverse and forward channels. When a connection is set up for a mobile user, the user is assigned two channels, at f and $f + \Delta$, for full-duplex communication. This arrangement is quite wasteful, because much of the time one or both of the channels are idle.

TDMA was also introduced in our discussion of satellite communications (e.g., see Figure 9.14). TDMA for cellular systems can be described as follows. As with FDMA, each cell is allocated a number of channels, half reverse and half forward. Again, for full-duplex communication, a mobile unit is assigned capacity on matching reverse and forward channels. In addition, each physical channel is further sub-

Table 10.5 Second-Generation Cellular Telephone Systems

	GSM	**IS-136**	**IS-95**
Year introduced	1990	1991	1993
Access method	TDMA	TDMA	CDMA
Base station transmission band	935 to 960 MHz	869 to 894 MHz	869 to 894 MHz
Mobile station transmission band	890 to 915 MHz	824 to 849 MHz	824 to 849 MHz
Spacing between forward and reverse channels	45 MHz	45 MHz	45 MHz
Channel bandwidth	200 kHz	30 kHz	1250 kHz
Number of duplex channels	125	832	20
Mobile unit maximum power	20 W	3 W	0.2 W
Users per channel	8	3	35
Modulation	GMSK	$\pi/4$ DQPSK	QPSK
Carrier bit rate	270.8 kbps	48.6 kbps	9.6 kbps
Speech coder	RPE-LTP	VSELP	QCELP
Speech coding bit rate	13 kbps	8 kbps	8, 4, 2, 1 kbps
Frame size	4.6 ms	40 ms	20 ms
Error control coding	Convolutional 1/2 rate	Convolutional 1/2 rate	Convolutional 1/2 rate forward; 1/3 rate reverse

divided into a number of logical channels. Transmission is in the form of a repetitive sequence of frames, each of which is divided into a number of time slots. Each slot position across the sequence of frames forms a separate logical channel. We saw an example of this in Figure 9.13.

Mobile Wireless TDMA Design Considerations

Before turning to the specific example of GSM, it will be useful to consider some general design guidelines by looking at a simple analysis, based on one in [JONE93]. This analysis motivates some of the design decisions made for GSM. The overall objective is to determine the length and composition of the traffic channel time slot that will provide effective speech and data transmission with efficient use of the radio spectrum. Let us consider the following set of requirements:

- **Number of logical channels (number of time slots in TDMA frame):** 8; this appears to be the minimum to justify the additional costs of multiplexing.
- **Maximum cell radius (R):** 35 km, to give a sufficiently high traffic level in rural areas.
- **Frequency:** Region around 900 MHz; this is commonly allocated to mobile radio applications.

- **Maximum vehicle speed (V_m):** 250 km/hr, or 69.4 m/s, to accommodate mobile units on high-speed trains.
- **Maximum coding delay:** Approximately 20 ms, to avoid adding unduly to delays within the fixed network, which may involve satellite links.
- **Maximum delay spread (Δ_m):** 10 (s (in mountainous regions); this is the difference in propagation delay among different multipath signals arriving at the same antenna.
- **Bandwidth:** Not to exceed 200 kHz, corresponding to 25 kHz per channel (the current spacing for analog FM cellular systems in Europe).

Figure 10.12 suggests the steps to be considered in designing the TDMA time slot. We use this as a guide in the following discussion.

The speech coder must provide satisfactory speech quality at minimum data rate. The traditional form of speech coding to produce a digital bit stream is pulse code modulation (PCM), which, as we saw in Section 6.4, results in a data rate of 64 kbps. This rate is undesirably high for use in cellular radio. With current technology, a data rate of 12 kbps is reasonable for producing good-quality speech reproduction.

If we restrict the coding delay to 20 ms, then it would be acceptable to form the encoded speech into blocks of 20 ms duration, or speech samples of 240 bits.

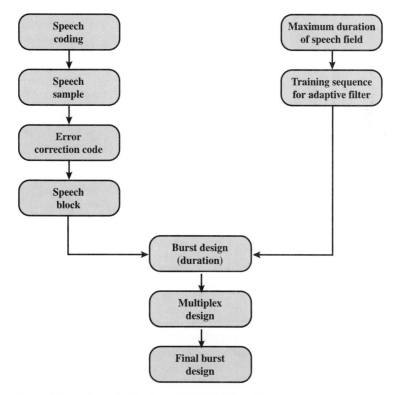

Figure 10.12   Steps in Design of TDMA Time Slot

Data at 12 kbps could also be blocked in 240-bit units. Error correction can then be applied to the 240-bit blocks.

For second-generation digital systems, convolutional error-correcting codes are commonly used with a code rate of 1/2. This overhead raises the number of bits in a block to 480. In addition, there is a constraint factor of 5, meaning that 4 bits must be added to the data block to account for the length of the shift register (see Section 8.3). This brings the speech block length to 488 bits.

With the parameters chosen so far, the minimum bit rate for an eight-channel system is

$$\frac{8 \text{ channels } \times 488 \text{ bits/channel}}{20 \times 10^{-3} \text{ s}} = 195.2 \text{ kbps}$$

In fact, the bit rate will be somewhat higher to take care of other design considerations, discussed subsequently. This means that a data rate of greater than 200 kbps will need to be carried in the available bandwidth of 200 kHz. In practice, such data rates cannot be achieved without the use of adaptive equalization. As was discussed in Section 5.4, in a mobile environment, adaptive equalization will require the inclusion of a new training sequence each time the mobile unit moves a distance sufficient to potentially cause changes in transmission path characteristics. Let us assume that a training sequence is included in each time slot. A rough criterion suggested in [JONE93] is that the phase angle of the carrier signal should be restricted to a change of 1/20th of a wavelength (an angle of $\pi/10$) after the training sequence. At 900 MHz, the wavelength is 0.333m. We can calculate

$$\text{Maximum transmission duration} = \frac{\lambda/20}{V_m} = \frac{0.333/20}{69.4} = 0.24 \text{ ms}$$

We can take better advantage of the training sequence by transmitting 0.24 ms of speech or data both before and after the training sequence and using the training sequence on the combined 0.48 ms of data.

Next, we need to determine the length of the training sequence. In the design of an equalizer for a multipath signal whose bandwidth is about equal to the bit rate (200 kHz, 200 kbps), a rule of thumb is that the number of taps on the equalizer (Figure 5.14) should be equal to 6 times the number of bits transmitted in the maximum dispersal time ($\Delta_m = 0.01$ ms). Thus, the amount of time in the time slot devoted to the training sequence is 0.06 ms.

Now consider that a guard interval is needed at the end of each time slot to account for the differing amounts of delay between different mobile units and the base station. Because eight mobile units share the same TDMA frame, it is necessary to adjust the timing of the transmissions of the mobile units so that the transmission from one unit does not interfere with adjacent time slots. It is the responsibility of the base station to provide synchronization information to each mobile unit to adjust relative delays to enforce the time slot structure of the TDMA frame. However, the mobile units may be moving relative to the base station and relative to each other, so a guard time is inserted in each time slot to account for these discrepancies. When a mobile first makes a connection through the base station, the base station can provide the mobile unit with timing information based on the current propagation delay between the mobile unit and the base station. We would also like to add a guard time sufficient to avoid the need to frequently update this synchronization information. We can calculate the guard time as follows. The average telephone call is about 130 seconds [JONE93], so the radial distance toward or away from the base station that a mobile could cover is (130 s) × (69.4 m/s) = 9022 m. The change in propagation delay caused by a movement of this distance is $9022/(3 \times 10^8 \text{ m/s}) = 0.03$ ms.

Figure 10.13a shows the tentative time slot design. The next step is to fit a coded data block into a convenient number of time slots, together with the training sequence and guard bits. We have a maximum duration of a time slot of approximately 0.57 ms. With 8 time slots per frame, that gives a frame time of about 4.6 ms. We said that we wanted to send data with a coding delay of 20 ms, so if we round the frame time down to 4 ms (time slot = 0.5 ms), then we could conveniently send a block of speech in five successive slots on the same channel. A speech block consists of 488 bits, so each time slot would need to hold 488/5 or about 98 data bits. This yields a bit rate of 98/0.4 = 245 kbps. At this data rate, the minimum number of training bits required is (0.06 ms) × (245 kbps) = 14.7, which on rounding becomes 15 bits. Similarly, the minimum number of guard bits is (0.03 ms) × (245 kbps) = 7.35, which on rounding becomes 8 bits.

(a) Approximate field durations

(b) Approximate field sizes

Figure 10.13   TDMA Time Slot

The resulting frame structure is shown in Figure 10.13b. We have 121 bits transmitted in 0.5 ms for a channel bit rate of 242 kbps.

Global System for Mobile Communications

Before the Global System for Mobile Communications (GSM) was developed, the countries of Europe used a number of incompatible first-generation cellular phone technologies. GSM was developed to provide a common second-generation technology for Europe so that the same subscriber units could be used throughout the continent. The technology has been extremely successful and is probably the most popular standard, worldwide, for new implementations. GSM first appeared in 1990 in Europe. Similar systems have now been implemented in North and South America, Asia, North Africa, the Middle East, and Australia. The GSM Association claimed nearly three-quarters of a billion subscribers worldwide at the end of 2000, the bulk of these in Europe and Asia Pacific, but with over 8 million in North America.

GSM Network Architecture

Figure 10.14 shows the key functional elements in the GSM system. The boundaries at Um, Abis, and A refer to interfaces between functional elements that are standardized in the GSM documents. Thus, it is possible to buy equipment from different vendors with the expectation that they will successfully interoperate. Additional interfaces are also defined in the GSM standards but need not concern us here.

Mobile Station

A mobile station communicates across the Um interface, also known as the **air interface**, with a base station transceiver in the same cell in which the mobile unit is located. The **mobile equipment** (ME) refers to the physical terminal, such as a telephone or PCS (personal communications service) device, which includes the radio transceiver, digital signal processors, and the **subscriber identity module** (SIM). The SIM is a portable device in the form of a smart card or plug-in module that stores the subscriber's identification number, the networks the subscriber is authorized to use, encryption keys, and other information specific to the subscriber. The GSM subscriber units are totally generic until an SIM is inserted. Therefore, a subscriber need only carry his or her SIM to use a wide variety of subscriber devices in many countries simply by inserting the SIM in the device to be used. In fact, except for certain emergency communications, the subscriber units will not work without a SIM inserted. Thus, the SIMs roam, not necessarily the subscriber devices.

Base Station Subsystem

A base station subsystem (BSS) consists of a base station controller and one or more base transceiver stations. Each **base transceiver station** (BTS) defines a single cell; it includes a radio antenna, a radio transceiver, and a link to a base station controller. A GSM cell can have a radius of between 100 m and 35 km, depending on the environment. A **base station controller** (BSC) may be collocated with a BTS or may control multiple BTS units and hence multiple cells. The BSC

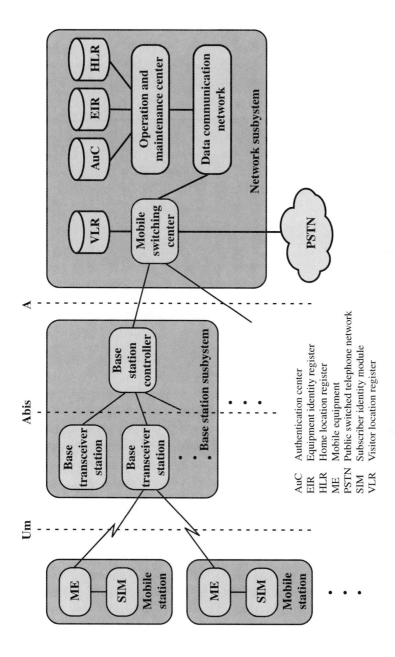

AuC   Authentication center
EIR   Equipment identity register
HLR   Home location register
ME   Mobile equipment
PSTN   Public switched telephone network
SIM   Subscriber identity module
VLR   Visitor location register

Figure 10.14   Overall GSM Architecture

313

reserves radio frequencies, manages the handoff of a mobile unit from one cell to another within the BSS, and controls paging.

Network Subsystem

The network subsystem (NS) provides the link between the cellular network and the public switched telecommunications networks. The NS controls handoffs between cells in different BSSs, authenticates users and validates their accounts, and includes functions for enabling worldwide roaming of mobile users. The central element of the NS is the **mobile switching center** (MSC). It is supported by four databases that it controls:

- **Home location register (HLR) database:** The HLR stores information, both permanent and temporary, about each of the subscribers that "belongs" to it (i.e., for which the subscriber has its telephone number associated with the switching center).

- **Visitor location register (VLR) database:** One important, temporary piece of information is the location of the subscriber. The location is determined by the VLR into which the subscriber is entered. The visitor location register maintains information about subscribers that are currently physically in the region covered by the switching center. It records whether or not the subscriber is active and other parameters associated with the subscriber. For a call coming to the subscriber, the system uses the telephone number associated with the subscriber to identify the home switching center of the subscriber. This switching center can find in its HLR the switching center in which the subscriber is currently physically located. For a call coming from the subscriber, the VLR is used to initiate the call. Even if the subscriber is in the area covered by its home switching center, it is also represented in the switching center's VLR, for consistency.

- **Authentication center database (AuC):** This database is used for authentication activities of the system; for example, it holds the authentication and encryption keys for all the subscribers in both the home and visitor location registers. The center controls access to user data as well as being used for authentication when a subscriber joins a network. GSM transmission is encrypted, so it is private. A stream cipher, A5, is used to encrypt the transmission from subscriber to base transceiver. However, the conversation is in the clear in the landline network. Another cipher, A3, is used for authentication.

- **Equipment identity register database (EIR):** The EIR keeps track of the type of equipment that exists at the mobile station. It also plays a role in security (e.g., blocking calls from stolen mobile stations and preventing use of the network by stations that have not been approved).

Radio Link Aspects

The GSM spectral allocation is 25 MHz for base transmission (935–960 MHz) and 25 MHz for mobile transmission (890–915 MHz). Other GSM bands have also been defined outside Europe. Users access the network using a combination of frequency division multiple access (FDMA) and time division multiple access (TDMA) (both are discussed in the next section). There are radio-frequency carriers every 200 kHz, which provide for 125 full-duplex channels. The channels are modulated at a data rate of 270.833 kbps. As with AMPS, there are two types of channels, traffic and control.

TDMA Format

GSM uses a complex hierarchy of TDMA frames to define logical channels (Figure 10.15). Fundamentally, each 200-kHz frequency band is divided into 8 logical channels defined by the repetitive occurrence of time slots.

At the lowest level is the time slot, also called a burst period, which has a duration of 15/26 ms, or approximately 0.577 ms. With a bit rate of 270.833 kbps, each time slot has a length of 156.25 bits. The time slot includes the following fields:

- **Trail bits:** Allow synchronization of transmissions from mobile units located at different distances from the base station, as explained subsequently.
- **Encrypted bits:** Data is encrypted in blocks by conventional encryption of 114 plaintext bits into 114 ciphertext bits; the encrypted bits are then placed in two 57-bit fields in the time slot.
- **Stealing bit:** Used to indicate whether this block contains data or is "stolen" for urgent control signaling.
- **Training sequence:** Used to adapt the parameters of the receiver to the current path propagation characteristics and to select the strongest signal in case of multipath propagation. The training sequence is a known bit pattern that differs for different adjacent cells. It enables the mobile units and base stations to determine that the received signal is from the correct transmitter and not a strong interfering transmitter. In addition, the training sequence is used for multipath equalization, which is used to extract the desired signal from unwanted reflections. By determining how the known training sequence is modified by multipath fading, the rest of the signal is processed to compensate for these effects.
- **Guard bits:** Used to avoid overlapping with other bursts due to different path delays.

The time slot format shown in Figure 10.15 is called a normal burst and carries user data traffic (compare Figure 10.13b). Other burst formats are used for control signaling.

Moving up the frame format hierarchy, 8-slot TDMA frames are typically organized into a 26-frame multiframe. One of the frames in the multiframe is used for control signaling and another is currently unused, leaving 24 frames for data traffic. Thus, each traffic channel receives one slot per frame and 24 frames per 120-ms multiframe. The resulting data rate is

$$\frac{114 \text{ bits/slot} \times 24 \text{ slots/multiframe}}{120 \text{ ms/multiframe}} = 22.8 \text{ kbps}$$

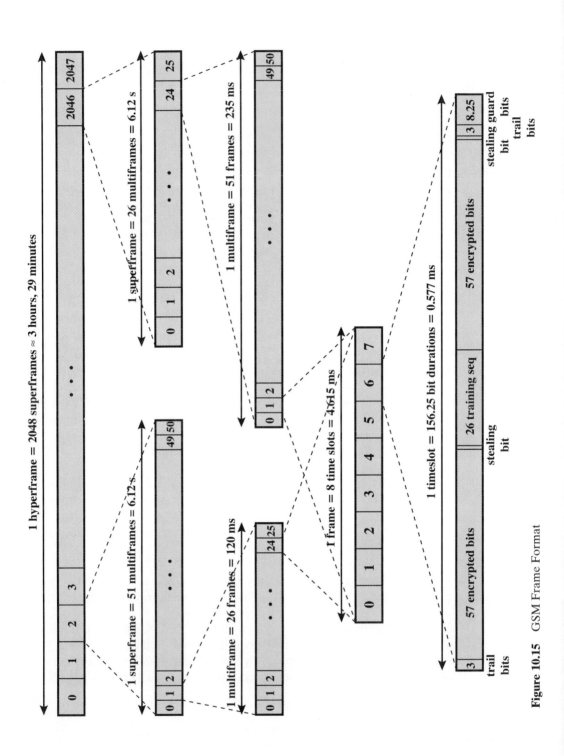

Figure 10.15 GSM Frame Format

316

The GSM specification also allows half-rate traffic channels, with two traffic channels each occupying one time slot in 12 of the 26 frames. With the use of half-rate speech coders, this effectively doubles the capacity of the system. There is also a 51-frame multiframe used for control traffic.

Speech coding

Figure 10.16 provides an overview of the processing of speech signals for transmission over a logical traffic channel. We look at each of these steps in turn.

The speech signal is compressed using an algorithm known as Regular Pulse Excited—Linear Predictive Coder (RPE-LPE) [KROO86]. In essence, data from previous samples are used to predict the current sample. Each sample is then encoded to consist of bits representing the coefficients of the linear combination of previous samples plus an encoded form of the difference between the predicted and actual sample. The result of the use of this code is to produce 260 bits every 20 ms, for a raw

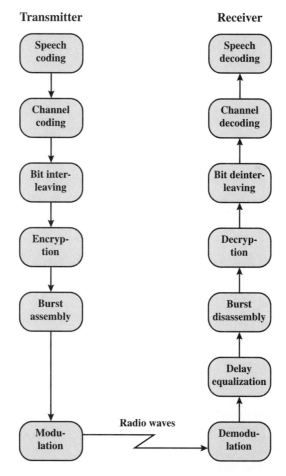

Figure 10.16 GSM Speech Signal Processing

data rate of 13 kbps. From the point of view of the quality of the speech produced by this encoding, the bits in the 260-bit block can be divided into three classes:

- **Class Ia:** 50 bits, most sensitive to bit errors
- **Class Ib:** 132 bits, moderately sensitive to bit errors
- **Class II:** 78 bits, least sensitive to bit errors

The first 50 bits are protected by a 3-bit cyclic redundancy check (CRC) error detection code. If an error is detected, the entire sample is discarded and replaced by a modified version of the preceding block. These 53 bits plus the 132 class 1b bits, plus a 4-bit tail sequence, are then protected by a convolutional (1, 2, 5) error-correcting code, resulting in $189 \times 2 = 378$ bits. The remaining 78 bits are unprotected and are appended to the protected bit to produce a block of 456 bits, with a resulting data rate of 456/20 ms = 22.8 kbps, which is the GSM traffic channel data rate.

To add protection against burst errors, each 456-bit block is divided into eight 57-bit blocks, which are transmitted in eight consecutive time slots. Because each time slot can carry two 57-bit blocks, each burst carries data from two different speech samples.

Following these steps, the speech data are encrypted 114 bits at a time, assembled into time slots (burst assembly), and finally modulated for transmission. The modulation scheme, Gaussian minimum shift keying (GMSK), is a form of frequency shift keying (FSK).

Data Encoding

Digital data are processed in a similar fashion as applied to speech signals. Data are processed in blocks of 240 bits every 20 ms, for a data rate of 12 kbps. Depending on the way logical channels are defined, the actual supported data rates are 9.6, 4,8, and 2.4 kbps. Each block is augmented by four tail bits. A (1, 2, 5) convolutional code is used to produce a block of $244 \times 2 = 488$ bits. Then 32 bits of this block are dropped (puncturing), leaving a block of 456 bits. A bit interleaving scheme is then used to spread the data over multiple bursts, again to reduce the effects of burst noise. The 488 bits are spread over 22 bursts in the following fashion:

- The 1st and 22nd bursts carry 6 bits each
- The 2nd and 21st bursts carry 12 bits each
- The 3rd and 20th bursts carry 18 bits each
- The 4th through 19th bursts carry 24 bits each

The result is that each burst carries information from 5 or 6 consecutive data blocks.

Slow Frequency Hopping

We have said that a given traffic channel is assigned a given frequency channel for transmission and reception. This is not strictly correct. GSM and many other cellular schemes use a technique known as slow frequency hopping to improve signal quality. Each successive TDMA frame in a given channel is carried on a different carrier frequency. Thus, the transmission frequency is changed once every 4.615 ms. Because multipath fading is dependent on carrier frequency, slow frequency hopping helps to compensate. Slow frequency hopping also reduces the effects of cochannel interference. Note that this is a form of spread spectrum communication.

Delay Equalization

Because mobile units are at different distances from the base station within a cell, their transmissions suffer differing amounts of delay. This phenomenon creates a design issue, because up to eight mobile units share the same TDMA frame. Thus, the timing of frame slots is critical. The base station provides a control signal to synchronize the timing of the various mobile units. Within the slot format, the tail bits and guard bits provide a margin to prevent the overlap of data bits from one time slot to another. The base station can adjust the timing of any active mobile by control signals that instruct the mobile to increment or decrement its timing.

GSM Signaling Protocol Architecture

A number of control messages are exchanged between the key entities in Figure 10.14 that deal with mobility, radio resources, and connection management. A detailed look at the various message formats and semantics could fill a book. Here we give an overview of the structure, which suggests the complexity of second-generation design.

Figure 10.17 summarizes the protocols used between the main elements of the network architecture. The lowest layer of the architecture is tailored to the physical link between entities. Between the mobile station and the base transceiver station,

BSSMAP	=	BSS mobile application part	MM	=	mobility management
BTSM	=	BTS management	MTP	=	message transfer part
CM	=	connection management	RRM	=	radio resources management
LAPD	=	link access protocol, D channel	SCCP	=	signal connection control part

Figure 10.17   GSM Signaling Protocol Architecture

the radio link discussed in preceding subsections carries higher-level data inside the TDMA format. Between other entities a standard 64-kbps digital channel is used.

At the link layer, a data link control protocol (see Figure 4.3) known as LAPDm is used. This is a modified version of the LAPD protocol defined for the Integrated Services Digital Network (ISDN). The remaining links use the normal LAPD protocol. In essence, LAPD is designed to convert a potentially unreliable physical link into a reliable data link. It does this by using a cyclic redundancy check to perform error detection (discussed in Section 8.1) and automatic repeat request (ARQ) to retransmit damaged frames (discussed in Section 8.4).[3]

Above the link layer are a number of protocols that provide specific functions. These include the following:

- **Radio resource management:** Controls the setup, maintenance, and termination of radio channels, including handoffs.
- **Mobility management:** Manages the location updating and registration procedures, as well as security and authentication.
- **Connection management:** Handles the setup, maintenance, and termination of calls (connections between end users).
- **Mobile application part (MAP):** Handles most of the signaling between different entities in the fixed part of the network, such as between the HLR and VLR.
- **BTS management:** Performs various management and administrative functions at the base transceiver station, under the control of the base station controller.

The MAP does not run directly on top of the link layer but rather on top of two intermediate protocols, SCCP and MTP. These latter protocols are part of Signaling System Number 7, which is a set of protocols designed to provide control signaling within digital circuit-switching networks, such as digital public telecommunications networks. These protocols provide general functions used by various applications, including MAP.

10.4 SECOND-GENERATION CDMA

Code division multiple access (CDMA) is a spread spectrum–based technique for multiplexing, introduced in Section 7.4, that provides an alternative to TDMA for second-generation cellular networks. We begin this section with an overview of the advantages of the CDMA approach and then look at the most widely used scheme, IS-95.

Code Division Multiple Access

CDMA for cellular systems can be described as follows. As with FDMA, each cell is allocated a frequency bandwidth, which is split into two parts, half for reverse

---

[3]See Appendix D for a discussion of data link control protocols.

(mobile unit to base station) and half for forward (base station to mobile unit). For full-duplex communication, a mobile unit uses both reverse and forward channels. Transmission is in the form of direct-sequence spread spectrum (DS-SS), which uses a chipping code to increase the data rate of the transmission, resulting in an increased signal bandwidth. Multiple access is provided by assigning orthogonal chipping codes to multiple users, so that the receiver can recover the transmission of an individual unit from multiple transmissions.

CDMA has a number of advantages for a cellular network:

- **Frequency diversity:** Because the transmission is spread out over a larger bandwidth, frequency-dependent transmission impairments, such as noise bursts and selective fading, have less effect on the signal.

- **Multipath resistance:** In addition to the ability of DS-SS to overcome multipath fading by frequency diversity, the chipping codes used for CDMA not only exhibit low cross correlation but also low autocorrelation. Therefore, a version of the signal that is delayed by more than one chip interval does not interfere with the dominant signal as much as in other multipath environments.

- **Privacy:** Because spread spectrum is obtained by the use of noiselike signals, where each user has a unique code, privacy is inherent.

- **Graceful degradation:** With FDMA or TDMA, a fixed number of users can access the system simultaneously. However, with CDMA, as more users access the system simultaneously, the noise level and hence the error rate increases; only gradually does the system degrade to the point of an unacceptable error rate.

A number of drawbacks of CDMA cellular should also be mentioned:

- **Self-jamming:** Unless all of the mobile users are perfectly synchronized, the arriving transmissions from multiple users will not be perfectly aligned on chip boundaries. Thus the spreading sequences of the different users are not orthogonal and there is some level of cross correlation. This is distinct from either TDMA or FDMA, in which for reasonable time or frequency guardbands, respectively, the received signals are orthogonal or nearly so.

- **Near-far problem:** Signals closer to the receiver are received with less attenuation than signals farther away. Given the lack of complete orthogonality, the transmissions from the more remote mobile units may be more difficult to recover. Thus, power control techniques are very important in a CDMA system.

- **Soft handoff:** As is discussed subsequently, a smooth handoff from one cell to the next requires that the mobile acquires the new cell before it relinquishes the old. This is referred to as a soft handoff and is more complex than the hard handoff used in FDMA and TDMA schemes.

Mobile Wireless CDMA Design Considerations

Before turning to the specific example of GSM, it will be useful to consider some general design elements of a CDMA cellular system.

RAKE Receiver

In a multipath environment, which is common in cellular systems, if the multiple versions of a signal arrive more than one chip interval apart from each other, the receiver can recover the signal by correlating the chip sequence with the dominant incoming signal. The remaining signals are treated as noise. However, even better performance can be achieved if the receiver attempts to recover the signals from multiple paths and then combine them, with suitable delays. This principle is used in the RAKE receiver.

Figure 10.18 illustrates the principle of the RAKE receiver. The original binary signal to be transmitted is spread by the exclusive-OR (XOR) operation with the transmitter's chipping code. The spread sequence is then modulated for transmission over the wireless channel. Because of multipath effects, the channel generates multiple copies of the signal, each with a different amount of time delay (τ_1, τ_2, etc), and each with a different attenuation factors (a_1, a_2, etc.). At the receiver, the combined signal is demodulated. The demodulated chip stream is then fed into multiple correlators, each delayed by a different amount. These signals are then combined using weighting factors estimated from the channel.

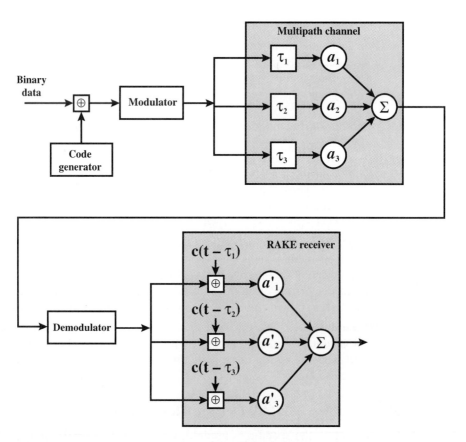

Figure 10.18 Principle of RAKE Receiver [PRAS98]

Soft Handoff

In an FDMA or TDMA system, neighboring cells use different portions of the available frequency spectrum (i.e., the frequency reuse factor N is greater than 1, typically 7). When the signal strength of a neighboring cell exceeds that of the current cell, plus a threshold, the mobile station is instructed to switch to a new frequency band that is within the allocation of the new cell. This is referred to as a **hard handoff**. In a typical CDMA cellular system, spatial separation of frequencies is not used (i.e., $N = 1$), because most of the time the interference from neighboring cells will not prohibit correct reception of a DS-SS signal.

In soft handoff, a mobile station is temporarily connected to more than one base station simultaneously. A mobile unit may start out assigned to a single cell. If the unit enters a region in which the transmissions from two base stations are comparable (within some threshold of each other), the mobile unit enters the soft handoff state in which it is connected to the two base stations. The mobile unit remains in this state until one base station clearly predominates, at which time it is assigned exclusively to that cell.

While in the soft handoff state, the transmissions from the mobile unit reaching the two base stations are both sent on to the mobile switching center, which estimates the quality of the two signals and selects one. The switch sends data or digitized speech signals to both base stations, which transmit them to the mobile unit. The mobile unit combines the two incoming signals to recover the information.

IS-95

The most widely used second-generation CDMA scheme is IS-95, which is primarily deployed in North America. Table 10.5 lists some key parameters of the IS-95 system. The transmission structures on the forward and reverse links differ and are described separately.

IS-95 Forward Link

Table 10.6 lists forward link channel parameters. The forward link consists of up to 64 logical CDMA channels each occupying the same 1228-kHz bandwidth (Figure 10.19a). The forward link supports four types of channels:

- **Pilot (channel 0):** A continuous signal on a single channel. This channel allows the mobile unit to acquire timing information, provides phase reference for the demodulation process, and provides a means for signal strength comparison for the purpose of handoff determination. The pilot channel consists of all zeros.
- **Synchronization (channel 32):** A 1200-bps channel used by the mobile station to obtain identification information about the cellular system (system time, long code state, protocol revision, etc.).
- **Paging (channels 1 to 7):** Contain messages for one or more mobile stations.
- **Traffic (channels 8 to 31 and 33 to 63):** The forward channel supports 55 traffic channels. The original specification supported data rates of up to 9600 bps. A subsequent revision added a second set of rates up to 14,400 bps.

Table 10.6 IS-95 Forward Link Channel Parameters

Channel	Sync	Paging		Traffic Rate Set 1						Traffic Rate Set 2			
Data rate (bps)	1200	4800	9600	1200	2400	4800	9600	1800	3600	7200	14400
Code repetition	2	2	1	8	4	2	1	8	4	2	1
Modulation symbol rate (sps)	4800	19,200	19,200	19,200	19,200	19,200	19,200	19,200	19,200	19,200	19,200
PN chips/ modulation symbol	256	64	64	64	64	64	64	64	64	64	64
PN chips/bit	1024	256	128	1024	512	256	128	682.67	341.33	170.67	85.33

Figure 10.19 IS-95 Channel Structure

Note that all of these channels use the same bandwidth. The chipping code is used to distinguish among the different channels. For the forward channel, the chipping codes are the 64 orthogonal 64-bit codes derived from a 64 × 64 Walsh matrix (discussed in Section 7.5; see Figure 7.17).

Figure 10.20 shows the processing steps for transmission on a forward traffic channel using rate set 1. For voice traffic, the speech is encoded at a data rate of 8550 bps. After additional bits are added for error detection, the rate is 9600 bps. The full channel capacity is not used when the user is not speaking. During quiet periods the data rate is lowered to as low as 1200 bps. The 2400-bps rate is used to transmit transients in the background noise, and the 4800 bps rate is used to mix digitized speech and signaling data.

The data or digitized speech is transmitted in 20-ms blocks with forward error correction provided by a convolutional encoder with rate 1/2, thus doubling the effective data rate to a maximum of 19.2 kbps. For lower data rates, the encoder output bits (called code symbols) are replicated to yield the 19.2-kbps rate. The data are then interleaved in blocks to reduce the effects of errors by spreading them out.

Following the interleaver, the data bits are scrambled. The purpose of this is to serve as a privacy mask and also to prevent the sending of repetitive patterns, which in turn reduces the probability of users sending at peak power at the same time. The scrambling is accomplished by means of a long code that is generated as a pseudorandom number from a 42-bit long shift register. The shift register is initialized with the user's electronic serial number. The output of the long code generator is at a rate of 1.2288 Mbps, which is 64 times the rate of 19.2 kbps, so only one bit in 64 is selected (by the decimator function). The resulting stream is XORed with the output of the block interleaver.

The next step in the processing inserts power control information in the traffic channel. The power control function of the base station robs the traffic channel of bits at a rate of 800 bps. These are inserted by stealing code bits. The 800-bps channel carries information directing the mobile unit to increment, decrement, or keep stable its current output level. This power control stream is multiplexed into the 19.2 kbps by replacing some of the code bits, using the long code generator to encode the bits.

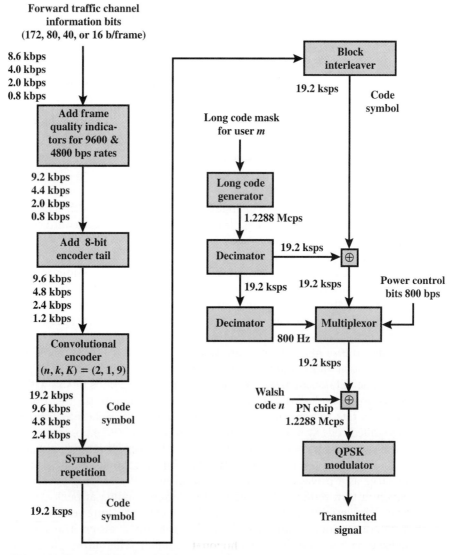

Figure 10.20 IS-95 Forward Link Transmission

The next step in the process is the DS-SS function, which spreads the 19.2 kbps to a rate of 1.2288 Mbps using one row of the 64 × 64 Walsh matrix. One row of the matrix is assigned to a mobile station during call setup. If a 0 bit is presented to the XOR function, then the 64 bits of the assigned row are sent. If a 1 is presented, then the bitwise XOR of the row is sent. Thus, the final bit rate is 1.2288 Mbps. This digital bit stream is then modulated onto the carrier using a QPSK modulation scheme. Recall from Chapter 6 that QPSK involves creating two bits streams that are separately modulated (see Figure 6.6). In the IS-95 scheme, the data are split into I and Q (in-phase and quadrature) channels and the data in each channel are XORed with a unique short code. The short codes are generated as pseudorandom numbers from a 15-bit long shift register.

IS-95 Reverse Link

Table 10.7 lists reverse link channel parameters. The reverse link consists of up to 94 logical CDMA channels each occupying the same 1228-kHz bandwidth (Figure 10.19b). The reverse link supports up to 32 access channels and up to 62 traffic channels.

The traffic channels in the reverse link are mobile unique. Each station has a unique long code mask based on its electronic serial number. The long code mask is a 42-bit number, so there are $2^{42} - 1$ different masks. The access channel is used by a mobile to initiate a call, to respond to a paging channel message from the base station, and for a location update.

Figure 10.21 shows the processing steps for transmission on a reverse traffic channel using rate set 1. The first few steps are the same as for the forward channel. For the reverse channel, the convolutional encoder has a rate of 1/3, thus tripling the effective data rate to a maximum of 28.8 kbps. The data are then block interleaved.

The next step is a spreading of the data using the Walsh matrix. The way in which the matrix is used, and its purpose, are different than that of the forward channel. In the reverse channel, the data coming out of the block interleaver are grouped in units of 6 bits. Each 6-bit unit serves as an index to select a row of the 64 × 64 Walsh matrix ($2^6 = 64$), and that row is substituted for the input. Thus the data rate is expanded by a factor of 64/6 to 307.2 kbps. The purpose of this encoding is to improve reception at the base station. Because the 64 possible codings are orthogonal, the block coding enhances the decision-making algorithm at the receiver and is also computationally efficient (see [PETE95] for details). We can view this Walsh modulation as a form of block error-correcting code with $(n, k) = (64, 6)$ and $d_{min} = 32$. In fact, all distances are 32.

The data burst randomizer is implemented to help reduce interference from other mobile stations (see [BLAC99] for a discussion). The operation involves using the long code mask to smooth the data out over each 20-ms frame.

The next step in the process is the DS-SS function. In the case of the reverse channel, the long code unique to the mobile is XORed with the output of the randomizer to produce the 1.2288-Mbps final data stream. This digital bit stream is then modulated onto the carrier using an orthogonal QPSK modulation scheme. This differs from the forward channel in the use of a delay element in the modulator (Figure 6.6) to produce orthogonality. The reason the modulators are different is that in the forward channel, the spreading codes are orthogonal, all coming from

Table 10.7 IS-95 Reverse Link Channel Parameters

Channel	Access	Traffic-Rate Set 1				Traffic-Rate Set 2			
Data rate (bps)	4800	1200	2400	4800	9600	1800	3600	7200	14400
Code rate	1/3	1/3	1/3	1/3	1/3	1/2	1/2	1/2	1/2
Symbol rate before repetition (sps)	14,400	3600	7200	14,400	28,800	3600	7200	14,400	28,800
Symbol repetition	2	8	4	2	1	8	4	2	1
Symbol rate after repetition (sps)	28,800	28,800	28,800	28,800	28,800	28,800	28,800	28,800	28,800
Transmit duty cycle	1	1/8	1/4	1/2	1	1/8	1/4	1/2	1
Code symbols/modulation symbol	6	6	6	6	6	6	6	6	6
PN chips/ modulation symbol	256	256	256	256	256	256	256	256	256
PN chips/bit	256	128	128	128	128	256/3	256/3	256/3	256/3

Figure 10.21 IS-95 Reverse Link Transmission

the Walsh matrix, whereas in the reverse channel, orthogonality of the spreading codes is not guaranteed.

10.5 THIRD-GENERATION SYSTEMS

The objective of the third-generation (3G) of wireless communication is to provide fairly high-speed wireless communications to support multimedia, data, and video in addition to voice. The ITU's International Mobile Telecommunications for the year 2000 (IMT-2000) initiative has defined the ITU's view of third-generation capabilities as follows:

- Voice quality comparable to the public switched telephone network
- 144 kbps data rate available to users in high-speed motor vehicles over large areas
- 384 kbps available to pedestrians standing or moving slowly over small areas
- Support (to be phased in) for 2.048 Mbps for office use
- Symmetrical and asymmetrical data transmission rates
- Support for both packet switched and circuit switched data services
- An adaptive interface to the Internet to reflect efficiently the common asymmetry between inbound and outbound traffic
- More efficient use of the available spectrum in general
- Support for a wide variety of mobile equipment
- Flexibility to allow the introduction of new services and technologies

More generally, one of the driving forces of modern communication technology is the trend toward universal personal telecommunications and universal communications access. The first concept refers to the ability of a person to identify himself or herself easily and use conveniently any communication system in an entire country, over a continent, or even globally, in terms of a single account. The second refers to the capability of using one's terminal in a wide variety of environments to connect to information services (e.g., to have a portable terminal that will work in the office, on the street, and on airplanes equally well). This revolution in personal computing will obviously involve wireless communication in a fundamental way. The GSM cellular telephony with its subscriber identity module, for example, is a large step toward these goals.

Personal communications services (PCSs) and personal communication networks (PCNs) are names attached to these concepts of global wireless communications, and they also form objectives for third-generation wireless.

Generally, the technology planned is digital using time division multiple access or code-division multiple access to provide efficient use of the spectrum and high capacity.

PCS handsets are designed to be low power and relatively small and light. Efforts are being made internationally to allow the same terminals to be used worldwide.

Alternative Interfaces

Figure 10.22 shows the alternative schemes that have been adopted as part of IMT-2000. The specification covers a set of radio interfaces for optimized performance in different radio environments. A major reason for the inclusion of five alternatives was to enable a smooth evolution from existing first- and second-generation systems.

The five alternatives reflect the evolution from the second-generation. Two of the specifications grow out of the work at the European Telecommunications Standards Institute (ETSI) to develop a UMTS (universal mobile telecommunications system) as Europe's 3G wireless standard. UMTS includes two standards. One of

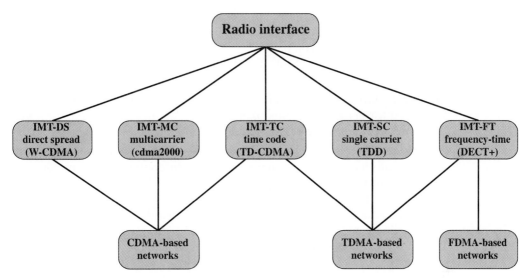

Figure 10.22 IMT-2000 Terrestrial Radio Interfaces

these is known as Wideband CDMA, or W-CDMA. This scheme fully exploits CDMA technology to provide high data rates with efficient use of bandwidth. Table 10.8 shows some of the key parameters of W-CDMA. The other European effort under UMTS is known as IMT-TC, or TD-CDMA. This approach is a combination of W-CDMA and TDMA technology. IMT-TC is intended to provide an upgrade path for the TDMA-based GSM systems.

Another CDMA-based system, known as cdma2000, has a North American origin. This scheme is similar to, but incompatible with, W-CDMA, in part because the standards use different chip rates. Also, cdma2000 uses a technique known as multicarrier, not used with W-CDMA.

We have looked at some of the technologies that appear in these 3G systems elsewhere in the book. These include turbo codes (Section 8.3), and Gold codes and variable-length spreading codes (Section 7.5).

Two other interface specifications are shown in Figure 10.22. IMT-SC is primarily designed for TDMA-only networks. IMT-FC can be used by both TDMA and FDMA carriers to provide some 3G services; it is an outgrowth of the Digital European Cordless Telecommunications (DECT) standard, discussed in Chapter 11.

CDMA Design Considerations

The dominant technology for 3G systems is CDMA. Although three different CDMA schemes have been adopted, they share some common design issues. [OJAN98] lists the following:

- **Bandwidth:** An important design goal for all 3G systems is to limit channel usage to 5 MHz. There are several reasons for this goal. On the one hand, a bandwidth of 5 MHz or more improves the receiver's ability to resolve multi-path when compared to narrower bandwidths. On the other hand, available spectrum is limited by competing needs, and 5 MHz is a reasonable upper limit on what can be allocated for 3G. Finally, 5 MHz is adequate for supporting data rates of 144 and 384 kHz, the main targets for 3G services.

- **Chip rate:** Given the bandwidth, the chip rate depends on desired data rate, the need for error control, and bandwidth limitations. A chip rate of 3 Mcps or more is reasonable given these design parameters.
- **Multirate:** The term *multirate* refers to the provision of multiple fixed-data-rate logical channels to a given user, in which different data rates are provided on different logical channels. Further, the traffic on each logical channel can be switched independently through the wireless and fixed networks to different destinations. The advantage of multirate is that the system can flexibly support multiple simultaneous applications from a given user and can efficiently use available capacity by only providing the capacity required for each service.

Table 10.8 W-CDMA Parameters

Channel bandwidth	5 MHz
Forward RF channel structure	Direct spread
Chip rate	3.84 Mcps
Frame length	10 ms
Number of slots/frame	15
Spreading modulation	Balanced QPSK (forward) Dual channel QPSK (reverse) Complex spreading circuit
Data modulation	QPSK (forward) BPSK (reverse)
Coherent detection	Pilot symbols
Reverse channel multiplexing	Control and pilot channel time multiplexed. I and Q multiplexing for data and control channels
Multirate	Various spreading and multicode
Spreading factors	4 to 256
Power control	Open and fast closed loop (1.6 kHz)
Spreading (forward)	Variable length orthogonal sequences for channel separation. Gold sequences 2^{18} for cell and user separation.
Spreading (reverse)	Same as forward, different time shifts in I and Q channels
Handover	Soft handover

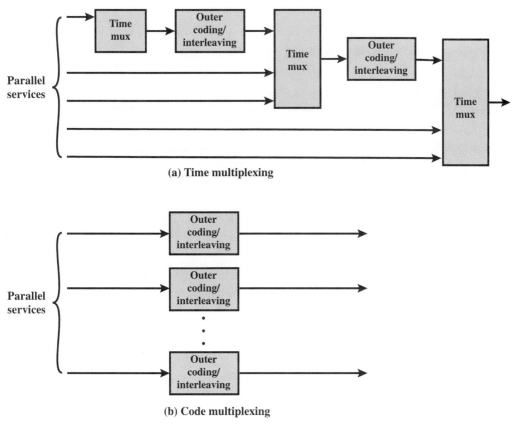

(a) Time multiplexing

(b) Code multiplexing

Figure 10.23   Time and Code Multiplexing Principles [OJAN98]

Multirate can be achieved with a TDMA scheme within a single CDMA channel, in which a different number of slots per frame are assigned to achieve different data rates. All the subchannels at a given data rate would be protected by error correction and interleaving techniques (Figure 10.23a). An alternative is to use multiple CDMA codes, with separate coding and interleaving, and map them to separate CDMA channels (Figure 10.23b).

10.6 RECOMMENDED READING AND WEB SITES

[BERT94] and [ANDE95] are instructive surveys of cellular wireless propagation effects. [POLL96] covers the handoff problem in depth. [EVER94] and [ORLI98] provide good accounts of cellular traffic analysis. [BLAC99] is one of the best technical treatments of second-generation cellular systems. A good survey of GSM concepts is [RAHN93]; for more detail see [GARG99].

[TANT98] contains reprints of numerous important papers dealing with CDMA in cellular networks. [DINA98] provides an overview of both PN and orthogonal spreading codes for cellular CDMA networks.

[OJAN98] provides an overview of key technical design considerations for 3G systems. Another useful survey is [ZENG00]. [PRAS00] is a much more detailed analysis.

ANDE95   Anderson, J.; Rappaport, T.; and Yoshida, S. "Propagation Measurements and Models for Wireless Communications Channels." *IEEE Communications Magazine*, January 1995.

BERT94   Bertoni, H.; Honcharenko, W.; Maciel, L.; and Xia, H. "UHF Propagation Prediction for Wireless Personal Communications." *Proceedings of the IEEE*, September 1994.

BLAC99   Black, U. *Second-generation Mobile and Wireless Networks.* Upper Saddle River, NJ: Prentice Hall, 1999.

DINA98   Dinan, E., and Jabbari, B. "Spreading Codes for Direct Sequence CDMA and Wideband CDMA Cellular Networks." *IEEE Communications Magazine*, September 1998.

EVER94   Everitt, D. "Traffic Engineering of the Radio Interface for Cellular Mobile Networks." *Proceedings of the IEEE*, September 1994.

GARG99   Garg, V., and Wilkes, J. *Principles and Applications of GSM.* Upper Saddle River, NJ: Prentice Hall, 1999.

OJAN98   Ojanpera, T., and Prasad, G. "An Overview of Air Interface Multiple Access for IMT-2000/UMTS." *IEEE Communications Magazine*, September 1998.

ORLI98   Orlik, P., and Rappaport, S. "Traffic Performance and Mobility Modeling of Cellular Communications with Mixed Platforms and Highly Variable Mobilities." *Proceedings of the IEEE*, July 1998.

POLL96   Pollini, G. "Trends in Handover Design." *IEEE Communications Magazine*, March 1996.

PRAS00   Prasad, R.; Mohr, W.; and Konhauser, W., eds. *Third-Generation Mobile Communication Systems.* Boston: Artech House, 2000.

RAHN93   Rahnema, M. "Overview of the GSM System and Protocol Architecture." *IEEE Communications Magazine*, April 1993.

TANT98   Tantaratana, S, and Ahmed, K., eds. *Wireless Applications of Spread Spectrum Systems: Selected Readings.* Piscataway, NJ: IEEE Press, 1998.

ZENG00   Zeng, M.; Annamalai, A.; and Bhargava, V. "Harmonization of Global Third-generation Mobile Systems. *IEEE Communications Magazine*, December 2000.

 Recommended Web sites:

- **Cellular Telecommunications and Internet Association:** An industry consortium that provides information on successful applications of wireless technology
- **GSM World:** Lots of information and links concerning GSM
- **CDMA Development Group:** Information and links for IS-95 and CDMA generally
- **WOW-com:** Site of the Cellular Telecommunications Industry Association

10.7 KEY TERMS, REVIEW QUESTIONS, AND PROBLEMS

Key Terms

Advanced Mobil Phone Service (AMPS)	forward channel	power control
base station	frequency reuse	reuse factor
blocking network	Global System for Mobile Communications (GSM)	reverse channel
cellular network	handoff	second-generation (2G) network
closed-loop power control	handover	soft handoff
code division multiple access (CDMA)	hard handoff	third-generation (3G) network
first-generation (1G) network	mobile radio	time division multiple access (TDMA)
	nonblocking network	
	open-loop power control	

Review Questions

1 What geometric shape is used in cellular system design?

2 What is the principle of frequency reuse in the context of a cellular network?

3 List five ways of increasing the capacity of a cellular system.

4 Explain the paging function of a cellular system.

5 List and briefly define different performance metrics that may be used to make the handoff decision.

6 As a mobile unit in communication with base station moves, what factors determine the need for power control and the amount of power adjustment?

7 Explain the difference between open-loop and closed-loop power control.

8 What is the difference between traffic intensity and the mean rate of calls in a system?

9 What are the key differences between first- and second-generation cellular systems?

10 What are the advantages of using CDMA for a cellular network?

11 What are the disadvantages of using CDMA for a cellular network?

12 Explain the difference between hard and soft handoff.

13 What are some key characteristics that distinguish third-generation cellular systems from second-generation cellular systems?

Problems

1 Consider four different cellular systems that share the following characteristics. The frequency bands are 825 to 845 MHz for mobile unit transmission and 870 to 890 MHz for base station transmission. A duplex circuit consists of one 30-kHz channel in each direction. The systems are distinguished by the reuse factor, which is 4, 7, 12, and 19, respectively.

    a. Suppose that in each of the systems, the cluster of cells (4, 7, 12, 19) is duplicated 16 times. Find the number of simultaneous communications that can be supported by each system.

    b. Find the number of simultaneous communications that can be supported by a single cell in each system.

    c. What is the area covered, in cells, by each system?

    d. Suppose the cell size is the same in all four systems and a fixed area of 100 cells is covered by each system. Find the number of simultaneous communications that can be supported by each system.

2 Describe a sequence of events similar to that of Figure 10.6 for

    a. a call from a mobile unit to a fixed subscriber.

    b. a call from a fixed subscriber to a mobile unit.

3 In the discussion of the handoff procedure based on relative signal strength with threshold, it was pointed out that if the threshold is set quite low, such as Th_3, the mobile may move far into the new cell (L_4). This reduces the quality of the communication link and may result in a dropped call. Can you suggest another drawback to this scheme?

4 Hysteresis is a technique commonly used in control systems. As an example, describe the hysteresis mechanism used in a household thermostat.

5 A telephony connection has a duration of 23 minutes. This is the only connection made by this caller during the course of an hour. How much is the amount of traffic, in Erlangs, of this connection?

6 Using Table 10.3, approximate the answers to the following. Also, in each case, give a description in words of the general problem being solved. *Hint:* Straight-line interpolation is adequate.

    a. Given $N = 20$, $A = 10.5$, find P.

    b. Given $N = 20$, $P = 0.015$, find A.

    c. Given $P = 0.005$, $A = 6$, find N.

7 An analog cellular system has a total of 33 MHz of bandwidth and uses two 25-kHz simplex (one-way) channels to provide full duplex voice and control channels.

    a. What is the number of channels available per cell for a frequency reuse factor of (1) 4 cells, (2) 7 cells, and (3) 12 cells?

    b. Assume that 1 MHz is dedicated to control channels but that only one control channel is needed per cell. Determine a reasonable distribution of control channels and voice channels in each cell for the three frequency reuse factors of part (a).

8 As was mentioned, the one-way bandwidth available to a single operator in the AMPS system is 12.5 MHz with a channel bandwidth of 30 kHz and 21 control channels. We would like to calculate the efficiency with which this system utilizes bandwidth for a particular installation. Use the following parameters:

- Cell area = 8 km^2
- Total coverage area = 4000 km^2
- Frequency reuse factor = 7
- Average number of calls per user during the busy hour = 1.2
- Average holding time of a call = 100 s
- Call blocking probability = 2%

    a. How many voice channels are there per cell?

    b. Use Table 10.3 and a simple straight-line interpolation to determine the total traffic carried per cell, in Erlangs/cell. Then convert that to Erlangs/km^2.

    c. Calculate the number of calls/hour/cell and the number of calls/hour/km^2.

    d. Calculate the number of users/hour/cell and the number of users/hour/channel.

    e. A common definition of spectral efficiency with respect to modulation, or modulation efficiency, in Erlangs/MHz/km^2, is

$$\eta = \frac{(\text{Total traffic carried by the system})}{(\text{Bandwidth})(\text{Total coverage area})}$$

Determine the modulation efficiency for this system.

9 A cellular system uses FDMA with a spectrum allocation of 12.5 MHz in each direction, a guard band at the edge of the allocated spectrum of 10 kHz, and a channel bandwidth of 30 kHz. What is the number of available channels?

10 If 8 speech channels are supported on a single radio channel, and if no guard band is assumed, what is the number of simultaneous users that can be accommodated in GSM?

11 a. What is the duration of a bit in GSM?

   b. If a user is allocated one time slot per frame, what is the delay between successive transmissions in successive frames?

12 If we consider the trailing bits, stealing bits, guard bits, and training bits in a GSM frame as overhead, and the rest of the bits as data, then what is the percentage overhead in a GSM frame?

13 Using the definition of slow frequency hopping from Chapter 7, demonstrate that GSM uses slow frequency hopping.

14 For a cellular system, FDMA spectral efficiency is defined as $\eta_a = \dfrac{B_c N_T}{B_w}$, where

   B_c = channel bandwidth
   B_w = total bandwidth in one direction
   N_T = total number of voice channels in the covered area

   a. What is an upper bound on η_a?

   b. Determine η_a for the system of Problem 8.

15 Consider a 7-cell system covering an area of 3100 km². The traffic in the seven cells is as follows:

Cell number	1	2	3	4	5	6	7
Traffic (Erlangs)	30.8	66.7	48.6	33.2	38.2	37.8	32.6

Each user generates an average of 0.03 Erlangs of traffic per hour, with a mean holding time of 120 s. The system consists of a total of 395 channels and is designed for a grade of service of 0.02.

   a. Determine the number of subscribers in each cell.

   b. Determine the number of calls per hour per subscriber.

   c. Determine the number of calls per hour in each cell.

   d. Determine the number of channels required in each cell. *Hint:* You will need to extrapolate using Table 10.3.

   e. Determine the total number of subscribers.

   f. Determine the average number of subscribers per channel.

   g. Determine the subscriber density per km².

   h. Determine the total traffic (total Erlangs).

   i. Determine the Erlangs per km².

   j. What is the radius of a cell?

CHAPTER 11

CORDLESS SYSTEMS AND WIRELESS LOCAL LOOP

I n this chapter, we look at two technologies that bring wireless access into the residence and office: cordless systems and wireless local loop (WLL).

11.1 CORDLESS SYSTEMS

Standardized cordless systems have evolved from cordless telephone technology. Originally, cordless telephones were developed to provide users with mobility within a residence or small office by separating the handset from the rest of the telephone (called the base station) and providing a simple analog wireless link. As technology improved, digital cordless telephones were developed. The products on the market used proprietary wireless interfaces. Because the same manufacturer sold the base station and the handset as a unit, there was no need for standards.

Standards-making bodies became interested in standardizing cordless technology to widen its range of applicability, in two directions. First, cordless systems can support multiple users from the same base station, which could include either multiple telephone handsets or both voice and data devices (e.g., fax or printer). Second, cordless systems can operate in a number of environments:

- **Residential:** Within a residence a single base station can provide voice and data support, enabling in-house communications as well as providing a connection to the public telephone network.
- **Office:** A small office can be supported by a single base station that provides service for a number of telephone handsets and data devices. In a larger office, multiple base stations can be used in a cellular configuration, with the base stations connected to a PBX (private branch exchange) switch. Such a configuration can serve hundreds or even thousands of users.
- **Telepoint:** Telepoint refers to the provision of a base station in a public place, such as a shopping mall or airport. This application has not succeeded in the marketplace.

A number of design considerations have driven the development of cordless standards. [WEBB00] lists the following:

1. The range of the handset from the base station is modest, up to about 200 m. Thus, low-power designs are used. Typically, the power output is one or two orders of magnitude lower than for cellular systems.
2. The handset and the base station need to be inexpensive. This dictates the use of simple technical approaches, such as in the area of speech coding and channel equalization.
3. Frequency flexibility is limited, because the user owns the base station as well as the mobile portion and can install these in a variety of environments. Hence, the system needs to be able to seek a low-interference channel wherever it is used.

Table 11.1 DECT and PWT Parameters

	DECT	**PWT**
Bandwidth	20 MHz	20 MHz
Band	1.88 to 1.9 GHz	1.91 to 1.92 GHz
Access method	TDD/TDMA/FDMA	TDD/TDMA/FDMA
Carrier bandwidth	1.728 MHz	1.25 MHz
Number of carriers	10	8
Channels per carrier	12	12
Number of channels	120	120
Handoff	Yes	Yes
Transmitted data rate	1.152 Mbps	1.152 Mbps
Speech rate	32 kbps	32 kbps
Speech coding technique	ADPCM	ADPCM
Modulation technique	Gaussian FSK	$\pi/4$ DQPSK
Peak output power	250 mW	90 mW
Mean output power	10 mW	10 mW
Maximum cell radius	30 to 100 m	30 to 100 m

Although a number of different standards have been proposed for cordless systems, the most prominent is DECT (digital enhanced cordless telecommunications),[1] developed in Europe. The U.S. equivalent is known as PWT (personal wireless telecommunications). Table 11.1 shows some of the key parameters for DECT and PWT. These systems use an approach referred to as time division duplex (TDD). We begin with a general discussion of TDD and then turn to the details of DECT.

Time Division Duplex

In the technique of TDD, also known as time-compression multiplexing (TCM), data are transmitted in one direction at a time, with transmission alternating between the two directions. We first look at simple TDD and then discuss TDMA TDD.

Simple TDD

To achieve the desired subscriber data rate with simple TDD, the transmitter's bit stream is divided into equal segments, compressed in time to a higher transmission rate, and transmitted in bursts, which are expanded at the other end to the original rate. A short quiescent period is used between bursts going in opposite directions to allow the channel to settle down. Thus, the actual data rate on the channel must be greater than twice the data rate required by the two end systems.

---

[1]DECT formerly stood for digital European cordless telephone.

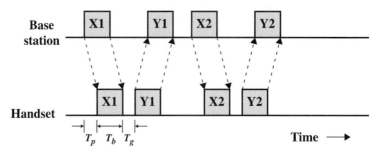

T_p = Propagation delay
T_b = Burst transmission time
T_g = Guard time

Figure 11.1   Transmission Using Time Division Duplex

The timing implications are shown in Figure 11.1. The two sides alternate in the transmission of data. Each side sends blocks of some fixed length, which take a time T_b to transmit; this time is a linear function of the number of bits in a block. In addition, a time T_p is required for the propagation of a signal from transmitter to receiver; this time is a linear function of the distance between transmitter and receiver. Finally, a guard time T_g is introduced to turn the channel around. Thus, the time to send one block is $(T_p + T_b + T_g)$. However, because the two sides must alternate transmissions, the rate at which blocks can be transmitted by either side is only $1/2(T_p + T_b + T_g)$. We can relate this to the effective data rate, R, as seen by the two end points as follows. Let B be the size of a block in bits and R be the desired data rate in bits per second. Then the effective number of bits transmitted per second is

$$R = B/2(T_p + T_b + T_g)$$

The actual data rate, A, on the medium can easily be seen to be

$$A = B/T_b$$

Combining the two, we have

$$A = 2R\left(1 + \frac{T_p + T_g}{T_b}\right)$$

Thus, the actual data rate on the link is more than double the effective data rate seen by the two sides. The choice of block size, B, is a compromise between competing requirements. If B is increased, there is a decrease in the actual data rate, A. This makes the task of implementation easier. On the other hand, this is accompanied by an increase in the signal delay due to buffering, which is undesirable for voice traffic.

Example. One of the standard interfaces defined for ISDN (Integrated Services Digital Network) is the basic interface, which provides a data rate of 192 kbps and uses a frame size of 48 bits. Suppose we use TDD with a block size equal to the frame size. Assume the distance between the subscriber and the network switch is 1 km and a guard time 10 μs is used. What is the actual data rate?

The burst transmission time is (48 bits)/(192 kbps) = 250 μs. The propagation delay is $(1 \text{ km})/(3 \times 10^8 \text{ m/s}) = 3.33$ μs. Thus

$$A = 2 \times 192 \times [1 + (3.33 + 10)/250)] = 404 \text{ kbps}$$

TDMA TDD

TDD was developed for use on wired subscriber systems but has now found application in wireless configurations. In a wireless configuration, TDD involves transmitting and receiving on the same carrier frequency but at different times. Wireless TDD is typically used with TDMA, in which a number of users receive forward (base to handset) channel signals in turn and then transmit reverse (handset to base) channel signals in turn, all on the same carrier frequency.

Two important advantages of TDD over using a TDMA system with two different carriers, one in each direction, are improved ability to cope with fast fading and improved capacity allocation.

With respect to **fast fading**, the pattern of fading changes as the frequency changes.[2] It is possible for a mobile receiving on one frequency and transmitting on another to experience strong fade in one direction only. One way to cope with fast fading is spatial diversity of the antennas. In this scheme a receiver employs two antennas, spaced ideally at least one wavelength apart. With such a configuration there is a good chance that if one of the antennas is experiencing significant fade, the other is not. The receiver can then select the strongest incoming signal for demodulation. This approach is fine for the base station but is not practical for small, inexpensive handsets. Further, we wish to avoid complex adaptive equalization algorithms or forward error control algorithms. With TDD, however, spatial diversity can still be used. For each forward channel burst arriving at the base station, the base station selects the antenna with the stronger signal for reception. The base station then uses that same antenna for the next transmission on the corresponding forward channel. Because the same frequency is used in both directions, this antenna should provide the strongest signal back at the handset.

The other advantage of TDMA/TDD over TDMA/FDMA is in the area of **capacity allocation**. For many data-oriented (as opposed to voice-oriented) applications, it is likely that the volume of traffic will be greater in the forward direction than in the reverse direction. If a conventional FDMA scheme is used, with equal bandwidth on forward and reverse channels, then the system must be sized for the forward channel and capacity on the reverse channel is wasted. On a TDD system,

---

[2]See Section 5.4 for a discussion of fast fading.

it is possible for a controller to allocate dynamically the number of TDMA slots in each direction so that more slots are available on the forward channel when needed.

DECT Frame Format

A good place to begin in explaining DECT is the TDMA/TDD frame format, illustrated in Figure 11.2. A single frame occupies 10 ms and consists of 24 TDMA time slots. For the default configuration, the first 12 time slots define 12 logical channels for transmission from base station to handset (forward direction), and the remaining

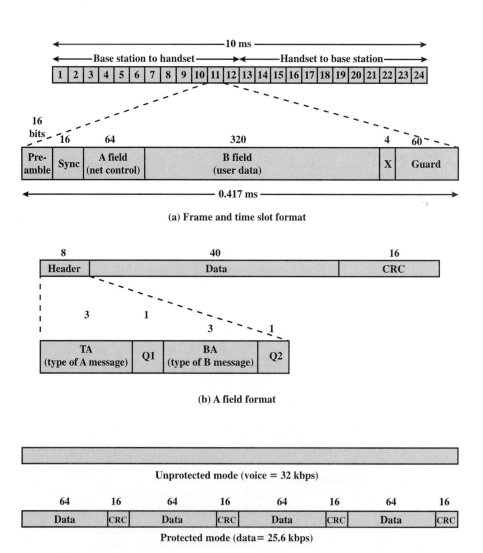

Figure 11.2 DECT Formats

12 time slots define 12 logical channels for transmission from handset to base station (reverse direction). Thus, a single carrier supports 12 full-duplex logical channels. Transmission alternates between bursts of 12 time slots in the forward direction followed by 12 time slots in the reverse direction.

Each time slot occupies $10/24 = 0.417$ ms and can be viewed as consisting of 6 fields and a total of 480 bits. Thus, the raw data rate is $480/0.417 = 1.152$ Mbps. The six fields are as follows:

- **Preamble (16 bits):** Serves to alert receiver and allow it to "warm up."
- **Sync (16 bits):** Used to enable the receiver to synchronize on the beginning of the time slot.
- **A field (64 bits):** Used for network control.
- **B field (320 bits):** Contains user data.
- **X field (4 bits):** Consists of four parity check bits, which enables terminals and base stations to monitor the quality of signal transmission.
- **Guard (60 bits):** This is a 52-µs guard time, corresponding to T_g in Figure 11.1.

A Field

The A field carries control information and consists of three subfields:

- **Header (8 bits):** Indicates the type of information carried in the A and B fields.
- **Data (40 bits):** Contains a network control message.
- **CRC (16 bits):** A 16-bit error detecting code covering the header and data (see Section 8.1 for a discussion of CRC).

The A field multiplexes five logical control channels, denoted as C, M, N, P, and Q (Table 11.2). The first three bits in the header define the type of information in the 40-bit data field. The Q1 and Q2 bits form a signaling channel that provides information on signal quality at the other device.

Table 11.2 DECT Logical Channels [GOOD97]

Channel	Data rate (kbps)		Purpose
	Base Transmit	**Terminal Transmit**	
I_N	2	2	Unprotected user information (telephone)
I_P	Variable	Variable	Protected user information (data)
C	0 to 2	0 to 2	Call management
M	0 to 2	0 to 2	Physical layer control
N	0.25 to 3.75	2 to 4	Handshaking
P	0 to 1.5	0	Paging
Q	0.25	0	System information

The **Q channel** is used to broadcast general system information from the base station to all terminals. Q channel information is carried in one frame out of a 16-frame multiframe. Therefore, the bit rate of the Q channel is 40 bits per 160 ms, or 250 bps. The **P channel** provides paging from the base station to the terminals. As in a cellular system, a paging message notifies a specific user of an incoming call. The P channel can occupy up to 6 frames per multiframe, for a maximum data rate of 1.5 kbps. In response to a page and at the time of handoff, a terminal uses the two-way **M channel** to exchange medium access control messages with the base station. These messages coordinate channel allocation and handoff operations. Up to 8 frames per multiframe in each direction, or half the capacity of the A field, can be used for M channel messages. Once a connection is established, the **N channel** provides a handshaking protocol. The base station transmits an identification code on the forward channel and the terminal echoes the code on the corresponding reverse N channel. This allows both sides to detect strong signals arriving from interfering sources using the same physical channel. From 1 to 15 of the 16 frames in a forward multiframe are used for the N channel traffic, depending on the needs of the M, C, and P channels. In the reverse direction, the N channel occupies from 8 to 16 frames per multiframe, depending on the needs of the M and C channels. Finally, the **C channel** provides call management for active connections and can occupy up to 8 frames per multiframe in each direction.

B Field

The B field transmits data in one of two modes. The **unprotected mode** is used to transmit digitized voice. This provides a data rate on each channel, in each direction, of 320 bits per 10 ms, or 32 kbps. This dictates the use of a voice encoding scheme that yields the 32-kbps rate, as discussed subsequently.

Protected mode transmits nonvoice data traffic. In this case, the B field is organized into four blocks of 64 data bits, with each block protected by a 16-bit CRC field. Notice that error correction is not provided, merely error detection. It is up to a higher layer, using an ARQ protocol (Section 8.4) to recover from detected errors. The protected mode can support a data rate of up to 25.6 kbps for a channel that occupies one time slot per frame. DECT allows for flexible assignment of time slots to logical channels, in both directions, so that this represents a base data rate.

DECT Operation

Figure 11.3 indicates the protocol architecture that supports DECT operations. At the **physical layer**, data are transmitted in the TDMA-TDD frames (Figure 11.2) over one of 10 RF carriers. The modulation method is Gaussian-filtered FSK, with a nominal deviation of 288 kHz. This is essentially the same as the GMSK technique used for GSM (Chapter 10). The ratio of data rate to transmission bandwidth is 2 (compare Table 6.2), and the data rate is 1.152 Mbps.

The **medium access control (MAC) layer** selects the physical channels and then establishes or releases connections on those channels. It also multiplexes information into the TDMA-TDD frame format. The MAC layer supports three services:

- **Broadcast:** Broadcast messages sent in the A field.
- **Connection oriented:** Transfer of user data in the B field.
- **Connectionless:** Supports individual DECT messages sent in the A field.

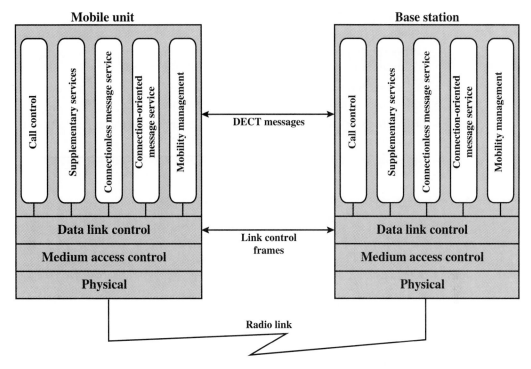

Figure 11.3 DECT Protocol Architecture

The data link control layer provides for the reliable transmission of messages using traditional data link control procedures, including error detection and automatic repeat request.[3]

Above the data link control layer are a set of services:

- **Call control:** Manages circuit-switched calls, including connection setup and release.
- **Supplementary services:** Services independent of any call that support operations.
- **Connectionless message service:** Support of connectionless messages. This service will segment longer messages into smaller blocks for transmission and reassemble at reception, if necessary.
- **Connection-oriented message service:** Support of connection-oriented messages.
- **Mobility management:** Handles functions necessary for the secure provision of DECT services. Mobility management is organized into seven groups of services:
  - **—Identity procedures:** Used for the mobile unit to identify itself to the base station.
  - **—Authentication procedure:** Establishes that the mobile unit is a valid network user.

---

[3]See Appendix D for a general discussion of data link control protocols.

—**Location procedure:** Used in systems with multiple base stations to track location of mobile unit.

—**Access rights procedure:** Establishes that the mobile unit has the right to gain access to a specific type of local or global network.

—**Key allocation procedure:** Distributes encryption keys for protecting network control information and user information.

—**Parameter retrieval procedure:** Used to exchange information about the parameters of the mobile unit and network operation.

—**Ciphering-related procedure:** Encryption and decryption operations.

Adaptive Differential Pulse Code Modulation

For voice digitization, DECT makes use of a procedure known as adaptive differential pulse code modulating (ADPCM). ADPCM has been standardized by ITU-T and is used in a number of applications, including digital circuit-switched networks such as ISDN, and in a number of wireless local loop implementations. We first look at the basic principles involved, then describe the simpler differential PCM (DPCM) scheme, and finally examine ADPCM.[4]

Differential Quantization

Differential quantization is based on the principle that speech signals tend not to change much between two samples. Thus, with ordinary PCM, the quantized values of adjacent samples will generally be near to one another and the transmitted PCM values contain considerable redundancy. Hence, it might make sense to transmit only the difference value between adjacent samples rather than the actual value, leading to the use of fewer bits per sample (Figure 11.4). Thus, if $m(k)$ is the kth sample, we transmit the difference $d(k) = m(k) - m(k - 1)$. If the receiver starts with the correct initial value, then on the basis of the sequence of difference samples $d(k)$, it can reconstruct the sequence of samples $m(k)$.

However, if we merely transmit the difference between the current and the immediately preceding samples, using fewer bits, there is the danger that the output at the receiver will begin to drift away from the true value at an increasing amount. If the difference value between two samples exceeds that which can be represented by the bits transmitted, then the receiver will err in reproducing the input and there is no way to make a correction subsequently. As a way to address this problem, the encoder could not only transmit a difference value; it could also replicate the decoding function that takes place at the receiver. The encoder could then transmit the difference between the current sample and what the encoder knows is the receiver's output from the previous transmission. In effect, the encoder is instructing the decoder to make incremental adjustments to its previous output, thus automatically providing a correction.

---

[4]Before proceeding, the reader may wish to review the discussion of PCM in Section 6.4.

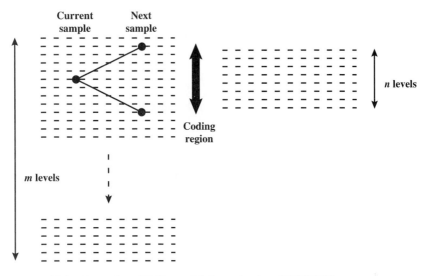

Figure 11.4 Normal and Differential Quantization [BUCH99]

Differential PCM

The scheme that has just been described is based on the assumption that difference values will be less than sample values. We can do even better than that by recognizing that voice signals change relatively slowly and therefore we can fairly accurately estimate, or predict, the value of the kth sample $m(k)$ from the values of the preceding samples. For an estimate of the kth sample, $\hat{m}(k)$, we then transmit the difference $d(k) = m(k) - \hat{m}(k)$. If we use an accurate estimator, this difference value should be less than the difference between successive samples. At the receiver, the same estimation function is used and the incoming difference value is added to the estimate of the current sample. This is the principle behind differential PCM (DPCM). Note that the simple difference scheme of the preceding paragraph is just a special case of DPCM in which we use the estimator $\hat{m}(k) = m(k - 1)$.

Figure 11.5a is a block diagram of the transmitter. An understanding of this diagram takes some discussion. To begin, an analog sample $m(k)$ is taken of the voice signal $g(t)$; this is a pulse amplitude modulation (PAM) sample. We are now faced with a difficulty. We could construct a predicted value $\hat{m}(k)$, take the difference, and transmit that. However, at the receiving end, instead of the past analog samples $m(k - 1)$, $m(k - 2)$, etc., what we have are the sequence of quantized differences from which we could construct a sequence of quantized samples, $m_q(k)$. So we cannot reconstruct $\hat{m}(k)$ but can only determine $\hat{m}_q(k)$, the estimate of the quantized sample $m_q(k)$, with the estimate based on the preceding quantized samples $m_q(k - 1)$, $m_q(k - 2)$, etc. If the transmitter is basing its prediction on values of $m(k)$ and the receiver is basing its prediction on values of $m_q(k)$, there is an error introduced in reconstruction. Instead, the transmitter should also determine $m_q(k)$ and transmit the difference $d(k) = m(k) - \hat{m}_q(k)$. As we have just seen, the receiver can also generate $\hat{m}_q(k)$, and from the received $d(k)$, the receiver can reconstruct $m_q(k)$.

It remains to show that Figure 11.5a produces the desired quantized differences. The output of the predictor is designated $\hat{m}_q(k)$, the predicted value of $m(k)$. The difference is taken to produce

$$d(k) = m(k) - \hat{m}_q(k)$$

This difference is then quantized to produce $d_q(k)$. We can express this as

$$d_q(k) = d(k) + e(k)$$

where $e(k)$ is the quantization error that results from approximating the analog $d(k)$ by the digital $d_q(k)$. The input to the predictor consists of this quantized difference plus the predictor output, which is fed back to become part of the input:

$$\begin{aligned} m_q(k) &= \hat{m}_q(k) + d_q(k) \\ &= [m(k) - d(k)] + [d(k) + q(k)] \\ &= m(k) + q(k) \end{aligned}$$

This demonstrates that $m_q(k)$ is a quantized version of $m(k)$. Therefore, the input to the predictor is the desired $m_q(k)$, which is what is needed for operation at the receiver. Figure 11.5b shows the logic at the receiver. The portion of the receiver in the dashed box is the same as the portion of the transmitter in the dashed box. The two dashed boxes have the same input, $d_q(k)$, and therefore produce the same

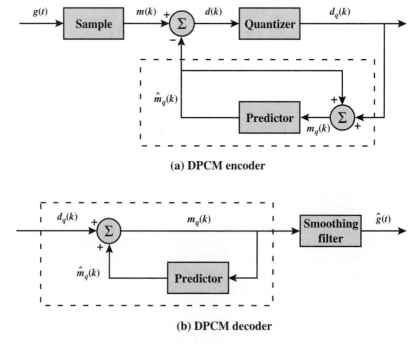

(a) DPCM encoder

(b) DPCM decoder

Figure 11.5 DPCM Transmitter and Receiver

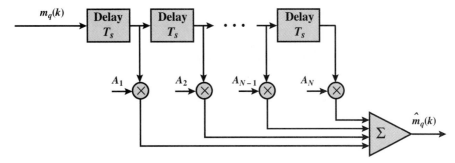

Figure 11.6 Linear Predictor Circuit

output, $m_q(k)$. At the receiver, this output is passed through a filter to produce an analog output that is an estimate of the original analog source.

The predictor is often the linear weighted sum of previous samples, implemented using shift registers, and a delay equal to the sample interval (Figure 11.6). The predictor implements the equation

$$\hat{m}_q(k) = \sum_{i=1}^{N} A_i m_q(k - i) \tag{11.1}$$

For a further discussion of linear predictors, see Appendix 11A.

Adaptive Differential PCM

The performance of DPCM can be improved by using adaptive prediction and quantization, so that the predictor and difference quantizer adapt to the changing characteristics of the speech being coded. In this subsection, we describe the ACPCM scheme standardized by ITU-T in Recommendation G.726,[5] which is used in DECT and in a number of wireless local loop schemes.

Figure 11.7 shows the basic ADPCM logic. The transmitter converts a 64-kbps digitized voice stream into a compressed 32-kbps stream. The overall block diagram is the same as that for DPCM. In this case, the adaptive predictor makes use not only of previous predictor output values but also previous quantized difference values. In both the predictor and the quantizer, parameter values of the algorithms are dynamically adjusted based on the statistical properties of previous samples. As with DPCM, the heart of the decoder is a replication of part of the logic of the encoder.

The **adaptive quantizer** takes as input the difference $d(k)$ between the PCM signal $s(k)$ and the signal estimate $s_e(k)$ and produces a 4-bit output ADPCM $I(k)$. The first two columns of Table 11.3 show the mapping. Prior to quantization, $d(k)$ is converted to a base 2 logarithmic representation and scaled by $y(k)$, which is an adaptation factor based on the rate of change of the signal over recent samples. The result is then mapped into 4 bits for transmission as the ADPCM signal.

[5]*General Aspects of Digital Transmission Systems; Terminal Equipments: 40, 32, 20, 16 kbit/s ADPCM.* 1990.

(a) ADPCM encoder

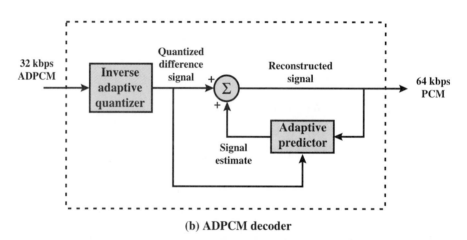

(b) ADPCM decoder

Figure 11.7 Simplified ADPCM Transmitter and Receiver

The **inverse adaptive quantizer** takes the 4-bit signal $I(k)$ and produces a difference signal $d_q(k)$ to serve as input to the adaptive predictor. The second and third columns of Table 11.3 show the mapping.

The **adaptive predictor** has the structure of a linear predictor (Figure 11.6) but is more complex than for DPCM. For ADPCM, the structure is a combination of a second-order recursive filter and a sixth-order nonrecursive filter. The equation is [compare Equation (11.1)]

$$s_e(k) = \sum_{i=1}^{2} A_i(k - i)s_e(k - i) + \sum_{i=1}^{6} B_i(k - i)d_q(k - i) \qquad (11.2)$$

Table 11.3 ADPCM Quantizer Normalized Input/Output Characteristics

Normalized quantizer input range $\log_2 |d(k)| - y(k)$	Adapter quantizer output $I(k)$	Inverse adapter quantizer output $d_q(k)$
$[3.12, +\infty)$	7	3.32
$[2.72, 3.12)$	6	2.91
$[2.34, 2.72)$	5	2.52
$[1.91, 2.34)$	4	2.13
$[1.38, 1.91)$	3	1.66
$[0.62, 1.38)$	2	1.05
$[-0.98, 0.62)$	1	0.031
$(-\infty, -0.98)$	0	$-\infty$

where the coefficients A and B are updated using algorithms that adapt to the rate of change of the s_e and d_q samples. Thus, the adaptive predictor is adjusted to adapt to the rate of change of the difference samples as well as the rate of change of the signal estimates.

Subject Measurement of Coder Performance

The goal of speech coding is to exploit signal redundancies, signal structure, and knowledge of human perception to code the signal to various bit rates while maintaining as high a quality as possible. In assessing the performance of a speech coder, subjective measurements of quality are more relevant than objective measures such as SNR or the mean square error. However, reliable values of subjective measurements are in general more difficult to obtain.

The most widely used subjective measurement as a standard for determining quality of service is the mean opinion score (MOS), obtained from formal subjective testing [DAUM82]. For the MOS measurement, a group of subjects listens to a sample of coded speech, and each classifies the output on a 5-point scale. To enhance the reliability of the test, it is repeated with various speech samples and

Table 11.4 Mean Opinion Score (MOS) Values

Number Score	Quality Scale	Impairment Scale
5	Excellent	Imperceptible
4	Good	(Just) perceptible but not annoying
3	Fair	(Perceptible and) slightly annoying
2	Poor	Annoying (but not objectionable)
1	Unsatisfactory	Very annoying (objectionable)

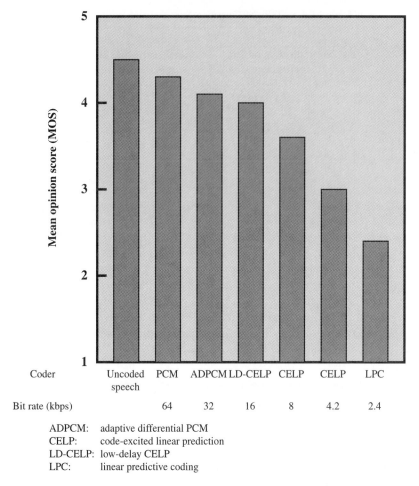

Figure 11.8   Subjective Speech Quality for Various Speech Coders

with various groups of subjects. The MOS scale is used in a number of specifications as a standard for quality (e.g., IEEE 802.16; described in Section 11.3).

Table 11.4 shows the scale that is used, with two alternative but equivalent interpretations. Figure 11.8 illustrates the MOS results reported in [RABI95] for various speech coders, including ADPCM. Note that even uncoded speech does not get a full rating of 5. This is because subjects may sometimes award a score of 4 to a sample that ideally deserves a 5 [JAYA84]. With this phenomenon in mind, a score of 4.0 to 4.5 is a very useful indicator of high-quality digitization.

11.2 WIRELESS LOCAL LOOP

Traditionally, the provision of voice and data communications to the end user, over the local loop, or subscriber loop, has been provided by wired systems. For

Table 11.5 Alternative Providers for End User Access

Entity	Technology	Application		
		Telephony	**Broadcast**	**Computer**
Public telephone	Twisted pair, ISDN, xDSL	One and two lines	Video on demand	High-speed asymmetrical access
Cable operator	Coaxial cable	One and two lines	50+ channels	High-speed asymmetrical
Cellular provider	Cellular and cordless	One line	No	Limited but mobility
3G Cellular provider	Cellular	One line	No	High-speed asymmetrical access
Narrowband WLL operator	Wireless	Two lines	No	64-kbps access
Broadband WLL operator	Wireless	Yes	50+ channels	High-speed asymmetrical or symmetrical access
Terrestrial broadcast	Analog and digital TV	No	5 to 10 channels	Some download potential
Satellite broadcast	Analog and digital	No	50+ channels	No

residential subscribers, twisted pair has been and continues to be the standard means of connection. For business and government subscribers, twisted pair, coaxial cable, and optical fiber are in use.

As subscribers have demanded greater capacity, particularly to support Internet use, traditional twisted pair technology has become inadequate. Telecommunications providers have developed a number technologies to meet the need, including ISDN (Integrated Services Digital Network), and a family of digital subscriber loop technologies, known as xDSL. In addition, cable operators have introduced two-way high-speed service using cable modem technology. Thus, wired technologies are responding to the need for reliable, high-speed access by residential, business, and government subscribers.

However, increasing interest is being shown in competing wireless technologies for subscriber access. These approaches are generally referred to as **wireless local loop (WLL)**, or **fixed wireless access**. WLL alternatives are narrowband, which offer a replacement for existing telephony services, and broadband,[6] which provide high-speed two-way voice and data service. Table 11.5, based on one in [WEBB00], compares WLL and other alternatives for fixed subscriber support.

In this section, we provide an overview of WLL, then a look at some technical issues, and finally examine two specific WLL approaches. Section 11.3 is devoted to an evolving standard for WLL known as IEEE 802.16.

---

[6]The term *broadband* is not precise. Generally, it refers to systems that provide user data rates of greater than 2 Mbps, up to 100s of Mbps.

The Role of WLL

Figure 11.9 illustrates a simple WLL configuration. A WLL provider services one or more cells. Each cell includes a base station antenna, mounted on top of a tall building or tower. Individual subscribers have a fixed antenna mounted on a building or pole that has an unobstructed line of sight to the base station antenna. From the base station, there is a link, which may either be wired or wireless, to a switching center. The switching center is typically a telephone company local office, which provides connections to the local and long-distance telephone networks. An internet service provider (ISP) may be collocated at the switch or connected to the switch by a high-speed link.

Figure 11.9 shows what amounts to a two-level hierarchy. More complex configurations have also been implemented, in which a base station may serve a number of subordinate base station antennas, each of which supports a number of subscribers.

The WLL has a number of advantages over a wired approach to subscriber loop support:

- **Cost:** Wireless systems are less expensive than wired systems. Although the electronics of the wireless transmitter/receiver may be more expensive than those used for wired communications, with WLL the cost of installing kilometers of cable, either underground or on poles, is avoided, as well as the cost of maintaining the wired infrastructure.
- **Installation time:** WLL systems typically can be installed rapidly. The key stumbling blocks are obtaining permission to use a given frequency band and finding a suitable elevated site for the base station antennas. Once these hurdles are cleared, a WLL system can be installed in a small fraction of the time required for a new wired system.

Figure 11.9 WLL Configuration

- **Selective installation:** Radio units are installed only for those subscribers who want the service at a given time. With a wired system, typically cable is laid out in anticipation of serving every subscriber in a local area.

WLL needs to be evaluated with respect to two alternatives:

- **Wired scheme using existing installed cable:** A large fraction of the earth's inhabitants do not have a telephone line. For high-speed applications, many subscribers with telephone lines do not have a line of sufficient quality or are too far from the central office to effectively use xDSL. Many of these same subscribers also do not have cable TV or their cable provider does not offer two-way data services. Finally, because WLL has become cost-competitive with wired schemes, new installations face a genuine choice between the wired and wireless approaches.
- **Mobile cellular technology:** Current cellular systems are too expensive and do not provide sufficient facilities to act as a realistic alternative to WLL. Even when 3G systems become available, they are likely to be more expensive and less functional than broadband WLL alternatives. A major advantage of WLL over mobile cellular is that, because the subscriber unit is fixed, the subscriber can use a directional antenna pointed at the base station antenna, providing improved signal quality in both directions.

In the United States, the Federal Communications Commission has set aside 15 frequency bands for use in commercial fixed wireless service, at frequencies of 2 to 40 GHz. In other countries, similar frequency bands have been allocated. Note that these frequencies are considerably higher than those used for cellular systems. At these frequencies, often referred to as millimeter wave frequencies, propagation characteristics are quite different from those in the MHz ranges. We look at propagation considerations next. Then we introduce a technique that is used in a number of WLL systems, known as orthogonal FDM (OFDM). Finally, we examine the two approaches of most interest for the WLL application: local multipoint distribution service (LMDS) and multichannel multipoint distribution service (MMDS).

Propagation Considerations for WLL

For most high-speed WLL schemes, frequencies in what is referred to as the millimeter wave region are used. Although the term *millimeter wave* is not precisely defined, a common boundary is 10 GHz; that is, frequencies above 10 GHz, up to about 300 GHz, are considered to be in the millimeter wave region.[7] The reasons for using frequencies in this range for WLL include the following:

1. There are wide unused frequency bands available above 25 GHz.
2. At these high frequencies, wide channel bandwidths can be used, providing high data rates.
3. Small size transceivers and adaptive antenna arrays can be used.

---

[7]The free space wavelength at 10 GHz is 30 mm, and at 300 GHz is 1 mm.

However, millimeter wave systems have some undesirable propagation characteristics:

1. Free space loss increases with the square of the frequency [Equation (5.2)]; thus losses are much higher in this range than in the ranges used for traditional microwave systems.
2. Generally, below 10 GHz, we can ignore attenuation due to rainfall and atmospheric or gaseous absorption. Above 10 GHz, these attenuation effects are large.
3. Multipath losses can be quite high. As was pointed out in Chapter 5, reflection occurs when an electromagnetic signal encounters a surface that is large relative to the wavelength of the signal; scattering occurs if the size of an obstacle is on the order of the wavelength of the signal or less; diffraction occurs when the wavefront encounters the edge of an obstacle that is large compared to the wavelength.

Because of these negative propagation characteristics, WLL systems can only serve cells of a limited radius, usually just a few km. Also, obstructions, including foliage, must be avoided along or near the line of sight. Finally, rainfall and humidity effects limit the range and availability of WLL systems.

Fresnel Zone

For effective communication at millimeter wavelengths, there should be an unobstructed line of sight between transmitter and receiver. The question then arises as to how much space around the direct path between transmitter and receiver should be clear of obstacles. A useful criterion relates to the concept of the Fresnel zone.

The definition of Fresnel zones is based on the theory that any small element of space in the path of an electromagnetic wave may be considered the source of a secondary wavelet, and that the radiated field can be built up by the superposition of all these wavelets. On the basis of this theory, it can be shown that objects lying within a series of concentric circles around the direct line of sight between two transceivers have constructive or destructive effects on communication. Those that fall within the first circle, the first Fresnel zone, have the most serious negative effects.

Consider a point along the direct path between a transmitter and receiver—that is, a distance S from the transmitter and a distance D from the receiver—with the total distance along the path equal to $S + D$ (Figure 11.10). Then the radius of the first Fresnel zone at that point is

$$R = \sqrt{\frac{\lambda SD}{S + D}}$$

where R, S, and D are in the same units, and λ is the wavelength of the signal along the path. For convenience, this can be restated as

$$R_m = 17.3\sqrt{\frac{1}{f_{GHz}} \frac{S_{km}D_{km}}{S_{km} + D_{km}}}$$

where R is expressed in meters, the two distances are in kilometers, and the signal frequency is in gigahertz.

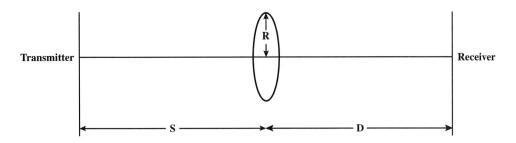

Figure 11.10   The First Fresnel Zone

> **Example.** Suppose the distance between the two transceivers is 10 km and the carrier frequency is 2.4 GHz. Then the radius of the first Fresnel zone at the midpoint between the two transceivers is 17.66 m. If the signal frequency is 28 GHz, then the radius at the same point is reduced to 5.17 m. Now consider a point along the path that is 1 km from one of the transceivers. Then, at 28 GHz, the radius is 3.1 m.

It has been found that if there is no obstruction within about 0.6 times the radius of the first Fresnel zone at any point between the two transceivers, then attenuation due to obstructions is negligible [FREE97]. One noteworthy example of an obstruction is the ground. Hence, the height of the two antennas must be such that there is no point along the path at which the ground is within 0.6 times the radius of the first Fresnel zone.

Atmospheric Absorption

At frequencies above 10 GHz, radio waves propagating through the atmosphere are subject to molecular absorption. The absorption as a function of frequency is very uneven, as shown in Figure 11.11. There is a peak of water vapor absorption at around 22 GHz and a peak of oxygen absorption near 60 GHz. This figure suggests that there is a favorable window for communication roughly from 28 GHz to 42 GHz, where the attenuation is on the order of 0.13 dB/km, and another favorable window from 75 GHz to 95 GHz, where the attenuation is on the order of 0.4 dB/km.

However, Figure 11.11 only shows the absorption effects at a particular temperature, relative humidity, and atmospheric pressure. Although the shape of these two curves remain the same, the actual values vary, especially with temperature and relative humidity. Table 11.6, taken from [DALK96], shows the effects of temperature and humidity.

> **Example.** Consider a 6-km communication link at 28 GHz. What is the free space loss? What is the additional loss due to atmospheric absorption on a hot, muggy day with a temperature of 30° and a relative humidity of 100%?
> From Equation (5.2), free space loss is $20 \log(f) + 20 \log(d) - 147.56 = 136.95$ dB. The additional loss due to atmospheric absorption is $6 \times 0.44 = 2.64$ dB.

Effect of Rain

One of the most serious concerns for millimeter wave propagation is attenuation due to rain. The presence of raindrops can severely degrade the reliability and performance of communication links and, during periods of heavy rain, may outweigh all other factors. The effect of rain on millimeter wave propagation is complex, depending on drop shape, drop size, rain rate, and frequency. A widely used formula for estimating attenuation due to rain is

$$A = aR^b \tag{11.3}$$

Figure 11.11 Absorption Due to Atmospheric Gas
(atmospheric pressure: 1013 mb; temperature: 15°C; water vapor: 7.5 g/m^3)

Table 11.6 Clear Air Absorption at 28 GHz (dB/km)

Relative Humidity

		0%	50%	100%
Temperature (°C)	0°	0.02	0.05	0.08
	10°	0.02	0.08	0.14
	20°	0.02	0.12	0.25
	30°	0.02	0.20	0.44
	40°	0.01	0.33	0.79

where the attenuation is in units of dB/km, the rain rate R is measured in mm/hr, and the parameters a and b depend on the distribution of drop sizes and on frequency. Further, attenuation is affected by whether the electromagnetic wave is horizontally or vertically polarized. Table 11.7, extracted from [FREE97], gives typical values for a and b as a function of frequency for horizontal and vertical waves.

Having determined a and b, attenuation then depends on the rain rate R. The principal concern is the percentage of time the rain rate exceeds a certain threshold. This depends on the climate zone. Table 11.8, developed by ITU, divides the earth into 15 climate zones based on precipitation patterns and shows the value of R that is exceeded for various percentages of time over the course of a year. Such information can be used to determine availability of a radio link.

Example. At a frequency of 30 GHz, with a vertically polarized wave, in climate zone P, 0.01% of the time, rainfall exceeds 145 mm/hr. At that rain rate, the attenuation that must be added to free space loss is A = 0.167 × 145 = 24.2 dB/km.

Table 11.7 Coefficients for Estimating Attenuation Due to Rain

Frequency (GHz)	a_h	a_v	b_h	b_v
1	0.0000387	0.0000352	0.912	0.880
2	0.000154	0.000138	0.963	0.923
6	0.00175	0.00155	1.308	1.265
10	0.0101	0.00887	1.276	1.264
20	0.0751	0.0691	1.099	1.065
30	0.187	0.167	1.021	1.000
40	0.350	0.310	0.939	0.929
50	0.536	0.479	0.873	0.868

Table 11.8 Rainfall Intensity Exceeded (mm/hr) for Various Rain Regions

		A	B	C	D	E	F	G	H	J	K	L	M	N	P	Q
	1	0.1	0.5	1	2.1	0.6	2	3	2	8	1.5	2	4	5	12	24
Outage Percentage of Time	**0.3**	0.8	2	3	4.5	2.4	5	7	4	13	4.2	7	11	15	34	49
	0.1	2	3	5	8	6	8	12	10	20	12	15	22	35	64	72
	0.01	8	12	15	19	22	28	30	32	35	42	60	63	95	145	115

*(Header spanning columns A–Q: **Rain Climate Zone**)*

Effects of Vegetation

Through part of its path, a WLL link may run through vegetation, particularly foliage of tall trees. In some suburban and small town areas, such obstacles may be unavoidable for some subscribers, even with rooftop subscriber antennas. A study reported in [PAPA97] reached the following conclusions:

1. The presence of trees near subscriber sites can lead to multipath fading.
2. The principal multipath effects from the tree canopy are diffraction and scattering.
3. Measurements in regularly planted orchards have found attenuation values between 12 and 20 dB per tree for deciduous trees and up to 40 dB for 1 to 3 coniferous trees, when the foliage is within 60% of the first Fresnel zone.
4. The multipath effects are highly variable due to wind.

Thus, when installing a WLL system, efforts should be made to avoid the presence of tree foliage within 60% of the first Fresnel zone for each subscriber. However, the presence of trees does not preclude communications, but means that adequate countermeasures, such as forward error correction, are required.

Orthogonal Frequency Division Multiplexing

OFDM, also called multicarrier modulation, uses multiple carrier signals at different frequencies, sending some of the bits on each channel. This is similar to FDM. However, in the case of OFDM, all of the subchannels are dedicated to a single data source.

Figure 11.12 illustrates OFDM. Suppose we have a data stream operating at R bps and an available bandwidth of $N\Delta f$, centered at f_0. The entire bandwidth could be used to send the data stream, in which case each bit duration would be $1/R$. The alternative is to split the data stream into N substreams, using a serial-to-parallel converter. Each substream has a data rate of R/N bps and is transmitted on a separate subcarrier, with a spacing between adjacent subcarriers of Δf. Now the bit duration is N/R.

OFDM has several advantages. First, frequency selective fading only affects some subchannels and not the whole signal. If the data stream is protected by a forward error-correcting code, this type of fading is easily handled. More important, OFDM overcome intersymbol interference (ISI) in a multipath environment. As discussed in Chapter 5, ISI has a greater impact at higher bit rates, because the distance between bits, or symbols, is smaller. With OFDM, the data rate is reduced by

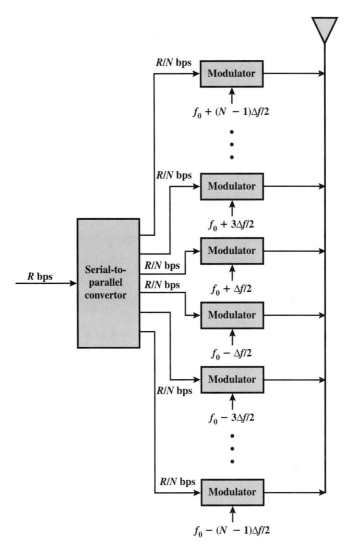

Figure 11.12   Orthogonal Frequency Division Multiplexing

a factor of N, which increases the symbol time by a factor of N. Thus, if the symbol period is T_s for the source stream, the period for the OFDM signals is NT_s. This dramatically reduces the effect of ISI. As a design criterion, N is chosen so that NT_s is significantly greater than the root-mean-square delay spread of the channel.

As a result of these considerations, with the use of OFDM, it may not be necessary to deploy equalizers, which are complex devices whose complexity increases with the number of symbols over which ISI is present.

A common modulation scheme used with OFDM is quadrature phase shift keying (QPSK). In this case, each transmitted symbol represents two bits. An example of an OFDM/QPSK scheme, used in a MMDS system [CISC00], occupies 6 MHz made up of 512 individual carriers, with a carrier separation of a little under 12 kHz. To minimize ISI, data are transmitted in bursts, with each burst consisting of a cyclic prefix followed by data symbols. The cyclic prefix is used to absorb transients from previous bursts caused by multipath. For this system, 64 symbols constitute the cyclic prefix, followed by 512 QPSK symbols per burst. On each subchannel, therefore, QPSK symbols are separated by a prefix of duration 64/512 symbol times. In general, by the time the prefix is over, the resulting waveform created by the combined multipath signals is not a function of any samples from the previous burst. Hence there is no ISI.

Multichannel Multipoint Distribution Service

Table 11.9 shows five frequency bands in the range 2.15 GHz to 2.68 GHz that have been allocated in the United States for fixed wireless access using MMDS. The first two bands were licensed in the 1970s when they were called multipoint distributions services (MDSs), for broadcast of 6-MHz TV channels. In 1996, the FCC increased the allocation to its present range and allowed for multichannel services, called MMDS. MMDS has been used to compete with cable TV providers and to provide service in rural areas not reached by broadcast TV or cable. For this reason, MMDS is also referred to as *wireless cable*.

Table 11.9   Fixed Wireless Communications Bands, FCC Allocation

Frequency (GHz)	Usage
2.1500 to 2.1620	Licensed MDS and MMDS; two bands of 6 MHz each
2.4000 to 2.4835	Unlicensed ISM
2.5960 to 2.6440	Licensed MMDS; eight bands of 6 MHz each
2.6500 to 2.6560	Licensed MMDS
2.6620 to 2.6680	Licensed MMDS
2.6740 to 2.6800	Licensed MMDS
5.7250 to 5.8750	Unlicensed ISM-UNII
24.000 to 24.250	Unlicensed ISM
24.250 to 25.250	Licensed
27.500 to 28.350	Licensed LMDS (Block A)
29.100 to 29.250	Licensed LMDS (Block A)
31.000 to 31.075	Licensed LMDS (Block B)
31.075 to 31.225	Licensed LMDS (Block A)
31.225 to 31.300	Licensed LMDS (Block B)
38.600 to 40.000	Licensed

ISM   = industrial, scientific, and medical
LMDS = local multipoint distribution service
MDS   = multichannel distribution service
MMDS = multichannel multipoint distribution service
UNII = unlicensed national information infrastructure

The transmitted power allowed by the FCC enables an MMDS base station to service an area with a radius of 50 km, but subscriber antennas must be in the line of sight. MMDS can be used to support two-way services. MMDS is also used in other countries for two-way access. Thus, MMDS is an alternative for broadband data services, such as Internet access.

The principal disadvantage of MMDS, compared to LMDS, which we discuss next, is that at the lower frequency of MMDS, it offers much less bandwidth than LMDS. With current technology, a single MMDS channel can offer upstream (subscriber to base station) transfer rates of 27 Mbps, with individual subscriber rates of 300 kbps to 3 Mbps [ORTI00]. However, developments in OFDM may allow higher data rates or more subscriber support for upstream MMDS. In any case, because of its lesser bandwidth, MMDS is likely to be used mainly by residential subscribers and small businesses, whereas LMDS appeals to larger companies with greater bandwidth demands.

The advantages of MMDS over LMDS include the following:

1. MMDS signals have larger wavelengths (greater than 10 cm) and can travel farther without losing significant power. Hence MMDS can operate in considerably larger cells, thereby lowering base station equipment costs.
2. Equipment at lower frequencies is less expensive, yielding cost savings at both the subscriber and base station.
3. MMDS signals don't get blocked as easily by objects and are less susceptible to rain absorption.

Local Multipoint Distribution Service

LMDS is a relatively new WLL service to deliver TV signals and two-way broadband communications, operating at millimeter frequencies. In the United States, LMDS will be offered at frequencies near 30 GHz; in Europe and some other areas, frequencies near 40 GHz will be used. Table 11.9 shows frequency bands that have been allocated in the United States for fixed wireless access using LMDS.

LMDS has the following advantages:

• Relatively high data rates, in the Mbps range
• Capable of providing video, telephony, and data
• Relatively low cost in comparison with cable alternatives

The principal disadvantage of LMDS is the short range from the base station, requiring a relatively large number of base stations to service a given area.

In a typical system, the base station antenna is located on top of a tall building or high pole overlooking the service area, with line of sight to subscribers with the possible exception of tree canopies. The base station antenna covers a sector 60° to 90° wide. Thus, full coverage requires 4 to 6 antennas. A radius of 2 to 4 km is typical. With the bandwidths available, an upstream data rate to the subscriber of up to 1 Mbps is reasonable, with a downstream capacity of 36 Mbps.

An important consideration is that LMDS's short-wavelength signals cannot pass around or penetrate objects like buildings, walls, or thick foliage. A certain amount of foliage can be tolerated, as is discussed earlier in this section, but dense foliage may require other countermeasures. By overlapping cell coverage, it may be possible to obtain coverage in shielded areas in one cell from the base station of a neighboring cell. Use of repeaters or reflectors is another possibility.

11.3 IEEE 802.16 FIXED BROADBAND WIRELESS ACCESS STANDARD

With the growing interest in LMDS WLL services, a need was recognized within the industry to develop standards for this service. In response to this need the IEEE 802 committee set up the 802.16 working group in 1999 to develop broadband wireless standards. The charter for the group is to develop standards that [MARK99]

- Use wireless links with microwave or millimeter wave radios
- Use licensed spectrum (typically)
- Are metropolitan in scale
- Provide public network service to fee-paying customers (typically)
- Use point-to-multipoint architecture with stationary rooftop- or tower-mounted antennas
- Provide efficient transport of heterogeneous traffic supporting quality of service (QoS)
- Are capable of broadband transmissions (>2 Mbps)

In essence, IEEE 802.16 standardizes the air interface and related functions associated with LMDS. As of this writing, three working groups have been chartered to produce standards:

- **IEEE 802.16.1:** Air Interface for 10 to 66 GHz
- **IEEE 802.16.2:** Coexistence of Broadband Wireless Access Systems
- **IEEE 802.16.3:** Air Interface for Licensed Frequencies, 2 to 11 GHz

Tables 11.10 through 11.12 define the scope and purpose of these three groups, as provided by their project authorizations. Figure 11.13 indicates where 802.16.1 and 802.16.3 fit into a larger context of wireless services.

The work of 802.16.1 is the farthest along and is the one most likely to generate the most industry interest, as it is targeted at available LMDS frequency bands. In this section, we provide an overview of 802.16 architecture and services and then look in more detail at the 802.16.1 specification.

IEEE 802.16 Architecture

System Reference Architecture

The 802.16 standards are designed with respect to the abstract system reference model shown in Figure 11.14. An 802.16 wireless service provides a communications path between a subscriber site, which may be either a single subscriber device or a network on the subscriber's premises (e.g., a LAN, PBX, IP-based net-

Table 11.10   IEEE 802.16.1: Air Interface for 10-66 GHz

Scope of Proposed Project

This standard specifies the physical layer and media access control layer of the air interface of interoperable fixed point-to-multipoint broadband wireless access systems. The specification enables transport of data, video, and voice services. It applies to systems operating in the vicinity of 30 GHz but is broadly applicable to systems operating between 10 and 66 GHz.

Purpose of Proposed Project

To enable rapid worldwide deployment of innovative, cost-effective, and interoperable multi-vendor broadband wireless access products. To facilitate competition in broadband access by providing alternatives to wireline broadband access. To facilitate coexistence studies, encourage consistent worldwide allocation, and accelerate the commercialization of broadband wireless access spectrum.

Table 11.11   IEEE 802.16.1: Air Interface for 10-66 GHz

Scope of Proposed Project

This project covers development of a Recommended Practice for the design and coordinated deployment of broadband wireless access (BWA) systems to minimize interference so as to maximize system performance and/or service quality. This practice will provide for coexistence using frequency and spatial separation and will cover three areas. First, it will recommend limits of in-band and out-of-band emissions from BWA transmitters through parameters including radiated power, spectral masks and antenna patterns. Second, it will recommend receiver tolerance parameters, including noise floor degradation and blocking performance, for interference received from other BWA systems as well as from other terrestrial and satellite systems. Third, it will provide coordination parameters, including band plans, separation distances, and power flux density limits, to enable successful deployment of BWA systems with tolerable interference. The scope includes interference between systems deployed across geographic boundaries in the same frequency band and systems deployed in the same geographic area in different frequency bands (including different systems deployed by a single license-holder in sub-bands of the licensees authorized bandwidth). The scope does not cover coexistence issues due to intra-system frequency re-use within the operator's licensed band, and it does not consider the impact of interference created by BWA systems on non-BWA terrestrial and satellite systems.

Purpose of Proposed Project

The purpose of this recommended practice is to provide coexistence guidelines to license holders, service providers, deployment groups, and system integrators. The equipment parameters contained within this practice will benefit equipment and component vendors and industry associations by providing design targets. The benefits of this practice will include:

- Coexistence of different systems with higher assurance that system performance objectives will be met.
- Minimal need for case-by-case interference studies and coordination between operators to resolve interference issues.
- Preservation of a favorable electromagnetic environment for deployment and operation of BWA systems, including future systems compliant to the 802.16 interoperability standard.
- Optimization of coverage and spectrum utilization.
- Cost-effective system deployment.

Table 11.12   IEEE 802.16.3: Air Interface for Licensed Frequencies, 2-11 GHz

---

Scope of Proposed Project

This standard specifies the physical layer and media access control layer of the air interface of interoperable fixed point-to-multipoint broadband wireless access systems (e.g., those supporting data rates of DS1/E1 or greater). The specification enables access to data, video, and voice services with a specified quality of service in licensed bands designated for public network access. It applies to systems operating between 2 and 11 GHz.

Purpose of Proposed Project

To enable rapid worldwide deployment of innovative, cost-effective, and interoperable multi-vendor broadband wireless access products. To facilitate competition in broadband access by providing wireless alternatives to wireline broadband access. To facilitate coexistence studies, encourage consistent worldwide allocation, and accelerate the commercialization of broadband wireless access spectrum. Utilization of frequencies from 2 to 11 GHz will address a market that includes residences, Small Office-Home Office (SOHO), telecommuters, and Small and Medium Enterprises (SME).

---

work) and a core network (the network to which 802.16 is providing access). Examples of a core network are the public telephone network and the Internet. Three interfaces are defined in this model. IEEE 802.16 standards are concerned with the air interface between the subscriber's transceiver station and the base transceiver station. The standards specify all the details of that interface, as discussed subsequently in this subsection. The system reference model also shows interfaces between the transceiver stations and the networks behind them (SNI and BNI). The details of these interfaces are beyond the scope of the 802.16 standards. The reason for showing these interfaces in the system reference model is that the subscriber and core network technologies (such as voice, ATM, etc.) have an impact

Characteristics and Applications		Options and Issues	Wireless Solution
2 Mbps to 644 Mbps Intercell links Fiber replacement	**I** **Transport**	μwave TDM; core IP Priced to beat fiber	P-P radio
2 Mbps to 155 Mbps Small/medium business Bandwidth-on-demand access	**II** **High-cap access**	mm wave PMP Systems LOS constrained Moderate cost pressures	IEEE 802.16.1 PMP radio
< 2Mbps Residential/small business Highly shared access	**III** **Mass market access**	μwave PMP Systems Extremely cost sensitive Must overcome LOS	IEEE 802.16.3 PMP radio
Wireless Ethernet The "IP" home	**IV** **In-building wireless networks**	Multiple applications High cost sensitivity Noisy environment	IEEE 802.11 wireless LAN

Figure 11.13   A Multitier Perspective of Wireless Transmission and Distribution Systems [IEEE 802.16]

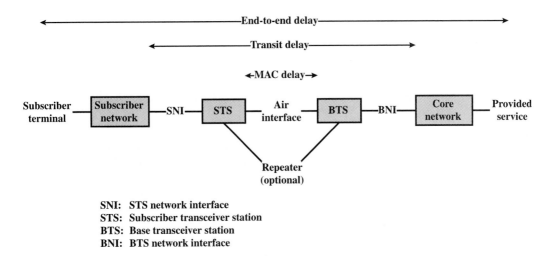

SNI: STS network interface
STS: Subscriber transceiver station
BTS: Base transceiver station
BNI: BTS network interface

Figure 11.14   IEEE 802.16 System Reference Points

on the technologies used in the air interface and the services provided by the transceiver stations over the air interface.

Finally, the system reference model includes the optional use of some sort of repeater. The air interface specification allows for the possibility of repeaters or reflectors to bypass obstructions and extend cell coverage.

Protocol Architecture

Protocols defined specifically for wireless transmission address issues relating to the transmission of blocks of data over the network. In OSI terms, higher-layer protocols (layer 3 or 4 and above; see Figure 4.3) are independent of network architecture and are applicable to a variety of networks and communications interfaces. Thus, a discussion of 802.16 protocols is concerned with lowest two layers of the OSI model.

Figure 11.15 relates the four protocol layers defined in the 802.16 protocol architecture to the OSI model. Working from the bottom up, the lowest two layers of the 802.16 protocol model correspond to the physical layer of the OSI model and include such functions as

- Encoding/decoding of signals
- Preamble generation/removal (for synchronization)
- Bit transmission/reception

In addition, the physical layer of the 802 model includes a specification of the transmission medium and the frequency band. Generally, this is considered "below" the lowest layer of the OSI model. However, the choice of transmission medium and frequency band is critical in wireless link design, and so a specification of the medium is included. In general, the 802.16 physical layer is concerned with these medium-dependent issues, and the transmission layer is concerned with the bulleted items listed previously.

Above the physical and transmission layers are the functions associated with providing service to subscribers. These include

- On transmission, assemble data into a frame with address and error detection fields.
- On reception, disassemble frame, and perform address recognition and error detection.
- Govern access to the wireless transmission medium.

These functions are grouped into a medium access control (MAC) layer. The protocol at this layer, between the base station and the subscriber station, is responsible for sharing access to the radio channel. Specifically, the MAC protocol defines how and when a base station or subscriber station may initiate transmission on the channel. Because some of the layers above the MAC layer, such as ATM, require specified service levels (QoS), the MAC protocol must be able to allocate radio channel capacity so as to satisfy service demands. In the downstream direction (base station to subscriber stations), there is only one transmitter and the MAC protocol is relatively simple. In the upstream direction, multiple subscriber stations are competing for access, resulting in a more complex MAC protocol.

Above the MAC layer is a convergence layer that provides functions specific to the service being provided. A convergence layer protocol may do the following:

- Encapsulate PDU (protocol data unit) framing of upper layers into the native 802.16 MAC/PHY frames.
- Map an upper layer's addresses into 802.16 addresses.
- Translate upper layer QoS parameters into native 802.16 MAC format.
- Adapt the time dependencies of the upper layer traffic into the equivalent MAC service.

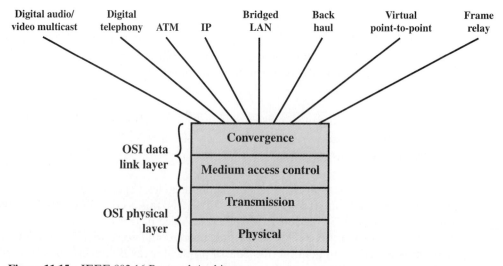

Figure 11.15 IEEE 802.16 Protocol Architecture

In some cases, such as digital audio and video, no convergence layer is needed and the stream of digital data is presented to the transmission layer. Upper-layer services that make use of a PDU structure do require a convergence layer.

An example of the protocol structure supported by the convergence layer is the handling of TCP/IP based traffic, as shown in Figure 11.16 (compare Figure 4.2). Higher-level data are passed down to LLC (logical link control), which appends control information as a header, creating an *LLC protocol data unit (PDU)*. This control information is used in the operation of the LLC protocol, which is a form of data link control protocol (see Appendix D). The entire LLC PDU is then passed down to the MAC layer, which appends control information at the front and back of the packet, forming a *MAC frame*. Again, the control information in the frame is needed for the operation of the MAC protocol. The figure shows the use of TCP/IP and an application layer above the 802.16 protocols.

Services

Requirements for the IEEE 802.16 standards are defined in terms of bearer services that the 802.16 systems must support. A bearer service refers to the type of traffic generated by a subscriber network or core network in Figure 11.14. For example, an 802.16 interface must be able to support the data rate and QoS required by an ATM network or an IP-based network, or support the data rate and delay requirements of voice or video transmissions. Separate bearer service requirements have been defined for 802.16.1 and 802.16.3.

IEEE 802.16.1 Services

IEEE 802.16.1 is designed to support the following bearer services:

- **Digital audio/video multicast:** Transports one-way digital audio/video streams to subscribers. The principal example of this service is a broadcast radio and video similar to digital broadcast cable TV and digital satellite TV. A special case of this service is two-way video such as in teleconferencing. In this latter case, delay requirements are stringent because of the interactivity involved.
- **Digital telephony:** Supports multiplexed digital telephony streams. This service is a classic WLL service that provides a replacement for wired access to the public telephone network.
- **ATM:** Provides a communications link that supports the transfer of ATM cells as part of an overall ATM network. The 802.16 link must support the various QoS services defined for ATM.
- **Internet protocol:** Supports the transfer of IP datagrams. The 802.16 link must provide efficient timely service. In addition, a variety of QoS services are now defined for IP-based networks, and 802.16 should support these.
- **Bridged LAN:** Similar to the IP-based support. A bridge LAN service enables transfer of data between two LANs with switching at the MAC layer.
- **Back-haul:** For cellular or digital wireless telephone networks. An 802.16 system may be a convenient means to provide wireless trunks for wireless telephony base stations.

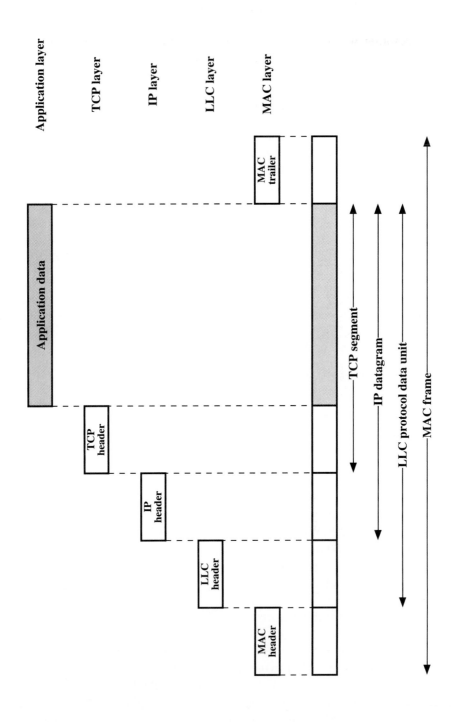

Figure 11.16 IEEE 802.16 Protocols in Context

372

- **Frame relay:** Similar to ATM. Frame relay uses variable-length frames in contrast to the fixed-length cells of ATM.

Another way of viewing the service requirements for 802.16.1 is shown in Table 11.13, which is taken from the 802.16.1 functional requirements document. Bearer services are grouped in three broad categories:

- **Circuit based:** These services provide a circuit-switching capability, in which connections are set up to subscribers across a core network.
- **Variable packet:** IP and frame relay are examples of services that make use of variable-length PDUs. Another example is MPEG video, which is a video

Table 11.13 IEEE 802.16.1 Services and QoS Requirements

	Bearer Service	**MAC Payload Rate**	**Maximum Ratio**	**Maximum Delay (one way)**
Circuit Based	High-quality narrowband/ Voice frequency telephony (Vocoder MOS (4.0)	32 to 64 kbps	BER 10^{-6}	5 ms
	Lower-quality narrowband/ Voice frequency telephony (Vocoder MOS < 4.0)	6 to 16 kbps	BER 10^{-4}	10 ms
	Trunking	$\leq$ 155 Mbps	BER 10^{-6}	5 ms
Variable Packet	Time-critical packet services	4 to 13 kbps (voice) 32 kbps to 1.5 Mbps (video)	BER 10^{-6}	10 ms
	Non-time-critical services: IP, IPX, frame relay, audio/video streaming, bulk data transfer, etc.	$\leq$ 155 Mbps	BER 10^{-8}	N/A
	MPEG video	$\leq$ 8Mbps	BER 10^{-11}	TBD
Fixed-length Cell/Packet	ATM Cell Relay—CBR	16 kbps to 155 Mbps	CLR 3×10^{-8} CER 4×10^{-6} CMR 1/day SEBCR 10^{-4}	10 ms
	ATM Cell Relay—rt-VBR	16 kbps to 155 Mbps	CLR 10^{-5} CER 4×10^{-6} CMR 1/day SEBCR 10^{-4}	10 ms
	ATM Cell Relay—other	$\leq$ 155 Mbps	CLR 10^{-5} CER 4×10^{-6} CMR 1/day SEBCR 10^{-4}	N/A

compression scheme in which successive blocks of digital video information may be of varying sizes.

- **Fixed-length cell/packet:** This service is for ATM.

The table summarizes requirements in three categories. The first category is the data rate that must be supported. The second category refers to error performance. For most services an upper limit on the bit error ration (BER) is defined. For ATM, various specific QoS error parameters are also used.

The final category is maximum one-way delay. To place this delay in context, Figure 11.14 shows three categories of delay defined in the 802.16 standards:

- **Medium access delay:** Once a transceiver station is ready to transmit, the medium access delay measures the amount of time that the station must wait before it can transmit.
- **Transit delay:** This is the delay from SNI to BNI or BNI to SNI. It includes the medium access delay plus the processing at the MAC layer for preparing transmission (from the STS or BTS) and at the Mac layer for reception (at the BTS or STS).
- **End-to-end delay:** The total delay between a terminal in the subscriber network, to the ultimate service beyond the core network. This includes the transit delay.

The maximum one-way delay category specified in Table 11.13 refers to transit delay.

IEEE 802.16.3 Services

IEEE 802.16.3 is designed to support the following bearer services:

- **Voice transport:** A packet-based (as opposed to circuit switched) service that provides equivalent service to that of the public switched telephone network.
- **Data transport:** Provides support for IP-based traffic, including IP-based QoS requirements.
- **Bridged LAN:** Similar to the IP-based support. A bridge LAN service enables transfer of data between two LANs with switching at the MAC layer.

Table 11.14 provides numerical requirements for these services.

Table 11.14   IEEE 802.16.3 Services and QoS Requirements

Service	Maximum Ratio	Maximum Delay (one way)
Full-quality telephony (Vocoder MOS $\geq$ 4.0)	BER 10^{-6}	20 ms
Standard-quality telephony (Vocoder MOS < 4.0)	BER 10^{-4}	40 ms
Time-critical packet services Non-time-critical services	BER 10^{-6} BER 10^{-9}	20 ms N/A

IEEE 802.16.1 MAC Layer

Data transmitted over the 802.16.1 air interface from or to a given subscriber are structured as a sequence of MAC frames. The term **MAC frame** as used in this context refers to the PDU that includes MAC protocol control information and higher-level data. This is not to be confused with a **TDMA frame**, which consists of a sequence of time slots, each dedicated to a given subscriber. A TDMA time slot may contain exactly one MAC frame, a fraction of a MAC frame, or multiple MAC frames. The sequence of time slots across multiple TDMA frames that is dedicated to one subscriber forms a logical channel, and MAC frames are transmitted over that logical channel.

Connections and Service Flow

The 802.16.1 MAC protocol is connection oriented. That is, a logical connection is set up between peer entities (MAC users) prior to the exchange of data between those entities. Each MAC frame includes a connection ID, which is used by the MAC protocol to deliver incoming data to the correct MAC user. In addition, there is a one-to-one correspondence between a connection ID and service flow. The service flow defines the QoS parameters for the PDUs that are exchanged on the connection.

The concept of a service flow on a connection is central to the operation of the MAC protocol. Service flows provide a mechanism for upstream and downstream QoS management. In particular, they are integral to the bandwidth allocation process. The base station allocates both upstream and downstream bandwidth on the basis of the service flow for each active connection. Examples of service flow parameters are latency (maximum acceptable delay), jitter (maximum acceptable delay variation), and throughput (minimum acceptable bit rate).

Frame Format

A good way to get a grasp of the MAC protocol is to examine the frame format (Figure 11.17). The frame consists of three sections:

- **Header:** Contains protocol control information needed for the functioning of the MAC protocol.
- **Payload:** The payload may be either higher-level data (e.g., an ATM cell, an IP packet, a block of digital speech) or a MAC control message.
- **CRC:** The cyclic redundancy check field contains an error-detecting code (discussed in Section 8.1).

48 or 56 bits	≥ 0 bits	32 bits
MAC Header	Payload (optional)	CRC

Figure 11.17   IEEE 802.16.1 Frame Format

Three header formats are defined. There is a generic header format in both the uplink (toward the base station) and downlink (toward the subscriber) directions. These formats are used for frames that contain either higher-level data or a MAC control message. The third format is used for a bandwidth request frame.

The **downlink header** format is shown in Figure 11.18a. It consists of the following fields:

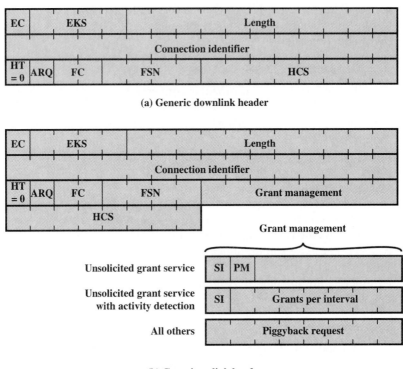

(a) Generic downlink header

(b) Generic uplink header

(c) Bandwidth request header

ARQ: Automatic repeat request   HCS: Header check sequence
EC: Encryption control   HT: Header type
EKS: Encryption key sequence   PM: Poll me bit
FC: Fragment control   SI: Slip indicator
FSN: Fragment sequence number

Figure 11.18 IEEE 802.16 MAC Header Formats

- **Encryption control (1 bit):** Indicates whether the payload is encrypted.
- **Encryption key sequence (4 bits):** An index into a vector of encryption key information, to be used if the payload is encrypted.
- **Length (11 bits):** Length in bytes of the entire MAC frame.
- **Connection identifier (16 bits):** A unidirectional, MAC-layer address that identifies a connection to equivalent peers in the subscriber and base station MAC. A CID maps to a SFID, which defines the QoS parameters to the service flow associated with that connection.
- **Header type (1 bit):** Indicates whether this is a generic or bandwidth request header.
- **ARQ indicator (1 bit):** Indicates whether the frame belongs to an ARQ enabled connection. If so, the ARQ mechanism described in Section 8.4 is used, and a 2-byte control field is prepended at the beginning of the frame. The control bit structure contains a 4-bit retry number and a 12 -bit sequence number. The retry number field is reset when a packet is first sent, and is incremented whenever it is retransmitted (up to the terminal value of 15). The sequence number field is assigned to each packet on its first transmission and then incremented.
- **Fragment control (2 bits):** Used in fragmentation and reassembly, as explained subsequently.
- **Fragment sequence number (4 bits):** Sequence number of the current fragment.
- **Header check sequence (8 bits):** An 8-bit CRC used to detect errors in the header.

Fragmentation is used to divide a higher-level block of data into two or more fragments in order to reduce the size of MAC frames. This is done to allow efficient use of available bandwidth relative to the QoS requirements of a connection's service flow. If fragmentation is not used, then the fragment control (FC) field is set to 00. If fragmentation is used, then the all of the fragments are assigned the same fragment sequence number (FSN) and the FC field has the following interpretation: first fragment (10); intermediate fragment (11); last fragment (01). The MAC user at the destination is responsible for reassembling all of the fragments with the same FSN.

The **uplink header** format is shown in Figure 11.18b. It contains all of the fields of the downlink header, plus an 8-bit grant management field. This field is used by the subscriber to convey bandwidth management needs to the base station. There are three different encodings of this field, depending on the type of connection. The subfields within the GM field include the following:

- **Slip indicator (1 bit):** If set, indicates a slip of uplink grants relative to the uplink queue depth.
- **Poll-me (1 bit):** If set, requests a poll by the base station.
- **Grants per interval (7 bits):** The number of grants required by a connection.
- **Piggyback request (8 bits):** The number of bytes of uplink capacity requested by the subscriber for this connection.

The first two formats for the GM field are associated with the unsolicited grant service (UGS). This service is designed to support real-time service flows. In essence, the base station periodically, using MAC management messages, grants an allocation of bytes to the subscriber on a given connection. The allocation is designed to keep up with the real time demands. If a subscriber finds that its queue of data to send has exceeded a threshold, the subscriber sends a GM field with the SI bit set and either requests a poll for bandwidth by setting the PM bit or requests that a given number of bandwidth grants be executed in the next time interval. The latter technique is used if this is a UGS with activity detection; this simply means that the flow may become inactive for substantial periods of time. For other types of service, the GM field may be used to make a request for capacity. This is referred to as a piggyback request because the request is made as part of a MAC frame carrying user data rather than in a separate bandwidth request management MAC frame.

Finally, the **bandwidth request header** is used by the subscriber to request additional bandwidth. This header is for a MAC frame with no payload. The 15-bit bandwidth request field indicates the number of bytes of capacity requested for uplink transmission.

MAC Management Messages

IEEE 802.16.1 defines a number of control messages that are used by the base station and the subscriber to manage the air interface and manage the exchange of data over the various connections. Messages are used to exchange operating parameters and status and encryption-related information, and for capacity management. The following is a brief summary of the messages currently defined:

- **Uplink and downlink channel descriptor:** Transmits characteristics of the physical channel.

- **Uplink and downlink access definition:** Allocates access to the uplink and downlink channels.

- **Ranging request and response:** The request is used by the subscriber to determine network delay and to request power and/or modulation adjustment. The response from the BS contains the requested parameters.

- **Registration request, response, and acknowledge:** The request is transmitted by the subscriber at initialization time and contains various relevant parameters. The base station replies with a response, and the subscriber sends an acknowledge to complete the handshake.

- **Privacy key management request and response:** Used to exchange information about encryption keys.

- **Dynamic service addition request, response, and acknowledge:** The request is sent by a subscriber to request a new service flow.

- **Dynamic service change request, response, and acknowledge:** The request is sent by a subscriber or the base station to dynamically change the parameters of an existing service flow.

- **Dynamic service deletion request and response:** The request is sent by the base station or subscriber to delete an existing service flow.

- **Multicast polling assignment request and response:** Sent by a subscriber to request inclusion in a multicast polling group.

- **Downlink data grant type request:** Sent by the base station to the subscriber to dictate the modulation method and FEC technique to be used on a particular connection, to enhance performance.

- **ARQ acknowledgment:** Used to acknowledge successful receipt of one or more packets from the peer MAC entity.

IEEE 802.16.1 Physical Layer

The 802.16.1 physical layer supports a different structure for the point-to-multipoint downstream channels and the multipoint-to-point upstream channels (Table 11.15). These structures reflect the differing requirements in the two directions. In general, most systems will require greater downstream capacity to individual subscribers to support asymmetric data connections such as Web applications over the Internet. For the upstream direction, the issue of medium access needs to be addressed, because there are a number of subscribers competing for the available capacity. These requirements are reflected in the physical layer specification.

Upstream Transmission

Upstream transmission uses a DAMA-TDMA (demand assignment multiple access—time division multiple access) technique. As was defined in Chapter 9, DAMA is a capacity assignment technique that adapts as needed to optimally respond to demand changes among the multiple stations. TDMA is simply the technique of dividing time on a channel into a sequence of frames, each consisting of a number of slots, and allocating one or more slots per frame to form a

Table 11.15 IEEE 801.16.1 Physical Layer Modes

	Upstream	Continuous Downstream (Mode A)	Burst Downstream (Mode B)
Access method	DAMA-TDMA	TDM	DAMA-TDMA
Duplexing technique	Matches downstream	FDD	FDD with adaptive modulation; FSDD; TDD

DAMA-TDMA: Demand assignement multiple access, time division multiple access
FDD: Frequency division duplexing
FSDD: Frequency shift division duplexing
TDD: Time division duplexing
TDM: Time division multiplexing

logical channel. With DAMA-TDMA, the assignment of slots to channels varies dynamically.

Upstream transmission makes use of a Reed-Solomon code for error correction and a modulation scheme based on QPSK.

Downstream Transmission

In the downstream direction, the standard specifies two modes of operation, one targeted to support a continuous transmission stream (mode A), such as audio or video, and one targeted to support a burst transmission stream (mode B), such as IP-based traffic.

For the **continuous downstream mode**, a simple TDM scheme is used for channel access. The duplexing technique that is used for allocating capacity between upstream and downstream traffic is known as FDD (frequency division duplex). FDD simply means that a different frequency band is used for transmission in each direction. This is equivalent to a FAMA-FDMA (fixed assignment multiple access—frequency division multiple access) scheme. FDD implies that all subscribers can transmit and receive simultaneously, each on their own assigned frequencies.

For the **burst downstream mode**, the DAMA-TDMA scheme is used for channel access. Three alternative techniques are available for duplexing traffic between upstream and downstream:

- **FDD with adaptive modulation:** This is the same FDD scheme used in the upstream mode, but with a dynamic capability to change the modulation and forward error correction schemes.
- **Frequency shift division duplexing (FSDD):** This is similar to FDD, but some or all of the subscribers are not capable of transmitting and receiving simultaneously.
- **Time division duplexing (TDD):** This technique is discussed in Section 11.1. A TDMA frame is used, with part of the time allocated for upstream transmission and part for downstream transmission.

The availability of these alternative techniques provides considerable flexibility in designing a system that optimizes the use of capacity.

11.4 RECOMMENDED READING AND WEB SITES

[PHIL98] is a detailed treatment of DECT and PWT.

A thorough analysis of propagation effects at millimeter wavelengths is found in [FREE97]. A briefer but useful survey of the same topic is [DALK96].

[NORD00] is a general overview of LMDS technology and applications. [FUNG98] focuses on some detailed transmitter/receiver design issues for MMDS. [WEBB00] is a good overall survey of wireless local loop technology. [KELL00] provides a thorough analysis of OFDM. [BOLC01] surveys design issues related to broadband wireless access.

BOLC01   Bolcskei, H., et al. "Fixed Broadband Wireless Access: State of the Art, Challenges, and Future Directions." *IEEE Communications Magazin*, January 2001.

DALK96   Dalke, R.; Hufford, G.; and Ketchum, R. *Radio Propagation Considerations for Local Multipoint Distribution Systems.* National Telecommunications and Information Administration Publication PB97116511, August 1996.

FREE97   Freeman, R. *Radio System Design for Telecommunications.* New York: Wiley, 1997.

FUNG98   Fung, P. "A Primer on MMDS Technology." *Communication Systems Design,* April 1998. Available at csdmag.com.

KELL00   Keller, T., and H. "Adaptive Multicarrier Modulation: A Convenient Framework for Time-Frequency Processing in Wireless Communication." *Proceedings of the IEEE,* May 2000.

NORD00   Nordbotten, A. "LMDS Systems and Their Application." *IEEE Communications Magazine,* June 2000.

PHIL98   Phillips, J., and Namee, G. *Personal Wireless Communications with DECT and PWT.* Boston: Artech House, 1998.

WEBB00   Webb, W. *Introduction to Wireless Local Loop: Broadband and Narrowband Systems.* Boston: Artech House, 2000.

Recommended Web sites:

- **Wireless Communications Association International:** represents the fixed broadband wireless access industry worldwide. Good set of links.
- **The IEEE 802.16 Working Group on Broadband Wireless Access Standards:** Contains working group documents plus discussion archives.
- **U.S. National Wireless Electronic Systems Testbed:** A measurements and standards resource for the broadband wireless access industry. Useful documents and links.

11.5 KEY TERMS, REVIEW QUESTIONS, AND PROBLEMS

Key Terms

adaptive differential PCM (ADPCM)	Fresnel zone	multicarrier modulation
cordless	linear predictive filter	multichannel multipoint distribution service (MMDS)
differential quantization	local multipoint distribution service (LMDS)	
digital enhanced cordless telecommunications (DECT)	logical link control (LLC)	orthogonal frequency division multiplexing (OFDM)
fixed broadband wireless	MAC frame	time division duplex (TDD)
fixed wireless access	medium access control (MAC)	wireless cable
		wireless local loop (WLL)

Review Questions

1 In what ways has traditional cordless telephony been extended by standardization?
2 What is the difference between TDD and TDM?
3 List and briefly define the DECT logical channels.
4 What are some key advantages of WLL over a wired subscriber loop?
5 What are the principal advantages of millimeter wave transmission compared to transmission at longer wavelengths?
6 What are the principal disadvantages of millimeter wave transmission compared to transmission at longer wavelengths?
7 What are the principal advantages of OFDM?
8 What are the relative advantages of MMDS compared to LMDS?
9 What are the key differences among IEEE 802.16.1, IEEE 802.16.2, and IEEE 802.16.3?

Problems

1 GSM, described in Chapter 10, makes use of a TDMA scheme in which there are a number of duplex channels, with each channel consisting of two dedicated frequency bands, one for transmission in each direction. Suppose that we wished to design a comparable system, using the same total amount of bandwidth, but using TDD. List the key parameters of a TDD-GSM system and compares these to the real GSM parameters.

2 A LOS microwave link 12 km long is planned for installation in Germany, which is in climate zone H (Table 11.8). The operational frequency is 38 GHz and the desired time availability is 99.99%. Local rain rate statistics are not available. The antenna polarization is horizontal.

   a. What amount of attenuation is to be anticipated?

   b. Repeat for 99.9% and 99% and comment on the practicality of the requirement for various availabilities.

APPENDIX 11A   LINEAR PREDICTIVE FILTERS[8]

The linear predictive filter is based on using an approximation of the Taylor series. For a function $g(t)$ that has derivatives of all orders at t, the function can be represented by its Taylor series:

$$g(x) = \sum_{n=0}^{\infty} \frac{(x - t)^n}{n!} g^{(n)}(t) \tag{11.4}$$

where $g^{(n)}(t)$ is the nth derivative of $g(t)$. Now, suppose we are going to sample $g(t)$ with a sampling interval of T_s. Then, defining $T_s = x - t$, we can restate Equation (11.4) as

$$g(t + T_s) = \sum_{n=0}^{\infty} \frac{(T_s)^n}{n!} g^{(n)}(t) \tag{11.5}$$

---

[8]The development in this appendix is based on material in [LATH98].

Equation (11.5) shows that from the value of the signal at time $t + T_s$ can be predicted from the value of its signal and its derivatives at time t. In fact, for small values of T_s (much less than one), we can produce a good approximation with just the first derivative:

$$g(t + T_s) \approx g(t) + T_s\, g'(t) \tag{11.6}$$

Let us denote the kth sample of $g(t)$ taken at time $t = kT_s$ as $m(k)$; then $m(k \pm 1) = g(kT_s \pm T_s)$. Further, we can approximate $g'(kT_s)$ by $[g(kT_s) - g(kT_s - T_s)]/T_s$. Therefore, from Equation (11.6), we have

$$m(k + 1) \approx m(k) + T_s\left[\frac{m(k) - m(k - 1)}{T_s}\right]$$
$$= 2m(k) - m(k - 1)$$

Thus, we can compute an approximate predication of the sample at $(k + 1)$ from the preceding two samples. The approximation improves as we add more samples. If N samples are used, the approximation formula becomes

$$m(k) \approx A_1 m(k - 1) + A_2 m(k - 2) + \ldots + A_N m(k - N) \tag{11.7}$$

The right-hand side of Equation (11.7) is $\hat{m}(k)$, the predicted value of $m(k)$. Thus,

$$\hat{m}(k) = A_1 m(k - 1) + A_2 m(k - 2) + \ldots + A_N m(k - N) \tag{11.8}$$

This is the linear predictor illustrated in Figure 11.6. The prediction coefficients A_i are determined from the statistical properties of the samples.

CHAPTER 12

MOBILE IP AND WIRELESS APPLICATION PROTOCOL

I n this chapter, we look at two standards that provide application-level support for wireless networking: Mobile IP and Wireless Application Protocol (WAP).

12.1 MOBILE IP

In response to the increasing popularity of palm-top and other mobile computers, mobile IP was developed to enable computers to maintain Internet connectivity while moving from one Internet attachment point to another. Although Mobile IP can work with wired connections, in which a computer is unplugged from one physical attachment point and plugged into another, it is particularly suited to wireless connections.

The term *mobile* in this context implies that a user is connected to one or more applications across the Internet, that the user's point of attachment changes dynamically, and that all connections are automatically maintained despite the change. This is in contrast to a user, such as a business traveler, with a portable computer of some sort who arrives at a destination and uses the computer's notebook to dial into an ISP (Internet service provider). In this latter case, the user's Internet connection is terminated each time the user moves and a new connection is initiated when the user dials back in. Each time an Internet connection is established, software in the point of attachment (typically an ISP) is used to obtain a new, temporarily assigned IP address. For each application-level connection (e.g., FTP, Web connection), this temporary IP address is used by the user's correspondent. A better term for this kind of use is *nomadic*.

We begin with a general overview of Mobile IP and then look at some of the details.

Operation of Mobile IP

As was described in Chapter 4, routers make use of the IP address in an IP datagram to perform routing. In particular, the **network portion** of an IP address (Figure 4.13) is used by routers to move a datagram from the source computer to the network to which the target computer is attached. Then the final router on the path, which is attached to the same network as the target computer, uses the **host portion** of the IP address to deliver the IP datagram to the destination. Further, this IP address is known to the next higher layer in the protocol architecture (Figure 4.4). In particular, most applications over the Internet are supported by TCP connections. When a TCP connection is set up, the TCP entity on each side of the connection knows the IP address of the correspondent host. When a TCP segment is handed down to the IP layer for delivery, TCP provides the IP address, and IP creates an IP datagram with that IP address in the IP header and sends the datagram out for routing and delivery. However, with a mobile host, the IP address may change while one or more TCP connections are active.

Figure 12.1 shows in general terms how Mobile IP deals with the problem of dynamic IP addresses. A mobile node is assigned to a particular network, known as its **home network**. Its IP address on that network, known as its **home address**, is

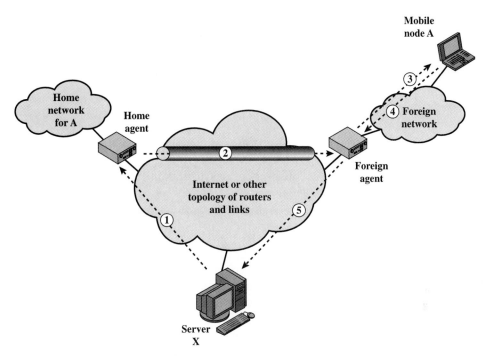

Figure 12.1   Mobile IP Scenario

static. When the mobile node moves its attachment point to another network, that is considered a **foreign network** for this host. Once the mobile node is reattached, it makes its presence known by registering with a network node, typically a router, on the foreign network known as a **foreign agent**. The mobile node then communicates with a similar agent on the user's home network, known as a **home agent**, giving the home agent the **care-of address** of the mobile node; the care-of address identifies the foreign agent's location. Typically, one or more routers on a network will implement the roles of both home and foreign agents.

When IP datagrams are exchanged over a connection between the mobile node and another host (a server in Figure 12.1), the following operations occur:

1. Server X transmits an IP datagram destined for mobile node A, with A's home address in the IP header. The IP datagram is routed to A's home network.
2. At the home network, the incoming IP datagram is intercepted by the home agent. The home agent encapsulates the entire datagram inside a new IP datagram which has the A's care-of address in the header, and retransmits the datagram. The use of an outer IP datagram with a different destination IP address is known as **tunneling**. This IP datagram is routed to the foreign agent.
3. The foreign agent strips off the outer IP header, encapsulates the original IP datagram in a network-level PDU (e.g., a LAN LLC frame), and delivers the original datagram to A across the foreign network.
4. When A sends IP traffic to X, it uses X's IP address. In our example, this is a fixed address; that is, X is not a mobile node. Each IP datagram is sent by A

to a router on the foreign network for routing to X. Typically, this router is also the foreign agent.

5. The IP datagram from A to X travels directly across the Internet to X, using X's IP address.

To support the operations illustrated in Figure 12.1, Mobile IP includes three basic capabilities:

- **Discovery:** A mobile node uses a discovery procedure to identify prospective home agents and foreign agents.
- **Registration:** A mobile node uses an authenticated registration procedure to inform its home agent of its care-of address.
- **Tunneling:** Tunneling is used to forward IP datagrams from a home address to a care-of address.

Figure 12.2 indicates the underlying protocol support for the Mobile IP capability. The registration protocol communicates between an application on the mobile node and an application in the home agent, and hence uses a transport-level protocol. Because registration is a simple request-response transaction, the overhead of the connection-oriented TCP is not required, and therefore UDP is used as the transport protocol. Discovery makes use of the existing ICMP (Internet control message protocol) by adding the appropriate extensions to the ICMP header. ICMP, which is described in Appendix 12A, is a connectionless protocol well suited for the discovery operation. Finally, tunneling is performed at the IP level.

Mobile IP is specified in a number of RFCs. The basic defining document is RFC 2002. Table 12.1 lists some useful terminology from RFC 2002.

Discovery

The discovery process in Mobile IP is very similar to the router advertisement process defined in ICMP (see Appendix 12A). Accordingly, agent discovery makes use of ICMP router advertisement messages, with one or more extensions specific to Mobile IP.

The mobile node is responsible for an ongoing discovery process. It must determine if it is attached to its home network, in which case IP datagrams may be

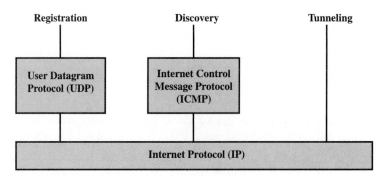

Figure 12.2 Protocol Support for Mobile IP

Table 12.1 Mobile IP Terminology (RFC 2002)

Mobile node	A host or router that changes its point of attachment from one network or subnetwork to another. A mobile node may change its location without changing its IP address; it may continue to communicate with other Internet nodes at any location using its (constant) IP address, assuming link-layer connectivity to a point of attachment is available
Home address	An IP address that is assigned for an extended period of time to a mobile node. It remains unchanged regardless of where the node is attached to the Internet.
Home agent	A router on a mobile node's home network which tunnels datagrams for delivery to the mobile node when it is away from home, and maintains current location information for the mobile node.
Home network	A network, possibly virtual, having a network prefix matching that of a mobile node's home address. Note that standard IP routing mechanisms will deliver datagrams destined to a mobile node's Home Address to the mobile node's Home Network.
Foreign agent	A router on a mobile node's visited network which provides routing services to the mobile node while registered. The foreign agent detunnels and delivers datagrams to the mobile node that were tunneled by the mobile node's home agent. For datagrams sent by a mobile node, the foreign agent may serve as a default router for registered mobile nodes.
Foreign network	Any network other than the mobile node's Home Network.
Care-of address	The termination point of a tunnel toward a mobile node, for datagrams forwarded to the mobile node while it is away from home. The protocol can use two different types of care-of address: a "foreign agent care-of address" is an address of a foreign agent with which the mobile node is registered, and a "co-located care-of address" is an externally obtained local address which the mobile node has associated with one of its own network interfaces.
Correspondent node	A peer with which a mobile node is communicating. A correspondent node may be either mobile or stationary.
Link	A facility or medium over which nodes can communicate at the link layer. A link underlies the network layer.
Node	A host or a router.
Tunnel	The path followed by a datagram while it is encapsulated. The model is that, while it is encapsulated, a datagram is routed to a knowledgeable decapsulating agent, which decapsulates the datagram and then correctly delivers it to its ultimate destination.

received without forwarding, or if it is attached to a foreign network. Because handoff from one network to another occurs at the physical layer, a transition from the home network to a foreign network can occur at any time without notification to the network layer (i.e., the IP layer). Thus, discovery for a mobile node is a continuous process.

For the purpose of discovery, a router or other network node that can act as an agent periodically issues a router advertisement ICMP message (see Figure 12.20d in Appendix 12A) with an advertisement extension. The router advertisement portion of the message includes the IP address of the router. The advertisement extension includes additional information about the router's role as an agent, as discussed subsequently. A mobile node listens for these **agent advertisement messages**. Because a foreign agent could be on the mobile node's home network (set up to serve visiting mobile nodes), the arrival of an agent advertisement does not necessarily tell the mobile node that it is on a foreign network. The mobile node must compare the network portion of the router's IP address with the network portion of its own home address. If these network portions do not match, then the mobile node is on a foreign network.

The **agent advertisement extension** follows the ICMP router advertisement fields and consists of the following fields (Figure 12.3):

- **Type:** 16, indicates that this is an agent advertisement.
- **Length:** $(6 + 4N)$, where N is the number of care-of addresses advertised.
- **Sequence number:** The count of agent advertisement messages sent since the agent was initialized.
- **Lifetime:** The longest lifetime, in seconds, that this agent is willing to accept a registration request from a mobile node.
- **R:** Registration with this foreign agent is required (or another foreign agent on this network). Even those mobile nodes that have already acquired a care-of address from this foreign agent must re-register.
- **B:** Busy. The foreign agent will not accept registrations from additional mobile nodes.

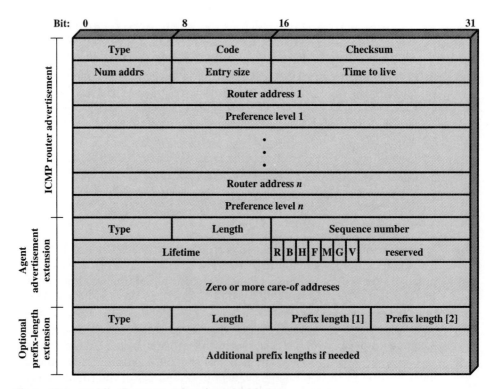

Figure 12.3 Mobile IP Agent Advertisement Message

- **H:** This agent offers services as a home agent on this network.
- **F:** This agent offers services as a foreign agent on this network.
- **M:** This agent can receive tunneled IP datagrams that use minimal encapsulation, explained subsequently.
- **G:** This agent can receive tunneled IP datagrams that use GRE encapsulation, explained subsequently.
- **V:** This agent supports the use of Van Jacobson header compression. This is an algorithm defined in RFC 1144 for compressing fields in the TCP and IP headers.
- **Care-of address:** The care-of address or addresses supported by this agent on this network. There must be at least one such address if the F bit is set. There may be multiple addresses.

There may also be an optional **prefix-length extension** following the advertisement extension. This extension indicates the number of bits in the router's address that define the network number (Figure 4.13). The mobile node uses this information to compare the network portion of its own IP address with the network portion of the router. The fields are as follows:

- **Type:** 19, indicates that this is a prefix-length advertisement.
- **Length:** N, where N is the value of the Num Addrs field in the ICMP router advertisement portion of this ICMP message. In other words, this is the number of router addresses listed in this ICMP message.
- **Prefix length:** The number of leading bits that define the network number of the corresponding router address listed in the ICMP router advertisement portion of this message. The number of prefix length fields matches the number of router address fields (N).

Agent Solicitation

Foreign agents are expected to issue agent advertisement messages periodically. If a mobile node needs agent information immediately, it can issue an ICMP router solicitation message (see Figure 12.20e in Appendix 12A). Any agent receiving this message will then issue an agent advertisement.

Move Detection

As was mentioned, a mobile node may move from one network to another due to some handoff mechanism, without the IP level being aware of it. The agent discovery process is intended to enable the agent to detect such a move. The agent may use one of two algorithms for this purpose:

- **Use of lifetime field:** When a mobile node receives an agent advertisement from a foreign agent that it is currently using or that it is now going to register with, it records the lifetime field as a timer. If the timer expires before the agent receives another agent advertisement from the agent, then the node assumes that it has lost contact with that agent. If, in the meantime, the mobile node has received an agent advertisement from another agent and that advertisement has not yet expired, the mobile node can register with this new agent. Otherwise, the mobile node should use agent solicitation to find an agent.

- **Use of network prefix:** The mobile node checks whether any newly received agent advertisement is on the same network as the node's current care-of address. If it is not, the mobile node assumes that it has moved and may register with the agent whose advertisement the mobile node has just received.

Co-Located Addresses

The discussion so far has involved the use of a care-of address associated with a foreign agent; that is, the care-of address is an IP address for the foreign agent. This foreign agent will receive datagrams at this care-of address, intended for the mobile node, and then forward them across the foreign network to the mobile node. However, in some cases a mobile node may move to a network that has no foreign agents or on which all foreign agents are busy. As an alternative, the mobile node may act as its own foreign agent by using a co-located care-of address. A co-located care-of address is an IP address obtained by the mobile node that is associated with the mobile node's current interface to a network.

The means by which a mobile node acquires a co-located address is beyond the scope of Mobile IP. One means is to dynamically acquire a temporary IP address through an Internet service such as DHCP (Dynamic Host Configuration Protocol). Another alternative is that the co-located address may be owned by the mobile node as a long-term address for use only while visiting a given foreign network.

Registration

Once a mobile node has recognized that it is on a foreign network and has acquired a care-of address, it needs to alert a home agent on its home network and request that the home agent forward its IP traffic. The registration process involves four steps:

1. The mobile node requests the forwarding service by sending a registration request to the foreign agent that the mobile node wants to use.
2. The foreign agent relays this request to the mobile node's home agent.
3. The home agent either accepts or denies the request and sends a registration reply to the foreign agent.
4. The foreign agent relays this reply to the mobile node.

If the mobile node is using a co-located care-of address, then it registers directly with its home agent, rather than going through a foreign agent.

The registration operation uses two types of messages, carried in UDP segments (Figure 12.4). The **registration request message** consists of the following fields:

- **Type:** 1, indicates that this is a registration request.
- **S:** Simultaneous bindings. The mobile node is requesting that the home agent retain its prior mobility bindings. When simultaneous bindings are in effect, the home agent will forward multiple copies of the IP datagram, one to each care-of address currently registered for this mobile node. Multiple simultaneous bindings can be useful in wireless handoff situations, to improve reliability.
- **B:** Broadcast datagrams. Indicates that the mobile node would like to receive copies of broadcast datagrams that it would have received if it were attached to its home network.

(a) Registration request message

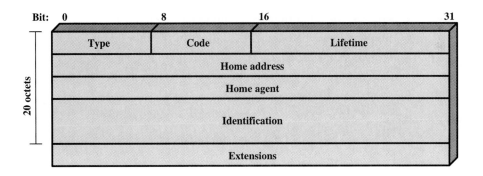

(b) Registration reply message

Figure 12.4 Mobile IP Registration Messages

- **D:** Decapsulation by mobile node. The mobile node is using a co-located care-of address and will decapsulate its own tunneled IP datagrams.
- **M:** Indicates that the home agent should use minimal encapsulation, explained subsequently.
- **V:** Indicates that the home agent should use Van Jacobson header compression.
- **G:** Indicates that the home agent should use GRE encapsulation, explained subsequently.
- **Lifetime:** The number of seconds before the registration is considered expired. A value of zero is a request for de-registration.
- **Home address:** The home IP address of the mobile node. The home agent can expect to receive IP datagrams with this as a destination address, and must forward those to the care-of address.
- **Home agent:** The IP address of the mobile node's home agent. This informs the foreign agent of the address to which this request should be relayed.

- **Care-of address:** The IP address at this end of the tunnel. The home agent should forward IP datagrams that it receives with mobile node's home address to this destination address.
- **Identification:** A 64-bit number generated by the mobile node, used for matching registration requests to registration replies and for security purposes, as explained subsequently.
- **Extensions:** The only extension so far defined is the authentication extension, explained subsequently.

The **registration reply message** consists of the following fields:

- **Type:** 3, indicates that this is a registration reply.
- **Code:** Indicates result of the registration request (Table 12.2).
- **Lifetime:** If the code field indicates that the registration was accepted, the number of seconds before the registration is considered expired. A value of zero indicates that the mobile node has been de-registered.
- **Home address:** The home IP address of the mobile node.
- **Home agent:** The IP address of the mobile node's home agent.
- **Identification:** A 64-bit number used for matching registration requests to registration replies.
- **Extensions:** The only extension so far defined is the authentication extension, explained subsequently.

Table 12.2 Code Values for a Mobile IP Registration Reply

Registration Successful	Registration Denied by the Foreign Agent
0 registration accepted	64 reason unspecified
1 registration accepted, but simultaneous mobility bindings unsupported	65 administratively prohibited
	66 insufficient resources
Registration Denied by the Home Agent	67 mobile node failed authentication
	68 home agent failed authentication
128 reason unspecified	69 requested Lifetime too long
129 administratively prohibited	70 poorly formed Request
130 insufficient resources	71 poorly formed Reply
131 mobile node failed authentication	72 requested encapsulation unavailable
132 foreign agent failed authentication	73 requested Van Jacobson compression unavailable
133 registration Identification mismatch	80 home network unreachable (ICMP error received)
134 poorly formed Request	81 home agent host unreachable (ICMP error received)
135 too many simultaneous mobility bindings	82 home agent port unreachable (ICMP error received)
136 unknown home agent address	88 home agent unreachable (other ICMP error received)

Securing the Registration Procedure

A key concern with the registration procedure is security. Mobile IP is designed to resist two types of attacks:

1. A node may pretend to be a foreign agent and send a registration request to a home agent so as to divert traffic intended for a mobile node to itself.
2. A malicious agent may replay old registration messages, effectively cutting the mobile node from the network.

The technique that is used to protect against such attacks involves the use of message authentication and the proper use of the identification field of the registration request and reply messages (Figure 12.4).

For purposes of message authentication, each registration request and reply contains an **authentication extension** (Figure 12.5) with the following fields:

- **Type:** Used to designate the type of this authentication extension.
- **Length:** 4 plus the number of bytes in the authenticator.
- **Security parameter index (SPI):** An index that identifies a security context between a pair of nodes. This security context is configured so that the two nodes share a secret key and parameters relevant to this association (e.g., authentication algorithm).
- **Authenticator:** A code used to authenticate the message. The sender inserts this code into the message using a shared secret key. The receiver uses the code to ensure that the message has not been altered or delayed. The authenticator protects the entire registration request or reply message, any extensions prior to this extension, and the type and length fields of this extension.

The default authentication algorithm uses keyed-MD5 to produce a 128-bit message digest. Appendix 12B describes this algorithm. For Mobile IP, a "prefix+ suffix" mode of operation is used. The MD5 digest is computed over the shared secret key, followed by the protected fields from the registration message, followed by the shared secret key again.

Figure 12.5 Mobile IP Authentication Extension

Three types of authentication extensions are defined:

- **Mobile-home:** This extension must be present and provides for authentication of the registration messages between the mobile node and the home agent.
- **Mobile-foreign:** The extension may be present when a security association exists between the mobile node and the foreign agent. The foreign agent will strip this extension off before relaying a request message to the home agent and add this extension to a reply message coming from a home agent.
- **Foreign-home:** The extension may be present when a security association exists between the foreign agent and the home agent.

Note that the authenticator protects the identification field in the request and reply messages. As a result, the identification value can be used to thwart replay types of attacks. As was mentioned, the identification value enables the mobile node to match a reply to a request. Further, if the mobile node and the home agent maintain synchronization, so that the home agent can distinguish between a reasonable identification value from a suspicious one, then the home agent can reject suspicious messages. One way to do this is to use a timestamp value. As long as the mobile node and home agent have reasonably synchronized values of time, the timestamp will serve the purpose. Alternatively, the mobile node could generate values using a pseudorandom number generator. If the home agent knows the algorithm, then it knows what identification value to expect next.

Tunneling

Once a mobile node is registered with a home agent, the home agent must be able to intercept IP datagrams sent to the mobile node's home address so that these datagrams can be forwarded via tunneling. The standard does not mandate a specific technique for this purpose but references ARP (Address Resolution Protocol) as a possible mechanism. The home agent needs to inform other nodes on the same network (the home network) that IP datagrams with a destination address of the mobile node in question should be delivered (at the link level) to this agent. In effect, the home agent steals the identity of the mobile node in order to capture packets destined for that node that are transmitted across the home network.

For example, suppose that R3 in Figure 12.6 is acting as the home agent for a mobile node that is attached to a foreign network elsewhere on the Internet. That is, there is a host H whose home network is LAN Z that is now attached to some foreign network. If host D has traffic for H, it will generate an IP datagram with H's home address in the IP destination address field. The IP module in D recognizes that this destination address is on LAN Z and so passes the datagram down to the link layer with instructions to deliver it to a particular MAC-level address on Z. Prior to this time, R3 has informed the IP layer at D that datagrams destined for that particular address should be sent to R3. Thus, the MAC address of R3 is inserted by D in the destination MAC address field of the outgoing MAC frame. Similarly, if an IP datagram with the mobile node's home address arrives at router R2, it recognizes that the destination address is on LAN Z and will attempt to deliver the datagram to a MAC-level address on Z. Again, R2 has previously been informed that the MAC-level address it needs corresponds to R3.

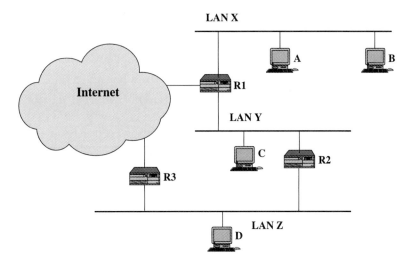

Figure 12.6 A Simple Internetworking Example

For traffic that is routed across the Internet and arrives at R3 from the Internet, R3 must simply recognize that for this destination address, the datagram is to be captured and forwarded.

To forward an IP datagram to a care-of address, the home agent puts the entire IP datagram into an outer IP datagram. This is a form of encapsulation, just as placing an IP header in front of a TCP segment encapsulates the TCP segment in an IP datagram. Three options for encapsulation are allowed for Mobile IP:

- **IP-within-IP encapsulation:** This is the simplest approach, defined in RFC 2003.
- **Minimal encapsulation:** This approach involves fewer fields, defined in RFC 2004.
- **Generic routing encapsulation (GRE):** This is a generic encapsulation procedure that was developed prior to the development of Mobile IP, defined in RFC 1701.

We review the first two of these methods.

IP-within-IP Encapsulation

With this approach, the entire IP datagram becomes the payload in a new IP datagram (Figure 12.7a). The inner, original IP header is unchanged except to decrement TTL by 1. The outer header is a full IP header. Two fields (indicated as unshaded in the figure) are copied from the inner header: The version number is 4, which is the protocol identifier for IPv4, and the type of service requested for the outer IP datagram is the same as that requested for the inner IP datagram.

In the inner IP header, the source address refers to the host that is sending the original datagram, and the destination address is the home address of the intended recipient. In the outer IP header, the source and destination addresses refer to the entry and exit points of the tunnel. Thus, the source address typically is the IP address of the home agent, and the destination address is the care-of address for the intended destination.

(a) IP-within-IP encapsulation

New IP header:

Version = 4	IHL	Type of service		Total length	
Identification			Flags	Fragment offset	
Time to live		Protocol = 4		Header checksum	
Source address (home agent address)					
Destination address (care-of address)					

Old IP header:

Version = 4	IHL	Type of service		Total length	
Identification			Flags	Fragment offset	
Time to live		Protocol		Header checksum	
Source address (original sender)					
Destination address (home address)					

IP payload (e.g., TCP segment)

Unshaded fields are copied from the inner IP header to the outer IP header.

(b) Minimal encapsulation

Modified IP header:

Version = 4	IHL	Type of service		Total length	
Identification			Flags	Fragment offset	
Time to live		Protocol = 55		Header checksum	
Source address (home agent address)					
Destination address (care-of address)					

Minimal forwarding header:

Protocol	S	reserved	Header checksum	
Destination address (home address)				
Source address (original sender; may not be present)				

IP payload (e.g., TCP segment)

Unshaded fields in the inner IP header are copied from the original IP header. Unshaded fields in the outer IP header are modified from the original IP header.

Figure 12.7   Mobile IP Encapsulation

> **Example.** Consider an IP datagram that originates at server X in Figure 12.1 and that is intended for mobile node A. The original IP datagram has a source address equal to the IP address of X and a destination address equal to the IP home address of A. The network portion of A's home address refers to A's home network, and so the datagram is routed through the Internet to A's home network, where it is intercepted by the home agent. The home agent encapsulates the incoming datagram with an outer IP header, which includes a source address equal to the IP address of the home agent and a destination address equal to the IP address of the foreign agent on the foreign network to which A is currently attached. When this new datagram reaches the foreign agent, it strips off the outer IP header and delivers the original datagram to A.

Minimal Encapsulation

Minimal encapsulation results in less overhead and can be used if the mobile node, home agent, and foreign agent all agree to do so. With minimal encapsulation, the new header is inserted between the original IP header and the original IP payload (Figure 12.7b). It includes the following fields:

- **Protocol:** Copied from the destination address field in the original IP header. This field identifies the protocol type of the original IP payload and thus identifies the type of header than begins the original IP payload.
- **S:** If 0, the original source address is not present, and the length of this header is 8 octets. If 1, the original source address is present, and the length of this header is 12 octets.
- **Header checksum:** Computed over all the fields of this header.
- **Original destination address:** Copied from the destination address field in the original IP header.
- **Original source address:** Copied from the source address field in the original IP header. This field is present only if the S bit is 1. The field is not present if the encapsulator is the source of the datagram (i.e., the datagram originates at the home agent).

The following fields in the original IP header are modified to form the new outer IP header:

- **Total length:** Incremented by the size of the minimal forwarding header (8 or 12).
- **Protocol:** 55; this is the protocol number assigned to minimal IP encapsulation.
- **Header checksum:** Computed over all the fields of this header; because some of the fields have been modified, this value must be recomputed.
- **Source address:** The IP address of the encapsulator, typically the home agent.
- **Destination address:** The IP address of the exit point of the tunnel. This is the care-of address and may either be the IP address of the foreign agent or the IP address of the mobile node (in the case of a co-located care-of address).

The processing for minimal encapsulation is as follows. The encapsulator (home agent) prepares the encapsulated datagram with the format of Figure 12.7b. This datagram is now suitable for tunneling and is delivered across the Internet to the care-of address. At the care-of address, the fields in the minimal forwarding header are restored to the original IP header and the forwarding header is removed from the datagram. The total length field in the IP header is decremented by the size of the minimal forwarding header (8 or 12) and the header checksum field is recomputed.

12.2 WIRELESS APPLICATION PROTOCOL

The Wireless Application Protocol (WAP) is a universal, open standard developed by the WAP Forum to provide mobile users of wireless phones and other wireless terminals such as pagers and personal digital assistants (PDAs) access to telephony and information services, including the Internet and the Web. WAP is designed to work with all wireless network technologies (e.g., GSM, CDMA, and TDMA). WAP is based on existing Internet standards, such as IP, XML, HTML, and HTTP, as much as possible. It also includes security facilities. Ericsson, Motorola, Nokia, and Phone.com established the WAP Forum in 1997, which now has several hundred members. The WAP Forum released v1.2 of WAP in June 2000.

Strongly affecting the use of mobile phones and terminals for data services are the significant limitations of the devices and the networks that connect them. The devices have limited processors, memory, and battery life. The user interface is also limited, and the displays small. The wireless networks are characterized by relatively low bandwidth, high latency, and unpredictable availability and stability compared to wired connections. Moreover, all these features vary widely from terminal device to terminal device and from network to network. Finally, mobile, wireless users have different expectations and needs from other information systems users. For instance, mobile terminals must be extremely easy to use, much easier than workstations and personal computers. WAP is designed to deal with these challenges. The WAP specification includes the following:

- A programming model based on the WWW Programming Model
- A markup language, the Wireless Markup Language, adhering to XML
- A specification of a small browser suitable for a mobile, wireless terminal
- A lightweight communications protocol stack
- A framework for wireless telephony applications (WTAs)

The WAP specification consists of a number of different protocols and modules, whose relationship is depicted in Figure 12.8.

Architectural Overview

The WAP Programming Model is based on three elements: the *client*, the *gateway*, and the *original server* (Figure 12.9). HTTP is used between the gateway and the original server to transfer content. The gateway acts as a proxy server for the wireless domain. Its processor(s) provide services that offload the limited capabilities of the hand-held, mobile, wireless terminals. For example, the gateway provides DNS services, converts between WAP protocol stack and the WWW stack (HTTP and TCP/IP), encodes information from the Web into a more compact form that minimizes

Figure 12.8 WAP Protocol Stack

wireless communication, and, in the other direction, decodes the compacted form into standard Web communication conventions. The gateway also caches frequently requested information.

Figure 12.10 illustrates key components in a WAP environment. Using WAP, a mobile user can browse Web content on an ordinary Web server. The Web server provides content in the form of HTML-coded pages that are transmitted using the standard Web protocol stack (HTTP/TCP/IP). The HTML content must go through an HTML filter, which may either be co-located with the WAP proxy or in a separate physical module. The filter translates the HTML content into WML content. If the filter is separate from the proxy, HTTP/TCP/IP is used to deliver the WML to the proxy. The proxy converts the WML to a more compact form known as binary WML and delivers it to the mobile user over a wireless network using the WAP protocol stack.

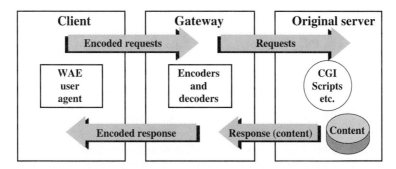

Figure 12.9 The WAP Programming Model

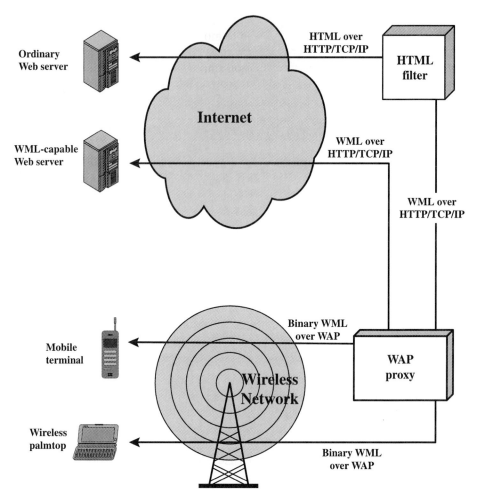

Figure 12.10 WAP Infrastructure

If the Web browser is capable of directly generating WML content, then the WML is delivered using HTTP/TCP/IP to the proxy, which converts the WML to binary WML and then delivers it to the mobile node using WAP protocols.

The WAP architecture is designed to cope with the two principal limitations of wireless Web access: the limitations of the mobile node (small screen size, limited input capability) and the low data rates of wireless digital networks. Even with the introduction of 3G wireless networks, which will provide broadband data rates, the small hand-held mobile nodes will continue to have limited input and display capabilities. Thus WAP or a similar capability will be needed for the indefinite future.

Wireless Markup Language

Wireless Markup Language (WML) was designed to describe content and format for presenting data on devices with limited bandwidth, limited screen size, and limited user input capability. It is designed to work with telephone keypads, styluses, and other input devices common to mobile, wireless communication. WML permits the scaling of displays for use on two-line screens found in some small devices, as well as the larger screens found on smart phones.

For an ordinary PC, a Web browser provides content in the form of Web pages coded with the Hypertext Markup Language (HTML). To translate an HTML-coded Web page into WML with content and format suitable for wireless devices, much of the information, especially graphics and animation, must be stripped away. WML presents mainly text-based information that attempts to capture the essence of the Web page and that is organized for easy access for users of mobile devices.

Important features of WML include the following:

- **Text and image support:** Formatting and layout commands are provided for text and limited image capability.
- **Deck/card organizational metaphor:** WML documents are subdivided into small, well-defined units of user interaction called *cards*. Users navigate by moving back and forth between cards. A card specifies one or more units of interaction (a menu, a screen of text, or a text-entry field). A WML deck is similar to an HTML page in that it is identified by a Web address (URL) and is the unit of content transmission.
- **Support for navigation among cards and decks:** WML includes provisions for event handling, which is used for navigation or executing scripts.

In an HTML-based Web browser, a user navigates by clicking on links. At a WML-capable mobile device, a user interacts with cards, moving forward and back through the deck.

WML is a tagged language, similar to HTML, in which individual language elements are delineated by lowercase tags enclosed in angle brackets. Typically, the WML definition of a card begins with the nonvisible portion, which contains executable elements, followed by the visible content. As an example, consider the following simple deck with one card, from [MANN99]:

```
<wml>
  <card id='card1'>
  <p>
     Hello WAP World.
  </p>
  </card>
</wml>
```

The tags <wml>, <card>, and <p> enclose the deck, card, and paragraph, respectively. Like HMTL, most elements end with a terminating tag that is identical to the starting tag with the addition of the character "/". When a wireless device receives this code, it will display the message "Hello WAP World" on the terminal's screen.

Table 12.3 lists the full set of WML tags, which are divided into eight functional groups.

Table 12.3 WML Tags

Tag	Description
	Deck Structure
<access>	Access control
<card>	Card definition
<head>	Deck-level information (meta, access, template)
<meta>	Meta information
<template>	Deck-level event bindings
<wml>	Deck definition
	Content
<img>	Image
<p>	Paragraph, visiblecontent
<table>	Table
<td>	Table data
<tr>	Table row
	Formatting
<b>	Bold
<big>	Large font
 	Line break
<em>	Emphasis
<i>	Italic
<small>	Small font
<strong>	Strong font
<u>	Underline

Tag	Description
	User Input
<fieldset>	Data entry items grouping
<input>	Data entry
<optgroup>	Subset of a choice list
<option>	Single choice in a list
<select>	Choice list
	Variables
<postfield>	Set an http request variable
<setvar>	Set a variable in a task
	Timers
<Timer>	Set a timer
	Tasks
<go>	Go to a URL
<noop>	No action
<prev>	Go to previous card
<refresh>	Screen redraw
	Task/Event Bindings
<a>	Abbreviated anchor
<anchor>	Anchor
<do>	Response to user button press
<onevent>	Intrinsic event binding

WMLScript

WMLScript is a scripting language with similarities to JavaScript. It is designed for defining script-type programs in a user device with limited processing power and memory. Table 12.4 shows valid WMLScript statements. Important capabilities of WMLScript include the following:

- Check the validity of user input before it is sent to the content server
- Access device facilities and peripherals.
- Interact with the user without introducing round trips to the origin server (e.g., display an error message).

Key WMLScript features include the following [WAPF98]:

- **JavaScript-based scripting language:** WMLScript is a subset of JavaScript, with some extensions.
- **Procedural logic:** WMLScript adds the power of procedural logic to the Wireless Application Environment (WAE), discussed subsequently.
- **Event-based:** WMLScript may be invoked in response to certain user or environmental events.
- **Compiled implementation:** WMLScript can be compiled down to a more efficient bytecode that is transported to the client.
- **Integrated into WAE:** WMLScript is fully integrated with the WML browser. This allows authors to construct their service using both WML and WMLScript.
- **Efficient extensible library support:** WMLScript can be used to expose and extend device functionality without changes to the device software.

Wireless Application Environment

The WAE specifies an application framework for wireless devices such as mobile telephones, pagers, and PDAs. In essence, the WAE consists of tools and formats

Table 12.4 WMLScript Statements

Statement	Description
=	Assignment
break	Terminate the current loop
continue	Current loop iteration
for	Indexed loop
function	Function declaration
if . . . else	Conditional test
return	Exit the current function
var	Variable declaration
while	Boolean-controlled loop

that are intended to ease the task of developing applications and devices supported by WAP. The major elements of the WAE model are as follows (Figure 12.11):

- **WAE User agents:** Software that executes in the user's wireless device and that provides specific functionality (e.g., display content) to the end user.
- **Content generators:** Applications (or services) on origin servers (e.g., CGI scripts) that produce standard content formats in response to requests from user agents in the mobile terminal. WAE does not specify any standard content generators but expects that there will be a variety available running on typical HTTP origin servers commonly used in WWW today.
- **Standard content encoding:** Defined to allow a WAE user agent (e.g., a browser) to conveniently navigate Web content.
- **Wireless telephony applications (WTA):** A collection of telephony-specific extensions for call and feature control mechanisms that provide authors advanced mobile network services. Using WTA, applications developers can use the microbrowser to originate telephone calls and to respond to events from the telephone network.

Wireless Session Protocol

WSP provides applications with an interface for two session services. The connection-oriented session service operates above the reliable transport protocol WTP, and the connectionless session service operates above the unreliable transport protocol WDP. In essence, WSP is based on HTTP with some additions and modifications to optimize its use over wireless channels. The principal limitations addressed are low data rate and susceptibility to loss of connection due to poor coverage or cell overloading.

Figure 12.11   WAE Client Components [WAPF98]

WSP is a transaction-oriented protocol based on the concept of a request and a reply. Each WSP protocol data unit (PDU) consists of a body, which may contain WML, WMLScript, or images, and a header, which contains information about the data in the body and about the transaction. WSP also defines a server Push operation, in which the server sends unrequested content to a client device. This may be used for broadcast messages or for services, such as news headlines or stock quotes, that may be tailored to each client device.

WSP Service

In general, a connection-mode WSP provides the following services:

- Establish a reliable session from client to server and release that session in an orderly manner.
- Agree on a common level of protocol functionality using capability negotiation.
- Exchange content between client and server using compact encoding.
- Suspend and resume a session.
- Push content from server to client in an unsynchronized manner.

At the service level, WSP is defined in terms of a collection of service primitives, with associated parameters. These service primitivres define the interface between WSP and users of WSP in the WAE.[1] At the protocol level, the WSP specification defines a PDU format used to exchange data between peer WSP entities (see Figures 4.5 and 4.6).

Figure 12.12 shows the key WSP transaction types in terms of the primitives and parameters that are exchanged. There are other transaction types, but these are sufficient to give a feel for the operation of WSP.

Session establishment involves the exchange of S-Connect primitives (Figure 12.12a). A WSP user acting as a client (mobile node side of the transaction) requests a session with a WSP user acting as a server (Web Server) on a remote system by issuing an S-Connect.req to WSP. Four parameters accompany the request:

- **Server address:** The peer with which the session is to be established.
- **Client address:** The originator of the session.
- **Client headers:** Contain attribute information that can be used for application-level parameters to be communicated to the peer. This information is passed without modification by WSP and is not processed by WSP.
- **Requested capabilities:** A set of capabilities for this session requested by the client; these are listed in Table 12.5.

The client's WSP then prepares a WSP PDU, containing these parameters, to convey the request to the peer WSP at the server. The server address, client address, and client headers are unchanged. However, the WSP service provider at the client or the WSP service provider at the server, or both, may modify the set of requested

---

[1]See Appendix 12C for a brief discussion of the concept of service primitives and parameters.

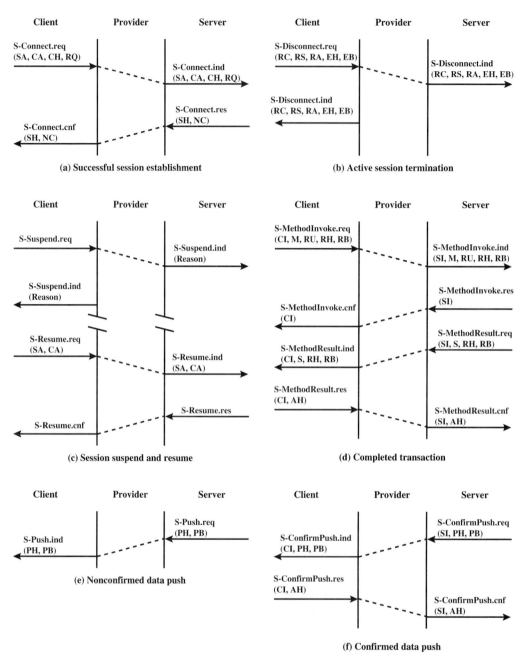

Figure 12.12 Wireless Session Protocol Primitives and Parameters

capabilities so that they do not imply a higher level of functionality than the provider can support. With this possible modification, an S-Connect.ind containing the same parameters as in the request is delivered to the WSP user at the server side. If the WSP user at the server accepts the session request, it responds by invoking WSP with an S-Connect.rsp containing server headers and negotiated capabilities.

Table 12.5 Wireless Session Protocol Capabilities

Name	Class	Type	Description
Aliases	I	List of addresses	Indicates which alternative addresses the peer may use to access this session service user. Can be used to facilitate a switch to a new bearer when a session is resumed.
Client SDU size	N	Positive integer	The size of the largest transaction service data unit that may be sent to the client during the session.
Extended methods	N	Set of method names	The set of extended methods (beyond HTTP/1.1) that are supported by both client and server peers.
Header code pages	N	Set of code page names	The set of extension header code pages that are supported by both client and server peers.
Maximum outstanding method requests	N	Positive integer	The maximum number of method invocations that can be active at the same time during the session.
Maximum outstanding push requests	N	Positive integer	The maximum number of confirmed push invocations that can be active at the same time during the session.
Protocol options	N	Set of facilities and features	May include Push, Confirmed Push, Session Resume, and Acknowledgment Headers.
Server SDU size	N	Positive integer	The size of the largest transaction SDU that may be sent to the server during the session.

I = informational
N = negotiable

The negotiated capabilities parameter is optional. If it is absent, the WSP user agrees to the set of capabilities proposed in the S-Connect.ind. If it is present, it reflects the level of functionality that the WSP user will accept. Finally, an S-Connect.ind is delivered to the original requester, containing the server headers and the final set of negotiated capabilities.

The S-Disconnect primitive is used for **session termination**. Figure 12.12b shows the case in which the client WSP user initiates the termination. The request primitive includes the following parameters:

- **Reason code:** Cause of disconnection. If the cause is that the client is being redirected to contact a new server address, the next two parameters must be present.
- **Redirect security:** Indicates whether or not the client may reuse the current secure session when redirecting.
- **Redirect addresses:** Alternate addresses to be used to establish a session.
- **Error headers and error body:** If the termination is due to an error, these parameters may be included to provide information to the server WSP user about the error.

WSP acknowledges the receipt of the request by returning an S-Disconnect.ind to the client WSP user and conveying an S-Disconnect.ind to the server WSP user.

WSP supports **session suspend and resume**. An example of the use of this feature is when the client knows that it may be temporarily unavailable, due to roaming or disconnect and reconnect of the client device to the network. When a session is suspended, the state of the session is saved on both the client and server side and any in-transit data are lost. Figure 12.12c shows the sequence involved when the suspend and resume are initiated by the client. For suspension, the only parameter is a reason code in the S-Suspend.ind primitive. When a resume request is issued, the server address and client address are present in the request and indication primitives.

A **transaction** involves an exchange of data between a client and server using the S-MethodInvoke and S-MethodResult primitives (Figure 12.12d). S-MethodInvoke is used to request an operation to be executed by the server. The request contains the following parameters:

- **Client Transaction ID:** Used to distinguish between pending transactions.
- **Method:** Identifies the requested operation.
- **Request URI (uniform resource identifier):** Specifies the entity to which the operation applies.
- **Request headers and body:** Attribute information and data associated with the request.

The indication conveyed to the server includes the same parameters except that the client transaction ID is replaced by a server transaction ID. The response and confirm primitives are used to confirm that the request has been conveyed and contain transaction IDs.

S-MethodResult is used to return a response to an operation request. The request issued by the server includes the server transaction ID, the status associated with this response, and response headers and body containing attribute information and data associated with the response. The response and confirm primitives are used to confirm that the request has been conveyed and contain transaction IDs. These two primitives may also contain acknowledgment headers used to return some information to the server.

The **nonconfirmed data push** is used to send unsolicited information from the server to the client (Figure 12.12e). The only parameters associated with these primitives are push headers and a push body containing attributes and the information to be conveyed. With **confirmed data push**, the server receives a confirmation that the push data have been delivered to the client. In addition to push headers and a push body, the confirmed data push primitives include a push ID; the respond and confirm primitives may also include acknowledgment headers.

The connectionless session service provides a nonconfirmed capability for exchanging content entities between WSP users. Only the method invocation and push facilities are available.

WSP Protocol Data Units

WSP conveys service requests and responses in WSP PDUs. Each PDU is passed down to the transport layer to be included as the body of a transport-level

PDU. At the top level, the WSP PDU consists of three fields. The TID field is used to associated requests with replies in the connectionless WSP service and is not present in the connection-mode service. The Type field specifies the type and function of the PDU and basically corresponds to the type of service primitive that invoked WSP. Finally, the Type-Specific Contents contain all of the information to be conveyed as a result of a WSP service primitive.

Wireless Transaction Protocol

WTP manages transactions by conveying requests and responses between a user agent (such as a WAP browser) and an application server for such activities as browsing and e-commerce transactions. WTP provides a reliable transport service but dispenses with much of the overhead of TCP, resulting in a lightweight protocol that is suitable for implementation in "thin" clients (e.g. mobile nodes) and suitable for use over low-bandwidth wireless links. WTP includes the following features:

- Three classes of transaction service.
- Optional user to user reliability: WTP user triggers the confirmation of each received message.
- Optional out-of-band data on acknowledgments.
- PDU concatenation and delayed acknowledgment to reduce the number of messages sent.
- Asynchronous transactions.

WTP is transaction oriented rather than connection oriented. With WTP, there is no explicit connection setup or teardown but rather a reliable connectionless service.

WTP Transaction Classes

WTP provides three transaction classes that may be invoked by WSP or another higher-layer protocol:

- **Class 0:** Unreliable invoke message with no result message
- **Class 1:** Reliable invoke message with no result message
- **Class 2:** Unreliable invoke message with one reliable result message

Class 0 provides an unreliable datagram service, which can be used for an unreliable push operation. Data from a WTP user are encapsulated by WTP (the initiator, or client) in an Invoke PDU and transmitted to the target WTP (the responder, or server), with no acknowledgment. The responder WTP delivers the data to the target WTP user.

Class 1 provides a reliable datagram service, which can be used for a reliable push operation. Data from an initiator are encapsulated in an Invoke PDU and transmitted to the responder. The responder delivers the data to the target WTP user and acknowledges receipt of the data by sending back an ACK PDU to the WTP entity on the initiator side, which confirms the transaction to the source WTP user. The responder WTP maintains state information for some time after the ACK has been sent to handle possible retransmission of the ACK if it gets lost and/or the initiator retransmits the Invoke PDU.

Class 2 provides a request/response transaction service and supports the execution of multiple transactions during one WSP session. Data from an initiator are encapsulated in an Invoke PDU and transmitted to the responder, which delivers the data to the target WTP user. The target WTP user prepares response data, which are handed down to the local WTP entity. The responder WTP entity sends these data back in a result PDU. If there is a delay in generating the response data beyond a timer threshold, the responder may send an ACK PDU before sending the result PDU. This prevents the initiator from unnecessarily retransmitting the Invoke message.

Protocol Formats and Operation

WTP makes use of six types of PDUs. Each PDU begins with a fixed header portion (Figure 12.13) and may be followed by a variable header portion that contains supplementary control information. The supplementary information is in the form of one or more transaction protocol items (TPIs).

The **Invoke PDU** is used to convey a request from an initiator to a responder; it is four bytes long and includes the following fixed header fields:

- **Continue flag:** If this flag is set, there are one or more TPIs following the fixed header. In turn, each TPI begins with a continue flag bit to indicate whether there are more TPIs to follow or this is the last TPI.
- **PDU type:** Indicates that this is an Invoke PDU.
- **Group trailer flag:** Used when segmentation and reassembly are employed, as explained subsequently.
- **Transmission trailer flag:** Also used with segmentation and reassembly.
- **Retransmission indicator:** Indicates whether this is a retransmission. The initiator will retransmit an Invoke PDU if it does not receive an acknowledgment within a specified time.
- **Transaction identifier:** Used to associate a PDU with a particular transaction.
- **Version:** Version of WTP.
- **TIDnew flag:** Set when the initiator has "wrapped" the TID value; that is, the next TID will be lower then the previous one.
- **U/P flag:** When set, it indicates that the initiator require a user acknowledgment from the server WTP user. This means the WTP user confirms every received message. When this flag is clear, the responding WTP entity may acknowledge an incoming PDU without a confirmation from its user.
- **Transaction class:** Indicates the desired transaction class to be used in processing this Invoke PDU.

If the message to be sent by WTP (the block of data from WSP) is too large for the current bearer, WTP may segment that message and send it in multiple packets, one per Invoke PDU. When a message is sent in a large number of small

(a) Invoke PDU

CON	PDU Type = Invoke	GTR	TTR	RID
	Transaction identifier (TID)			
Version	TIDnew	U/P	reserved	TCL

(a) Invoke PDU

(b) ACK PDU

CON	PDU Type = Ack	Tve/Tok	rsvd	RID
	Transaction identifier (TID)			

(b) ACK PDU

(c) Result PDU

CON	PDU Type = Result	GTR	TTR	RID
	Transaction identifier (TID)			

(c) Result PDU

(d) Abort PDU

CON	PDU Type = Abort	Abort Type
	Transaction identifier (TID)	
	Abort reason	

(d) Abort PDU

(e) Segmented Invoke or Result PDU

CON	PDU Type	GTR	TTR	RID
	Transaction identifier (TID)			
	Packet sequence number			

(e) Segmented Invoke or Result PDU

(f) Negative Acknowledgment PDU

CON	PDU Type = Negative ACK	reserved	RID
	Transaction identifier (TID)		
	Number of missing packets = N		
5	Packet sequence number(s)		
...	of missing packets		
4+N			

(f) Negative Acknowledgment PDU

CON = continue flag   TIDnew = TIDnew flag
GTR = group trailer   U/P = user/provider acknowledgment flag
TTR = transmission trailer   TCL = transaction class
RID = retransmission indicator Tve/Tok = TID verify/TID OK flag

Figure 12.13   WTP PDU Fixed Header Formats

413

packets, the packets may be sent and acknowledged in groups. Table 12.6 Shows how the GTR and TTR flags are used to manage the process.

The **ACK PDU** is used to acknowledge an Invoke or Result PDU. It is three bytes long. The PDU includes a Tve/Tok flag, whose interpretation depends on the direction of the PDU. In the direction from the responder to the initiator, this is a Tve flag. If the Tve flag is set, it has the interpretation "Do you have an outstanding transaction with this TID?" In the other direction, if the Tok flag is set, it means "I have an outstanding transaction with this TID."

The **Result PDU** is a 3-byte PDU used to convey the response of the server to the client.

The **Abort PDU** is used to abort a transaction. Two abort types are defined: user and provider. If the abort is generated by the WTP user (e.g., WSP), then the user's reason for the abort is conveyed in the body of the PDU and provided to the WTP user at the destination of the abort PDU. If the abort is generated by the WTP provider (the WTP entity that is sending this abort PDU), then the abort reason field in the PDU indicates one of the following reasons:

- **Unknown:** Unexplained error.
- **Protocol error:** The received PDU could not be interpreted.
- **Invalid TID:** Used by the initiator as a negative result to the TID verification.
- **Not implemented Class 2:** The respondent does not support class 2, which was requested.
- **Not implemented SAR:** The respondent does not support segmentation and reassembly.
- **Not implemented user acknowledgment:** The responder does not support user acknowledgment.
- **WTP version 1:** The initiator requested a version of WTP that is not supported; current version is 1.
- **Capacity temporarily exceeded:** Due to an overload situation, transaction cannot be completed.

The **segmented invoke PDU** and the **segmented result PDU** may be used for segmentation and reassembly. When they are used, each packet is numbered sequentially. The **negative acknowledgment PDU** is used to indicate that one or more packets in a sequence did not arrive.

Table 12.6   Group Trailer (GTR) and Transmission Trailer (TTR) Combinations

GTR	TTR	Description
0	0	Not last packet
0	1	Last packet of message
1	0	Last packet of packet group
1	1	Segmentation and reassembly not supported

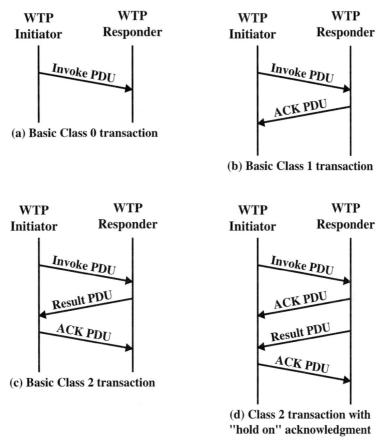

Figure 12.14 Examples of WTP Operation

Figure 12.14 shows some basic examples of the time sequence of the use of TWP PDUs for the three classes of operation.

WTP Service

The WTP service is defined by three primitives. TR-Invoke is used to initiate a new transaction. TR-Result is used to send back a result of a previously initiated transaction. And Tr-Abort is used to abort an existing transaction. Figure 12.15 shows the relationship between these primitives and a class 2 transaction with "hold on" acknowledgment. Compare with Figure 12.14d.

Figure 12.15 also shows how the WTP service supports the WSP service. The sequence of WSP service primitives provides for a completed transaction and is identical to the sequence shown in Figure 12.12d.

Wireless Transport Layer Security

WTLS provides security services between the mobile device (client) and the WAP gateway. WTLS is based on the industry-standard Transport Layer Security (TLS)

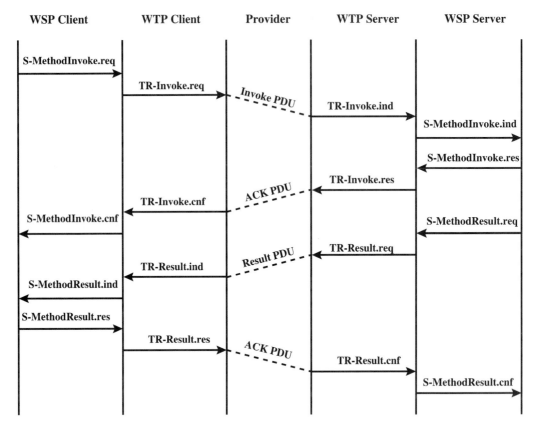

Figure 12.15 WSP-WTP Timing Diagram

Protocol, which is a refinement of the secure sockets layer (SSL). TLS is the standard security protocol used between Web browsers and Web servers.[2] WTLS is more efficient that TLS, requiring fewer message exchanges. To provide end-to-end security, WTLS is used between the client and the gateway, and TLS is used between the gateway and the target server. WAP systems translate between WTLS and TLS within the WAP gateway. Thus, the gateway is a point of vulnerability and must be given a high level of security from external attacks.

WTLS provides the following features:

- **Data integrity:** Ensures that data sent between the client and the gateway are not modified, using message authentication.
- **Privacy:** Ensures that the data cannot be read by a third party, using encryption.
- **Authentication:** Establishes the authentication of the two parties, using digital certificates.

---

[2]For a detailed description of TLS, see [STAL99].

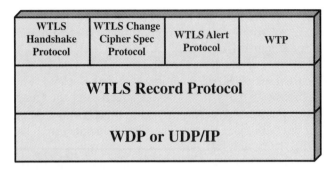

Figure 12.16 WTLS Protocol Stack

- **Denial-of-service protection:** Detects and rejects messages that are replayed or not successfully verified.

WTLS is not a single protocol but rather two layers of protocols, as illustrated in Figure 12.16. The WTLS Record Protocol provides basic security services to various higher-layer protocols. In particular, the hypertext transfer protocol (HTTP), defined in RFC 2068 and which provides the transfer service for Web client/server interaction, can operate on top of WTLS. Three higher-layer protocols are defined as part of WTLS: the Handshake Protocol, The Change Cipher Spec Protocol, and the Alert Protocol.

WTLS Record Protocol

The WTLS Record Protocol takes user data from the next higher layer (WTP, WTLS handshake protocol, WTLS alert protocol, WTLS change cipher spec protocol) and encapsulates these data in a PDU. The following steps occur (Figure 12.17):

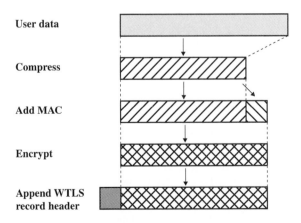

Figure 12.17 WTLS Record Protocol Operation

1. The payload is compressed using a lossless compression algorithm.
2. A message authentication code (MAC) is computed over the compressed data, using HMAC. HMAC is a keyed hash code similar to (but more complex than) the one described in Appendix 12B. One of several hash algorithms can be used with HMAC, including MD-5 and SHA-1. The length of the hash code is 0, 5, or 10 bytes. The MAC is added after the compressed data.
3. The compressed message plus the MAC code are encrypted using a symmetric encryption algorithm. The allowable encryption algorithms are DES, triple DES, RC5, and IDEA.
4. The Record Protocol prepends a header to the encrypted payload.

The Record Protocol header consists of the following fields (Figure 12.18):

- **Content type (8 bits):** The higher-layer protocol above the WTLS Record Protocol.
- **Cipher spec indicator (1 bit):** If this bit is zero, it indicates that no compression, MAC protection, or encryption is used.
- **Sequence number field indicator (1 bit):** Indicates whether a sequence number field is present.
- **Record length field indicator (1 bit):** Indicates whether a record length field is present.

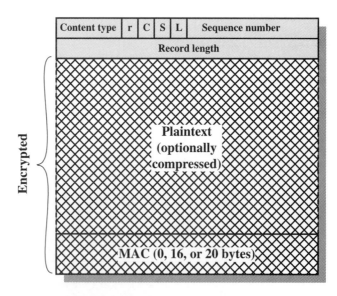

r = reserved
C = cipher spec indicator
S = sequence number field indicator
L = record length field indicator
MAC = message authentication code

Figure 12.18   WTLS Record Format

- **Sequence number (16 bits):** A sequence number associated with this PDU. This provides reliability over an unreliable transport service.
- **Record length (32 bits):** The length in bytes of the plaintext data (or compressed data if compression is used).

Change Cipher Spec Protocol

Associated with the current transaction is a cipher spec, which specifies the encryption algorithm, the hash algorithm used as part of HMAC, and cryptographic attributes, such as MAC code size. There are actually a two states associated with each session. Once a session is established, there is a current operating state for both read and write (i.e., receive and send). In addition, during the Handshake Protocol, pending read and write states are created.

The Change Cipher Spec Protocol is one of the three WTLS-specific protocols that use the WTLS Record Protocol, and it is the simplest. This protocol consists of a single message, which consists of a single byte with the value 1. The sole purpose of this message is to cause the pending state to be copied into the current state, which updates the cipher suite to be used on this connection.

Alert Protocol

The Alert Protocol is used to convey WTLS-related alerts to the peer entity. As with other applications that use WTLS, alert messages are compressed and encrypted, as specified by the current state.

Each message in this protocol consists of 2 bytes. The first byte takes the value warning(1), critical(2), or fatal(3) to convey the severity of the message. If the level is fatal, WTLS immediately terminates the connection. Other connections on the same session may continue, but no new connections on this session may be established. The second byte contains a code that indicates the specific alert. Examples of fatal alerts include the following:

- **unexpected_message:** An inappropriate message was received.
- **bad_record_mac:** An incorrect MAC was received.
- **decompression_failure:** The decompression function received improper input (e.g., unable to decompress or decompress to greater than maximum allowable length).
- **handshake_failure:** Sender was unable to negotiate an acceptable set of security parameters given the options available.
- **illegal_parameter:** A field in a handshake message was out of range or inconsistent with other fields.

Examples of nonfatal alerts include the following:

- **bad_certificate:** A received certificate was corrupt (e.g., contained a signature that did not verify).
- **unsupported_certificate:** The type of the received certificate is not supported.
- **certificate_revoked:** A certificate has been revoked by its signer.

- **certificate_expired:** A certificate has expired.
- **certificate_unknown:** Some other unspecified issue arose in processing the certificate, rendering it unacceptable.

Handshake Protocol

The most complex part of WTLS is the Handshake Protocol. This protocol allows the server and client to authenticate each other and to negotiate an encryption and MAC algorithm and cryptographic keys to be used to protect data sent in a WTLS record. The Handshake Protocol is used before any application data are transmitted.

The Handshake Protocol consists of a series of messages exchanged by client and server. Figure 12.19 shows the initial exchange needed to establish a logical connection between client and server. The exchange can be viewed as having four phases.

The **first phase** is used to initiate a logical connection and to establish the security capabilities that will be associated with it. The exchange is initiated by the client. The client sends a client_hello message that includes a session ID and a list of cryptographic and compression algorithms supported by the client (in decreasing order of preference for each algorithm type). After sending the client_hello message, the client waits for the server_hello message. This message indicates which cryptographic and compression algorithms will be used for the exchange.

The **second phase** is used for server authentication and key exchange. The server begins this phase by sending its public-key certificate, if it needs to be authenticated. Next, a server_key_exchange message may be sent if it is required. This message is needed for certain public-key algorithms used for symmetric key exchange. Next, the server can request a public-key certificate from the client, using the certificate_request message. The final message in Phase 2, and one that is always required, is the server_hello_done message, which is sent by the server to indicate the end of the server hello and associated messages. After sending this message, the server will wait for a client response. This message has no parameters.

The **third phase** is used for client authentication and key exchange. Upon receipt of the server_hello_done message, the client should verify that the server provided a valid certificate if required and check that the server_hello parameters are acceptable. If all is satisfactory, the client sends one or more messages back to the server. If the server has requested a certificate, the client sends a certificate message. Next is the client_key_exchange message, which must be sent in this phase. The content of the message depends on the type of key exchange. Finally, in this phase, the client may send a certificate_verify message to provide explicit verification of a client certificate.

The **fourth phase** completes the setting up of a secure connection. The client sends a change_cipher_spec message and copies the pending CipherSpec into the current CipherSpec. Note that this message is not considered part of the Handshake Protocol but is sent using the Change Cipher Spec Protocol. The client then immediately sends the finished message under the new algorithms, keys, and secrets. The finished message verifies that the key exchange and authentication processes were successful. In response to these two messages, the server sends its own change_cipher_spec message, transfers the pending to the current CipherSpec, and sends its finished message. At this point the handshake is complete and the client and server may begin to exchange application layer data.

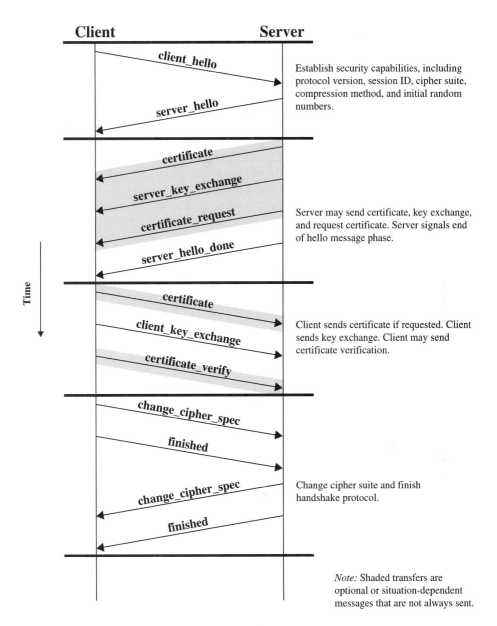

Figure 12.19 WTLS Handshake Protocol Action

Wireless Datagram Protocol

WDP is used to adapt a higher-layer WAP protocol to the communication mechanism (called the bearer) used between the mobile node and the WAP gateway. Adaptation may include partitioning data into segments of appropriate size for the bearer and interfacing with the bearer network. WDP hides details of the various bearer networks from the other layers of WAP. In some instances, WAP is implemented on top of IP.

WDP Service

The WDP service is defined by two service primitives. The T-DUnitdata primitive provides a nonconfirmed service with the following parameters:

- **Source address:** Address of the device making a request to the WDP layer
- **Source port:** Application address associated with the source address
- **Destination address:** Destination address for the data submitted to WDP
- **Destination port:** Application address associated with the destination address
- **User data:** User data from the next higher layer, submitted to WDP for transmission to the destination port

The T-Derror.ind primitive is used to alert a WDP user of a failure to deliver a WDP datagram. In addition to the source address, source port, destination address, and destination port parameters, T-Derror.ind includes an error code parameter with local significance.

WDP Protocol

The following fields are necessary in a WDP PDU:

- Destination port.
- Source port.

If the underlying bearer does not provide segmentation and reassembly, the feature is implemented in WDP in a bearer-independent way.

For example, GSM (Global System for Mobile Communications) dictates a format for a user data header, in which the header consists of a sequence of information elements, and each element is defined by an identifier, a length, and one or more bytes of value. The WDH PDU for GSM has the following structure:

- **Header length (1 byte):** Length of header.
- **Port numbers identifier (1 byte):** The value 5 indicates that this information element consists of two port numbers.
- **Port numbers length (1 byte):** The value 4 indicates that the value portion of this information element is 4 bytes long.
- **Destination port (2 bytes)**
- **Source port (2 bytes)**
- **SAR identifier (1 byte):** The value 0 indicates that this information element consists of information for segmentation and reassembly.
- **SAR length (1 byte):** The value 3 indicates that the value portion of this information element is 3 bytes long.
- **Datagram reference number (1 bytes):** An identifier assigned to all of the segments that make up a block of user data.
- **Number of segments (1 byte):** The total number of segments that need to be reassembled.

Table 12.7 WCMP Messages

WCMP Message	WCMP Type	WCMP Code	WDP Node	WAP Gateway
Destination Unreachable	51			
• No route to destination		0	N/A	O
• Communication administratively prohibited		1	N/A	O
• Address unreachable		3	N/A	O
• Port unreachable		4	M	N/A
Parameter Problem	54			
• Erroneous header field		0	O	O
Message Too Big	60	0	M	N/A
Reassembly Failure	61			
• Reassembly time exceeded		1	O	N/A
• Buffer overflow		2	O	N/A
Echo Request	178	0	O	N/A
Echo Reply	179	0	M	N/A

M = mandatory
O = optional
N/A = not applicable

- **Segment count:** A sequence number that identifies this segment within the sequence of all segments that need to be reassembled to form the block of user data.
- **User data (1 to n bytes)**

Wireless Control Message Protocol

WCMP performs the same support function for WDP as ICMP does for IP (see Appendix 12A). WCMP is used in environments that do not provide an IP bearer and therefore do not lend themselves to the use of ICMP. WCMP is used by wireless nodes and WAP gateways to report errors encountered in processing WDP datagrams. WCMP can also be used for informational and diagnostic purposes.

Table 12.7 lists the WCMP messages and associated error codes.

12.3 RECOMMENDED READING AND WEB SITES

[PERK97] is a good survey article on Mobile IP; a somewhat less technical, more business-oriented description from the same author is [PERK98]. For greater detail, see [SOLO98]. The August 2000 issue of *IEEE Personal Communications* contains a number of articles on enhancements to the current Mobile IP standard.

[MANN99] is an overview of WAP, while [PASS00] discusses building applications for wireless communications using WAP. [HEIJ00] provides detailed coverage of WAP.

HEIJ00 Heijden, M., and Taylor, M., eds. *Understanding WAP: Wireless Applications, Devices, and Services.* Boston: Artech House, 2000.

MANN99 Mann, S. "The Wireless Application Protocol." *Dr. Dobb's Journal*, October 1999.

PASS00 Passani, L. "Creating WAP Services." *Dr. Dobb's Journal*, July 2000.

PERK97 Perkins, C. "Mobile IP." *IEEE Communications Magazine*, May 1997.

PERK98 Perkins, C. "Mobile Networking Through Mobile IP." *IEEE Internet Computing*, January–February 1998.

SOLO98 Solomon, J. *Mobile IP: The Internet Unplugged.* Upper Saddle River, NJ: Prentice Hall PTR, 1998.

Recommended Web sites:

- **IP Routing for Wireless/Mobile Hosts:** IETF Working Group on Mobile IP. Contains current RFCs and Internet drafts.
- **Wireless Application Protocol Forum:** WAP technical specifications and industry links.

12.4 KEY TERMS, REVIEW QUESTIONS, AND PROBLEMS

Key Terms

care-of address	internet control message	wireless datagram protocol (WDP)
encapsulation	protocol (ICMP)	wireless session protocol (WSP)
foreign agent	mobile IP	wireless transaction
foreign network	tunneling	protocol (WTP)
hash function	wireless application	wireless transport layer
home address	environment (WAE)	security (WTLS)
home agent	wireless application	wireless markup
home network	protocol (WAP)	language (WML)

Review Questions

1 Explain the distinction between a mobile user and a nomadic user.

2 What is tunneling?

3 List and briefly define the capabilities provided by mobile IP.

4 What is the relationship between mobile IP discovery and ICMP?

5 What are the two different types of destination addresses that can be assigned to a mobile node while it is attached to a foreign network?

6 Under what circumstances would a mobile node choose to use each of the types of address referred to in Question 5?

7 What is the difference between an HTML filter and a WAP proxy?

8 What are the functional areas supported by WML?

9   What services are provided by WSP?

10   When would each of the three WTP transaction classes be used?

11   List and briefly define the security services provided by WTLS.

Problems

1   This problem refers to Figure 12.6. Suppose that LAN Z is the home network for host E and that D sends a block of data to E via IP.

   a. Show the PDU structure, including the fields of the IP header and the lower-level headers (MAC, LLC) with the contents of address fields indicated for the case in which E is on its home network.

   b. Repeat part a for the case in which E is on a foreign network reachable via the Internet through R3. Show formats for the MAC frame leaving D and the IP datagram leaving R3. Assume that IP-to-IP encapsulation is used.

   c. Repeat part (b) for the IP datagram leaving R3, but now assume that minimal encapsulation is used.

2   Again referring to Figure 12.6, assume that A is a mobile node and that LAN X is a foreign network for A. Assume that an IP datagram arrives at R1 from the Internet to be delivered to A. Show the format of the IP datagram arriving at R1 and the MAC frame leaving R1 (include the IP header or headers) for the following cases:

   a. IP-to-IP encapsulation is used and R1 is the care-of address.

   b. Minimal encapsulation is used and R1 is the care-of address.

   c. IP-to-IP encapsulation is used and A is the care-of address.

   d. Minimal encapsulation is used and A is the care-of address.

3   In a typical mobile IP implementation in a home agent, the agent maintains a mobility binding table to map a mobile node's home address to its care-of address for packet forwarding. What entries are essential for each row of the table?

4   In a typical mobile IP implementation in a foreign agent, the agent maintains a visitor table that contains information about the mobile nodes currently visiting this network. What entries are essential for each row of the table?

5   In WTLS, why is there a separate Change Cipher Spec Protocol, rather than including a change_cipher_spec message in the Handshake Protocol?

APPENDIX 12A   INTERNET CONTROL MESSAGE PROTOCOL

The IP standard specifies that a compliant implementation must also implement ICMP (RFC 792, RFC 950, RFC 1256). ICMP provides a means for transferring messages from routers and other hosts to a host. In essence, ICMP provides feedback about problems in the communication environment. Examples of its use are when a datagram cannot reach its destination, when the router does not have the buffering capacity to forward a datagram, and when the router can direct the station to send traffic on a shorter route. In most cases, an ICMP message is sent in response to a datagram, either by a router along the datagram's path or by the intended destination host.

    ICMP is a user of IP. An ICMP message is constructed and then passed down to IP, which encapsulates the message with an IP header and then transmits the resulting datagram in the usual fashion. Because ICMP messages are transmitted in IP datagrams, their delivery is not guaranteed and their use cannot be considered reliable.

Figure 12.20 shows the format of the various ICMP message types. An ICMP message starts with a 64-bit header consisting of the following:

- **Type (8 bits):** Specifies the type of ICMP message.
- **Code (8 bits):** Used to specify parameters of the message that can be encoded in one or a few bits.

Type	Code	Checksum
Unused		
IP header + 64 bits of original datagram		

(a) Destination unreachable; time exceeded; source quench

Type	Code	Checksum
Pointer	Unused	
IP header + 64 bits of original datagram		

(b) Parameter problem

Type	Code	Checksum
Router IP address		
IP header + 64 bits of original datagram		

(c) Redirect

Type	Code	Checksum
Num addrs	Entry size	Lifetime
Router address 1		
Preference level 1		
•		
•		
•		
Router address n		
Preference level n		

(d) Router advertisement

Type	Code	Checksum
Unused		

(e) Router solicitation

Type	Code	Checksum
Identifer	Sequence number	
Originate timestamp		

(f) Timestamp

Type	Code	Checksum
Identifer	Sequence number	
Originate timestamp		
Receive timestamp		
Transmit timestamp		

(g) Timestamp reply

Type	Code	Checksum
Identifier	Sequence number	
Optional data		

(h) Echo; echo reply

Type	Code	Checksum
Identifer	Sequence number	

(i) Address mask request

Type	Code	Checksum
Identifer	Sequence number	
Address mask		

(j) Address mask reply

Figure 12.20 ICMP Message Formats

- **Checksum (16 bits):** Checksum of the entire ICMP message. This is the same checksum algorithm used for IP.
- **Parameters (32 bits):** Used to specify more lengthy parameters.

For some message types, these fields are followed by additional information fields that further specify the content of the message.

In those cases in which the ICMP message refers to a prior datagram, the information field includes the entire IP header plus the first 64 bits of the data field of the original datagram. This enables the source host to match the incoming ICMP message with the prior datagram. The reason for including the first 64 bits of the data field is that this will enable the IP module in the host to determine which upper-level protocol or protocols were involved. In particular, the first 64 bits would include a portion of the TCP header or other transport-level header.

The **destination unreachable** message covers a number of contingencies. A router may return this message if it does not know how to reach the destination network. In some networks, an attached router may be able to determine if a particular host is unreachable and return the message. The destination host itself may return this message if the user protocol or some higher-level service access point is unreachable. This could happen if the corresponding field in the IP header was set incorrectly. If the datagram specifies a source route that is unusable, a message is returned. Finally, if a router must fragment a datagram but the Don't Fragment flag is set, the datagram is discarded and a message is returned.

A router will return a **time exceeded** message if the lifetime of the datagram expires. A host will send this message if it cannot complete reassembly within a time limit.

A syntactic or semantic error in an IP header will cause a **parameter problem** message to be returned by a router or host. For example, an incorrect argument may be provided with an option. The parameter field contains a pointer to the octet in the original header where the error was detected.

The **source quench** message provides a rudimentary form of flow control. Either a router or a destination host may send this message to a source host, requesting that it reduce the rate at which it is sending traffic to the internet destination. On receipt of a source quench message, the source host should cut back the rate at which it is sending traffic to the specified destination until it no longer receives source quench messages. The source quench message can be used by a router or host that must discard datagrams because of a full buffer. In that case, the router or host will issue a source quench message for every datagram that it discards. In addition, a system may anticipate congestion and issue source quench messages when its buffers approach capacity. In that case, the datagram referred to in the source quench message may well be delivered. Thus, receipt of a source quench message does not imply delivery or nondelivery of the corresponding datagram.

A router sends a **redirect** message to a host on a directly connected router to advise the host of a better route to a particular destination. The following is an example, using Figure 12.6. Router R1 receives a datagram intended for D from host C on network Y, to which R1 is attached. R1 checks its routing table and obtains the address for the next router, R2, on the route to the datagram's internet destination network, Z. Because R2 and the host identified by the internet source address of the datagram are on the same network, R1 sends a redirect message to C. The redirect message advises the host to send its traffic for network Z directly to router R2, because this is a shorter path to the destination. The router forwards the original datagram to its internet destination (via R2). The address of R2 is contained in the parameter field of the redirect message.

The **echo** and **echo reply** messages provide a mechanism for testing that communication is possible between entities. The recipient of an echo message is obligated to return the message in an echo reply message. An identifier and sequence number are associated with the echo message to be matched in the echo reply message. The identifier might be used like a service access point to identify a particular session, and the sequence number might be incremented on each echo request sent.

The **timestamp** and **timestamp reply** messages provide a mechanism for sampling the delay characteristics of the internet. The sender of a timestamp message may include an identifier and sequence number in the parameters field and include the time that the message is sent (originate timestamp). The receiver records the time it received the message and the time that it transmits the reply message in the timestamp reply message. If the timestamp message is sent using strict source routing, then the delay characteristics of a particular route can be measured.

The **address mask request** and **address mask reply** messages are useful in an environment that includes subnets. The address mask request and reply messages allow a host to learn the address mask for the LAN to which it connects. The host broadcasts an address mask request message on the LAN. The router on the LAN responds with an address mask reply message that contains the address mask.

Router Discovery

A router discovery capability was added to ICMP with RFC 1256. The objective of the router discovery capability is to automate the process by which a host determines a router address. In order for a host to send an IP datagram beyond the network to which it is attached, the host must have the address of at least one router attached to that network. These router addresses can be preconfigured in the host, but this approach has limitations. In particular, for newly attached hosts, including mobile hosts, such configuration files may not be available. RFC 1256 provides a way by which hosts may discover router addresses. It is applicable on networks that provide a multicast and/or broadcast capability.[3]

RFC 1256 defines two new ICMP message types: router advertisement and router solicitation. Periodically, each router that conforms to RFC 1256 issues a **router advertisement** message. The message includes the following fields:

- **Num addrs:** The number of router addresses advertised in this message.
- **Addr entry size:** The number of 32-bit words per each router address; the value must be 2.

---

[3]A multicast address is an address that designates a group of entities within a domain (e.g., network, internet). A broadcast address is an address that designates all entities within a domain (e.g., network, internet). Multicast and broadcast are easily done on a local area network, because all stations share the same transmission medium. Multicast and broadcast are also available on a number of wireless and switched network technologies.

- **Lifetime:** The maximum number of seconds that the router advertisement may be considered valid; the default value is 1800 (30 minutes).
- **Router address *i*, for 1 ≤ *i* ≤ num addrs:** The sending router's IP address(es) on the interface from which the message was sent.
- **Preference level *i*, for 1 ≤ *i* ≤ num addrs:** The preferability of each router address *i* as a default router address, relative to other router addresses on this network. This is a signed value in twos complement representation; a higher value indicates more preferable.

Typically, a router will have a single IP address on a network, but multiple IP addresses are allowed. There will be multiple IP addresses for a router if the router has multiple physical connections (interfaces) to the network. Multiple IP addresses may also be assigned to a single interface to serve multiple subnets; this latter use need not concern us here. The preference level is used by a host to determine a default router to use when the host does not have sufficient routing information to determine which router is best for a given destination address. For example, in Figure 12.6, an IP datagram from host D addressed to host C is best sent through router R2, whereas a datagram addressed to a remote host elsewhere in the network should be sent through R3. But initially, if D has no information about which router to use, it needs to send the datagram to a default router. In this example, if the network administrator determines that most internet traffic from LAN Z is local (to other LANs at this location), then R2 should be assigned a higher preference level; and if most of the traffic is remote, then R3 should be assigned a higher preference level.

As a default, routers should issue router advertisement messages once every 7 to 10 minutes. If all hosts on this network support the IP multicast feature, then the messages should be sent on the all-systems multicast address of 224.0.0.1. Otherwise the broadcast address of 255.255.255.255 must be used.

If a host is just becoming active on a network, it can solicit router advertisements from all attached routers by issues a **router solicitation** message. Note from Figure 12.20e that this message contains no information other than identifying the type of message. Its purpose is simply to stimulate all routers to issue advertisements; hence no additional information is needed. If all routers on this network support the IP multicast feature, then the messages should be sent on the all-routers multicast address of 224.0.0.2. Otherwise the broadcast address of 255.255.255.255 must be used.

APPENDIX 12B   MESSAGE AUTHENTICATION

One of the requirements for the Mobile IP registration protocol is message authentication. This appendix provides a brief overview. For more detail, see [STAL99].

A message, file, document, or other collection of data is said to be authentic when it is genuine and came from its alleged source. Message authentication is a procedure that allows communicating parties to verify that received messages are authentic. The two important aspects are to verify that the contents of the message have not been altered and that the source is authentic. We may also wish to verify a message's timeliness (it has not been artificially delayed and replayed) and sequence relative to other messages flowing between two parties.

A common technique used for message authentication is based on a keyed one-way hash function.

One-Way Hash Function

A hash function maps a variable-length block of data into a smaller fixed-length block. The purpose of a hash function is to produce a "fingerprint" of a file, message, or other block of data. To be useful for message authentication, a hash function H must have the following properties:

1. H can be applied to a block of data of any size.
2. H produces a fixed-length output.
3. $H(x)$ is relatively easy to compute for any given x, making both hardware and software implementations practical.
4. For any given code h, it is computationally infeasible to find x such that $H(x) = h$.
5. For any given block x, it is computationally infeasible to find $y \neq x$ with $H(y) = H(x)$.
6. It is computationally infeasible to find any pair (x, y) such that $H(x) = H(y)$.

The first three properties are requirements for the practical application of a hash function to message authentication. The fourth property is the "one-way" property: It is easy to generate a code given a message, but virtually impossible to generate a message given a code. This property is important if the authentication technique involves the use of a secret value, as described subsequently.

The fifth property guarantees that it is impossible to find an alternative message with the same hash value as a given message.

A hash function that satisfies the first five properties in the preceding list is referred to as a **weak hash function**. If the sixth property is also satisfied, then it is referred to as a **strong hash function**. The sixth property protects against a sophisticated class of attack known as the birthday attack.

In addition to providing authentication, a message digest also provides error detection. It performs the same function as an error detection code such as CRC: If any bits in the message are accidentally altered in transit, the message digest will be in error.

A widely used hash function is MD5, which produces a 128-bit message digest. MD5 is the default hash function for Mobile IP.

Keyed Hash Code

Figure 12.21 shows a technique that uses a hash function for message authentication. This technique assumes that two communicating parties, say A and B, share a common secret value S_{AB}. When A has a message to send to B, it calculates the hash function over the concatenation of the secret value and the message:

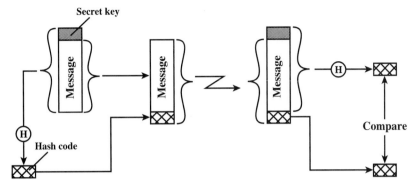

Figure 12.21   Message Authentication Using a One-Way Hash Function

$MD_M = H(S_{AB}\|M)$.[4] It then sends $[M\|MD_M]$ to B. Because B possesses S_{AB}, it can recompute $H(S_{AB}\|M)$ and verify MD_M. Because the secret value itself is not sent, it is not possible for an attacker to modify an intercepted message. As long as the secret value remains secret, it is also not possible for an attacker to generate a false message.

The keyed hash code approach depends on the hash function being one way. If the hash function is not one way, an attacker can easily discover the secret value: If the attacker can observe or intercept a transmission, the attacker obtains the message M and the hash code $MD_M = H(S_{AB}\|M)$. The attacker then inverts the hash function to obtain $S_{AB}\|M = H^{-1}(MD_M)$. Because the attacker now has both M and $S_{AB}\|M$, it is a trivial matter to recover S_{AB}.

APPENDIX 12C   SERVICE PRIMITIVES AND PARAMETERS

In a communications architecture, such as the OSI model or the TCP/IP architecture (Figure 4.4), each layer is defined in two parts: the protocol between peer (at the same level) entities in different systems, and the services provided by one layer to the next higher layer in the same system.

The services between adjacent layers in a protocol architecture are expressed in terms of primitives and parameters. A primitive specifies the function to be performed, and the parameters are used to pass data and control information. The actual form of a primitive is implementation dependent. An example is a procedure call.

Four types of primitives are used in standards to define the interaction between adjacent layers in the architecture. These are defined in Table 12.8. The layout of Figure 12.22a suggests the time ordering of these events. For example, consider the transfer of a connection request from WSP user A to a peer entity B in another system. The following steps occur:

---

[4] $\|$ denotes concatenation.

Table 12.8 Service Primitive Types

REQUEST	A primitive issued by a service user to invoke some service and to pass the parameters needed to specify fully the requested service.

INDICATION	A primitive issued by a service provider either to
	   1. indicate that a procedure has been invoked by the peer service user on the connection and to provide the associated parameters, or
	   2. notify the service user of a provider-initiated action.

RESPONSE	A primitive issued by a service user to acknowledge or complete some procedure previously invoked by an indication to that user.
CONFIRM	A primitive issued by a service provider to acknowledge or complete some procedure previously invoked by a request by the service user.

1. A invokes the services of WSP with an S-Connect.req primitive. Associated with the primitive are the parameters needed, such as the destination address.

2. The WSP entity in A's system prepares an WSP PDU to be sent to its peer WSP entity in B. This PDU is then sent encapsulated in a WTP PDU.

3. The destination WSP entity receives the WSP PDU and delivers the data to B via an S-Connect.ind, which includes the source address and other parameters.

4. B issues an S-Connect.res to its WSP entity.

5. B's WSP entity conveys the acknowledgment to A's WSP entity in a PDU.

6. The acknowledgment is delivered to A via an S-Connect.cnf.

This sequence of events is referred to as a **confirmed service**, as the initiator receives confirmation that the requested service has had the desired effect at the other end. If only request and indication primitives are involved (corresponding to steps 1 through 3), then the service dialogue is a **nonconfirmed service**; the initiator receives no confirmation that the requested action has taken place (Figure 12.22b).]

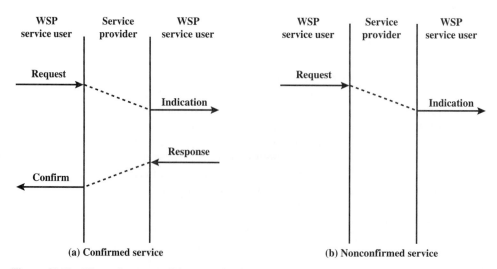

Figure 12.22 Times Sequence Diagrams for Service Primitives

PART FOUR

Wireless LANs

CHAPTER 13

WIRELESS LAN TECHNOLOGY

In just the past few years, wireless LANs have come to occupy a significant niche in the local area network market. Increasingly, organizations are finding that wireless LANs are an indispensable adjunct to traditional wired LANs, to satisfy requirements for mobility, relocation, ad hoc networking, and coverage of locations difficult to wire.

This chapter provides a survey of wireless LANs. We begin with an overview that looks at the motivations for using wireless LANs and summarizes the various approaches in current use. The next three sections examine in more detail the three principal types of wireless LANs, classified according to transmission technology: infrared, spread spectrum, and narrowband microwave.

13.1 OVERVIEW

As the name suggests, a wireless LAN is one that makes use of a wireless transmission medium. Until relatively recently, wireless LANs were little used. The reasons for this included high prices, low data rates, occupational safety concerns, and licensing requirements. As these problems have been addressed, the popularity of wireless LANs has grown rapidly.

In this section, we first look at the requirements for and advantages of wireless LANs and then preview the key approaches to wireless LAN implementation.

Wireless LAN Applications

[PAHL95] lists four application areas for wireless LANs: LAN extension, cross-building interconnect, nomadic access, and ad hoc networks. Let us consider each of these in turn.

LAN Extension

Early wireless LAN products, introduced in the late 1980s, were marketed as substitutes for traditional wired LANs. A wireless LAN saves the cost of the installation of LAN cabling and eases the task of relocation and other modifications to network structure. However, this motivation for wireless LANs was overtaken by events. First, as awareness of the need for LANs became greater, architects designed new buildings to include extensive prewiring for data applications. Second, with advances in data transmission technology, there is an increasing reliance on twisted pair cabling for LANs and, in particular, Category 3 and Category 5 unshielded twisted pair. Most older building are already wired with an abundance of Category 3 cable, and many newer buildings are prewired with Category 5. Thus, the use of a wireless LAN to replace wired LANs has not happened to any great extent.

However, in a number of environments, there is a role for the wireless LAN as an alternative to a wired LAN. Examples include buildings with large open areas, such as manufacturing plants, stock exchange trading floors, and warehouses; historical buildings with insufficient twisted pair and where drilling holes for new

Figure 13.1 Example Single-Cell Wireless LAN Configuration

wiring is prohibited; and small offices where installation and maintenance of wired LANs is not economical. In all of these cases, a wireless LAN provides an effective and more attractive alternative. In most of these cases, an organization will also have a wired LAN to support servers and some stationary workstations. For example, a manufacturing facility typically has an office area that is separate from the factory floor but that must be linked to it for networking purposes. Therefore, typically, a wireless LAN will be linked into a wired LAN on the same premises. Thus, this application area is referred to as LAN extension.

Figure 13.1 indicates a simple wireless LAN configuration that is typical of many environments. There is a backbone wired LAN, such as Ethernet, that supports servers, workstations, and one or more bridges or routers to link with other networks. In addition, there is a control module (CM) that acts as an interface to a wireless LAN. The control module includes either bridge or router functionality to link the wireless LAN to the backbone. It includes some sort of access control logic, such as a polling or token-passing scheme, to regulate the access from the end systems. Note that some of the end systems are standalone devices, such as a workstation or a server. Hubs or other user modules (UMs) that con-

Figure 13.2 Example Multiple-Cell Wireless LAN Configuration

trol a number of stations off a wired LAN may also be part of the wireless LAN configuration.

The configuration of Figure 13.1 can be referred to as a single-cell wireless LAN; all of the wireless end systems are within range of a single control module. Another common configuration, suggested by Figure 13.2, is a multiple-cell wireless LAN. In this case, there are multiple control modules interconnected by a wired LAN. Each control module supports a number of wireless end systems within its transmission range. For example, with an infrared LAN, transmission is limited to a single room; therefore, one cell is needed for each room in an office building that requires wireless support.

Cross-Building Interconnect

Another use of wireless LAN technology is to connect LANs in nearby buildings, be they wired or wireless LANs. In this case, a point-to-point wireless link is used between two buildings. The devices so connected are typically bridges or routers. This single point-to-point link is not a LAN per se, but it is usual to include this application under the heading of wireless LAN.

Nomadic Access

Nomadic access provides a wireless link between a LAN hub and a mobile data terminal equipped with an antenna, such as a laptop computer or notepad computer. One example of the utility of such a connection is to enable an employee returning from a trip to transfer data from a personal portable computer to a server in the office. Nomadic access is also useful in an extended environment such as a campus or a business operating out of a cluster of buildings. In both of these cases, users may move around with their portable computers and may wish access to the servers on a wired LAN from various locations.

Ad Hoc Networking

An ad hoc network is a peer-to-peer network (no centralized server) set up temporarily to meet some immediate need. For example, a group of employees, each with a laptop or palmtop computer may convene in a conference room for a business or classroom meeting. The employees link their computers in a temporary network just for the duration of the meeting.

Figure 13.3 suggests the differences between a wireless LAN that supports LAN extension and nomadic access requirements and an ad hoc wireless LAN. In the former case, the wireless LAN forms a stationary infrastructure consisting of one or more cells with a control module for each cell. Within a cell, there may be a number of stationary end systems. Nomadic stations can move from one cell to another. In contrast, there is no infrastructure for an ad hoc network. Rather, a peer collection of stations within range of each other may dynamically configure themselves into a temporary network.

Wireless LAN Requirements

A wireless LAN must meet the same sort of requirements typical of any LAN, including high capacity, ability to cover short distances, full connectivity among attached stations, and broadcast capability. In addition, there are a number of requirements specific to the wireless LAN environment. The following are among the most important requirements for wireless LANs:

- **Throughput:** The medium access control protocol should make as efficient use as possible of the wireless medium to maximize capacity.
- **Number of nodes:** Wireless LANs may need to support hundreds of nodes across multiple cells.
- **Connection to backbone LAN:** In most cases, interconnection with stations on a wired backbone LAN is required. For infrastructure wireless LANs, this is easily accomplished through the use of control modules that connect to both types of LANs. There may also need to be accommodation for mobile users and ad hoc wireless networks.
- **Service area:** A typical coverage area for a wireless LAN has a diameter of 100 to 300 m.
- **Battery power consumption:** Mobile workers use battery-powered workstations that need to have a long battery life when used with wireless adapters.

(a) Infrastructure wireless LAN

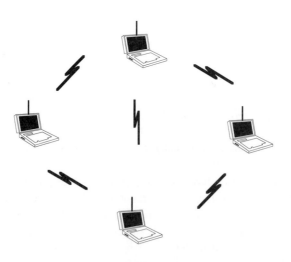

(b) Ad hoc LAN

Figure 13.3 Wireless LAN Configurations

This suggests that a MAC protocol that requires mobile nodes to monitor access points constantly or engage in frequent handshakes with a base station is inappropriate. Typical wireless LAN implementations have features to reduce power consumption while not using the network, such as a sleep mode.

- **Transmission robustness and security:** Unless properly designed, a wireless LAN may be interference prone and easily eavesdropped. The design of a wireless LAN must permit reliable transmission even in a noisy environment and should provide some level of security from eavesdropping.

- **Collocated network operation:** As wireless LANs become more popular, it is quite likely for two or more wireless LANs to operate in the same area or in some area where interference between the LANs is possible. Such interference may thwart the normal operation of a MAC algorithm and may allow unauthorized access to a particular LAN.

- **License-free operation:** Users would prefer to buy and operate wireless LAN products without having to secure a license for the frequency band used by the LAN.

- **Handoff/roaming:** The MAC protocol used in the wireless LAN should enable mobile stations to move from one cell to another.

- **Dynamic configuration:** The MAC addressing and network management aspects of the LAN should permit dynamic and automated addition, deletion, and relocation of end systems without disruption to other users.

It is instructive to compare wireless LANs to wired LANs and mobile data networks using Kiviat graphs,[1] as shown in Figure 13.4.

Wireless LAN Technology

Wireless LANs are generally categorized according to the transmission technique that is used. All current wireless LAN products fall into one of the following categories:

- **Infrared (IR) LANs:** An individual cell of an IR LAN is limited to a single room, because infrared light does not penetrate opaque walls.

- **Spread spectrum LANs:** This type of LAN makes use of spread spectrum transmission technology. In most cases, these LANs operate in the ISM (Industrial, Scientific, and Medical) bands so that no FCC licensing is required for their use in the United States.

- **Narrowband microwave:** These LANs operate at microwave frequencies but do not use spread spectrum. Some of these products operate at frequencies that require FCC licensing, while others use one of the unlicensed ISM bands.

Table 13.1 summarizes some of the key characteristics of these three technologies; the details are explored in the next three sections.

---

[1]A Kiviat graph provides a pictorial means of comparing systems along multiple variables. The variables are laid out at equal angular intervals. A given system is defined by one point on each variable; these points are connected to yield a shape that is characteristic of that system.

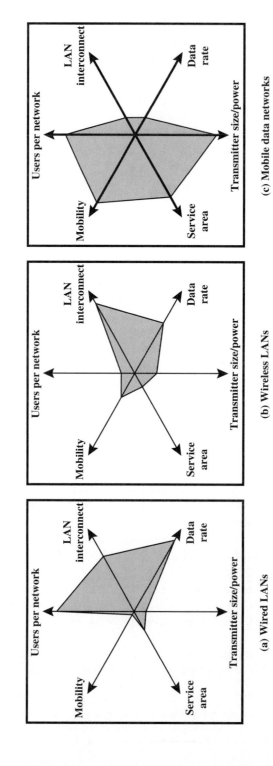

(a) Wired LANs

(b) Wireless LANs

(c) Mobile data networks

Figure 13.4 Kiviat Graphs for Data Networks

440

Table 13.1 Comparison of Wireless LAN Technologies

	Infrared		Spread Spectrum		Radio
	Diffused Infrared	**Directed Beam Infrared**	**Frequency Hopping**	**Direct Sequence**	**Narrowband Microwave**
Data Rate (Mbps)	1 to 4	1 to 10	1 to 3	2 to 20	10 to 20
Mobility	Stationary/mobile	Stationary with LOS	Mobile	Stationary/mobile	
Range (m)	15 to 60	25	30 to 100	30 to 250	10 to 40
Detectability	Negligible		Little		Some
Wavelength/ frequency	λ: 800 to 900 nm		902 to 928 MHz 2.4 to 2.4835 GHz 5.725 to 5.85 GHz		902 to 928 MHz 5.2 to 5.775 GHz 18.825 to 19.205 GHz
Modulation technique	ASK		FSK	QPSK	FS/QPSK
Radiated power	—		<1W		25 mW
Access method	CSMA	Token Ring, CSMA	CSMA		Reservation ALOHA, CSMA
License required	No		No		Yes unless ISM

13.2 INFRARED LANs

Optical wireless communication in the infrared portion of the spectrum is commonplace in most homes, where it used for a variety of remote control devices. More recently, attention has turned to the use of infrared technology to construct wireless LANs. In this section, we begin with a comparison of the characteristics of infrared LANs with those of radio LANs and then look at some of the details of infrared LANs.

Strengths and Weaknesses

The two competing transmission media for wireless LANs are microwave radio, using either spread spectrum or narrowband transmission, and infrared. Infrared offers a number of significant advantages over the microwave radio approaches. First, the spectrum for infrared is virtually unlimited, which presents the possibility of achieving extremely high data rates. The infrared spectrum is unregulated worldwide, which is not true of some portions of the microwave spectrum.

In addition, infrared shares some properties of visible light that make it attractive for certain types of LAN configurations. Infrared light is diffusely reflected by light-colored objects; thus it is possible to use ceiling reflection to achieve coverage of an entire room. Infrared light does not penetrate walls or other opaque objects. This has two advantages: First, infrared communications can be more easily secured against eavesdropping than microwave; and second, a separate infrared installation can be operated in every room in a building without interference, enabling the construction of very large infrared LANs.

Another strength of infrared is that the equipment is relatively inexpensive and simple. Infrared data transmission typically uses intensity modulation, so that IR receivers need to detect only the amplitude of optical signals, whereas most microwave receivers must detect frequency or phase.

The infrared medium also exhibits some drawbacks. Many indoor environments experience rather intense infrared background radiation, from sunlight and indoor lighting. This ambient radiation appears as noise in an infrared receiver, requiring the use of transmitters of higher power than would otherwise be required and also limiting the range. However, increases in transmitter power are limited by concerns of eye safety and excessive power consumption.

Transmission Techniques

There are three alternative transmission techniques commonly used for IR data transmission: the transmitted signal can be focused and aimed (as in a remote TV control); it can be radiated omnidirectionally; or it can be reflected from a light-colored ceiling.

Directed Beam Infrared

Directed-beam IR can be used to create point-to-point links. In this mode, the range depends on the emitted power and on the degree of focusing. A focused

IR data link can have a range of kilometers. Such ranges are not needed for constructing indoor wireless LANs. However, an IR link can be used for cross-building interconnect between bridges or routers located in buildings within a line of sight of each other.

One indoor use of point-to-point IR links is to set up a token ring LAN (Figure 13.5). A set of IR transceivers can be set up so that data circulate around them in a ring configuration. Each transceiver supports a workstation or a hub of stations, with the hub providing a bridging function.

Ominidirectional

An omnidirectional configuration involves a single base station that is within line of sight of all other stations on the LAN. Typically, this station is mounted on the ceiling (Figure 13.6a). The base station acts as a multiport repeater. The ceiling transmitter broadcasts an omnidirectional signal that can be received by all of the other IR transceivers in the area. These other transceivers transmit a directional beam aimed at the ceiling base unit.

Diffused

In this configuration, all of the IR transmitters are focused and aimed at a point an a diffusely reflecting ceiling (Figure 13.6b). IR radiation striking the ceiling is reradiated omnidirectionally and picked up by all of the receivers in the area.

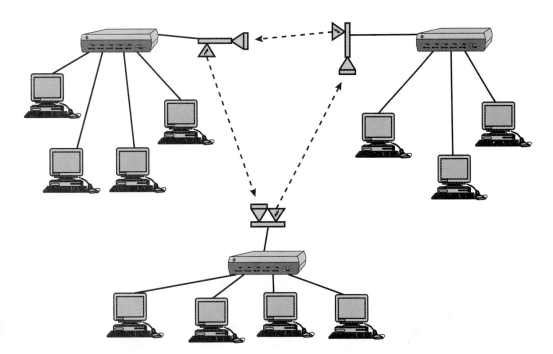

Figure 13.5   Token Ring LAN Using Point-to-Point Infrared Links

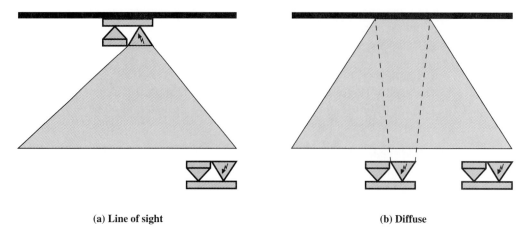

(a) Line of sight   (b) Diffuse

Figure 13.6 Configuration for Omnidirectional Infrared LANs

Figure 13.7 shows a typical configuration for a wireless IR LAN installation. There are a number of ceiling-mounted base stations, one to a room. Each station provides connectivity for a number of stationary and mobile workstations in its area. Using ceiling wiring, the base stations are all connected back to a server that can act as an access point to a wired LAN or a WAN. In addition, there may be conference rooms without a base station where ad hoc networks may be set up.

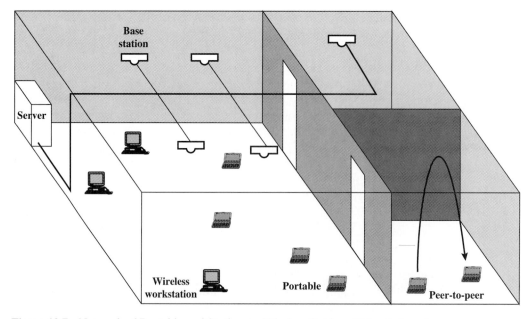

Figure 13.7 Network of Portable and Stationary Wireless Stations Using Infrared

13.3 SPREAD SPECTRUM LANs

Currently, the most popular type of wireless LAN uses spread spectrum techniques.

Configuration

Except for quite small offices, a spread spectrum wireless LAN makes use of a multiple-cell arrangement, as was illustrated in Figure 13.2. Adjacent cells make use of different center frequencies within the same band to avoid interference.

Within a given cell, the topology can be either hub or peer to peer. The hub topology is indicated in Figure 13.2. In a hub topology, the hub is typically mounted on the ceiling and connected to a backbone wired LAN to provide connectivity to stations attached to the wired LAN and to stations that are part of wireless LANs in other cells. The hub may also control access, as in the IEEE 802.11 point coordination function. The hub may also control access by acting as a multiport repeater with similar functionality to the multiport repeaters of 10 Mbps and 100 Mbps Ethernet. In this case, all stations in the cell transmit only to the hub and receive only from the hub. Alternatively, and regardless of access control mechanism, each station may broadcast using an omnidirectional antenna so that all other stations in the cell may receive; this corresponds to a logical bus configuration.

One other potential function of a hub is automatic handoff of mobile stations. At any time, a number of stations are dynamically assigned to a given hub based on proximity. When the hub senses a weakening signal, it can automatically hand off to the nearest adjacent hub.

A peer-to-peer topology is one in which there is no hub. A MAC algorithm such as CSMA is used to control access. This topology is appropriate for ad hoc LANs.

Transmission Issues

A desirable, though not necessary, characteristic of a wireless LAN is that it be usable without having to go through a licensing procedure. The licensing regulations differ from one country to another, which complicates this objective. Within the United States, the Federal Communications Commission (FCC) has authorized two unlicensed applications within the ISM band: spread spectrum systems, which can operate at up to 1 watt, and very low power systems, which can operate at up to 0.5 watts. Since this band was opened up by the FCC, its use for spread spectrum wireless LANs has become popular.

In the United States, three microwave bands have been set aside for unlicensed spreadspectrum use: 902–928 MHz (915-MHz band), 2.4–2.4835 GHz (2.4-GHz band), and 5.725–5.825 GHz (5.8-GHz band). Of these, the 2.4 GHz is also used in this manner in Europe and Japan. The higher the frequency, the higher the potential bandwidth, so the three bands are of increasing order of attractiveness from a capacity point of view. In addition, the potential for interference must be considered. There are a number of devices that operate at around 900 MHz, including cordless telephones, wireless microphones, and amateur radio. There are fewer devices operating at 2.4 GHz; one notable example is the microwave oven, which tends to have greater leakage of radiation with increasing age. At present there is little competition at the 5.8-Ghz band; however, the higher the frequency band, in general the more expensive the equipment.

Until recently, typical spread spectrum wireless LANs were limited to just 1 to 3 Mbps. As is discussed in Chapter 14, newer standards options provide for 5.5 and 11 Mbps. Some proprietary systems provide even higher data rates.

13.4 NARROWBAND MICROWAVE LANs

The term *narrowband microwave* refers to the use of a microwave radio frequency band for signal transmission, with a relatively narrow bandwidth—just wide enough to accommodate the signal. Until recently, all narrowband microwave LAN products have used a licensed microwave band. More recently, at least one vendor has produced a LAN product in the ISM band.

Licensed Narrowband RF

Microwave radio frequencies usable for voice, data, and video transmission are licensed and coordinated within specific geographic areas to avoid potential interference between systems. Within the United States, licensing is controlled by the FCC. Each geographic area has a radius of 28 km and can contain five licenses, with each license covering two frequencies. Motorola holds 600 licenses (1200 frequencies) in the 18-GHz range that cover all metropolitan areas with populations of 30,000 or more.

A narrowband scheme typically makes use of the cell configuration illustrated in Figure 13.2. Adjacent cells use nonoverlapping frequency bands within the overall 18-GHz band. In the United States, because Motorola controls the frequency band, it can assure that independent LANs in nearby geographical locations do not interfere with one another. To provide security from eavesdropping, all transmissions are encrypted.

One advantage of the licensed narrowband LAN is that it guarantees interference-free communication. Unlike unlicensed spectrum, such as ISM, licensed spectrum gives the license holder a legal right to an interference-free data communications channel. Users of an ISM-band LAN are at risk of interference disrupting their communications, for which they may not have a legal remedy.

Unlicensed Narrowband RF

In 1995, RadioLAN became the first vendor to introduce a narrowband wireless LAN using the unlicensed ISM spectrum. This spectrum can be used for narrowband transmission at low power (0.5 watts or less). The RadioLAN product operates at 10 Mbps in the 5.8-GHz band. The product has a range of 50 m in a semiopen office and 100 m in an open office.

The RadioLAN product makes use of a peer-to-peer configuration with an interesting feature. As a substitute for a stationary hub, the RadioLAN product automatically elects one node as the Dynamic Master, based on parameters such as location, interference, and signal strength. The identity of the master can change automatically as conditions change. The LAN also includes a dynamic relay function, which allows each station to act as a repeater to move data between stations that are out of range of each other.

13.5 RECOMMENDED READING AND WEB SITES

[PAHL95] and [BANT94] are detailed survey articles on wireless LANs. [KAHN97] provides good coverage of infrared LANs.

BANT94   Bantz, D., and Bauchot, F. "Wireless LAN Design Alternatives." *IEEE Network*, March/April, 1994.

KAHN97   Kahn, J., and Barry, J. "Wireless Infrared Communications." *Proceedings of the IEEE*, February 1997.

PAHL95   Pahlavan, K.; Probert, T.; and Chase, M. "Trends in Local Wireless Networks." *IEEE Communications Magazine*, March 1995.

 Recommended Web sites:

- **Wireless LAN Alliance:** Gives an introduction to the technology, including a discussion of implementation considerations and case studies from users. Links to related sites.

13.6 KEY TERMS AND REVIEW QUESTIONS

Key Terms

ad hoc networking infrared	Kiviat graph LAN extension	nomadic access wireless LAN

Review Questions

1 List and briefly define four application areas for wireless LANs.
2 List and briefly define key requirements for wireless LANs.
3 What is the difference between a single-cell and a multiple-cell wireless LAN?
4 What is a Kiviat graph?
5 What are some key advantages of infrared LANs?
6 What are some key disadvantages of infrared LANs?
7 List and briefly define three transmission techniques for infrared LANs.

CHAPTER 14

IEEE 802.11 WIRELESS LAN STANDARD

T he most prominent specification for wireless LANs was developed by the IEEE 802.11 working group. We look first at the overall architecture of IEEE 802 standards and then at the specifics of IEEE 802.11.

14.1 IEEE 802 ARCHITECTURE

The architecture of a LAN is best described in terms of a layering of protocols that organize the basic functions of a LAN. This section opens with a description of the standardized protocol architecture for LANs, which encompasses physical, medium access control, and logical link control layers. We then look in more detail at medium access control and logical link control.

Protocol Architecture

Protocols defined specifically for LAN and MAN (metropolitan area network) transmission address issues relating to the transmission of blocks of data over the network. In OSI terms, higher-layer protocols (layer 3 or 4 and above) are independent of network architecture and are applicable to LANs, MANs, and WANs. Thus, a discussion of LAN protocols is concerned principally with lower layers of the OSI model.

Figure 14.1 relates the LAN protocols to the OSI architecture (Figure 4.3). This architecture was developed by the IEEE 802 committee and has been adopted by all organizations working on the specification of LAN standards. It is generally referred to as the IEEE 802 reference model.[1]

Working from the bottom up, the lowest layer of the IEEE 802 reference model corresponds to the **physical layer** of the OSI model and includes such functions as

- Encoding/decoding of signals
- Preamble generation/removal (for synchronization)
- Bit transmission/reception

In addition, the physical layer of the 802 model includes a specification of the transmission medium and the topology. Generally, this is considered "below" the lowest layer of the OSI model. However, the choice of transmission medium and topology is critical in LAN design, and so a specification of the medium is included.

Above the physical layer are the functions associated with providing service to LAN users. These include the following:

- On transmission, assemble data into a frame with address and error detection fields.
- On reception, disassemble frame, and perform address recognition and error detection.

---

[1]See Appendix A for a discussion of the IEEE 802 Standards Committee.

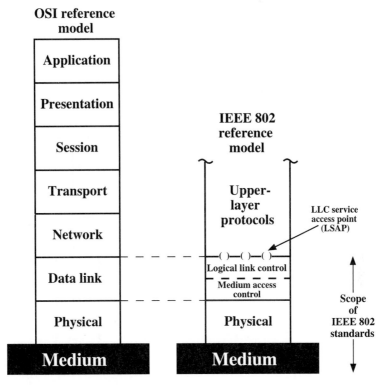

Figure 14.1   IEEE 802 Protocol Layers Compared to OSI Model

- Govern access to the LAN transmission medium.
- Provide an interface to higher layers and perform flow and error control.

These are functions typically associated with OSI layer 2. The set of functions in the last bullet item are grouped into a **logical link control (LLC)** layer. The functions in the first three bullet items are treated as a separate layer, called **medium access control (MAC)**. The separation is done for the following reasons:

- The logic required to manage access to a shared-access medium is not found in traditional layer 2 data link control.
- For the same LLC, several MAC options may be provided.

Figure 14.2, which reproduces Figure 11.16, illustrates the relationship between the levels of the architecture. Higher-level data are passed down to LLC, which appends control information as a header, creating an *LLC protocol data unit (PDU)*. This control information is used in the operation of the LLC protocol. The entire LLC PDU is then passed down to the MAC layer, which appends control information at the front and back of the packet, forming a *MAC frame*. Again, the control information in the frame is needed for the operation of the MAC protocol. For context, the figure also shows the use of TCP/IP and an application layer above the LAN protocols.

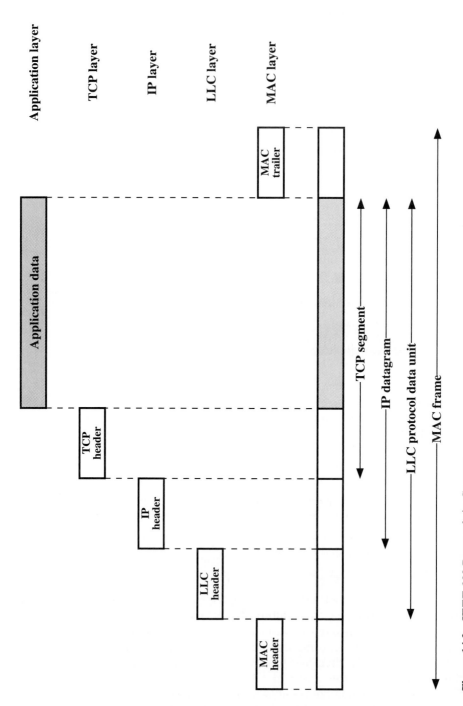

Figure 14.2 IEEE 802 Protocols in Context

452

MAC Frame Format

The MAC layer receives a block of data from the LLC layer and is responsible for performing functions related to medium access and for transmitting the data. As with other protocol layers, MAC implements these functions making use of a protocol data unit at its layer. In this case, the PDU is referred to as a MAC frame.

The exact format of the MAC frame differs somewhat for the various MAC protocols in use. In general, all of the MAC frames have a format similar to that of Figure 14.3. The fields of this frame are as follows:

- **MAC control:** This field contains any protocol control information needed for the functioning of the MAC protocol. For example, a priority level could be indicated here.
- **Destination MAC address:** The destination physical attachment point on the LAN for this frame.
- **Source MAC address:** The source physical attachment point on the LAN for this frame.
- **Data:** The body of the MAC frame. This may be LLC data from the next higher layer or control information relevant to the operatoin of the MAC protocol.
- **CRC:** The cyclic redundancy check field (also known as the frame check sequence, FCS, field). This is an error-detecting code, as we have seen in HDLC and other data link control protocols (Section 8.1).

In most data link control protocols, the data link protocol entity is responsible not only for detecting errors using the CRC but for recovering from those errors by retransmitting damaged frames. In the LAN protocol architecture, these two functions are split between the MAC and LLC layers. The MAC layer is responsible for detecting errors and discarding any frames that are in error. The LLC layer optionally keeps track of which frames have been successfully received and retransmits unsuccessful frames.

Logical Link Control

The LLC layer for LANs is similar in many respects to other link layers in common use. Like all link layers, LLC is concerned with the transmission of a link-level PDU between two stations, without the necessity of an intermediate switching node. LLC has two characteristics not shared by most other link control protocols:

1. It must support the multiaccess, shared-medium nature of the link (this differs from a multidrop line in that there is no primary node).
2. It is relieved of some details of link access by the MAC layer.

Addressing in LLC involves specifying the source and destination LLC users. Typically, a user is a higher-layer protocol or a network management function in the station. These LLC user addresses are referred to as service access points (SAPs), in keeping with OSI terminology for the user of a protocol layer.

We look first at the services that LLC provides to a higher-level user, and then at the LLC protocol.

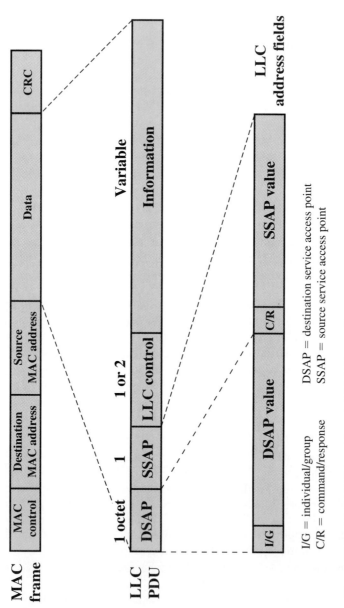

Figure 14.3 LLC PDU in a Generic MAC Frame Format

I/G = individual/group   DSAP = destination service access point
C/R = command/response   SSAP = source service access point

LLC Services

LLC specifies the mechanisms for addressing stations across the medium and for controlling the exchange of data between two users. The operation and format of this standard is based on HDLC. Three services are provided as alternatives for attached devices using LLC:

- **Unacknowledged connectionless service:** This service is a datagram-style service. It is a very simple service that does not involve any of the flow- and error-control mechanisms. Thus, the delivery of data is not guaranteed. However, in most devices, there will be some higher layer of software that deals with reliability issues.
- **Connection-mode service:** This service is similar to that offered by HDLC. A logical connection is set up between two users exchanging data, and flow control and error control are provided.
- **Acknowledged connectionless service:** This is a cross between the previous two services. It provides that datagrams are to be acknowledged, but no prior logical connection is set up.

Typically, a vendor will provide these services as options that the customer can select when purchasing the equipment. Alternatively, the customer can purchase equipment that provides two or all three services and select a specific service based on application.

The **unacknowledged connectionless service** requires minimum logic and is useful in two contexts. First, it will often be the case that higher layers of software will provide the necessary reliability and flow-control mechanism, and it is efficient to avoid duplicating them. For example, TCP could provide the mechanisms needed to ensure that data are delivered reliably. Second, there are instances in which the overhead of connection establishment and maintenance is unjustified or even counterproductive (for example, data collection activities that involve the periodic sampling of data sources, such as sensors and automatic self-test reports from security equipment or network components). In a monitoring application, the loss of an occasional data unit would not cause distress, as the next report should arrive shortly. Thus, in most cases, the unacknowledged connectionless service is the preferred option.

The **connection-mode service** could be used in very simple devices, such as terminal controllers, that have little software operating above this level. In these cases, it would provide the flow control and reliability mechanisms normally implemented at higher layers of the communications software.

The **acknowledged connectionless service** is useful in several contexts. With the connection-mode service, the logical link control software must maintain some sort of table for each active connection, to keep track of the status of that connection. If the user needs guaranteed delivery but there are a large number of destinations for data, then the connection-mode service may be impractical because of the large number of tables required. An example is a process control or automated factory environment where a central site may need to communicate with a large number of processors and programmable controllers. Another use of this is the handling of important and time-critical alarm or emergency control signals in a factory. Because of their importance, an acknowledgment is needed so that the sender can be assured that the signal got through. Because of the urgency of the signal, the user might not want to take the time first to establish a logical connection and then send the data.

LLC Protocol

The basic LLC protocol is modeled after HDLC and has similar functions and formats. The differences between the two protocols can be summarized as follows:

- LLC makes use of the asynchronous balanced mode of operation of HDLC, to support connection-mode LLC service; this is referred to as type 2 operation. The other HDLC modes are not employed.
- LLC supports an unacknowledged connectionless service using the unnumbered information PDU; this is known as type 1 operation.
- LLC supports an acknowledged connectionless service by using two new unnumbered PDUs; this is known as type 3 operation.
- LLC permits multiplexing by the use of LLC service access points (LSAPs).

All three LLC protocols employ the same PDU format (Figure 14.3), which consists of four fields. The DSAP and SSAP fields each contain a 7-bit address, which specify the destination and source users of LLC. One bit of the DSAP indicates whether the DSAP is an individual or group address. One bit of the SSAP indicates whether the PDU is a command or response PDU. The format of the LLC control field is identical to that of HDLC (Figure D.1, Appendix D), using extended (7-bit) sequence numbers.

For **type 1 operation**, which supports the unacknowledged connectionless service, the unnumbered information (UI) PDU is used to transfer user data. There is no acknowledgment, flow control, or error control. However, there is error detection and discard at the MAC level.

Two other PDU types, XID and TEST, are used to support management functions associated with all three types of operation. Both PDU types are used in the following fashion. An LLC entity may issue a command (C/R bit = 0) XID or TEST. The receiving LLC entity issues a corresponding XID or TEST in response. The XID PDU is used to exchange two types of information: types of operation supported and window size. The TEST PDU is used to conduct a loopback test of the transmission path between two LLC entities. Upon receipt of a TEST command PDU, the addressed LLC entity issues a TEST response PDU as soon as possible.

With **type 2 operation**, a data link connection is established between two LLC SAPs prior to data exchange. Connection establishment is attempted by the type 2 protocol in response to a request from a user. The LLC entity issues a SABME PDU[2] to request a logical connection with the other LLC entity. If the connection is accepted by the LLC user designated by the DSAP, then the destination LLC entity returns an unnumbered acknowledgment (UA) PDU. The connection is henceforth

---

[2]This stands for Set Asynchronous Balanced Mode Extended. It is used in HDLC to choose ABM and to select extended sequence numbers of 7 bits. Both ABM and 7-bit sequence numbers are mandatory in type 2 operation.

uniquely identified by the pair of user SAPs. If the destination LLC user rejects the connection request, its LLC entity returns a disconnected mode (DM) PDU.

Once the connection is established, data is exchanged using information PDUs, as in HDLC. The information PDUs include send and receive sequence numbers, for sequencing and flow control. The supervisory PDUs are used, as in HDLC, for flow control and error control. Either LLC entity can terminate a logical LLC connection by issuing a disconnect (DISC) PDU.

With **type 3 operation**, each transmitted PDU is acknowledged. A new (not found in HDLC) unnumbered PDU, the acknowledged connectionless (AC) information PDU, is defined. User data are sent in AC command PDUs and must be acknowledged using an AC response PDU. To guard against lost PDUs, a 1-bit sequence number is used. The sender alternates the use of 0 and 1 in its AC command PDU, and the receiver responds with an AC PDU with the opposite number of the corresponding command. Only one PDU in each direction may be outstanding at any time.

14.2 IEEE 802.11 ARCHITECTURE AND SERVICES

Work on wireless LANs within the IEEE 802 committee began in 1987 within the IEEE 802.4 group. The initial interest was in developing an ISM-based wireless LAN using the equivalent of a token-passing bus MAC protocol. After some work, it was decided that token bus was not suitable for controlling a radio medium without causing inefficient use of the radio frequency spectrum. IEEE 802 then decided in 1990 to form a new working group, IEEE 802.11, specifically devoted to wireless LANs, with a charter to develop a MAC protocol and physical medium specification. Table 14.1 briefly defines key terms used in the IEEE 802.11 standard.

Table 14.1 IEEE 802.11 Terminology

Access point (AP)	Any entity that has station functionality and provides access to the distribution system via the wireless medium for associated stations
Basic service set (BSS)	A set of stations controlled by a single coordination function.
Coordination function	The logical function that determines when a station operating within a BSS is permitted to transmit and may be able to receive PDUs.
Distribution System (DS)	A system used to interconnect a set of BSSs and integrated LANs to create an ESS.
Extended service set (ESS)	A set of one or more interconnected BSSs and integrated LANs that appear as a single BSS to the LLC layer at any station associated with one of these BSSs.
MAC protocol data unit (MPDU)	The unit of data exchanged between two peer MAC entites using the services of the physical layer.
MAC service data unit (MSDU)	Information that is delivered as a unit between MAC users.
Station	Any device that contains an IEEE 802.11 conformant MAC and physical layer.

IEEE 802.11 Architecture

Figure 14.4 illustrates the model developed by the 802.11 working group. The smallest building block of a wireless LAN is a basic service set (BSS), which consists of some number of stations executing the same MAC protocol and competing for access to the same shared wireless medium. A BSS may be isolated or it may connect to a backbone distribution system (DS) through an access point (AP). The access point functions as a bridge. The MAC protocol may be fully distributed or controlled by a central coordination function housed in the access point. The BSS generally corresponds to what is referred to as a cell in the literature. The DS can be a switch, a wired network, or a wireless network.

The simplest configuration is shown in Figure 14.4, in which each station belongs to a single BSS; that is, each station is within wireless range only of other stations within the same BSS. It is also possible for two BSSs to overlap geographically, so that a single station could pariticipate in more than one BSS. Further, the association between a station and a BSS is dynamic. Stations may turn off, come within range, and go out of range.

An extended service set (ESS) consists of two or more basic service sets interconnected by a distribution system. Typically, the distribution system is a wired backbone LAN but can be any communications network. The extended service set appears as a single logical LAN to the logical link control (LLC) level.

Figure 14.4 indicates that an access point (AP) is implemented as part of a station; the AP is the logic within a station that provides access to the DS by providing DS services in addition to acting as a station. To integrate the IEEE 802.11 architecture with a traditional wired LAN, a portal is used. The portal logic is imple-

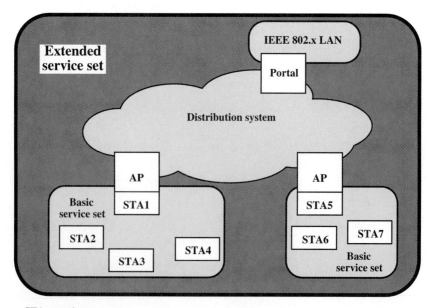

STA = station

Figure 14.4   IEEE 802.11 Architecture

mented in a device, such as a bridge or router, that is part of the wired LAN and that is attached to the DS.

IEEE 802.11 Services

IEEE 802.11 defines nine services that need to be provided by the wireless LAN to provide functionality equivalent to that which is inherent to wired LANs. Table 14.2 lists the services and indicates two ways of categorizing them.

1. The service provider can be either the station or the distribution system (DS). Station services are implemented in every 802.11 station, including access point (AP) stations. Distribution services are provided between basic service sets (BSSs); these services may be implemented in an AP or in another special-purpose device attaced to the distribution system.

2. Three of the services are used to control IEEE 802.11 LAN access and confidentiality. Six of the services are used to support delivery of MAC service data units (MSDUs) between stations. The MSDU is a the block of data passed down from the MAC user to the MAC layer; typically this is a LLC PDU. If the MSDU is too large to be transmitted in a single MAC frame, it may be fragmented and transmitted in a series of MAC frames. Fragmentation is discussed in Section 14.3.

Following the IEEE 802.11 document, we next discuss the services in an order designed to clarify the operation of an IEEE 802.11 ESS network. **MSDU delivery**, which is the basic service, has already been mentioned.

Distribution of Messages Within a DS

The two services involved with the distribution of messages within a DS are distribution and integration. **Distribution** is the primary service used by stations to exchange MAC frames when the frame must traverse the DS to get from a station in one BSS to a station in another BSS. For example, suppose a frame is to be sent

Table 14.2 IEEE 802.11 Services

Service	Provider	Used to support
Association	Distribution system	MSDU delivery
Authentication	Station	LAN access and security
Deauthentication	Station	LAN access and security
Dissassociation	Distribution system	MSDU delivery
Distribution	Distribution system	MSDU delivery
Integration	Distribution system	MSDU delivery
MSDU delivery	Station	MSDU delivery
Privacy	Station	LAN access and security
Reassociation	Distribution system	MSDU delivery

from station 2 (STA 2) to STA 7 in Figure 14.4. The frame is sent from STA 2 to STA 1, which is the AP for this BSS. The AP gives the frame to the DS, which has the job of directing the frame to the AP associated with STA 5 in the target BSS. STA 5 receives the frame and forwards it to STA 7. How the message is transported through the DS is beyond the scope of the IEEE 802.11 standard.

If the two stations that are communicating are within the same BSS, then the distribution service logically goes through the single AP of that BSS.

The **integration** service enables transfer of data between a station on an IEEE 802.11 LAN and a station on an integrated IEEE 802.x LAN. The term *integrated* refers to a wired LAN that is physically connected to the DS and whose stations may be logically connected to an IEEE 802.11 LAN via the integration service. The integration service takes care of any address translation and media conversion logic required for the exchange of data.

Association-Related Services

The primary purpose of the MAC layer is to transfer MSDUs between MAC entities; this purpose is fulfilled by the distribution service. For that service to function, it requires information about stations within the ESS that is provided by the association-related services. Before the distribution service can deliver data to or accept data from a station, that station must be *associated*. Before looking at the concept of association, we need to describe the concept of mobility. The standard defines three transition types of based on mobility:

- **No transition:** A station of this type is either stationary or moves only within the direct communication range of the communicating stations of a single BSS.
- **BSS transition:** This is defined as a station movement from one BSS to another BSS within the same ESS. In this case, delivery of data to the station requires that the addressing capability be able to recognize the new location of the station.
- **ESS transition:** This is defined as a station movement from a BSS in one ESS to a BSS within another ESS. This case is supported only in the sense that the station can move. Maintenance of upper-layer connections supported by 802.11 cannot be guaranteed. In fact, disruption of service is likely to occur.

To deliver a message within a DS, the distribution service needs to know where the destination station is located. Specifically, the DS needs to know the identity of the AP to which the message should be delivered in order for that message to reach the destination station. To meet this requirement, a station must maintain an association with the AP within its current BSS. Three services relate to this requirement:

- **Association:** Establishes an initial association between a station and an AP. Before a station can transmit or receive frames on a wireless LAN, its identity and address must be known. For this purpose, a station must establish an association with an AP within a particular BSS. The AP can then communicate this information to other APs within the ESS to facilitate routing and delivery of addressed frames.

- **Reassociation:** Enables an established association to be transferred from one AP to another, allowing a mobile station to move from one BSS to another.

- **Disassociation:** A notification from either a station or an AP that an existing association is terminated. A station should give this notification before leaving an ESS or shutting down. However, the MAC management facility protects itself against stations that disappear without notification.

Access and Privacy Services

There are two characteristics of a wired LAN that are not inherent in a wireless LAN.

1. In order to transmit over a wired LAN, a station must be physically connected to the LAN. On the other hand, with a wireless LAN, any station within radio range of the other devices on the LAN can transmit. In a sense, there is a form of authentication with a wired LAN, in that it requires some positive and presumably observable action to connect a station to a wired LAN.

2. Similarly, in order to receive a transmission from a station that is part of a wired LAN, the receiving station must also be attached to the wired LAN. On the other hand, with a wireless LAN, any station within radio range can receive. Thus, a wired LAN provides a degree of privacy, limiting reception of data to stations connected to the LAN.

IEEE 802.11 defines three services that provide a wireless LAN with these two features:

- **Authentication:** Used to establish the identity of stations to each other. In a wired LAN, it is generally assumed that access to a physical connection conveys authority to connect to the LAN. This is not a valid assumption for a wireless LAN, in which connectivity is achieved simply by having an attached antenna that is properly tuned. The authentication service is used by stations to establish their identity with stations they wish to communicate with. IEEE 802.11 supports several authentication schemes and allows for expansion of the functionality of these schemes. The standard does not mandate any particular authentication scheme, which could range from relatively unsecure handshaking to public-key encryption schemes. However, IEEE 802.11 requires mutually acceptable, successful authentication before a station can establish an association with an AP.

- **Deathentication:** This service is invoked whenever an existing authentication is to be terminated.

- **Privacy:** Used to prevent the contents of messages from being read by other than the intended recipient. The standard provides for the optional use of encryption to assure privacy. The algorithm specified in the standard is WEP, which is described in Section 14.3.

14.3 IEEE 802.11 MEDIUM ACCESS CONTROL

The IEEE 802.11 MAC layer covers three functional areas: reliable data delivery, access control, and security. We look at each of these in turn.

Reliable Data Delivery

As with any wireless network, a wireless LAN using the IEEE 802.11 physical and MAC layers is subject to considerable unreliability. Noise, interference, and other propagation effects result in the loss of a significant number of frames. Even with error-correction codes, a number of MAC frames may not successfully be received. This situation can be dealt with by reliability mechanisms at a higher layer, such as TCP. However, timers used for retransmission at higher layers are typically on the order of seconds. It is therefore more efficient to deal with errors at the MAC level. For this purpose, IEEE 802.11 includes a frame exchange protocol. When a station receives a data frame from another station it returns an acknowledgment (ACK) frame to the source station. This exchange is treated as an atomic unit, not to be interrupted by a transmission from any other station. If the source does not receive an ACK within a short period of time, either because its data frame was damaged or because the returning ACK was damaged, the source retransmits the frame.

Thus, the basic data transfer mechanism in IEEE 802.11 involves an exchange of two frames. To further enhance reliability, a four-frame exchange may be used. In this scheme, a source first issues a request to send (RTS) frame to the destination. The destination then responds with a clear to send (CTS). After receiving the CTS, the source transmits the data frame, and the destination responds with an ACK. The RTS alerts all stations that are within reception range of the source that an exchange is under way; these stations refrain from transmission in order to avoid a collision between two frames transmitted at the same time. Similarly, the CTS alerts all stations that are within reception range of the destination that an exchange is under way. The RTS/CTS portion of the exchange is a required function of the MAC but may be disabled.

Access Control

The 802.11 working group considered two types of proposals for a MAC algorithm: distributed access protocols, which, like Ethernet, distribute the decision to transmit over all the nodes using a carrier-sense mechanism; and centralized access protocols, which involve regulation of transmission by a centralized decision maker. A distributed access protocol makes sense for an ad hoc network of peer workstations and may also be attractive in other wireless LAN configurations that consist primarily of bursty traffic. A centralized access protocol is natural for configurations in which a number of wireless stations are interconnected with each other and some sort of base station that attaches to a backbone wired LAN; it is especially useful if some of the data is time sensitive or high priority.

The end result for 802.11 is a MAC algorithm called DFWMAC (distributed foundation wireless MAC) that provides a distributed access control mechanism with an optional centralized control built on top of that. Figure 14.5 illustrates the

Figure 14.5   IEEE 802.11 Protocol Architecture

architecture. The lower sublayer of the MAC layer is the distributed coordination function (DCF). DCF uses a contention algorithm to provide access to all traffic. Ordinary asynchronous traffic directly uses DCF. The point coordination function (PCF) is a centralized MAC algorithm used to provide contention-free service. PCF is built on top of DCF and exploits features of DCF to assure access for its users. Let us consider these two sublayers in turn.

Distributed Coordination Function

The DCF sublayer makes use of a simple CSMA (carrier sense multiple access) algorithm. If a station has a MAC frame to transmit, it listens to the medium. If the medium is idle, the station may transmit; otherwise the station must wait until the current transmission is complete before transmitting. The DCF does not include a collision detection function (i.e., CSMA/CD) because collision detection is not practical on a wireless network. The dynamic range of the signals on the medium is very large, so that a transmitting station cannot effectively distinguish incoming weak signals from noise and the effects of its own transmission.

To ensure the smooth and fair functioning of this algorithm, DCF includes a set of delays that amounts to a priority scheme. Let us start by considering a single delay known as an interframe space (IFS). In fact, there are three different IFS values, but the algorithm is best explained by initially ignoring this detail. Using an IFS, the rules for CSMA access are as follows (Figure 14.6):

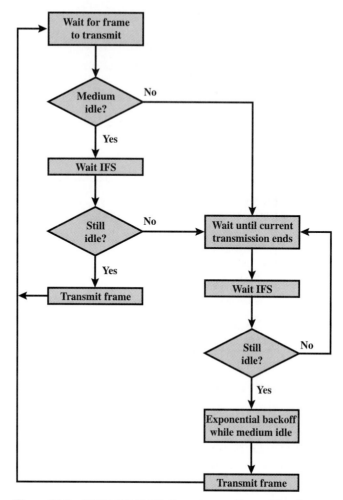

Figure 14.6 IEEE 802.11 Medium Access Control Logic

1. A station with a frame to transmit senses the medium. If the medium is idle, it waits to see if the medium remains idle for a time equal to IFS. If so, the station may transmit immediately.

2. If the medium is busy (either because the station initially finds the medium busy or because the medium becomes busy during the IFS idle time), the station defers transmission and continues to monitor the medium until the current transmission is over.

3. Once the current transmission is over, the station delays another IFS. If the medium remains idle for this period, then the station backs off a random amount of time and again senses the medium. If the medium is still idle, the station may transmit. During the backoff time, if the medium becomes busy, the backoff timer is halted and resumes when the medium becomes idle.

To ensure that backoff maintains stability, a technique known as binary exponential backoff is used. A station will attempt to transmit repeatedly in the face of repeated collisions, but after each collision, the mean value of the random delay is doubled. The binary exponential backoff provides a means of handling a heavy load. Repeated failed attempts to transmit result in longer and longer backoff times, which helps to smooth out the load. Without such a backoff, the following situation could occur. Two or more stations attempt to transmit at the same time, causing a collision. These stations then immediately attempt to retransmit, causing a new collision.

The preceding scheme is refined for DCF to provide priority-based access by the simple expedient of using three values for IFS:

- **SIFS (short IFS):** The shortest IFS, used for all immediate response actions, as explained in the following discussion
- **PIFS (point coordination function IFS):** A midlength IFS, used by the centralized controller in the PCF scheme when issuing polls
- **DIFS (distributed coordination function IFS):** The longest IFS, used as a minimum delay for asynchronous frames contending for access

Figure 14.7a illustrates the use of these time values. Consider first the SIFS. Any station using SIFS to determine transmission opportunity has, in effect, the highest

(a) Basic access method

(b) PCF superframe construction

Figure 14.7 IEEE 802.11 MAC Timing

priority, because it will always gain access in preference to a station waiting an amount of time equal to PIFS or DIFS. The SIFS is used in the following circumstances:

- **Acknowledgment (ACK):** When a station receives a frame addressed only to itself (not multicast or broadcast) it responds with an ACK frame after waiting only for an SIFS gap. This has two desirable effects. First, because collision detection is not used, the likelihood of collisions is greater than with CSMA/CD, and the MAC-level ACK provides for efficient collision recovery. Second, the SIFS can be used to provide efficient delivery of an LLC protocol data unit (PDU) that requires multiple MAC frames. In this case, the following scenario occurs. A station with a multiframe LLC PDU to transmit sends out the MAC frames one at a time. Each frame is acknowledged after SIFS by the recipient. When the source receives an ACK, it immediately (after SIFS) sends the next frame in the sequence. The result is that once a station has contended for the channel, it will maintain control of the channel until it has sent all of the fragments of an LLC PDU.
- **Clear to Send (CTS):** A station can ensure that its data frame will get through by first issuing a small Request to Send (RTS) frame. The station to which this frame is addressed should immediately respond with a CTS frame if it is ready to receive. All other stations receive the RTS and defer using the medium.
- **Poll response:** This is explained in the following discussion of PCF.

The next longest IFS interval is the PIFS. This is used by the centralized controller in issuing polls and takes precedence over normal contention traffic. However, those frames transmitted using SIFS have precedence over a PCF poll.

Finally, the DIFS interval is used for all ordinary asynchronous traffic.

Point Coordination Function

PCF is an alternative access method implemented on top of the DCF. The operation consists of polling by the centralized polling master (point coordinator). The point coordinator makes use of PIFS when issuing polls. Because PIFS is smaller than DIFS, the point coordinator can seize the medium and lock out all asynchronous traffic while it issues polls and receives responses.

As an extreme, consider the following possible scenario. A wireless network is configured so that a number of stations with time-sensitive traffic are controlled by the point coordinator while remaining traffic contends for access using CSMA. The point coordinator could issue polls in a round-robin fashion to all stations configured for polling. When a poll is issued, the polled station may respond using SIFS. If the point coordinator receives a response, it issues another poll using PIFS. If no response is received during the expected turnaround time, the coordinator issues a poll.

If the discipline of the preceding paragraph were implemented, the point coordinator would lock out all asynchronous traffic by repeatedly issuing polls. To prevent this, an interval known as the superframe is defined. During the first part of this interval, the point coordinator issues polls in a round-robin fashion to all stations configured for polling. The point coordinator then idles for the remainder of the superframe, allowing a contention period for asynchronous access.

Figure 14.7b illustrates the use of the superframe. At the beginning of a super-frame, the point coordinator may optionally seize control and issues polls for a give period of time. This interval varies because of the variable frame size issued by responding stations. The remainder of the superframe is available for contention-based access. At the end of the superframe interval, the point coordinator contends for access to the medium using PIFS. If the medium is idle, the point coordinator gains immediate access and a full superframe period follows. However, the medium may be busy at the end of a superframe. In this case, the point coordinator must wait until the medium is idle to gain access; this results in a foreshortened superframe period for the next cycle.

MAC Frame

Figure 14.8a shows the 802.11 frame format. This general format is used for all data and control frames, but not all fields are used in all contexts. The fields are as follows:

- **Frame control:** Indicates the type of frame and provides control information, as explained presently.
- **Duration/connection ID:** If used as a duration field, indicates the time (in microseconds) the channel will be allocated for successful transmission of a MAC frame. In some control frames, this field contains an association, or connection, identifier.

FC = Frame control
D/I = Duration/Connection ID
SC = Sequence control

(a) MAC frame

DS = Distribution system   MD = More data
MF = More fragments   W = Wired equivalent privacy bit
RT = Retry   O = Order
PM = Power management

(b) Frame control field

Figure 14.8   IEEE 802.11 MAC Frame Format

- **Addresses:** The number and meaning of the address fields depend on context. Address types include source, destination, transmitting station, and receiving station.
- **Sequence control:** Contains a 4-bit fragment number subfield, used for fragmentation and reassembly, and a 12-bit sequence number used to number frames sent between a given transmitter and receiver.
- **Frame body:** Contains an MSDU or a fragment of an MSDU. The MSDU is a LLC protocol data unit or MAC control information.
- **Frame check sequence:** A 32-bit cyclic redundancy check.

The frame control field, shown in Figure 14.8b, consists of the following fields:

- **Protocol version:** 802.11 version, currently version 0.
- **Type:** Identifies the frame as control, management, or data.
- **Subtype:** Further identifies the function of frame. Table 14.3 Defines the valid combinations of type and subtype.
- **To DS:** The MAC coordination sets this bit to 1 in a frame destined to the distribution system.
- **From DS:** The MAC coordination sets this bit to 1 in a frame leaving the distribution system.
- **More fragments:** Set to 1 if more fragments follow this one.
- **Retry:** Set to 1 if this is a retransmission of a previous frame.
- **Power management:** Set to 1 if the transmitting station is in a sleep mode.
- **More data:** Indicates that a station has additional data to send. Each block of data may be sent as one frame or a group of fragments in multiple frames.
- **WEP:** Set to 1 if the optional wired equivalent protocol is implemented. WEP is used in the exchange of encryption keys for secure data exchange.
- **Order:** Set to 1 in any data frame sent using the Strictly Ordered service, which tells the receiving station that frames must be processed in order.

We now look at the various MAC frame types.

Control Frames

Control frames assist in the reliable delivery of data frames. There are six control frame subtypes:

- **Power save-poll (PS-Poll):** This frame is sent by any station to the station that includes the AP (access point). Its purpose is to request that the AP transmit a frame that has been buffered for this station while the station was in power-saving mode.
- **Request to send (RTS):** This is the first frame in the four-way frame exchange discussed under the subsection on reliable data delivery at the beginning of Section 14.3. The station sending this message is alerting a potential destination, and all other stations within reception range, that it intends to send a data frame to that destination.

Table 14.3 Valid Type and Subtype Combinations

Type Value	Type Description	Subtype Value	Subtype Description
00	Management	0000	Association request
00	Management	0001	Assocation response
00	Management	0010	Reassociation request
00	Management	0011	Reassociation response
00	Management	0100	Probe request
00	Management	0101	Probe response
00	Management	1000	Beacon
00	Management	1001	Announcement traffic indication message
00	Management	1010	Dissociation
00	Management	1011	Authentication
00	Management	1100	Deauthentication
01	Control	1010	Power save - poll
01	Control	1011	Request to send
01	Control	1100	Clear to send
01	Control	1101	Acknowledgment
01	Control	1110	Contention-free (CF)-end
01	Control	1111	CF-end + CF-ack
10	Data	0000	Data
10	Data	0001	Data + CF-Ack
10	Data	0010	Data + CF-Poll
10	Data	0011	Data + CF-Ack + CF-Poll
10	Data	0100	Null function (no data)
10	Data	0101	CF-Ack (no data)
10	Data	0110	CF-poll (no data)
10	Data	0111	CF-Ack + CF-poll (no data)

- **Clear to send (CTS):** This is the second frame in the four-way exchange. It is sent by the destination station to the source station to grant permission to send a data frame.
- **Acknowledgment:** Provides an acknowledgment from the destination to the source that the immediately preceding data, management, or PS-Poll frame was received correctly.
- **Contention-free (CF)-end:** Announces the end of a contention-free period that is part of the point coordination function.

- **CF-end + CF-ack:** Acknowledges the CF-end. This frame ends the contention-free period and releases stations from the restrictions associated with that period.

Data Frames

There are eight data frame subtypes, organized into two groups. The first four subtypes define frames that carry upper-level data from the source station to the destination station. The four data-carrying frames are as follows:

- **Data:** This is the simplest data frame. It may be used in both a contention period and a contention-free period.
- **Data + CF-Ack:** May only be sent during a contention-free period. In addition to carrying data, this frame acknowledges previously received data.
- **Data + CF-Poll:** Used by a point coordinator to deliver data to a mobile station and also to request that the mobile station send a data frame that it may have buffered.
- **Data + CF-Ack + CF-Poll:** Combines the functions of the Data + CF-Ack and Data + CF-Poll into a single frame.

The remaining four subtypes of data frames do not in fact carry any user data. The Null Function data frame carries no data, polls, or acknowledgments. It is used only to carry the power management bit in the frame control field to the AP, to indicate that the station is changing to a low-power operating state. The remaining three frames (CF-Ack, CF-Poll, CF-Ack + CF-Poll) have the same functionality as the corresponding data frame subtypes in the preceding list (Data + CF-Ack, Data + CF-Poll, Data + CF-Ack + CF-Poll) but without the data.

Management Frames

Management frames are used to manage communications between stations and APs. The following subtypes are included:

- **Association request:** Sent by a station to an AP to request an association with this BSS. This frame includes capability information, such as whether encryption is to be used and whether this station is pollable.
- **Association response:** Returned by the AP to the station to indicate whether it is accepting this association request.
- **Reassociation request:** Sent by a station when it moves from one BSS to another and needs to make an association with the AP in the new BSS. The station uses reassociation rather than simply association so that the new AP knows to negotiate with the old AP for the forwarding of data frames.
- **Reassociation response:** Returned by the AP to the station to indicate whether it is accepting this reassociation request.
- **Probe request:** Used by a station to obtain information from another station or AP. This frame is used to locate an IEEE 802.11 BSS.

- **Probe response:** Response to a probe request.
- **Beacon:** Transmitted periodically to allow mobile stations to locate and identify a BSS.
- **Announcement traffic indication message:** Sent by a mobile station to alert other mobile stations that may have been in low power mode that this station has frames buffered and waiting to be delivered to the station addressed in this frame.
- **Dissociation:** Used by a station to terminate an association.
- **Authentication:** Multiple authentication frames are used in an exchange to authenticate one station to another, as described subsequently.
- **Deauthentication:** Sent by a station to another station or AP to indicate that it is terminating secure communications.

Security Considerations

IEEE 802.11 provides both privacy and authentication mechanisms.

The Wired Equivalent Privacy Algorithm

With a wireless LAN, eavesdropping is a major concern because of the ease of capturing a transmission. IEEE 802.11 incorporates WEP to provide a modest level of security. To provide privacy, as well as data integrity, WEP uses an encryption algorithm based on the RC4 encryption algorithm.

Figure 14.9a shows the encryption process. The integrity algorithm is simply the 32-bit CRC that is appended to the end of the MAC frame (Figure 14.8a). For the encryption process, a 40-bit secret key is shared by the two participants in the exchange. An initialization vector (IV) is concatenated to the secret key. The resulting block forms the seed that is input to the pseudorandom number generator (PRNG) defined in RC4. The PRNG generates a bit sequence of the same length as the MAC frame plus its CRC. A bit-by-bit exclusive-OR between the MAC frame and the PRNG sequence produces the ciphertext. The IV is attached to the ciphertext and the resulting block is transmitted. The IV is changed periodically (as often as every transmission). Every time the IV is changed, the PRNG sequence is changed, which complicates the task of an eavesdropper.

At the receiving end (Figure 14.9b), the receiver retrieves the IV from the data block and concatenates this with the shared secret key to generate the same key sequence used by the sender. This key sequence is then XORed with the incoming block to recover the plaintext. This technique makes use of the following property of XOR:

$$A \oplus B \oplus B = A$$

Thus, if we take the plaintext, XOR it with the key sequence, and then XOR the result with the key sequence, we get back the plaintext. Finally, the receiver compares the incoming CRC with the CRC calculated at the receiver to validate integrity.

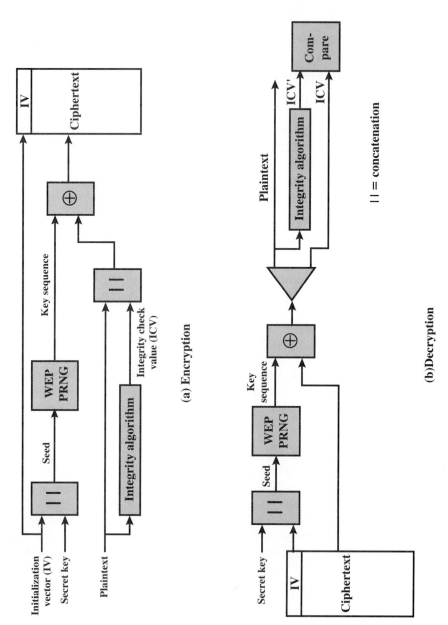

(a) Encryption

(b) Decryption

|| = concatenation

Figure 14.9 WEP Block Diagram

Authentication

IEEE 802.11 provides two types of authentication: open system and shared key. **Open system authentication** simply provides a way for two parties to agree to exchange data and provides no security benefits. In open system authentication, one party sends a MAC control frame, known as an authentication frame, to the other party. The frame indicates that this is an open system authentication type. The other party responds with its own authentication frame and the process is complete. Thus, open system authentication consists simply of the exchange of the identities between the parties.

Shared key authentication requires that the two parties share a secret key not shared by any other party. This key is used to assure that both sides are authenticated to each other. The procedure for authentication between two parties, A and B, is as follows:

1. A sends a MAC authentication frame with an authentication algorithm identification of "Shared Key" and with a station identifier that identifies the sending station.
2. B responds with an authentication frame that includes a 128-octet *challenge text*. The challenge text is generate using the WEP PRNG. The key and IV used in generating this challenge text are unimportant because they do not play a role in the remainder of the procedure.
3. A transmits an authentication frame that includes the challenge text just received from B. The entire frame is encrypted using WEP.
4. B receives the encrypted frame and decrypts it using WEP and the secret key shared with A. If decryption is successful (matching CRCs), then B compares the incoming challenge text with the challenge text that it sent in the second message. B then sends an authentication message to A with a status code indicating success or failure.

14.4 IEEE 802.11 PHYSICAL LAYER

The physical layer for IEEE 802.11 has been issued in three stages; the first part was issued in 1997 and the remaining two parts in 1999. The first part, simply called IEEE 802.11, includes the MAC layer and three physical layer specifications, two in the 2.4-GHz band and one in the infrared, all operating at 1 and 2 Mbps. IEEE 802.11a operates in the 5-GHz band at data rates up to 54 Mbps. IEEE 802.11b operates in the 2.4-Ghz band at 5.5 and 11 Mbps. We look at each of these in turn.

Original IEEE 802.11 Physical Layer

Three physical media are defined in the original 802.11 standard:

- Direct-sequence spread spectrum operating in the 2.4-GHz ISM band, at data rates of 1 Mbps and 2 Mbps

- Frequency-hopping spread spectrum operating in the 2.4-GHz ISM band, at data rates of 1 Mbps and 2 Mbps
- Infrared at 1 Mbps and 2 Mbps operating at a wavelength between 850 and 950 nm

Table 14.4 summarizes key details.

Table 14.4 IEEE 802.11 Physical Layer Specifications

(a) Direct sequence spread spectrum

Data rate	Chipping code length	Modulation	Symbol rate	Bits/symbol
1 Mbps	11 (Barker sequence)	DBPSK	1 Msps	1
2 Mbps	11 (Barker sequence)	DQPSK	1 Msps	2
5.5 Mbps	8 (CCK)	DBPSK	1.375 Msps	4
11 Mbps	8 (CCK)	DQPSK	1.375 Msps	8

(b) Frequency-hopping spread spectrum

Data rate	Modulation	Symbol rate	Bits/symbol
1 Mbps	Two-level GFSK	1 Msps	1
2 Mbps	Four-level GFSK	1 Msps	2

(c) Infrared

Data rate	Modulation	Symbol rate	Bits/symbol
1 Mbps	16-PPM	4 Msps	0.25
2 Mbps	4-PPM	4 Msps	0.5

(d) Orthogonal FDM

Data rate	Modulation	Coding rate	Coded bits per subcarrier	Code bits per OFDM symbol	Data bits per OFDM symbol
6 Mbps	BPSK	1/2	1	48	24
9 Mbps	BPSK	3/4	1	48	36
12 Mbps	QPSK	1/2	2	6	48
18 Mbps	QPSK	3/4	2	96	72
24 Mbps	16-QAM	1/2	4	192	96
36 Mbps	16-QAM	3/4	4	192	144
49 Mbps	64-QAM	2/3	6	288	192
54 Mbps	16-QAM	3/4	6	288	216

Direct-Sequence Spread Spectrum

Up to seven channels, each with a data rate of 1 Mbps or 2 Mbps, can be used in the DS-SS system. The number of channels available depends on the bandwidth allocated by the various national regulatory agencies. This ranges from 13 in most European countries to just one available channel in Japan. Each channel has a bandwidth of 5 Mhz. The encoding scheme that is used is DBPSK for the 1-Mbps rate and DQPSK for the 2-Mbps rate.

Recall from Chapter 7 that a DS-SS system makes use of a chipping code, or pseudonoise sequence, to spread the data rate and hence the bandwidth of the signal. For IEEE 802.11, a Barker sequence is used.

A Barker sequence is a binary $\{-1, +1\}$ sequence $\{s(t)\}$ of length n with the property that its autocorrelation values $R(\tau)$ satisfy $|R(\tau)| \leq 1$ for all $|\tau| \leq (n - 1)$. Further, the Barker property is preserved under the following transformations.

$$s(t) \rightarrow -s(t) \qquad s(t) \rightarrow (-1)^t s(t) \qquad \text{and} \qquad s(t) \rightarrow -s(n - 1 - t)$$

as well as under compositions of these transformations. Only the following Barker sequences are known:

$n =$	2	+ +
$n =$	3	+ + −
$n =$	4	+ + + −
$n =$	5	+ + + − +
$n =$	7	+ + + − − + −
$n =$	11	+ − + + − + + + − − −
$n =$	13	+ + + + + − − + + − + − +

The 11-chip Barker sequence is used. Thus, each data binary 1 is mapped into the sequence $\{+ - + + - + + + - - -\}$, and each binary 0 is mapped into the sequence $\{- + - - + - - - + + +\}$.

Important characteristic of Barker sequences are their robustness against interference and their insensitivity to multipath propagation.

Frequency-Hopping Spread Spectrum

Recall from Chapter 7 that a FH-SS system makes use of a multiple channels, with the signal hopping from one channel to another based on a pseudonoise sequence. In the case of the IEEE 802.11 scheme, 1-MHz channels are used. The number of channels available ranges from 23 in Japan to 70 in the United States.

The details of the hopping scheme are adjustable. For example, the minimum hop rate for the United States is 2.5 hops per second. The minimum hop distance in frequency is 6 MHz in North America and most of Europe and 5 MHz in Japan.

For modulation, the FH-SS scheme uses two-level Gaussian FSK for the 1-Mbps system. The bits zero and one are encoded as deviations from the current carrier frequency. For 2 Mbps, a four-level GFSK scheme is used, in which four different deviations from the center frequency define the four 2-bit combinations.

Infrared

The IEEE 802.11 infrared scheme is omnidirectional (Figure 13.6) rather than point to point. A range of up to 20 m is possible. The modulation scheme for the 1-Mbps data rate is known as 16-PPM (pulse position modulation). In this scheme, each group of 4 data bits is mapped into one of the 16-PPM symbols; each symbol is a string of 16 bits. Each 16-bit string consists of fifteen 0s and one binary 1. For the 2-Mbps data rate, each group of 2 data bits is mapped into one of four 4-bit sequences. Each sequence consists of three 0s and one binary 1. The actual transmission uses an intensity modulation scheme, in which the presence of a signal corresponds to a binary 1 and the absence of a signal corresponds to binary 0.

IEEE 802.11a

The IEEE 802.11a specification makes use of the 5-GHz band. Unlike the 2.4-GHz specifications, IEEE 802.11 does not use a spread spectrum scheme but rather uses orthogonal frequency division multiplexing (OFDM). Recall from Section 11.2 that OFDM, also called multicarrier modulation, uses multiple carrier signals at different frequencies, sending some of the bits on each channel. This is similar to FDM. However, in the case of OFDM, all of the subchannels are dedicated to a single data source.

The possible data rates for IEEE 802.11a are 6, 9, 12, 18, 24, 36, 48, and 54 Mbps. The system uses up to 52 subcarriers that are modulated using BPSK, QPSK, 16-QAM, or 64-QAM, depending on the rate required. Subcarrier frequency spacing is 0.3125 MHz. A convolutional code at a rate of 1/2, 2/3, or 3/4 provides forward error correction.

IEEE 802.11b

IEEE 802.11b is an extension of the IEEE 802.11 DS-SS scheme, providing data rates of 5.5 and 11 Mbps. The chipping rate is 11 MHz, which is the same as the original DS-SS scheme, thus providing the same occupied bandwidth. To achieve a higher data rate in the same bandwidth at the same chipping rate, a modulation scheme known as complementary code keying (CCK) is used.

The CCK modulation scheme is quite complex and is not examined in detail here. Figure 14.10 provides an overview of the scheme for the 11-Mbps rate. Input data are

Figure 14.10   11-Mbps CCK Modulation Scheme

treated in blocks of 8 bits at a rate of 1.375 MHz (8 bits/symbol $\times$ 1.375 MHz = 11 Mbps). Six of these bits are mapped into one of 64 codes sequences based on the use of the 8×8 Walsh matrix (Figure 7.17). The output of the mapping, plus the two additional bits, forms the input to a QPSK modulator.

14.5 RECOMMENDED READING AND WEB SITES

[OHAR99] is an excellent technical treatment of IEEE 802.11. [GEIE99] also provides detailed coverage of the IEEE 802.11 standards, and numerous case studies. [CROW97] is a good survey article on the 802.11 standards. Neither of the last two references covers IEEE 802.11a and IEEE 802.11b. [GEIE01] has a good discussion of IEEE 802.11a.

CROW97 Crow, B., et al. "IEEE 802.11 Wireless Local Area Networks." *IEEE Communications Magazine*, September 1997.

GEIE99 Geier, J. *Wireless LANs.* New York: Macmillan Technical Publishing, 1999.

GEIE01 Geier, J. "Enabling Fast Wireless Networks with OFDM." *Communications System Design*, February 2001. (www.csdmag.com)

OHAR99 Ohara, B., and Petrick, A. *IEEE 802.11 Handbook: A Designer's Companion.* New York: IEEE Press, 1999.

 Recommended Web sites:

- **The IEEE 802.11 Wireless LAN Working Group:** Contains working group documents plus discussion archives.
- **Wireless Ethernet Compatibility Alliance:** An industry group promoting the interoperability of 802.11 products with each other and with Ethernet.

14.6 KEY TERMS AND REVIEW QUESTIONS

Key Terms

access point (AP)	distribution system (DS)	open system authentication
Barker sequence	extended service set (ESS)	point coordination function (PCF)
basic service set (BSS)	logical link control (LLC)	shared key authentication
binary exponential backoff	MAC protocol data unit (MPDU)	wired equivalent privacy (WEP)
complementary code keying (CCK)	MAC service data unit (MSDU)	
coordination function	medium access control (MAC)	
distributed coordination function (DCF)		

Review Questions

1 List and briefly define the IEEE 802 protocol layers.
2 What is the difference between a MAC address and an LLC address?
3 List and briefly define LLC services.
4 What is the difference between an access point and a portal?
5 Is a distribution system a wireless network?
6 List and briefly define IEEE 802.11 services.
7 How is the concept of an association related to that of mobility?
8 What characteristics of a wireless LAN present unique security challenges not found in wired LANs?
9 Which form of authentication is more secure and why: open system authentication or shared key authentication?

CHAPTER 15

BLUETOOTH

Bluetooth[1] is an always-on, short-range radio hookup that resides on a microchip. It was initially developed by Swedish mobile-phone maker Ericsson in 1994 as a way to let laptop computers make calls over a mobile phone. Since then, several thousand companies have signed on to make Bluetooth the low-power short-range wireless standard for a wide range of devices. Industry observers expect Bluetooth to be installed in billions of devices by 2005 (*Business Week*, 18 September 2000).

The Bluetooth standards are published by an industry consortium known as the Bluetooth SIG (special interest group). This chapter provides an overview.

15.1 OVERVIEW

The concept behind Bluetooth is to provide a universal short-range wireless capability. Using the 2.4-GHz band, available globally for unlicensed low-power uses, two Bluetooth devices within 10 m of each other can share up to 720 kbps of capacity. Bluetooth is intended to support an open-ended list of applications, including data (e.g., schedules and telephone numbers), audio, graphics, and even video. For example, audio devices can include headsets, cordless and standard phones, home stereos, and digital MP3 players. Bluetooth can provide consumers with the ability to do the following:

- Make calls from a wireless headset connected remotely to a cell phone.
- Eliminate cables linking computers to printers, keyboards, and the mouse.
- Hook up MP3 players wirelessly to other machines to download music.
- Set up home networks so that a couch potato can remotely monitor air conditioning, the oven, and childrens' Internet surfing.
- Call home from a remote location to turn appliances on and off, set the alarm, and monitor activity.

Bluetooth Applications

Bluetooth is designed to operate in an environment of many users. Up to eight devices can communicate in a small network called a **piconet**. Ten of these piconets can coexist in the same coverage range of the Bluetooth radio. To provide security, each link is encoded and protected against eavesdropping and interference.

Bluetooth provides support for three general application areas using short-range wireless connectivity:

- **Data and voice access points:** Bluetooth facilitates real-time voice and data transmissions by providing effortless wireless connection of portable and stationary communications devices.

---

[1]The name comes from King Harald Blaatand (Bluetooth) of Denmark, who lived in the tenth century A.D. Unlike his Viking counterparts, King Harald had dark hair (thus the name Bluetooth, meaning a dark complexion) and is credited with bringing Christianity to Scandiavia along with uniting Denmark and Norway. The blue logo that identifies Bluetooth-enabled devices is derived from the runes of his initials.

- **Cable replacement:** Bluetooth eliminates the need for numerous, often proprietary, cable attachments for connection of practically any kind of communication device. Connections are instant and are maintained even when devices are not within line of sight. The range of each radio is approximately 10 m, but can be extended to 100 m with an optional amplifier.
- **Ad hoc networking:** A device equipped with a Bluetooth radio can establish instant connection to another Bluetooth radio as soon as it comes into range.

Table 15.1 gives some examples of Bluetooth uses.

Bluetooth Standards Documents

The Bluetooth standards present a formidable bulk: well over 1500 pages, divided into two groups: core and profile. The **core specifications** describe the details of the various layers of the Bluetooth protocol architecture, from the radio interface to link control. Related topics are covered, such as interoperability with related technologies, testing requirements, and a definition of various Bluetooth timers and their associated values.

Table 15.1 Bluetooth User Scenarios [HAAR98]

Three-in-one phone When you are in the office, your phone functions as an intercom (no telephony charge). At home, it functions as a cordless phone (fixed-line charge). When you are on the move, it functions as a mobile phone (cellular charge).	**Briefcase e-mail** Access e-mail while your portable PC is still in the briefcase. When your PC receives an e-mail message, you are notified by your mobile phone. You can also use the phone to browse incoming e-mail and read messages.
Internet bridge Use your portable PC to surf the Internet anywhere, whether you are connected wirelessly through a mobile phone (cellular) or through a wired connection (PSTN, ISDN, LAN, xDSL).	**Delayed messages** Compose e-mail on your PC while you are on an airplane. When you land and are allowed to switch on your mobile phone, the messages are sent immediately.
Interactive conference In meetings and at conferences, you can share information instantly with other participants. You can also operate a projector remotely without wire connectors.	**Automatic synchronization** Automatically synchronize your desktop computer, portable PC, notebook, and mobile phone. As soon as you enter the office, the address list and calendar in your notebook automatically updates the files on your desktop computer or vice versa.
The ultimate headset Connect a headset to your mobile PC or to any wired connection and free your hands for more important tasks at the office or in your car.	**Instant digital postcard** Connect a camera cordlessly to your mobile phone or to any wire-bound connection. Add comments from you mobile phone, a notebook, or portable PC and send them instantly.
Portable PC speakerphone Connect cordless headsets to your portable PC, and use it as a speaker phone regardless of whether you are in the office, your car, or at home.	**Cordless desktop** Connect your desktop/laptop computer cordlessly to printers, scanner, keyboard, mouse, and the LAN.

The **profile specifications** are concerned with the use of Bluetooth technology to support various applications. Each profile specification discusses the use of the technology defined in the core specifications to implement a particular usage model. The profile specification includes a description of which aspects of the core specifications are mandatory, optional, and not applicable. The purpose of a profile specification is to define a standard of interoperability, so that products from different vendors that claim to support a given usage model will work together. In general terms, profile specifications fall into one of two categories: cable replacement or wireless audio. The cable replacement profiles provide a convenient means for logically connecting devices in proximity to one another and for exchanging data. For example, when two devices first come within range of one another, they can automatically query each other for a common profile. This might then cause the end users of the device to be alerted, or cause some automatic data exchange to take place. The wireless audio profiles are concerned with establishing short-range voice connections.

Figure 15.1, from [WILS00], provides a useful guide for a developer in wading through the many documents with a particular application in mind. The reading list begins with coverage of some essential core specifications plus the general access profile. This profile is one of a number of profiles that serve as a foundation for other profiles and do not specify independently usable functionality. The general access profile specifies how the Bluetooth baseband architecture, defined in the core specifications, is to be used between devices that implement one or multiple profiles. Following a basic set of documents, the reading list splits along two lines, depending on whether the reader's interest is in cable replacement or wireless audio.

Protocol Architecture

Bluetooth is defined as a layered protocol architecture (Figure 15.2) consisting of core protocols, cable replacement and telephony control protocols, and adopted protocols.

The **core protocols** form a five-layer stack consisting of the following elements:

- **Radio:** Specifies details of the air interface, including frequency, the use of frequency hopping, modulation scheme, and transmit power.
- **Baseband:** Concerned with connection establishment within a piconet, addressing, packet format, timing, and power control.
- **Link manager protocol (LMP):** Responsible for link setup between Bluetooth devices and ongoing link management. This includes security aspects such as authentication and encryption, plus the control and negotiation of baseband packet sizes.
- **Logical link control and adaptation protocol (L2CAP):** Adapts upper-layer protocols to the baseband layer. L2CAP provides both connectionless and connection-oriented services.
- **Service discovery protocol (SDP):** Device information, services, and the characteristics of the services can be queried to enable the establishment of a connection between two or more Bluetooth devices.

RFCOMM is the **cable replacement protocol** included in the Bluetooth specification. RFCOMM presents a virtual serial port that is designed to make replacement of cable technologies as transparent as possible. Serial ports are one of the

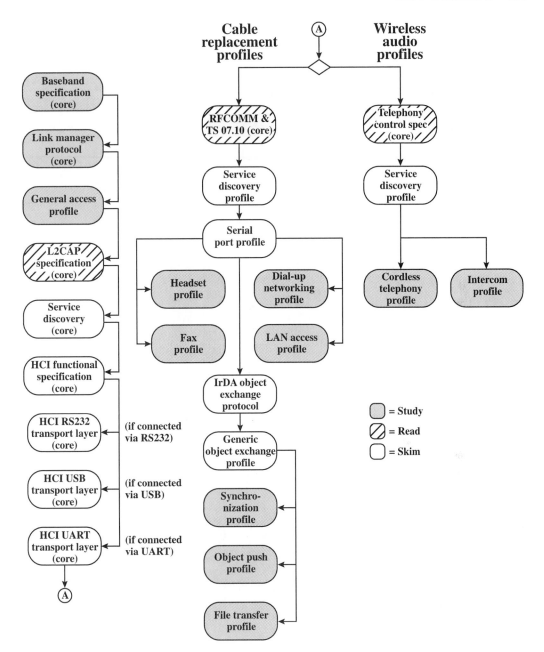

Figure 15.1   Bluetooth Reading List

most common types of communications interfaces used with computing and communications devices. Hence, RFCOMM enables the replacement of serial port cables with the minimum of modification of existing devices. RFCOMM provides for binary data transport and emulates EIA-232 control signals over the Bluetooth baseband layer. EIA-232 (formerly known as RS-232) is a widely used serial port interface standard.

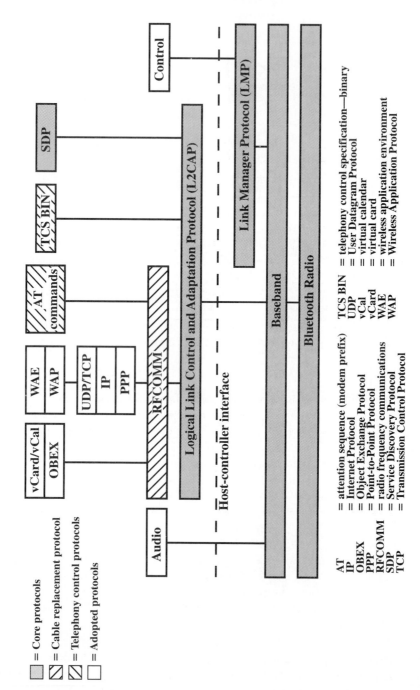

Figure 15.2 Bluetooth Protocol Stack

▨	= Core protocols
▨	= Cable replacement protocol
▨	= Telephony control protocols
▢	= Adopted protocols

AT	=	attention sequence (modem prefix)
IP	=	Internet Protocol
OBEX	=	Object Exchange Protocol
PPP	=	Point-to-Point Protocol
RFCOMM	=	radio frequency communications
SDP	=	Service Discovery Protocol
TCP	=	Transmission Control Protocol

TCS BIN	=	telephony control specification—binary
UDP	=	User Datagram Protocol
vCal	=	virtual calendar
vCard	=	virtual card
WAE	=	wireless application environment
WAP	=	Wireless Application Protocol

Bluetooth specifies a **telephony control protocol**. TCS BIN (telephony control specification—binary) is a bit-oriented protocol that defines the call control signaling for the establishment of speech and data calls between Bluetooth devices. In addition, it defines mobility management procedures for handling groups of Bluetooth TCS devices.

The **adopted protocols** are defined in specifications issued by other standards-making organizations and incorporated into the overall Bluetooth architecture. The Bluetooth strategy is to invent only necessary protocols and use existing standards whenever possible. The adopted protocols include the following:

- **PPP:** The point-to-point protocol is an Internet standard protocol for transporting IP datagrams over a point-to-point link.
- **TCP/UDP/IP:** These are the foundation protocols of the TCP/IP protocol suite (described in Chapter 4).
- **OBEX:** The object exchange protocol is a session-level protocol developed by the Infrared Data Association (IrDA) for the exchange of objects. OBEX provides functionality similar to that of HTTP, but in a simpler fashion. It also provides a model for representing objects and operations. Examples of content formats transferred by OBEX are vCard and vCalendar, which provide the format of an electronic business card and personal calendar entries and scheduling information, respectively.
- **WAE/WAP:** Bluetooth incorporates the wireless application environment and the wireless application protocol into its architecture (described in Chapter 12).

Usage Models

A number of usage models are defined in Bluetooth profile documents. In essence, a usage model is set of protocols that implement a particular Bluetooth-based application. Each profile defines the protocols and protocol features supporting a particular usage model. Figure 15.3, taken from [METT99], illustrates the highest-priority usage models. These are as follows:

- **File transfer:** The file transfer usage model supports the transfer of directories, files, documents, images, and streaming media formats. This usage model also includes the capability to browse folders on a remote device.
- **Internet bridge:** With this usage model, a PC is wirelessly connected to a mobile phone or cordless modem to provide dial-up networking and fax capabilities. For dial-up networking, AT commands are used to control the mobile phone or modem, and another protocol stack (e.g., PPP over RFCOMM) is used for data transfer. For fax transfer, the fax software operates directly over RFCOMM.
- **LAN access:** This usage model enables devices on a piconet to access a LAN. Once connected, a device functions as if it were directly connected (wired) to the LAN.
- **Synchronization:** This model provides a device-to-device synchronization of PIM (personal information management) information, such as phone book, calendar, message, and note information. IrMC (Ir mobile communications) is an IrDA protocol that provides a client/server capability for transferring updated PIM information from one device to another.

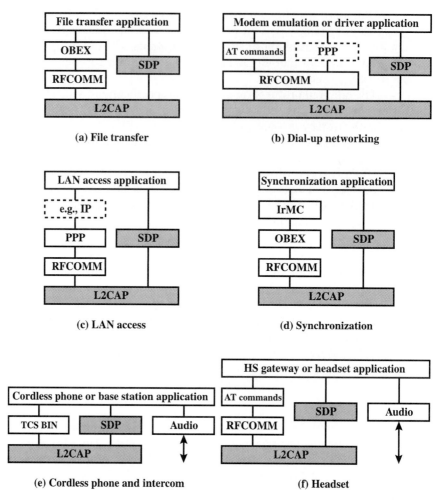

Figure 15.3 Bluetooth Usage Models

- **Three-in-one phone:** Telephone handsets that implement this usage model may act as a cordless phone connecting to a voice base station, as an intercom device for connecting to other telephones, and as a cellular phone.
- **Headset:** The headset can act as a remote device's audio input and output interface.

Piconets and Scatternets

As was mentioned, the basic unit of networking in Bluetooth is a **piconet**, consisting of a master and from one to seven active slave devices. The radio designated as the master makes the determination of the channel (frequency-hopping sequence) and phase (timing offset, i.e., when to transmit) that shall be used by all devices on this piconet. The radio designated as master makes this determination using its own device address as a parameter, while the slave devices must tune to the same channel and phase. A slave may only communicate with the master and may only communicate when granted permission by the master. A device in one piconet may also exist as part of another piconet and may function as either a slave or master in each piconet (Figure 15.4). This form of overlapping is called a **scatternet**. Figure 15.5, based on one in [HAAR00a], contrasts the piconet/scatternet architecture with other forms of wireless networks.

The advantage of the piconet/scatternet scheme is that it allows many devices to share the same physical area and make efficient use of the bandwidth. A Bluetooth system uses a frequency-hopping scheme with a carrier spacing of 1 MHz. Typically, up to 80 different frequencies are used for a total bandwidth of 80 MHz. If frequency hopping were not used, then a single channel would correspond to a single 1-MHz band. With frequency hopping a logical channel is defined by the frequency-hopping sequence. At any given time, the bandwidth available is 1 MHz, with a maximum of eight devices sharing the bandwidth. Different logical channels (different hopping sequences) can simultaneously share the same 80-MHz bandwidth. Collisions will occur when devices in different piconets, on different logical channels, happen to use the same hop frequency at the same time. As the number of piconets in an area increases, the number of collisions increases, and performance degrades. In summary, the physical area and total bandwidth are shared by the scatternet. The logical channel and data transfer are shared by a piconet.

Figure 15.4 Master/Slave Relationships

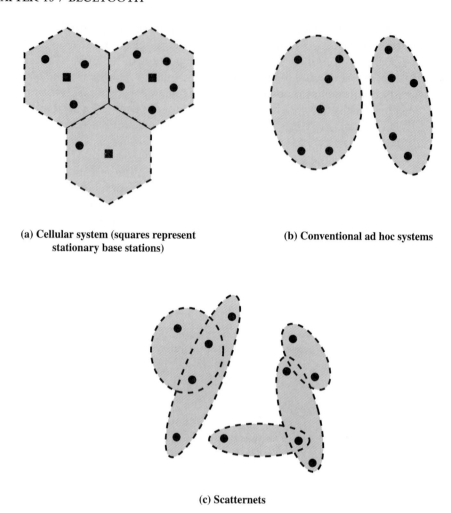

(a) Cellular system (squares represent stationary base stations)

(b) Conventional ad hoc systems

(c) Scatternets

Figure 15.5 Wireless Network Configurations

15.2 RADIO SPECIFICATION

The Bluetooth radio specification is a short document that gives the basic details of radio transmission for Bluetooth devices. Some of the key parameters are summarized in Table 15.2.

One aspect of the radio specification is a definition of three classes of transmitters based on output power:

- **Class 1:** Outputs 100 mW (+20 dBm) for maximum range, with a minimum of 1 mW (0 dBm). In this class, power control is mandatory, ranging from 4 to 20 dBm. This mode provides the greatest distance.

Table 15.2   Bluetooth Radio and Baseband Parameters

Topology	Up to 7 simultaneous links in a logical star
Modulation	GFSK
Peak data rate	1 Mbps
RF bandwidth	220 kHz (-3 dB), 1 MHz (-20 dB)
RF band	2.4 GHz, ISM band
RF carriers	23/79
Carrier spacing	1 MHz
Transmit power	0.1 W
Piconet access	FH-TDD-TDMA
Frequency hop rate	1600 hops/s
Scatternet access	FH-CDMA

- **Class 2:** Outputs 2.4 mW ($+4$ dBm) at maximum, with a minimum of 0.25 mW (-6 dBm). Power control is optional.
- **Class 3:** Lowest power. Nominal output is 1 mW.

Bluetooth makes use of the 2.4-GHz band within the ISM (Industrial, Scientific, and Medical) band. In most countries, the bandwidth is sufficient to define 79 1-MHz physical channels (Table 15.3). Power control is used to keep the devices from emitting any more RF power than necessary. The power control algorithm is implemented using the link management protocol between a master and the slaves in a piconet.

Modulation for Bluetooth is Gaussian FSK, with a binary one represented by a positive frequency deviation and a binary zero represented by a negative frequency deviation from the center frequency. The minimum deviation is 115 kHz.

Table 15.3   International Bluetooth Frequency Allocations

Area	Regulatory Range	RF Channels
U.S., most of Europe, and most other countries	2.4 to 2.4835 GHz	$f = 2.402 + n$ MHz, $n = 0,..., 78$
Japan	2.471 to 2.497 GHz	$f = 2.473 + n$ MHz, $n = 0,..., 22$
Spain	2.445 to 2.475 GHz	$f = 2.449 + n$ MHz, $n = 0,..., 22$
France	2.4465 to 2.4835 GHz	$f = 2.454 + n$ MHz, $n = 0,..., 22$

15.3 BASEBAND SPECIFICATION

One of the most complex of the Bluetooth documents is the baseband specification. In this section we provide an overview of the key elements.

Frequency Hopping

Frequency hopping (FH) in Bluetooth serves two purposes:

1. It provides resistance to interference and multipath effects.
2. It provides a form of multiple access among co-located devices in different piconets.

The FH scheme works as follows. The total bandwidth is divided into 79 (in almost all countries) **physical channels**, each of bandwidth 1 MHz. FH occurs by jumping from one physical channel to another in a pseudorandom sequence. The same hopping sequence is shared by all of the devices on a single piconet; we will refer to this as an **FH channel**.[2] The hop rate is 1600 hops per second, so that each physical channel is occupied for a duration of 0.625 ms. Each 0.625-ms time period is referred to as a slot, and these are numbered sequentially.

Bluetooth radios communicate using a time division duplex (TDD) discipline. Recall from Chapter 11 that TDD is a link transmission technique in which data are transmitted in one direction at a time, with transmission alternating between the two directions. Because more than two devices share the piconet medium, the access technique is TDMA. Thus piconet access can be characterized as FH-TDD-TDMA. Figure 15.6 illustrates the technique. In the figure, k denotes the slot number, and $f(k)$ is the physical channel selected during slot period k.

Transmission of a packet starts at the beginning of a slot. Packet lengths requiring 1, 3, or 5 slots are allowed. For multislot packets, the radio remains at the same frequency until the entire packet has been sent (Figure 15.7). In the next slot after the

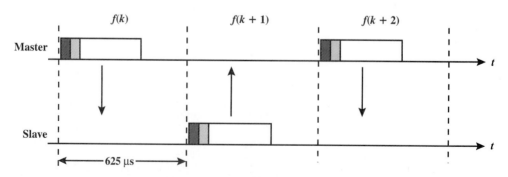

Figure 15.6 Frequency-Hop Time Division Duplex

---

[2]The term FH *channel* is not used in the Bluetooth documents but is introduced here for clarity.

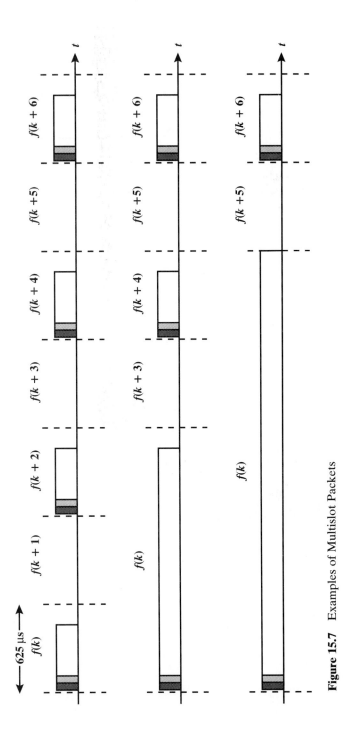

Figure 15.7 Examples of Multislot Packets

multislot packet, the radio returns to the frequency required for its hopping sequence, so that during transmission, two or four hop frequencies have been skipped.

Using TDD prevents crosstalk between transmit and receive operations in the radio transceiver, which is essential if a one-chip implementation is desired. Note that because transmission and reception take place at different time slots, different frequencies are used.

The FH sequence is determined by the master in a piconet and is a function of the master's Bluetooth address. A rather complex mathematical operation involving permutations and exclusive-OR (XOR) operations is used to generate a pseudo-random hop sequence.

Because different piconets in the same area will have different masters, they will use different hop sequences. Thus, most of the time, transmissions on two devices on different piconets in the same area will be on different physical channels. Occasionally, two piconets will use the same physical channel during the same time slot, causing a collision and lost data. However, because this will happen infrequently, it is readily accommodated with forward error correction and error detection/ARQ techniques. Thus, a form of code division multiple access (CDMA) is achieved between devices on different piconets in the same scatternet; this is referred to as FH-CDMA.

Physical Links

Two types of links can be established between a master and a slave:

- **Synchronous connection oriented (SCO):** Allocates a fixed bandwidth between a point-to-point connection involving the master and a single slave. The master maintains the SCO link by using reserved slots at regular intervals. The basic unit of reservation is two consecutive slots (one in each transmission direction). The master can support up to three simultaneous SCO links while a slave can support two or three SCO links. SCO packets are never retransmitted.

- **Asynchronous connectionless (ACL):** A point-to-multipoint link between the master and all the slaves in the piconet. In slots not reserved for SCO links, the master can exchange packets with any slave on a per-slot basis, including a slave already engaged in an SCO link. Only a single ACL link can exist. For most ACL packets, packet retransmssion is applied.

SCO links are used primarily to exchange time-bounded data requiring guaranteed data rate but without guaranteed delivery. One example, used in a number of Bluetooth profiles, is digitally encoded audio data with built-in tolerance to lost data. The guaranteed data rate is achieved through the reservation of a particular number of slots.

ACL links provide a packet-switched style of connection. No bandwidth reservation is possible and delivery may be guaranteed through error detection and retransmission. A slave is permitted to return an ACL packet in the slave-to-master slot if and only if it has been addressed in the preceding master-to-slave slot. For ACL links, 1-slot, 3-slot, and 5-slot packets have been defined. Data can be sent either unprotected (although ARQ can be used at a higher layer) or protected with a 2/3 forward error correction code. The maximum data rate that can be achieved is with a 5-slot unprotected packet with asymmetric capacity allocation, resulting in 721 kbps in the forward direction and 57.6 kbps in the reverse direction. Table 15.4 summarizes all of the possibilities.

Packets

The packet format for all Bluetooth packets is shown in Figure 15.8. It consists of three fields:

- **Access code:** Used for timing synchronization, offset compensation, paging, and inquiry
- **Header:** Used to identify packet type and to carry protocol control information
- **Payload:** If present, contains user voice or data and, in most cases, a payload header

Access Code

There are three types of access codes:

- **Channel access code (CAC):** Identifies a piconet (unique for a piconet)
- **Device access code (DAC):** Used for paging and its subsequent responses
- **Inquiry access code (IAC):** Used for inquiry purposes

An access code consists of a preamble, a sync word, and a trailer. The **preamble** is used for DC compensation. It consists of the pattern 0101 if the least significant (leftmost) bit in the sync word is 0 and the pattern 1010 if the least significant bit in the sync word is 1. Similarly, the **trailer** is 0101 if the most significant bit (rightmost) of the sync word is 1 and 1010 if the most significant bit is 0.

Table 15.4   Achievable Data Rates on the ACL Link

Type	Symmetric (kbps)	Asymmetric (kbps)	
DM1	108.8	108.8	108.8
DH1	172.8	172.8	172.8
DM3	256.0	384.0	54.4
DH3	384.0	576.0	86.4
DM5	286.7	477.8	36.3
DH5	432.6	721.0	57.6

DMx = x-slot FEC-encoded
DHx = x-slot unprotected

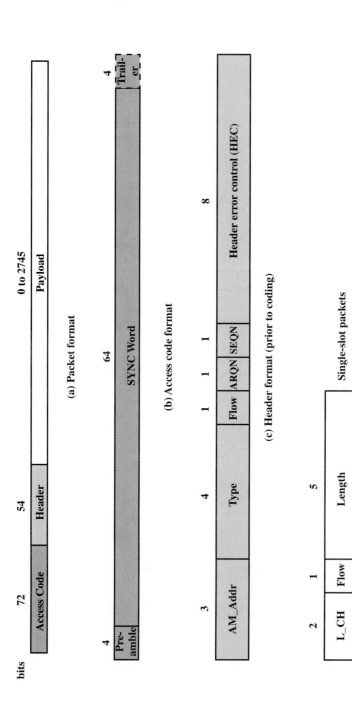

bits

(a) Packet format

72	54	0 to 2745
Access Code	Header	Payload

(b) Access code format

4	64	4
Pre-amble	SYNC Word	Trail-er

(c) Header format (prior to coding)

3	4	1	1	1	8
AM_Addr	Type	Flow	ARQN	SEQN	Header error control (HEC)

(d) Data payload header format

Single-slot packets

2	1	5
L_CH	Flow	Length

Multislot packets

2	1	9	4
L_CH	Flow	Length	Undefined

Figure 15.8 Bluetooth Baseband Formats

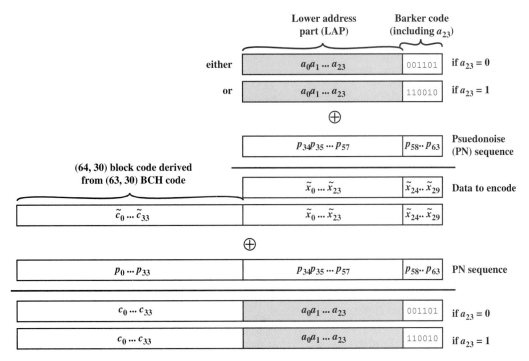

Figure 15.9 Construction of Sync Word

The 64-bit **sync word** consists of three components (Figure 15.9) and is worth examining in some detail. Each Bluetooth device is assigned a globally unique 48-bit address. The 24 least significant bits are referred to as the lower address part (LAP) and are used in forming the sync word. For a CAC, the LAP of the master is used; for a DAC, the LAP of the paged unit. There are two different IACs. The general IAC (GIAC) is a general inquiry message used to discover which Bluetooth devices are in range, and for this a special reserved value of LAP is available. A dedicated IAC (DIAC) is common for a dedicated group of Bluetooth units that share a common characteristic, and a previously defined LAP corresponding to that characteristic is used.

Using the appropriate LAP, the sync word is formed as follows:

1. To the LAP, append the 6 bits 001101 if the most significant bit (MSB) of the LAP is 0, and append 110010 if the MSB is 1. This forms a 7-bit Barker sequence.[3] The purpose of including a Barker sequence is to further improve the autocorrelation properties of the sync word.

2. Generate a 64-bit pseudonoise (PN) sequence, $p_0, p_1, \ldots, p_{63}$. The sequence is defined by the equation $P(X) = 1 + X + X^3$, and can be implemented with a 6-bit linear feedback shift register. The seed value for the PN sequence is 100000.[4]

---

[3]See Section 14.4 for a discussion of Barker sequences.
[4]See Section 7.5 for a discussion of PN sequence generation and generating equations [e.g., Equation (7.9)].

3. Take the bitwise XOR of $p_{34}, p_{35}, \ldots, p_{63}$ and the 30-bit sequence produced in step 1. This "scrambles" the information, removing unwanted regularities.

4. Generate a 34-bit error-correcting code for the scrambled information block and place this at the beginning to form a 64-bit codeword. Thus, we have a (64, 30) code. To generate this code, start with a (63, 30) BCH code.[5] Then define the generator polynomial $g(X) = (1 + X)g'(X)$, where $g'(X)$ is the generator polynomial for the (63, 30) BCH code. This produces the desired 34-bit code.

5. Take the bitwise XOR of $p_0, p_a, \ldots, p_{63}$ and the 64-bit sequence produced in step 4. This step descrambles the information part of the codeword so that the original LAP and Barker sequence are transmitted. The step also scrambles the block code.

The scrambling of the information part of the codeword in step 3 is designed to strengthen the error-correcting properties of the block code. The subsequent descrambling enables the receiver to recover the LAP easily. In the words of the specification, the scrambling of the 34-bit error code removes the cyclic properties of the underlying code. This might give better transmission spectral qualities and also improve autocorrelation properties.

Packet Header

The header format for all Bluetooth packets is shown in Figure 15.8c. It consists of six fields:

- **AM_ADDR:** Recall that a piconet includes at most seven active slaves. The 3-bit AM_Addr contains the "active mode" address (temporary address assigned to this slave in this piconet) of one of the slaves. A transmission from the master to a slave contains that slave's address; a transmission from a slave contains its address. The 0 value is reserved for a broadcast from the master to all slaves in the piconet.

- **Type:** Identifies the type of packet (Table 15.5). Four type codes are reserved for control packets common to both SCO and ACL links. The remaining packet types are used to convey user information. For SCO links, the HV1, HV2, HV3 packets each carry 64-kbps voice. The difference is the amount of error protection provided, which dictates how frequently a packet must be sent to maintain the 64-kbps data rate. The DV packet carries both voice and data. For ACL links, 6 different packets are defined. These, together with the DM1 packet, carry user data with different amounts of error protection and different data rates (Table 15.4). There is another packet type common to both physical links; it consists of only the access code, with a fixed length of 68 bits (does not include trailer). This is referred to as the ID packet and is used in the inquiry and access procedures.

---

[5] See Section 8.2 for a discussion of BCH codes.

Table 15.5 Bluetooth Packet Types

Type Code	Physical Link	Name	Number of Slots	Description
0000	Common	NULL	1	Has no payload. Used to return link information to the source regarding the success of the previous transmission (ARQN), or the status of the RX buffer (FLOW). Not acknowledged.
0001	Common	POLL	1	Has no payload. Used by master to poll a slave. Acknowledged.
0010	Common	FHS	1	Special control packet for revealing device address and the clock of the sender. Used in page master response, inquiry response, and frequency hop synchronization. 2/3 FEC encoded.
0011	Common	DM1	1	Supports control messages and can also carry user data. 16-bit CRC. 2/3 FEC encoded.
0101	SCO	HV1	1	Carries 10 information bytes; typically used for 64-kbps voice. 1/3 FEC encoded.
0110	SCO	HV2	1	Carries 20 information bytes; typically used for 64-kbps voice. 2/3 FEC encoded.
0111	SCO	HV3	1	Carries 30 information bytes; typically used for 64-kbps voice. Not FEC encoded.
1000	SCO	DV	1	Combined data (150 bits) and voice (50 bits) packet. Data field 2/3 FEC encoded.
0100	ACL	DH1	1	Carries 28 information bytes plus 16-bit CRC. Not FEC encoded. Typically used for high-speed data.
1001	ACL	AUX1	1	Carries 30 information bytes with no CRC or FEC. Typically used for high-speed data.
1010	ACL	DM3	3	Carries 123 information bytes plus 16-bit CRC. 2/3 FEC encoded.
1011	ACL	DH3	3	Carries 185 information bytes plus 16-bit CRC. Not FEC encoded.
1110	ACL	DM5	5	Carries 226 information bytes plus 16-bit CRC. 2/3 FEC encoded.
1111	ACL	DH5	5	Carries 341 information bytes plus 16-bit CRC. Not FEC encoded.

- **Flow:** Provides a 1-bit flow control mechanism for ACL traffic only. When a packet with Flow = 0 is received, the station receiving the packet must temporarily halt the transmission of ACL packets on this link. When a packet with Flow = 1 is received, transmission may resume.
- **ARQN:** Provides a 1-bit acknowledgment mechanism for ACL traffic protected by a CRC (Table 15.5). If the reception was successful, an ACK (ARQN=1) is returned; otherwise a NAK (ARQN=0) is returned. When no

return message regarding acknowledge is received, a NAK is assumed implicitly. If a NAK is received, the relevant packet is retransmitted.

- **SEQN:** Provides a 1-bit sequential numbering schemes. Transmitted packets are alternately labeled with a 1 or 0. This is required to filter out retransmissions at the destination; if a retransmission occurs due to a failing ACK, the destination receives the same packet twice.
- **Header error control (HEC):** An 8-bit error detection code used to protect the packet header.

Payload Format

For some packet types, the baseband specification defines a format for the payload field. For voice payloads, no header is defined. For all of the ACL packets and for the data portion of the SCO DV packet, a header is defined. For data payloads, the payload format consists of three fields:

- **Payload header:** An 8-bit header is defined for single-slot packets, and a 16-bit header is defined for multislot packets.
- **Payload body:** Contains user information.
- **CRC:** A 16-bit CRC code is used on all data payloads except the AUX1 packet.

The payload header, when present, consists of three fields (Figure 15.8d):

- **L_CH:** Identifies the logical channel (described subsequently). The options are LMP message (11); an unfragmented L2CAP message or the start of a fragmented L2CAP message (10); the continuation of a fragmented L2CAP message (01); or other (00).
- **Flow:** Used to control flow at the L2CAP level. This is the same on/off mechanism provided by the Flow field in the packet header for ACL traffic.
- **Length:** The number of bytes of data in the payload, excluding the payload header and CRC.

Error Correction

At the baseband level, Bluetooth makes use of three error correction schemes:

- 1/3 rate FEC (forward error correction)
- 2/3 rate FEC
- ARQ (automatic repeat request)

These error correction schemes are designed to satisfy competing requirements. The error correction scheme must be adequate to cope with the inherently unreliable wireless link but must also be streamlined and efficient.

The **1/3 rate FEC** is used on the 18-bit packet header and also for the voice field in an HV1 packet. The scheme simply involves sending three copies of each bit. A majority logic is used: Each received triple of bits is mapped into whichever bit is in the majority.

The **2/3 rate FEC** is used in all DM packets, in the data field of the DV packet, in the FHS packet, and in the HV2 packet. The encoder is a form of Hamming code with parameters (15, 10). This code can correct all single errors and detect all double errors in each codeword.

The **ARQ scheme** is used with DM and DH packets, and the data field of DV packets. The scheme is similar to ARQ schemes used in data link control protocols (Section 8.4). Recall that ARQ schemes have the following elements:

- **Error detection:** The destination detects errors and discards packets that are in error. Error detection is achieved with a CRC error-detecting code supplemented with the FEC code.
- **Positive acknowledgment:** The destination returns a positive acknowledgment to successfully received, error-free packets.
- **Retransmission after timeout:** The source retransmits a packet that has not been acknowledged after a predetermined amount of time.
- **Negative acknowledgment and retransmission:** The destination returns a negative acknowledgment to packets in which an error is detected. The source retransmits such packets.

Bluetooth uses what is referred to as a *fast ARQ* scheme, which takes advantage of the fact that a master and slave communicate in alternate time slots. Figure 15.10 illustrates the technique. When a station receives a packet, it determines if an error has occurred using a 16-bit CRC. If so, the ARQN bit in the header set to 0 (NAK); if no error is detected, then ARQN is set to 1 (ACK). When a station receives a NAK, it retransmits the same packet as it sent in the preceding slot, using the same 1-bit SEQN in the packet header. With this technique, a sender is notified in the next time slot if a transmission has failed and, if so, can retransmit. The use

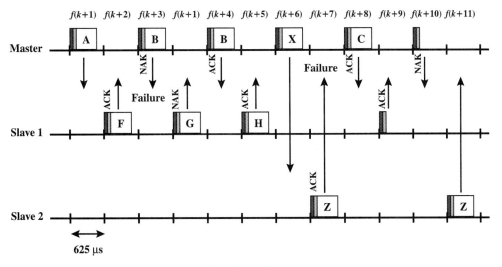

Figure 15.10 An Example of Retransmission Operation

of 1-bit sequence numbers and immediate packet retransmission minimizes over-head and maximizes responsiveness.

Figure 15.11 shows the ARQ mechanism in more detail. On reception of a packet (Figure 15.11a), the device first checks that the header is valid, using the HEC; if not the packet is rejected and ARQN is set to NAK in the next time slot. Then the device does an address match and checks whether this is the type of packet that uses the ARQ mechanisms. Having passed these tests, the device next checks whether this is a new sequence number (SEQN) or the same as the last SEQN. If the SEQNs are the same, then this is a retransmission, which is ignored. If the SEQN is new, then the device checks the CRC. If no error is detected, the next outgoing packet has ARQN = ACK, and if an error is detected, the next outgoing packet has ARQN = NAK.

On the transmit side (Figure 15.11b), the next DM, DH, or DV packet to be transmitted is determined by the value of the immediately preceding incoming ARQN. So long as ACKs are received, the device sends out new payload, alter-nating SEQN values between 0 and 1. If a NAK or no acknowledgment at all is received, the device will retransmit the old payload repeatedly until an ACK is received or until some threshold is reached, at which time the old payload is flushed from the transmit buffer and a new payload is transmitted.

Logical Channels

Bluetooth defines five types of logical data channels designted to carry different types of payload traffic.

- **Link control (LC):** Used to manage the flow of packets over the link interface. The LC channel is mapped onto the packet header. This channel carries low-level link control information like ARQ, flow control, and payload character-ization. The LC channel is carried in every packet except in the ID packet, which has no packet header.
- **Link manager (LM):** Transports link management information between par-ticipating stations. This logical channel supports LMP traffic and can be car-ried over either an SCO or ACL link.
- **User asynchronous (UA):** Carries asynchronous user data. This channel is normally carried over the ACL link but may be carried in a DV packet on the SCO link.
- **User isochronous (UI):** Carries isochronous user data.[6] This channel is nor-mally carried over the ACL link but may be carried in a DV packet on the SCO link. At the baseband level, the UI channel is treated the same way as a UA channel. Timing to provide isochronous properties is provided at a higher layer.
- **User synchronous (US):** Carries synchronous user data. This channel is car-ried over the SCO link.

---

[6]The term *isochronous* refers to blocks of data that recur with known periodic timing.

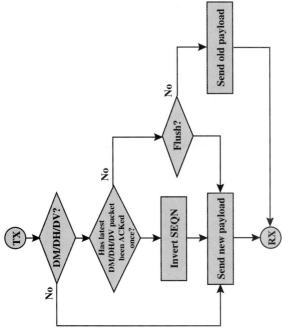

(b) Retransmit filtering for packets with CRC.

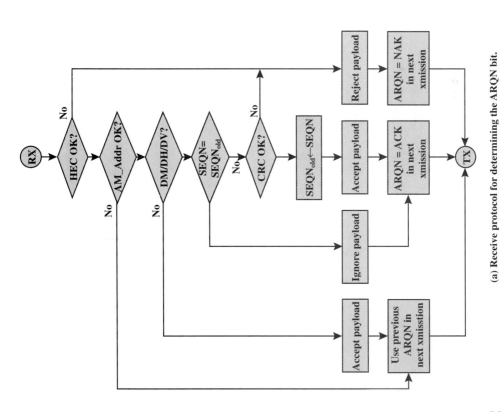

(a) Receive protocol for determining the ARQN bit.

Figure 15.11 Bluetooth ARQ Scheme

501

Channel Control

The operation of a piconet can be understood in terms of the states of operation during link establishment and maintenance (Figure 15.12). There are two major states:

- **Standy:** The default state. This is a low-power state in which only the native clock is running.
- **Connection:** The device is connected to a piconet as a master or a slave.

In addition, there are seven interim substates that are used to add new slaves to a piconet. To move from one state to the other, either commands from the Bluetooth link manager are used or internal signals in the link controller are used. The substates are as follows:

- **Page:** Device has issued a page. Used by the master to activate and connect to a slave. Master sends page message by transmitting slave's device access code (DAC) in different hop channels.
- **Page scan:** Device is listening for a page with its own DAC.

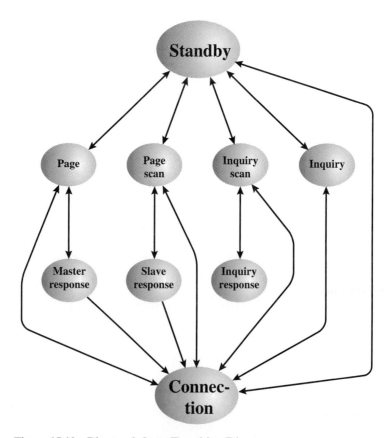

Figure 15.12 Bluetooth State Transition Diagram

- **Master response:** A device acting as a master receives a page response from a slave. The device can now enter the connection state or return to the page state to page for other slaves.
- **Slave response:** A device acting as a slave responds to a page from a master. If connection setup succeeds, the device enters the connection state; otherwise it returns to the page scan state.
- **Inquiry:** Device has issued an inquiry, to find the identity of the devices within range.
- **Inquiry scan:** Device is listening for an inquiry.
- **Inquiry response:** A device that has issued an inquiry receives an inquiry response.

Inquiry Procedure

The first step in establishing a piconet is for a potential master to identify devices in range that wish to participate in the piconet. A device begins an inquiry procedure for this purpose under the impetus of a user or application on the device. The inquiry procedure begins when the potential master transmits an ID packet with an inquiry access code (IAC), which is a code common to all Bluetooth devices. Recall that the ID packet has no header and no payload.

Of the 79 radio carriers, 32 are considered wake-up carriers. The master broadcasts the IAC over each of the 32 wake-up carriers in turn. This occurs in the Inquiry state (Figure 15.12). Meanwhile, devices in the Standby state periodically enter the Inquiry Scan state to search for IAC messages on the wake-up carriers. When a device receives the inquiry, it enters the Inquiry Response state and returns an FHS packet (Table 15.5) containing its device address and timing information required by the master to initiate a connection. The master does not respond to the FHS packet and may remain in the Inquiry state until it is satisfied that all radios have been found.

Once a device has responded to an Inquiry, it moves to the page scan state to await a page from the master in order to establish a connection. However, if a collision occurred in the Inquiry Response phase (two or more devices simultaneously respond to an inquiry), no page will be received and the device may need to return to the Inquiry Scan state to attempt another inquiry and response.[7]

Page Procedure

Once the master has found devices within its range, it is able to establish connections to each device, setting up a piconet. For each device to be paged, the master uses that device's address (BD_ADDR) to calculate a page frequency-hopping sequence, the aim of which is to contact the device during paging. The master pages by using an ID packet, this time with a device access code (DAC) of the specific slave. Recall that the DAC is the lower address part of the slave's device address. The slave responds by returning the same DAC ID packet to the master in the same hopping sequence (known as the page-mode-hopping sequence) that was used by

---

[7]The state diagram of Figure 15.12 is taken from the baseband specification and does not show a transition from Inquiry Response to Page Scan, but does show a transition from Inquiry Response to Inquiry Scan. However, the accompanying text in the specification corresponds to the explanation we give.

the master. The master responds to this in the next master-to-slave slot with its own FHS packet, containing its device address and its real-time Bluetooth clock value. Once again, the slave sends a response DAC ID packet to the master to confirm the receipt of the master's FHS packet. The slave at this point transitions from the Slave Response state to the Connection state and begins to use the connection-hopping sequence defined in the master's FHS packet. Meanwhile, the master may continue to page until it has connected to all the desired slaves; the master then enters the Connection state.

Connection State

For each slave, the Connection state starts with a Poll packet sent from the master to verify that the slave has switched to the master's timing and channel frequency hopping. The slave can respond with any type of packet.

Once the slave is in the Connection state, it can be in one of four modes of operation:

- **Active:** The slave actively participates in the piconet by listening, transmitting, and receiving packets. The master periodically transmits to the slaves to maintain synchronization.
- **Sniff:** The slave does not listen on every receive slot (every other slot) but only on specified slots for its messages. The slave can operate in a reduced-power status the rest of the time. For sniff mode to operate, the master designates a reduced number of time slots for transmission to a specific slave.
- **Hold:** The device in this mode does not support ACL packets and goes to reduced power status. The slave may still participate in SCO exchanges. During periods of no activity, the slave is free to idle in a reduced power status or possibly participate in another piconet.
- **Park:** When a slave does not need to participate on the piconet but still is to be retained as part of the piconet, it can enter the park mode, which is a low-power mode with very little activity. The device is given a parking member address (PM_ADDR) and loses its active member (AM_ADDR) address. With the use of the park mode, a piconet may have more than seven slaves.

Bluetooth Audio

The baseband specification indicates that either of two voice encoding schemes can be used: pulse code modulation (PCM) or continuously variable slope delta (CVSD) modulation. The choice is made by the link managers of the two communicating devices, which negotiate the most appropriate scheme for the application.

PCM was discussed in Section 6.4. CVSD is a form of delta modulation (DM), also discussed in Section 6.4. Recall that with delta modulation, an analog input is approximated by a staircase function that moves up or down by one quantization level (δ) at each sampling interval (T_s). Thus, the output of the delta modulation process can be represented as a single binary digit for each sample. In essence, a bit stream is produced by approximating the derivative of an analog signal rather than its amplitude: A 1 is generated if the staircase function is to go up during the next interval; a 0 is generated otherwise.

As was discussed, there are two forms of error in a DM scheme: quantizing noise, which occurs when the waveform is changing very slowly, and slope overload noise, when the waveform is changing rapidly (Figure 6.18). CVSD is designed to minimize both these types of error by using a variable quantization level, one that is small when the waveform is changing slowly and large when the waveform is changing rapidly (Figure 15.13; based on one in [HAAR98]). The slope is monitored by considering the K most recent output bits. The resulting scheme is more resistant to bit errors than PCM and more resistant to quantizing and slope overload errors than DM.

Figure 15.14 illustrates the CVSD encoding and decoding (compare Figure 6.19). As with DM, a binary output is converted into a staircase function that tracks the original waveform as closely as possible. For encoding, the following occurs: The input to the encoder is 64-kbps PCM. At each sampling time, the PCM input is compared to the most recent value of the approximating staircase function, expressed as $\hat{x}(k - 1)$. The output of the comparator $b(k)$ is defined as:

$$b(k) = \begin{cases} 1 & x(k) - \hat{x}(k) \geq 0 \\ -1 & x(k) - \hat{x}(k) < 0 \end{cases}$$

For transmission, these numbers are represented by the sign bit (negative numbers are mapped to binary 1; positive numbers are mapped to 0). The output $b(k)$ is used as to produce the magnitude of the next step in the staircase, $\delta(k)$, as follows:

$$\delta(k) = \begin{cases} \min[\delta_{min} + \delta(k - 1), \delta_{max}] & \text{if at least } J \text{ of the last } K \text{ output bits are the same} \\ \max[\beta \times \delta(k - 1), \delta_{min}] & \text{otherwise} \end{cases}$$

0 0 0 1 1 1 1 1 1 0 1 0 0 0 0 0 1 0 1 1 1 1 0 0 1 1 1 1 0 1 0 1 0 1 0 0 0 0 0 0 1 1 0 1 1 1 1 0 0

Figure 15.13   Example of Continuously Variable Slope Delta Modulation

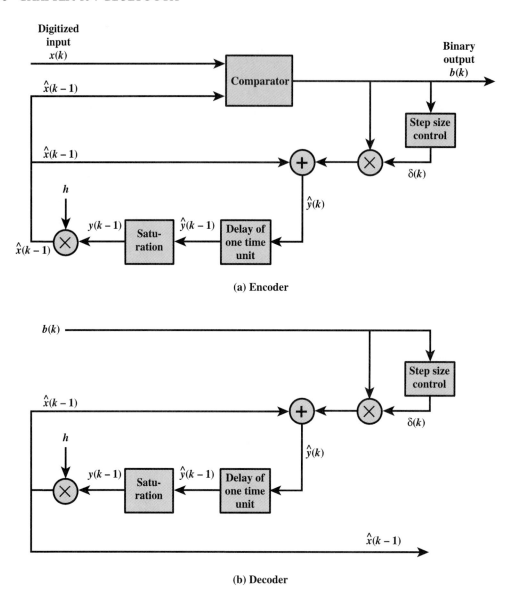

(a) Encoder

(b) Decoder

Figure 15.14 Continuously Variable Slope Delta Modulation

Table 15.6 shows the default parameter values. The effect of the preceding definition is that if the waveform is changing rapidly (at least J of the last K steps have been in the same direction), then the magnitude of the step change, $\delta(k)$, increases in a linear fashion by a constant amount δ_{min}, up to some maximum magnitude δ_{max}. On the other hand, if the waveform is not changing rapidly, then the magnitude of the step change gradually decays by a *decay factor* β, down to a minimum value of δ_{min}. The sign of the step change is determined by the sign of the output $b(t)$.

Table 15.6 CVSD Parameter Values

Parameter	Value
H	$1 - \dfrac{1}{32} = .0.96875$
β	$1 - \dfrac{1}{1024} \approx 0.999$
J	4
K	4
δ_{min}	10
δ_{max}	1280
Y_{min}	-2^{15} or $-2^{15} + 1$
y_{max}	$2^{15} - 1$

The step change is then added to the most recent value of the staircase function to produce $\hat{y}(k)$. This value is then delayed one sample time, yielding $\hat{y}(k - 1)$. Then a *saturation function* is applied, defined as

$$y(k) = \begin{cases} \min[\hat{y}(k), y_{max}] & \hat{y}(k) \geq 0 \\ \max[\hat{y}(k), y_{min}] & \hat{y}(k) < 0 \end{cases}$$

where y_{min} and y_{max} are the negative and positive saturation values for the encoder, limiting the total range of the staircase function.

Finally, $y(k - 1)$ is multiplied by the decay factor h to yield the waveform estimate $\hat{x}(k - 1)$.

Bluetooth Security

The Bluetooth baseband specification defines a facility for link security between any two Bluetooth devices, consisting of the following elements:

- Authentication
- Encryption (privacy)
- Key management and usage

The security algorithms make use of four parameters:

- **Unit address:** The 48-bit device address, which is publicly known
- **Secret authentication key:** A secret 128-bit key
- **Secret privacy key:** A secret key of length from 4 to 128 bits
- **Random number:** A 128-bit random number derived from a pseudorandom generation algorithm executed in the Bluetooth unit

The two secret keys are generated and configured with the unit and not disclosed.

The purpose of **authentication** is to verify the claimed identity of one of the two Bluetooth devices involved an exchange. Figure 15.15 shows the procedure in which unit A is authenticating unit B. Authentication is performed by verifying that the two devices share the same preconfigured authentication key. To begin, A generates a random number AU_RAND_A and transmits this value to B. Both sides use the authentication algorithm E_1 to generate a 32-bit signed response SRES. E_1 takes as input the value AU_RAND_A, the 48-bit device address of B, and the shared secret key, and produces a 128-bit output; 32 bits of this output form SRES. The algorithm E_1 is based on the encryption algorithm SAFER, and generates a message authentication code (MAC), which is a hash code of the input based on the secret key. After B has generated SRES, it returns this value to A. A compares the incoming value of SRES with the value that it has generated. If the two match, B is authenticated.

Figure 15.15 shows authentication in one direction only. Mutual authentication is achieved by performing the same exchange with B initiating the challenge.

User information can be protected by **encryption** of the packet payload; the access code and the packet header are never encrypted. Encryption is performed using an encryption algorithm known as E_0. Figure 15.16 illustrates the process. When encryption is enabled, the master sends a random number RAND to the slave. For each packet transmission, a new encryption key is generated as follows. First, a one-time payload key is generated by combining in a complex fashion RAND, the master's address, the current clock value, and a shared secret key. This payload key is used as input to E_0 to produce a continuous stream of bits labeled z in Figure 15.16. E_0 is in the form of a linear feedback shift register (LFSR) that uses the payload key for initialization of the LFSR. For encryption (and decryption), the payload is bitwise XORed with the output of E_0. Because the clock value changes for each encryption, a different encryption key is used each time, enhancing security.

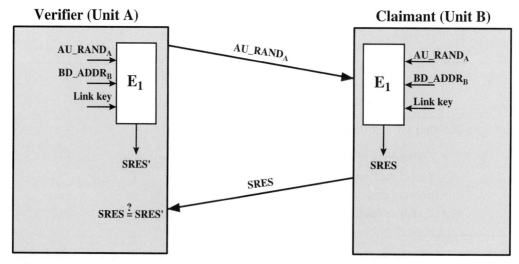

Figure 15.15 Authentication Using Challenge-Response

Figure 15.16 Stream Ciphering for Bluetooth

15.4 LINK MANAGER SPECIFICATION

LMP manages various aspects of the radio link between a master and a slave. The protocol involves the exchange of messages in the form of LMP PDUs (protocol data units) between the LMP entities in the master and slave. Messages are always sent as single slot packets with a 1-byte payload header that identifies the message type and a payload body that contains additional information pertinent to this message.

The procedures defined for LMP are grouped into 24 functional areas, each of which involves the exchange of one or more messages. Table 15.7 lists these areas, together with the PDUs involved in each area.[8] We briefly look at each area in turn.

The two **general response** messages are used to reply to other PDUs in a number of different procedures. The accepted PDU includes the opcode of the message that is accepted. The not_accepted PDU includes the opcode of the message that is not accepted and the reason why it is not accepted.

LMP supports various security services with mechanisms for managing authentication, encryption, and key distribution. These services include the following:

- **Authentication:** Authentication is defined in the baseband specification but involves the exchange of two LMP PDUs, one containing the random number and one containing the signed response (Figure 15.15).
- **Pairing:** This service allows mutually authenticated users to automatically establish a link encryption key. As a first step, an initialization key is generated by both sides and used in the authentication procedure to authenticate that the two sides have the same key. The initialization key is generated from a common personal identification number (PIN) entered in both devices. The two sides then exchange messages to determine if the link key to be used for future encryptions will be a secret key already configured or a combination key that is calculated based on the master's link key.

---

[8]In the LMP specification, each PDU name begins with LMP_. For example, the first PDU listed in Table 15.7 has the name LMP_ accepted. For brevity, we omit the LMP_ prefix.

Table 15.7 LMP PDUs

Function	PDUs
General response	accepted, not_accepted
Security Service	
Authentication	au_rand, sres
Pairing	in_rand, au_rand, sres, comb_key, unit_key
Change link key	comb_key
Change current link key	temp_rand, temp_key, use_semi_permanent_key
Encryption	encryption_mode_req, encryption_key_size_req, start_encryption_req, stop_encryption_req
Time/synchronization	
Clock offset request	clkoffset_req, clkoffset_res
Slot offset information	Slot_offset
Timing accuracy information request	timing_accuracy_req, timing_accuracy_res
Station Capability	
LMP version	version_req, version_res
Supported features	features_req, features_res
Mode Control	
Switch master/slave role	Switch_req
Name request	name_req, name_res
Detach	detach
Hold mode	hold, hold_req
Sniff mode	sniff, sniff_req, unsniff_req
Park mode	park_req, park, set_broadcast_window, modify_beacon, unpark_PM_ADDR_req, unpark_BD_ADDR_req
Power control	incr_power_req, decr_power_req, max_power, min_power
Channel quality-driven change between DM and DH	auto_rate, preferred_rate
Quality of service	quality_of_service, quality_of_service_req
SCO links	SCO_link_req, remove_SCO_link_req
Control of multislot packets	max_slot, max_slot_req
Paging scheme	page_mode_req, page_scan_mode_req
Link supervision	supervision_timeout

- **Change link key:** If two devices are paired and use a combination key, then that key can be changed. One side generates a new key and sends it to the other side XORed with the old link key. The other side accepts or rejects the key.
- **Change current link key:** The current link key can be changed temporarily. The exchange involves the use of random numbers and XOR calculations to generate the temporary key, which is used for a single session.
- **Encryption:** LMP is not directly involved in link **encryption** but provides services to manage the encryption process. A number of parameters may be negotiated, including the operating encryption mode (no encryption, point-to-point only, point-to-point and broadcast), size of the key, and the random seed key use to start a new encryption session. LMP is also used to begin and end the use of encryption.

LMP provides mechanisms for synchronizing the clocks in the various piconet participants:

- **Clock offset request:** When a slave receives the FHS packet, the difference is computed between its own clock and the master's clock value included in the payload of the FHS packet. The clock offset is also updated each time a packet is received from the master. The master can request this clock offset anytime during the connection. By saving this clock offset, the master knows on what RF channel the slave wakes up to PAGE SCAN after it has left the piconet. This can be used to speed up the paging time the next time the same device is paged.
- **Slot offset information:** An initiating device can transmit a message that describes timing differences (time difference between slot boundaries) between two adjacent piconets.
- **Timing accuracy information request:** Used by a device to retrieve the accuracy parameters of another device's timing subsystem. Parameters include long-term clock drift and clock jitter.

LMP includes two PDUs that are used to exchange information about the communicating devices:

- **LMP version:** Allows each LMP entity to determine the LMP version implemented in the other. So far, there is only one version.
- **Supported features:** The Bluetooth radio and link controller may support only a subset of the packet types and features described in Baseband Specification and Radio Specification. The PDU LMP_features_req and LMP_features_res are used to exchange this information. Table 15.8 lists the features that may be exchanged.

A Bluetooth device has a number of states and modes that it can occupy. LMP provides the following PDUs to manage these modes.

- **Switch master/slave role:** Allows a slave to become the master of the piconet. For example, this is needed when a paging device must be the master. If a new device needs to issue a page, it can use this service.
- **Name request:** Enables a device to request the text name of another device.

Table 15.8 LMP Supported Feature List

3-slot packets
5-slot packets
encryption
slot offset
timing accuracy
switch
hold mode
sniff mode
park mode
RSSI
channel quality-driven data rate
SCO link
HV2 packets
HV3 packets
μ-law log
A-law log
CVSD
paging scheme
power control

- **Detach:** Enables a device to remove itself from a connection. This can be issued by either master or slave.
- **Hold mode:** Places the link between a master and slave in hold mode for a specified time.
- **Sniff mode:** To enter sniff mode, master and slave negotiate a sniff interval T sniff and a sniff offset, D sniff, which specifies the timing of the sniff slots. The offset determines the time of the first sniff slot; after that the sniff slots follows periodically with the sniff interval T sniff.
- **Park mode:** Places a slave in park mode.
- **Power control:** Used by a device to direct another device to increase or decrease the second device's transmit power.
- **Channel quality-driven change between DM and DH:** A device is configured to use DM packets always or to use DH packets always or to adjust its packet type automatically according to the quality of the channel. This service allows an explicit change among these three alternatives. The difference between DM and DH is that the payload in a DM packet is protected with a 2/3 FEC code, whereas the payload of a DH is not protected with any FEC.
- **Quality of service:** Two parameters define Bluetooth QoS. The *poll interval*, which is the maximum time between transmissions from a master to a particular slave, is used for capacity allocation and latency control. The *number of repetitions for broadcast packets* (NBC). Broadcast packets are not acknowledged and so the automatic retransmission of all broadcast packets improves reliability.
- **SCO links:** Used to establish an SCO link.
- **Control of multislot packets:** Arbitrates the maximum number of time slots a packet can cover. The default value is one. This mechanism can be used to select 3 or 5.

- **Paging scheme:** Controls the type of paging scheme to be used between devices on the piconet. There is a default scheme that is mandatory for implementation. Additional optional schemes may be defined.
- **Link supervision:** Controls the maximum time a device should wait before declaring the failure of a link.

15.5 LOGICAL LINK CONTROL AND ADAPTATION PROTOCOL

Like logical link control (LLC) in the IEEE 802 specification, L2CAP provides a link-layer protocol between entities across a shared-medium network. As with LLC, L2CAP provides a number of services and relies on a lower layer (in this case, the baseband layer) for flow and error control.

L2CAP makes use of ACL links; it does not provide support for SCO links. Using ACL links, L2CAP provides two alternative services to upper-layer protocols:

- **Connectionless service:** This is a reliable datagram style of service.
- **Connection-mode service:** This service is similar to that offered by HDLC. A logical connection is set up between two users exchanging data, and flow control and error control are provided.

L2CAP Channels

L2CAP provides three types of logical channels:

- **Connectionless:** Supports the connectionless service. Each channel is unidirectional. This channel type is typically used for broadcast from the master to multiple slaves.
- **Connection-oriented:** Supports the connection-oriented service. Each channel is bidirectional (full duplex). A quality of service (QoS) flow specification is assigned in each direction.
- **Signaling:** Provides for the exchange of signaling messages between L2CAP entities.

Figure 15.17 provides an example of the use of L2CAP logical channels. Associated with each logical channel is a channel identifier (CID). For connection-oriented channels, a unique CID is assigned at each end of the channel to identify this connection and associate it with an L2CAP user on each end. Connectionless channels are identified by a CID value of 2, and signaling channels are identified by a CID value of 1. Thus, between the master and any slave, there is only one connectionless channel and one signaling channel, but there may be multiple connection-oriented channels.

L2CAP Packets

Figure 15.18 shows the format of L2CAP packets. For the connectionless service, the packet format consists of the following fields:

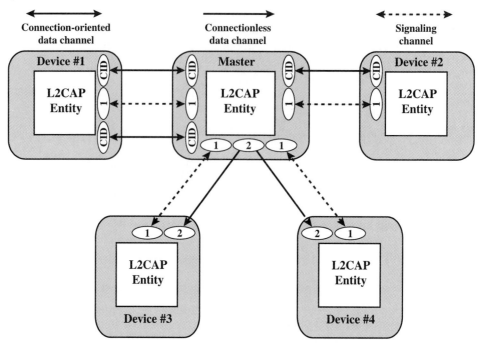

Figure 15.17 L2CAP Channels

- **Length:** Length of the information payload plus PSM fields, in bytes.
- **Channel ID:** A value of 2, indicating the connectionless channel.
- **Protocol/service multiplexer (PSM):** Identifies the higher-layer recipient for the payload in this packet.
- **Information payload:** Higher-layer user data. This field may be up to 65533 ($2^{16} - 3$) bytes in length.

Connection-oriented packets have the same format as connectionless packets, but without the PSM field. The PSM field is not needed because the CID identifies the upper-layer recipient of the data. The information payload field may be up to 65535 ($2^{16} - 1$) bytes in length.

Signaling command packets have the same header format as the connection-oriented packets. In this case, the CID value is 1, indicating the signaling channel. The payload of a signaling packet consists of one or more L2CAP commands, each of which consists of four fields:

- **Code:** Identifies the type of command.
- **Identifier:** Used to match a request with its reply. The requesting device sets this field and the responding device uses the same value in its response. A different identifier must be used for each original command.
- **Length:** Length of the data field for this command, in bytes.
- **Data:** Additional data, if necessary, relating to this command.

Signaling Commands

There are eleven commands in five categories (Table 15.9). The **command reject command** can be sent in response to any command to reject it. Reasons for rejection include invalid CID or length exceeded.

Connection commands are used to establish a new logical connection. The request command includes a PSM value indicating the L2CAP user for this connection. Three values are so far defined, for the service discovery protocol, RFCOMM, and the telephony control protocol. Other PSM values are assigned dynamically and are implementation dependent. The request command also includes the CID value that will be assigned to this connection by the source. The response command includes the source CID and the destination CID, the latter assigned to this channel by the respondent. The result parameter indicates the outcome (successful, pending, rejected) and, if the result is pending, the status field indicates the current status that makes this a pending connection (e.g., authentication pending, authorization pending).

Configure commands are sent to establish an initial logical link transmission contract between two L2CAP entities and to renegotiate this contract whenever appropriate. Each configuration parameter in a configuration request is related exclusively to either the outgoing or the incoming data traffic. The request command includes a flags field; currently the only flag is an indicator of whether additional configuration commands will be sent. The options field contains a list

Figure 15.18 L2CAP Formats

Table 15.9 L2CAP Signaling Command Codes

Code	Description	Parameters
0x01	Command reject	Reason
0x02	Connection request	PSM, Source CID
0x03	Connection response	Destination CID, Source CID, Result, Status
0x04	Configure request	Destination CID, Flags, Options
0x05	Configure response	Source CID, Flags, Result, Options
0x06	Disconnection request	Destination CID, Source CID
0x07	Disconnection response	Destination CID, Source CID
0x08	Echo request	Data (optional)
0x09	Echo response	Data (optional)
0x0A	Information request	InfoType
0x0B	Information response	InfoType, Result, Data (optional)

of parameters and their values to be negotiated. Each parameter is defined by three fields:

- **Type (1 byte):** The 7 least significant bits of this byte identify the option. If the most significant bit is set to 0, the option is mandatory and, if not recognized, the recipient must refuse the configuration request. If the most significant bit is set to 1, the option is optional and may be ignored by the recipient.
- **Length (1 byte):** The length of the option payload. A length of 0 indicates no payload.
- **Option payload:** Further information about this option.

The following parameters may be negotiated:

- **Maximum transmission unit (MTU):** The largest L2CAP packet payload, in bytes, that the originator of the request can accept for that channel. The MTU is asymmetric and the sender of the request shall specify the MTU it can receive on this channel if it differs from the default value. L2CAP implementations must support a minimum MTU size of 48 bytes. The default value is 672 bytes. This is not a negotiated value but simply informs the recipient of the size of MTU that the sender of this request can accept.
- **Flush timeout option:** Recall in our discussion of the baseband specification that as part of the ARQ mechanism, a payload will be flushed after failure on repeated attempts to retransmit. The flush timeout is the amount of time the originator will attempt to transmit an L2CAP packet successfully before giving up and flushing the packet.
- **Quality of service (QoS):** Identifies the traffic flow specification for the local device's traffic (outgoing traffic) over this channel. This parameter is described in the following subsection.

In the latter two cases, a negotiation takes place, in which the recipient can accept the flush timeout and QoS parameters or request an adjustment. The initial sender can then accept or reject the adjustment.

The configure response command also includes a flags field with the same meaning as in the configuration request command. The result field in the response command indicates whether the preceding request is accepted or rejected. The options field contains the same list of parameters as from the corresponding request command. For a successful result, these parameters contain the return values for any wild card parameters (see discussion of QoS, subsequently). For an unsuccessful result, rejected parameters should be sent in the response with the values that would have been accepted if sent in the original request.

The **disconnection commands** are used to terminate a logical channel.

The **echo commands** are used to solicit a response from a remote L2CAP entity. These commands are typically used for testing the link or passing vendor-specific information using the optional data field.

The **information commands** are used to solicit implementation-specific information from a remote L2CAP entity.

Quality of Service

The QoS parameter in L2CAP defines a traffic flow specification based on RFC 1363.[9] In essence, a **flow specification** is a set of parameters that indicate a performance level that the transmitter will attempt to achieve.

When included in a Configuration Request, this option describes the outgoing traffic flow from the device sending the request to the device receiving it. When included in a positive Configuration Response, this option describes the incoming traffic flow agreement as seen from the device sending the response. When included in a negative Configuration Response, this option describes the preferred incoming traffic flow from the perspective of the device sending the response.

The flow specification consists of the following parameters:

- Service type
- Token rate (bytes/second)
- Token bucket size (bytes)
- Peak bandwidth (bytes/second)
- Latency (microseconds)
- Delay variation (microseconds)

The **service type** parameter indicates the level of service for this flow. A value of 0 indicates that no traffic will be transmitted on this channel. A value of 1 indicates a best effort service; the device will transmit data as quickly as possible but with no guarantees about performance. A value of 2 indicates a guaranteed service; the sender will transmit data that conform to the remaining QoS parameters.

---

[9]*A Proposed Flow Specification*, RFC 1363, September 1992.

The **token rate** and **token bucket size** parameters define a token bucket scheme that is often used in QoS specifications. The advantage of this scheme is that it provides a concise description of the peak and average traffic load the recipient can expect and it also provides a convenient mechanism by which the sender can implement the traffic flow policy.

A token bucket traffic specification consists of two parameters: a token replenishment rate R and a bucket size B. The token rate R specifies the continually sustainable data rate; that is, over a relatively long period of time, the average data rate to be supported for this flow is R. The bucket size B specifies the amount by which the data rate can exceed R for short periods of time. The exact condition is as follows: During any time period T, the amount of data sent cannot exceed $RT + B$.

Figure 15.19 illustrates this scheme and explains the use of the term *bucket*. The bucket represents a counter that indicates the allowable number of bytes of data that can be sent at any time. The bucket fills with *byte tokens* at the rate of R (i.e., the counter is incremented R times per second), up to the bucket capacity (up to the maximum counter value). Data arrive from the L2CAP user and are assembled into packets, which are queued for transmission. A packet may be transmitted if there are sufficient byte tokens to match the packet size. If so, the packet is transmitted and the bucket is drained of the corresponding number of tokens. If there are insufficient tokens available, then the packet exceeds the specification for this flow. The treatment for such packets is not specified in the document; typically, the packet will simply be queued for transmission until sufficient tokens are available.

Over the long run, the rate of data allowed by the token bucket is R. However, if there is an idle or relatively slow period, the bucket capacity builds up, so that at most an additional B bytes above the stated rate can be accepted. Thus, B is a measure of the degree of burstiness of the data flow that is allowed.

For L2CAP, a value of zero for the two parameters implies that the token scheme is not needed for this application and will not be used. A value of all 1s is

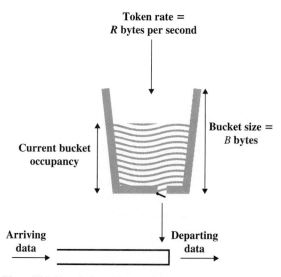

Figure 15.19   Token Bucket Scheme

the wild card value. For best effort service, the wild card indicates that the requestor wants as large a token or as large a token bucket size, respectively, as the responder will grant. For guaranteed service, the wild card indicates that the maximum data rate or bucket size, respectively, is available at the time of the request.

The **peak bandwidth**, expressed in bytes per second, limits how fast packets may be sent back-to-back from applications. Some intermediate systems can take advantage of this information, resulting in more efficient resource allocation. Consider that if the token bucket is full, it is possible for the flow to send a series of back-to-back packets equal to the size of the token bucket. If the token bucket size is large, this back-to-back run may be long enough to exceed the recipient's capacity. To limit this effect, the maximum transmission rate bounds how
fast successive packets may be placed on the network.

The **latency** is the maximum acceptable delay between transmission of a bit by the sender and its initial transmission over the air, expressed in microseconds.

The **delay variation** is the difference, in microseconds, between the maximum and minimum possible delay that a packet will experience. This value is used by applications to determine the amount of buffer space needed at the receiving side in order to restore the original data transmission pattern. If a receiving application requires data to be delivered in the same pattern that the data were transmitted, it may be necessary for the receiving host briefly to buffer data as they are received so that the receiver can restore the old transmission pattern. An example of this is a case where an application wishes to send and transmit data such as voice samples, which are generated and played at regular intervals. The amount of buffer space that the receiving host is willing to provide determines the amount of variation in delay permitted for individual packets within a given flow.

15.6 RECOMMENDED READING AND WEB SITES

[HAAR00a] and [HAAR00b] provide good overviews of Bluetooth. Two other surveys, both multipart, are also of interest: [WILS00] and [RODB00]. There are two good book-length technical treatments: [BRAY01] and [MILL01]; the former provides somewhat more technical detail than the latter.

BRAY01   Bray, J., and Sturman, C. *Bluetooth: Connect Without Cables.* Upper Saddle River, NJ: Prentice Hall, 1992.

HAAR00a   Haartsen, J. "The Bluetooth Radio System." *IEEE Personal Communications*, February 2000.

HAAR00b   Haartsen, J., and Mattisson, S. "Bluetooth—A New Low-Power Radio Interface Providing Short-Range Connectivity." *Proceedings of the IEEE*, October 2000.

MILL01   Miller, B., and Bisdikian, C. *Bluetooth Revealed.* Upper Saddle River, NJ: Prentice Hall, 2001.

RODB00   Rodbell, M. "Bluetooth: Wireless Local Access, Baseband and RF Interfaces, and Link Management." *Communications System Design*, March, April, May 2000. (www.csdmag.com)

WILS00   Wilson, J., and Kronz, J. "Inside Bluetooth: Part I and Part II." *Dr. Dobb's Journal*, March, April 2000.

Recommended Web sites:

- **Bluetooth SIG:** Contains all the standards, numerous other documents, and news and information on Bluetooth companies and products.
- **Infotooth:** An excellent supplementary source of information on Bluetooth.

15.7 KEY TERMS AND REVIEW QUESTIONS

Key Terms

Bluetooth	link manager (LM)	profile specification
cable replacement	logical link control and	RFCOMM
protocol	adaptation protocol	scatternet
core specification	(L2CAP)	service discovery protocol
flow specification	piconet	usage model

Review Questions

1 In general terms, what application areas are supported by Bluetooth?
2 What is the difference between a core specification and a profile specification?
3 What is a usage model?
4 What is the relationship between master and slave in a piconet?
5 How is it possible to combine frequency hopping and time division duplex?
6 How does FH-CDMA differ from DS-CDMA?
7 List and briefly define the types of links that can be established between a master and a slave.
8 What error correction schemes are used in Bluetooth baseband?
9 List and briefly define Bluetooth baseband logical channels.
10 What security services are provided by Bluetooth?
11 List and briefly define L2CAP logical channels.
12 What is a flow specification?

APPENDIX A

STANDARDS AND STANDARDS-SETTING ORGANIZATIONS

An important concept that recurs frequently in this book is standards. This appendix provides some background on the nature and relevance of standards and looks at the key organizations involved in developing standards for networking and communications.

A.1 THE IMPORTANCE OF STANDARDS

It has long been accepted in the telecommunications industry that standards are required to govern the physical, electrical, and procedural characteristics of communication equipment. In the past, this view has not been embraced by the computer industry. Whereas communication equipment vendors recognize that their equipment will generally interface to and communicate with other vendors' equipment, computer vendors have traditionally attempted to monopolize their customers. The proliferation of computers and distributed processing has made that an untenable position. Computers from different vendors must communicate with each other and, with the ongoing evolution of protocol standards, customers will no longer accept special-purpose protocol conversion software development. The result is that standards now permeate all the areas of technology discussed in this book.

There are a number of advantages and disadvantages to the standards-making process. The principal advantages of standards are as follows:

- A standard assures that there will be a large market for a particular piece of equipment or software. This encourages mass production and, in some cases, the use of large-scale-integration (LSI) or very-large-scale-integration (VLSI) techniques, resulting in lower costs.
- A standard allows products from multiple vendors to communicate, giving the purchaser more flexibility in equipment selection and use.

The principal disadvantages of standards are as follows:

- A standard tends to freeze the technology. By the time a standard is developed, subjected to review and compromise, and promulgated, more efficient techniques are possible.
- There are multiple standards for the same thing. This is not a disadvantage of standards per se, but of the current way things are done. Fortunately, in recent years the various standards-making organizations have begun to cooperate more closely. Nevertheless, there are still areas where multiple conflicting standards exist.

A.2 STANDARDS AND REGULATION

It is helpful for the reader to distinguish three concepts:

- Voluntary standards
- Regulatory standards
- Regulatory use of voluntary standards

Voluntary standards are developed by standards-making organizations, such as those described in this appendix. They are voluntary in that the existence of the standard does not compel its use. That is, manufacturers voluntarily implement a product that conforms to a standard if they perceive a benefit to themselves; there is no legal requirement to conform. These standards are also voluntary in the sense that they are developed by volunteers who are not paid for their efforts by the standards-making organization that administers the process. These volunteers are employees of interested organizations, such as manufacturers and government agencies.

Voluntary standards work because they are generally developed on the basis of broad consensus and because the customer demand for standard products encourages the implementation of these standards by the vendors.

In contrast, a regulatory standard is developed by a government regulatory agency to meet some public objective, such as economic, health, and safety objectives. These standards have the force of regulation behind them and must be met by providers in the context in which the regulations apply. Familiar examples of regulatory standards are in areas such as fire codes and health codes. But regulations can apply to a wide variety of products, including those related to computers and communications. For example, the Federal Communications Commission regulates electromagnetic emissions.

A relatively new, or at least newly prevalent, phenomenon is the regulatory use of voluntary standards. A typical example of this is a regulation that requires that the government purchase of a product be limited to those that conform to some referenced set of voluntary standards. This approach has a number of benefits:

- It reduces the rule-making burden on government agencies.
- It encourages cooperation between government and standards organizations to produce standards of broad applicability.
- It reduces the variety of standards that providers must meet.

A.3 THE INTERNATIONAL TELECOMMUNICATIONS UNION

The International Telecommunication Union (ITU) is a United Nations specialized agency. Hence the members of ITU-T are governments. The U.S. representation is housed in the Department of State. The charter of the ITU is that it "is responsible for studying technical, operating, and tariff questions and issuing Recommendations on them with a view to standardizing telecommunications on a worldwide basis." Its primary objective is to standardize, to the extent necessary, techniques and operations in telecommunications to achieve end-to-end compatibility of international telecommunication connections, regardless of the countries of origin and destination.

ITU Radio Communication Sector

The ITU Radiocommunication (ITU-R) Sector was created on 1 March 1993 and comprises the former CCIR and IFRB (founded 1927 and 1947, respectively). ITU-R is responsible for all ITU's work in the field of radio communications. The main activities of ITU-R are as follows:

- Develop draft ITU-R Recommendations on the technical characteristics of, and operational procedures for, radiocommunication services and systems.
- Compile Handbooks on spectrum management and emerging radiocommunication services and systems.

ITU-R is organized into the following study groups:

- SG 1 Spectrum management
- SG 3 Radiowave propagation
- SG 4 Fixed-satellite service
- SG 6 Broadcasting service (terrestrial and satellite)
- SG 7 Science services
- SG 8 Mobile, radiodetermination, amateur and related satellite services
- SG 9 Fixed service

- SC Special Committee on Regulatory/Procedural Matters
- CCV Coordination Committee for Vocabulary
- CPM Conference Preparatory Meeting

ITU Telecommunication Standardization Sector

The ITU-T was created on 1 March 1993 as one consequence of a reform process within the ITU. It replaces the International Telegraph and Telephone Consultative Committee (CCITT), which had essentially the same charter and objectives as the new ITU-T. The ITU-T fulfils the purposes of the ITU relating to telecommunications standardization by studying technical, operating and tariff questions and adopting Recommendations on them with a view to standardizing telecommunications on a worldwide basis.

ITU-T is organized into 14 study groups that prepare Recommendations, numbered as follows:

2. Network and Service Operation
3. Tariff and Accounting Principles
4. Telecommunications Management Network and Network Maintenance
5. Protection Against Electromagnetic Environment Effects
6. Outside Plant
7. Data Networks and Open System Communications
8. Characteristics of Telematic Systems
9. Television and Sound Transmission
10. Languages and General Software Aspects for Telecommunication Systems
11. Signalling Requirements and Protocols
12. End-to-End Transmission Performance of Networks and Terminals
13. General Network Aspects
15. Transport Networks, Systems, and Equipment
16. Multimedia Services and Systems

Schedule

Work within ITU-R and ITU-T is conducted in four-year cycles. Every four years, a World Telecommunications Standardization Conference is held. The work program for the next four years is established at the assembly in the form of questions submitted by the various study groups, based on requests made to the study groups by their members. The conference assesses the questions, reviews the scope of the study groups, creates new or abolishes existing study groups, and allocates questions to them.

Based on these questions, each study group prepares draft Recommendations. A draft Recommendation may be submitted to the next conference, four years hence, for approval. Increasingly, however, Recommendations are approved when they are ready, without having to wait for the end of the four-year study period. This accelerated procedure was adopted after the study period that ended in 1988. Thus,

1988 was the last time that a large batch of documents was published at one time as a set of Recommendations.

A.4 INTERNET STANDARDS AND THE INTERNET SOCIETY

Many of the protocols that make up the TCP/IP protocol suite have been standardized or are in the process of standardization. By universal agreement, an organization known as the Internet Society is responsible for the development and publication of these standards. The Internet Society is a professional membership organization that oversees a number of boards and task forces involved in Internet development and standardization.

This section provides a brief description of the way in which standards for the TCP/IP protocol suite are developed.

The Internet Organizations and RFC Publication

The Internet Society is the coordinating committee for Internet design, engineering, and management. Areas covered include the operation of the Internet itself and the standardization of protocols used by end systems on the Internet for interoperability. Three organizations under the Internet Society are responsible for the actual work of standards development and publication:

- **Internet Architecture Board (IAB):** Responsible for defining the overall architecture of the Internet, providing guidance and broad direction to the IETF.
- **Internet Engineering Task Force (IETF):** The protocol engineering and development arm of the Internet.
- **Internet Engineering Steering Group (IESG):** Responsible for technical management of IETF activities and the Internet standards process.

The actual development of new standards and protocols for the Internet is carried out by working groups chartered by the IETF. Membership in a working group is voluntary; any interested party may participate. During the development of a specification, a working group will make a draft version of the document available as an Internet Draft, which is placed in the IETF's "Internet Drafts" online directory. The document may remain as an Internet Draft for up to six months, and interested parties may review and comment on the draft. During that time, the IESG may approve publication of the draft as an RFC (Request for Comment). If the draft has not progressed to the status of an RFC during the six-month period, it is withdrawn from the directory. The working group may subsequently publish a revised version of the draft.

The IETF is responsible for publishing the RFCs, with approval of the IESG. The RFCs are the working notes of the Internet research and development community. A document in this series may be on essentially any topic related to computer communications and may be anything from a meeting report to the specification of a standard.

The Standardization Process

The decision of which RFCs become Internet standards is made by the IESG, on the recommendation of the IETF. To become a standard, a specification must meet the following criteria:

- Be stable and well understood
- Be technically competent
- Have multiple, independent, and interoperable implementations with substantial operational experience
- Enjoy significant public support
- Be recognizably useful in some or all parts of the Internet

The key difference between these criteria and those used for international standards from ITU is the emphasis here on operational experience.

The left-hand side of Figure A.1 shows the series of steps, called the *standards track*, that a specification goes through to become a standard; this process is defined in RFC 2026. The steps involve increasing amounts of scrutiny and testing. At each step, the IETF must make a recommendation for advancement of the protocol, and the IESG must ratify it. The process begins when the IESG approves the publication of an Internet Draft document as an RFC with the status of Proposed Standard.

The white boxes in the diagram represent temporary states, which should be occupied for the minimum practical time. However, a document must remain a Proposed Standard for at least six months and a Draft Standard for at least four months

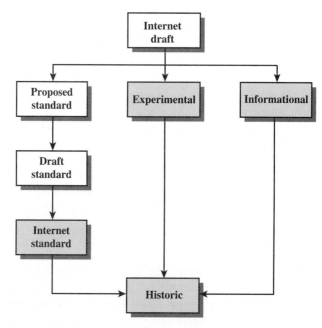

Figure A.1   Internet RFC Publication Process

to allow time for review and comment. The gray boxes represent long-term states that may be occupied for years.

For a specification to be advanced to Draft Standard status, there must be at least two independent and interoperable implementations from which adequate operational experience has been obtained.

After significant implementation and operational experience has been obtained, a specification may be elevated to Internet Standard. At this point, the Specification is assigned an STD number as well as an RFC number.

Finally, when a protocol becomes obsolete, it is assigned to the Historic state.

Non-Standards Track Documents

A protocol or other specification that is not considered ready for standardization may be published as an Experimental RFC. After further work, the specification may be resubmitted. If the specification is generally stable, has resolved known design choices, is believed to be well understood, has received significant community review, and appears to enjoy enough community interest to be considered valuable, then the RFC will be designated a Proposed Standard.

Finally, an Informational Specification is published for the general information of the Internet community.

A.5 THE IEEE 802 STANDARDS

The key to the development of the LAN market is the availability of a low-cost interface. The cost to connect equipment to a LAN must be much less than the cost of the equipment alone. This requirement, plus the complexity of the LAN logic, dictates a solution based on the use of chips and very-large-scale integration (VLSI). However, chip manufacturers are reluctant to commit the necessary resources unless there is a high-volume market. A widely accepted LAN standard assures that volume and also enables equipment from a variety of manufacturers to intercommunicate. This is the rationale of the IEEE 802 committee.

The committee issued a set of standards, which were subsequently adopted in 1985 by the American National Standards Institute (ANSI) as American National Standards. These standards were subsequently revised and reissued as international standards by the International Organization for Standardization (ISO) in 1987, with the designation ISO 8802. Since then, the IEEE 802 committee has continued to revise and extend the standards, which are ultimately then adopted by ISO.

Two conclusions were quickly reached by the committee. First, the task of communication across the local network is sufficiently complex that it needs to be broken up into more manageable subtasks. This resulted in the IEEE 802 reference model introduced in Chapter 14 (Figure 14.1).

Second, no single technical approach will satisfy all requirements. The second conclusion was reluctantly reached when it became apparent that no single standard would satisfy all committee participants. There was support for various topologies, access methods, and transmission media. The response of the committee was to standardize all serious proposals rather than to attempt to settle on just one.

LAN Implementation Model

In addition to developing a protocol reference model to structure the work of the committee, the committee also introduced an implementation model to guide the development of specific standards. The two models are compared in Figure A.2. The difference is that the implementation model highlights the complexity of physical layer standardization. For a given MAC layer, a number of different physical medium options are available. In most cases, there is a medium-independent portion of the physical layer specification, which deals with signal encoding, synchronization, and other design issues that are common across multiple media. There is, in addition, a medium-dependent portion that deals with electrical and mechanical issues specific to a particular medium. Depending on implementation, these two parts may be implemented separately with an interface in between.

Organization of IEEE 802

The work of the IEEE 802 committee is currently organized into the following working groups:

- **802.1 Higher Layer LAN Protocols Working Group:** Chartered to concern itself with and develop standards and recommended practices in the following areas: 802 LAN/MAN architecture, internetworking among 802 LANs,

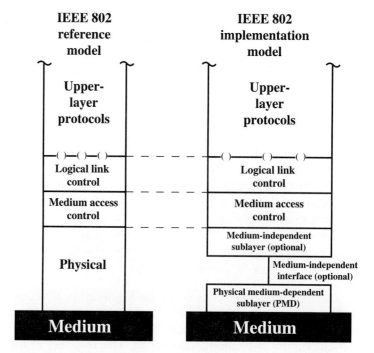

Figure A.2 IEEE 802 Reference and Implementation Models

MANs, and other wide area networks, 802 overall network management, and protocol layers above the MAC and LLC layers.

- **802.2 Logical Link Control (LLC) Working Group:** Currently inactive.
- **802.3 Ethernet Working Group:** Develops standards for CSMA/CD (Ethernet) based LANs.
- **802.4 Token Bus Working Group:** Develops standards for token bus LANs. Currently inactive.
- **802.5 Token Ring Working Group:** Develops standards for token ring LANs.
- **802.6 Metropolitan Area Network Working Group:** Develops standards for MANs. Currently inactive.
- **802.7 Broadband TAG:** Technical advisory group that developed a recommended practice, IEEE Std 802.7-1989, IEEE Recommended Practices for Broadband Local Area Networks (Reaffirmed 1997). This group is inactive with no ongoing projects. The maintenance effort for IEEE Std 802.7-1989 is supported by 802.14.
- **802.8 Fiber Optic TAG:** Develops recommended practices for fiber optics.
- **802.9 Isochronous LAN Working Group:** Develops standards for isochronous LANs.
- **802.10 Security Working Group:** Develops standards for interoperable LAN/MAN security.
- **802.11 Wireless LAN Working Group:** Develops standards for wireless LANs.
- **802.12 Demand Priority Working Group:** Develops standards for demand priority LANs (100VG-AnyLAN).
- **802.13:** Not used.
- **802.14 Cable Modem Working Group:** Chartered to create standards for data transport over traditional cable TV networks. The reference architecture specifies a hybrid fiber/coax plant with an 80-km radius from the headend. The primary thrust of the network protocol in design is to transport IEEE 802.2 LLC traffic types (exemplified by Ethernet). There is, however, a strong feeling within the group that the network should also support ATM networking to carry various types of multimedia traffic.
- **802.15 Wireless Personal Area Networks Working Group:** Develops personal area network standards for short-distance wireless networks.
- **802.16 Broadband Wireless Access Working Group:** Develops standards for broadband wireless access.
- **802.17 Resilient Packet Ring Working Group:** The standard will define a very high-speed network protocol that is optimized for packet transmission in resilient optical fiber ring topologies.

APPENDIX B

TRAFFIC ANALYSIS

Section 10.1 introduced the concept of traffic analysis. This appendix provides more detail.[1]

B.1 BASIC TRAFFIC CONCEPTS

Traffic engineering concepts were developed in the design of telephone switches and circuit-switching telephone networks, but the concepts equally apply to cellular networks. Consider a cell able to handle N simultaneous users (capacity of N channels) that has L potential subscribers (L mobile units). If $L < N$, the system is referred to as *nonblocking*; all calls can be handled all the time. If $L > N$, the system is *blocking*; a subscriber may attempt a call and find the capacity fully in use and therefore be blocked. For a blocking system, the fundamental performance questions we wish to answer are as follows:

1. What is the degree of blocking; that is, what is the probability that a call request will be blocked? Alternatively, what capacity (N) is needed to achieve a certain upper bound on the probability of blocking?
2. If blocked calls are queued for service, what is the average delay? Alternatively, what capacity is needed to achieve a certain average delay?

---

[1]This appendix makes use of concepts from queuing analysis. A basic refresher on queuing analysis can be found at the Computer Science Student Support Site at WilliamStallings.com/StudentSupport.html.

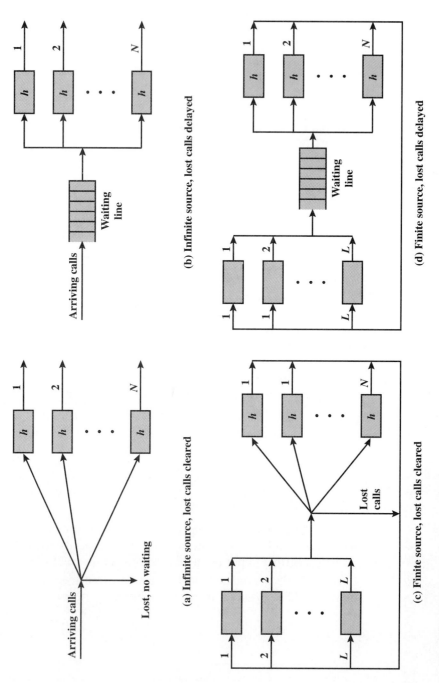

(a) Infinite source, lost calls cleared

(b) Infinite source, lost calls delayed

(c) Finite source, lost calls cleared

(d) Finite source, lost calls delayed

Figure B.1 Multiserver Queuing Models

Two parameters determine the amount of load presented to a system:

- λ: the mean rate of calls (connection requests) attempted per unit time
- h: the mean holding time per successful call

The basic measure of traffic is the traffic intensity, expressed in a dimensionless unit, the Erlang:

$$A = \lambda h$$

The parameter A, as a measure of busy-hour traffic (discussed in Section 10.1), serves as input to a traffic model. The model is then used to answer questions such as those posed in the beginning of this subsection. There are two key factors that determine the nature of the model:

- The manner in which blocked calls are handled
- The number of traffic sources

Blocked calls may be handle in one of two ways. First, blocked calls can be put in a queue awaiting a free channel; this is referred to as **lost calls delayed** (LCD), although in fact the call is not lost, merely delayed. Second, a blocked call can be rejected and dropped. This in turn leads to two assumptions about the action of the user. If the user hangs up and waits some random time interval before another call attempt, this is known as **lost calls cleared** (LCC). If the user repeatedly attempts calling, it is known as **lost calls held** (LCH). For each of these blocking options, formulas have been developed that characterize the performance of the system. For cellular systems, the LCC model is generally used and is generally the most accurate.

The second key element of a traffic model is whether the number of users is assumed to be finite or infinite. Figure B.1 illustrates this difference. For an **infinite source** model, there is assumed to be a fixed mean arrival rate. For the **finite source** case, the arrival rate will depend on the number of sources already engaged. In particular, if the total pool of users is L, each of which generates calls at an average rate of λ/L, then, when the cell is totally idle, the arrival rate is λ. However, if there are K users occupied at time t, then the instantaneous arrival rate at that time is $\lambda(L - K)/L$. Infinite source models are analytically easier to deal with. The infinite source assumption is reasonable when the number of sources is at least 5 to 10 times the capacity of the system.

B.2 MULTISERVER MODELS

We are now ready to turn to the use of the various traffic models for system sizing. For each of the four models of Figure B.1, formulas have been derived for the quantities of interest. The most important relationships are summarized in Table B.1. These formulas are based on the following assumptions:

- Poisson arrivals
- Exponential holding time (not needed for infinite sources, LCC)

Table B.1 Traffic Formulas

Table B.1 Traffic Formulas	(c) Finite sources, lost calls cleared

(a) Infinite sources, lost calls cleared

$$P = \frac{\dfrac{A^N}{N!}}{\displaystyle\sum_{x=0}^{N} \dfrac{A^x}{x!}}$$

(b) Infinite sources, lost calls delayed

$$P(> 0) = \frac{\dfrac{A^N}{N!}\dfrac{N}{N - A}}{\displaystyle\sum_{x=0}^{N-1} \dfrac{A_x}{x!} + \dfrac{A^N}{N!}\dfrac{N}{N - A}}$$

$$P(> t) = P(> 0)e^{-(N - A)t/h}$$

$$D_1 = P(> 0)\frac{h}{N - A}$$

$$D_2 = \frac{h}{N - A}$$

$$P_2(> t) = e^{-(N - A)t/h}$$

(c) Finite sources, lost calls cleared

$$P = \frac{\dbinom{L - 1}{N}M^N}{\displaystyle\sum_{x=0}^{N}\dbinom{L - 1}{x}M^x}$$

where

$$\binom{L - 1}{x} = \frac{(L - 1)!}{x!(L - 1 - x)!}$$

$$M = \frac{A}{L - A(1 - P)}$$

(d) Finite sources, lost calls delayed

$$P(> 0) = \frac{\displaystyle\sum_{x=N}^{L} \dfrac{L!}{N!}\dfrac{M^x}{(L - x)!N^{x-N}}}{\displaystyle\sum_{x=0}^{N-1}\dbinom{L}{x}M^x + \sum_{x=N}^{L}\dfrac{L!}{N!}\dfrac{M^x}{(L - x)!N^{x-N}}}$$

where

$$M = \frac{A}{L + 1 - A(1 - P)} \approx \frac{A}{L + 1 - A}$$

A = offered traffic, Erlangs
N = number of servers
L = number of sources
h = mean holding time
P = probability of loss (blocking, delay)

$P(>0)$ = Probability of delay greater than 0
$P(>t)$ = Probability of delay greater than t
$P_2(>t)$ = Probability of delay greater than t on calls delayed
D_1 = mean delay, all calls
D_2 = mean delay, delayed calls

- Equal traffic intensity per source
- Calls served in order of arrival (for delay calculations)

Even with these assumptions, it can be seen that the formulas involve lengthy summations. In earlier days, much of the work of traffic theorist lay in simplifying assumptions to the point that the equations could be calculated at all. The results were and are published in tables (e.g., [MART94]). Unfortunately, the tendency would be to try to use the available tables in situations whose assumptions did not fit any of the tables. The problem is now alleviated with the use of the computer. Nevertheless, the tabular results are still useful for quick and rough sizing.

Several parameters in Table B.1 warrant comment. For LCC systems, P is the probability that a call request will be cleared, or lost. This is the ratio of calls unable to obtain service to the total call requests; in telephone traffic, it is also called **grade of service**. For LCD systems, an arriving call will be delayed rather than cleared. In this case, $P(>0)$ is the probability that a call request will find the system fully utilized and hence be delayed. $P(>t)$ is the probability that any call request is delayed by an amount greater than t, whereas $P_2(>t)$ is the probability that a call that is delayed will be delayed by an amount greater than t.

Infinite Sources, Lost Calls Cleared

This case is discussed in Section 10.1. As was mentioned, the equation of Table B.1a is referred to as *Erlang B*. Table 10.3 provides an extract of an Erlang B table. Figure B.2 plots the probability of loss as a function of offered load with the number of servers as a parameter.

Finite Sources, Lost Calls Cleared

In reality, the number of sources is not infinite, and Table B.1c applies. This is a more complicated formula and, because of the extra parameter L, the tables are more unwieldy than for Erlang B. In many cases, the infinite source assumption will suffice.

To get a handle on the relative size of the difference between finite and infinite source assumptions, let us compare two systems. One is infinite source with a calling rate of λ; the other is a finite source with a calling rate per source of λ/L. We then have

$$A_\infty = \lambda h$$

$$A_L = \frac{\lambda}{L}(L - K)h$$

$$= \lambda h\left(1 - \frac{K}{L}\right) \geq \lambda h\left(1 - \frac{N}{L}\right)$$

where

A_∞ = offered traffic, infinite source case
A_L = offered traffic, L sources
K = number of sources currently engaged in a call

The inequality results from the fact that the number of sources engaged cannot exceed the total capacity N of the system.

We have

$$A_\infty > A_L > A_\infty\left(1 - \frac{N}{L}\right)$$

Thus, for L much larger than N, A_∞ is a good approximation of A_L.

This conclusion is confirmed by Table B.2, which shows that as the number of sources gets large compared to capacity, the effective capacity approaches the value

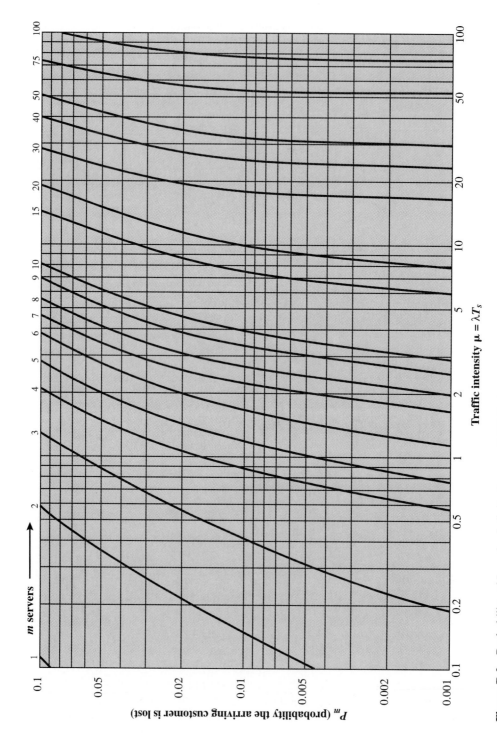

Figure B.2   Probability of Loss for Infinite Sources, LCC Systems

Table B.2 Lost Calls Cleared, Finite and Infinite Sources (number of servers = 10)

Number of sources	Offered load (Erlangs)		
	$p = 0.005$	$p = 0.01$	$p = 0.05$
∞	2.8	4.46	6.22
50	4.16	4.64	6.4
25	4.6	5.1	6.81
20	4.81	5.32	7.06
15	5.27	5.78	7.41
12	5.97	6.47	8.02
10	10	10	10

of the infinite source case. Note that as the probability of loss decreases, the approximation becomes relatively less accurate. You should also be able to deduce from Table B.2 that the probability of loss is always less for a finite system than for a similar system with an infinite source. Thus the infinite source model gives conservative estimates for sizing.

Lost Calls Delayed

When queuing is allowed, the designer may be more interested in the delay characteristics than the blocking characteristics of the switch. Table B.1b shows several formulas for the infinite source, LCD case. The designer might be interested in the probability of any delay (Erlang C formula), the probability of delay greater than a given amount, or the mean value of delay.

The probability of delay, the probability of delay greater than a given amount, and the average delay on all offered calls are complex functions of A and N and can be solved only with the aid of a computer or the appropriate tables. Fortunately, the average delay and the probability of delay greater than a given amount, for calls that are delayed, are easily calculated and of some interest.

Example. What is the load that can be offered to a switch of capacity 1500 with a mean holding time of 1000 s if the fraction of delayed calls waiting longer then 1 minute is not to exceed 10%? We have $N = 1500$, $h = 1000$, $t = 60$, and $P_2(>60) = 0.1$. Substituting, we have

$$\ln(0.1) = -(1500 - A) \times (0.06)$$

Solving for A yields $A = 1462$. Therefore, for these requirements, the load on the system may be very near to the total capacity.

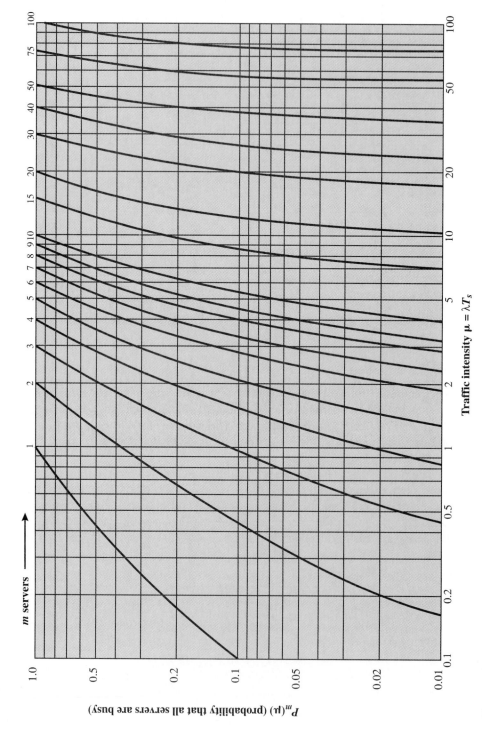

Figure B.3 Probability of Delay for Infinite Sources, LCD Systems

Example. This example makes use of Figure B.3, which shows the probability of delay for infinite sources, LCD. Consider a switch with capacity 20 that experiences an average call holding time of 5 minutes. If the load on the system is 16 Erlangs, what is the fraction of all calls that will be delayed greater than 2.5 minutes? First, we need the fraction of calls that will be delayed at all. From Figure B.3, with $A = 16$ and $N = 20$, we have that $P(>0)$ is approximately 0.25. Then

$$\begin{aligned}
P(>150) &= P(>0) \times e^{-(N-A)t/h} \\
&= 0.25 \times e^{-(20-16)(150/300)} \\
&= 0.03
\end{aligned}$$

The average delay on calls delayed is $h/(N-A) = 75$ s. The average delay for all calls is $P(>0) \times 75 = 18.75$ s.

Table B.1d shows the formula for finite source, LCD. This is the most complicated analytically, and the infinite source case should be used for a first approximation.

Summary

Using either tables or computer programs, the equations of Table B.1 can be used in a variety of ways. For infinite sources, LCC, there are three variables: P, N, and A (which can be determined from λ and h). Given any two variables, one can solve for the third. Example questions are as follows:

- Given a measured value of P for a particular N, how much must N be increased to reduce P to a given level?
- Given λ, h, and a desired value for P, what capacity (N) is required?

For infinite source, LCD, there is the additional parameter of the delay. As before, among the variables $P(>0)$, N, and A, given any two the third can be found. To determine D, h must be known.

The same considerations apply for the finite source cases (LCC and LCD). For finite sources, a fixed L is used and then the same types of questions can be addressed.

B.3 RECOMMENDED READING

A good practical reference to the queuing theory underlying the concepts of this appendix is [TANN95]; it provides detailed guidance for the application of queuing analysis plus a number of worked-out examples. The book also contains a disk with an extensive library of subroutines in Pascal for calculating the characteristics of many queuing situations. Another excellent practical reference is [GUNT00]. [MART94] provides a good overview of traffic analysis and contains a number of graphs and tables that can be used to perform quick analyses.

GUNT00 Gunther, N. *The Practical Performance Analyst.* Lincoln, NE: Authors Choice Press, 2000.
MART94 Martine, R. *Basic Traffic Analysis.* Englewood Cliffs, NJ: Prentice-Hall, 1994.
TANN95 Tanner, M. *Practical Queueing Analysis.* New York: McGraw-Hill, 1995.

APPENDIX C

FOURIER ANALYSIS

In this appendix, we provide an overview of key concepts in Fourier analysis.

C.1 FOURIER SERIES REPRESENTATION OF PERIODIC SIGNALS

With the aid of a good table of integrals, it is a remarkably simple task to determine the frequency domain nature of many signals. We begin with periodic signals. Any periodic signal can be represented as a sum of sinusoids, known as a Fourier series:[1]

$$x(t) = \frac{A_0}{2} + \sum_{n=1}^{\infty} \left[A_n \cos(2\pi n f_0 t) + B_n \sin(2\pi n f_0 t) \right]$$

where f_0 is the reciprocal of the period of the signal ($f_0 = 1/T$). The frequency f_0 is referred to as the *fundamental frequency or fundamental harmonic;* integer multiples of f_0 are referred to as *harmonics.* Thus a periodic signal with period T consists of the fundamental frequency $f_0 = 1/T$ plus integer multiples of that frequency. If $A_0 \neq 0$, then $x(t)$ has a *dc component.*

---

[1]Mathematicians typically write Fourier series and transform expressions using the variable w_0, which has a dimension of radians per second and where $w_0 = 2\pi f_0$. For physics and engineering, the f_0 formulation is preferred; it makes for simpler expressions, and it is intuitively more satisfying to have frequency expressed in Hz rather than radians per second.

	Signal	**Fourier Series**

| **Square wave** | $(4A/\pi) \times [\cos(2\pi f_1 t) - (1/3)\cos(2\pi(3f_1)t)$ $+ (1/5)\cos(2\pi(5f_1)t) - (1/7)\cos(2\pi(7f_1)t)$ $+ \ldots]$ |

| **Triangular wave** | $C_0 = 0$ $C_n = 0 \quad$ for n even $C_n = 8A/(n\pi)^2 \quad$ for n odd |

| **Sawtooth wave** | $A_0 = 0$ $A_n = 0 \quad$ for n even $B_n = -(-1)^{(n)} \times (2A/\pi n)$ |

| **Half-wave rectified cosine** | $C_0 = 2A/\pi$ $C_n = 0 \,$ for n odd $C_n = (2A/\pi) \times (-1)^{(1+n/2)} \times (2/(n^2 - 1))$ for n even |

| **Full-wave rectified cosine** | $C_0 = 4A/\pi$ $C_n = (4A/\pi) \times (-1)^n \times (1/(4n^2 - 1))$ |

| **Pulse train** | $C_n = (2A\tau/T) \times (\sin(n\pi\tau/T)/(n\pi\tau/T)$ |

Figure C.1 Some Common Periodic Signals and Their Fourier Series

The values of the coefficients are calculated as follows:

$$A_0 = \frac{2}{T}\int_0^T x(t)\, dt$$

$$A_n = \frac{2}{T}\int_0^T x(t)\cos(2\pi n f_0 t)\, dt$$

$$B_n = \frac{2}{T}\int_0^T x(t)\sin(2\pi n f_0 t)\, dt$$

This form of representation, known as the sine-cosine representation, is the easiest form to compute but suffers from the fact that there are two components at each frequency. A more meaningful representation, the amplitude-phase representation, takes the form

$$x(t) = \frac{C_0}{2} + \sum_{n=1}^{\infty} C_n \cos(2\pi n f_0 t + \theta_n)$$

This relates to the earlier representation as follows:

$$C_0 = A_0$$
$$C_n = \sqrt{A_n^2 + B_n^2}$$
$$\theta_n = tan^{-1}\left(\frac{-B_n}{A_n}\right)$$

Examples of the Fourier series for periodic signals are shown in Figure C.1.

C.2 FOURIER TRANSFORM REPRESENTATION OF APERIODIC SIGNALS

For a periodic signal, we have seen that its spectrum consists of discrete frequency components, at the fundamental frequency and its harmonics. For an aperiodic signal, the spectrum consists of a continuum of frequencies. This spectrum can be defined by the Fourier transform. For a signal $x(t)$ with a spectrum $X(f)$, the following relationships hold:

$$x(t) = \int_{-\infty}^{\infty} X(f)e^{j2\pi ft}df$$
$$X(f) = \int_{-\infty}^{\infty} x(t)e^{-j2\pi ft}dt$$

where $j = \sqrt{-1}$. The presence of an imaginary number in the equations is a matter of convenience. The imaginary component has a physical interpretation having to do with the phase of a waveform, and a discussion of this topic is beyond the scope of this book.

Figure C.2 presents some examples of Fourier transform pairs.

Power Spectral Density and Bandwidth

The absolute bandwidth of any time-limited signal is infinite. In practical terms, however, most of the power in a signal is concentrated in some finite band, and the effective bandwidth consists of that portion of the spectrum that contains most of the power. To make this concept precise, we need to define the power spectral density (PSD). In essence, the PSD describes the power content of a signal as a function of frequency, so that it shows how much power is present over various frequency bands.

First, we observe the power in the time domain. A function $x(t)$ usually specifies a signal in terms of either voltage or current. In either case, the instantaneous power in the signal is proportional to $|x(t)|^2$. We define the average power of a time-limited signal as

$$P = \frac{1}{t_1 - t_2} \int_{t_1}^{t_2} |x(t)|^2 dt$$

For a periodic signal the average power in one period is

$$P = \frac{1}{T} \int_0^T |x(t)|^2 dt$$

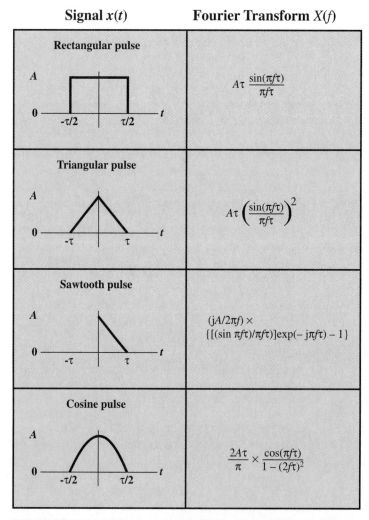

Signal $x(t)$	Fourier Transform $X(f)$
Rectangular pulse	$A\tau \dfrac{\sin(\pi f \tau)}{\pi f \tau}$
Triangular pulse	$A\tau \left(\dfrac{\sin(\pi f \tau)}{\pi f \tau} \right)^2$
Sawtooth pulse	$(jA/2\pi f) \times \{[(\sin \pi f \tau)/\pi f \tau]\exp(-j\pi f \tau) - 1\}$
Cosine pulse	$\dfrac{2A\tau}{\pi} \times \dfrac{\cos(\pi f \tau)}{1 - (2f\tau)^2}$

Figure C.2　Some Common Aperiodic Signals and Their Fourier Transforms

We would like to know the distribution of power as a function of frequency. For periodic signals, this is easily expressed in terms of the coefficients of the exponential Fourier series. The power spectral density $S(f)$ obeys

$$S(f) = \sum_{n=-\infty}^{\infty} |C_n|^2 \delta(f - nf_0)$$

where f_0 is the inverse of the period of the signal ($f_0 = 1/T$), C_n is the coefficient in the amplitude-phase representation of a Fourier series, and $\delta(t)$ is the unit impulse, or delta, function, defined as

$$\delta(t) = \begin{cases} 0 & \text{if } t \neq 0 \\ \infty & \text{if } t = 0 \end{cases}$$

$$\int_{-\infty}^{\infty} \delta(t)\, dt = 1$$

The power spectral density $S(f)$ for aperiodic functions is more difficult to define. In essence, it is obtained by defining a "period" T_0 and allowing T_0 to increase without limit.

For a continuous valued function $S(f)$, the power contained in a band of frequencies, $f_1 < f < f_2$, is

$$P = 2\int_{f_1}^{f_2} S(f)\, df$$

For a periodic waveform, the power through the first j harmonics is

$$P = C_0^2 + \frac{1}{2}\sum_{n=1}^{j} C_n^2$$

With these concepts, we can now define the half-power bandwidth, which is perhaps the most common bandwidth definition. The half-power bandwidth is the interval between frequencies at which $S(f)$ has dropped to half of its maximum value of power, or 3 dB below the peak value.

C.3 RECOMMENDED READING

A very accessible treatment of Fourier series and Fourier transforms is [JAME95]. Another worthwhile treatment is [HSU84]. For a thorough understanding of Fourier series and transforms, the book to read is [KAMM00].

HSU84 Hsu, H. *Applied Fourier Analysis*. New York: Harcourt Brace, 1984.

JAME95 James, J. *A Student's Guide to Fourier Transforms*. Cambridge, England: Cambridge University Press, 1995.

KAMM00 Kammler, D. *A First Course in Fourier Analysis*. Upper Saddle River, NJ: Prentice Hall, 2000.

APPENDIX D

DATA LINK CONTROL PROTOCOLS

Throughout this book, a number of references have been made to the use of data link control protocols as part of a protocol architecture. A key mechanism that is part of most data link control protocols is error control using automatic repeat request (ARQ), which is discussed in Section 8.4. This appendix looks at HDLC, which is representative of data link control protocols and indeed is the base from which most such protocols have been derived.

D.1 HIGH-LEVEL DATA LINK CONTROL

The most important data link control protocol is HDLC (ISO 3009, ISO 4335). Not only is HDLC widely used, but it is the basis for many other important data link control protocols, which use the same or similar formats and the same mechanisms as employed in HDLC.

HDLC Frame Structure

Perhaps the best way to begin an explanation of HDLC is to look at the frame structure. The operation of HDLC involves the exchange of two sorts of information between the two connected stations. First, HDLC accepts user data from some higher layer of software and delivers that user data across the link to the other side. On the other side, HDLC accepts the user data and delivers it to a higher layer of software on that side. Second, the two HDLC modules must exchange control information, to provide for flow control, error control, and other control functions. The method by which this is done is to format the information that is exchanged into a **frame**. A frame is a predefined structure that provides a specific location for various kinds of control information and for user data.

Figure D.1 depicts the format of the HDLC frame. The frame has the following fields:

- **Flag:** Used for synchronization. It appears at the beginning and end of the frame and always contains the pattern 01111110.
- **Address:** Indicates the secondary station for this transmission. It is needed in the case of a multidrop line, where a primary may send data to one of a number of secondaries, and one of a number of secondaries may send data to the primary. This field is usually 8 bits long, but can be extended (Figure D.1b).
- **Control:** Identifies the purpose and functions of the frame. It is described later in this subsection.
- **Information:** Contains the user data to be transmitted.
- **Frame check sequence:** Contains a 16- or 32-bit cyclic redundancy check, used for error detection.

HDLC defines three types of frames, each with a different control field format. Information frames (I frames) carry the user data to be transmitted for the station. Additionally, the information frames contain control information for flow control and error control. Supervisory frames (S frames) provide another means of exercising flow control and error control. Unnumbered frames (U frames) provide supplemental link control functions.

The first one or two bits of the control field serve to identify the frame type. The remaining bit positions are organized into subfields, as indicated in Figures D.1c and D.1d. Their use is explained in the discussion of HDLC operation, which follows. Note that the basic control field for S and I frames uses 3-bit sequence numbers. With the appropriate set-mode commands, an extended control field can be used that employs 7-bit sequence numbers.

All of the control field formats contain the poll/final (P/F) bit. Its use depends on context. Typically, in command frames, it is referred to as the P bit and is set to 1 to solicit (poll) a response frame from the peer HDLC entity. In response frames, it is referred to as the F bit and is set to 1 to indicate the response frame transmitted as a result of a soliciting command.

HDLC Operation

HDLC operation consists of the exchange of I frames, S frames, and U frames between two stations. The various commands and responses defined for these frame types are listed in Table D.1. In describing HDLC operation, we will discuss these three types of frames.

The operation of HDLC involves three phases. First, one side or another initializes the data link so that frames may be exchanged in an orderly fashion. During this phase, the options that are to be used are agreed upon. After initialization, the

(a) Frame format

(b) Extended address field

(c) 8-bit control field format

(d) 16-bit control field format

Figure D.1 HDLC Frame Structure

two sides exchange user data and the control information to exercise flow and error control. Finally, one of the two sides signals the termination of the operation.

Initialization

Initialization may be requested by either side by issuing one of the six set-mode commands. This command serves three purposes:

1. It signals the other side that initialization is requested.
2. It specifies which of the three modes is requested; these modes have to do with whether one side acts as a primary and controls the exchange or whether the two sides are peers and cooperate in the exchange.
3. It specifies whether 3- or 7-bit sequence numbers are to be used.

Table D.1 HDLC Commands and Responses

Name	Command/ Response	Description
Information (I)	C/R	Exchange user data
Supervisory (S)		
Receive ready (RR)	C/R	Positive acknowledgment; ready to receive I frame
Receive not ready (RNR)	C/R	Positive acknowledgment; not ready to receive
Reject (REJ)	C/R	Negative acknowledgment; go back N
Selective reject (SREJ)	C/R	Negative acknowledgment; selective reject
Unnumbered (U)		
Set normal response/extended mode (SNRM/SNRME)	C	Set mode; extended = 7-bit sequence numbers
Set asynchronous response/extended mode (SARM/SARME)	C	Set mode; extended = 7-bit sequence numbers
Set asynchronous balanced/extended mode (SABM, SABME)	C	Set mode; extended = 7-bit sequence numbers
Set initialization mode (SIM)	C	Initialize link control functions in addressed station
Disconnect (DISC)	C	Terminate logical link connection
Unnumbered Acknowledgment (UA)	R	Acknowledge acceptance of one of the set-mode commands
Disconnected mode (DM)	R	Responder is in disconnected mode
Request disconnect (RD)	R	Request for DISC command
Request initialization mode (RIM)	R	Initialization needed; request for SIM command
Unnumbered information (UI)	C/R	Used to exchange control information
Unnumbered poll (UP)	C	Used to solicit control information
Reset (RSET)	C	Used for recovery; resets N(R), N(S)
Exchange identification (XID)	C/R	Used to request/report status
Test (TEST)	C/R	Exchange identical information fields for testing
Frame reject (FRMR)	R	Report receipt of unacceptable frame

If the other side accepts this request, then the HDLC module on that end transmits an Unnumbered Acknowledged (UA) frame back to the initiating side. If the request is rejected, then a Disconnected Mode (DM) frame is sent.

Data Transfer

When initialization has been requested and accepted, a logical connection is established. Both sides may begin to send user data in I frames, starting with sequence number 0. The N(S) and N(R) fields of the I frame are sequence numbers that support flow control and error control. An HDLC module sending a sequence of I frames will number them sequentially, modulo 8 or 128, depending on whether 3- or 7-bit sequence numbers are used, and place the sequence number in N(S). N(R) is the acknowledgment for I frames received; it enables the HDLC module to indicate which number I frame it expects to receive next.

S frames are also used for flow control and error control. The Receive Ready (RR) frame is used to acknowledge the last I frame received by indicating the next I frame expected. The RR is used when there is no reverse user data traffic (I frames) to carry an acknowledgment. Receive Not Ready (RNR) acknowledges an I frame, as with RR, but also asks the peer entity to suspend transmission of I frames. When the entity that issued RNR is again ready, it sends an RR. REJ initiates the go-back-N ARQ. It indicates that the last I frame received has been rejected and that retransmission of all I frames beginning with number N(R) is required. Selective reject (SREJ) is used to request retransmission of just a single frame.

Disconnect

Either HDLC module can initiate a disconnect, either on its own initiative if there is some sort of fault or at the request of its higher-layer user. HDLC issues a disconnect by sending a Disconnect (DISC) frame. The other side must accept the disconnect by replying with a UA.

Examples of Operation

To better understand HDLC operation, several examples are presented in Figure D.2. In the example diagrams, each arrow includes a legend that specifies the frame name, the setting of the P/F bit, and, where appropriate, the values of N(R) and N(S). The setting of the P or F bit is 1 if the designation is present and 0 if absent.

Figure D.2a shows the frames involved in link setup and disconnect. The HDLC entity for one side issues an SABM command[1] to the other side and starts a timer. The other side, upon receiving the SABM, returns a UA response and sets local variables and counters to their initial values. The initiating entity receives the UA response, sets its variables and counters, and stops the timer. The logical connection is now active, and both sides may begin transmitting frames. Should the

---

[1]This stands for Set Asynchronous Balanced Mode. The SABM command is a request to start an exchange. The ABM part of the acronym refers to the mode of transfer, a detail that need not concern us here.

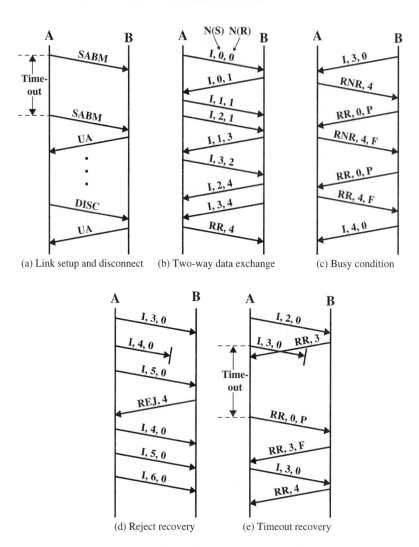

Figure D.2 Examples of HDLC Operation

timer expire without a response, the originator will repeat the SABM, as illustrated. This would be repeated until a UA or DM is received or until, after a given number of tries, the entity attempting initiation gives up and reports failure to a management entity. In such a case, higher-layer intervention is necessary. The same figure (Figure D.2a) shows the disconnect procedure. One side issues a DISC command, and the other responds with a UA response.

Figure D.2b illustrates the full-duplex exchange of I frames. When an entity sends a number of I frames in a row with no incoming data, then the receive sequence number, N(R), is simply repeated (e.g., I,1,1; I,2,1 in the A-to-B direction). When an entity receives a number of I frames in a row with no outgoing frames, then the receive sequence number in the next outgoing frame must reflect the cumulative activity (e.g., I,1,3 in the B-to-A direction). Note that, in addition to I frames, data exchange may involve supervisory frames.

Figure D.2c shows an operation involving a busy condition. Such a condition may arise because an HDLC entity is not able to process I frames as fast as they are arriving, or the intended user is not able to accept data as fast as they arrive in I frames. In either case, the entity's receive buffer fills up and it must halt the incoming flow of I frames, using an RNR command. In this example, station A issues an RNR, which requires the other side to halt transmission of I frames. The station receiving the RNR will usually poll the busy station at some periodic interval by sending an RR with the P bit set. This requires the other side to respond with either an RR or an RNR. When the busy condition has cleared, A returns an RR, and I frame transmission from B can resume.

An example of error recovery using the REJ command is shown in Figure D.2d. In this example, A transmits I frames numbered 3, 4, and D. Frame 4 suffers an error. B detects the error and discards the frame. When B receives I frame 5, it discards this frame because it is out of order and sends an REJ with an N(R) of 4. This causes A to initiate retransmission of all I frames sent, beginning with frame 4. It may continue to send additional frames after the retransmitted frames.

An example of error recovery using a timeout is shown in Figure D.2e. In this example, A transmits I frame number 3 as the last in a sequence of I frames. The frame suffers an error. B detects the error and discards it. However, B cannot send an REJ. This is because there is no way to know if this was an I frame. If an error is detected in a frame, all of the bits of that frame are suspect, and the receiver has no way to act upon it. A, however, started a timer as the frame was transmitted. This timer has a duration long enough to span the expected response time. When the timer expires, A initiates recovery action. This is usually done by polling the other side with an RR command with the P bit set, to determine the status of the other side. Because the poll demands a response, the entity will receive a frame containing an N(R) field and be able to proceed. In this case, the response indicates that frame 3 was lost, which A retransmits.

These examples are not exhaustive. However, they should give the reader a good feel for the behavior of HDLC.

GLOSSARY

Some of the definitions in this glossary are from *The New IEEE Standard Dictionary of Electrical and Electronics Terms*, IEEE Std 100-1992, 1993. These are marked with an asterisk.

amplitude modulation   A form of modulation in which the amplitude of a carrier wave is varied in accordance with some characteristic of the modulating signal.

amplitude-shift keying   Modulation in which the two binary values are represented by two different amplitudes of the carrier frequency.

analog data*   Data represented by a physical quantity that is considered to be continuously variable and whose magnitude is made directly proportional to the data or to a suitable function of the data.

analog signal   A continuously varying electromagnetic wave that may be propagated over a variety of media.

analog transmission   The transmission of analog signals without regard to content. The signal may be amplified, but there is no intermediate attempt to recover the data from the signal.

angle modulation*   Modulation in which the angle of a sine wave carrier is varied. Phase and frequency modulation are particular forms of angle modulation.

antenna*   That part of a transmitting or receiving system that is designed to radiate or to receive electromagnetic waves.

attenuation   The reduction of strength of a signal as a function of distance traveled.

aperiodic   A function or signal that is not periodic.

application layer   Layer 7 of the OSI model. This layer determines the interface of the system with the user.

asynchronous transfer mode (ATM)   A form of packet transmission using fixed-size packets, called cells.

atmospheric absorption*   The loss of energy in transmission of radio waves, due to dissipation in the atmosphere.

automatic repeat request   A feature that automatically initiates a request for retransmission when an error in transmission is detected.

bandwidth   The difference in Hertz between the limiting (upper and lower) frequencies of a spectrum.

bit error rate   The probability that a transmitted bit is received in error.

block error correction code   A technique in which a k-bit block of data is mapped into an n-bit block ($n > k$) called a **codeword**, using an FEC (forward error correction) encoder

broadband   In data communications generally refers to systems that provide user data rates of greater than 2 Mbps, up to 100s of Mbps.

burst error   A burst error of length B is a contiguous sequence of B bits in which the first and last bits and any number of intermediate bits are received in error

carrier frequency   A continuous frequency capable of being modulated or impressed with a second (information-carrying) signal.

cell relay   The packet-switching mechanism used for the fixed-size packets called cells. ATM is based on cell relay technology.

cellular network   A wireless communications network in which fixed antennas are arranged in a hexagonal pattern and mobile stations communicate through nearby fixed antennas.

channel*   A single path for transmitting electric signals. *Note:* The word *path* is to be interpreted in a broad sense to include separation by frequency division or time division. The term *channel* may signify either a one-way or a two-way path.

channel capacity*   The maximum possible information rate through a channel subject to the constraints of that channel.

checksum   An error-detecting code based on a summation operation performed on the bits to be checked.

circuit switching   A method of communicating in which a dedicated communications path is established between two devices through one or more intermediate switching nodes. Unlike packet switching, digital data are sent as a continuous stream of bits. Bandwidth is guaranteed, and delay is essentially limited to propagation time. The telephone system uses circuit switching.

crosstalk*   Undesired energy appearing in one signal path as a result of coupling from other signal paths.

cyclic redundancy check   An error detecting code in which the code is the remainder resulting from dividing the bits to be checked by a predetermined binary number.

datagram   In packet switching, a packet, independent of other packets, that carries information sufficient for routing from the originating data terminal equipment (DTE) to the destination DTE without the necessity of establishing a connection between the DTEs and the network.

decibel   A measure of the relative strength of two signals. The number of decibels is 10 times the log of the ratio of the power of two signals, or 20 times the log of the ratio of the voltage of two signals.

diffraction* Deviation of part of a beam, determined by the wave nature of radiation, and occurring when the radiation passes the edge of an opaque obstacle.

digital data Data consisting of a sequence of discrete elements.

digital signal A discrete or discontinuous signal, such as voltage pulses.

digital transmission The transmission of digital data, using either an analog or digital signal, in which the digital data are recovered and repeated at intermediate points to reduce the effects of noise.

dipole antenna* Any one of a class of antennas producing a radiation pattern approximating that of an elementary electric dipole.

direct sequence spread spectrum A form of spread spectrum in which each bit in the original signal is represented by multiple bits in the transmitted signal, using a spreading code.

Doppler shift* The effective change of frequency of a received signal due to the relative velocity of a transmitter with respect to the receiver.

downlink The communications link from satellite to earth station.

electric dipole* An elementary radiator consisting of a pair of equal and opposite oscillating electric charges an infinitesimal distance apart.

encapsulation The addition of control information by a protocol entity to data obtained from a protocol user.

error correction code* A code in which each expression conforms to specific rules of construction, so that departures from this construction can be automatically detected, and permits the automatic correction of some or all of the errors.

error-detecting code* A code in which each expression conforms to specific rules of construction, so that if certain errors occur in an expression, the resulting expression will not conform to the rules of construction and thus the presence of the errors is detected.

fading* The time variation of received signal power caused by changes in the transmission medium or path(s).

flat fading* That type of fading in which all frequency components of the received signal fluctuate in the same proportions simultaneously.

flow control The function performed by a receiving entity to limit the amount or rate of data that is sent by a transmitting entity.

forward channel In a cellular or cordless network, the communications link from the base station to the mobile unit.

forward error correction Procedures whereby a receiver, using only information contained in the incoming digital transmission, a receiver corrects bit errors in the data

frame check sequence An error-detecting code inserted as a field in a block of data to be transmitted. The code serves to check for errors upon reception of the data.

free space loss   Loss in signal energy caused by the dispersion of the signal over distance.

frequency   Rate of signal oscillation in hertz.

frequency division multiplexing   The division of a transmission facility into two or more channels by splitting the frequency band transmitted by the facility into narrower bands, each of which is used to constitute a distinct channel.

frequency domain   A characterization of a function or signal in terms of its component frequencies.

frequency-hopping spread spectrum   A form of spread spectrum in which the signal is broadcast over a seemingly random series of radio frequencies, hopping from frequency to frequency at fixed intervals.

frequency modulation   Modulation in which the frequency of an alternating current is the characteristic varied.

frequency-shift keying   Modulation in which the two binary values are represented by two different frequencies near the carrier frequency.

fundamental frequency*   The lowest frequency component in the Fourier representation of a periodic quantity.

gain (of an antenna)*   The ratio of the radiation intensity, in a given direction, to the radiation intensity that would be obtained if the power accepted by the antenna were radiated isotropically.

geostationary   Refers to a geosynchronous satellite angle with zero inclination. so the satellite appears to hover over one spot on the earth's equator.

geosynchronous   The Clarke circular orbit above the equator. For a planet the size and mass of the earth, this point is 35,863 miles above the surface.

ground wave*   A radio wave propagated over the earth and is ordinarily affected by the presence of the ground and troposphere. *Notes*: (1) The ground wave include all components of a radio wave over the earth except ionospheric and tropospheric waves. (2) The ground wave is refracted because of variations in the dielectric constant of the troposphere.

guided medium   A transmission medium in which the waves are guided along a solid medium, such as copper twisted pair, copper coaxial cable, or optical fiber.

half-wave dipole*   A wire antenna consisting of two straight collinear conductors of equal length, separated by a small feeding gap, with each conductor approximately a quarter-wavelength long.

Hamming distance*   The number of digit positions in which two binary numbers of the same length are different.

hash function   A function that maps a variable length data block or message into a fixed-length value called a hash code. The function is designed in such a way that, when protected, it provides an authenticator to the data or message. Also referred to as a message digest.

header   System-defined control information that precedes user data.

impulse noise   A high-amplitude, short-duration noise pulse.

infrared   Electromagnetic waves whose frequency range is above that of micro-wave and below the visible spectrum: 3×10^{11} to 4×10^{14} Hz.

intermodulation noise   Noise due to the nonlinear combination of signals of different frequencies.

internet   A collection of packet-switched networks connected via routers.

Internet Protocol   An internetworking protocol that provides connectionless service across multiple packet-switching networks.

ionosphere   That part of the earth's outer atmosphere where ionization caused by incoming solar radiation affects the transmission of radio waves. It generally extends from a height of about 50 km to about 400 km above the earth's surface.

isochronous*   The time characteristic of an event or signal recurring at known, periodic time intervals.

local area network (LAN)   A general-purpose local network that can serve a variety of devices. Typically used for terminals, microcomputers, and minicomputers.

local loop   Transmission path, generally twisted pair, between the individual subscriber and the nearest switching center of the public telecommunications network.

medium access control   For broadcast networks, the method of determining which device has access to the transmission medium at any time.

microwave   Electromagnetic waves in the frequency range 1 to 40 GHz.

millimeter wave   An imprecise term. Generally, millimeter wave systems operate in a region between 10 GHz (wavelength = 30 mm) and 300 GHz (wavelength = 1 mm).

modulation*   A process whereby certain characteristics of a wave, called a carrier, are varied or selected in accordance with a modulating function.

multipath*   The propagation phenomenon that results in signals reaching the receiving antenna by two or more paths.

multiplexing   In data transmission, a function that permits two or more data sources to share a common transmission medium such that each data source has its own channel.

network layer   Layer 3 of the OSI model. Responsible for routing data through a communication network.

noise   Unwanted signals that combine with and hence distort the signal intended for transmission and reception.

packet   A group of bits that includes data plus source and destination addresses. Generally refers to a network layer (layer 3) protocol.

packet switching A method of transmitting messages through a communications network, in which long messages are subdivided into short packets. The packets are then transmitted as in message switching. Usually, packet switching is more efficient and rapid than message switching.

parity bit* A binary digit appended to an array of binary digits to make the sum of all the binary digits, including the parity bit, always odd (odd parity) or always even (even parity).

peak amplitude The maximum value or strength of a signal over time; typically, this value is measured in volts.

period The absolute value of the minimum interval after which the same characteristics of a periodic waveform recur.

periodic waveform A waveform $f(t)$ that satisfies $f(t) = f(t + nk)$ for all integers n, with k being a constant.

phase For a periodic signal $f(t)$, the fractional part t/P of the period P through which t has advanced relative to an arbitrary origin. The origin is usually taken at the last previous passage through zero from the negative to the positive direction.

phase modulation Modulation in which the phase angle of a carrier is the characteristic varied.

phase-shift keying Modulation in which the phase of the carrier signal is shifted to represent digital data.

physical layer Layer 1 of the OSI model. Concerned with the electrical, mechanical, and timing aspects of signal transmission over a medium.

presentation layer Layer 6 of the OSI model. Provides for the selection of a common syntax for representing data and for transformation of application data into and from the common syntax.

protocol A set of rules governing the exchange of data between two entities.

protocol data unit A set of data specified in a protocol of a given layer and consisting of protocol control information of that layer, and possibly user data of that layer.

pseudonoise A sequence of numbers that are apparently statistically random.

pulse code modulation A process in which a signal is sampled, and the magnitude of each sample with respect to a fixed reference is quantized and converted by coding to a digital signal.

radiation pattern A graphical representation of the radiation properties of an antenna as a function of space coordinates. Typically, the distance from the antenna to each point on the radiation pattern is proportional to the power radiated from the antenna in that direction.

reflection Occurs when an electromagnetic signal encounters a surface that is large relative to the wavelength of the signal; the angle of incidence equals the angle of reflection.

refraction* The bending of a beam in transmission through an interface between two dissimilar media or in a medium whose refractive index is a continuous function of position.

reverse channel In a cellular or cordless network, the communications link from the mobile unit to the base station.

router A device used to link two or more networks. The router makes use of an internet protocol, which is a connectionless protocol operating at layer 3 of the OSI model.

scattering* The production of waves of changed direction, frequency, or polarization when radio waves encounter matter.

selective fading* Fading that affects unequally the different spectral components of a radio signal.

service access point A means of identifying a user of the services of a protocol entity. A protocol entity provides one or more SAPs for use by higher-level entities.

session layer Layer 5 of the OSI model. Manages a logical connection (session) between two communicating processes or applications.

sky wave* A radio wave propagated obliquely toward, and returned from, the ionosphere.

spectrum Refers to an absolute range of frequencies. For example, the spectrum of infrared is 3×10^{11} to 4×10^{14} Hz.

spread spectrum A technique in which the information in a signal is spread over a wider bandwidth using a spreading code.

spreading code A sequence of digits used to spread bandwidth in a spread spectrum system. Also called a spreading sequence or a chipping code.

subscriber loop Synonymous with local loop.

synchronous time division multiplexing A method of TDM in which time slots on a shared transmission line are assigned to I/O channels on a fixed, predetermined basis.

thermal noise Statistically uniform noise due to the temperature of the transmission medium.

time division duplex A link transmission technique in which data are transmitted in one direction at a time, with transmission alternating between the two directions.

time division multiplexing The division of a transmission facility into two or more channels by allotting the facility to several different information channels, one at a time.

time domain A characterization of a function or signal in terms of value as a function of time.

transmission medium The physical path between transmitters and receivers in a communications system.

transport layer   Layer 4 of the OSI model. Provides reliable, transparent transfer of data between end points.

troposphere*   That portion of the earth's atmosphere in which temperature generally decreases with altitude, clouds form, and convection is active. The troposphere occupies the space from the earth's surface up to a height ranging from about 6 km at the poles to about 18 km at the equator.

unguided medium   A transmission medium, such as air, vacuum, or water, in which an antenna is employed for transmission and reception.

uplink   The communications link from earth station to satellite.

virtual circuit   A packet-switching service in which a connection (virtual circuit) is established between two stations at the start of transmission. All packets follow the same route, need not carry a complete address, and arrive in sequence.

wavelength*   The distance between two points in a periodic wave that have the same phase.

wireless   Refers to transmission through air, vacuum, or water by means of an antenna.

REFERENCES

Abbreviations

ACM   Association for Computing Machinery
IEEE   Institute of Electrical and Electronics Engineers

ADAM91   Adamek, J. *Foundations of Coding.* New York: Wiley, 1991.

AGRA99   Agrawal, P., and Sreenan, C. "Get Wireless: A Mobile Technology Spectrum." *IT Pro*, August 1999

ANDE95   Anderson, J.; Rappaport, T.; and Yoshida, S. "Propagation Measurements and Models for Wireless Communications Channels." *IEEE Communications Magazine*, January 1995.

ASH90   Ash, R. *Information Theory.* New York: Dover, 1990.

BANT94   Bantz, D., and Bauchot, F. "Wireless LAN Design Alternatives." *IEEE Network*, March/April, 1994.

BELL00   Bellamy, J. *Digital Telephony.* New York: Wiley, 2000.

BERL80   Berlekamp, E. "The Technology of Error-Correcting Codes." *Proceedings of the IEEE*, May 1980.

BERL87   Berlekamp, E.; Peile, R.; and Pope, S. "The Application of Error Control to Communications." *IEEE Communications Magazine*, April 1987.

BERR96   Berrou, C., and Glavieux, A. "Near Optimum Error Correcting Codes and Decoding: Turbo Codes." *IEEE Transactions on Communications*, October 1996.

BERT92   Bertsekas, D., and Gallager, R. *Data Networks.* Englewood Cliffs, NJ: Prentice Hall, 1992.

BERT94   Bertoni, H.; Honcharenko, W.; Maciel, L.; and Xia, H. "UHF Propagation Prediction for Wireless Personal Communications." *Proceedings of the IEEE*, September 1994.

BERT00   Bertoni, H. *Radio Propagation for Modern Wireless Systems.* Upper Saddle River, NJ: Prentice Hall, 2000.

BHAR83   Bhargava, V. "Forward Error Correction Schemes for Digital Communications." *IEEE Communications Magazine*, January 1983.

BLAC99a   Black, U. *Second-generation Mobile and Wireless Networks.* Upper Saddle River, NJ: Prentice Hall, 1999.

BLAC99b   Black, U. *ATM Volume I: Foundation for Broadband Networks.* Upper Saddle River, NJ: Prentice Hall, 1992.

BOLC01   Bolcskei, H., et al. "Fixed Broadband Wireless Access: State of the Art, Challenges, and Future Directions." *IEEE Communications Magazine*, January 2001.

BRAY01   Bray, J., and Sturman, C. *Bluetooth: Connect Without Cables.* Upper Saddle River, NJ: Prentice Hall, 1992.

BUCH99   Buchanan, B. *Handbook of Data and Communication Networks.* Boston: Kluwer Academic Publishers, 1999.

CARN99a   Carne, E. *Telecommunications Primer: Data, Voice, and Video Communications.* Upper Saddle River, NJ: Prentice Hall, 1999.

CARN99b Carne, E. *Telecommunications Topics: Applications of Functions and Probabilities in Electronic Communications.* Upper Saddle River, NJ: Prentice Hall, 1999.

CISC00 Cisco Systems, Inc. *Overcoming Multipath in Non-Line-of-Sight High-Speed Microwave Communication Links.* White Paper, 2000. (www.cisco.com)

COTT00 Cottrell, R.; Langhammer, M.; and Mauer, V. "Turbo Decoding for Comm Apps." *Communication Systems Design,* August 2000.

COUC01 Couch, L. *Digital and Analog Communication Systems.* Upper Saddle River, NJ: Prentice Hall, 2001.

CROW97 Crow, B., et al. "IEEE 802.11 Wireless Local Area Networks." *IEEE Communications Magazine,* September 1997.

DALK96 Dalke, R.; Hufford, G.; and Ketchum, R. *Radio Propagation Considerations for Local Multipoint Distribution Systems.* National Telecommunications and Information Administration Publication PB97116511, August 1996.

DAUM82 Daumer, W. "Subjective Evaluation of Several Efficient Speech Coders." *IEEE Transactions on Communications,* April 1982.

DINA98 Dinan, E., and Jabbari, B. "Spreading Codes for Direct Sequence CDMA and Wideband CDMA Cellular Networks." *IEEE Communications Magazine,* September 1998.

DIXO94 Dixon, R. *Spread Spectrum Systems with Commercial Applications.* New York: Wiley, 1994.

ECON99 "The World in Your Pocket." *The Economist,* October 1999.

EDEL82 Edelson, B.; Marsten, R.; and Morgan, W. "Greater Message Capacity for Satellites.' *IEEE Spectrum,* March 1982.

ELBE99 Elbert, B. *Introduction to Satellite Communication.* Boston: Artech House, 1999.

ENGE00 Engelmann, R. "The Origins of Radio." *IEEE Potentials,* October/November 2000.

EVAN98 Evans, J. "New Satellites for Personal Communications." *Scientific American,* April 1998.

EVER94 Everitt, D. "Traffic Engineering of the Radio Interface for Cellular Mobile Networks." *Proceedings of the IEEE,* September 1994.

FREE96 Freeman, R. *Telecommunication System Engineering.* New York: Wiley, 1996.

FREE97 Freeman, R. *Radio System Design for Telecommunications.* New York: Wiley, 1997.

FREE98a Freeman, R. *Telecommunication Transmission Handbook.* New York: Wiley, 1998.

FREE98b Freeman, R. "Bits, Symbols, Baud, and Bandwidth." *IEEE Communications Magazine,* April 1998.

FREE99 Freeman, R. *Fundamentals of Telecommunications.* New York: Wiley, 1999.

FUNG98 Fung, P. "A Primer on MMDS Technology." *Communication Systems Design,* April 1998. Available at csdmag.com.

GARG99 Garg, V., and Wilkes, J. *Principles and Applications of GSM.* Upper Saddle River, NJ: Prentice Hall, 1999.

GEIE99 Geier, J. *Wireless LANs.* New York: Macmillan Technical Publishing, 1999.

GEIE01 Geier, J. "Enabling Fast Wireless Networks with OFDM." *Communications System Design,* February 2001. (www.csdmag.com)

GIBS93 Gibson, J. *Principles of Digital and Analog Communications.* New York: Macmillan, 1993.

GIBS97 Gibson, J. ed. *The Communications Handbook.* Boca Raton, FL: CRC Press, 1997.

GLOV98 Glover, I., and Grant, P. *Digital Communications.* Upper Saddle River, NJ: Prentice Hall, 1998.

GOOD97   Goodman, D. *Wireless Personal Communications Systems.* Reading, MA: Addison-Wesley, 1997.

GUNT00   Gunther, N. *The Practical Performance Analyst.* Lincoln, NE: Authors Choice Press, 2000.

HAAR98   Harrtsen, J. "Bluetooth: The Universal Radio Interface for ad hoc, Wireless Connectivity." *Ericsson Review*, No. 3, 1998. (www.ericsson.se)

HAAR00a   Haartsen, J. "The Bluetooth Radio System." *IEEE Personal Communications*, February 2000.

HAAR00b   Haartsen, J., and Mattisson, S. "Bluetooth—A New Low-Power Radio Interface Providing Short-Range Connectivity." *Proceedings of the IEEE*, October 2000.

HAAS00   Haas, Z. "Wireless and Mobile Networks." In [TERP00].

HATA80   Hata, M. "Empirical Formula for Propagation Loss in Land Mobile Radio Services." *IEEE Transactions on Vehicular Technology*, March 1980.

HAYK94   Haykin, S. *Communication Systems.* New York: Wiley, 1994.

HEIJ00   Heijden, M., and Taylor, M., eds. *Understanding WAP: Wireless Applications, Devices, and Services.* Boston: Artech House, 2000.

HSU84   Hsu, H. *Applied Fourier Analysis.* New York: Harcourt Brace, 1984.

INGL97   Inglis, A., and Luther, A. *Satellite Technology: An Introduction.* Boston: Focal Press, 1997.

JAIN90   Jain, Y. "Convolutional Codes Improve Bit-Error Rate in Digital Systems." *EDN*, August 20, 1990.

JAME95   James, J. *A Student's Guide to Fourier Transforms.* Cambridge, England: Cambridge University Press, 1995.

JAYA84   Jayant, N., and Noll, P. *Digital Coding of Waveforms.* Englewood Cliffs, NJ: Prentice Hall, 1984.

JONE93   Jones, E. *Digital Transmission.* New York: McGraw-Hill, 1993.

KAHN97   Kahn, J., and Barry, J. "Wireless Infrared Communications." *Proceedings of the IEEE*, February 1997.

KAMM00   Kammler, D. *A First Course in Fourier Analysis.* Upper Saddle River, NJ: Prentice Hall, 2000.

KELL00   Keller, T., and H. "Adaptive Multicarrier Modulation: A Convenient Framework for Time-Frequency Processing in Wireless Communication." *Proceedings of the IEEE*, May 2000.

KNUT98   Knuth, D. *The Art of Computer Programming, Volume 2: Seminumerical Algorithms.* Reading, MA: Addison-Wesley, 1998.

KROO86   Kroon, P, and Deprettere, E. "Regular Pulse Excitation—A Novel Approach to Effective Multipulse Coding of Speech." *IEEE Transactions on Acoustics, Speech, and Signal Processing*, No. 5, 1986.

LATH98   Lathi, B. *Modern Digital and Analog Communication Systems.* New York: Oxford University Press, 1998.

LEBO98   Lebow, I. *Understanding Digital Transmission and Recording.* New York: IEEE Press, 1998.

MACW76   Macwilliams, F., and Sloane, N. "Pseudo-Random Sequences and Arrays." *Proceedings of the IEEE*, December 1976. Reprinted in [TANT98].

MANN99   Mann, S. "The Wireless Application Protocol." *Dr. Dobb's Journal*, October 1999.

MARK99   Marks, R. "The IEEE 802.16 Working Group on Broadband Wireless." *IEEE Network*, March/April 1999.

MART94   Martine, R. *Basic Traffic Analysis.* Upper Saddle River, NJ: Prentice Hall, 1994.

MCDY99   McDysan, D., and Spohn, D. *ATM: Theory and Application.* New York: McGraw-Hill, 1999.

METT99   Mettala, R., et al. *Bluetooth Protocol Architecture Version 1.0.* Bluetooth Whitepaper 1.C.120/1.0, 25 August 1999. (www.bluetooth.com)

MILL01   Miller, B., and Bisdikian, C. *Bluetooth Revealed.* Upper Saddle River, NJ: Prentice Hall, 2001.

MOSH89   Moshos, G. *Data Communications: Principles and Problems.* New York: West Publishing Co., 1989.

MURH98   Murhammer, M., et al. *TCP/IP: Tutorial and Technical Overview.* Upper Saddle River: NJ: Prentice Hall, 1998.

NORD00   Nordbotten, A. "LMDS Systems and Their Application." *IEEE Communications Magazine,* June 2000.

OHAR99   Ohara, B., and Petrick, A. *IEEE 802.11 Handbook: A Designer's Companion.* New York: IEEE Press, 1999.

OJAN98   Ojanpera, T., and Prasad, G. "An Overview of Air Interface Multiple Access for IMT-2000/UMTS." *IEEE Communications Magazine,* September 1998.

OKUM68   Okumura, T., et. al., "Field Strength and Its Variability in VHF and UHF Land Mobile Radio Service." *Rev. Elec. Communication Lab.* 1968.

ORLI98   Orlik, P., and Rappaport, S. "Traffic Performance and Mobility Modeling of Cellular Communications with Mixed Platforms and Highly Variable Mobilities." *Proceedings of the IEEE,* July 1998.

ORTI00   Ortiz, S. "Broadband Fixed Wireless Travels the Last Mile." *Computer,* July 2000.

PAHL95   Pahlavan, K.; Probert, T.; and Chase, M. "Trends in Local Wireless Networks." *IEEE Communications Magazine,* March 1995.

PAPA97   Papazian, P.; Hufford, G.; Aschatz, R.; and Hoffman, R. "Study of the Local Multipoint Distribution Service Radio Channel." *IEEE Transactions on Broadcasting,* June 1997.

PARK88   Park, S., and Miller, K. "Random Number Generators: Good Ones are Hard to Find." *Communications of the ACM,* October 1988.

PASS00   Passani, L. "Creating WAP Services." *Dr. Dobb's Journal,* July 2000.

PEAR92   Pearson, J. *Basic Communication Theory.* Englewood Cliffs, NJ: Prentice Hall, 1992.

PERK97   Perkins, C. "Mobile IP." *IEEE Communications Magazine,* May 1997.

PETE61   Peterson, W., and Brown, D. "Cyclic Codes for Error Detection." *Proceedings of the IEEE,* January 1961.

PETE95   Peterson, R.; Ziemer, R.; and Borth, D. *Introduction to Spread Spectrum Communications.* Englewood Cliffs, NJ: Prentice Hall, 1995.

PHIL98   Phillips, J., and Namee, G. *Personal Wireless Communications with DECT and PWT.* Boston: Artech House, 1998.

PICH97   Pichna, R., and Wang, Q. "Power Control." In [GIBS97].

PICK82   Pickholtz, R.; Schilling, D.; and Milstein, L. "Theory of Spread Spectrum Communications—A Tutorial." *IEEE Transactions on Communications,* May 1982. Reprinted in [TANT98].

POLL96   Pollini, G. "Trends in Handover Design." *IEEE Communications Magazine,* March 1996.

POOL98   Polle, I. *Your Guide to Propagation.* Potters Bar, Herts., U.K.: Radio Society of Great Britain, 1998.

PRAS98   Prasad, R., and Ojanpera, T. "An Overview of CDMA Evolution: Toward Wideband CDMA." *IEEE Communications Surveys,* Fourth Quarter 1998. Available at www.comsoc.org.

PRAS00   Prasad, R.; Mohr, W.; and Konhauser, W., eds. *Third Generation Mobile Communication Systems.* Boston: Artech House, 2000.

PROA01   Proakis, J. *Digital Communications.* New York: McGraw-Hill, 2001.

RABI95   Rabiner, L. "Toward Vision 2001: Voice and Audio Processing Considerations." *AT&T Technical Journal*, March/April 1995.

RAHN93   Rahnema, M. "Overview of the GSM System and Protocol Architecture." *IEEE Communications Magazine*, April 1993.

RAMA88   Ramabadran, T., and Gaitonde, S. "A Tutorial on CRC Computations." *IEEE Micro*, August 1988.

RAPP97   Rappaport, T.; Rias, M.; and Kapoor, V. "Propagation Models." In [GIBS97].

RODB00   Rodbell, M. "Bluetooth: Wireless Local Access, Baseband and RF Interfaces, and Link Management." *Communications System Design*, March, April, May 2000. (www.csdmag.com)

SCHI00   Schiller, J. *Mobile Communications*. Reading, MA: Addison-Wesley, 2000.

SKLA93   Sklar, B. "Defining, Designing, and Evaluating Digital Communication Systems." *IEEE Communications Magazine*, November 1993.

SKLA97a   Sklar, B. "Rayleigh Fading Channels in Mobile Digital Communication Systems." *IEEE Communications Magazine*, July 1997.

SKLA97b   Sklar, B. "A Primer on Turbo Code Concepts." *IEEE Communications Magazine*, December 1997.

SKLA01   Sklar, B. *Digital Communications: Fundamentals and Applications*. Upper Saddle River, NJ: Prentice Hall, 2001.

SOLO98   Solomon, J. *Mobile IP: The Internet Unplugged*. Upper Saddle River, NJ: Prentice Hall PTR, 1998.

SPOH97   Spohn, D. *Data Network Design*. New York: McGraw-Hill, 1997.

SPRA91   Spragins, J,; Hammond, J.; and Pawlikowski, K. *Telecommunications Protocols and Design*. Reading, MA: Addison-Wesley, 1991.

STAL99   Stallings, W. *Cryptography and Network Security: Principles and Practice, 2nd ed.* Upper Saddle River, NJ: Prentice Hall, 1999.

STAL00   Stallings, W. *Data and Computer Communications, Sixth Edition.* Upper Saddle River, NJ: Prentice Hall, 2000.

TANN95   Tanner, M. *Practical Queueing Analysis.* New York: McGraw-Hill, 1995.

TANT98   Tantaratana, S., and Ahmed, K., eds. *Wireless Applications of Spread Spectrum Systems: Selected Readings.* Piscataway, NJ: IEEE Press, 1998.

TERP00   Terplan, K., and Morreale, P. eds. *The Telecommunications Handbook.* Boca Raton, FL: CRC Press, 2000.

THUR00   Thurwachter, C. *Data and Telecommunications: Systems and Applications.* Upper Saddle River, NJ: Prentice Hall, 2000.

VUCE00   Vucetic, B., and Yuan, J. *Turbo Codes: Principles and Applications.* Boston: Kluwer Academic Publishers, 2000.

WAPF98   WAP Forum. *Wireless Application Environment Overview.* WAP Forum document, April 1998.

WEBB00   Webb, W. *Introduction to Wireless Local Loop: Broadband and Narrowband Systems.* Boston: Artech House, 2000.

WILS00   Wilson, J., and Kronz, J. "Inside Bluetooth: Part I and Part II." *Dr. Dobb's Journal*, March, April 2000.

XION00   Xiong, F. *Digital Modulation Techniques.* Boston: Artech House, 2000.

ZENG00   Zeng, M.; Annamalai, A.; and Bhargava, V. "Harmonization of Global Third-Generation Mobile Systems. *IEEE Communications Magazine*, December 2000.

INDEX

ACRONYMS

2G	Second Generation
3G	Third Generation
AM	Amplitude Modulation
AMPS	Advanced Mobile Phone Service
ARQ	Automatic Repeat Request
ASK	Amplitude-Shift Keying
ATM	Asynchronous Transfer Mode
BER	Bit Error Rate
bps	Bits Per Second
CDMA	Code Division Multiple Access
CRC	Cyclic Redundancy Check
DAMA	Demand Assignment Multiple Access
dBm	decibel-milliWatt
dBW	decibel-Watt
DECT	Digital Enhanced Cordless Telecommunications
DM	Delta Modulation
DSSS	Direct Sequence Spread Spectrum
ECC	Error Correction Code
EHF	Extremely High Frequency
ELF	Extremely Low Frequency
FAMA	Fixed Assignment Multiple Access
FCC	Federal Communications Commission
FCS	Frame Check Sequence
FDM	Frequency Division Multiplexing
FDMA	Frequency Division Multiple Access
FEC	Forward Error Correction
FHSS	Frequency-Hopping Spread Spectrum
FSK	Frequency-Shift Keying
FM	Frequency Modulation
HDLC	High-Level Data Link Control
GEO	Geostationary; Geosynchronous
GSM	Global System for Mobile Communications
GW	Ground Wave
HF	High Frequency
IAB	Internet Architecture Board
ICMP	Internet Control Message Protocol
IEEE	Institute of Electrical and Electronics Engineers
IETF	Internet Engineering Task Force
IP	Internet Protocol
ISO	International Organization for Standardization
ITU	International Telecommunication Union
ITU-T	ITU Telecommunication Standardization Sector
LAN	Local Area Network
LEO	Low Earth Orbit
LF	Low Frequency
LFSR	Linear Feedback Shift Register
LLC	Logical Link Control
LMDS	Local Multipoint Distribution Service
LOS	Line of Sight
MAC	Medium Access Control
MAN	Metropolitan Area Network
MEO	Medium Earth Orbit
MF	Medium Frequency
MMDS	Multichannel Multipoint Distribution Service
MOS	Mean Opinion Score
MSS	Mobile Service Satellite
OFDM	Orthogonal Frequency Division Multiplexing
OSI	Open Systems Interconnection
PCM	Pulse Code Modulation
PDU	Protocol Data Unit
PM	Phase Modulation
PN	Pseudonoise
PRN	Pseudorandom Number
PSK	Phase-Shift Keying
PWT	Personal Wireless Telecommunications
QAM	Quadrature Amplitude Modulation
QoS	Quality of Service
RF	Radio Frequency
SAP	Service Access Point
SDU	Service Data Unit
SHF	Super High Frequency
SS	Spread Spectrum
SW	Sky Wave; Short Wave
TCP	Transmission Control Protocol
TDD	Time Division Duplex
TDM	Time Division Multiplexing
TDMA	Time Division Multiple Access
UDP	User Datagram Protocol
UHF	Ultra High Frequency
VF	Voice Frequency
VHF	Very High Frequency
VLF	Very Low Frequency
WAN	Wide Area Network
WAP	Wireless Application Protocol
WLL	Wireless Local Loop
XOR	Exclusive OR